Land Grants in Missouri Territory

1805–1812

❧ ● ☙

James L. Douthat

Heritage Books
2024

HERITAGE BOOKS
AN IMPRINT OF HERITAGE BOOKS, INC.

Books, CDs, and more—Worldwide

For our listing of thousands of titles see our website
at
www.HeritageBooks.com

Published 2024 by
HERITAGE BOOKS, INC.
Publishing Division
5810 Ruatan Street
Berwyn Heights, MD 20740

Originally published 2021

International Standard Book Number
Paperbound: 978-0-7884-9341-6

INTRODUCTION

The Missouri Territory might be misleading as this is really the territory purchased in the Louisiana Purchase lying above Missouri and goes upward to Canada. The Territory is between the Arkansas River and the Canadian border. Most of the area was settled by the French in the early 18th century and the other end the Spanish from the 16th century, therefore many of the names are French or Spanish in origin with about as many English names and the other two.

In reading this collection of land claims being filed under the American flag, the Commissioners require witnesses to verify the claim of the occupant who is requesting a grant. The witness gives more details on the family and the background of the settler. It is worth while to research every entry for each person of interest as additional information might be given. In one case the names of the children are given at this early date and therefore is of interest to the McCourtney [Page 81] descendants. In other claim for tens of thousands of acres, a man from Montgomery County, Kentucky is seeking the grant to establish a colony for settlers from that county. Another is filling a claim for a similar grant to establish a colony for the Irish who wish to come to America. Too many similar claims to mention her.

When reading the index each name on a page is referenced only once as the index is large in total context. We did not index the names of the government officials as many of these are mentioned multiple times on each page. If any of these are your ancestors, they are mentioned all through these pages. There are officials for the Spanish population and the French population as well as the United States' representatives.

Good luck with your ancestors and your search.

James L. Douthat
Mountain Press
2021

12th Congress.]   No. 206.   [2d Session

LAND CLAIMS IN THE MISSOURI TERRITORY.

COMMUNICATED TO THE HOUSE OF REPRESENTATIVES, DECEMBER 1, 1812.

GENERAL LAND OFFICE, *December* 1, 1812.

SIR:

In obedience to the requisitions of an act of Congress respecting claims to land in the Territories of Orleans and Louisiana, I have the honor to transmit a report of the commissioners for ascertaining and adjusting the titles and claims to land in the Territory of Louisiana, (now Missouri,) of all the claims filed with the Recorder which have not been confirmed or granted, in two large bound books, marked and numbered 1 and 2. It is respectfully requested that, when wanted, they may be furnished the Senate, and, at the close of the session, be returned to this office for safe keeping.

I have the honor to be, with great respect, sir, your obedient servant,

EDWARD TIFFIN, *Commissioner.*

The Hon. the SPEAKER *of the House of Representatives of the U. S.*

Report of the commissioners for ascertaining and adjusting the titles and claims to land in the Territory of Louisiana, of all the claims filed with the Recorder which have not been confirmed or granted.

JOHN SMITH T., assignee of Seth Hunt, who was assignee of Henry Dodge, deputy sheriff of the district of St. Genevieve, who sold the same as the property of Pierre Belote, claiming five hundred arpents of land, situate on Grande river, in the district of St. Genevieve, produces to the Board a concession from Charles Dehault Delassus, Lieutenant Governor, to Pierre Belote, dated 5th September, 1799; a deed of transfer from Henry Dodge, deputy sheriff, to Seth Hunt, dated 25th April, 1805; a deed of transfer from Seth Hunt to claimant, dated 15th June, 1805.

Bernard Pratte, being duly sworn, says that he wrote the petition annexed to said concession, and believes it to be antedated; believes the same to have been granted in 1801 or 1802; knows positively it was granted before 1803; that Belote did not apply to him for the writing of said petition; does not recollect whether he wrote the same in St. Louis or St. Genevieve, but believes he wrote it at the request of his (the witness's) brother; that the application was a verbal one; that he does not know of having heard of orders being sent to the Lieutenant Governor not to give any concessions.

Marie Phillipe Leduc, being also duly sworn, says that, in 1803, orders were received from the Intendant to the Lieutenant Governor not to give any grants for lands.

The foregoing testimony was taken by the Board on the 19th July, 1806; and on the 9th October, 1809, the foregoing claim was decided on. Present, John B. C. Lucas, Clement B. Penrose, and Frederick Bates, commissioners, who are unanimously of opinion that it ought not to be confirmed.

NATHAN SULLINS.—A claim for nine hundred and fifty-six arpents of land, situate on the waters of Missouri, district of St. Louis. Produces a survey of said land, dated 29th November, 1805, and certified the 20th January, 1806.
Testimony taken. August 9th, 1806. Edy Musick, being duly sworn, says that claimant prepared for putting up a cabin in 1801; that in 1804 he completed the same, and has actually inhabited and cultivated it to this day.
November 1st, 1809. This claim was decided on: Present, John B. C. Lucas, Clement B. Penrose, and Frederick Bates, commissioners, who are unanimously of opinion that this claim ought not to be granted.

JACQUES CHAUVIN.—A claim for a tract of land, containing, by survey, ten hundred and sixty-three arpents, situate on the Missouri, district of St. Louis. Produces a concession from Charles Dehault Delassus, Lieutenant Governor, to him, for such quantity of land as shall be found within certain boundaries therein described, dated the 3d September, 1799; also a survey of the aforesaid quantity, taken the 26th January, and certified the 17th May, 1800.
Testimony taken. July 26th, 1806. James Mackay, being duly sworn, says that the said tract of land was settled by claimant in the year 1799, and that he, the said claimant, did, prior to and on the 1st day of October, 1800, actually inhabit and cultivate the same; and was then the head of a family.
Testimony taken. November 9th, 1808. Louis Marc, being duly sworn, says that eight years ago claimant inhabited and cultivated said tract, and that the same has been actually inhabited and cultivated by or for him ever since.
November 1st, 1809. This claim was decided on: Present, John B. C. Lucas, Clement B. Penrose, and Frederick Bates, commissioners. It is the opinion of a majority of the Board that this claim ought not to be confirmed; Clement B. Penrose, commissioner, voting for the confirmation thereof. The said majority declare, that if the above claim had not exceeded eight hundred arpents, they would have voted for its confirmation.

MARIE PHILLIPE LEDUC.—A claim for fifteen thousand arpents of land, situate in the district of St. Charles. Produces a concession for the same from Charles Dehault Delassus, Lieutenant Governor, dated 7th January, 1800, and a certificate of survey of the same, dated 5th March, 1804.
Testimony taken. May 3d, 1806. Louis Lebeaume, being duly sworn, says that the claimant arrived in the country in the year 1792, and took up his residence at New Madrid; that, about the end of 1793, he was employed by Government in the arrangement and regulating of the militia of that place; that he remained so about twelve months, and never received any compensation for the same; that Government was then in daily expectation of an attempt by the French to invade the country, and preparing to oppose them; that he afterwards was employed by Government in writing and translating; that he never did receive any compensation for his services in that capacity; that witness, on his return from New Orleans, in the year 1796, found said claimant in Charles D. Delassus's employ, the said Delassus being then commandant of New Madrid; that the said Delassus having come to St. Louis, and taken the command of that post, claimant followed him, and was by him employed as his private secretary, for which witness believes he received some compensation, but cannot tell what it was.
Auguste Choteau, being also sworn, says that he knew claimant in 1799; that he was then employed with the Lieutenant Governor, Charles D. Delassus, both on public and private business, and acted then as his interpreter; that Delassus sent him to New Madrid on public business; and further, that the Lieutenant Governor, Delassus, informed him (the witness) prior to his (the claimant's) arrival at this place, that he would interfere with Government in his favor.
Albert Tison, being also duly sworn, says that he knew the above claimant at New Madrid, when in the employ of Delassus; that claimant did, some time towards the latter end of 1799, or the beginning of 1800, show him (the witness) a concession, which he informed him he had received from the Lieutenant Governor; that a few days afterwards he again saw the said concession; that the quantity therein specified was that above claimed, and that he verily believes it the one showed him by claimant at the time above mentioned.
Opinion and remarks of the Board. May 3, 1806: Present, John B. C. Lucas, Clement B. Penrose, and James L. Donaldson. The Board apply to this claim the questions put to Antoine Soulard, and his answers to the same in the claim of David Delausuy; for a copy of which see appendix to this report.
The Board reject this claim. They are, however, satisfied that the concession is neither antedated nor fraudulent.
July 25, 1807: Present, John B. C. Lucas, Clement B. Penrose, and Frederick Bates, commissioners. On the suggestion of the agent of the United States that there had been an erasure on the above concession, this case was laid over to enable the claimant to produce further proof.
October 8th, 1808: Present, Clement B. Penrose and Frederick Bates, commissioners. The Board, on a re-examination of the erasure alleged to have been made in the concession, are of opinion that the same was given it the time it bears date, 7th January, 1800.
October 30th, 1809: Present, John B. C. Lucas, Clement B. Penrose, and Frederick Bates, commissioners. It is the unanimous opinion of the Board that this claim ought not to be confirmed.
For a translation of the concession in this claim, see appendix to this report.

JAMES MACKAY.—A claim for four hundred arpents of land, situate on the rivers Sabine and Bonne Femme, district of St. Charles. Produces a concession from Zenon Trudeau, Lieutenant Governor, dated 31st May, 1797; also a plat of said land, dated December 2d, 1804, and signed Mackay.
Opinion and remarks of the Board. July 31st, 1807. It appears to the Board that, on the petition of the aforesaid concession, the name of the claimant, the place of his residence, the quantity granted, and the situation of the land, have been altered and written on erasure; and that the concession refers to the petition, especially as to the situation, name, and quantity granted; and also the aforesaid petition declares that the land prayed for is situate on a saline, which part of said petition appears to be altered and written on erasure. Present, John B. C. Lucas, Clement B. Penrose, and Frederick Bates, commissioners. The agent of the United States being also present, objects to the aforesaid concession, on the ground of its being antedated, and otherwise fraudulent; whereupon the Board require further proof of the party.
November 4th, 1809. This claim was decided on: Present, John B. C. Lucas and Clement B. Penrose, commissioners. It is the opinion of the Board that this claim ought not to be confirmed.

JAMES MACKAY.—A claim for a lot in the town of St. Louis, three hundred feet front, and three hundred feet in depth. Produces a concession from Charles Dehault Delassus, Lieutenant Governor, dated the 5th of September, 1799

Opinion of the Board. November 4th, 1809. This claim was decided on: Present, John B. C. Lucas and Clement B. Penrose, commissioners. It is the opinion of the Board that this claim ought not to be confirmed.

JAMES MACKAY.—A claim for two hundred and eighty-two arpents, situate in the common of St. Louis. Produces a concession from Charles Dehault Delassus, Lieutenant Governor, dated the 9th of October, 1799; survey and certificate dated the 17th of December, 1802.

Testimony taken. July 22d, 1806. Auguste Chouteau, being duly sworn, says that the said tract of land was surveyed in 1804 or 1805; that he never heard of a concession having been granted for the same until the survey was taken; that the said tract is adjoining a tract claimed by the witness; and that the same interferes with a tract claimed by the inhabitants of St. Louis as a common.

Opinion of the Board. November 4th, 1809. This claim was decided on: Present, John B. C. Lucas and Clement B. Penrose, commissioners. It is the opinion of the Board that this claim ought not to be confirmed.

JAMES MACKAY, assignee of James McDonald.—A claim for eighteen hundred arpents, situate in the district of St. Louis, on the river Desperes. Produces a copy of a deed, certified by claimant to be from an original in his office, dated the 13th of February, 1802, and a plat of survey for the same, dated the 29th of ———— 1802, and certified the 15th of March, 1803.

Opinion of the Board. November 4th, 1809. This claim was decided on: Present, John B. C. Lucas and Clement B. Penrose, commissioners. It is the opinion of the Board that this claim ought not to be confirmed.

CLAIBOURNE THOMAS, assignee of Edward Butler.—A claim as aforesaid for seven hundred and fifty-six and a half arpents, situate on the waters of the Grand Glaize, district of St. Louis. Produces a certificate of survey, dated February 7, 1806; also a quit-claim from said Butler to claimant, dated June 19, 1804.

Testimony taken. April 7, 1806. William Drennen, being duly sworn, says that the said Edward Butler did, prior to and on the 20th day of December, 1803, actually inhabit and cultivate the said tract of land, and was then of the age of twenty-one years and upwards.

Opinion of the Board. April 7, 1806: Present, John B. C. Lucas and Clement B. Penrose, commissioners. The Board grant to Claibourne Thomas, assignee as aforesaid, seven hundred and fifty arpents of land, situate as aforesaid, provided so much be found vacant there.

Testimony taken. November 11, 1809. Benjamin Johnston, being duly sworn, says that Edward Butler first settled on the tract claimed in the year 1801; inhabited and cultivated the same in the years 1802 and 1803; inhabited and cultivated by or for claimant ever since.

Opinion of the Board. November 11, 1809. This claim was decided on: Present, John B. C. Lucas, Clement B. Penrose, Frederick Bates, commissioners. The Board is unanimously of opinion that said tract ought not to be granted.

JOHN MULLANPHY, assignee of Joseph Robidoux, deceased.—A claim as aforesaid for one thousand one hundred and fifty and a half arpents, situate in the fields of St. Ferdinand, district of St. Louis. Produces a concession from Zenon Trudeau, Lieutenant Governor, to Joseph Robidoux, for the said tract of land, dated April 15, 1796; a certificate of survey of the same, dated April 10, 1797; and a deed of transfer of said land, executed by Joseph Robidoux and his wife, to the said J. Mullanphy, dated January 30, 1805.

Testimony taken. February 4, 1806. Francis Dunegan, being duly sworn, says that he was commandant of the village of St. Ferdinand when the tract of land above mentioned was first settled; that all his grants for lands to individuals were merely verbal, as were also his orders of surveys for the same; that, when the said Joseph Robidoux surveyed said land, he met with no opposition, it being generally understood in the village that the same was said Robidoux's property; that he began the settling of the same in the year 1794, and that one Louis Lafleur undertook the cultivating of the same for the said Joseph Robidoux, and did, prior to and on the 1st day of October, 1800, actually inhabit and cultivate the same as his agent; and further, that the said tract is composed of several small tracts, purchased by the said Joseph Robidoux from individuals, inhabitants of the said village of St. Ferdinand, by virtue of grants for the same.

Opinion of the Board. February 4, 1806: Present, John B. C. Lucas, Clement B. Penrose, and James L. Donaldson, commissioners. It being proved to the Board that the above concession was granted to the said Joseph Robidoux, in consequence of a purchase by him of several lots originally granted to a number of the inhabitants of the said village of St. Ferdinand, the Board confirm to the said John Mullanphy the aforesaid tract of land, bounded as aforesaid, as per the said concession.

Opinion and remarks of the Board. November 13, 1809. This claim was decided on: Present, John B. C. Lucas, Clement B. Penrose, and Frederick Bates, commissioners. It is the opinion of a majority of the Board that this claim ought not to be confirmed; Clement B. Penrose, commissioner, voting for the confirmation thereof.

JOHN MULLANPHY, assignee of James St. Vrain.—A claim as aforesaid for four thousand arpents of land, situate on the river Cuivre, district of St. Charles. Produces a concession from Charles Dehault Delassus, dated November 18, 1799; a survey of the same, dated February 14, 1804, and certified 5th March, 1804; and a deed of transfer of the same from the said James St. Vrain to the claimant, dated November 12, 1804.

Testimony taken. May 3, 1806. Marie Philippe Le Duc, being duly sworn, says that the aforesaid concession is his own hand-writing; that he arrived at St. Louis on the 22d November, 1799, and was on his way from New Madrid at the time the same bears date; that, about eight or ten days after his arrival, he entered with Mr. Delassus as his secretary; that, when with Delassus in that capacity, he was in the habit of writing decrees or concessions; that he wrote several in 1800, '1, and '2, and was then informed by the Lieutenant Governor that such had been promised some time towards the latter end of 1799, and they were accordingly dated of that date. Being asked whether he had written any decrees or concessions in 1803, bearing date prior to the 1st of October, 1800, answered he did not recollect he had; he further said that petitions would remain some time with the Lieutenant Governor before he gave his decree thereon; and that James St. Vrain was, for about ten years, captain of a galley up the Mississippi.

Louis Labeaume, being also sworn, says that he believes the petition annexed to the aforesaid concession to be his hand-writing, and that he did, about the time the same bears date, write one for him for the same quantity of arpents; that he saw the aforesaid concession in the possession of the said James St. Vrain some time about October or November, 1800, when he, the said St. Vrain, was preparing to send the same down to New Orleans to have his title completed.

St. Vrain is brother to the Lieutenant Governor Delassus, and holds no other claim of that quantity of land.

Opinion of the Board. November 15, 1809. This claim was decided on: Present, John B. C. Lucas and Clement B. Penrose, commissioners. It is the opinion of the Board that this claim ought not to be confirmed.

JOHN MULLANPHY, assignee of Hiacinthe Egliz.—A claim as aforesaid for a piece of land, situate on the Mississippi, district of St. Louis, the quantity of which is not specified. Produces a concession from Charles Dehault Delassus, Lieutenant Governor, dated October 22, 1799; a certificate of survey of twelve arpents ninety-four perches, dated March 10, 1803; and a deed of transfer of the same, dated February 9, 1805.

Opinion and remarks of the Board. June 14, 1806: Present, John B. C. Lucas, Clement B. Penrose, and James L. Donaldson, commissioners. This claim being unsupported by actual inhabitation and cultivation, the Board reject the same, and remark that the aforesaid concession is not duly registered, but believe it to bear date with the day it was granted.

Opinion of the Board. November 15, 1809. This claim was decided on: Present, John B. C. Lucas and Clement B. Penrose, commissioners. It is the opinion of the Board that this claim ought not to be confirmed.

JOHN MULLANPHY, assignee of Toussaint Gendron.—A claim as aforesaid for eight hundred arpents of land, situate on the river Cuivre, in the district of St. Charles. Produces to the Board a concession from Don Carlos Dehault Delassus, Lieutenant Governor, dated the 5th of April, 1800; also a conveyance from the said Gendron to claimant, dated the 5th of September, 1803.

Opinion of the Board. November 15, 1809. This claim was decided on: Present, John B. C. Lucas and Clement B. Penrose, commissioners. It is the opinion of the Board that this claim ought not to be confirmed.

JOHN MULLANPHY, assignee of Hiacinthe Egliz.—A claim as aforesaid for eight hundred arpents of land, situate at the point of the rivers Mississippi and Merimeck, in the district of St. Louis. Produces a concession from Charles Dehault Delassus, Lieutenant Governor, dated December 16, 1799; a certificate of survey of three hundred and six arpents, dated 20th February, 1806; and a deed of transfer of the same, dated 9th February, 1805.

Testimony taken. September 6, 1806. Antoine Soulard, being duly sworn, says that he knows of nothing contradicting the date of the concession; and further, that he knows of Zenon Trudeau having promised said Hiacinthe Egliz a concession.

Opinion and remarks of the Board. June 14 1806. This claim being unsupported by actual habitation and cultivation, the Board reject the same, and require further proof of the date of said concession; they observe that the same is not duly registered: Present, John B. C. Lucas, Clement B. Penrose, and James L. Donaldson, commissioners.

Opinion of the Board. November 15, 1809. This claim was decided on: Present, John B. C. Lucas and Clement B. Penrose, commissioners. It is the opinion of the Board that this claim ought not to be confirmed.

JOHN MULLANPHY, assignee of Madame (veuve) Rigauche.—A claim as aforesaid for one thousand six hundred arpents of land, situate on the river Mississippi, in the district of St. Louis. Produces to the Board a concession for the same from Don Charles Dehault Delassus, Lieutenant Governor, dated the 1st January, 1800, to the said veuve Rigauche; also a plat of survey, dated the 19th of February, 1804, and certified the 8th of March, 1804.

Testimony taken. August 23, 1806. Antoine Soulard, being duly sworn, says that claimant was appointed a tutoress to the young ladies of this place, in which capacity she received the promise from the Baron de Carondelet of a compensation of fifteen dollars per month; that she never received it; that he verily believes the above concession to have been granted prior to the 1st day of October, 1800, and as a compensation for her services.

Louis Labeaume, being duly sworn, says that he wrote the decree of the above concession, and verily believes it was granted at the time it bears date.

Opinion of the Board. November 15, 1809. This claim was decided on: Present, John B. C. Lucas and Clement B. Penrose, commissioners. It is the opinion of the Board that this claim ought not to be confirmed.

JOHN MULLANPHY, assignee of Andrew and Baptiste Blondeau Duzey.—A claim as aforesaid for four hundred and eighty arpents of land, situate on the waters of the river Dardennes, in the district of St. Charles. Produces to the Board a concession for the same from Don Zenon Trudeau, Lieutenant Governor, dated the 18th of March, 1799; also a plat of survey, dated the 10th of April, 1805, signed Mackay; and a deed of conveyance from Charles Tayon, dated 6th July, 1805.

Testimony taken. August 25, 1806. Isidore Savoye, being duly sworn, says that the aforesaid Jean Baptiste Blondeau settled the said tract of land in the beginning of 1796, raised a crop on it, and lived thereon until the fall of that year, when, his wife being very ill, he removed to the village of St. Charles, in order to procure that medical assistance which her situation required; that she died some time after, leaving him with a large family of children; that, in that situation, he determined upon remaining in the said village, and gave up the said tract.

Opinion of the Board. November 15, 1809. This claim was decided on: Present, John B. C. Lucas and Clement B. Penrose, commissioners. It is the opinion of the Board that this claim ought not to be confirmed.

JOHN MULLANPHY, assignee of Joseph La Pierre and Joseph Aubuchon.—A claim as aforesaid for an island of eight hundred arpents of land, in the river Missouri. Produces a concession from Zenon Trudeau, Lieutenant Governor, to the said Joseph La Pierre and Joseph Aubuchon, said to be granted for pasture, and declared by him, the said Lieutenant Governor, to be unfit for cultivation; said concession dated 23d April, 1798; and a deed of transfer of said land to claimant, dated May 17, 1805.

Opinion and remarks of the Board. May 12, 1806: Present, Clement B. Penrose and James L. Donaldson, commissioners. The Board reject this claim, for want of actual inhabitation and cultivation; they are satisfied that said concession is neither antedated nor fraudulent.

Opinion of the Board. November 15, 1809. This claim was decided on: Present, John B. C. Lucas and Clement B. Penrose, commissioners. It is the opinion of the Board that this claim ought not to be confirmed.

JOHN MULLANPHY, assignee of Gabriel Cerre.—A claim as aforesaid for an island of eight hundred arpents of land, situate at the mouth of the river Cuivre, in the Mississippi, in the district of St. Charles. Produces a concession from Charles Dehault Delassus, Lieutenant Governor, dated May 25, 1800; and an act of public sale of the effects and property of said Gabriel Cerre, deceased, dated July 28, 1805.

Opinion and remarks of the Board. July 8, 1806: Present, Clement B. Penrose and James L. Donaldson, commissioners. The Board reject this claim, and require further proof.

Opinion of the Board. November 15, 1809. This claim was decided on: Present, John B. C. Lucas and Clement B. Penrose, commissioners. It is the opinion of the Board that this claim ought not to be confirmed.

JOHN MULLANPHY, assignee of Augustin Trudell, assignee of Hiacinthe Dehaitre.—A claim for one hundred and fifty acres of land, situate near St. Ferdinand, in the district of St. Louis. Produces to the Board a conveyance from Hiacinthe Dehaitre to Augustin Trudell, for one arpent and a half front, on the river St. Ferdinand, and from thence to the river Missouri, dated 20th March, 1805; also, a conveyance from said Augustin Trudell to claimant, for three arpents in front, from said river St. Ferdinand to the said river Missouri, dated 20th of March, 1805.

Opinion of the Board. November 17, 1809. This claim was decided on: Present, John B. C. Lucas, Clement B. Penrose, and Frederick Bates, commissioners. It is the opinion of the Board that this claim ought not to be confirmed.

JOHN MULLANPHY, assignee of Dennis Tool, assignee of George Fallis.—A claim for seventy-six arpents of land, situate in the fields of St. Ferdinand, in the district of St. Louis. Produces to the Board a conveyance from said Fallis to said Tool, dated the 13th June, 1809; also, a conveyance from said Tool to claimant, dated the 25th March, 1805.

Opinion of the Board. November 17, 1809. This claim was decided on: Present, John B. C. Lucas, Clement B. Penrose, and Frederick Bates, commissioners. It is the opinion of the Board that this claim ought not to be confirmed.

ABRAHAM KEITHLEY.—A claim for three hundred arpents of land, situate on the river Cuivre, in the district of St. Charles. Produces, as a special permission to settle, a concession from Charles Dehault Delassus, dated February 4, 1801; also, a plat and certificate of survey of the same, dated the 10th of February, 1804.

Testimony taken. February 21, 1806. Isaac Hostetter, being duly sworn, says that the above claimant did actually cultivate the said tract of land, and raised crops thereon, in the years 1800 and 1801; that, in the spring of 1803, he was obliged to abandon the said tract of land, for fear of the Indians, who, at that time, committed depredations in that neighborhood; that, in the fall of the same year, he returned to the same, proceeded to the cultivating of it, living then with the witness, at a distance of about three miles; that, in the course of that year, he dug three wells, there being no water on said land; and that, about two years ago, to wit, in the beginning of 1804, he put up a cabin thereon, and has actually inhabited and cultivated the same to this day.

Opinion and remarks of the Board. February 21, 1806: Present, John B. C. Lucas and Clement B. Penrose, commissioners. The Board are unanimously of opinion that this is a case coming within the spirit of the law and their equity powers; and therefore they grant the above claimant three hundred arpents of land, as per the aforesaid concession.

Testimony taken. August 3, 1807. Isaac Hostetter, being duly sworn, says that the claimant had a wife and two children in the year 1803.

Opinion and remarks of the Board. November 20, 1809. This claim was decided on: Present, John B. C. Lucas and Clement B. Penrose, commissioners. It is the opinion of a majority of the Board that this claim ought not to be confirmed; Frederick Bates, commissioner, voting for the granting thereof.

SAMUEL LEWIS.—A claim, under the second section of the act, for one thousand and fifty arpents of land, situate on the river Peruque, in the district of St. Charles. Produces a certificate of a permission to settle from Charles Tayon, dated 27th February, 1806, together with a plat and certificate of survey of the same, dated 7th of December, 1805, certified to have been surveyed on the 15th of February, 1806.

Testimony taken. July 14, 1806. David Edwards, being duly sworn, says that one John Burnet settled the said tract of land in the year 1801; that, in 1803, towards the latter end of that year, he sold the same to claimant, having previously raised two crops; that claimant then moved on it, and actually inhabited it on the 20th day of December, 1803, and had then a very large stock on the same; and further, that he had, on the said 20th December, 1803, a wife, one child, and one slave.

Opinion and remarks of the Board. July 14, 1806: Present, John B. C. Lucas and Clement B. Penrose, commissioners. The Board reject this claim, for want of actual cultivation by claimant prior to and on the 20th December, 1803.

Opinion of the Board. November 20th, 1809. This claim was decided on: Present, John B. C. Lucas and Clement B. Penrose, commissioners. It is the opinion of the Board that this claim ought not to be granted.

CHRISTOPHER ZOOMALT.—A claim for seven hundred and fifty-six arpents of land, situate on the river Peruque, in the district of St. Charles. Produces a certificate of survey of said land, dated 20th January, 1806; also, for permission to settle, a certificate, sworn by James Mackay, commandant, the 21st of October, 1808.

Testimony taken. February 6, 1806. Angus Gellis, being duly sworn, says that the above claimant arrived in this country in the year 1799; that he begun the settlement of said land in the year 1801; that, when engaged in cultivating the same, he would inhabit it, but resided with his father after the gathering of his crops; that he had, in the year 1803, about ten arpents of land under fence, and raised one hundred bushels of corn on the same in that year; that his father is advanced in years, and has with him but one son, of about thirteen years of age; and that the distance from his establishment to his father's house is about two miles.

Opinion and remarks of the Board. February 6, 1806: Present, John B. C. Lucas and James L. Donaldson, commissioners. The Board reject this claim, said land not being actually inhabited on the 20th day of December, 1803; but think it a very hard case.

Testimony taken. August 4, 1807. Henry Zoomalt, being duly sworn, says that the claimant kept his stock of cattle, &c. on the aforesaid land in the year 1801, and has continued to keep and feed the same there until this day; and the deponent further saith that he and the claimant lived and slept on the land aforesaid in the year 1802, while making their crop.

Opinion of the Board. November 18, 1809. This claim was decided on: Present, John B. C. Lucas, Clement B. Penrose, and Frederick Bates, commissioners. It is the opinion of a majority of the Board that this claim ought not to be confirmed; Frederick Bates voting for the granting thereof.

DAVID COONRAD.—A claim for eight hundred and fifty arpents of land, situate on the river Peruque, in the district of St. Charles. Produces a plat and survey of the same, certified to have been made on the 24th January, 1806, and recorded with the surveyor the 14th of February, 1806.

Testimony taken. February 21, 1806. Christopher Zoomalt, being duly sworn, says that the said claimant begun his settlement of said tract of land some time in the fall of 1803, moved thereon with his family in the spring of 1804, and has actually inhabited and cultivated the same to this day.

Opinion of the Board. November 20, 1809. This claim was decided on: Present, John B. C. Lucas and Clement B. Penrose, commissioners. It is the opinion of the Board that this claim ought not to be granted.

PETER TIGUE.—A claim, under the second section of the act of Congress, for seven hundred and fifty-six arpents of land, situate on the Dardennes. district of St. Charles. Produces a certificate of permission to settle, granted by Charles Tayon, commandant of St. Charles, dated February 10, 1806, and a certificate of survey, dated the 3d December, 1805, and recorded with the surveyor on the 10th February, 1806.

Testimony taken. February 14, 1806. William McConnell, being duly sworn, says that the said claimant did cultivate said land in 1802, and did also, prior to and on the 20th day of December, 1803, actually cultivate the same; that he was then of the age of twenty-one years and upwards, had a cabin built on said land, and six arpents of the same cleared.

Opinion and remarks of the Board. February 14, 1806: Present, John B. C. Lucas, Clement B. Penrose, and James L. Donaldson, commissioners. The Board reject this claim, and think it a case of equity.

November 20, 1809. This claim was decided on: Present, John B. C. Lucas and Clement B. Penrose, commissioners. It is the opinion of the Board that this claim ought not to be granted.

JOHN McCONNELL (claiming, under the second section of the act of Congress, nine hundred and fifty-six arpents of land, situate on the river Dardennes, district of St. Charles,) produces a certificate of a permission to settle, granted by J. Mackay, commandant, dated February 10, 1806, and a certificate of survey of the said land, dated 27th January, 1806.

Testimony taken. February 12, 1806. James Boldridge, being duly sworn, says that the above claimant was, some time in September, 1803, of the age of twenty-one, and did then cultivate said tract of land.

Peter Tigue, being also sworn, says that the said land was actually cultivated prior to and on the 20th day of December, 1803, when he resided with his father; that his improvement and that of his father are joining, and under the same enclosures; that, about two years ago, the claimant married, moved on said land with his family, and has resided thereon to this day.

Opinion of the Board. November 20, 1809. This claim was decided on: Present, John B. C. Lucas and Clement B. Penrose, commissioners. It is the opinion of the Board that this claim ought not to be granted.

FRANCIS SMITH.—A claim, under the second section of the act of Congress, for four hundred arpents of land, situate on the Missouri, district of St. Charles. Produces a certificate of a permission to settle from J. Mackay, commandant of St. Andrew's, dated February 16, 1806; also a certificate of survey of the same, bearing the same date.

Opinion and remarks of the Board. February 17, 1806: Present, Clement B. Penrose and James L. Donaldson, commissioners. In consequence of a grant of two hundred and fifty arpents to claimant, the Board reject this claim.

November 20, 1809. This claim was decided on: Present, John B. C. Lucas and Clement B. Penrose, commissioners. It is the opinion of the Board that this claim ought not to be granted.

WILLIAM MEEK, assignee of Francis Woods.—A claim as aforesaid for two hundred and forty arpents of land, situate on the river Peruque, in the district of St. Charles. Produces a concession from Charles Dehault Delassus, Lieutenant Governor, dated 21st September, 1799, and a plat and certificate of the same, dated 27th December, 1803, certified to have been made the 14th of March, 1803; also a deed of transfer from Francis Woods to claimant dated the 13th of June, 1804.

Testimony taken. April 17th, 1806. John Home, being duly sworn, says that one William Linx did, in the spring of 1800, proceed to the improving of said land; cleared a few acres of the same, and moved on it in the month of May of that year, and remained thereon until the ensuing spring, when one Grosjean moved on the same, and made a garden.

David Bryan, being duly sworn, says that he was in company with the aforesaid Francis Woods in the year 1803, when he applied to James Mackay for a concession; that the said James Mackay promised him one; that the said Francis Woods arrived in the country in the year 1800, and that he (the witness) never heard of his, (the said Woods) or any one for him, having applied for a concession before, neither does he know whether the said Woods holds any other claim to lands in his own name in the Territory; and further, that he (the witness) knew the before-named Grosjean on said land, in the spring of 1801, when he sold the same to the said Francis Woods; in the spring of 1802 the said Woods exchanged the said tract for another tract, the property of one Crow; that, in the month of December, 1803, he (the said Woods) made a second exchange of the tract he had from said Crow for the one he formerly held, and gave said Crow forty dollars to boot; the said tract having augmented in value by the improvements made on the same.

Being interrogated whether said Woods was one of Colonel Boone's followers, he said no, but came into the country with one Hancock; and further, that he (the witness) was present when one Stockdale, who arrived in the country in 1800, applied for a concession, witness believes about the time the said Woods made his application; and that he obtained one, but does not know when.

James Mackay, being also sworn, and being interrogated as to the hand-writing of the petition of the said Woods, said he believed it to be his.

Being asked whether the said concession was signed at the time it bears date, refused to answer; but said that the facts stated in the petition, as ground for concession, were a mere routine.

Opinion of the Board and remarks. April 17, 1806: Present, John B. C. Lucas and James L. Donaldson, commissioners. The Board being satisfied that the aforesaid concession is a fraudulent and an antedated one, reject this claim; they however think it a case of hardship.

November 20, 1809. This claim was decided on: Present, John B. C. Lucas and Clement B. Penrose, commissioners. It is the opinion of the Board that this claim ought not to be confirmed.

DAVID McKINNEY.—A claim for five hundred and ninety arpents of land, situate on Femme Osage, district of St. Charles. Produces a concession from Charles Dehault Delassus, Lieutenant Governor, dated June 20, 1800, together with a plat and certificate of survey of the same, dated the 27th December, 1803, and certified to have been made on the 8th of November, 1803.

Testimony taken. April 14th, 1806. Kinkaid Caldwell, being duly sworn, says, that some time in the year 1800, being at James Mackay's, he was by him informed that one Francis Wayat had arrived from the county of Montgomery, in the State of Kentucky, and had applied for lands in behalf of a number of persons of that country, wishing to remove to this; and that the said Mackay showed the witness a list of the names of the applicants, of whom the said claimant was one. David Bryan, being also sworn, says that the said claimant improved the said land in the year 1804, and raised a crop thereon.

Opinion of the Board. November 29th, 1809. This claim was decided on: Present, John B. C. Lucas and Clement B. Penrose, commissioners. It is the opinion of the Board that this claim ought not to be granted.

DAVID KINCAID.—A claim, under the second section of the act of Congress, for five hundred arpents of land, situate on the forks of the river Charrette, district of St. Charles. Produces a special permission to settle a concession from Charles Dehault Delassus, Lieutenant Governor, dated the 14th of January, 1803, and certified to have been surveyed the 27th February, 1806.

Testimony taken. April 2d, 1806. Kinkaid Caldwell, being duly sworn, says, that the claimant, having purchased the right of one Francis Woods to the said land, who had then a cabin on the same, did, in the year 1803, proceed to the building of a house; that he had then a family, consisting of himself, wife, and eight children; and that, early in the spring of 1804, he moved on the said land, and has actually inhabited and cultivated it to this day.

Opinion of the Board. November 20th, 1809: Present, John B. C. Lucas and Clement B. Penrose, commissioners. It is the opinion of the Board that this claim ought not to be granted.

NOEL ANTOINE PRIEUR.—A claim for two lots of land, situate in the village of St. Charles, containing one hundred and twenty feet front, and three hundred back, by virtue of an order of survey from Zenon Trudeau, Lieutenant Governor, dated the 17th June, 1797.

Testimony taken. August 4th, 1807. Francis Duquette, being duly sworn, says that he knows the lots above described, and that he assisted M. Mackay in surveying the same for the claimant, and that he, the witness, gave the claimant a small house; and that, while in the act of pulling it down, he had one of his legs broken, in consequence of which it was amputated; and the deponent further says that the aforesaid claimant was chaunter of the church in said village, and clerk to the commandant of the same.

Opinion of the Board. November 20th 1809: Present, John B. C. Lucas and Clement B. Penrose, commissioners. It is the opinion of the Board that this claim ought not to be confirmed.

NOEL ANTOINE PRIEUR.—A claim, under the second section of the act of Congress, for four hundred arpents of land, on the Dardennes, district of St. Charles. Produces a limited permission to settle from Charles Dehault Delassus, Lieutenant Governor, dated the 3d September, 1801, and a survey of the same taken the 23d December, 1803, and certified the 23d January, 1804.

Testimony taken. August 8th 1806. Etienne Bernard, being duly sworn, says, that in 1804 claimant began the building of a house on said land, cleared a field, raised a crop, and has actually inhabited and cultivated the same to this day; and further, that he had, on the 20th day of December, 1803, a wife and two children.

Opinion and remarks of the Board. August 8th 1806: Present, John B. C. Lucas, commissioner. The Board reject this claim for want of actual inhabitation and cultivation prior to and on the 20th December, 1803, and observe that claimant was, under the Spanish Government, a public officer; that, when in the act of preparing for building on said land, in the year 1801, a large piece of timber fell on his leg, and broke it; that, in that situation, he was then obliged to relinquish his plan of building, having no person to assist him, and not being in a situation to employ any one to do it for him. Approved, August 12th, 1806.

November, 20th 1809: Present, John B. C. Lucas and Clement B. Penrose, commissioners. It is the opinion of the Board that this claim ought not to be confirmed

JOSEPH VOISARD.—A claim of eight hundred and fifty arpents of land, near the river Dardennes, in the district of St. Charles, by virtue of inhabitation the 20th of December, 1803.

Testimony taken. August 4th, 1807. Noel Antoine Prieur, being duly sworn, says, that he knows a piece of land owned by claimant which is situate on the river Dardennes, near one George Girtie's land, and that the said claimant cultivated the aforesaid land in the year 1803, and that in the year 1804 he raised corn on said land, and that there have been four crops raised there; and further, that the claimant has about twelve arpents in cultivation.

Opinion of the Board. November 21st, 1809: Full Board. It is the opinion of the Board that this claim ought not to be granted.

GEORGES HOFFMAN, SEN.—A claim, under the second section of the act of Congress, for eight hundred and fifty-six arpents of land, situate on the river Peruque, district of St. Charles. Produces a certificate of a permission to settle from Charles Tayon, commandant, dated 5th February, 1806; also a plat of survey of the same, dated the 5th of December, 1805, and certificate of the same, dated the 11th February, 1806.

Testimony taken. February 14th, 1806. Nicholas Coontz, being duly sworn, says that one William Harrington put up a cabin on said land, and settled the same in the year 1800.

John Scott, being also duly sworn, says that the above claimant did actually inhabit and cultivate said land in the years 1801 and 1802, and that in that year the above-named William Harrington acknowledged before him that he had sold his right to said land by virtue of his improvement to the above claimant; that, in the said year, 1802, he moved out of it; that, having married in 1804, he returned on said land with his family; has resided thereon to this day. He renounces any other claim to land in his own name in this Territory.

Opinion and remarks of the Board. February 14, 1806: Full Board. The Board reject this claim, and think it a case of equity.

November 21, 1809: Full Board. It is the opinion of the Board that this claim ought not to be granted.

EDWARD HEMPSTEAD, assignee of John Cook.—A claim for two arpents of front, by forty arpents in depth, of land, situate adjoining the field lots of the village of St. Charles, in pursuance of a permission from Charles Tayon, Spanish commandant of St. Charles, to said T. Cook, dated September 18, 1800, which has been produced; also a plat of survey of the same, dated the 16th of February, 1806, and certified to have been recorded with the surveyor the 28th February, 1806; and also a deed of conveyance from John Cook to claimant, dated May 31, 1805.

Testimony taken. August 5, 1807. Nicholas Coontz, being duly sworn, says that, in the year 1798, he, the witness, ploughed part of said tract of land for the use of said Cook, the original claimant; that said Cook did raise corn on the land aforesaid, either in the year 1797 or 1798, and did continue to raise corn during four or five years from that time; and that said Cook was the head of a family at that time, and had a wife and six children.

William McConnel, also sworn, says that the aforesaid land was cultivated in the year 1797, and was cultivated from that time until the year 1804.

Opinion of the Board. November 21, 1809: Full Board. It is the opinion of the Board that this claim ought not to be granted.

STEPHEN JACKSON.—Claiming, under the second section of the act of Congress, four hundred and twenty arpents of land, situate on the river Tuque, district of St. Charles. Produces, as a special permission to settle, a concession from Charles Dehault Delassus, Lieutenant Governor, dated February 15, 1803, together with a plat and certificate of survey of the same, dated the 12th of November, 1803, and certified the 13th April, 1804.

Testimony taken. February 10, 1806. William Hancock, being duly sworn, says that he knows the said land; that the same was not cultivated until the fall of 1802, when the said claimant made a garden thereon, and raised turnips; that the said claimant was, in the spring of 1803, prevented from cultivating said land by sickness; and that, having recovered from the same, he was obliged to hire himself to work, in order to be enabled to pay James Mackay the amount of a note he had given him, amounting to forty-eight dollars, dated November 12, 1803, being the price of said concession; that the said James Mackay told the witness, who had applied to him for a concession in favor of said claimant, that the times were changed, and that he was very sorry for it, but that he should have to charge him ten dollars per hundred arpents for said concession; and further, that he, the claimant, had rented from the witness a piece of land on which he resided, being distant from the tract above claimed of one half mile; and that the said Jackson has actually inhabited and cultivated said tract of land from the fall of 1804 to this day. He claims no other land in his own name in this Territory.

Opinion and remarks of the Board. February 10, 1806: Full Board. The Board reject this claim, but think it a hard case.

November 21, 1809: Full Board. It is the opinion of the Board that this claim ought not to be granted.

ARTHUR BURNS.—Claiming, under the second section of the act of Congress, eight hundred arpents of land, situate on the Femme Osage, district of St. Charles. Produces a survey certified the 15th of February, 1806, and entered on the surveyor's books the 24th February, 1806.

Testimony taken. July 14, 1806. Albert Tison, being duly sworn, says that he saw, held, and read, a special permission to settle, granted by Charles Dehault Delassus, Lieutenant Governor, to claimant.

Squire Boon, being duly sworn, says that claimant settled the said tract of land in the year 1800, and did, prior to and on the 20th day of December, 1803, actually inhabit and cultivate the said tract of land, and had then a wife and eleven children.

Opinion and remarks of the Board. July 14, 1806: Present, John B. C. Lucas and Clement B. Penrose, commissioners. The Board grant the said claimant seven hundred and fifty arpents of land, situate as aforesaid, provided so much be found vacant there.

November 21, 1819: Full Board. It is the opinion of a majority of the Board that this claim ought not to be granted; Frederick Bates, commissioner, voting for the granting thereof.

ARTHUR BURNS.—A claim of eight hundred arpents of land, situate on the waters of the river Mississippi, in the district of St. Louis. Produces to the Board a concession for the same, from Don Carlos Dehault Delassus, Lieutenant Governor, dated the 25th May, 1800; also a plat of survey of the same, dated the 1st of February, 1804, and certified the 20th March, 1804.

Opinion of the Board. November 21, 1809: Full Board. It is the opinion of the Board that this claim ought not to be confirmed.

JULIUS EMMONS, assignee of John Linsey, who was assignee of William Ewing.—A claim, under the second section of the act of Congress, for seven hundred and forty-four arpents of land, situate on the waters of the river Mississippi, in the district of St. Charles. Produces a survey of the same, dated 11th February, 1806; a deed of transfer from one William Ewing to said John Lindsey, dated October 16th, 1804; and another deed of transfer from said Linsey to claimant, dated January 6, 1806.

Testimony taken. July 15, 1806. William Ewing, being duly sworn, says that the said William Ewing settled the said tract of land in the year 1801, and did, prior to and on the 20th day of December, 1803, actually inhabit and cultivate the said tract of land, and had then a wife and three children.

Opinion and remarks of the Board. July 15, 1806: Present, John B. C. Lucas, commissioner. The Board reject this claim for want of permission to settle. Approved the above minutes, July 17, 1806.

November 22, 1809: Present, John B. C. Lucas, Clement B. Penrose, and Frederick Bates, commissioners. It is the opinion of the Board that this claim ought not to be granted.

JAMES MACKAY.—A claim of thirty thousand arpents of land. Produces a concession from Charles Dehault Delassus, Lieutenant Governor, dated the 13th of October, 1799; a survey of thirteen thousand eight hundred and thirty-five arpents of land, on the river Cuivre, taken May 25th, 1801, and certified 8th March, 1802; a survey of five hundred and forty-five arpents of land, situate on same river, taken 29th December, 1802, and certified 28th February, 1806; another survey of five thousand two hundred and eighty arpents of land, situate on the Missouri, taken the 20th December, 1804, and certified the 28th February, 1806; and, lastly, a survey of ten thousand three hundred and forty arpents of land, taken the 7th February, 1803. The Board having required further proof, the said claimant produced a passport from Zenon Trudeau to him, as agent of the commercial company of the river Missouri, on a voyage of discovery up said river, undertaken by the orders of the Baron de Carondelet, and which was to last six years; a letter from Don Manuel Gayoso de Lemos, the Intendant General at New Orleans, dated the 20th May, 1799, wherein he much approves of the conduct of claimant as commandant, commends the steps taken by him for the opening of roads and establishing good police regulations, both military and civil, with the view to the aggrandizement of his post, and informing further that he has recommended him very particularly to the then Lieutenant Governor of the province, Charles Dehault Delassus.

Testimony taken. July 22, 1806. George Fallis, being duly sworn, says that, in the year 1799, one John Wealthy built a cabin on a small piece of land, which he fenced in; that he lived on the same for about one year, when he made a present of his improvement to one Keithley, who, having remained on it until Christmas of the year 1801, gave it up to one Rhodes, who afterwards gave it to witness; that the same was afterwards surveyed by claimant, in consequence of a purchase from the said Rhodes; that he, the witness, never heard of a concession for the said tract of land, and that the same was surveyed after his, the witness's, removal from the same; and further, that the said small improvement was surveyed in the aforesaid tract of ———— on the ————.

Objections of the agent of the United States. The agent of the United States objects to the aforesaid concession, on the grounds of its being antedated, and otherwise fraudulent; he also objects to two surveys made on part of the aforesaid concession, one for thirteen thousand eight hundred and thirty-five, the other for ten thousand three hundred and forty, on the grounds aforesaid. Further proof is required of the party.

Opinion of the Board. November 4, 1809: Present, John B. C. Lucas and Clement B. Penrose, commissioners. It is the opinion of the Board that this claim ought not to be confirmed.

BENJAMIN SPENCER.—A claim, under the second section of the act of Congress, for eight hundred arpents of land, situate on the river Grand Glaize, district of St. Charles. Produces, as a special permission to settle, a concession from Charles Dehault Delassus, Lieutenant Governor, dated the 5th of May, 1801, and a plat and certificate of survey of the same, dated 20th March, 1804.

Testimony taken. July 14, 1806. Charles Tremont, being duly sworn, says that claimant settled said tract of land in November 1803, built a house on the same, dug a well, and actually inhabited it on the 20th day of December, 1803; that, in the year 1804, he had a field under enclosure, and was then working at a saline on said land; and further, that he has actually inhabited and cultivated the same to this day; and had, on the 20th day of December, 1803, three children.

Opinion of the Board. July 14th, 1806: Present, John B. C. Lucas and Clement B. Penrose, commissioners. The Board reject this claim for want of actual cultivation on the 20th day of December, 1803.

November 22d, 1809: Present, John B. C. Lucas and Clement B. Penrose, commissioners. It is the opinion of the Board that this claim ought not to be confirmed.

JAMES KERR.—A claim for twelve hundred arpents of land, situate on the river Dardennes, district of St. Charles. Produces a concession from Don Zenon Trudeau, Lieutenant Governor, dated March 4th, 1798; and a certificate of survey of the same, dated January 11th, 1800.

Testimony taken. June 14th, 1806. Andrew Sommalt, being duly sworn, says that one-half of the aforesaid tract of land so conceded is of a very bad quality, and on the frontiers; that the said claimant begun his settlement of the same in the year 1799; that he did, prior to and on the 1st day of October, 1800, actually inhabit and cultivate the same, and was, at the time of obtaining said concession, the head of a family.

August 6th, 1807. Henry Zomalt, being duly sworn, says that the claimant actually inhabited and cultivated the aforesaid twelve hundred arpents of land since the year 1799 until this day.

Opinion and remarks of the Board. June 14th, 1806: Full Board. The Board, being of opinion that, from a strict interpretation of the act of Congress, and the letter of the Spanish regulations, the quantity of land which could be lawfully granted by the Lieutenant Governor to a new settler cannot exceed the quantity of eight hundred arpents, confirm to the said claimant eight hundred arpents of land, situate as aforesaid, and reject four hundred arpents, the remaining quantity of said concession.

November 22d, 1809: Present, full Board. It is the opinion of a majority of the Board that this claim ought not to be confirmed; Clement B. Penrose, commissioner, voting for the confirmation thereof. The said majority do declare that, if the above claim had not exceeded eight hundred arpents, they would have voted for its confirmation.

JAMES JONES, assignee of George Ayrey, assignee of Thomas Howell, who was assignee of Timothy Kibby.— A claim for six hundred and forty arpents of land, situate on the river Dardennes, district of St. Charles. Produces a notice to the recorder, dated the 5th of August, 1807.

Testimony taken. August 6th, 1807. John Wildan, being duly sworn, says that in the spring of the year 1803 Timothy Kibby built a cabin, and settled on the aforesaid claim on the 17th of November of the same year, and also raised a crop on said claim in the year 1803, and that there have been crops raised on the same every year since. The witness also says that he saw the claimant living on said land in the latter part of the winter of 1805, and that he has been living there ever since.

Opinion of the Board. November 22d, 1809: Full Board. It is the opinion of the Board that this claim ought not to be granted.

HENRY STEPHENSON, assignee of Arthur Burns.—A claim, under the second section of the act of Congress, for one thousand and eighty arpents of land, situate on the river Peruque, district of St. Charles. Produces a survey of the same, dated the 7th of December, 1805. The claimant declares that he only purchased the labor of said Burns on said land, and does not claim any title to the aforesaid land through him.

Testimony taken. July 29th, 1806. John Lafleur, being duly sworn, says that one Burns, having raised two or three crops on said land, sold his right to the same to the said claimant, who moved on it in March, 1804, and has actually inhabited and cultivated the same to this day. The said Burns had a wife and five children.

Adam Martin, being duly sworn, says that he was present, in July, 1803, when claimant applied for and received permission to settle, from James Mackay, who was then a commandant.

Opinion of the Board. November 22d, 1809: Full Board. It is the opinion of the Board that this claim ought not to be granted.

CLAIBOURNE RHODES.—A claim, under the second section of the act of Congress, for six hundred arpents of land, situate on the waters of the river Mississippi, in the district of St. Charles. Produces a special permission to settle, from Charles Dehault Delassus, Lieutenant Governor, dated the 17th February, 1800; and a survey of the same, taken the 30th of December, 1803, and certified the 20th of January, 1804.

Testimony taken. July 16th, 1806. William Ewing, being duly sworn, says that the said claimant did, some time in the fall of 1803, cut house logs, with the intent of building a distillery; that, at that period, the Indians seeming inclined to hostilities, he did not think it prudent to proceed any further in the same.

Samuel Griffith, being also duly sworn, says that, about the time claimant was preparing for the aforesaid distillery, three young men were killed by the Indians at a very small distance from the aforesaid tract; that claimant, fearing a repetition of the same, gave up his plan of said building; that the first knowledge he, the witness, had of claimant's intention of building said distillery, was derived from the persons whom he had engaged for the building of the same; that he had, prior to that period, improved another tract of land, situate at the Portage des Sioux; that he cultivated the same for three years consecutively, to wit, in the years 1798, 1799, and 1800; that he did afterwards, at the request of the Lieutenant Governor, and upon the promise of another tract, move out of the same, and relinquish his right thereto, having prior to that complied with the Spanish law and regulations, whereby three years of cultivation vested in the cultivator the right of domain.

Opinion and remarks of the Board. July 16, 1806: Present, John B. C. Lucas, commissioner. The Board reject this claim, and observe that claimant lived in the Territory on the 20th December, 1803.

Approved the above minutes, July 22d, 1806.

November 24th, 1809: Present, John B. C. Lucas and Frederick Bates, commissioners. It is the opinion of the Board that this claim ought not to be confirmed.

ANDREW REED.—A claim for seven hundred and fifty arpents of land, situate on the waters of the river St. François, in the district of Cape Girardeau. Produces a certificate of survey of the same, dated January 29th, 1806.

Testimony taken. May 5th, 1806. Jesse Smith, being duly sworn, says that the claimant is by trade a blacksmith; that he settled the said tract of land in 1801; that in 1802 he went out of the country; that, having returned in 1803, he raised on said tract of land a crop; that he had a house built on the same, which he did actually inhabit

10   LAND GRANTS IN MISSOURI TERRITORY - 1805 - 1812

****

when cultivating the said tract of land; that he went out hunting, but always left in said house or cabin his said utensils or implements of husbandry, and always considered said house as his actual residence; and further, that he raised on said land seventy or eighty bushels of corn in 1803; was then of the age of twenty-one years and upwards.

Opinion and remarks of the Board. May 5th, 1806: Present, Clement B. Penrose and James L. Donaldson, commissioners. The Board grant the claimant one hundred arpents of land, situated as aforesaid, provided so much be found vacant there.

November 25th, 1809. On application, the Board agree to take testimony in the above claim.

Testimony taken. November 25th, 1809. Joseph Coke, being duly sworn, says that, in the year 1801, he went with claimant to a commandant of Cape Girardeau, whom he believes to be Lorimier, but will not be positive as to his name; that said commandant gave permission at that time to claimant to settle.

Opinion of the Board. November 25th, 1809: Full Board. It is the opinion of the Board that this claim ought not to be granted.

John Mullanphy, assignee of Joseph Lacroix, assignee of François St. Cir, by a public sale.—A claim for six hundred arpents of land, situate on the river Philip, in the district of St. Louis. Produces a concession for the same from Don Carlos Dehault Delassus, Lieutenant Governor, to François St. Cir, dated the 1st of December, 1800; also a plat of survey of the same, dated the 9th of January, 1802, and certified the 2d of March, 1802; and a conveyance from Joseph Lacroix to claimant, dated the 31st of June, 1805.

Opinion of the Board. November 25th, 1809: Full Board. It is the opinion of the Board that this claim ought not to be confirmed.

James Morrison, assignee of James Batey, assignee of John Littlejohn.—A claim for seven hundred and fifty arpents of land, situate on the river Femme Osage, district of St. Charles. Produces a plat and certificate of survey, dated the 3d, and certified the 12th February, 1806; also a deed of conveyance from said Littlejohn to James Batey, dated the 24th October, 1804; and a deed from said Batey to said Morrison, dated the 18th February, 1806.

Testimony taken. August 6th, 1807. James Vanbibber, being duly sworn, says that Daniel Boon, commandant of Femme Osage district, gave permission to claimant to settle about the last of October, 1803.

David Kinkaid, being duly sworn, says that, on the 23d of October, 1803, he saw the said Littlejohn had a cabin built, and was clearing land on the above claim; and that he was raising corn in 1804.

Opinion of the Board. November 25th, 1809: Full Board. It is the opinion of the Board that this claim ought not to be granted.

David Darst, Junior.—A claim for two hundred and sixty arpents of land, situate on the Femme Osage, district of St. Charles. Produces a concession from Don Zenon Trudeau, dated 1st June, 1797, and a certificate of survey of two hundred and sixty-four arpents, dated the 8th of July, 1798.

Testimony taken. February 11th, 1806. William McConnell, being duly sworn, says that he is well acquainted with the above claimant; that he is a cripple, and weakly, and of the age of about fourteen; he further says that he was present when the above concession was granted to claimant; that it was intended as a support for said child. The above tract joins the land conceded to David Darst, the father of the claimant.

Opinion of the Board. November 29th, 1809: Full Board. It is the opinion of the Board that this claim ought not to be confirmed.

Isaac Darst.—A claim for three hundred and fifty arpents of land. Produces a concession from Charles Dehault Delassus, Lieutenant Governor, dated the 10th of March, 1803, and a plat and certificate of survey, certified the 28th of March, 1804.

Opinion of the Board. November 29th, 1809: Full Board. It is the opinion of the Board that this claim ought not to be confirmed.

James Vanbibber.—A claim for four hundred and twenty-six arpents of land, situate on the waters of the Missouri, district of St. Charles. Produces a certificate of survey, dated February 27th, 1806.

Testimony taken. April 7th, 1806: Jonathan Bryan, being duly sworn, says that claimant did, prior to and on the 20th day of December, 1803, actually inhabit and cultivate the said tract of land, and had then a wife and three children.

Opinion and remarks of the Board. April 7, 1806: Present, John B. C. Lucas and Clement B. Penrose, commissioners. The Board grant the said claimant one thousand arpents of land, situate as aforesaid, provided so much be found vacant there.

November 29, 1804: Full Board. It is the opinion of the Board that this claim ought not to be granted.

Nathan Boone, assignee of Robert Hall.—A claim for eight hundred arpents of land, situate on Femme Osage, district of St. Charles. Produces, as a special permission to settle, a concession from Don Zenon Trudeau, Lieutenant Governor, dated January 26, 1798, to said Robert Hall, and a certificate of survey of said land, dated 10th January, 1800.

Testimony taken. February 3, 1806. Jonathan Bryan, being duly sworn, says that the said tract of land was settled by the above Robert Hall in December, 1799; that he, the said Hall left the country prior to 1st October, 1800, and has never returned, and that the above claimant did, prior to and on the 28th day of December, 1803, actually inhabit and cultivate the same, being then the head of a family.

August 6, 1807. Isaac Vanbibber, being duly sworn, says that, immediately after Robert Hall left said land, Nathan Boone settled on it, raised a crop in 1800, and has inhabited and cultivated it ever since.

Opinion and remarks of the Board. February 13, 1806: Full Board. The Board grant the above claimant eight hundred arpents of land, as per the above concession.

December 1, 1809: Full Board. It is the opinion of a majority of the Board that this claim ought not to be granted; Frederick Bates, commissioner, being of opinion that this claim ought to be confirmed to Robert Hall, or his legal representatives, under the fourth section of the act of 1807.

Jeremiah Grojean, assignee of George Weiland.—A claim of three hundred arpents of land, situate on the river Cuivre, district of St. Charles. Produces a concession from Don Charles Dehault Delassus, Lieutenant Governor, dated the 10th of October, 1799, together with a plat and certificate of survey, dated 20th January, 1804; also, a certified copy of a deed of conveyance from said Weiland to claimant, dated the 20th of January, 1804.

LAND GRANTS IN MISSOURI TERRITORY - 1805 - 1812   11

****

Testimony taken. August 6, 1807. James Lewis, being duly sworn, says that he knows the fields near Christopher Clark's, and that the claimant has cultivated the aforesaid land two or three year's; and that the field cultivated contains eight or ten acres.

Objection of the agent of the United States. August 6, 1807. The agent of the United States alleges fraud and antedate. The Board require further proof.

Opinion of the Board. December 1, 1809: Full Board. It is the opinion of the Board that this claim ought not to be confirmed.

Colonel DANIEL BOONE.—A claim for one thousand arpents of land, situate on Femme Osage, district of St. Charles. Produces a concession from Don Zenon Trudeau, Lieutenant Governor, dated January 24th, 1798, and a certificate of survey of the same, dated January 9, 1800; also, a letter from Don Zenon Trudeau to him, dated in the year 1798, inviting him to remove, with his family, to Louisiana, with the promise of a grant of land; and also a commission from Don Charles D. Delassus, Lieutenant Governor, to him, said claimant, dated 11th July, 1800, appointing him commandant of the district of the Femme Osage.

Colonel D. Boone stated to the Board, that, on his arrival in Louisiana, he took up his residence, with his lady, at his son Daniel M. Boone's, in the said district of Femme Osage, and adjoining the lands he now claims; that they remained there until about two years ago, when he moved to a younger son's, Nathan Boone, where he now lives It is proved that the said claimant is of the age of about seventy years, and his wife about sixty-eight. He further stated, that, having inquired of Charles D. Delassus as to the propriety of improving and settling his land within a year and a day from the date of the concession, as directed by the Spanish laws, he was informed by said Delassus, that, being commandant of the said district, he need not trouble himself about the cultivating of the same as, by the commission he held of commandant of said district, he was not considered as coming within the meaning of said laws.

Testimony taken. February 13, 1806. Jonathan Bryan, being duly sworn, says that he knew Colonel Dania Boone in this country in the year 1800.

Opinion of the Board. December 1, 1809: Full Board. It is the opinion of the Board that this claim ought not to be confirmed.

JAMES LEWIS.—A claim of four hundred arpents of land, situate on the river Cuivre, district of St. Charles Produces, as a special permission to settle, a concession from Don Charles Dehault Delassus, Lieutenant Governor, dated September 21, 1799, and a certificate of survey of the same, dated January 20, 1804.

Testimony taken. February 17, 1806. William Linn, being duly sworn, says that the aforesaid tract of land lies on the frontiers, and at great distance from any other plantations; that the claimant actually inhabited and cultivated the same in the beginning of 1804; that, in the spring of that year, he was obliged to leave it, the Indians having about that time killed three white men in that neighborhood; and that he returned on the same in the fall of that year, and has actually inhabited and cultivated it to this day.

Objection of the agent of the United States. August 6, 1807. The agent of the United alleges against said concession fraud and antedate. The Board require further proof.

Opinion of the Board. December 1, 1809: Full Board. It is the opinion of the Board that this claim ought not to be confirmed.

JACOB GROJEAN.—A claim for four hundred arpents of land, situate on the river Cuivre, district of St. Charles. Produces, as a special permission to settle, a concession from Don Charles Dehault Delassus, Lieutenant Governor, dated September the 20th, 1799; and a certificate of survey of the same, January 20, 1804.

Testimony taken. February 15, 1806. William Linn, being duly sworn, says that the above claimant had a small cabin on said land in December, 1803; that, in the beginning of 1804, he built up a larger one, moved his family on said land, and has to this day actually inhabited and cultivated the same.

Opinion and remarks of the Board. February 15, 1806: Present, John B. C. Lucas and Clement B. Penrose, commissioners. The Board reject this claim, but think it a case of equity.

Objection of the agent of the United States. August 6, 1807. The agent of the United States alleges fraud and antedate.

Opinion of the Board. December 1, 1809: Full Board. It is the opinion of the Board that this claim ought not to be confirmed.

JOSEPH CHARTRAN.—A claim for nine hundred and ninety-eight arpents of land, situate on the river Charrette, district of St. Charles. Produces a survey of the same, dated the 1st February, 1805.

Testimony taken. July 31, 1806. Charles Tayon, being duly sworn, says that, when he was commandant of St. Charles, the above claimant applied to him for permission to settle on vacant lands; that he then submitted the said application to Zenon Trudeau, Lieutenant Governor, who told him he might grant the said permission; that the said claimant settled the said tract of land in the year 1801, and did, prior to and on the 20th day of December, 1803, actually inhabit and cultivate the same, and had then a wife and four or five orphan children, entirely destitute of the means of subsistence, and looking up to the claimant for the same.

August 7, 1807. John B. Leauzon, being duly sworn, says that he knows the land claimed by the said Chartran, situate at the village Charrette; that the same was settled by claimant in the year 1801, and that he has continued to inhabit and cultivate the same ever since; that the said claimant has generally had four orphan children with him looking up to him for support, and whom he has treated with tenderness, and in every respect as a good father would treat his own; that, in 1803, he had three of them with him.

Opinion of the Board. July 31, 1806: John B. C. Lucas attended the Board. The Board grant the said claimant two hundred arpents of land, situate as aforesaid.

December 1, 1809: Full Board. It is the opinion of the Board that this claim ought not to be granted.

JAMES MORRISON, assignee of William McHugh.—A claim for one thousand three hundred and twenty arpents of land. Produces a deed from the said McHugh and his wife, dated 23d April, 1803; and a plat and certificate of survey, dated February 14, 1806, and certified 21st February, 1806.

Testimony taken. August 7, 1807. Jonathan Bryant, being duly sworn, says that he knows the above claim, and that William McHugh settled on it in 1801, and lived in a camp until some time in July of the same year; planted about two acres of corn and tended it; and that he and the greatest part of his family were taken sick and moved away, and that he had a wife and nine children at that time.

William Ewing, being duly sworn, says that the said McHugh had some of his cattle killed by the Indians, and the witness says he saw the Indians carrying away some beef they had killed at the same time; and that he was living in the house with said McHugh, and that he was alarmed, and believes that said McHugh and the rest of his family were also; that, in consequence, they all moved off; and that they were ten or twelve miles beyond any other settlement; and that the said McHugh had three children killed by the Indians at the place of his last removal, about the year 1804.

Opinion of the Board. December 2, 1809: Full Board. It is the opinion of the Board that this claim ought not to be granted.

ABRAHAM DARST.—A claim for four hundred arpents of land, situate on the waters of Charrette, district of St. Charles. Produces a concession from Don Charles Dehault Delassus, Lieutenant Governor, dated 10th of October, 1799; also a plat and certificate of survey, dated the 2d of December, 1801, and certified the 17th of September, 1802.

Testimony taken. August 7, 1807. Thomas Smith, being duly sworn, says, that in January, 1804, he went with claimant to said tract, and aided him in clearing some land and planting an apple orchard; and the next fall went back with claimant, built a house, fenced the orchard, and planted turnips; and that there has been nothing done on said land since.

Objection of the agent of the United States. August 7, 1807. The agent of the United States alleges fraud and antedate. The Board require further proof.

Opinion of the Board. December 2, 1809: Present, John B. C. Lucas and Frederick Bates, commissioners. It is the opinion of the Board that this claim ought not to be confirmed.

JOHN BAPTISTE BELLAND, in the right of his wife, the widow of Peter Peltier, who was assignee of Joseph Robidoux.—A claim for a lot in the village of St. Charles, bounded by the first high street, on one side by Duplessis, on the other by a parade ground, and in the rear by the Missouri. Produces a certified copy of a deed of sale from Robidoux and wife to claimant, dated 26th July, 1804.

Testimony taken. July 31st, 1806. Charles Tayon, being duly sworn, says that a house was built on said lot about ten years ago, by one John B. Senecal, and that the same has been actually inhabited and cultivated to this day.

Opinion of the Board. July 31st, 1806. The honorable John B. C. Lucas attended the Board. The Board reject this claim for want of a duly registered warrant of survey.

December 2d, 1809: Present, John B. C. Lucas and Frederick Bates, commissioners. It is the opinion of the Board that this claim ought not to be granted.

NATHANIEL SIMONDS.—A claim for four hundred and ten arpents of land, situate on the river Cuivre, district of St. Charles. Produces a special permission to settle, from Charles Dehault Delassus, dated February 4, 1801; and a survey of the same, dated January 3, and certified February 10, 1804.

Testimony taken. July 15, 1806: Zadock Woods, being duly sworn, says that the claimant settled said tract of land in the year 1802; and did, prior to and on the 20th day of December, 1803, actually inhabit and cultivate the same; and had then three children.

August 7, 1807. Isaac Cottle, being duly sworn, says that the claimant moved on the aforesaid land in 1802; raised a crop that year; and that in 1802 his wife died there, and that the claimant did not reside on said land, he believes, for two years after; residing in the intermediate time at St. Louis and St. Charles.

William Farnsworth, being duly sworn, says that the claimant was living on his land in December, 1803, and that the witness heard him chopping wood; also says that the claimant had a son living with him at that time.

Silvenius Cottle, being duly sworn, says that the claimant went on the land claimed in May, 1802, with his family, and built a cabin, and broke up some ground, and that the claimant's wife died in September following; and that he continued to inhabit until the next spring; and that he then left his place, and was absent about one year, and returned to the place in 1804, and has inhabited and cultivated the same ever since.

Jonathan Woods, being duly sworn, says that the claimant moved on his land about the 25th of May, 1802; that he, the witness, saw ground ploughed, corn planted and coming up on said land; that he, the witness, was sick the remaining part of this season; and further says, that the claimant's wife died about the 4th of September, and that he, the witness, was convalescent, and went to the house at that time, and saw claimant there residing, and the claimant brought his family to the witness's house to reside, where one of them died fifteen days after; and that the claimant, with the rest of his family, removed to Warran Cottle's; and that said claimant was, during the greatest part of the summer of 1803, at St. Louis; and that he returned to his land in the latter part of November, 1803, but had no crop growing that fall; and that it has been the place of his residence ever since.

Ira Cottle, being duly sworn, says that, to the best of his knowledge, the claimant resided on said land on the 20th of December, 1803.

Opinion of the Board. July 15, 1806: Present, John B. C. Lucas, commissioner. The Board grant the said claimant two hundred and fifty arpents of land, situate as aforesaid, provided so much be found vacant there. Approved the above minutes, July 22d, 1806.

December 2d, 1809: Full Board. It is the opinion of the Board that this claim ought not to be granted.

FRANCIS ROY.—A claim for eight hundred arpents of land, situate on the river Mississippi, district of St. Charles.

LOUIS ROY.—A claim for eight hundred arpents of land, situate as aforesaid.

BAPTISTE ROY.—A claim for eight hundred arpents of land, situate as aforesaid.

JOSEPH ROY.—A claim for eight hundred arpents of land, situate as aforesaid. Produces a concession from Charles Dehault Delassus, Lieutenant Governor, dated 29th December, 1799; also a plat and certificate of survey dated 20th January, 1804.

Testimony taken. August 7, 1807: Toussaint Cerre, being duly sworn, says that he knows the above four claimants; that the oldest of them is now twenty-five years of age, and that the youngest is seventeen years of age, and that the above claimants claim no other land in the Territory.

Objection of the agent of the United States. August 7, 1807. The agent objects on account of the claimants being under age at the time the grant bears date. The Board require other proof.

Opinion of the Board. December 2, 1809: Full Board. It is the opinion of the Board that the above four claims ought not to be confirmed.

TOUSSAINT CERRE.—A claim for one thousand arpents of land, situate on the river Mississippi, district of St. Charles. Produces a concession from Charles Dehault Delassus, Lieutenant Governor, dated 28th of October, 1799; also a plat and certificate of survey, dated 20th of January, 1804.

Opinion of the Board. December 2, 1809: Full Board. It is the opinion of the Board that this claim ought not to be confirmed.

TOUSSAINT CERRE.—A claim for one hundred and sixty arpents, situate on the river Dardennes, district of St. Charles. Produces a concession from Don Zenon Trudeau, Lieutenant Governor, dated 1st of July, 1796; together with a plat and certificate of survey, dated 1st December, 1799, and certified 8th January, 1800.
Opinion of the Board. December 2d, 1809: Full Board. It is the opinion of the Board that this claim ought not to be confirmed.

JOHN COOK, assignee of John Vallet.—A claim for four hundred arpents of land, situate in the district of St. Charles. Produces a survey of the same, taken the 20th February, 1806, and certified the 28th of the same month; and a deed of transfer of the same, dated May 12th, 1803.
Testimony taken. August 29th, 1806. Noel Hebert, being duly sworn, says that he saw the said John Vallet on the said tract of land in the year 1802; that he was then ploughing.
August 8th, 1807. Joseph Sorain, being duly sworn, says that, eight years ago, the said Vallet moved on said land, and continued there about one week; after which he left it, and went to reside in St. Charles; that, in the fall of the same year, he, the said Vallet, went back to the same place, gathered his corn, and took it to St. Charles.
June 29th, 1808. John Vallet, being duly sworn, says that he has no interest in this claim; that he, witness, is the father of seven children, and improved said land in the beginning of the year 1800, and worked thereon until May, 1803, when he sold the same to claimant; and resided thereon during the time of raising his crops, with his wife and children; that, after having been one year on the land, he applied to Don Carlos Dehault Delassus, Lieutenant Governor, for permission to settle; said Lieutenant Governor told him, deponent, to take his plough and go on with his work, and nobody should disturb him.
Antoine Marechal, sworn, says that he was on the place claimed in the spring of 1803; then saw corn stalks in a field, which appeared to have been cultivated the year before; and also, at the same time, saw about three-fourths of an acre of land ploughed round the houses for a garden; that he, deponent, inhabited and cultivated the land claimed the last year, 1807.
Opinion of the Board. December 5, 1809: Present, John B. C. Lucas and Clement B. Penrose, commissioners. It is the opinion of the Board that this claim ought not to be granted.

FRANCIS DUQUETTE.—A claim of four hundred and thirty arpents, situate in the district of St. Charles. Produces a duly registered warrant of survey, dated the 22d December, 1795; a certificate from A. Soulard, that the same does not belong to the domain, having been surveyed by another person, the same dated the 17th October, 1799; and an additional warrant of survey of Charles Dehault Delassus, Lieutenant Governor, also duly registered, and dated 10th of November, 1799; together with a survey of four hundred and thirty arpents, taken the 6th, and certified the 28th of March, 1804.
Opinion of the Board. August 15, 1806: Present, John B. C. Lucas and Clement B. Penrose, commissioners. This claim being unsupported by actual inhabitation and cultivation, the Board reject it.
December 5, 1809. It is the opinion of the Board that this claim ought not to be confirmed. Present, John B. C. Lucas, and Clement B. Penrose, commissioners.

FRANCIS DUQUETTE.—A claim for four hundred arpents, situate in the district of St. Charles. Produces a warrant of survey from Don Zenon Trudeau, Lieutenant Governor, dated July 1, 1796; and a survey of the same, taken the 26th July, 1800, and certified February 17, 1804.
December 5, 1809: Present, John B. C. Lucas and Clement B. Penrose, commissioners. It is the opinion of the Board that this claim ought not to be confirmed.

FRANCIS DUQUETTE, assignee of Isadore La Croix, a foreigner.—A claim of a town lot, situate in St. Charles. Produces a warrant of survey for the same, from Don Zenon Trudeau, Lieutenant Governor, dated the 23d January, 1797; a figurative plat of the same, dated the 10th December, 1799, and certified the 22d December, 1803; together with a deed of transfer of the same, dated the 6th September, 1800.
Testimony taken. August 15, 1806. Francis Fabien, being duly sworn, says that, about seven years ago, the said lot was cleared, and house logs hauled on it for the purposes of building.
Opinion of the Board. December 5, 1809: Present, John B. C. Lucas and Clement B. Penrose, commissioners. It is the opinion of the Board that this claim ought not to be confirmed.

FRANCIS DUQUETTE, assignee of Isadore La Croix, a foreigner.—A claim for six thousand arpents of land, in the district of St. Charles, and adjoining the town. Produces a petition for a tract contained within certain natural boundaries therein described; a certificate from Charles Tayon, the then commandant of St. Charles, stating his belief that the land petitioned for will not exceed ten arpents in breadth; a warrant of survey from Zenon Trudeau, Lieutenant Governor, dated January 23, 1797, for such a quantity as may be found in breadth, between a tract, the property of said claimant, and the Marais *Temsclair*, by a depth of forty arpents; together with a survey of four thousand four hundred arpents, taken the 5th December, 1799, and certified May 30, 1803; and a deed of transfer of the same, dated 6th September, 1800.
Testimony taken. August 15, 1806. François Fabien, being duly sworn, says that the said tract of land was cultivated about nine years ago.
Opinion of the Board. August 15, 1806: Present, John B. C. Lucas and Clement B. Penrose, commissioners. The Board reject this claim, and remark that, from the papers upon record, it appears that four hundred arpents were intended to be granted by the aforesaid concessions.
December 5, 1809: Present, John B. C. Lucas and Clement B. Penrose, commissioners. It is the opinion of the Board that this claim ought not to be confirmed.

ALMOND COTTEL.—A claim for eight hundred and fifty-six arpents of land, situate in the district of St. Charles, on the river Peruque. Produces a notice to the recorder, dated August 8, 1807.
Testimony taken. August 8, 1807. Ira Cottle, being duly sworn, says that claimant, in the year 1803, lived on the above land, and raised a crop; had also his family with him, but cannot say whether he was there the 20th day of December, 1803; he, said claimant, having moved off said land about that time, and has not returned; and believes he was not there on the 20th December, 1803.
Opinion of the Board. December 5, 1809: Present, John B. C. Lucas and Clement B. Penrose, commissioners. It is the opinion of the Board that this claim ought not to be granted.

LOUIS BARRADA, assignee of Francis Saucier.—A claim for a lot in the village of St. Charles, one hundred and thirty feet by three hundred feet. Produces a deed of conveyance from said Francis Saucier to claimant, dated April 24, 1804.

Testimony taken. August 8, 1807. Louis La Marche, being duly sworn, says that eleven years ago said Saucier built a house on said land, and that it has been inhabited and cultivated until this day.
Opinion of the Board. December 13, 1809: Full Board. It is the opinion of the Board that this claim ought not to be granted.

Louis Barrada, assignee of Francis Saucier.—A claim for a lot in the village of St. Charles, one hundred and twenty feet by one hundred and fifty feet.
Testimony taken. August 8, 1807. Louis La Marche, being duly sworn, says that about ten years ago said Saucier enclosed said lot for a garden, and that it has been cultivated ever since.
Opinion of the Board. December 13, 1809: Full Board. It is the opinion of the Board that this claim ought not to be granted.

Robert Spincer.—A claim for seven hundred and fifty arpents of land, situate in the district of St. Charles. Produces a plat and certificate of survey, dated September 5, 1805, and certified to be received for record February 28, 1806.
Testimony taken. August 8, 1807. Etienne Bernard, being duly sworn, says that in 1802 the above land was inhabited and cultivated by claimant, and until this day; and that in 1803 he had a wife and one child.
Opinion of the Board. December 13, 1809: Full Board. It is the opinion of the Board that this claim ought not to be granted.

Ira Cottle, assignee of Henry McLaughlin, assignee of William Hays.—A claim for six hundred arpents of land, situate on rive. Cuivre, district of St. Charles. Produces, as a special permission to settle, a concession from Zenon Trudeau, Lieutenant Governor, for the same, to said William Hays, dated January 24, 1798; and a certificate of survey, dated January 8, 1800; a deed of transfer of said land, from said William Hays to the said H. McLaughlin, dated May 16, 1800; and another deed of transfer from the said McLaughlin to claimant, dated 31st January, 1805.
Testimony taken. March 24, 1806. Martin Woods, being duly sworn, says that said McLaughlin did, prior to and on the 20th day of December, 1803, actually inhabit and cultivate the said tract of land.
August 8, 1807. Bazile Proulx, being duly sworn, says that Henry McLaughlin lived in 1799 on the land claimed, and remained on the same until 1804.
Opinion of the Board. March 24, 1806: Present, John B. C. Lucas and James L. Donaldson, commissioners. The Board grant the said claimant, assignee as aforesaid, six hundred arpents of land, situate as aforesaid, as per said concession.
December 15, 1809: Full Board. It is the opinion of the Board that this claim ought not to be confirmed.

John Stephenson, Jun.—A claim of three hundred arpents of land, situate on the Missouri river, in the district of St. Charles. Produces a concession from Charles D. Delassus, Lieutenant Governor, dated October 10, 1799; and a survey of the same, taken the 9th of February, and certified the 1st March, 1804.
Testimony taken. August 7, 1806: Antoine Soulard, being duly sworn, says that the above concession was granted in the year 1803, as a relief to claimant's father, in consequence of the great loss he met with by the burning of his house; that, in consequence of that, Charles D. Delassus, Lieutenant Governor, directed him, the witness, to antedate the same, in order to make it agree with the claim of the father.
Auguste Chouteau, being duly sworn, says that, about five years ago, to the best of his recollection, the father of claimant having been robbed by the Indians of all he possessed, and left without even the necessary clothing, he came to this place, where the commandant drew out an instrument of writing, recommending him as an object of charity to the inhabitants.
Colonel Daniel Boone, being some time ago before the Board, when the aforesaid claim was first produced, and being requested to tell what he knew respecting the situation of claimant's father, said that, about three or four years ago, James Stephenson, senior, the father of claimant, having had his house destroyed by fire, and his property taken away by the Indians, he did, at his request, inform the Lieutenant Governor of the same, praying, at the same time, that he might grant him an additional concession of some two or three hundred arpents of land; that said Stephenson, on his return from St. Louis, informed him, the said Boone, of his success, and told him that the commandant had granted him a concession in the name of his son.
Opinion of the Board. December 15th, 1799: Full Board. It is the opinion of the Board that this claim ought not to be confirmed.

Alexander Clark.—A claim for eighty arpents of land, situate on Marais des Liards, district of St. Louis. Produces a concession from Zenon Trudeau, Lieutenant Governor, dated September 14th, 1799; and a certificate of survey of the same, dated April 19th, 1803.
Testimony taken. February 1st, 1806. James Richardson, being duly sworn, says that the tract of land above claimed is adjoining the land on which the said Alexander Clark now resides; that he, the said Alexander, having no water on his land, and having found a spring on the said adjoining land, he applied to Zenon Trudeau, Lieutenant Governor, for a concession of the same, which was accordingly granted him.
Opinion and remarks of the Board. February 1st, 1806: Full Board. The Board reject this claim; the said land not being actually inhabited and cultivated prior to and on the 1st day of October, 1800, nor prior to and on the 20th day of December, 1803; they, however, think the case very hard.
December 15th, 1809: Full Board. It is the opinion of the Board that this claim ought not to be confirmed.

John Bollinger.—A claim for three hundred arpents of land, situate on White waters, district of Cape Girardeau. Produces, as a special permission to settle, a concession from Charles D. Delassus, Lieutenant Governor, dated January 20th, 1800; and a plat and certificate of survey of the same, dated March 5th, 1801.
Opinion of the Board. December 22d, 1809: Full Board. It is the opinion of the Board that this claim ought not to be confirmed.

Jacob Miller.—A claim for three hundred and fifty arpents of land, situate on White river, district of Cape Girardeau. Produces to the Board, as a certificate of permission to settle, list B, on which said claimant is No. 32; and a plat of survey, signed B. Cousin, and signed by Antoine Soulard, as received for record.
Testimony taken. February 11th, 1809. Joseph Neyswanger, being duly affirmed, says that claimant settled in the year 1804, cleared five or six acres, and built a cabin; on the same or the following year claimant sold this im-

provement, and removed to another tract which he had purchased; which latter has an enclosure and cultivation of about ten acres, a cabin, and stable; inhabitation and cultivation to the present day. Claimant has a wife and one child.

Opinion of the Board. December 22d, 1809: Full Board. It is the opinion of the Board that this claim ought not to be granted.

Enos Randall, Sen.—A claim for three hundred and fifty arpents of land, and eighty five and a quarter perches, situate on the waters of Cape La Cruche. Produces to the Board, as a permission to settle, list A, on which claimant is No. 149; a plat of survey, dated 7th December, 1805, and certified 21st February, 1806.

Testimony taken. February 11th, 1809. Thomas Bull, being duly affirmed, says that said land is situate on the waters of Cape La Cruche; that claimant settled in the year 1806 or 1807, built a cabin, and enclosed five or six acres, and has continued to cultivate and inhabit to the present day; has a wife and one child.

Opinion of the Board. December 22d, 1809: Full Board. It is the opinion of the Board that this claim ought not to be granted.

Abraham Randall.—A claim for seven hundred and seventy-eight arpents twenty-nine perches of land, situate on Hubble's and Randall's creeks, district of Cape Girardeau. Produces, as a special permission to settle, list A, on which said claimant is No. 52; a plat of survey, dated March 2d, 1805, and certified February 13th, 1806.

Testimony taken. May 30th, 1808. (By Frederick Bates, commissioner, authorized from the Board to take testimony at Cape Girardeau.) Thomas Bull, duly affirmed, says that said land was first improved by the establishment of a cabin by witness's brother-in-law, who abandoned the same in two or three months, as public land; in 1801, or 1802, Peter Bellew took possession of and lived in the said cabin for a short time, who, in 1803, left the same; after which claimant made a settlement, in 1804, repaired the roof of the cabin, and planted peach trees, who has ever since inhabited and cultivated the premises; about seven or eight acres now in cultivation; claimant has a wife and two children.

May 31st, 1808. John Abernathee, duly sworn, says that when Peter Bellew left the premises, in September, 1803, he offered for sale merely his labor, disclaiming all right to the soil, intending to place, or having previously placed, his head right on or near White water.

Medad Randall, being duly sworn, says that Peter Bellew left the premises with an intention to keep a stock for witness; some little time after that, claimant observed to Bellew that he wished to settle on this tract thus abandoned; Bellew replied that he might do so, for that he, Bellew, had no claim to it; he was welcome.

Opinion of the Board. December 22d, 1809. Full Board: It is the opinion of the Board that this claim ought not to be granted.

John Miller.—A claim for thirteen hundred and twenty-four arpents twenty-one perches of land, situate on White river, district of Cape Girardeau. Produces to the Board, as a special permission to settle, list B, on which claimant is No. 19, and a plat of survey dated January 3d, 1806.

Testimony taken. May 1st, 1806. George F. Bollinger, being duly sworn, says that the said claimant settled the said tract of land in October, 1803, built a cabin thereon, and has actually inhabited and cultivated it to this day; that, in 1804, he cleared about forty acres of the same, and moved his family thereon; and further, that he had, on the 20th December, 1803, a wife and nine children, and claims no other lands in his own name in the Territory.

May 30th 1808. (By Frederick Bates, commissioner, authorized from the Board to take testimony at Cape Girardeau.) Joseph Neyswanger affirmed, says that claimant settled in the year 1803, built a dwelling, cabin, and stable, and cleared and cultivated between fifteen and twenty acres; said improvements have been improved and extended from year to year until the present day; claimant has a wife and twelve children.

Opinion of the Board. December 22d, 1809: Full Board. It is the opinion of the Board that this claim ought not to be granted.

Isaac Miller.—A claim for three hundred arpents of land, situate on White Water creek, district of Cape Girardeau. Produces, as a special permission to settle, list B, on which claimant is No. 30; and a plat of survey dated January 9th, 1806, countersigned Antoine Soulard, Surveyor General.

Testimony taken. May 30th, 1808. (By Frederick Bates, commissioner, authorized from the Board to take testimony at Cape Girardeau, &c.) Joseph Neyswanger, affirmed, says that claimant settled the land in 1804, and it has been uninterruptedly inhabited and cultivated until the present day; claimant had a wife and two children; his wife lately died.

Opinion of the Board. December 23d, 1809: Full Board. It is the opinion of the Board that this claim ought not to be granted.

Frederick Limbaugh, Senior.—A claim for eight hundred and fourteen arpents forty-two perches of land, situate on White waters, district of Cape Girardeau. Produces, as a special permission to settle, list B, on which claimant is No. 16, and a certificate of survey of the same, dated January 17th 1806.

Testimony taken. May 1st, 1806. George F. Bollinger, being duly sworn, says that claimant did, in the beginning of 1803, cut house logs; that he cultivated the same in the year 1804; that he was a schoolmaster, and had, on the 20th day of December, 1803, a child; claims no other lands in his own name in the Territory.

May 30th, 1808. (By Frederick Bates, commissioner, authorized from the Board to take testimony at Cape Girardeau, &c.) Joseph Neyswanger, affirmed, says that said land was first cultivated in 1800, and the following year; claimant, under the above-mentioned permission, settled said land in October, 1803, and during the following winter built a cabin thereon, and has inhabited and cultivated the premises every successive year to this day; claimant has two sons in Louisiana.

Opinion of the Board. December 23d, 1809: Full Board. It is the opinion of the Board that this claim ought not to be granted.

Urban Asherbrauner.—A claim for three hundred and fifty arpents and ninety five perches of land, situate on Castor creek, district of Cape Girardeau. Produces to the Board a plat of survey, certified to be received for record February 27th, 1806, by Antoine Soulard, Surveyor General.

Testimony taken. May 30th, 1808. (By Frederick Bates, commissioner, authorized from the Board to take testimony at Cape Girardeau, &c.) Daniel Asherbrauner, being duly sworn, says that claimant improved a tract of land in the year 1800; that the survey of Philip Bollinger afterwards took in the spring of the claimant, which induced him to abandon his improvement, and leave the country in the following year; he again returned in the year 1805, and in that year improved the premises now claimed; settled in the following year, erected a cabin, a mill for the grinding of corn and wheat, and cultivated about three or four acres of land; claimant has continued to inhabit, cultivate, and improve till the present day; has a wife and one child.

Opinion of the Board. December 23d, 1809: Full Board. It is the opinion of the Board that this claim ought not to be granted.

JOHN BOLLINGER, son of John.—A claim for five hundred and sixty-one arpents and fifty-one and a half perches of land, situate on White waters, district of Cape Girardeau. Produces, as a special permission to settle, list A, on which claimant is No. 105; and a plat of survey, certified to be received for record February 27, 1806, by Antoine Soulard, Surveyor General.

Testimony taken. May 30, 1808. (By Frederick Bates, commissioner, authorized from the Board to take testimony at Cape Girardeau, &c.) Daniel Asherbrauner, being sworn, says that said land was first improved in 1803, and inhabited in the following year; he left said tract in the spring of 1805, and again removed thereon in the fall of the same year, since which time he has constantly inhabited and cultivated ten or twelve acres; he has a good dwelling-house, stable, and spring-house, and has a wife and three children.

Opinion of the Board. December 23, 1809: Full Board. It is the opinion of the Board that this claim ought not to be granted.

CHARLES TAYON, Jun.—A claim for forty-three arpents of land, situate adjoining Charrette village, district of St. Charles. Produces a plat of survey, dated February 17, 1806, and certified February 28, 1806.

Testimony taken. December 28, 1809. Joseph Chartrand, being duly sworn, says that the land claimed has been inhabited and cultivated for claimant for seven years last past; and that he, witness, as syndic of Charrette village, did, in 1802, give permission to Charles Tayon, Sen. to settle this land; that his permission was to settle on two hundred and forty feet front, by forty arpents in depth, provided so much could be found vacant there; that the survey of Ramsay bounds in the rear the present claim, and interferes with it; said Ramsay commenced cultivation on his claim about two and a half or three years after claimant.

Opinion of the Board. December 28, 1809: Full Board. It is the opinion of the Board that this claim ought not to be granted.

FREDERICK LIMBAUGH, Jun.—A claim for five hundred and twenty-nine arpents of land, situate on White waters, district of Cape Girardeau. Produces, as a special permission to settle, list B, on which claimant is No. 17; and a plat of survey, dated January 21, 1806, countersigned Antoine Soulard, Surveyor General.

Testimony taken. May 31, 1808. (By Frederick Bates, commissioner, authorized from the Board to take testimony at Cape Girardeau, &c.) Joseph Neyswanger, duly affirmed, says that claimant settled said land in the month of November, 1803, at which time he commenced the building of a house and the clearing of the land, and has inhabited and cultivated the premises to the present day; about fifteen or twenty acres are now in cultivation; claimant had a wife and six or seven children in 1803.

Opinion of the Board. December 29, 1809: Full Board. It is the opinion of a majority of the Board that this claim ought not to be granted; Frederick Bates, commissioner, voting for the granting thereof.

MARTIN COTHNER.—A claim for seven hundred and seven arpents seventy-four perches of land, situate on White waters, district of Cape Girardeau. Produces to the Board, as a special permission to settle, list B, on which claimant is No. 25; and a plat of survey, certified to be received for record February 27, 1806, by Antoine Soulard, Surveyor General.

Testimony taken. May 2, 1806. George F. Bollinger, being duly sworn, says that claimant settled said tract of land in November, 1803, put up a cabin, and moved his family on the same; and that he did, in 1804, raise a crop thereon, and has actually inhabited and cultivated it to this day; had, on the 20th December, 1803, a wife and two children, and about fifteen acres cleared.

Opinion of the Board. December 29, 1809: Full Board. It is the opinion of a majority of the Board that this claim ought not to be granted; Frederick Bates, commissioner, voting for the granting of three hundred arpents.

MARTIN THOMAS.—A claim for three hundred and fifty arpents ninety-five perches of land, situate on White waters, district of Cape Girardeau. Produces to the Board, as a special permission to settle, list B, on which claimant is No. 33; and a plat of survey, certified to be received for record February 27, 1806, by Antoine Soulard, Surveyor General.

Testimony taken. May 31, 1808. (By Frederick Bates, commissioner, authorized from the Board to take testimony at Cape Girardeau, &c.) Joseph Neyswanger, affirmed, says that claimant, in 1806, enclosed about one-fourth of an acre of land, and planted turnip and apple seed.

Opinion of the Board. December 29, 1809: Full Board. It is the opinion of the Board that this claim ought not to be granted.

JOSEPH NEYSWANGER, Jun.—A claim for five hundred arpents of land, situate on White waters, district of Cape Girardeau. Produces to the Board, as a special permission to settle, list A, on which claimant is No. 103; and a plat of survey, certified to be received for record February 27, 1806, by Antoine Soulard, Surveyor General.

Testimony taken. May 31, 1809. (By Frederick Bates, commissioner, authorized from the Board to take testimony at Cape Girardeau, &c.) Frederick Limbaugh, Sen., being duly sworn, says that said land was first settled in 1804 for claimant, at which time a cabin was built, and stables, and five or six acres were cleared and cultivated; and the premises have been uninterruptedly inhabited and cultivated by or for claimant to the present time; claimant has a wife and one child.

Opinion of the Board. December 29, 1809: Full Board. It is the opinion of the Board that this claim ought not to be granted.

JOSEPH NEYSWANGER, Sen.—A claim for one hundred and sixteen arpents fifty-four and one-third perches of land, situate on White waters, district of Cape Girardeau. Produces to the Board, as a special permission to settle, list A, on which claimant is No. 162; and a plat of survey, certified to be received for record February 27, 1806, by Antoine Soulard, Surveyor General.

Testimony taken. May 31, 1808. (By Frederick Bates, commissioner, authorized from the Board to take testimony at Cape Girardeau, &c.) John Bollinger, duly sworn, says that claimant settled and cultivated said land in 1804, and has, either himself or by tenants, constantly inhabited and cultivated to this day; eight or ten acres of land are enclosed and cultivated; claimant has a wife and three children.

Opinion of the Board. December 29, 1809: Full Board. It is the opinion of the Board that this claim ought not to be granted.

CONRAD STOTLER.—A claim for two hundred and thirty-three arpents ninety-six perches of land, situate on White waters, district of Cape Girardeau. Produces to the Board, as a special permission to settle, list A, on which claimant is No. 164; and a plat of survey, certified to be received for record February 27, 1806, by Antoine Soulard, Surveyor General.
Testimony taken. May 31, 1808. (By Frederick Bates, commissioner, authorized from the Board to take testimony at Cape Girardeau, &c.) Joseph Neyswanger, Sen., affirmed, says that there is no cultivation; two years ago a house was built, which still remains; no other improvement.
Opinion of the Board. December 29, 1809: Full Board. It is the opinion of the Board that this claim ought not to be granted.

VALENTINE LORR.—A claim for three hundred and fifty arpents ninety-five perches of land, situate on White waters, district of Cape Girardeau. Produces to the Board, as a special permission to settle, list A, on which claimant is No. 110; and a plat of survey, certified to be received for record February 27, 1806, by Antoine Soulard, Surveyor General.
Testimony taken. May 31, 1809. (By Frederick Bates, commissioner, authorized from the Board to take testimony at Cape Girardeau, &c.) Joseph Neyswanger, Sen., affirmed, says that claimant, in the year 1804, made preparations for building, but never established his cabin; no enclosure, no cultivation.
Opinion of the Board. December 29, 1809: Full Board. It is the opinion of the Board that this claim ought not to be granted.

DANIEL BOLLINGER, son of John.—A claim for seven hundred and one arpents eighty-nine perches of land, situate on White waters, district of Cape Girardeau. Produces to the Board, as a special permission to settle, list A, on which claimant is No. 104; and a plat of survey, certified to be received for record February 27, 1806, by Antoine Soulard, Surveyor General.
Testimony taken. May 1, 1806. Adam Stotler, being duly sworn, says that claimant proceeded to settling of said land in the fall of 1803, cut house logs, and began to put up his cabin, which having completed in the spring of 1804, he moved on said land, and has actually inhabited and cultivated it to this day; that he was of the age of twenty-one years and upwards on the 20th December, 1803, and claims no other lands in his own name in this Territory.
Opinion of the Board. December 29, 1809: Full Board. It is the opinion of the Board that this claim ought not to be granted.

HENRY BOLLINGER, son of Daniel.—A claim for seven hundred and one arpents eighty-nine perches of land, situate on White waters, district of Cape Girardeau. Produces, as a special permission to settle, list A, on which claimant is No. 97; and a plat of survey, certified to be received for record February 27, 1806, by A. Soulard, Surveyor General.
Testimony taken. May 31, 1808. (By Frederick Bates, commissioner, authorized by the Board to take testimony at Cape Girardeau, &c.) John Bollinger, sworn, says that claimant improved said land in the fall of the year 1803, built a cabin, cleared six or seven acres in the first year, moved on said tract the following year, and has continued till the present time to inhabit and cultivate; wife and one child in the year 1803; ten or twelve acres now in cultivation.
Opinion of the Board. December 29, 1809: Full Board. It is the opinion of a majority of the Board that this claim ought not to be granted; Frederick Bates, commissioner, voting for the granting of three hundred arpents.

HANDEL BARKS.—A claim for five hundred and eighty-four arpents ninety-one perches of land, situate on White waters, district of Cape Girardeau. Produces to the Board, as a special permission to settle, list B, on which claimant is No. 18; and a plat of survey certified to be received for record February 27th, 1806, by Antoine Soulard, Surveyor General.
Testimony taken. May 1st, 1806. George F. Bollinger, being duly sworn, says that the said claimant settled the said tract of land about the middle of December, 1803, built a cabin thereon, and has actually inhabited and cultivated the same to this day; had, on the 20th December, 1803, a wife and five children; claims no other lands in his own name in this Territory.
Opinion of the Board. December 29th, 1809: Full Board. It is the opinion of a majority of the Board that this claim ought not to be granted; Frederick Bates, commissioner, voting for the granting of five hundred arpents.

PHILLIP BOLLINGER, son of Daniel.—A claim for three hundred and fifty arpents ninety-five perches of land, situate on White waters, district of Cape Girardeau. Produces to the Board, as a special permission to settle, list A, on which claimant is No. 99; and a plat of survey certified to be received for record February 27th, 1806, by Antoine Soulard, Surveyor General.
Opinion of the Board. December 29th, 1809: Full Board. It is the opinion of the Board that this claim ought not to be granted.

MICHAEL LIMBAUGH.—A claim for three hundred and fifty-one arpents ninety perches of land, situate on White waters, district of Cape Girardeau. Produces to the Board, as a special permission to settle, list B, on which claimant is No. 34; and a plat of survey, dated January 18th, 1806, countersigned Antoine Soulard, Surveyor General.
Testimony taken. May 31st, 1808. (By Frederick Bates, commissioner, authorized by the Board to take testimony at Cape Girardeau, &c.) Joseph Neyswanger, Sen., affirmed, says that in the year 1804 he marked a spring, but made no improvement.
Opinion of the Board. December 29th, 1809: Full Board. It is the opinion of the Board that this claim ought not to be granted.

JOHN HAND.—A claim for three hundred and sixty arpents twenty-one and two-thirds perches of land, situate on the waters of Hubble's creek, district of Cape Girardeau. Produces to the Board, as a special permission to settle, list A, on which claimant is No. 70; and a plat of survey, dated December 6th, 1805, countersigned Antoine Soulard, Surveyor General.
Testimony taken. May 31st, 1808. (By Frederick Bates, commissioner, authorized from the Board to take testimony at Cape Girardeau, &c.) Henry Hand, duly sworn, says that claimant improved or commenced im-

provement June 13th, 1803, cleared a small lot, and planted corn; since which he has enlarged his improvement, but has never inhabited; claimant was only turned of seventeen years when he commenced his improvement.

Opinion of the Board. December 29th, 1809: Full Board. It is the opinion of the Board that this claim ought not to be granted.

THOMAS BULL.—A claim for three hundred arpents of land, situate on the head waters of Hubble's creek, district of Cape Girardeau. Produces to the Board, as a special permission to settle, list A, on which claimant is No. 147; and a plat of survey for one hundred and eighty arpents twenty-seven perches, dated February 3d, 1806, and certified February 13th, same year.

Testimony taken. May 31st, 1808. (By Frederick Bates, commissioner, authorized from the Board to take testimony at Cape Girardeau, &c.) Anthony Randall says that a man of the name of Daniel Brant, five years ago made a small improvement on this land, cleared and enclosed one acre and a quarter, and built a dwelling-house and stable, and soon thereafter, same year, said Brant sold his improvement, and laid his head right in another place; a man of the name of Monday became the purchaser, who sold to a third person; after which the premises were comprehended in the survey. Abraham Randall, being duly sworn, says that in 1805 David Holey, son-in-law of claimant, was placed on the premises by (as witness was informed by Holey) claimant; said Holey has remained thereon to the present time as the tenant of claimant; witness does believe that this was the case, and that said Holey was moved to premises in claimant's wagon.

Opinion of the Board. December 29th, 1809: Full Board. It is the opinion of the Board that this claim ought not to be granted.

REUBEN NORMAN, assignee of Jacob Foster, Jun.—A claim for one hundred and fifty arpents of land, situate on White waters, district of Cape Girardeau.

THE SAME, assignee of Allen McKenzie.—A claim for one hundred arpents of land, situate on White waters, district of Cape Girardeau. Produces to the Board, as a special permission to settle, list A, on which Jacob Foster, Jun. is No. 140, and Allen McKenzie is No. 136; and a plat of survey of two hundred and fifty arpents, signed Bartholomew Cousin, and countersigned Antoine Soulard, Surveyor General.

Testimony taken. May 31st, 1808. (By Frederick Bates, commissioner, authorized from the Board to take testimony at Cape Girardeau, &c.) Dennis O'Sleecy, being duly sworn, says that in the year 1806 he saw claimant building a cabin on the land claimed, on the west side of the creek.

Opinion of the Board. January 13th, 1810: Present, John B. C. Lucas and Frederick Bates, commissioners. It is the opinion of the Board that these two claims ought not to be granted.

ISAAC WILLIAM.—A claim for nine hundred and twenty-four arpents fifteen perches of land, situate on Cape La Cruche, district of Cape Girardeau. Produces to the Board, as a special permission to settle, list A, on which claimant is No. 54; and a plat of survey, dated February 2d, 1806, and certified February 13th, 1806.

Testimony taken. May 31st, 1808. (By Frederick Bates, commissioner, authorized from the Board to take testimony at Cape Girardeau, &c.) Abraham Randall, being duly sworn, says that claimant improved said land in the summer of 1803, cleared some ground for building, and had logs cut for a cabin.

Medad Randall, being duly sworn, says that he assisted claimant to raise a house on said tract in 1804; house finished and inhabited same year; in the year 1805 claimant cleared, enclosed, and cultivated between four and five acres, and has constantly inhabited and cultivated to the present time. Claimant had a wife when he moved on said land.

Opinion of the Board. January 13th, 1810: Present, John B. C. Lucas and Frederick Bates, commissioners. It is the opinion of the Board that this claim ought not to be granted.

ANTHONY RANDALL.—A claim for one hundred and sixteen arpents ninety perches of land, situate on the waters of Randall's creek, district of Cape Girardeau. Produces to the Board, as a special permission to settle, list A, on which claimant is No. 132; and a plat of survey, dated February 27th, 1806, countersigned Antoine Soulard, Surveyor General.

Testimony taken. May 31st, 1808. (By Frederick Bates, commissioner, authorized from the Board to take testimony at Cape Girardeau, &c.) Thomas Morgan, being duly sworn, says he assisted in the survey of said land, on which there is no improvement.

Opinion of the Board. January 13th, 1810: Present, John B. C. Lucas and Frederick Bates, commissioners. It is the opinion of the Board that this claim ought not to be granted.

MORGAN BYRNES, assignee of Timothy Connelly.—A claim for one hundred and sixty-five arpents and forty-one perches of land, situate on Gibany's creek, district of Cape Girardeau. Produces to the Board, as a special permission to settle, list A, on which Timothy Connelly is No. 125; and a plat of survey, dated December 28th, 1805, countersigned Antoine Soulard, Surveyor General; also a deed of transfer from said Connelly to claimant, dated April 3d, 1804.

Opinion of the Board. January 13th, 1810: Present, John B. C. Lucas and Frederick Bates, commissioners. It is the opinion of the Board that this claim ought not to be granted.

THOMAS S. RODNEY.—A claim for three hundred and fifty arpents ninety-five perches of land, situate on the waters of Big Swamp, district of Cape Girardeau. Produces to the Board, as a special permission to settle, list A, on which claimant is No. 67; and a plat of survey, dated February 14th, 1806, countersigned February 28th, 1806, by Antoine Soulard, Surveyor General.

Testimony taken. May 31st, 1808. (By Frederick Bates, commissioner, authorized from the Board to take testimony at Cape Girardeau, &c.) Martin Rodney, being duly sworn, says, no improvement except deadening trees, &c.

Opinion of the Board. January 16th, 1810: Full Board. It is the opinion of the Board that this claim ought not to be granted.

ANDREW RAMSAY, Jun.—A claim for two hundred and fifty-seven arpents forty perches of land, situate on the waters of Big Swamp, district of Cape Girardeau. Produces to the Board, as a special permission to settle, list A, on which claimant is No. 123; and a plat of survey, dated December 28th, 1805, countersigned Antoine Soulard, Surveyor General. Said tract adjoins a cultivated tract of claimant.

Opinion of the Board. January 16th, 1810: Full Board. It is the opinion of the Board that this claim ought not to be granted.

LEMUEL CHENEY.—A claim for one hundred arpents of land, situate in the district of Cape Girardeau. Produces to the Board, as a special permission to settle, list A, on which claimant is No. 142.
Opinion of the Board. January 16th, 1810: Full Board. It is the opinion of the Board that this claim ought not to be granted.

WILLIAM BONER.—A claim for one hundred and eighty arpents of land, situate in the district of Cape Girardeau. Produces to the Board, as a special permission to settle, list A, on which claimant is No. 124.
Opinion of the Board. January 16, 1810: Full Board. It is the opinion of the Board that this claim ought not to be granted.

EDWARD F. BOND, assignee of John Hays, assignee of John Magee, assignee of Alexander Andrew.—A claim for two hundred and forty arpents of land, situate on Can's creek, fork of Byrd's creek, district of Cape Girardeau. Produces to the Board a concession from Zenon Trudeau, Lieutenant Governor, to Alexander Andrew, dated January 5, 1798; a plat of survey, dated March 30, 1802, and certified May 2, 1803; a deed of conveyance from Alexander Andrew to John Magee, dated March 9; a deed of conveyance from Michael Quin to John Hays, dated October 5, 1804; and a deed of conveyance from John Hays to claimant, dated October 21, 1805.
Testimony taken. May 31, 1808. (By Frederick Bates, commissioner, authorized from the Board to take testimony at Cape Girardeau, &c.) John Byrd, Esquire, being duly sworn, says that John Magee cultivated said land in 1803, at which time he also inhabited the same; believes the premises have been generally inhabited, and knows perfectly that a crop has been cultivated every year to the present day.
Opinion of the Board. January 16, 1810: Full Board. It is the opinion of the Board that this claim ought not to be confirmed.

ROBERT GIBANY.—A claim for three hundred and forty-eight arpents forty-two perches of land, situate on Gibany's creek, district of Cape Girardeau. Produces to the Board, as a special permission to settle, list A, on which claimant is No. 46; a plat of survey, dated December 24, 1805, countersigned Antoine Soulard, Surveyor General.
Testimony taken. May 31, 1808. (By Frederick Bates, commissioner, authorized from the Board to take testimony at Cape Girardeau, &c. Andrew Ramsay, Sen. sworn, says, claimant came to the country about the last of the year 1797, or beginning of the year 1798; that he has continued in the country ever since, and performed all those duties usually enjoined on subjects during the continuance of that Government; that claimant followed the business of a blacksmith, which witness presumes prevented a more early application for a concession.
Samuel Bradley, being duly sworn, says that he has seen claimant working on the tract claimed; that several acres, perhaps ten, were cleared, and a sufficiency of rails mauled to enclose it; the claimant also occupied a sugar camp on said land.
Opinion of the Board. January 16, 1810: Full Board. It is the opinion of the Board that this claim ought not to be granted.

JOSEPH YOUNG.—A claim for two hundred and thirty-three arpents ninety-six perches of land, situate on the waters of Byrd's creek, district of Cape Girardeau. Produces to the Board, as a special permission to settle, list A, on which claimant is No. 120; and a plat of survey, signed B. Cousin, countersigned Antoine Soulard, Surveyor General.
Opinion of the Board. January 16, 1810: Full Board. It is the opinion of the Board that this claim ought not to be granted.

JEREMIAH CONWAY, assignee of Peter Bellew.—A claim for seven hundred and twenty arpents of land, situate on the waters of White waters, district of Cape Girardeau. Produces to the Board, as a special permission to settle, list B, on which P. Bellew is No. 4, for four hundred arpents; and a deed of transfer from Peter Bellew to claimant, dated October 1, 1804.
Testimony taken. June 1, 1808. (By Frederick Bates, commissioner, authorized from the Board to take testimony at Cape Girardeau, &c.) Ithamar Hubble, duly sworn, says that Peter Bellew settled on said tract in October, 1803, built a cabin, cleared, enclosed, and, on the following year, cultivated about three acres; constantly inhabited and cultivated to the present time; about ten acres now in cultivation; Bellew had a wife and one child in 1803.
Opinion of the Board. January 16, 1810: Full Board. It is the opinion of a majority of the Board that this claim ought not to be granted; Frederick Bates, commissioner, voting for the granting of four hundred arpents.

ELIJAH WELSH.—A claim for three hundred and fifty arpents ninety-five perches of land, situate on the waters of the river White waters, district of Cape Girardeau. Produces to the Board, as a special permission to settle, list A, on which claimant is No. 62; a plat of survey, dated December 6, 1805; countersigned February 28, 1806, by Antoine Soulard, Surveyor General.
Testimony taken. August 29, 1806. Jeremiah Conway, being duly sworn, says that claimant settled the said tract of land in the fall of 1803, built a cabin on the same, and actually inhabited it prior to and on the 20th day of December of that year; that he had then a wife; and further, that he did, in the year 1804, raise a crop on it, and has actually inhabited and cultivated it to this day.
Opinions of the Board. August 29, 1806: Present, John B. C. Lucas and Clement B. Penrose, commissioners. The Board reject this claim for want of actual cultivation prior to and on the 20th day of December, 1803.
January 20, 1810: Full Board. It is the opinion of a majority of the Board that this claim ought not to be granted; Frederick Bates, commissioner, voting for the granting of three hundred arpents.

EBENEZER HUBBLE.—A claim for seven hundred and forty arpents sixty-eight perches of land, situate on White waters, district of Cape Girardeau. Produces to the Board, as a special permission to settle, list A, on which claimant is No. 51; and a plat of survey, dated December 5, 1805, countersigned February 28, 1806, by Antoine Soulard, Surveyor General.
Testimony taken. April 16, 1806. Athamar Hubble, being duly sworn, says that the said claimant was, at the time of obtaining said concession; of the age of twenty-one years and upwards; that he did proceed to the

improvement of said land in 1803, sowed one acre of said land in turnips, planted peach trees; that, in 1804, he put up a cabin, and hired a man in that year, who did cultivate the same for him.

June 1, 1808. (By Frederick Bates, commissioner, authorized from the Board to take testimony at Cape Girardeau, &c.) Athamar Hubble, duly sworn, says that a turnip field was sowed on this land in 1803; in the following March a cabin was built, and claimant's family moved into it, and have continued to inhabit and cultivate to the present day about twelve acres; in cultivation at this time; no children, but was twenty-one years of age.

Opinion of the Board. January 20, 1810: Full Board. It is the opinion of the Board that this claim ought not to be granted.

MARTIN RODNEY.—A claim for two hundred and thirty-six arpents seventy perches of land, situate on Hubble's creek, district of Cape Girardeau. Produces to the Board, as a special permission to settle, list A, on which claimant is No. 151; a plat of survey, dated December 19, 1805, countersigned by Antoine Soulard, Surveyor General.

Testimony taken. June 1, 1808. (By Frederick Bates, commissioner, authorized from the Board to take testimony at Cape Girardeau, &c.) B. Cousin, who acted principally for the late commandant, Louis Lorimier, states that this is a continuation to a former concession which was deemed too small.

Opinion of the Board. January 20, 1810: Full Board. It is the opinion of the Board that this claim ought not to be granted.

JOHN GUETHING.—A claim for five hundred and eighty-four arpents eighty-one and three-quarters perches of land, situate on Hubble's creek, district of Cape Girardeau. Produces to the Board, as a special permission to settle, list A, on which claimant is No. 37; a plat of survey, dated December 16, 1805, certified February 21, 1806.

Opinion of the Board. January 20, 1810: Full Board. It is the opinion of the Board that this claim ought not to be granted.

CHRISTOPHER AIDENGER.—A claim for four hundred and sixty-five arpents of land, situate on the waters of Little White river, district of Cape Girardeau. Produces to the Board, as a special permission to settle, list B, on which claimant is No. 35.

Testimony taken. May 2, 1806. George F. Bollinger, being duly sworn, says that claimant settled the said tract of land in 1801; that, in 1802, he cleared about two acres of the same, and raised a crop, and has actually cultivated it to this day; and further, that he did, in 1804, move his family on said tract, and has actually inhabited it to this day; had, on the 20th December, 1803, a wife and child.

Opinion of the Board. January 20, 1810: Full Board. It is the opinion of the Board that this claim ought not to be granted.

JONATHAN HUBBLE, son of Jonathan.—A claim, for the benefit of Robert English, for seven hundred and forty acres of land, situate on White Water creek, district of Cape Girardeau. Produces to the Board, as a special permission to settle, list A, on which said Jonathan Hubble is No. 50, for two hundred and fifty arpents; a plat of survey, dated December 18, 1805; a transfer from the said Hubble to John McCarty, dated May 8, 1805; and a transfer from said McCarty to said English, dated November 22, 1806.

Testimony taken. June 1, 1808. (By Frederick Bates, commissioner, authorized from the Board to take testimony at Cape Girardeau, &c.) Athamar Hubble, duly sworn, says that, in December, 1803, about a week before Christmas, claimant moved on this land, where a camp had been previously established; next spring he built a cabin, cleared, enclosed, and raised a crop of corn; remained two years, and raised two crops, after which he moved off, and no crops raised since; there has been occasionally a tenant on said land, who did not cultivate.

Opinion of the Board. January 20, 1810: Full Board. It is the opinion of the Board that this claim ought not to be granted.

PETER HARTLE.—A claim for six hundred arpents of land, situate on White waters, district of Cape Girardeau. Produces to the Board, as a special permission to settle, list B, on which claimant is No. 23, and a certificate of survey of three hundred and forty-five arpents, dated January 15, 1806.

Testimony taken. May 2, 1806. George F. Bollinger, being duly sworn, says that claimant settled said tract of land in November, 1803, cut house-logs, and fenced in a small piece of land; that his cabin being completed in January, 1804, he moved on said land, and has actually inhabited and cultivated it to this day; had, on the 20th December, 1803, a wife and six children.

Opinion of the Board. January 20, 1810: Full Board. It is the opinion of the Board that this claim ought not to be granted.

ANDREW RAMSAY, Sen., assignee of Solomon Thorn.—A claim for two hundred and forty arpents of land, situate on Big Swamp, district of Cape Girardeau. Produces to the Board a concession from Zenon Trudeau, Lieutenant Governor, to Solomon Thorn for the same, dated 5th January, 1798; a plat of survey, dated May 9, 1799, and certified October, 30, 1799; and a deed of conveyance from said Thorn to Andrew Ramsay, Sen., dated May 14, 1804.

Testimony taken. June 1, 1808. (By Frederick Bates, authorized from the Board to take testimony at Cape Girardeau, &c.) Robert Gibany, duly sworn, says, land was improved in the year 1801, a camp built, about twelve or fourteen acres were grubbed, chopped, and cleared in a body, about one-half of which belonged to the said premises; a nursery was cultivated, and an orchard planted; a garden was also made, and abandoned in the following year.

Opinion of the Board. January 20, 1810: Full Board. It is the opinion of the Board that this claim ought not to be confirmed.

ANDREW RAMSAY, Sen., assignee of Samuel Bradley.—A claim for three hundred arpents of land, situate on Big Swamp, district of Cape Girardeau. Produces to the Board a concession from Zenon Trudeau, Lieutenant Governor, to Samuel Bradley, dated December 15, 1797; a plat of survey, dated May 10, and certified November 2, 1799; and a deed of conveyance from said Bradley to claimant, dated May 14, 1804.

Testimony taken. June 1, 1808. (By Frederick Bates, commissioner, authorized from the Board to take testimony at Cape Girardeau, &c.) Robert Gibany, sworn, says, land was improved in 1801, a camp built, about twelve or fourteen acres cleared in a body, half of which belonged to the adjoining tract, and half to these premises; a nursery planted, and orchard; a garden made; abandoned in the following year.

Opinion of the Board. January 20, 1810: Full Board. It is the opinion of the Board that this claim ought not to be confirmed.

JOHN WEAVER.—A claim for three hundred arpents of land, situate on Ramsay creek, district of Cape Girardeau. Produces to the Board, as a special permission to settle, list A, on which claimant is No. 60; and a plat of survey, dated December 21, 1805, signed B. Cousin, and countersigned Antoine Soulard, Surveyor General.
Opinion of the Board. January 23, 1810: Full Board. It is the opinion of the Board that this claim ought not to be granted.

JACOB WELKER.—A claim for nine hundred and eighty-two arpents sixty-five perches of land, situate on waters of Caney creek, district of Cape Girardeau. Produces to the Board, as a special permission to settle, list A, on which the claimant is No. 109, for three hundred arpents; a plat of survey, signed B. Cousin, and certified to be received for record February 27, 1806, by Antoine Soulard, Surveyor General.,
Testimony taken. June 1, 1808. (By Frederick Bates, commissioner, authorized from the Board to take testimony at Cape Girardeau, &c.) Leonard Welker, duly sworn, says that claimant settled in November, 1804, and moved his family on in the spring following; built a cabin, and cultivated about six acres of ground; premises constantly inhabited and cultivated to this time.
Opinion of the Board. January 23, 1810: Full Board. It is the opinion of the Board that this claim ought not to be granted.

JOHN LORANCE.—A claim for three hundred arpents of land, situate in the district of Cape Girardeau. Produces to the Board, as a special permission to settle, list A, on which claimant is No. 106.
Testimony taken. June 1, 1808. (By Frederick Bates, commissioner, authorized from the Board to take testimony at Cape Girardeau, &c.) Christopher Aidenger, duly sworn, says that claimant made a small improvement in 1804, moved on to it in the following year, and continued to inhabit and cultivate it to the present time; between nine and eleven acres now in cultivation.
Opinion of the Board. January 23, 1810: Full Board. It is the opinion of the Board that this claim ought not to be granted.

DAVID GREEN.—A claim for three hundred and forty-seven arpents fifty-three and a half perches of land, situate on Byrd's creek, district of Cape Girardeau. Produces to the Board, as a special permission to settle, list A, on which the claimant is No. 81, for three hundred arpents; a plat of survey, dated November 28, 1805, signed B. Cousin, and countersigned Antoine Soulard, Surveyor General.
Opinion of the Board. January 24, 1810: Present, John B. C. Lucas and Clement B. Penrose, commissioners. It is the opinion of the Board that this claim ought not to be granted.

JAMES COWAN.—A claim for seven hundred and fifty-six arpents of land, situate on river Dubois, district of St. Louis. Produces to the Board a plat of survey, dated February 28, 1806, certified January 8, 1806, by Antoine Soulard, Surveyor General. For permission to settle, see Mackay's list.
Testimony taken. January 24, 1810. John Sullens, being duly sworn, says that the improvement of claimant was made in 1804; witness then saw turnips and corn growing on the place; not quite half an acre fenced in; the land was cultivated the next year; no house then built; claimant was a single man, and resided in the neighborhood, at his brother-in-law's.
Opinion of the Board. January 24, 1810: Present, John B. C. Lucas and Clement B. Penrose, commissioners. It is the opinion of the Board that this claim ought not to be granted.

ANDREW RAMSAY, assignee of Charles Bunch.—A claim for three hundred arpents of land, situate on Big Swamp, district of New Madrid. Produces to the Board a permission to settle, from Henry Peyroux, commandant of New Madrid district, to Charles Bunch, dated April 9, 1800; an order of survey from said commandant for three hundred arpents, in favor of said Bunch, dated September 9, 1800; a plat of survey, signed James Story, surveyor, New Madrid district; a certified copy of a deed of conveyance from Charles Bunch to claimant, dated November, 1803, and certified October 28, 1805.
Testimony taken. June 1, 1808. (By Frederick Bates, commissioner, authorized from the Board to take testimony at Cape Girardeau, &c.) Robert Gibany, duly sworn, says that, in the year 1802, Andrew Ramsay cultivated the premises; he had a house, and an enclosure of a few acres; premises have been constantly inhabited and cultivated to the present time; about twenty-five or thirty acres now in cultivation; a good nursery and small orchard.
Opinion of the Board. January 24, 1810: Present, John B. C. Lucas and Clement B. Penrose, commissioners. It is the opinion of the Board that this claim ought not to be confirmed.

DAVID DOWNARD.—A claim for three hundred arpents of land, situate on the river Mississippi, district of Cape Girardeau. Produces to the Board, as a special permission to settle, list A, on which claimant is No. 73.
Opinion of the Board. January 24, 1810: Present, John B. C. Lucas and Clement B. Penrose, commissioners. It is the opinion of the Board that this claim ought not to be granted.

JOHN DOUGHERTY.—A claim for four hundred arpents of land, situate on Byrd's creek, district of Cape Girardeau. Produces to the Board, as a special permission to settle, list A, on which claimant is No 39, for three hundred arpents; a plat of survey of four hundred arpents, dated February 28, 1806, signed Edward F. Bound, countersigned February 28, 1806, by Antoine Soulard, Surveyor General.
Testimony taken. June 1, 1808. (By Frederick Bates, commissioner, authorized from the Board to take testimony at Cape Girardeau, &c.) John Guething, Esq., duly sworn, says that claimant cleared a part of this land in the year 1800, but believes there were no other improvements.
Opinion of the Board. January 24, 1810: Present, John B. C. Lucas and Clement B. Penrose, commissioners. It is the opinion of the Board that this claim ought not to be granted.

ANDREW RAMSAY, Sen.—A claim for four hundred arpents of land, situate on Big Swamp, district of Cape Girardeau. Produces to the Board, as a special permission to settle, list A, on which claimant is No. 123.
Testimony taken. June 1, 1808: (By Frederick Bates, commissioner, authorized from the Board to take testimony at Cape Girardeau, &c.) John Simpson, duly sworn, says that claimant has made sugar on this land, but knows of no other improvements than the camp.
Opinion of the Board. January 24, 1810: Present, John B. C. Lucas and Clement B. Penrose, commissioners. It is the opinion of the Board that this claim ought not to be granted.

CHRISTOPHER HAYS.—A claim for one thousand arpents of land, situate on Hubble's creek, district of Cape Girardeau. Produces to the Board a permission from Don Casa Calvo, Governor General, to him, to settle on vacant land, dated January 28, 1800; a concession from Don Carlos Dehault Delassus, Lieutenant Governor, for one thousand arpents, dated July 25, 1800; a plat of survey of one thousand two hundred and ninety-three arpents eighty-seven perches, dated December 3, 1805, signed B. Cousin, and countersigned Antoine Soulard, Surveyor General.

Testimony taken. April 16, 1806. James Earl, being duly sworn, says that claimant settled the said tract of land in February, 1800, and did, prior to and on the 1st day of October in that year, actually inhabit and cultivate the said tract of land; and had then a wife and a child.

June 1, 1808. (By Frederick Bates, commissioner, authorized from the Board to take testimony at Cape Girardeau, &c.) James Earl, duly sworn, says that said tract was settled by claimant in 1800, who built a house, and cleared and cultivated several acres of land; premises inhabited and cultivated to the present time; about five hundred acres now in cultivation.

Opinions and remarks of the Board. April 16, 1806: Present, John B. C. Lucas and James L. Donaldson, commissioners. The Board confirm to the aforesaid claimant eight hundred arpents of land, situate as aforesaid, by virtue of and making part of the said concession.

January 27, 1810: Full Board. It is the opinion of a majority of the Board that this claim ought not to be confirmed. Frederick Bates, commissioner, does declare that, if this claim did not exceed eight hundred arpents, he would vote for its confirmation; Clement B. Penrose, commissioner, voting for its confirmation.

CHRISTOPHER HAYS.—A claim of five hundred arpents of land, situate on Table creek, district of Cape Girardeau. Produces to the Board, as a special permission to settle, list A, on which claimant is No. 146; a plat of survey for four hundred arpents, dated March 8, 1805, signed B. Cousin, countersigned Antoine Soulard, Surveyor General.

Testimony taken. April 16, 1806. James Earl, being duly sworn, says that claimant did proceed to the improving of said tract in 1803, and cleared about ten arpents.

June 1, 1808. (By Frederick Bates, commissioner, authorized from the Board to take testimony at Cape Girardeau, &c.) Benijah Lafferty, being duly sworn, says that, in 1803, in the fall, he saw Monday, a tenant of claimant, clearing land, which said Monday told witness was for claimant; witness passed in the following spring, and saw about ten acres cleared; no inhabitation.

Opinion of the Board. January 27, 1810: Full Board. It is the opinion of the Board that this claim ought not to be granted.

JAMES RAMSAY, Jun.—A claim for four hundred arpents of land, situate on White waters, district of Cape Girardeau. Produces to the Board, as a special permission to settle, list A, on which claimant is No. 36.

Testimony taken. June 1, 1808. (By Frederick Bates, commissioner, authorized from the Board to take testimony at Cape Girardeau, &c.) James Earle, duly sworn, says that in 1802 he saw a cabin and a small garden-spot made by the tenant of the claimant.

Elisha Welsh, duly sworn, says that the land was improved in October, 1800; a hut or cabin built; claimant then cleared, enclosed, and the following year cultivated, a small spot of ground; premises constantly cultivated (but not inhabited) till this time; three small spots of corn, peach trees and watermelons have been cultivated.

Opinion of the Board. February 3, 1810: Full Board. It is the opinion of the Board that this claim ought not to be granted.

BENJAMIN HELDEBRAND.—A claim for three hundred acres of land, situate on White waters, district of Cape Girardeau. Produces to the Board, as a special permission to settle, list A, on which claimant is No. 111, for three hundred arpents; a plat of survey, signed B. Cousin, and certified to be received for record February 27, 1806, by Antoine Soulard, Surveyor General.

Testimony taken. June 2, 1808. (By Frederick Bates, commissioner, authorized from the Board to take testimony at Cape Girardeau, &c.) Frederick Slinker, duly sworn, says that claimant settled in 1805, built a cabin, and cleared about four acres, and still inhabits and cultivates.

Opinion of the Board. February 3, 1810: Full Board. It is the opinion of the Board that this claim ought not to be granted.

WILLIAM PATTERSON.—A claim for nine hundred and seventy arpents of land, situate on White waters, district of Cape Girardeau. Produces to the Board, as a special permission to settle, list B, on which claimant is No. 24, for six hundred and fifty arpents; and a survey of nine hundred and seventy arpents, dated February 27, 1806.

Testimony taken. May 2, 1806. George F. Bollinger, being duly sworn, says that claimant settled the said tract of land in October, 1803; built a cabin thereon, and moved his family on the same; that he did, in the year 1804, clear ten acres, raised a crop that year, and has actually inhabited and cultivated it to this day; had, on the 23d December, 1803, a wife and nine children.

Opinion of the Board. February 3, 1810: Full Board. It is the opinion of a majority of the Board that this claim ought not to be granted; Frederick Bates, commissioner, voting for the granting of six hundred and fifty arpents.

DANIEL HELDEBRAND.—A claim for three hundred and fifty arpents ninety-five perches of land, situate on White waters, district of Cape Girardeau. Produces to the Board, as a special permission to settle, list A, on which claimant is No. 108, for three hundred arpents; a plat of survey for three hundred and fifty arpents ninety-five perches, signed B. Cousin, and countersigned Antoine Soulard, Surveyor General, February 27, 1806, as received for record.

Opinion of the Board. February 3, 1810: Full Board. It is the opinion of the Board that this claim ought not to be granted.

ABRAHAM BYRD.—A claim for two hundred and fifty arpents of land, situate on Byrd's creek, district of Cape Girardeau. Produces a concession from Charles Dehault Delassus, dated January 24, 1800, and a survey of the same, dated December, 25, 1805.

Testimony taken. June 2, 1808. (By Frederick Bates, commissioner, authorized from the Board to take testimony at Cape Girardeau, &c.) David Fenel, sworn, says that claimant had a pair of millstones cut on premises in 1803; a cabin built and inhabited; about forty acres are now enclosed, cultivated, and inhabited at this time by John Gibany.

Opinion of the Board. February 3, 1810: Full Board. It is the opinion of the Board that this claim ought not to be confirmed.

ABRAHAM BYRD, Jun.—A claim for two hundred and twenty-five arpents of land, situate on the Mississippi, district of Cape Girardeau. Produces a certificate of a warrant of survey from Henry Peyroux, commandant of New Madrid, dated March 21, 1804, and a certificate of survey dated January 11, 1806.

Testimony taken. May 1, 1806. George Hacker, being duly sworn, says that one Cown settled the said tract of land in 1802; that the same was, prior to and on the 20th day of December, 1803, actually inhabited and cultivated by claimant; that said claimant held another tract of land in the district of Cape Girardeau, of which he had disposed prior to the 20th December of that year. Abraham Byrd, Sen., the claimant's father, observed that he was in 1803 of the age of eighteen or nineteen, and was doing militia duty in 1802.

Solomon Thorn, being also sworn, says that claimant has done militia duty under him for upwards of six years.

Opinion of the Board. February 3, 1810: Full Board. It is the opinion of the Board that this claim ought not to be granted.

ABRAHAM BYRD, Sen., assignee of Jonathan Stoker, assignee of John Johnson, assignee of William Smith.—A claim for four hundred and forty-five arpents of land, situate on the Mississippi, district of New Madrid. Produces to the Board a permission to settle, from Henry Peyroux, commandant at New Madrid, to John Johnson, to settle on twelve or fifteen arpents of land, dated 26th August, 1800; a certificate of survey for the same, dated January 11, 1806; a deed of transfer from the said Jonathan Stoker to John Johnson, dated November 17, 1801; and a deed of transfer from said John Johnson to the above claimant, dated December, 29, 1802.

Testimony taken. May 1, 1806. Andrew Ramsay, being duly sworn, says that the said John Johnson settled the said tract of land in the fall of 1800; that he built a house on the same, and actually inhabited it.

Solomon Thorn, being duly sworn, says that crops were raised on said land in the years 1801 and 1802, and that claimant did, prior to and on the 20th December, 1803, actually inhabit and cultivate the same; and had then a wife, five children, and nineteen negroes.

June 2, 1808. (By Frederick Bates, commissioner, authorized from the Board to take testimony at Cape Girardeau, &c.) Andrew Ramsay, Jun., sworn, says that Johnson settled this land the last of the year 1800, or first of the year 1801; built a cabin; cleared, enclosed, and cultivated a small field; premises constantly inhabited and cultivated to the present time, a large field now in cultivation.

James Brady, duly sworn, says that he has been on the lands of the claimant, and supposes that sixty or seventy acres are enclosed and in cultivation.

Opinions of the Board. May 1, 1806: Present, Clement B. Penrose and James L. Donaldson, commissioners. The Board grant the said claimant seven hundred and fifty arpents, situate as aforesaid.

February 6, 1810: Full Board. It is the opinion of the Board that this claim ought not to be granted.

ABRAHAM BYRD, Sen, assignee of Jonathan Stoker.—A claim for two hundred and fifty arpents of land, situate on the Mississippi, district of New Madrid. Produces a certificate of a petition, and a permission to settle from Henry Peyroux, dated March 24th, 1802; a certificate of survey, dated January 11th, 1806; and a deed of transfer of the same executed to claimant by Abraham Byrd, Jun., attorney to the said Jonathan Stoker, dated January 11th, 1804; and the power of attorney of said Stoker to said Abraham Byrd, Junior, to sell said land, dated December 29th, 1802.

Testimony taken. May 1st, 1806. George Hacker, being duly sworn, says that the said Jonathan Stoker settled the said tract of land in the spring of 1802, and raised a crop thereon, and that the same was, prior to and on the 20th of December, 1803, actually inhabited and cultivated for the use of the claimant, by his negroes, and has been so to this day. This tract is adjoining the tract above claimed by said Abraham Byrd, Senior.

June 2d, 1808. (By Frederick Bates, commissioner, authorized from the Board to take testimony at Cape Girardeau, &c.) Andrew Ramsay, Junior, sworn, says that Stoker settled this land in 1802; cleared, enclosed, and cultivated a field, and inhabited a cabin, which had been previously built; premises constantly inhabited and cultivated to the present time.

Opinion of the Board. February 6th, 1810: Full Board. It is the opinion of the Board that this claim ought not to be granted.

ABRAHAM BYRD, Sen.—A claim for eight hundred arpents of land, situate on the Mississippi, district of New Madrid. Produces a duly certified copy of permission to settle, from Henry Peyroux, commandant of New Madrid, dated March 24th, 1802, and a certificate of survey, dated January 11th, 1806.

Testimony taken. May 1st, 1806. George Hacker, being duly sworn, says that claimant settled the said tract of land in 1803, and that the same was, prior to and on the 20th day of December, 1803, actually inhabited and cultivated by his negroes, and for his use.

June 2d, 1808. (By Frederick Bates, commissioner, authorized from the Board to take testimony at Cape Girardeau, &c.) Andrew Ramsay, Junior, duly sworn, says that claimant settled, cleared, enclosed, and cultivated in 1803; built a house; premises constantly inhabited and cultivated to the present time; upwards of twenty acres now in cultivation; claimant, in 1803, had six children and a wife.

Opinion of the Board. February 6th, 1810: Full Board. It is the opinion of the Board that this claim ought not to be granted.

ABRAHAM BYRD, Sen., assignee of Charles Fenley.—A claim for three hundred and twenty-five arpents of land, situate at Prairie St. Charles, district of New Madrid. Produces to the Board a certified copy of a petition for a concession, dated December 20th, 1800; a certificate of survey of said land; and a deed of transfer from the said Fenley to the said Abraham Byrd, Sen., dated January 17th, 1806.

Testimony taken. May 1st, 1806. Stephens Jones, being duly sworn, says that said Charles Fenley settled the said tract of land in the year 1801, and raised a crop thereon that year, and that he had, prior to his selling of the same to the said claimant, cleared about eight or nine acres; and further, that the same was, prior to and on the 20th day of December, 1803, actually inhabited and cultivated by claimant's negroes, and for his use; that he had on the same a good cabin and about fifteen acres in cultivation; and, lastly, that the said tract came to the said Fenley by virtue of an exchange, the property of one Bowee.

June 2d, 1808. (By Frederick Bates, commissioner, authorized from the Board to take testimony at Cape Girardeau, &c.) Robert Lane, being duly sworn, says that Fenley settled this land in 1801; cleared, enclosed, and cultivated six or seven acres; built a cabin; and premises have been constantly inhabited and cultivated to the present time; ten or twelve acres now in cultivation.

Opinion of the Board. February 6th, 1810: Full Board. It is the opinion of the Board that this claim ought not to be granted.

ABRAHAM BYRD, Jun.—A claim for three hundred and seventy-four arpents forty-nine perches of land, situate on Byrd's creek, district of Cape Girardeau. Produces to the Board as a special permission to settle, list A, on which claimant is No. 117; a plat of survey, dated December 11th, 1805, signed B. Cousin, countersigned Antoine Soulard, Surveyor General.

 Opinion of the Board. February 6th, 1810: Full Board. It is the opinion of the Board that this claim ought not to be granted.

MOSES BYRD.—A claim for three hundred and fifty-two arpents of land, situate on Byrd's creek, district of Cape Girardeau. Produces to the Board, as a special permission to settle, list A, on which claimant is No. 119; a plat of survey, dated December 11th, 1805, signed B. Cousin, countersigned Antoine Soulard, Surveyor General.

 Testimony taken. June 2d, 1808. (By Frederick Bates, commissioner, authorized from the Board to take testimony at Cape Girardeau, &c.) Abraham Byrd, Jun., duly affirmed, says, improvement was made in the year 1807; ten or twelve acres cultivated; a house, stable, spring house, &c.

 Opinion of the Board. February 6th, 1810: Full Board. It is the opinion of the Board that this claim ought not to be granted.

JOHN BYRD.—A claim for five hundred and eighty-five arpents and eighty-four perches of land, situate on the waters of Byrd's creek, district of Cape Girardeau. Produces to the Board, as a special permission to settle, list A, on which claimant is No. 118; a certificate of survey of five hundred and eighty-five arpents and twenty-four perches, dated December 30th, 1805; and a quit-claim from one Jacob Myers and Kesiah his wife, late widow of one Joseph Crutchlow, dated April 12th, 1802.

 Testimony taken. April 16th, 1806. Joseph Young, being duly sworn, says that the said Joseph Crutchlow did, prior to and on the 1st day of October, 1800, actually inhabit and cultivate the said tract of land; that he died on said land in the year 1801; that the said claimant did, in the year 1802, clear twelve or fifteen arpents of the said tract; cultivated that year, and to this day.

 Bartholomew Cousin, being also duly sworn, says that the aforesaid Kesiah Crutchlow, after the death of her husband, obtained from the commandant, Louis Lorimier, permission to cultivate the said land; that the said commandant had promised her a concession for the same; and further, that claimant, having purchased the said tract of land, applied for a concession for the same, and obtained the aforesaid concession, so dated as mentioned in list A.

 June 2d, 1808. (By Frederick Bates, commissioner, authorized from the Board to take testimony at Cape Girardeau, &c.) Joseph Young, being duly sworn, says that the premises were improved in the spring of 1800; a house was then built, a small field cleared, and a part cultivated. Since the year 1803 claimant has cultivated a part of this tract. No person was living on this land on the 20th December, 1803, though in cultivation.

 Opinions and remarks of the Board. April 16th, 1806: Present, John B. C. Lucas and James L. Donaldson, commissioners. The claimant having had a tract of eight hundred arpents of land confirmed to him under the first section of the act, and the same not being actually inhabited on the 20th December, 1803, the Board reject this claim. They, however, observe that they think it a hard case.

 February 6th, 1810: Full Board. It is the opinion of the Board that this claim ought not to be granted.

JOHN BYRD, assignee of Samuel S. Kennedy.—A claim for four hundred and sixty-eight arpents and fourteen perches of land, situate on the waters of Byrd's creek, district of Cape Girardeau. Produces to the Board, as a special permission to settle, list B, on which claimant is No. 2; a plat of survey of the same; and a transfer of said Samuel S. Kennedy to claimant, dated January 12th, 1805.

 Opinion of the Board. February 6th, 1810: Full Board. It is the opinion of the Board that this claim ought not to be granted.

JOHN BYRD, assignee of James Arrell.—A claim for two hundred and thirty-four arpents and five perches of land, situate on the waters of Byrd's creek, district of Cape Girardeau. Produces to the Board, as a special permission to settle, list A, on which James Arrell is No. 131, for three hundred arpents; a plat of survey, dated January 1st, 1806, signed B. Cousin, and countersigned Antoine Soulard, Surveyor General.

 Opinion of the Board. February 6th, 1810: Full Board. It is the opinion of the Board that this claim ought not to be granted.

JOHN BYRD, assignee of Josiah Lee, Junior.—A claim for two hundred and thirty-four arpents of land, situate on the waters of Byrd's creek, district of Cape Girardeau. Produces to the Board, as a special permission to settle, list A, on which said Lee is No. 121, for two hundred arpents; a plat of survey for two hundred and thirty-four arpents; and a conveyance from said Lee to claimant, dated October 3d, 1804.

 Opinion of the Board. February 6th, 1810: Full Board. It is the opinion of the Board that this claim ought not to be granted.

JOHN BYRD, assignee of William Jackson.—A claim for four hundred and eight arpents and eighty-six perches of land, situate on Byrd's creek, district of Cape Girardeau. Produces to the Board, as a special permission to settle, list A, on which claimant is No. 89; a plat of survey, dated December 30th, 1805, signed B. Cousin, and countersigned Antoine Soulard, Surveyor General.

 Testimony taken. June 2d, 1808. (By Frederick Bates, commissioner, authorized from the Board to take testimony at Cape Girardeau, &c.) Joseph Young, being duly sworn, says the premises were improved in the year 1803; a field of several acres cleared, enclosed, and cultivated to this day, but not inhabited; about seven or eight acres in cultivation at this time.

 Opinion of the Board. February 6th, 1810: Full Board. It is the opinion of the Board that this claim ought not to be granted.

AMOS BYRD, Senior.—A claim for one thousand arpents of land, situate on the waters of a fork of Byrd's creek, district of Cape Girardeau. Produces to the Board a concession from Zenon Trudeau, Lieutenant Governor, dated January 7th, 1798; a plat of survey, dated 29th and 30th November, 1799, and certified December 5th, 1799.

 Testimony taken. June 2d, 1808. (By Frederick Bates, commissioner, authorized from the Board to take testimony at Cape Girardeau, &c.) Abraham Byrd, being duly affirmed, says this land was first improved in 1801; in the following years, particularly in 1803, a field of several acres was cleared, enclosed, and cultivated, a house built, and the premises inhabited and cultivated to the present time. Upwards of fifty acres are now in cultivation.

 Opinion and remarks of the Board. February 6th, 1810: Full Board. It is the opinion of a majority of the Board that this claim ought not to be confirmed; Clement B. Penrose, commissioner, voting for the confirmation thereof: but the said majority do declare that, if the said claim had not exceeded eight hundred arpents, they would have voted for its confirmation.

ANDREW PATTERSON.—A claim for three hundred and fifty-one arpents and fifty perches of land, situate on Byrd's creek, district of Cape Girardeau. Produces to the Board, as a special permission to settle, list A, on which claimant is No. 72, for three hundred arpents; a plat of survey, dated December 2d, 1805, signed B. Cousin, and countersigned Antoine Soulard, Surveyor General.

Opinion of the Board. February 6th, 1810: Full Board. It is the opinion of the Board that this claim ought not to be granted.

EPHRAIM CARPENTER.—A claim for seven hundred and fifty arpents of land, situate on the river Saline, district of St. Genevieve. Produces a duly registered general permission to settle on any of the vacant lands, from Peter Delassus Deluziere, dated March 28th, 1798; and an order from the same to remove from the tract he had first settled on to any other part of the public lands.

Testimony taken. June 23d, 1806. Job Westover, being duly sworn, says that claimant had on said tract of land a house; that, in the year 1798, he, the witness, was employed by claimant to lay a floor in said house; that, about two months afterwards, about the time said claimant was preparing to improve and cultivate the said tract, a party of Indians fired at a Mr. Dodge, an inhabitant of that part of the country, and pursued him for several miles; that the settlers, among whom was claimant, being alarmed at the conduct of said Indians, left their settlement; and further, that about a year or eighteen months afterwards, one Philip Emdie moved on said land, and remained thereon during the years 1800 and 1801.

James F. Piller, being also duly sworn, says that he, the witness, arrived in the country in the year 1799; that he purchased said land from claimant, proceeded to the improvement of the same, and lived on it, and raised a crop in the year 1800; that, about the latter part of that year, to wit, Christmas, a Mr. Vallée, surveying a tract of land adjoining the same, surveyed it in, whereupon said witness lost the said improvement, and was obliged to move out; that the said Vallée never paid witness any thing for said improvement so surveyed in; that, in 1802, said witness cultivated again the said tract, raised a crop on the same, one-half of which he gathered, leaving the other half for the said Vallée; that Vallée told witness that the house on said land was the property of the above claimant. Said claimant had, on the 20th day of December, 1803, a wife and child.

Walter Fenwick, being also duly sworn, says that he knew said claimant in the country about nine years ago, and that he remained in it about three or four years.

February 10th, 1810. Stace McDonough sworn, says that the land claimed is situate on the north side of the north fork of the Saline creek, about six or seven miles from its mouth. Witness was on the place claimed in 1798; claimant was then with his family, consisting of a wife and child, and two hired men, and had a house built, which he was living in; had about four acres grubbed, and some fences mauled; that, while witness was at the house of claimant, an express came and informed them that the Indians were robbing the settlement, and had whipped three men in consequence of this information: the settlement was abandoned about a year and a half afterwards. Witness was present when claimant and one Jean F. Pillars made an agreement together, which was, that said Pillars might go and settle on the place claimed; that about Christmas of the year 1800, witness was on the place claimed, and found Jean F. Pillars, with his family, then inhabiting it. Witness saw corn stalks in the field adjoining the house, and appearances of its having been cultivated that year; that the year after, said Pillars, with his family, moved off this land, and went to a place about a mile further up the creek, and has continued to inhabit and cultivate the place moved to ever since.

Opinions of the Board. June 23d, 1806: Present, Clement B. Penrose and James L. Donaldson, commissioners. The Board reject this claim for want of actual inhabitation and cultivation by claimant, prior to and on the 20th day of December, 1803.

February 10th, 1810. Present, John B. C. Lucas and Frederick Bates, commissioners. It is the opinion of the Board that this claim ought not to be granted.

DANIEL BOLLINGER, Senior.—A claim for three hundred and seventy-two arpents of land, situate on White waters, district of Cape Girardeau. Produces to the Board, as a special permission to settle, list A, on which claimant is No. 161; a plat of survey of the same, signed B. Cousin, and countersigned the 27th February, 1806, by Antoine Soulard, Surveyor General.

Opinion of the Board. February 19th, 1810: Full Board. It is the opinion of the Board that this claim ought not to be granted.

DAWALT BOLLINGER, son of Daniel Bollinger.—A claim for three hundred and fifty arpents and ninety-five perches of land, situate on White waters, district of Cape Girardeau. Produces to the Board, as a special permission to settle, list A, on which claimant is No. 98, for three hundred arpents; a plat of survey, signed B. Cousin, and certified to be received for record February 27th, 1806 by Antoine Soulard, Surveyor General.

Testimony taken. June 2, 1808. (By Frederick Bates, commissioner, authorized from the Board to take testimony at Cape Girardeau, &c.) Philip Bollinger, being duly sworn, says that claimant cultivated the premises in 1804.

Opinion of the Board. February 19, 1810: Full Board. It is the opinion of the Board that this claim ought not to be granted.

PHILIP BOLLINGER.—A claim for three hundred arpents of land, situate on Crooked creek, water of White waters, district of Cape Girardeau. Produces to the Board, as a special permission to settle, list A, on which claimant is No. 99.

Opinion of the Board. February 19, 1810: Full Board. It is the opinion of the Board that this claim ought not to be granted.

MATTHIAS BOLLINGER, Senior.—A claim for three hundred and fifty arpents ninety-five perches of land, situate on White waters, district of Cape Girardeau. Produces to the Board, as a special permission to settle, list A, on which claimant is No. 160; a plat of survey, signed B. Cousin, and certified to be received for record February 27, 1806, by Antoine Soulard, Surveyor General.

Opinion of the Board. Febuary 19, 1810: Full Board. It is the opinion of the Board that this claim ought not to be granted.

STEPHEN BYRD.—A claim for four hundred and fifty-seven arpents twenty perches of land, situate on Cow creek, fork of Byrd's creek, district of Cape Girardeau. Produces to the Board, as a special permission to settle, list A, on which claimant is No. 116; a plat of survey, dated December 10, 1805, signed B. Cousin, countersigned Antoine Soulard, Surveyor General.

Opinion of the Board. February 19, 1810: Full Board. It is the opinion of the Board that this claim ought not to be granted.

HENRY HOWARD, assignee of Joseph Young, assignee of Jephtha Cornelius.—A claim for six hundred arpents of land, situate on Byrd's creek, district of Cape Girardeau. Produces to the Board, as a special permission to settle, list A, on which claimant is No. —; and a certificate of survey of five hundred and eighty-five arpents and forty-four perches, dated December 10, 1805; a deed of transfer from Jephtha Cornelius to Joseph Young, dated September 9, 1803, and another deed of transfer from said Young to claimant, dated May 21, 1804.
Testimony taken. April 12, 1806. James Earl, being duly sworn, says that the said Joseph Young did, prior to and on the 20th day of December, 1803, actually inhabit and cultivate the said tract of land.
Opinions of the Board. April 12, 1806: Present, John B. C. Lucas and James L. Donaldson, commissioners. The Board grant the said claimant, assignee of Joseph Young, six hundred arpents of land, situate as aforesaid, as per the said concession.
February 19, 1810: Full Board. It is the opinion of the Board that this claim ought not to be granted.

GEORGE F. BOLLINGER.—A claim for one hundred and eighty arpents and fifty perches of land, situate on White waters, district of Cape Girardeau. Produces to the Board a concession from Don Carlos Dehault Delassus, Lieutenant Governor, for two hundred and fifty arpents, dated January 20, 1800; and a plat of survey, dated January 8, 1806.
Opinion and remarks of the Board. February 19, 1810. The petitioner is styled George Frederick Bollinger, but signs his name, "Frederick Bollinger." A majority of the Board being of opinion that the signature "Frederick Bollinger" ought to be, and is actually, the criterion of the name of the claimant; therefore, it is considered by them that the notice and the style of the petition ought to have been in the name of Frederick Bollinger. It is the opinion of the Board that this claim ought not to be confirmed.

GEORGE HAYS, assignee of Rowland Meredith, assignee of Mary Fitzgibbons.—A claim for two hundred arpents of land, situate on Gibany's creek, district of Cape Girardeau. Produces to the Board a concession from Zenon Trudeau, Lieutenant Governor, to Mary Fitzgibbons, for the same, dated January 5, 1798; a plat of survey, dated May 10, 1799, certified April 13, 1801; a transfer from Mary Fitzgibbons to Rowland Meredith, dated January 15, 1805; and a transfer from said Meredith to claimant, dated February 28, 1805.
Testimony taken. June 2, 1808. (By Frederick Bates, commissioner, authorized from the Board to take testimony at Cape Girardeau, &c.) Andrew Ramsay, junior, being duly sworn, says that there was a sugar camp on this land in the year 1800; no other improvements; sugar still made on the premises.
Opinion of the Board. February 19, 1810: Full Board. It is the opinion of the Board that this claim ought not to be confirmed.

PETER KRYTZ.—A claim for one thousand one hundred and seventy arpents of land, situate on White waters, district of Cape Girardeau. Produces to the Board, as a special permission to settle, list A, on which claimant is No. 28, for five hundred arpents; a plat of survey, dated January 6, 1806, signed B. Cousin, countersigned Antoine Soulard, Surveyor General.
Testimony taken. June 2, 1809. (By Frederick Bates, commissioner, authorized from the Board to take testimony at Cape Girardeau, &c.) George F. Bollinger, being duly sworn, says that claimant commenced his improvement in the year 1803, and, having cultivated corn in that year, moved his family finally to the premises, in the year 1804; he had been occasionally there in the preceding year; thinks claimant raised his house in 1803; constantly inhabited and cultivated to this day; about sixteen or seventeen acres now in cultivation.
Opinion of the Board. February 19, 1810: Full Board. It is the opinion of the Board that this claim ought not to be granted.

PETER KRYTZ, legatee of Duwalt Kyrtz.—A claim for two hundred and thirty-four arpents and thirty-six perches of land, situate on waters of Byrd's creek, district of Cape Girardeau. Produces to the Board, as a special permission to settle, list B, on which Duwalt Krytz is No. 28, for two hundred arpents; a plat of survey, dated January 7, 1806, signed B. Cousin, countersigned Antoine Soulard, Surveyor General.
Testimony taken. June 2, 1808. (By Frederick Bates, commissioner, authorized from the Board to take testimony at Cape Girardeau, &c.) George F. Bollinger, duly sworn, says that this land was improved in the year 1804, in October or November; cabin built; a few acres, about twelve or fourteen, cleared, enclosed, and cultivated; constantly inhabited and cultivated to this day.
Opinion of the Board. February 19, 1810: Full Board. It is the opinion of the Board that this claim ought not to be granted.

JAMES RUSSELL.—A claim for three hundred and fifty arpents and ninety-five perches of land, situate on Byrd's creek, district of Cape Girardeau. Produces to the Board, as a special permission to settle, list A, on which claimant is No. 88; a plat of survey, dated February 20, 1806, signed Edward F. Bound, countersigned February 28, 1806, by Antoine Soulard, Surveyor General.
Testimony taken. June 2, 1808. (By Frederick Bates, commissioner, authorized from the Board to take testimony at Cape Girardeau, &c.) Abraham Byrd, duly affirmed, says that the premises were first settled in the fall of 1805; the following year put in sixteen acres of corn and other grain; constantly inhabited to this day; about thirty-two acres are now in cultivation.
Opinion of the Board. February 21, 1810: Full Board. It is the opinion of the Board that this claim ought not to be granted.

MORRIS YOUNG.—A claim for three hundred and fifty arpents and ninety-five perches of land, situate on a fork of Byrd's creek, district of Cape Girardeau. Produces to the Board, as a special permission to settle, list B, on which claimant is No. 41, for three hundred arpents; and a plat of survey, signed B. Cousin, countersigned Antoine Soulard, Surveyor General.
Opinion of the Board. February 21, 1810: Full Board. It is the opinion of the Board that this claim ought not to be granted.

AUSTIN YOUNG.—A claim for three hundred and thirty-eight arpents and ninety-five perches of land, situate on Byrd's creek, district of Cape Girardeau. Produces to the Board, as a special permission to settle, list A, on which claimant is No. 91, for three hundred arpents; and a certificate of survey of three hundred and thirty-three arpents, dated December 31, 1805.

Testimony taken. April 16, 1806. Joseph Young, being duly sworn, says that claimant was, at the time of obtaining said concession, of the age of twenty-one years and upwards; that he hired a person to improve said tract of land, in the year 1803, who raised a crop on the same in that year, when he had about nine arpents cleared; that the same has been cultivated to this day for the use of the claimant, who was working on the land of the witness and boarding with him.

Opinion of the Board. February 21, 1810: Full Board. It is the opinion of the Board that this claim ought not to be granted.

ZEBULON REED.—A claim for two hundred and fifty arpents of land, in the district of Cape Girardeau. Produces to the Board, as a special permission to settle, list A, on which claimant is No. 75.

Opinion of the Board. February 21, 1810: Full Board. It is the opinion of the Board that this claim ought not to be granted.

JAMES BEVINS.—A claim for two hundred arpents of land, situate on White waters, district of Cape Girardeau. Produces to the Board, as a special permission to settle, list B, on which claimant is No. 31.

Testimony taken. June 3, 1808. (By Frederick Bates, commissioner, authorized from the Board to take testimony at Cape Girardeau, &c.) Isaac Miller, duly sworn, says that this land was first settled in the year 1805, a cabin then built, and four or five acres enclosed and cultivated; constantly inhabited to this time; about fourteen acres now in cultivation; no family.

Opinion of the Board. February 21, 1810: Full Board. It is the opinion of the Board that this claim ought not to be granted.

JAMES CURRIN, assignee of Jacob Myers.—A claim for three hundred and fifty arpents of land, situate at Tewapite Bottom, district of Cape Girardeau. Produces to the Board a certificate from Henry Peyroux, commandant of New Madrid, that a special permission to settle had been granted, dated March 24, 1804; a survey of the same, by James Storry; and a deed of transfer, dated February 11, 1806.

Testimony taken. August 13, 1806. William Cox, being duly sworn, says that the said Myers did settle the said tract of land in March, 1801, and did also, prior to and on the 20th day of December, 1803, actually inhabit and cultivate the same; and had then a wife and seven children.

Opinion and remarks of the Board. August 13, 1806: Full Board. The Board grant the said claimant, assignee of Jacob Myers, five hundred and fifty arpents of land, situate as aforesaid, provided so much be found vacant there.

Opinion of the Board. February 21, 1810: Full Board. It is the opinion of a majority of the Board that this claim ought not to be granted; Frederick Bates, commissioner, voting for the granting thereof.

JAMES BOYD.—A claim for one hundred and eighteen arpents sixteen perches of land, situate on Caney creek, district of Cape Girardeau. Produces a plat of survey, dated December 9, 1805, signed B. Cousin, and countersigned Antoine Soulard, Surveyor General.

Opinion of the Board. February 27, 1810: Present, John B. C. Lucas and Clement B. Penrose, commissioners. It is the opinion of the Board that this claim ought not to be granted.

JOSEPH THOMSON, Sen., (the representatives of.)—A claim for two hundred and thirty-four arpents of land, situate on Ramsay creek, district of Cape Girardeau. Produces to the Board, as a special permission to settle, list A, on which claimant is No. 156, and a certificate of survey, (two hundred and thirty-four arpents,) dated December 20, 1805.

Testimony taken. April 17, 1806. Joseph Worthington, being duly sworn, says that claimant did improve the said tract of land in the year 1804.

June 3, 1808. (By Frederick Bates, commissioner, authorized from the Board to take testimony at Cape Girardeau, &c.) James Cottle, duly sworn, says that improvement commenced in 1807, in the spring; eight or ten acres now in cultivation, and a cabin built.

Opinion of the Board. February 27, 1810: Present, John B. C. Lucas and Clement B. Penrose, commissioners. It is the opinion of the Board that this claim ought not to be granted.

DAVID HARRIS.—A claim for two hundred and sixty-eight arpents ninety perches of land, situate on waters of Ramsay creek, district of Cape Girardeau. Produces to the Board, as a special permission to settle, list B, on which claimant is No. 50, for two hundred and fifty arpents, and a plat of survey, dated December 20, 1805, signed B. Cousin, countersigned Antoine Soulard, Surveyor General.

Testimony taken. April 17, 1806. Joseph Worthington, being duly sworn, says that claimant settled the said tract of land in 1804, and has actually inhabited and cultivated the same to this day.

June 3, 1808. (By Frederick Bates, commissioner, authorized from the Board to take testimony at Cape Girardeau, &c.) Solomon Thorn, sworn, says that, in the year 1803, claimant improved premises, inhabited same year, and has continued to inhabit and cultivate to this time; about sixteen acres in cultivation; two cabins, both built before the 20th December, 1803.

Opinion of the Board. February 28, 1810: Full Board. It is the opinion of the Board that this claim ought not to be granted.

ALEXANDER PARISH.—A claim for two hundred and fifty arpents of land, situate on waters of White waters, district of Cape Girardeau. Produces to the Board, as a special permission to settle, list B, on which claimant is No. 19.

Testimony taken. June 3, 1808. (By Frederick Bates, commissioner, authorized from the Board to take testimony at Cape Girardeau, &c.) Alexander Thorn, duly sworn, says that, in the year 1802, or about six years ago, he saw a small improvement made by claimant on the premises, a half-faced cabin, watermelons planted, and a few peach trees.

Opinion of the Board. February 28, 1810: Full Board. It is the opinion of the Board that this claim ought not to be granted.

LEVI WOLVERTON.—A claim for two hundred and fifty arpents of land, situate on the Mississippi, district of Cape Girardeau. Produces to the Board, as a special permission to settle, list A, on which claimant is No. 42.

Testimony taken. June 3, 1808. (By Frederick Bates, commissioner, authorized from the Board to take testimony at Cape Girardeau, &c.) John Seavers, duly sworn, says that in the year 1805 claimant cleared up some ground, planted vines, and built a half-faced cabin; about one acre now cleared.

Solomon Thorn, duly sworn, says that he cultivated watermelons on the premises eight years ago; in 1803 claimant cultivated, but did not inhabit in that year.

Opinion of the Board. February 28, 1810: Full Board. It is the opinion of the Board that this claim ought not to be granted.

ABRAHAM BYRD, assignee of Jeremiah Thomson, assignee of John Smith.—A claim for two hundred and forty-six arpents of land, situate on Byrd's creek, district of Cape Girardeau. Produces to the Board a permission to settle for John Smith, sworn to by Louis Lorimier, commandant of Cape Girardeau, June 3, 1808.

No improvement except a sugar camp.

Opinion of the Board. February 28, 1810: Full Board. It is the opinion of the Board that this claim ought not to be granted.

STEPHEN BYRD, assignee of Thompson Byrd.—A claim for one hundred and ninety-seven arpents two and a half perches of land, situate in the district of Cape Girardeau. Produces to the Board a concession from Don Zenon Trudeau, Lieutenant Governor, dated January 5, 1798; and a certificate of survey, dated October 1, 1799; and a deed of transfer of said land, dated June 1, 1805.

Testimony taken. April 12, 1806. Athamar Hubbell, being duly sworn, says that claimant was, at the time of obtaining said concession, and still is, under age, and claims no other lands in this Territory in his own name.

June 3, 1808. (By Frederick Bates, commissioner, authorized from the Board to take testimony at Cape Girardeau, &c.) Jacob Jacobs, duly sworn, says that this tract was improved in 1801; in that year, about one acre was cleared, enclosed, and cultivated in corn, tobacco, and vines; never inhabited, and no improvement since.

Opinion of the Board. February 28, 1810: Full Board. It is the opinion of the Board that this claim ought not to be confirmed.

WILLIAM GARNER, assignee of James Murphy.—A claim for seven hundred and ninety arpents of land, situate on the waters of White waters, district of Cape Girardeau. Produces to the Board, as a special permission to settle, list A, on which claimant is No. 68, for three hundred arpents; a survey of the same, taken the 2d December, 1805, and certified February 26, 1806; and a deed of transfer, dated September 6, 1805.

Testimony and acknowledgments taken. August 15, 1806. Elijah Franks, being duly sworn, says that the said Murphy settled the said tract of land in August, 1803, cleared a field, built a house, into which he moved in the fall of that year, and actually inhabited the same prior to and on the 20th day of December, 1803; that, in the spring of 1804, he made a nursery of peach trees, and raised a crop that year; and further, that the same has been actually inhabited and cultivated to this day; that the said Murphy had, on the 20th December, 1803, a wife and child.

June 7, 1808. (By Frederick Bates, commissioner, authorized from the Board to take testimony at Cape Girardeau, &c.) David Ferrell, duly sworn, says that James Murphy and his brother Frank improved this land in the fall of 1803, built a cabin, and lived in it, which said cabin was constantly inhabited until the year 1805; a field of a few acres was cleared, enclosed, and cultivated till the year 1806; between six and eight acres prepared for cultivation.

Ezekiel Able appears before the said commissioner, and relinquishes all claim to the foregoing tract, having sold the same to William Garner, or rather released the same to him, and suffered him to claim under the transfer of James Murphy.

Jeremiah Able also appears before the said commissioner, and relinquishes all claim to the foregoing tract of land to William Garner.

Ezekiel Able, duly sworn, says that there had been some dispute between Frank and James Murphy, both of whom wish to hold the same plantation. Witness was present when Frank agreed that James should keep possession of the land now claimed by Garner, adding that he would go to the other place; saying, at the same time, that he, (witness,) or any other person, might buy, as he (Frank) had no claims to the premises.

John Shields, duly sworn, says, in 1804 was out and settled near the place settled by James, when he heard Frank say that he had given up the premises now claimed to his brother James.

Opinion of the Board. March 2, 1810: Full Board. It is the opinion of a majority of the Board that this claim ought not to be granted; Frederick Bates, commissioner, voting for the granting of three hundred arpents.

DANIEL HUBBLE.—A claim for two hundred and fifty arpents of land, situate on Foster's creek, district of Cape Girardeau. Produces to the Board, as a special permission to settle, list A, on which claimant is No. 56.

Testimony taken. June 3, 1808. (By Frederick Bates, commissioner, authorized from the Board to take testimony at Cape Girardeau, &c.) Matthew Hubble, duly sworn, says that a small improvement was made on this land in the year 1805; a few peach and apple trees planted.

Opinion of the Board. March 2, 1810: Full Board. It is the opinion of the Board that this claim ought not to be granted.

JONATHAN FOREMAN.—A claim for three hundred and fifty three arpents and eighty-eight perches of land, situate on Hubble's creek, district of Cape Girardeau. Produces to the Board a concession from Don Carlos Dehault Delassus, Lieutenant Governor, dated April 27, 1803; a plat of survey, dated February 4, 1806, and certified February 12, same year.

Testimony taken. June 3, 1808. (By Frederick Bates, commissioner, authorized from the Board to take testimony at Cape Girardeau, &c.) John Guething, duly sworn, says that in the spring of 1802 Foreman employed him (witness) to work at his mill; worked seven days; that at this time James Campbell came to the mill, and told witness that he had sold his improvement (by which witness conceived that the mere labor and expense were intended) to Jonathan Foreman, for a cow with calf, or for a cow and calf together, with some other property; that witness gave a quantity of corn to Campbell for the cow, and, on said Campbell's order verbal, received her from Foreman.

David Patterson, duly sworn, says that about January or February, 1802, witness was present at the mill with Campbell and Foreman, who were conversing about the purchase by Foreman of Campbell's improvement, who appeared desirous to sell, on account of his apprehensions of Foreman's mill-dam; witness left them for a short time, and returned, when witness was told that they had bargained; that Foreman had purchased Campbell's improvement, for which he was to let Campbell have a cow with calf, or a cow and calf, and a quantity of corn;

witness understood that the land, as well as the labor and expense, was conveyed by Campbell to Foreman in this bargain.

John Guething, before sworn, in reply to the question of the interfering claimant, Jeremiah Able, answered: I understood it to be the intention of the parties, and the determination of Campbell, after this sale, to lay his head right on some other place.

Peter Burns, being duly sworn, says that he heard Campbell say he had sold his right of that land to Jonathan Foreman, the land lying above where the mill of Jonathan Foreman now stands; witness also heard said Foreman say that he bought said land; witness never understood that Campbell sold his head right to Foreman, and does not believe that he did. Campbell, after this sale, always believed that he had the privilege to lay his head right elsewhere. In 1801 Campbell lived on this land, and cultivated a small spot of ground in turnips and other vegetables; lived in a cabin which had been previously built.

Opinion of the Board. March 2, 1810: Full Board. It is the opinion of the Board that this claim ought not to be granted.

ALEXANDER SUMMERS.—A claim for two hundred and fifty arpents of land, situate on White waters, district of Cape Girardeau. Produces to the Board, as a special permission to settle, list A, on which claimant is No. 49.

Opinion of the Board. March 2, 1810: Full Board. It is the opinion of the Board that this claim ought not to be granted.

JOHN ZELLIFROW.—A claim for three hundred and forty-nine arpents and sixty-eight perches of land, situate on the waters of Byrd's creek, district of Cape Girardeau. Produces to the Board, as a special permission to settle, list A, on which claimant is No. 92, for three hundred arpents; a plat of survey, dated December 10, 1805, signed B. Cousin, countersigned Antoine Soulard, Surveyor General.

Opinion of the Board. March 2, 1810: Full Board. It is the opinion of the Board that this claim ought not to be granted.

DENNIS SULLIVAN.—A claim for three hundred and fifty arpents and ninety-three and one-third perches of land, situate on Byrd's creek, district of Cape Girardeau. Produces to the Board, as a special permission to settle, list A, on which claimant is No. 94, for three hundred arpents; a plat of survey, dated December 30, 1805, signed B. Cousin, countersigned Antoine Soulard, Surveyor General.

Testimony taken. June 4, 1808. (By Frederick Bates, commissioner, authorized from the Board to take testimony at Cape Girardeau, &c.) John McCarty, duly sworn, says that claimant came to Louisiana in the year 1802, and worked at the blacksmith's business for two years, since which he has taught a school. No improvement.

Opinion of the Board. March 2, 1810: Full Board. It is the opinion of the Board that this claim ought not to be granted.

JOHN BYRD, assignee of James Earl, alias Arrell.—A claim for two hundred arpents of land, situate on White waters, district of Cape Girardeau. Produces to the Board, as a special permission to settle, list A, on which claimant is No. 131; a plat of survey, dated January 1, 1806, signed B. Cousin, countersigned Antoine Soulard, Surveyor General; a transfer from James Earl to claimant, dated January 28, 1805.

Opinion of the Board. March 2, 1810: Full Board. It is the opinion of the Board that this claim ought not to be granted.

JOHN P. AIDENGER, assignee of James Earl, assignee of George Morgan.—A claim for three hundred arpents of land, situate on White waters, district of Cape Girardeau. Produces to the Board, as a special permission to settle, list A, on which George Morgan is No. 61, for three hundred arpents; a transfer from George Morgan to James Earl, dated January 27, 1807; and an assignment from said Earl to claimant, dated April 21, 1808.

Testimony taken. June 4, 1808. (By Frederick Bates, commissioner, authorized from the Board to take testimony at Cape Girardeau, &c.) Elisha Welsh, duly sworn, says that he saw Morgan on the land in 1803, but does not know that he lived there; there was no cabin, no cultivation.

Opinion of the Board. March 2, 1810: Full Board. It is the opinion of the Board that this claim ought not to be granted.

EZEKIEL ABLE, assignee of Daniel Brant.—A claim for seven hundred and ninety arpents of land, situate on White waters, district of Cape Girardeau. Produces to the Board a plat of survey of four thousand three hundred arpents, dated December 22, 1805, certified February 28, 1806, in which survey the tract claimed is included; also an assignment of Daniel Brant and others to Ezekiel Able, dated February 25, 1806.

Testimony taken. June 4, 1808. (By Frederick Bates, commissioner, authorized from the Board to take testimony at Cape Girardeau, &c.) Elisha Welsh, being duly sworn as to Brant's improvement, says, improvement made in 1802; a good cabin; about one acre cleared, enclosed, and cultivated; premises constantly inhabited and cultivated to this time; eight acres now in cultivation; a second cabin since built, also stables; and orchards planted.

Charles Sexton, sworn, says he knows the statement of Welsh, as to Brant's improvement, is true.

Opinion of the Board. March 8, 1810. Present: John B. C. Lucas and Clement B. Penrose, commissioners. It is the opinion of the Board that this claim ought not to be granted.

EZEKIEL ABLE, assignee of Rezin Bailey.—A claim for seven hundred and forty arpents of land, situate on White waters, district of Cape Girardeau. Produces to the Board a plat of survey of four thousand three hundred arpents, dated December 22, 1805, certified February 28, 1806, in which survey the tract claimed is included; also an assignment of Rezin Bailey and others to Ezekiel Able, dated February 25, 1806.

Testimony taken. June 4, 1808. (By Frederick Bates, commissioner, authorized from the Board to take testimony at Cape Girardeau, &c. Elisha Welsh, sworn, says, as to Bailey's improvement, cultivated in 1802; lived in a camp in 1803, and cultivated turnips; not inhabited, but cultivated in timothy and orchards, to the present time.

Opinion of the Board. March 8, 1810. Present: John B. C. Lucas and Clement B. Penrose, commissioners. It is the opinion of the Board that this claim ought not to be granted.

EZEKIEL ABLE, assignee of William Smith.—A claim for one thousand and forty arpents of land, situate on White waters, district of Cape Girardeau. Produces to the Board a plat of survey of four thousand three hundred arpents, dated December 22, 1805, certified February 28, 1806, in which survey the tract claimed is included; also an assignment of William Smith and others to Ezekiel Able, dated February 25, 1806.

Testimony taken. June 4, 1808. (By Frederick Bates, commissioner, authorized from the Board to take testimony at Cape Girardeau, &c.) Elisha Welsh, sworn as to William Smith's improvement, says, settled in 1802; built a cabin; cleared, enclosed, and cultivated three acres; inhabited and cultivated to this time; fifteen acres now in cultivation.

Opinion of the Board. March 8, 1810. Present: John B. C. Lucas and Clement B. Penrose, commissioners. It is the opinion of the Board that this claim ought not to be granted.

EZEKIEL ABLE, assignee of Francis Murphy.—A claim for seven hundred and ninety arpents of land, situate on White waters, district of Cape Girardeau. Produces to the Board a plat of survey of four thousand three hundred arpents, dated December 22, 1805, certified February 28, 1806; in which survey the tract claimed is included; also an assignment from Francis Murphy and others to Ezekiel Able, dated February 25, 1806.

Testimony taken. June 4, 1808. (By Frederick Bates, commissioner, authorized from the Board to take testimony at Cape Girardeau, &c.) Elisha Welsh, sworn as to Francis Murphy, says, improvements made in 1803; about one acre cleared, enclosed, and cultivated; built a cabin and lived in it; wife bore a child; these premises constantly inhabited and cultivated.

Opinion of the Board. March 8, 1810: Present, John B. C. Lucas and Clement B. Penrose, commissioners. It is the opinion of the Board that this claim ought not to be granted.

EZEKIEL ABLE, assignee of James Smith.—A claim for six hundred and forty acres of land, situate on White waters, district of Cape Girardeau. Produces to the Board a plat of survey of four thousand three hundred arpents, dated 22d December, 1805, certified 28th February, 1806; in which survey the tract claimed is included; also an assignment of James Smith and others to Ezekiel Able, dated February 25, 1806.

Testimony taken. June 4, 1808: (By Frederick Bates, commissioner, authorized from the Board to take testimony at Cape Girardeau, &c.) Elisha Welsh, sworn, says, James Smith improved in 1803; cultivated one-fourth of an acre; did not inhabit; cut up brush and piled it.

Opinion of the Board. March 8, 1810: Present, John B. C. Lucas and Clement B. Penrose, commissioners. It is the opinion of the Board that this claim ought not to be granted.

EZEKIEL ABLE, assignee of Jacob Sharadon.—A claim for six hundred and forty acres of land, situate on White waters, district of Cape Girardeau. Produces to the Board an assignment of Jacob Sharadon and others to Ezekiel Able, dated February 25, 1806.

Testimony taken. June 4, 1808. (By Frederick Bates, commissioner, authorized from the Board to take testimony at Cape Girardeau, &c.) Daniel Brant, sworn as to Sharadon's improvement, says, premises were improved in 1803; one-fourth of an acre chopped, trees deadened, brush piled.

Opinion of the Board. March 8, 1810: Present, John B. C. Lucas and Clement B. Penrose, commissioners. It is the opinion of the Board that this claim ought not to be granted.

JOHN MCCARTY, assignee of William Murphy, assignee of Alexander Andrews, Jun.—A claim for four hundred and forty arpents eighty perches of land, situate on waters of Byrd's creek, district of Cape Girardeau. Produces to the Board, as a special permission to settle, list A, on which Alexander Andrews, Junior, is No. 13, for three hundred arpents; a plat of survey, dated 9th December, 1805, signed B. Cousin, countersigned Antoine Soulard, Surveyor General; a deed of transfer from Alexander Andrews, Jun. to said William Murphy, dated 1st August, 1802; and another deed of transfer, from said William Murphy to claimant, dated the 11th February, 1806.

Testimony taken. August 18, 1806. Francis Murphy, being duly sworn, says that the said tract of land was settled in the year 1802, and was, also, prior to and on the 20th day of December, 1803, actually inhabited and cultivated by one Alexander Andrews, Sen., as tenant to the said William Murphy.

Opinions of the Board. August 18, 1806: Present, John B. C. Lucas and Clement B. Penrose, Esqrs. The Board reject this claim for want of actual inhabitation by the said William Murphy, and also of a permission to settle.

March 2, 1810: Full Board. It is the opinion of the Board that this claim ought not to be granted.

AQUILLA WATHEN, assignee of Polly Boyd.—A claim for two hundred arpents of land, situate on Caney creek, district of Cape Girardeau. Produces to the Board an affidavit of permission to settle, in favor of Polly Boyd, dated 6th June, 1808.

Testimony taken. June 4, 1808. (By Frederick Bates, commissioner, authorized from the Board to take testimony at Cape Girardeau, &c.) James Boyd, duly sworn, says that in 1803, before and after the 20th December, Polly Boyd lived on the premises, and in the following year witness, her father, cultivated flax on the premises for her use.

June 7, 1808. (By Frederick Bates, as aforesaid.) James Boyd, duly sworn, says that in the spring of 1802 witness helped to raise a cabin on that place, and also assisted in clearing about one acre and a half of ground, and in breaking it up and planting it; in the year 1803, old Mr. Andrews raised corn on the premises, by permission of witness, as Polly Boyd's father; in 1804, witness put part of it in flax, pulled and put the flax in the cabin which we had built in 1802, which, or a part of it, continued in said cabin until the present spring.

John Boyd, duly sworn, says that he knows very little more than what the foregoing witness, his father, has stated.

Robert Green, sworn, says that claimant employed witness's son, and paid him twenty dollars for raising a cabin on the premises in 1807.

Opinion of the Board. March 2, 1810: Full Board. It is the opinion of the Board that this claim ought not to be granted.

HUGH CRESWELL.—A claim for one hundred and one arpents thirty-one perches of land, situate on Randall's creek, district of Cape Girardeau. Produces to the Board, as a special permission to settle, list A, on which the claimant is No. 138, for one hundred arpents; a plat of survey, dated 3d February, 1806, certified 13th February of the same year.

Opinion of the Board. March 8, 1810: Present, John B. C. Lucas and Clement B. Penrose, commissioners. It is the opinion of the Board that this claim ought not to be granted.

JOHN GIBANY.—A claim for three hundred and fifty arpents ninety-five perches of land, situate on White waters, district of Cape Girardeau. Produces to the Board, as a special permission to settle, list A, on which claimant is No. 129; a plat of survey, dated December 3, 1805, signed Edward F. Bond, countersigned February 28, 1806, by Antoine Soulard, Surveyor General.

LAND GRANTS IN MISSOURI TERRITORY - 1805 - 1812   31

****

Testimony taken. June 4, 1808. (By Frederick Bates, commissioner, authorized from the Board to take testimony at Cape Girardeau, &c.) Elisha Welsh, duly sworn, says that a cabin was built on the premises in 1804; a small spot cleared, but no cultivation.

Opinion of the Board. March 8, 1810: Present, John B. C. Lucas and Clement B. Penrose, commissioners. It is the opinion of the Board that this claim ought not to be granted.

CHARLES SEXTON.—A claim for three hundred and fifty arpents ninety-five perches of land, situate on White waters, district of Cape Girardeau. Produces to the Board, as a special permission to settle, list A, on which claimant is No. 48, for three hundred arpents; a plat of survey, dated 3d December, 1805, certified to be received for record 28th February, 1806, by Antoine Soulard, Surveyor General.

Testimony taken. June 4, 1808. (By Frederick Bates, commissioner, authorized from the Board to take testimony at Cape Girardeau, &c.) Daniel Brant, duly sworn, says that claimant made a small improvement in the year 1803, but did not inhabit; this improvement being afterwards taken in by the survey of Ezekiel Able, the surveyor laid out a tract for claimant, in the woods adjoining the lands of the said Ezekiel, which has never been improved.

Opinion of the Board. March 8, 1810: Present, John B. C. Lucas and Clement B. Penrose, commissioners. It is the opinion of the Board that this claim ought not to be granted.

JOHN SIMPSON.—A claim for three hundred arpents of land, situate on waters of Hubble's creek, district of Cape Girardeau. Produces to the Board, as a special permission to settle, list A, on which claimant is No. 45.

Opinion of the Board. March 8, 1810: Present, John B. C. Lucas and Clement B. Penrose, commissioners. It is the opinion of the Board that this claim ought not to be granted.

BAPTISTE GODAIR.—A claim for two hundred and four arpents of land, situate on Ramsay's creek, district of Cape Girardeau. Produces to the Board, as a special permission to settle, list A, on which claimant is No. 41, for three hundred and fifty arpents; a plat of survey of two hundred and four arpents, dated 21st December, 1805, signed B. Cousin, countersigned Antoine Soulard, Surveyor General.

Testimony taken. June 4, 1808. (By Frederick Bates, commissioner, authorized from the Board to receive testimony at Cape Girardeau, &c.) Samuel Bradley, duly sworn, says that in 1803 a small brush heap was made, and logs cut for a cabin, and cabin raised in 1804; since which time, it has been constantly inhabited and cultivated; about two acres in cultivation in 1804.

Opinion of the Board. March 8, 1810: Present, John B. C. Lucas and Clement B. Penrose, commissioners. It is the opinion of the Board that this claim ought not to be granted.

WILLIAM MORRISON, assignee of Jeremiah Thompson, assignee of David McMoutrie.—A claim for four hundred and sixty-four arpents ninety-five perches of land, situate on Gibany's creek, district of Cape Girardeau. Produces to the Board, as a special permission to settle, list B, on which David McMoutrie is No. 3, for three hundred arpents; a plat of survey, dated 6th January, 1806, certified to be received for record 26th February, 1806, by Antoine Soulard, Surveyor General; a deed of transfer from said McMoutrie to said Thompson, dated 6th December, 1804; and a deed of transfer from said Thompson to claimant, dated 7th May, 1805.

Testimony taken. June 4, 1808. (By Frederick Bates, commissioner, authorized from the Board to take testimony at Cape Girardeau, &c.) Joseph Worthington, duly sworn, says that premises were first settled and cultivated in spring of 1803, and continued till the fall of same year; after which year it was left vacant.

Opinion of the Board. March 8, 1810: Present, John B. C. Lucas and Clement B. Penrose, commissioners. It is the opinion of the Board that this claim ought not to be granted.

THOMAS FOSTER.—A claim for two hundred and forty arpents of land, situate on Hubble's creek, district of Cape Girardeau. Produces to the Board a notice to the recorder, dated 1st June, 1808.

Testimony taken. June 6th 1808. (By Frederick Bates, commissioner, authorized from the Board to take testimony at Cape Girardeau, &c.) David Ferrell, sworn, says that claimant in 1803 built a cabin, cleared, enclosed, and cultivated a field of a few acres, inhabited and cultivated throughout the year 1803, and abandoned until the last winter, when he again took possession.

Opinion of the Board. March 13th, 1810: Full Board. It is the opinion of the Board that this claim ought not to be granted.

JOSEPH WORTHINGTON, assignee of Henry Hall.—A claim for two hundred and eighty-four arpents thirty-one and one-third perches of land, situate on Mill creek, district of Cape Girardeau. Produces to the Board a certificate of survey of the same, dated December 20th, 1805, and a deed of transfer of the same, dated December; 27th, 1804.

Testimony taken. April 17th, 1806. David Ferrell, being duly sworn, says that the said Henry Hall settled the said tract of land in the fall of 1803, and did actually inhabit and cultivate the same prior to and on the 20th of December, 1803, when he had a wife and three children.

Opinions of the Board. April 17th, 1806: Present, John B. C. Lucas and James L. Donaldson, commissioners. The Board grant the said claimant, assignee as aforesaid, one thousand arpents of land, situate as aforesaid, provided so much be found vacant there.

March 13th, 1810: Full Board. It is the opinion of the Board that this claim ought not to be granted.

JOSEPH WORTHINGTON.—A claim for one hundred and seventy arpents of land, situate on Ramsay's creek, district of Cape Girardeau. Produces to the Board, as a special permission to settle, list A, on which claimant is No. 155, for one hundred and fifty arpents; a plat of survey, dated 21st December, 1805, and certified to be received for record 27th February, 1806, by Antoine Soulard, Surveyor General.

Opinion of the Board. March 13th, 1810: Full Board. It is the opinion of the Board that this claim ought not to be granted.

JOSEPH THOMPSON, Junior.—A claim for two hundred and fifty arpents of land, situate on Caney creek, district of Cape Girardeau. Produces to the Board, as a special permission to settle, list A, on which claimant is No. 95.

Testimony taken. June 6th, 1808. (By Frederick Bates, commissioner, authorized from the Board to take testimony at Cape Girardeau, &c.) Joseph Worthington, duly sworn, says that claimant, in the fall of the year 1803, went on the premises, built a camp, and lived in it for a short time, (not till 23d of December;) deadened and marked trees, and planted peach stones; no other improvement.

Opinion of the Board. March 14th, 1810: Full Board. It is the opinion of the Board that this claim ought not to be granted.

SAMUEL DORSEY, assignee of Horace Austin.—A claim for eight hundred and sixty-five arpents sixty-six perches of land, situate on White waters, district of Cape Girardeau. Produces to the Board, as a special permission to settle, list A, on which Horace Austin is No. 55, for three hundred arpents; and a survey, dated 15th December, 1805, and certified to be received for record 26th February, 1806, by Antoine Soulard, Surveyor General; also, a deed of transfer from said Horace Austin to claimant, dated May 8th, 1805.

Testimony taken. June 6th, 1808. (By Frederick Bates, commissioner, authorized from the Board to take testimony at Cape Girardeau, &c.) Thomas Foster, duly sworn, says that Austin settled in the fall of 1803, and lived in a cabin previously built; cleared and enclosed a field of three or four acres, and cultivated it the following year, in the fall of which he moved away.

Opinion of the Board. March 14th, 1810: Full Board. It is the opinion of a majority of the Board that this claim ought not to be granted; Frederick Bates, commissioner, voting for the granting of three hundred arpents.

JENNY LOGAN, widow of John Logan.—A claim for four hundred and ninety-one arpents seventy-five perches of land, situate in the district of New Madrid. Produces to the Board a certificate of survey of said land, dated December 18th, 1805.

Testimony taken. April 18th, 1806. Jacob Friend, being duly sworn, says that claimant settled the said tract of land in the year 1802, and did prior to and on the 20th day of December, 1803, actually inhabit and cultivate the said tract of land, and had then three children.

June 6th, 1808. (By Frederick Bates, commissioner, authorized from the Board to take testimony at Cape Girardeau, &c.) Jeremiah Simpson, being duly sworn, says that in March, 1801, the widow went on this land, which her husband had in his life time chosen, finished a cabin which had been before commenced and abandoned, cleared one and a half or two acres of ground, enclosed and cultivated it in March or April, 1802; the widow was married and left the premises; since which time there has been neither inhabitation nor cultivation.

Opinions of the Board. April 18th, 1806: Present, John B. C. Lucas and James L. Donaldson, commissioners. The Board grant the said claimant ———, situate as aforesaid, provided so much be found vacant there.

March 14th 1810: Full Board. It is the opinion of the Board that this claim ought not to be granted.

WILLIAM HAND.—A claim for three hundred arpents of land, situate on the waters of Hubble's creek, district of Cape Girardeau. Produces to the Board, as a special permission to settle, list A, on which claimant is No. 69.

Testimony taken. June 2d, 1808. (By Frederick Bates, commissioner, authorized from the Board to take testimony at Cape Girardeau, &c.) Henry Hand, duly sworn, says that he made brush piles and cut logs on the 7th January, 1802; in the following year, July 4th, he commenced a clearing, and soon thereafter planted corn and turnips; July 7th, 1804, John Taylor took possession of the premises, for the removal of whom, he, witness, applied to Louis Lorimer, Esq., then commandant of Cape Girardeau.

John McCarty, duly sworn, says that a few years ago, perhaps in 1803, he saw an advertisement of claimant, warning all persons against trespassing or intruding on a tract of land which he claimed by improvement or head right, granted by Louis Lorimer, the commandant of the district. This advertisement was posted up at Foreman's mill.

Charles Demoss, duly sworn, says, in 1803, passing through the land now occupied by John Taylor, he saw brush heaps near a spring; same year, at same spring, saw an advertisement on a tree, forewarning all persons from occupying said land, as it was alleged to be the property of claimant; saw the advertisement alluded to in M'Carty's testimony at the mill.

Gilbert Hector, duly sworn, says that he, witness, went with claimant to premises in the year 1803 or 1804, to the camp of John Taylor, when claimant, in presence of witness, forewarned said Taylor from making any improvement on said land.

Question by interfering claimant, (Able.)—Did you see an improvement on this land in 1803? Answer.—I saw either turnips or corn cultivated on premises, or perhaps both, and enclosed by a brush fence, either in 1803 or 1804, and before Taylor occupied.

B. Cousin, Esq., states, from a registry which he brought to the Board, that William Hand desired him to annul an entry of location for three hundred arpents on Hubble's creek, for the reason that he should lay his head right arising from the general concession at Cape La Cruche; it further appears from the said registry, that the land thus vacated was then entered for John Taylor.

Opinion of the Board. March 14th, 1810: Full Board. It is the opinion of the Board that this claim ought not to be granted.

JOHN TAYLOR.—A claim for five hundred and sixty-two arpents seventy-three and a half perches of land, situate on Hubble's and Randall's creeks, district of Cape Girardeau. Produces to the Board, as a special permission to settle, list B, on which claimant is No. 20, for five hundred and fifty arpents, (this claim interfering with the foregoing;) a plat of survey, dated 6th December, 1805, signed B. Cousin, countersigned Antoine Soulard, Surveyor General.

Testimony taken. June 2d, 1808. (By Frederick Bates, commissioner, authorized from the Board to take testimony at Cape Girardeau, &c.) Samuel Pew, sworn, says he knows the land, lives near it, has passed through it, and knows of no cultivation on the premises in 1803.

David Paterson, sworn, says that he knows this tract of land, and was acquainted with it before Taylor moved to it, and verily believes that there were no improvements on the premises in the year 1803; at this time there are a good square log-house, stable, kitchen, smoke-house, and ten or twelve acres in cultivation.

Opinion of the Board. March 14th, 1810: Full Board. It is the opinion of the Board that this claim ought not to be granted.

PETER MENARD.—A claim for four hundred arpents. Produces to the Board a concession from Zenon Trudeau, Lieutenant Governor, for four hundred arpents, dated 5th November, 1798.

Opinion of the Board. March 19th, 1810: Full Board. It is the opinion of the Board that this claim ought not to be confirmed.

JOHN C. HARBISON, assignee of John Hays, sheriff of the district of Cape Girardeau, who sold the following property as belonging to Louis Largeau; produces to the Board a concession from Don Zenon Trudeau, Lieutenant Governor, to Louis Largeau, for the same, dated August 26, 1797; a plat of survey, dated December 1, 1797, certified January 1, 1798; and a deed of conveyance from said sheriff Hays to claimant, dated December 7, 1805; a claim for one thousand arpents of land.

LAND GRANTS IN MISSOURI TERRITORY - 1805 - 1812

33

****

Acknowledgments taken. June 7, 1808. (By Frederick Bates, authorized from the Board to take testimony &c. at Cape Girardeau, &c.) Claimant appeared personally before said commissioner, and acknowledges that, for valuable consideration, he has and does transfer to Anthony Hayden two hundred and fifty arpents of the tract now claimed; and claimant also acknowledges that, for valuable considerations, he has transferred, and does hereby transfer, to Rheineke and Steenback, two hundred and fifty arpents of the tract now claimed.

Opinion of the Board. March 19, 1810: Full Board. It is the opinion of the Board that this claim ought not to be confirmed.

LOUIS LORIMER.—A claim for eight thousand arpents of land, situate on the Mississippi, district of Cape Girardeau. Produces to the Board a petition for eighty by one hundred arpents; a concession thereon from the Baron de Carondelet, Governor General of Louisiana, for forty arpents front, by one hundred arpents depth, dated October 26, 1795; an official letter from the said Governor General to Zenon Trudeau, Lieutenant Governor, ordering him to put claimant in possession of the other forty arpents front, by one hundred arpents depth, petitioned for by him, dated January 26, 1797; a certified copy of a plat of survey of eight thousand arpents, taken October 26, 1797, certified December 11, 1797, signed Antoine Soulard, Surveyor General of the Territory of Louisiana, February 27, 1806.

Translations of the several papers produced by claimant in support of his claim.

Don Louis Lorimer, inhabitant of this district, with the greatest respect due to your lordship, represents, that wishing to establish himself in the same, petitions your lordship to be pleased to grant him eighty arpents of land in front, by one hundred in depth, front to Cypress island, in Cape Girardeau, bounded on its two extremities by the King's domain; a favor which he hopes to merit of your justice.

At the request of the party interested.

JUAN BARNO Y FERRUSOLA.

To His Lordship the GOVERNOR GENERAL.

NEW MADRID, *September 1, 1795.*

I consider the petitioner worthy of the favor which he solicits, for being vested with the circumstances required by the instruction.

THOMAS PORTELL.

NEW ORLEANS, *October 26, 1795.*

The Surveyor, Don Anthony Soulard, shall establish the petitioner on forty arpents in front of the eighty which he demands, by one hundred in depth, on the place mentioned by the above memorial, provided they are vacant, and do not prejudice the neighbors, under the express condition to make the road and regular improvements within the precise term of one year; and this concession to be declared null and void, if, at the precise term of three, the said land is not established; and not being in his power to alienate the same within the said term; under which provisions the diligence of survey shall be made at the continuation, which will be remitted to me in order to provide the petitioner with the corresponding title in form.

EL BARON DE CARONDELET.

NEW ORLEANS, *January 26, 1797.*

You will give orders to Anthony Soulard to survey for Louis Lorimer the forty arpents more of land which he petitioned for, on the place mentioned, and which will complete the eighty he had demanded; after which, he is to demand it by memorial, which you will recommend with reference to this official letter, in order to give him the decree of concession.

God preserve you many years.

EL BARON DE CARONDELET.

Don ZENON TRUDEAU.

ST. LOUIS, *February 26, 1806.*

No. 1.—Surveyed in virtue of the decree of His Lordship the Baron de Carondelet, Commandant General of the province, dated the 26th October, 1795, and of the official letter by him directed to the Lieutenant Governor, in date of the 26th February, 1797, by him transmitted to me. The said tract surveyed the 26th October, 1797; the certificate of survey delivered the 11th of December, same year.

I certify the present extract to be faithfully copied and translated from the register A, of the surveys in Cape Girardeau district, page 1, No. 1.

ANTOINE SOULARD,
Surveyor General of Territory of Louisiana.

Don LOUIS LORIMER.

Testimony taken. March 20, 1810: Auguste Chouteau, sworn, says that the claimant inhabited and cultivated the land claimed fifteen or twenty years ago, and continued so to do until eight years past; the last time witness saw the place claimed, claimant had made considerable improvements on the land.

Marie Philip Le Duc, sworn, says that he saw claimant on the place claimed, inhabiting and cultivating in 1799; that claimant was then erecting large buildings; witness has seen the place claimed several times since, the last time in 1808; always found claimant on the land inhabiting, and cultivating, and improving the same.

Anthony Soulard, sworn, says that the village of Cape Girardeau is on the tract claimed by Louis Lorimer, as proprietor, and that the inhabitants claim under him.

Opinion and remarks of the Board. March 20th, 1810: Full Board. The Board are unanimously of opinion that this claim ought not to be confirmed. Clement B. Penrose and Frederick Bates, commissioners, declaring that if this claim had not exceeded a league square, they would have voted for its confirmation. John B. C. Lucas, commissioner, states as reasons of his opinion, that the order of survey or concession under date of the 26th October, 1795, does not appear to be registered; that the letter of office, under date of the 26th January, 1797, directed to Don Zenon Trudeau, is not an order directed by said Zenon Trudeau to Anthony Soulard, even if it should be construed that the said order is of sufficient authority to make the survey. However, it does not appear that the said order bears registry. He further states, that the quantity of land claimed under these two orders is more than the quantity usually allowed, agreeably to the laws, usages, and customs of the Spanish Government; and that no ordinance or copy of ordinance has been shown or exhibited authorizing the Governor to make decrees or orders for such quantity.

LOUIS LORIMER.—A claim for one thousand arpents of land. Produces to the Board a petition to Don Carlos Dehault Delassus, Lieutenant Governor, and a recommendation from said Delassus to the Intendant, dated 31st July, 1800.

Opinion of the Board. March 22d, 1810: Full Board. It is the opinion of the Board that this claim ought not to be confirmed.

LOUIS LORIMER.—A claim for thirty thousand arpents. Produces to the Board a concession for the same from Don Carlos Dehault Delassus, Lieutenant Governor, dated 15th January, 1800; also an official letter from said Lieutenant Governor to claimant, dated 2d August, 1803.

Opinion of the Board. March 22d, 1810: Full Board. It is the opinion of the Board that this claim ought not to be confirmed.

LOUIS LORIMER, assignee of Francis Bertheaume.—A claim for four hundred and twenty arpents of land. Produces to the Board a concession from Don Carlos Dehault Delassus, Lieutenant Governor, to said Bertheaume for the same, dated 28th December, 1799; and a deed of transfer from Bertheaume to claimant, dated December 5th, 1804.

Opinion of the Board. March 22d, 1810: Full Board. It is the opinion of the Board that this claim ought not to be confirmed.

WILLIAM LORIMER.—A claim for one thousand arpents of land, situate on the forks of Cape La Cruche, district of Cape Girardeau. Produces to the Board a concession for the same from Don Carlos Dehault Delassus, Lieutenant Governor, dated 28th December, 1799.

Opinion of the Board. March 22d, 1810: Full Board. It is the opinion of the Board that this claim ought not to be confirmed.

LOUIS LORIMER, Jun.—A claim for one thousand and six arpents thirty-two perches of land, situate on Caney creek, district of Cape Girardeau. Produces to the Board a concession from Don Carlos Dehault Delassus, Lieutenant Governor, for one thousand arpents, dated 28th December, 1799; a plat of survey, dated November 25th, 1803, and certified 13th December, 1803.

Opinion of the Board. March 22d, 1810: Full Board. It is the opinion of the Board that this claim ought not to be confirmed.

AUGUSTE BOUGAINVILLE LORIMER.—A claim for seven hundred and forty arpents of land, situate on Caney creek, district of Cape Girardeau. Produces to the Board a concession from Don Carlos Dehault Delassus, Lieutenant Governor, for one thousand arpents, dated 28th December, 1799; a plat of survey, dated November 25th, 1803, and certified 13th December, 1803.

Opinion of the Board. March 22d, 1810: Full Board. It is the opinion of the Board that this claim ought not to be confirmed.

LOUIS LORIMER, assignee of Hypolite Mariot.—A claim for four hundred and sixty-one arpents of land, situate on Big Swamp, district of Cape Girardeau. Produces to the Board a concession from Don Carlos Dehault Delassus, Lieutenant Governor, to Hypolite Mariot, for two hundred and fifty arpents, dated December 10th, 1799; a plat of survey, dated 12th and 13th January, 1804, certified 7th February, 1804; also list A, on which said Mariot is No. 127, for three hundred arpents; a deed of transfer from said Mariot to claimant, dated February 18th, 1804.

Opinion of the Board. March 22d, 1810: Full Board. It is the opinion of the Board that this claim ought not to be confirmed.

JAMES EVANS, assignee of Hays, sheriff of the district of Cape Girardeau, assignee of Louis Largeau.—A claim for five hundred arpents of land. Produces to the Board a notice to the recorder, dated June 7th, 1808; also a deed from said sheriff, who sold the said land as the property of William Lorimer, as heir to Louis Largeau, to claimant; the said deed dated September 18th, 1807; the land claimed lying back of the Old Cape.

Opinion of the Board. March 22d, 1810: Full Board. It is the opinion of the Board that this claim ought not to be granted.

JOHN HAYS.—A claim for seven hundred and forty arpents of land, situate on the Mississippi, district of Cape Girardeau. Produces to the Board, as a special permission to settle, list A, on which claimant is No. 71, for four hundred arpents; a plat of survey, dated 18th February, 1806, signed Edward F. Bond, countersigned Antoine Soulard, Surveyor General, 28th February, 1806.

Testimony taken. June 7th, 1808. (By Frederick Bates, authorized from the Board to take testimony at Cape Girardeau, &c.) Solomon Thorn, duly sworn, says that in 1802 he was on this tract, and saw an improvement, to wit, a cabin and a field in cultivation, with corn, which said improvement witness has been frequently told by claimant was his property; witness has passed this tract every year since 1802, and always observed that it was in cultivation.

Opinion of the Board. March 22d, 1810: Full Board. It is the opinion of the Board that this claim ought not to be granted.

JOHN MCCARTY, assignee of Jacob Kelly.—A claim for five hundred and forty-six arpents forty-eight perches of land, situate on Byrd's creek, district of Cape Girardeau. Produces to the Board a concession from Don Carlos Dehault Delassus, Lieutenant Governor, to Jacob Kelly, dated 24th January, 1800, for five hundred and fifty arpents; a plat of survey, dated 18th April, 1803, certified May 2d, 1803; and a transfer from said Jacob Kelly to claimant, dated August 30th, 1803.

Testimony taken. June 7th, 1808. (By Frederick Bates, commissioner, authorized from the Board to take testimony at Cape Girardeau, &c.) Solomon Thorn, duly sworn, says that Cavender, son-in-law and tenant of claimant, lived on and cultivated this land in 1803, at which time about thirteen acres were cultivated; a good cabin and fences; premises inhabited and cultivated to the present day; fourteen or fifteen acres now in cultivation.

Opinion of the Board. March 22d, 1810: Full Board. It is the opinion of a majority of the Board that this claim ought not to be confirmed; Frederick Bates, commissioner, voting for a confirmation.

GEORGE HENDERSON.—A claim for three hundred arpents of land, situate on the big bend of the Mississippi, district of Cape Girardeau. Produces to the Board, as a special permission to settle, list A, on which claimant is No. 82; and also a certificate of permission to settle from Louis Lorimer, commandant of Cape Girardeau district, dated 7th June, 1808, sworn to before Robert Green; a plat of survey, dated 5th February, 1806, signed Edward F. Bond, and countersigned Antoine Soulard, Surveyor General, 28th February, 1806.

Opinion of the Board. March 22d, 1810: Full Board. It is the opinion of the Board that this claim ought not to be granted.

NICOLAS REVEILLE.—A claim for two hundred arpents of land, situate on Ramsay's creek, district of Cape Girardeau. Produces to the Board, as a special permission to settle, list A, on which claimant is No. 115.

Testimony taken. June 7th, 1808. (By Frederick Bates, commissioner, authorized from the Board to take testimony at Cape Girardeau, &c.) Solomon Thorn, duly sworn, says that in the year 1801 he saw a field enclosed, (of about one acre,) with a brush fence, and cultivated in corn, cucumbers, and other vegetables, at which time there was a cabin on this tract inhabited, but how long after the witness does not know; said cabin was below the Big Lick, about one hundred yards on the west side of the creek.

Opinion of the Board. March 22d, 1810: Full Board. It is the opinion of the Board that this claim ought not to be granted.

THOMAS HUFF.—A claim for five hundred arpents of land, situate on lake Le Bœuf, district of New Madrid. Produces to the Board an order of survey from Henry Peyroux, commandant of New Madrid district, for five hundred arpents, dated 22d May, 1801, and No. 1224; and a survey, signed Joseph Story, for four hundred and ninety-six arpents, without date.

Testimony taken. June 15, 1808. (By Frederick Bates, commissioner, authorized from the Board to take testimony at New Madrid, &c.) Edward Mathews, duly sworn, says that premises were cleared, enclosed, and cultivated in 1801; left the land some time in same year, when claimant left the country; he left also his property, to wit, working tools, &c., and appeared anxious to return, but never did that witness knows of.

William Smith, duly sworn, says, in the beginning of 1801, he came to the country with two negroes and other property, in which year he cleared, enclosed, and cultivated, to wit, four or five acres of land, and abandoned the premises after making one crop, leaving his working tools and some cattle; after removal, claimant wrote to witness, desiring him to take care of his plantation.

Opinion of the Board. March 26, 1810: Present, John B. C. Lucas and Clement B. Penrose, commissioners. It is the opinion of the Board that this claim ought not to be confirmed.

THOMAS HUFF, Jun.—A claim for two hundred arpents of land, situate on lake Le Bœuf, district of New Madrid. Produces to the Board an order of survey from Henry Peyroux, commandant of New Madrid district, dated 22d May, 1801, and No. 1224, for two hundred arpents; and a survey of the same, signed Joseph Story, without date.

Opinion of the Board. March 26, 1810: Present, John B. C. Lucas and Clement B. Penrose, commissioners. It is the opinion of the Board that this claim ought not to be confirmed.

CHARLES LUCAS, assignee of Phœbe Jones.—A claim for two hundred and fifty arpents of land, situate on Tywappety, district of New Madrid. Produces to the Board a certified copy of a permission to settle, from Henry Peyroux, commandant of New Madrid district, dated March 24, 1802; a survey, dated the 15th January, 1806; and a deed of transfer of Phœbe Jones to claimant, dated September 4, 1805.

Testimony taken. August 13, 1806. John Tucker, sworn, says that the said Phœbe Jones had, on the 20th day of December, 1803, a child and two slaves.

June 15, 1808. (By Frederick Bates, commissioner, authorized from the Board to take testimony at New Madrid, &c.) William Cox, sworn, says that a sugar camp was established on premises in 1802, and continued till 1804.

Opinion of the Board. March 26, 1810: Present, John B. C. Lucas and Clement B. Penrose, commissioners. It is the opinion of the Board that this claim ought not to be granted.

CHARLES LUCAS, assignee of Stephen Jones.—A claim for eight hundred and seventy arpents of land situate on Tywappety Bottom, district of New Madrid, on the Mississippi. Produces to the Board a certified list of permissions to settle, formerly given, No. 1369, on which Stephen Jones is No. 229, for four hundred arpents, dated 21st March, 1804, and signed Henry Peyroux, commandant of New Madrid; a plat of survey of eight hundred and seventy arpents, dated 24th January, 1806, signed Edward F. Bond; and a deed of conveyance from said Jones to claimant, dated 24th June, 1805.

Testimony taken. June 15, 1808. (By Frederick Bates, commissioner, authorized from the Board to take testimony at New Madrid, &c.) William Cox, duly sworn, says that a sugar camp was established in the year 1802, and continued until the year 1804.

Opinion of the Board. March 26, 1810: Present, John B. C. Lucas and Clement B. Penrose, commissioners. It is the opinion of the Board that this claim ought not to be granted.

CHARLES LUCAS, assignee of Rezin Bowie.—A claim for three hundred and eighty arpents of land, situate on Fish lake, district of New Madrid. Produces to the Board a special permission to settle, from Henry Peyroux, commandant of New Madrid district, dated the 19th December, 1800; a survey of the same, dated the 8th June, 1801; and a deed of transfer of Rezin Bowie to claimant, dated October 23, 1802.

Testimony taken. August 13, 1806. William Cox, being duly sworn, says that the said Rezin Bowie arrived in the country in August, 1800; that he immediately proceeded to the building of a house, which he completed; that he sowed turnips, and gathered the same.

John Tucker, being also duly sworn, says that when he, the witness, arrived in the country in the year 1802, he found the said Rezin Bowie on said land, and cultivating the same; that the said land was, prior to and on the 20th day of December, 1803, actually inhabited and cultivated for the use of the claimant, and has been so to this day; that he has about fifty acres of the same cleared and under cultivation, with an orchard of about eight or nine hundred fruit trees; had a wife and eight children.

Opinions of the Board. August 13, 1806: Full Board. The Board reject this claim; the said tract not being actually inhabited and cultivated by the claimant.

March 26, 1810: Present, John B. C. Lucas and Clement B. Penrose, commissioners. It is the opinion of the Board that this claim ought not to be confirmed.

CHARLES LUCAS, assignee of David Bowie.—A claim for two hundred arpents of land, situate on Big Swamp, district of New Madrid. Produces to the Board a certificate of a special permission to settle, from Henry Peyroux, commandant of New Madrid district, dated May 22, 1801, and a survey dated the 9th June, 1801; together with an acknowledgment of sale from said D. Bowie to claimant, dated October 23, 1802.

Testimony taken. August 13, 1806. William Cox, being duly sworn, says that the said tract of land was, prior to and on the 1st day of October, 1800, actually inhabited and cultivated by the said David Bowie.

John Tucker, being also duly sworn, says that the said tract of land was, prior to and on the 20th day of October, 1803, actually inhabited and cultivated for the use of the claimant, who had about four or five acres of the same sowed in oats; and further, that the said David was, on the 1st day of October, 1800, of the age of twenty-one years and upwards.

June 15, 1808. (By Frederick Bates, commissioner, authorized from the Board to take testimony at New Madrid, &c.) William Cox, duly sworn, says premises were inhabited and cultivated in 1800, and constantly till this day; about ten or fifteen acres now in cultivation. Bowie, in 1803, had three negroes.

Opinions of the Board. August 13, 1806: Full Board. The Board reject this claim, for want of a duly registered warrant of survey.

March 26, 1810. Present, John B. C. Lucas and Clément B. Penrose, commissioners. It is the opinion of the Board that this claim ought not to be confirmed.

ARUND RUTGERS.—A claim for seven thousand and fifty-six arpents of land, situate on the river Dardennes, district of St. Charles. Produces to the Board a concession from Zenon Trudeau, Lieutenant Governor, dated 14th April, 1799; a plat of survey for seven thousand and fifty-five arpents ninety-four perches, dated 1st February, 1800, and certified 5th March, same year. The concession in this claim was given for the building of a mill.

Testimony taken. Peter Provenchere, sworn, says that he (witness) was on the premises the 24th or 25th May, 1803; then saw a large dwelling house on premises, and a large field cleared and ready to be fenced in, timber cut, hewed, and hauled for a mill, and mill-dam; that, in the preceding November, he (witness) by order of claimant, paid Thomas Howell for doing a part of the above work; claimant returned to this country from the United States about the 2d June, 1803, with a number of workmen, and went immediately on the land claimed with said workmen; inhabited and cultivated the land that year, and has continued to inhabit and cultivate said land ever since; claimant has continually, from the 2d June, 1803, been working on premises, in erecting mills; said mills not yet completed, as the dam has been once or twice carried away by high waters; claimant's whole family moved on premises in July, 1805, and have continued on the same ever since; claimant himself, with his workmen and servants, resided on premises from June, 1803, to the present day.

John Alexander Mickau, sworn, says that he (witness) was on the premises about the 1st of December, 1803; that there were several houses actually built on the premises, and a great quantity of land cleared; that he saw a number of workmen then at work on the place; premises appeared to have been improved some time previous to this, as witness saw a store-house was built, and a store kept on premises; also saw a quantity of hewed timber, and the building of a mill far advanced; witness says that claimant was not on the premises at that time, but saw his overseer; thinks that claimant, with his family, resided on the place in 1804.

Antoine Soulard, sworn, says that he received a letter, dated 1799, from claimant, written at Red Banks, or Lexington, Kentucky; the concession in this claim was therein enclosed, and he was requested to survey the land; witness received said letter in the year 1800; that Mr. Mackay, witness's deputy, surveyed said land, whose return was dated at the time the survey was made; that, although the survey may not have been made at the time it bears date, it still bears date near the time application was made to him (witness;) that the returns of surveys were made by Mr. Mackay on loose sheets of paper; witness always recorded them on his books, and then destroyed them as useless; that he (witness) generally regarded the time in dating his certificates of survey when application was made to him for survey, if recollected, and did not regard the time of the return of his deputy.

Opinion and remark of the Board. April 3, 1810: Full Board. It is the opinion of a majority of the Board that this claim ought not to be confirmed; Clement B. Penrose voting for the confirmation of a league square; Frederick Bates, commissioner, declaring that he would have voted for a confirmation, had this claim not have exceeded eight hundred arpents.

JOHN WELDON.—A claim for five hundred arpents of land, situate in the district of St. Charles. Produces to the Board a notice of claim.

John Weldon, the claimant, personally appears before the Board, and renounces all claim to certain land, as surveyed in his name, on the river Missouri; survey dated 17th November, 1803, certified 27th December, 1803, and recorded in book D, page 108, of the Recorder's office.

Claimant produces also, as a permission to settle, a concession from Charles Dehault Delassus, Lieutenant Governor, to him, for five hundred arpents, dated 20th December, 1799.

Testimony taken. March 30, 1810. John McConnell, sworn, says that the claimant inhabited a tract of land, situate on the waters of the Dardennes, about one or two miles from the inhabitation of Arund Rutgers, in the winter of 1802; in the spring following cultivated, and has continued to inhabit and cultivate said land ever since; claimant had a wife and four children in 1802 and 1803.

Opinion and remarks of the Board. April 3, 1810: Full Board. It is the opinion of the Board that this claim ought not to be granted; but the Board do declare that they would have voted for the granting of five hundred arpents, had this claim not been embraced in the tract claimed by Arund Rutgers, under the first section of the act of 1805.

JOSEPH PARISH.—A claim for eight hundred arpents of land, situate on the waters of the river St. Francis, district of Cape Girardeau. Produces to the Board a certificate of survey of the same, dated January 28, 1806.

Testimony taken. May 5, 1806. Robert A. Logan, being duly sworn, says that claimant did, prior to and on the 20th day of December, 1803, actually inhabit and cultivate said tract of land, and had then a wife and seven children.

May 30, 1808. David Logan, sworn, says that in January, 1801, or 1802, he applied to Louis Lorimer, commandant of Cape Girardeau, for permission for claimant to settle on vacant land, who then gave the permission asked.

Opinions of the Board. May 5, 1806: Present, Clement B. Penrose and James L. Donaldson, commissioners. The Board grant the said claimant five hundred and fifty arpents of land, situate as aforesaid, provided so much be found vacant there.

April 5, 1810: Full Board. It is the opinion of the Board that this claim ought not to be granted.

WILLIAM HAYS, deceased, (the heirs of.)—A claim for one thousand arpents of land, situate on Femme Osage, district of St. Charles. Produces to the Board, as a special permission to settle, a concession from Don Zenon Trudeau, Lieutenant Governor, dated January 24, 1798; and a certificate of survey of the same, dated January 10, 1800.

Testimony taken. February 11, 1806. Joshua Dodson, being duly sworn, says that the said William Hays did clear and raise a crop on said land in the year 1799, and that he did, prior to and on the 20th day of December, 1803, actually inhabit and cultivate the same.

April 7, 1809. John B. Callaway, sworn, says that he, witness, came to this country in the fall of 1799; then found William Hays inhabiting and cultivating the land claimed, and he continued so to do until 1804, when witness left this country; returned again in 1806, and found the representatives of claimant inhabiting and cultivating the same, and they have continued so to do ever since.

Opinions of the Board. February 11, 1806: Full Board. The Board grant the heirs of William Hays, deceased, one thousand arpents of land, situate as aforesaid, provided so much be found vacant there.

April 10, 1810: Full Board. It is the opinion of a majority of the Board that this claim ought not to be confirmed; Clement B. Penrose, commissioner, voting for the confirmation; but the said majority do declare, that, if this claim had not exceeded eight hundred arpents, they would have voted for its confirmation.

LOUIS COURTOIS, Sen.—A claim for seven thousand and fifty-six arpents of land, situate on the river Merrimack, district of St. Louis. Produces to the Board a concession for the same from Don Carlos Dehault Delassus, Lieutenant Governor, dated 5th January, 1800; a plat of survey, dated 18th January, 1804, and certified 29th January, same year.

Testimony taken. October 25, 1808. Benito Vasquez, sworn, says that about twenty-eight years ago he often saw claimant and family going towards the Merrimack, where it was said, and then alleged, that they resided; saw them passing for six years, but never was at their improvement.

Opinion of the Board. April 10, 1810: Full Board. It is the opinion of the Board that this claim ought not to be confirmed.

JADUTHAN KENDALL, assignee of Richard Glover.—A claim for two hundred and fifty arpents of land, on Sandy creek, district of St. Louis. Produces to the Board a notice to the recorder, dated 30th June, 1808, and an assignment from Glover to claimant, dated 27th March, 1806.

Testimony taken. October 26, 1808. David Boyles, duly sworn, says Glover settled this tract in 1803; built a house, planted peach trees, and continued to inhabit and cultivate during that and the following years.

Opinion of the Board. April 10, 1810: Full Board. It is the opinion of the Board that this claim ought not to be granted.

AMABLE PARTENAY, assignee of Theresa Colman.—A claim for two thousand five hundred arpents of land, situate on the river Establishment, district of St. Genevieve. Produces to the Board an order from Manuel Perez, Lieutenant Governor, to Henry Peyroux, commandant of St. Genevieve, to concede, provided it is vacant, a tract of land of fifty arpents square, situate on the river Establishment, at the side towards the Mississippi, adjoining land of Thomas Clem, to Francis Colman, dated 12th May, 1788; a concession from said Henry Peyroux for the same to Francis Colman, dated May 15, 1788; a plat of survey, dated February 21, 1806, certified to be received for record 28th February, 1806; and a transfer from Theresa Colman to claimant, dated 29th January, 1806.

Testimony taken. November 14, 1808. Baptiste Bequet, sworn, says that twenty years ago Francis Colman had a house built on the tract claimed, and enclosed a field.

Opinion of the Board. April 11, 1810: Full Board. It is the opinion of the Board that this claim ought not to be confirmed.

JOHN FERRY.—A claim for eight hundred arpents of land, situate on the Missouri, district of St. Charles. Produces to the Board a concession from Don Carlos Dehault Delassus, Lieutenant Governor, dated 11th January, 1800; a plat of survey, dated 26th January, 1804, certified the 5th March, same year, in which survey the land is said to be situated on the Mississippi, but, on examination thereof, it appears evidently to be a mistake, since, if it were so, the land must be situated on the east side of the Mississippi.

Testimony taken. January 28, 1809. Warner Gilbert, sworn, says that he knows the land claimed, and that it is situated on the Missouri, about twelve miles above the mouth; and that, about three years ago, apple trees were planted on the same, and land cleared; that there was a nursery fenced in; claimant resided with witness on an adjoining tract of land in 1802, and raised a crop with him.

Objection of the agent of the United States. April 14, 1810. The agent of the United States objects to this concession, as being antedated.

Opinion of the Board. April 14, 1810: Present, John B. C. Lucas and Clement B. Penrose, commissioners. It is the opinion of the Board that this claim ought not to be confirmed.

WILLIAM RUSSELL, assignee of George Pursley.—A claim for one thousand one hundred arpents of land, situate on the waters of Point Labadie creek, district of St. Louis. Produces to the Board a notice to the recorder, and a deed of transfer from George Pursley to claimant, dated September 2, 1807.

Testimony taken. October 28, 1808. Aaron Colvin, sworn, says that George Pursley, seven years ago, built a cabin on the tract claimed, and commenced clearing some ground, but never finished it; he knows of nothing else being done on the land by or for him, said Pursley.

Ambrose Boles, sworn, says that George Pursley was living on the tract claimed in April, 1803; had a garden fenced in, and some things growing in it, when he was driven off by the Indians. For permission to settle, see Mackay's list.

January 17, 1810. Peter Pritchett, duly sworn, says that Pursley inhabited and cultivated the land claimed in the spring of 1803; that he, witness, saw vegetables growing at that time on said land; that, on or about the 3d of April, same year, the Indians killed a man by the name of Ridenhour in the same settlement; that the settlement, in consequence of said Ridenhour being killed, broke up. Witness says that George McFall, by permission of said Pursley, inhabited said land in the fall of said year; that Pursley's family, in the year 1803, consisted of his wife and four or five children; witness says that the inhabitants generally returned to the settlement in the fall of 1803.

Opinion of the Board. April 16, 1810: Present, John B. C. Lucas and Clement B. Penrose, commissioners. It is the opinion of the Board that this claim ought not to be granted.

SAMUEL HODGES, Jun.—A claim for two hundred and forty arpents of land, situate on the Missouri, district of St. Louis. Produces to the Board a concession for the same from Don Zenon Trudeau, Lieutenant Governor, dated March 2, 1798; and a plat of survey, dated October 20, 1802, certified December 17, same year.

Testimony taken. April 3, 1810. Jacob Seely, duly sworn, says that William Davis made an improvement to the east, adjoining Gilbert Hodge's survey, on the place claimed, in the fall of 1801, or spring of 1802; built a still-house in the fall of 1803; witness cut rail timber for William Davis, said William Davis living then on the premises, and carrying on his distillery; in 1804 a mill was built on the land for said Davis. Davis resided on premises in 1802, 1803, and 1804.

Elias Mills, sworn, says that in 1806 he was at the distillery of William Davis.

Opinion of the Board. April 16, 1810: Present, John B. C. Lucas and Clement B. Penrose, commissioners. It is the opinion of the Board that this claim ought not to be confirmed.

FRANCIS VALLE, Senior, (the representatives of.)—A claim for seven thousand and fifty-six arpents of land, situate on the waters of the river Saline, district of St. Genevieve. Produces to the Board a survey and plat of the same, taken September 15, 1797, and a certificate of the same, dated November 16, 1805; also a certificate from Anthony Soulard, Surveyor General, stating that he has seen, and had in his possession, a concession for the aforesaid tract of land; said concession granted by Zenon Trudeau, Lieutenant Governor, and bearing date the 9th day of September, 1796.

Testimony taken. June 20th, 1806. Baptiste Vallé, being duly sworn, says that about the year 1798, or 1799, he saw the aforesaid concession; and further, that the same having been sent down to New Orleans to procure a complete title, he saw the receipt of the person who took the same down to that effect; that about 1798, or 1799, two farms were laid out on said land, and a number of buildings erected on the same.

Israel Dodge, being also sworn, says that the said tract of land was settled in the year 1797, forty or fifty arpents cleared, and that the said tract has been actually inhabited and cultivated for the use of the said Francis Vallé, or his representatives, from that period to this day. A large stock has always been kept on the same.

December 1, 1807. Francis Vallé, Junior, one of the representatives aforesaid, being duly sworn, says that the concession was sent to New Orleans, and that Don Zenon Trudeau wrote to the deponent's father that he had made a search in the office at New Orleans for the concession, and that it could not be found; and that the said concession is not now in the possession of any of the said representatives, to the best of this deponent's knowledge and belief.

Opinions and remark of the Board. June 20, 1806: Present, Clement B. Penrose and James L. Donaldson, commissioners. The Board reject this claim for want of a duly registered warrant of survey.

April 17, 1810: Full Board. It is the opinion of a majority of the Board that this claim ought not to be confirmed; Clement B. Penrose, commissioner, voting for the confirmation of one league square; but the said majority declare, that if this claim had not exceeded eight hundred arpents, they would have voted for its confirmation.

FRANCIS VALLE, Senior, (the representatives of.)—A claim for one thousand arpents of land, situate on the waters of the river Saline, district of St. Genevieve. Produces to the Board a concession (not duly registered) from Charles Dehault Delassus, Lieutenant Governor, dated December 25, 1799. Said concession intended as a complement of the aforesaid seven thousand and fifty-six arpents, granted, as appears by reference to the foregoing claim, and whereof six thousand and fifty-six arpents only could be surveyed; the said one thousand arpents granted for cutting of woods to enable claimants to carry on salt works; also, produces a survey of said one thousand arpents, taken December 15, 1800, and certified the 15th of May, 1801.

Opinions and remarks of the Board. June 20, 1806: Present, Clement B. Penrose and James L. Donaldson, commissioners. The Board reject this claim; they are satisfied that it was granted at the time it bears date.

April 16, 1810: Present, John B. C. Lucas and Clement B. Penrose, commissioners. It is the opinion of the Board that this claim ought not to be confirmed.

FRANCIS VALLE, Senior, (the representatives of.)—A claim for a town lot of two arpents square in the town of St. Genevieve. Produces to the Board a permission to settle from Antonio Doro, dated September 22, 1785, (not duly registered.) Not inhabited and cultivated.

Opinion of the Board. April 17, 1810: Full Board. It is the opinion of the Board that this claim ought not to be granted.

FRANCIS VALLE, Junior.—A claim for seven thousand and fifty-six arpents of land, situate on the river Establishment, district of St. Genevieve. Produces to the Board a concession from Don Zenon Trudeau, Lieutenant Governor, (not duly registered,) dated July 4, 1796; and a survey of the same, dated April 4, 1799, and certified July 6, 1799.

Testimony taken. June 20, 1806. Joseph Pratt, being duly sworn, says that claimant did, in the year 1796, build a house and out-houses on said tract of land; that he cleared about forty acres of land, which he did actually cultivate, and has now about fifty acres under cultivation, in three separate parks; and further, that the same was, prior to and on the 1st day of October, 1800, actually inhabited and cultivated, and has continued to be so to this day.

Opinions and remarks of the Board. June 20, 1806: Present, Clement B. Penrose and James L. Donaldson, commissioners. The Board reject this claim, for want of a duly registered warrant of survey, and claimant being under age at the time he obtained said concession.

April 17, 1810. It is the opinion of a majority of the Board that this claim ought not to be confirmed; Clement B. Penrose, commissioner, voting for the confirmation of a league square. Frederick Bates, commissioner, declares that, if this claim had not exceeded eight hundred arpents, he would have voted for its confirmation. John B. C. Lucas, commissioner, states, as reasons of his opinion, 1st, that the warrant or order of survey does not bear registry; 2d, that the quantity is greater than that generally allowed by the known Spanish regulations; 3d, that the grantee was under age at the time the grant was made, and that the regulations contemplate no other persons to whom lands may be granted but families or heads of families. Clement B. Penrose, commissioner, refers to the first section of the act entitled " An act respecting claims to lands in the Territories of Orleans and Louisiana," passed the 3d of March, 1807.

FRANCIS VALLE, Jun.—A claim for seven thousand and fifty-six arpents of land, situate in the district of New Bourbon, on the river Aux Vases. Produces to the Board a petition to Don Morales, the Intendant General at New Orleans, for the above quantity of land, for the purpose of building a saw-mill; dated the 10th March, 1802, together with a recommendation from Pierre D. Deluziere, commandant of the district of New Bourbon, to the said Intendant General, stating that the claimant is worthy of the grant solicited; also, an order by the said Morales to Peter Derbigny, translator, to have the petition and recommendation translated, and then to be transmitted to the fiscal for examination.

Testimony taken. December 1, 1807. Thomas Dodge, being duly sworn, says that Francis Vallé, Jun. began to build a mill and a cabin on said tract in July, and finished it in November, 1802, and that it was inhabited from that time until this day for claimant; was cultivated in 1803, and ever since; that the mill has worked ever since it was completed, when there was a sufficiency of water.

Opinion of the Board. April 17, 1810: Full Board. It is the opinion of the Board that this claim ought not to be confirmed.

LAND GRANTS IN MISSOURI TERRITORY - 1805 - 1812 39

****

EZEKISL ESTES, alias EASTRIDGE.—A claim for six hundred and fifty arpents of land, situate on Grand river, district of St. Genevieve, by virtue of a verbal permission from Francis Vallé, commandant of St. Genevieve district. Produces to the Board a certificate of survey of said land, dated January 29, 1806.

Testimony taken. January 29, 1806. Michael Hart, being duly sworn, says that the said Ezekiel Eastridge did, prior to and on the 20th day of December, 1803, actually inhabit and cultivate the said tract of land, and that he was at that time the head of a family.

December 1, 1807. Robert Estes, being duly sworn, says that he knows the above claim of land, and that the same was inhabited and cultivated in the year 1802 by the claimant, and ever since, to the present day; that he had a wife and eight children.

The claimant declares that Francis Vallé, commandant, gave him verbal permission to settle on vacant lands, within the bounds of this district, in 1802.

Opinions of the Board. January 29, 1806: Full Board. The Board grant the said Ezekiel Eastridge six hundred and fifty arpents of land, situate as aforesaid, as his settlement right, provided the same be found vacant there.

April 17, 1810: Full Board. It is the opinion of the Board that this claim ought not to be granted.

ROBERT ESTES.—A claim for eight hundred and seventy arpents of land, situate on Terre Blue, district of St. Genevieve. Produces to the Board a certificate of survey, dated February 18, 1806.

Testimony and declaration taken. February 21, 1806. Jacob Mosteller, being duly sworn, says that the above claimant settled said land in 1801, and did, prior to and on the 20th day of December, 1803, actually inhabit and cultivate the same, when he had a wife and four children.

December 1, 1807. Robert Estes, the said claimant, being duly sworn, says that he applied to Francis Vallé, commandant of St. Genevieve district, in the year 1801, in the presence of a certain man named Crow, for permission to settle on the vacant land, and that said Crow was a stranger to said claimant; and that he never has, to his knowledge, seen him since, nor does he know where he is at this time.

Observation of the Board. December 1, 1807: The said commandant, Francis Vallé, has been dead some years.

Opinions of the Board. February 21, 1806: Present, John B. C. Lucas and Clement B. Penrose, commissioners. The Board grant Robert Estes one thousand and fifty arpents of land, situate as aforesaid, provided so much be found vacant there.

April 17, 1810: Full Board. It is the opinion of the Board that this claim ought not to be granted.

JOHN AUGUST.—A claim for seven hundred and eighty arpents of land, situate on Terre Blue, district of St. Genevieve. Produces to the Board a plat and certificate of survey, dated the 7th of January, 1806, and certified 20th February, same year. No permission to settle proven.

Testimony taken. December 1, 1807. John Andrews, being duly sworn, says that he knows the premises; that said land was inhabited by the claimant in the year 1802, and that in the year 1803 a small crop of corn was cultivated by him, perhaps one acre; witness also says that claimant gathered in his crop of corn in the autumn of the year 1803, and thinks he inhabited as late as the last of the month of December of that year.

Opinion of the Board. April 17, 1810: Full Board. It is the opinion of the Board that this claim ought not to be granted.

ROBERT ADAMS.—A claim for six hundred and sixty arpents of land, situate on Big river, district of St. Genevieve. Produces to the Board a plat and certificate of survey of said land, dated January 7, 1806, and received for record February 20, 1806. No permission to settle.

Testimony taken. February 22, 1806. Jacob Mosteller, being duly sworn, says that the said claimant did, prior to and on the 20th day of December, 1803, actually inhabit and cultivate the said tract of land, and had then a wife and two children.

Opinions of the Board. February 22, 1806: Full Board. The Board grant the said claimant nine hundred and fifty arpents of land, situate as aforesaid, provided so much be found vacant there.

April 17, 1810: Full Board. It is the opinion of the Board that this claim ought not to be granted.

JAMES HAWKINS.—A claim for seven hundred and forty-eight arpents sixty-eight perches of land, situate on Mill creek, near Mine à Breton, district of St. Genevieve. Produces to the Board a plat of survey, dated January 25, 1806, certified to be received for record February 28, 1806. Permission to settle on file.

Testimony taken. November 2, 1808. John Strickland, being duly sworn, says that, in the fall of 1803, claimant cut logs on this tract, and, in the spring of 1804, put up a cabin, and planted corn; lived in the same while raising his crop that year; has never done any thing on the tract since.

Opinion of the Board. April 10, 1810: Full Board. It is the opinion of the Board that this claim ought not to be granted.

JOHN HAWKINS, assignee of Alexander Murdock.—A claim for two hundred and ninety-nine arpents forty-six perches of land, situate on the Mississippi, opposite Pole island, district of St. Genevieve. Produces to the Board a survey taken December 5, 1805, and certified February 27, 1806; also, a petition to the Intendant General at New Orleans, dated February 24, 1803, praying for three hundred arpents of land; and a certificate from Pierre Delassus Deluziere, commandant of New Bourbon, that the petitioner merits the land solicited; also, a certified copy of a deed of conveyance from the aforesaid Alexander Murdock to said claimant, dated June 20, 1804.

Testimony taken. June 24, 1806. James Burns, being duly sworn, says that claimant settled the said tract of land in the beginning of 1803; raised a crop on the same; that he was a single man, and lived with his brother, whose tract is adjoining the aforesaid land; and that he actually cultivated the same on the 20th day of December of that year, and was then of the age of twenty-one years and upwards.

Opinion of the Board. April 18, 1810: Present, John B. C. Lucas and Clement B. Penrose, commissioners. It is the opinion of the Board that this claim ought not to be granted.

ISAAC DOGHEAD.—A claim for seven hundred and ninety-two arpents of land, situate on Big river, district of St. Genevieve. Produces to the Board a certificate of survey, of the same, dated February 18th, 1806.

Testimony taken. February 21st, 1806. Robert Estes, being duly sworn, says that the said claimant settled said tract of land in the spring of 1804, and has actually inhabited and cultivated the same to this day; and that his family did, on the 20th day of December, 1803, consist of himself, wife, and two children.

****

December 2d, 1807. Abraham Parker, being duly sworn, says that he was present at the commandant's of St. Genevieve about the year 1801, when the said claimant obtained permission to settle on the vacant land in the district of St. Genevieve.

Opinion of the Board. April 18th, 1810: Present, John B. C. Lucas and Clement B. Penrose, commissioners. It is the opinion of the Board that this claim ought not to be granted.

WILLIAM EADS.—A claim for four hundred arpents of land, situate on the waters of Big river, district of St. Genevieve. Produces to the Board a concession from Charles Dehault Delassus, Lieutenant Governor, dated September 8th, 1799; and a survey of three hundred and ninety-eight arpents eighty perches of land, taken November the 30th, 1803, and certified January 15th, 1804.

Testimony taken. June 25th, 1806. Aquila Low, being duly sworn, says that the said Eads acknowledged before him that he has sold the aforesaid tract of land to one James Keith; that the said Keith settled the said tract in the year 1804, and actually inhabited and cultivated it in 1804, and was then of the age of twenty-one years and upwards.

Opinion of the Board. April 18th, 1810: Present, John B. C. Lucas and Clement B. Penrose, commissioners. It is the opinion of the Board that this claim ought not to be confirmed.

ROBERT J. FRIEND,—A claim for eighteen hundred arpents of land, situate on the river St. François. Produces to the Board a concession from Don Zenon Trudeau, Lieutenant Governor, dated March 18th, 1798; and a certificate of survey, dated December 27th, 1803.

Testimony taken. December 2d, 1807. Joseph Pratt, being duly sworn, says that he has no interest in said claim, and that claimant told him, either in 1799 or 1800, he had obtained a concession from Don Zenon Trudeau, Lieutenant Governor.

Opinion of the Board. April 18th, 1810: Present, John B. C. Lucas and Clement B. Penrose, commissioners. It is the opinion of the Board that this claim ought not to be confirmed.

WILLIAM HOLMES.—A claim for eight hundred arpents of land. Produces to the Board a concession of Charles Dehault Delassus, Lieutenant Governor, dated March 29th, 1800; and a certificate of survey of the same, dated December 27th, 1803.

Testimony taken. December 2d, 1807. James Davis, being duly sworn, says that said tract was first cultivated in July, 1804; shortly after there was a house built on the same; that claimant moved into said house, and that this tract has been inhabited and cultivated ever since.

Opinion of the Board. April 18th, 1810: Present, John B. C. Lucas and Clement B. Penrose, commissioners. It is the opinion of the Board that this claim ought not to be confirmed.

MOSES BATES.—A claim for eight hundred arpents of land, situate on Bellevue, waters of Grand river, district of St. Genevieve. Produces to the Board a special permission to settle from Charles Dehault Delassus, Lieutenant Governor, dated September 8th, 1799; and a survey of the same, taken the 2d January, and certified the 28th May, 1800.

Testimony taken. August 29th, 1806. Benjamin Strother, being duly sworn, says that the said claimant settled the said tract of land in the spring of 1804, raised a crop on the same, built a house, and has actually inhabited and cultivated it to this day; that claimant is one of Moses Austin's followers, and arrived in the country in the year 1798; that claimant and his family arrived in the country sick, and continued so for upwards of a year and further; that he, the witness, did, about two years after claimant's arrival, hear of his having applied for a concession.

Opinions of the Board. August 29th, 1806: Present, John B. C. Lucas and Clement B. Penrose, commissioners. The Board reject this claim, and are satisfied that the concession was granted at the time it bears date.

April 18th, 1810: Present, John B. C. Lucas and Clement B. Penrose, commissioners. It is the opinion of the Board that this claim ought not to be confirmed.

ISAAC JACKSON and STEPHEN EVANS, assignees of Samuel J. Withero.—A claim for eight hundred and forty arpents of land, situate on the waters of Grand river, district of St. Genevieve. Produces to the Board a certificate of survey of said land, dated January 10th, 1806; an assignment of said land from the above Samuel J. Withero to one Abraham Baker, dated November 26th, 1803; an assignment from the above Abraham Baker to one Jacob Mosteller, dated February 10th, 1804; and an assignment from the said Jacob Mosteller to the said claimants, dated May 8th, 1804.

Testimony taken. February 18th, 1806. Robert Eastus, being duly sworn, says that the above-named Samuel J. Withero settled the said tract of land in the year 1803; that he raised a crop thereon, and moved out of it in October of that year; that he afterwards conveyed his right to the said land and crop to one Abraham Baker, who gathered the same; and, lastly, that the said claimants moved on said land in the spring of 1804, and have actually inhabited and cultivated it to this day.

Opinions and remarks of the Board. February 18th, 1806: Full Board. The Board reject this claim, and think it a case of equity.

April 18th, 1810: Present, John B. C. Lucas and Clement B. Penrose, commissioners. It is the opinion of the Board that this claim ought not to be granted.

PIERRE BOYER.—A claim for one hundred and sixty arpents of land, situate on *Terre Blue*. Produces to the Board a concession from Don Zenon Trudeau, Lieutenant Governor, dated June 10th, 1797; also, a plat and certificate of survey of the same, dated January 25th, 1800, and certified June 10th, 1800.

Opinion of the Board. April 18th, 1810: Present, John B. C. Lucas and Clement B. Penrose, commissioners. It is the opinion of the Board that this claim ought not to be confirmed.

JOSEPH JAMES.—A claim for seven hundred and forty-eight arpents and sixty-eight perches of land, situate on Obrazo creek, district of St. Genevieve. Produces to the Board a survey of the same, dated January 9th, 1806, and certified February 26th, 1806.

Testimony taken. June 21st, 1806. Samuel Hinch, Senior, being duly sworn, says that claimant settled said tract of land in the year 1801; that the same was actually cultivated and inhabited for the use of claimant, prior to and on the 20th day of December, 1803, at which time he had two cabins on the same; was of the age of twenty-one years and upwards, and had then a wife.

December 2, 1807. John Hawkins, being duly sworn, says that he was present when Samuel Hinch, Senior, (the witness formerly examined on this claim, and who is since dead,) was examined by the Board, and says that he was present at Mr. Deluziere's, commandant of New Bourbon, when the claimant received a verbal permission from said commandant to settle on vacant land.

Opinion of the Board. April 18, 1810: Present, John B. C. Lucas and Clement B. Penrose, commissioners. It is the opinion of the Board that this claim ought not to be granted.

EDWARD JOHNSTON.—A claim for nine hundred and fifty-four arpents of land, situate at Bellevue, district of St. Genevieve. Produces to the Board a survey of the same, dated January 3, 1806, and certified February 6, 1806.

Testimony taken. June 26, 1806. John Sinkler, being duly sworn, says that he was present when claimant obtained from the commandant permission to settle on vacant lands. .

John Lewis, being also duly sworn, says that he was on said land in February, 1804, when claimant was actually settled on and inhabited the said tract of land; that he raised a crop that year, and has actually inhabited and cultivated the same to this day.

Opinion of the Board. April 19, 1810: Full Board. It is the opinion of the Board that this claim ought not to be granted.

ABRAHAM PARKER.—A claim for one thousand arpents of land, situate on Big river, district of St. Genevieve. Produces to the Board a survey of the same, dated the 6th February, 1806, and certified the 29th of the same month and year.

Testimony taken. December 3, 1807. Abraham Baker, being duly sworn, says that he did, about five years ago, hear the claimant say that he had obtained permission to settle on vacant land, and the witness saw that he built a house on the same tract in 1801; that he moved into the same in 1802, raised a crop the same year, and has continued to inhabit and cultivate the same ever since: and had a wife and eight children in the year 1803.

Opinion of the Board. April 19, 1810: Full Board. It is the opinion of the Board that this claim ought not to be granted.

DARIUS SHAW.—A claim for seven hundred and forty-eight arpents and sixty-eight perches of land, (mine,) situate in the district of St. Genevieve. Produces to the Board a survey of the same, dated January 8, 1806, and certified the 28th February of the same year; also the oath of Joseph Deselle, syndic, at the Mine à Breton, taken before James Austin, a justice of the peace, dated November 28, 1807, declaring that he gave permission to said Darius Shaw to settle on said land the 12th of May, 1803.

Testimony taken. August 29, 1806. John McNeal, being duly sworn, says that claimant actually cultivated the said tract of land in the years 1801, 1802, and 1803, and raised crops on the same in the said years; that he moved on it in 1804, and has actually inhabited and cultivated it to this day, and was, on the 20th day of December, 1803, of the age of twenty-one years and upwards.

December 3, 1807. John McNeal, (the person formerly sworn) being now duly sworn, says that he is well acquainted with the tract claimed; that there has been some digging there, but no mineral found; that it is about half or three quarters of a mile from the mine called New Diggings, and about two miles from the Mine à Breton.

Opinion of the Board. April 19th, 1810: Full Board. It is the opinion of the Board that this claim ought not to be granted.

JOHN BAKER.—A claim for four hundred arpents of land, situate on Big river, district of St. Genevieve. Produces to the Board a survey of the same, dated February 26, 1806, and certified the 28th of the same month and year.

Testimony taken. June 25, 1806. William Alley, being duly sworn, says that he was informed that the Lieutenant Governor had promised to grant the above quantity of land to such persons as went with him as militiamen, on an expedition to New Madrid, where some Indians were to be executed. The above claimant was one of those who went on that expedition; that he settled the said tract of land in the year 1798, and has actually cultivated the same to this day; was, on the 1st of October, of the age of twenty-one years and upwards, and claims no other land in his own name in the Territory.

Opinion of the Board. April 19th, 1810: Full Board. It is the opinion of a majority of the Board that this claim ought not to be granted; Frederick Bates, commissioner, voting for the granting of one hundred arpents.

URIAH HULL.—A claim for eight hundred and fifty-three arpents and ninety-six perches of land, situate at Bellevue, district of St. Genevieve. Produces to the Board a survey of the same, dated February 22, 1806, and certified the 28th of the same month and year.

Testimony taken. June 26, 1806. Walter Crow, being duly sworn, says that claimant settled the said tract of land in 1804, raised a crop, and has actually inhabited and cultivated the same to this day; had, on the 20th day of December, 1803, a wife.

Opinion of the Board. April 19, 1810: Full Board. It is the opinion of the Board that this claim ought not to be granted.

JOHN SINCLAIR.—A claim for one thousand two hundred and eighty arpents of land, situate on the waters of the river of St. Francis, district of St. Genevieve. Produces to the Board a survey of the same, taken the 20th February, 1806, and certified the 26th of the same month and year.

Testimony taken. June 25, 1806. Edward Johnson, being duly sworn, says that he was present when claimant obtained permission to settle on vacant land.

William Crawford, being also duly sworn, says that about the 15th of December, 1803, he saw claimant on the said tract of land; that he was then actually inhabiting the same, and had with him his family, which then consisted of a wife and twelve children; and that a crop had been raised on said land, but gathered prior to claimant moving on it.

Opinion of the Board. April 19, 1810: Full Board. It is the opinion of the Board that this claim ought not to be granted.

This claim and James Campbell's are united, and one settlement.

WALTER CROW.—A claim for four hundred and forty-one arpents and fifteen perches of land, situate at Bellevue, district of St. Genevieve. Produces to the Board a survey of the same, dated January 30, 1806, and certified February 27, 1806.

Testimony taken. June 25, 1806. Thomas McLaughlin, being duly sworn, says that he, the witness, arrived in that settlement in 1803; that claimant was then actually cultivating the said tract of land, and raised a crop; that in the beginning of 1804 he built a house on the same, moved his family into it, and has actually inhabited and cultivated the same to this day; and further, that he, the witness, was present when claimant obtained permission to settle on vacant land; and that he had, on the 20th day of December, 1803, a wife and child.

December 3, 1807. Benjamin Crow, being duly sworn, says that in 1803 he was present when claimant obtained permission to settle, from Deselle, syndic at Mine à Breton.

Opinion of the Board. April 19, 1810: Full Board. It is the opinion of the Board that this claim ought not to be granted.

JAMES McLAUGHLIN.—A claim for seven hundred and seven arpents of land, situate at Bellevue, district of St. Genevieve. Produces to the Board a survey of the same, dated January 29, 1806, and certified February 5, 1806.

Testimony taken. June 27, 1806. Benjamin Crow, being duly sworn, says that the said claimant improved the said land in 1803, built a house in 1804, and has actually inhabited and cultivated the same to this day; and further, that he had obtained permission to settle on vacant lands from the commandant; had, on 20th December, 1803, a wife.

Opinion of the Board. April 19, 1810: Full Board. It is the opinion of the Board that this claim ought not to be granted.

WILLIAM REED, Senior.—A claim for one thousand and seventy-seven arpents of land, situate at Bellevue, district of St. Genevieve. Produces to the Board a survey of the same, dated the 4th February, 1806, and certified the 27th of the same month and year.

Testimony taken. June 27, 1806. Benjamin Crow, being duly sworn, says that claimant settled the said tract of land in February, 1803, and did, prior to and on the 20th December, 1803, actually inhabit and cultivate the same; and had a wife, three children, and four slaves.

Joseph Gerrard, being duly sworn, says that claimant had obtained from the commandant permission to settle on vacant lands.

Opinions of the Board. June 27, 1806: Present, Clement B. Penrose and James L. Donaldson, commissioners. The Board grant the said William Reed four hundred and thirty arpents of land, situate as aforesaid, provided so much be found vacant there.

April 19, 1810: Full Board. It is the opinion of the Board that this claim ought not to be granted.

JOHN ANDERSON.—A claim for seven hundred and forty-seven arpents and forty-six perches of land, situate at Bellevue, district of St. Genevieve. Produces to the Board a survey of the same, taken January 30, 1806, and certified February 27, 1806.

Testimony taken. June 25, 1806. Benjamin Crow, being duly sworn, says that claimant proceeded to improve the said tract of land in 1803, but never inhabited and cultivated the same.

Opinion of the Board. April 19, 1810: Full Board. It is the opinion of the Board that this claim ought not to be granted.

THOMAS BEAR.—A claim for three hundred and seventy-five arpents and thirty-five perches of land, situate at Bellevue, district of St. Genevieve. Produces to the Board a survey of the same, taken the 4th February, 1806, and certified the 27th of the same month and year.

Testimony taken. June 27, 1806. David Roza, being duly sworn, says that he was present when claimant obtained from the commandant permission to settle on vacant lands.

Benjamin Crow, being also duly sworn, says that the said claimant settled the said tract of land in the year 1804, raised a crop on the same in that year, and has actually inhabited and cultivated it to this day; and was, on the 20th day of December, 1803, of the age of twenty-one years and upwards.

Opinion of the Board. April 19, 1810: Full Board. It is the opinion of the Board that this claim ought not to be granted.

JOSEPH McMURTRY.—A claim for one thousand and twenty-four arpents of land, situate on Big river, district of St. Genevieve. Produces, in support of said claim, a plat and certificate of survey of the same, dated February 18, 1806, and certified to be received for record February 20, 1806.

Testimony taken. December 3, 1807. Benjamin Crow, being duly sworn, says that, in October, 1803, he went with claimant to choose a place; claimant fixed on one, and built a cabin on it in 1804, and raised a crop that year; and has inhabited and cultivated the same until this day.

Opinion of the Board. April 19, 1810: Full Board. It is the opinion of the Board that this claim ought not to be granted.

BERNARD ROGAN.—A claim for one hundred and sixty-one arpents and thirty perches of land, situate at Bellevue, district of St. Genevieve. Produces to the Board a survey of the same, dated January 25, 1806, and certified February 27, 1806.

Testimony taken. June 27, 1806. Benjamin Crow, being duly sworn, says that the above claimant settled the said tract of land in February, 1804, and has actually inhabited and cultivated the same to this day; and that he was, on the 20th day of December, 1803, of the age of twenty-one years and upwards.

Opinion of the Board. April 20, 1810: Full Board. It is the opinion of the Board that this claim ought not to be granted.

SARAH STARNATER.—A claim of seven hundred and sixty-one and a half arpents of land, situate on Big river, district of St. Genevieve. Produces to the Board a certificate of survey of the same, dated February 20, 1806.

Testimony taken. February 22, 1806. Jacob Mosteller, being duly sworn, says that the said claimant did, prior to and on the 20th day of December, 1803, actually inhabit and cultivate the said tract of land, having then five children.

Opinions of the Board. February 22, 1806: Full Board. The Board grant the said Sarah Starnater one thousand arpents of land, situate as aforesaid, provided so much be found vacant there.

April 20, 1810: Full Board. It is the opinion of the Board that this claim ought not to be granted.

WILLIAM REED.—A claim for one hundred and seventeen arpents and ninety-five perches of land, situate on the Mississippi, district of St. Genevieve. Produces to the Board a survey of the same, taken the 20th January, and certified the 25th February, 1805.

Testimony taken. June 25, 1806. Camille Delassus, being duly sworn, says that he was present when claimant applied for, and obtained, permission to settle on vacant lands.

****

Joseph Manning, being also duly sworn, says that claimant did, prior to and on the 20th day of December, 1800, actually inhabit and cultivate the said tract of land, and had then seven children.

Opinions of the Board. June 25, 1806: Present, Clement B. Penrose and James L. Donaldson, commissioners. The Board grant the said claimant four hundred and fifty arpents of land, situate as aforesaid, provided so much be found vacant there.

April 20, 1810: Full Board. It is the opinion of the Board that this claim ought not to be granted.

WILLIAM REED, Junior.—A claim for seven hundred and-twenty seven arpents and eleven perches of land, situate at Bellevue, district of St. Genevieve. Produces to the Board a survey of the same, dated February 26, 1806, and certified the 27th February, 1806.

Testimony taken. June 26, 1806. John Lewis, being duly sworn, says that he always understood from the neighbors of the claimant, that he had obtained a permission to settle, from some person authorized to grant the same; that he arrived in the country in November, 1803; settled said land in 1804; worked on the same occasionally, living then with his father-in-law; and further, that he was a single man, of the age of twenty-one years and upwards.

Opinion of the Board. April 20, 1810: Full Board. It is the opinion of the Board that this claim ought not to be granted.

WILLIAM BATES.—A claim for seven hundred and forty-eight arpents and sixty-eight perches of land, situate at Bellevue settlement, district of St. Genevieve. Produces to the Board a plat and certificate of survey, dated February 3, 1806, and certified to be received for record February 27, 1806.

Testimony and declaration taken. December 3, 1807. The claimant's brother declares that claimant was not of age in 1803; that he did not know of his having any permission to settle, but that he knows of his having no other claim in the Territory.

John McNeal, being duly sworn, says that claimant built a cabin on said tract in September, 1804.

Opinion of the Board. April 20, 1810: Full Board. It is the opinion of the Board that this claim ought not to be granted.

JOSEPH REED, JUN.—A claim for seven hundred and forty arpents and three perches of land, situate at Bellevue settlement, district of St. Genevieve. Produces to the Board, in support of said claim, a plat and certificate of survey, dated February 8th, 1806, and certified to be received for record February 28th, 1806.

Testimony taken. December 3d, 1807. Joseph Girard, being duly sworn, says that some time in 1802 he was present at Francis Valle, late commandant of St. Genevieve, when he gave a verbal permission to claimant to settle on vacant land.

William Reed, being also duly sworn, says that claimant built a cabin on the aforesaid tract in 1804, and that the same has never been inhabited nor cultivated.

Opinion of the Board. April 20th, 1810: Full Board. It is the opinion of the Board that this claim ought not to be granted.

THOMAS REED.—A claim for seven hundred and forty-seven arpents of land, situate at Bellevue, district of St. Genevieve. Produces to the Board a survey of the same, dated February 4, 1806, and certified the 27th of the same month and year.

Testimony taken. June 27, 1806. Joseph Gerrard, being duly sworn, says that he was present when claimant obtained from the commandant permission to settle on vacant lands.

Benjamin Crow, being also duly sworn, says that claimant began the improving of said land in 1803; built a cabin in 1804, and was, on the 20th day of December, 1803, of the age of twenty-one years and upwards.

Opinion of the Board. April 20, 1810: Full Board. It is the opinion of the Board that this claim ought not to be granted.

MICHAEL RABER.—A claim for nine hundred and twenty-two arpents of land, situate on the waters of the Joachim, district of St. Genevieve. Produces to the Board a survey of the same, dated February 26, 1806.

Testimony taken. July 5, 1806. Edward Butler, being duly sworn, says that he was present when the commandant granted the above claimant permission to settle on vacant lands; that the said claimant did, prior to and on the 20th day of December, 1803, actually inhabit and cultivate the said tract of land, and had then a wife and two children.

Opinions of the Board. July 5, 1806: Present James L. Donaldson, commissioner. The Board grant the said claimant three hundred arpents of land, situate as aforesaid, provided so much be found vacant there. Approved the above minutes July 7, 1806.

April 20, 1810: Full Board. It is the opinion of the Board that this claim ought not to be granted.

THOMAS DONAHOE, assignee of Rowland Meredith, assignee of Jesse Evans.—A claim for three hundred arpents of land, situate on the Mississippi, district of St. Genevieve. Produces to the Board a concession from Zenon Trudeau, Lieutenant Governor, to the said Jesse Evans, (not duly registered,) dated December 14, 1797, a survey of the same, taken September 28, 1799, and certified the 10th October of the same year; also a deed of transfer of the same from Jesse Evans to Rowland Meredith, dated April 19, 1804; and a deed of transfer from said Rowland Meredith to claimant, dated February 14, 1806.

Opinions and remarks of the Board. June 24, 1806: Present, Clement B. Penrose and James L. Donaldson, commissioners. This claim being unsupported by actual cultivation and inhabitation, the Board reject the same. They observe that the said Jesse Evans claims no other land in his own name in the Territory, and that the aforesaid concession (also not duly registered,) was granted at the time the same bears date.

April 20, 1810: Full Board. It is the opinion of the Board that this claim ought not to be confirmed.

BEDE MOORE.—A claim for nine hundred and thirty-five arpents and eighty-five perches of land, situate on the Saline, district of St. Genevieve. Produces to the Board a certificate from Pierre D. Deluziere, commandant of New Bourbon, that he had permitted said claimant to settle on vacant lands, dated December 3d, 1805; and a survey of said land taken the 4th of January, 1806, and certified February 26, same year.

Testimony taken. June 24, 1806. Peter Tucker, being duly sworn, says that claimant settled the said tract of land in the fall of 1803, moved his family on the same, and actually inhabited it for about three months of that year; that he cleared and fenced in a few acres; and claims no other land in his own name in this Territory; and had then a wife and two children.

Opinion of the Board. April 20, 1810: Full Board. It is the opinion of a majority of the Board that this claim ought not to be granted; Frederick Bates, commissioner, voting for the granting of three hundred arpents.

THOMAS McLAUGHLIN.—A claim for nine hundred and eight arpents of land, situate at Bellevue, district of St. Genevieve. Produces to the Board a survey of the same, dated 22d of January, 1806, and certified the 5th February, same year.

Testimony taken. June 27, 1806. Benjamin Crow, being duly sworn, says that he was present when claimant obtained from the commandant permission to settle on vacant lands; that he began the improving of said land in 1803; made a camp on the same, and had his family on it, but was obliged by sickness to remove from the same; that, in the beginning of 1804, he built a cabin, raised a crop on said land, and has actually inhabited and cultivated it to this day; had, on the 20th day of December, 1803, a wife and child.

Opinion of the Board. April 23, 1810: Present, John B. C. Lucas and Clement B. Penrose, commissioners. It is the opinion of the Board that this claim ought not to be granted.

WILLIAM MIDDLETON.—A claim for seven hundred and fifteen arpents forty-nine perches of land, situate on Cape Cinqhommes, district of St. Genevieve. Produces to the Board a survey of the same, dated the 19th February, 1806, and certified the 28th of the same month and year.

Testimony taken. June 26, 1806. Benjamin Cox, being duly sworn, says that claimant settled said tract of land in the year 1802, built a house on the same, and did, prior to and on the 20th day of December, 1803, actually inhabit and cultivate the same, and was twenty-one years of age and upwards. Camille Lassus, being also duly sworn, says that he was present when claimant obtained permission to settle from commandant.

Opinions of the Board. June 26, 1806: Present, Clement B. Penrose, and James L. Donaldson, commissioners. The Board grant the said claimant one hundred arpents of land, situate as aforesaid, provided so much be found vacant there.

April 23, 1810: Present, John B. C. Lucas and Clement B. Penrose, commissioners. It is the opinion of the Board that this claim ought not to be granted.

BERNARD LAYTON.—A claim for nine hundred and forty-seven arpents fifty-six and a half perches of land, situate on Cape Cinqhommes, district of St. Genevieve. Produces to the Board a special permission to settle, certified by Pierre D. Deluziere, dated December 14, 1805; and a survey of the same, taken the 18th February, 1806, and certified the 25th of the same month and year.

Testimony taken. June 25, 1806. Joseph Manning, being duly sworn, says that the said claimant settled the said tract of land in the year 1803; built a house on the same, and was preparing to move on it, when he was detained by sickness; that he moved his family on the same in the spring of 1804; raised a crop thereon, and has actually inhabited and cultivated it to this day; had a wife and two children.

Opinion of the Board. April 23, 1810: Present, John B. C. Lucas and Clement B. Penrose, commissioners. It is the opinion of the Board that this claim ought not to be granted.

LAKIN WALKER, assignee of Isaac Murphy.—A claim for one hundred arpents of land. Produces to the Board a notice of the recorder, and a relinquishment and sale from the said Isaac Murphy to claimant, dated January 16, 1805.

Testimony taken. December 3, 1807. William Murphy, being duly sworn, says that in 1802 Isaac Murphy cut house logs and made rails, and that in 1805 the present claimant built a cabin, and raised a crop in 1806, and has inhabited and cultivated the same ever since; and that he, the witness, obtained permission from Pierre D. Deluziere, commandant of New Bourbon, for Isaac Murphy to settle in the fall of 1800; and said Murphy was of the age of twenty-one years and upwards in 1803.

Opinion of the Board. April 23, 1810: Present, John B. C. Lucas and Clement B. Penrose, commissioners. It is the opinion of the Board that this claim ought not to be granted.

JAMES MANNING.—A claim for one hundred and eighty-two arpents of land, situate on the Mississippi, district of St. Genevieve. Produces to the Board a certificate of survey of the same, dated January 21, 1806.

Testimony taken. June 25, 1806. Camille Delassus, being duly sworn, says that he was present when claimant obtained from the commandant permission to settle on vacant lands.

Henry Riley, being also duly sworn, says that claimant settled the said tract of land in the year 1803, and did, prior to and on the 20th day of December in that year, actually inhabit and cultivate the same; and had then a wife and child.

Opinions of the Board. June 25th, 1806: Present, Clement B. Penrose and James L. Donaldson, commissioners. The Board grant the said claimant two hundred and fifty arpents of land, situate as aforesaid, provided so much be found vacant there.

April 23d, 1810: Present, John B. C. Lucas and Clement B. Penrose, commissioners. It is the opinion of the Board that this claim ought not to be granted.

MARK MANNING.—A claim for one hundred and fifty arpents of land, situate on the Mississippi, district of St. Genevieve. Produces to the Board a permission to settle, certified by Pierre D. Deluziere, commandant of New Bourbon, dated December, 5th, 1805, and a survey of the same, certified January 20th, 1806.

Testimony taken. June 25th, 1806. Joseph Manning being duly sworn, says, that claimant settled the said tract of land in 1803; built a house on the same; after which, being taken sick, and his family being also in a sickly state of health, he could not move on it until the spring of 1804; and that he has actually inhabited and cultivated the same to this day; had, on the 20th day of December, 1803, a wife and three children.

Opinion of the Board. April 23d, 1810: Present, Clement B. Penrose and John B. C. Lucas, commissioners. It is the opinion of the Board that this claim ought not to be granted.

BERNARD CECIL, claiming eight hundred and ninety-four arpents of land, situate on Saline creek, district of St. Genevieve; produces a certificate of permission to settle from Pierre Deluziere, commandant, dated 14th December, 1805; a plat of survey, certified 5th February, 1806.

Testimony taken. April 1st, 1806. Clement Haydon, being duly sworn, says that claimant had, on the 20th December, 1803, a wife and four children; that he was then preparing to build a house on said land; that in 1804 he raised a crop on the same, and has actually inhabited and cultivated it to this day; that prior to claimant moving on said land, there was a house on what he intended to survey; but that one Hawkins, in surveying the adjoining tract, had surveyed the same; and further, that the family of said claimant was, in the said year 1803, all sick, and thereby had it not in their power to cultivate the said tract.

April 23d, 1810: Present, Lucas and Penrose, commissioners. It is the opinion of the Board that this claim ought not to be granted.

JEREMIAH GROJEAN, claiming eight hundred and ninety-six arpents of land, as assignee of James Lewis; produces to the Board a plat of survey, certified the 26th February, 1806, district of St. Charles.

Testimony taken. August 6th, 1807. William Lynn, sworn, says that James Lewis settled on the aforesaid claim in 1802, raised a crop in 1803, and sold the same about September, 1803, to claimant, who moved on said land in the spring of 1804, and has inhabited and cultivated the same to this day; said Lewis had a wife and one child when he moved from said land; and that he remained on the same until spring of 1804.

November 24th, 1809: Present, Lucas and Bates, commissioners. It is the opinion of the Board that this claim ought not to be granted.

BARTHOLOMEW COUSIN, claiming seven hundred and sixty-seven arpents of land, situate on the Mississippi, Tywappity Bottom, district of Cape Girardeau; produces a grant for the same from Juan Ventura Morales, Intendant General of Louisiana, dated 28th April, 1802, and found in the abstract of all the concessions and patented grants of lands appertaining to the district of Louisiana, recorded in the registers kept by the Spanish and French Governments of the province of Louisiana since the 2d July, 1756, until the 23d of April 1802, transmitted to the Board by the Secretary of the Treasury, said grant also accompanied with a certified copy of a plat of survey taken the 13th April, and certified 2d November, 1799; said grant conditioned for the compliance with the 3d, 4th, 6th, 7th and 9th, articles of regulations published by the Intendancy the 17th July, 1799.

March 9th, 1810: Present, Lucas, Penrose, and Bates, commissioners. The Board ascertain that the alleged grant is not a title made and completed under the provisions of the act of Congress, entitled " An act for ascertaining and adjusting the titles and claims to land within the Territory of Orleans and district of Louisiana."

BARTHOLOMEW COUSIN, claiming six thousand arpents of land, situate on White waters, district of Cape Girardeau; produces to the Board a concession from Charles D. Delassus, dated 15th October, 1799; a plat of survey, certified 1st March, 1802: said land granted as a compensation to claimant for his services to Government. Claimant also produces a letter from Charles D. Delassus, Lieutenant Governor, dated 15th October, 1799, wherein he acknowledges his claim to the generosity and benevolence of the Spanish Government, for the many services he had rendered the country since his arrival in the same, showing a disposition to do more for him when occasion should offer, and promising to procure him the appointment of interpreter to the district of Cape Girardeau, with a fixed salary annexed to the same; an official letter from the same to the Governor General, dated 25th June, 1802, wherein, after reciting the services rendered by claimant to Government, he recommends him to the said Governor; and one other official letter, from the same to claimant, dated 30th March, 1803, wherein he dispenses him (as far as in his power) with the compliance with the 4th article of the regulations, to wit, settlement and inhabitation.

Testimony taken. August 30, 1806. Anthony Soulard, duly sworn, says that claimant was employed by Government as interpreter of the English language to Louis Lorimer, commandant of that district; that the object of Government was to extend the settlement of said district to the river St. Francis; that Zenon Trudeau, whose favorite claimant was, had recommended him to Delassus; that, some time after, having shown a desire to move from said district, Delassus persuaded him to remain, and promised him an office, with some salaries annexed to the same, together with other compensations for his former services to Government.

August 30, 1806: Present, Lucas, Penrose, and Donaldson, commissioners. The Board reject this claim, and remark that they are satisfied that the said concession was granted at the time the same bears date.

March 9, 1810: Present, Lucas, Penrose, and Bates, commissioners. On the motion of John B. C. Lucas, commissioner, as follows, to wit: Whereas, it appears in the minutes of the former Board that the said Board have remarked, that they are satisfied that the said concession was granted at the time the same bears date; and inasmuch as it does not appear that any suggestion of fraud and antedate was made, either by the agent of the United States, or any of the members of the Board, which, being the case, shows that no question did exist before the said Board as to fraud or antedate, to which this decision, by way of remark, can apply; and whereas any decision, without question, is in itself preposterous, and might be considered as officious, *Therefore, resolved,* That this remark and decision be rescinded. A question being taken on the motion, it was negatived; and on a question being taken on the claim, it is the unanimous opinion of the Board that this claim ought not to be confirmed.

BARTHOLOMEW COUSIN, claiming ten thousand arpents of land; produces a pre-emption right for fifty thousand arpents, granted by Charles D. Delassus, Lieutenant Governor, March 5, 1800; said land to be paid for in services, or otherwise; also a concession from said Delassus, dated 17th December, 1802, for ten thousand arpents, as compensation for services rendered, being part of the above fifty thousand arpents.

March 13, 1810: Present, Lucas, Penrose, and Bates, commissioners. It is the opinion of the Board that this claim ought not to be confirmed.

AQUILLA LOW, claiming two hundred and eighty-five arpents and fifty perches of land, situate in Bellevue, district of St. Genevieve.

Testimony taken. December 3, 1807. William Murphy sworn, says, that in the fall of 1800, witness obtained permission to settle from Deluziere, commandant, for Acquilla Low, to settle on vacant land.

Edward Johnson, sworn, says that the son of witness cut house logs on said tract in 1804; heard his son say that he gave up his improvement to said Low; claimant built and moved in a cabin on said tract in 1805; remained in said cabin about three months; moved in it again in 1816, and raised a crop; has continued to inhabit and cultivate the same ever since.

April 24, 1810: Present, Lucas, Penrose, and Bates, commissioners. It is the opinion of the Board that this claim ought not to be granted.

SAMUEL PIERCEALL, claiming one thousand and forty-nine and three-quarters arpents of land, situate on Flat river, district of St. Genevieve; produces a plat of survey, dated 18th February, 1806.

Testimony taken. February 20, 1806. Ezekiel Estes, duly sworn, says that the said claimant did, prior to and on the 20th day of December, 1803, actually inhabit and cultivate the said tract of land, and had then a wife and two children.

Testimony taken. December 3, 1807. James Cunningham, being duly sworn, says that, to the best of his recollection, in 1803 claimant built a house, but did not move therein; raised a crop of potatoes that year; that, in the year 1804, the claimant moved upon the said tract, raised a crop, and has inhabited and cultivated it ever since; was a single man in 1803.

James Davis, sworn, says that in April, 1803, he passed the cabin belonging to claimant; he was then residing therein; raised a crop that year, and has inhabited and cultivated it ever since, and had then a wife and two children.

February 20, 1806. Present: Lucas and Penrose, commissioners. The Board grant the above claimant nine hundred and fifty arpents of land, situate as aforesaid, provided so much be found vacant there.

April 24, 1810: Present Lucas, Penrose, and Bates, commissioners. It is the opinion of the Board that this claim ought not to be granted.

GIDEON W. TREAT, claiming seven hundred and forty-eight arpents of land, situate on the west-fork of Prairie Spring creek, district of St. Genevieve; produces a plat of survey, certified 28th February, 1806.

Testimony taken. August 29, 1806. John McNeal, sworn, says that one Francis Tibaut actually cultivated and raised crops on the said tract of land, in the years 1801 and 1802; that, having sold the same to claimant, he, the said claimant, in the year 1803, had a person who actually cultivated the same on shares, prior to and on the 20th of December of said year; and further, that the said claimant, who was then of the age of twenty-one years and upwards, lived with one Darius Shaw; that he has a tan-yard established on said tract.

Testimony taken. December 3, 1807. Darius Shaw, sworn, says that he was present when Mr. Deselle gave permission, in 1803, to claimant to settle on vacant land; that the land lies about three-quarters of a mile from the New Diggings, but does not know of any mineral having been discovered; said tract adjoins witness.

April 24, 1810. Present: Lucas, Penrose, and Bates, commissioners. It is the opinion of the Board that this claim ought not to be granted.

WILLIAM DILLON, assignee of Christopher Anthony, claiming one thousand one hundred arpents of land, situate on waters of St. François, district of St. Genevieve; produces a certificate of permission to settle for Christopher Anthony from Delassus Deluziere, dated 7th December, 1805; a plat of survey dated 13th February, 1806, a deed of transfer from Anthony to claimant, dated August 13, 1804.

Testimony taken. February 15, 1806. John Callaway, duly sworn, says that Christopher Anthony did, in January, 1802, cut logs for and laid the foundation of a house; that the said Christopher did that year raise a crop on said land; that the said Anthony's family not having then arrived in the country, he had taken his board with the witness, about a mile distant from said land; that, in the year 1803, one Matthew Logan, a tenant of said Anthony, did actually cultivate said land, and raised a crop thereon, said crop being intended by said Anthony as a compensation to Logan, for work done by him, said Logan, for said Anthony; that, about the latter end of 1803, the said Anthony having completed a house on said land, moved thereon, and did actually inhabit and cultivate the same until about the middle of 1804; that he had, on the 20th December, 1803, a wife and three children.

April 24, 1810: Present, Lucas, Penrose, and Bates, commissioners. It is the opinion of a majority of the Board that this claim ought not to be granted. Frederick Bates, commissioner, voting for the granting of three hundred and fifty arpents.

JOHN COOPER, claiming seven hundred and forty-eight arpents and sixty-eight perches of land, situate in Bellevue, district of St. Genevieve; produces a plat of survey, certified 28th February, 1806.

Testimony taken. June 27, 1806. Elisha Baker, duly sworn, says claimant settled said tract of land in 1804, raised a cabin, and cultivated a small spot; had, on 20th December, 1803, a wife and child.

April 24, 1810: Present, Lucas, Penrose, and Bates, commissioners. It is the opinion of the Board that this claim ought not to be granted.

JOHN McNEAL, claiming seven hundred and forty-eight arpents of land, situate in the district of St. Genevieve; produces two plats of surveys; one for five hundred and forty-four arpents and sixty-two perches, and the other for two hundred and three arpents and fifty-five perches; said surveys certified 28th February, 1806.

Testimony taken. August 29, 1806. William Bates, duly sworn, says that the said claimant settled the aforesaid tract of two hundred and three arpents and fifty-five perches in the month of March, 1804; raised a crop on the same that year; that in 1805 he moved on it, and has actually inhabited and cultivated it to this day.

April 24, 1810: Present, Lucas, Penrose, and Bates, commissioners. It is the opinion of the Board that this claim ought not to be granted.

NICHOLAS MOORE, claiming two hundred and eighty-five arpents and fifty perches of land, situate on south fork of Saline creek, district of St. Genevieve; produces a notice to the recorder.

Testimony taken. December 3, 1807. Peter Tucker, being duly sworn, says, that claimant went on the land claimed in 1805, and raised a crop; it was inhabited and cultivated that year, and in the year 1806 by claimant; and present year inhabited and cultivated for him.

Clement Hayden, sworn, says, that he, witness, applied to Deluziere, commandant of New Bourbon, in 1803, and obtained for claimant permission to settle.

April 24, 1810: Present, Lucas, Penrose, and Bates, commissioners. It is the opinion of the Board that this claim ought not to be granted.

JAMES MOORE, Sen., claiming nine hundred and fifty-one arpents of land, situate on Saline creek, district of St. Genevieve; produces a certificate from Pierre Deluziere that he had permitted claimant to settle on vacant land, dated 14th December, 1805; a plat of survey, certified 1st February, 1806.

Testimony taken. June 24, 1806. Tunis Quich, being duly sworn, says that claimant settled said tract of land in November, 1803; had then a house built on the same; that he moved on it in the beginning of 1804, and has actually inhabited and cultivated the same to this day; had, 20th December, 1803, three children.

April 24, 1810: Present, Lucas, Penrose, and Bates, commissioners. It is the opinion of the Board that this claim ought not to be granted.

HUMPHREY GIBSON, Jun., claiming eight hundred and fifty-three arpents fifteen perches of land, situate on river Plattin, district of St. Genevieve; produces a plat of survey, certified 20th February, 1806.

Testimony taken. June 27, 1806. Thomas Bear, being duly sworn, says that the said claimant settled the said tract of land in the year 1802, and did, prior to and on the 20th day of December, 1803, actually inhabit and cultivate the same, and had then a wife, three children, and three slaves.

Joseph Jerred, being duly sworn, says that he was present when the commandant permitted claimant to settle on vacant lands.

****

June 27, 1806: Present, Penrose and Donaldson, commissioners. The Board grant the said claimant four hundred and ten arpents of land, situate as aforesaid, provided so much be found vacant there.

April 24, 1810: Present, Lucas, Penrose, and Bates, commissioners. It is the opinion of the Board that this claim ought not to be granted.

JOAB LINE, claiming one hundred arpents of land, situate on the western fork of the river St. François, district of St. Genevieve; produces to the Board a permission to settle, from Pierre Deluziere, dated 6th December, 1800.

Testimony taken. September 9, 1806. Michael Hart, being duly sworn, says that claimant settled a tract of land in the spring of 1801, on the waters of the river St. François; that said tract is distant about four miles from said river; that he raised two crops on the same, to wit, in 1801 and 1802, but did not actually inhabit the same; that, in the fall of 1802, he sowed a crop, which witness believes he did not gather; that, in the beginning of the winter of that year he left his house, his wife having eloped from him; had about sixteen or seventeen arpents under fence; that, when absent, he still kept on said tract his goods, furniture, and stock, and would often call to see the same; that he, the witness, was present when a survey of one Murphy, taken by virtue of a concession, took in said improvement; that claimant objected to the same, threatening to sue him, but all without effect; that, when said survey took place, he had a crop of grain in his fields.

James Cunningham being also duly sworn, says that he saw the claimant in full possession of said land, in the spring of 1802; that he remained so until the year following, when the survey of said Murphy, by virtue of the aforesaid concession, took in all his improvement to about three arpents, and also that his house was surveyed in, and was taken possession of; he claims no other land in his own name in the territory, and had, on the 20th December, 1803, a wife.

May 2, 1810: Present, Lucas, Penrose, and Bates, commissioners. It is the opinion of the Board that this claim ought not to be granted.

SARAH MURPHY, widow and representative of William Murphy, Sen., claiming eight hundred arpents of land, situate on waters of St. François, district of St. Genevieve; produces a concession from Zenon Trudeau, to William Murphy, Sen., her deceased husband, dated 1st March, 1798; a certificate from Pierre Delassus Deluziere, dated December 20th, 1805, whereby it appears that a special permission of settlements had been granted to the above claimant, a certificate of survey of seven hundred and ninety-nine and a half arpents of land, dated April 10, 1800.

Testimony taken. January 14, 1806. William Murphy, Jun., duly sworn, says that William Murphy, Sen., the husband of the above claimant, having obtained from the Spanish Government a special permission to establish himself and family on such spot of His Majesty's land as he might think the most suitable to his purposes, and being since dead, the above claimant, in consequence thereof, determined upon availing herself of the above permission so granted as aforesaid; that, accordingly, she sent a younger son to this country with instructions to settle on a certain tract of land, situate on the waters of the river St. François; that the young man accordingly began a settlement, and raised a crop on said land, and put a family on the same; that said family did actually reside upon and cultivate the said tract of land, for the said claimant on the 20th day of December, 1803; that the above claimant and her family, together with three slaves, did arrive in this country some time in the year 1804.

January 14, 1806: Present, Lucas and Donaldson, commissioners. The Board refer this case to Congress, and are of opinion that the above claimant, Sarah Murphy, must have experienced a great hardship in leaving a situation in all probability comfortable, in the State of Tennessee, her former place of abode, in expectation of availing herself of the special permission granted to her late husband, and in pursuance of the then Spanish commandant's promises of encouragement to her other sons in this country.

May 2, 1810: Present, Lucas, Penrose, and Bates, commissioners. It is the opinion of the Board that this claim ought not to be confirmed.

JOSEPH MILES, claiming twelve hundred arpents of land, situate on the Saline creek, district of St. Genevieve; produces a certified permission to settle, by Pierre Delassus Deluziere, dated December the 14th, 1805; a plat of survey, certified 3d of February, 1806.

Testimony taken. June 24, 1806. Peter Tucker, sworn, says, that the aforesaid claimant settled the said tract of land in the year 1803, built a house on the same, made hay, and actually inhabited it prior to and on the 20th day of December, of that year; and further, that he raised a crop on the same, in the year 1804, and has actually inhabited and cultivated it to this day; had, 20th December, 1803, a wife and seven children.

June 24, 1806: Present, Clement B. Penrose, and James L. Donaldson, commissioners. The Board grant the above claimant five hundred and fifty arpents of land, situate as aforesaid, provided so much be found vacant there.

May 3, 1810: Present, Lucas, Penrose, and Bates, commissioners. It is the opinion of a majority of the Board, that this claim ought not to be granted, Frederick Bates, commissioner, voting for the granting of five hundred and fifty arpents.

JOHN CARRAWAY and HENRY DODGE, assignees of James James, claiming nine hundred and fifty arpents of land, situate on the waters of the river St. François, district of St. Genevieve; produces a plat of survey, certified the 13th of February, 1806.

Testimony taken. August 29, 1806. William Johnson, being duly sworn, says that one James James, did, sometime in the month of October, 1803, clear a piece of land, part of said tract, planted the same in chalottes, and did, prior to and on the 20th day of December, of that year, actually inhabit and cultivate the same, having then a wife and child; that he claims no other land in his own name in the territory.

May 3, 1810: Present, Lucas, Penrose, and Bates, commissioners. It is the opinion of the Board that this claim ought not to be granted.

MARY OWSLEY, widow of Jonathan Owsley, claiming twelve hundred arpents of land, situate on waters of the St. François, district of St. Genevieve; produces to the Board a concession from Don Carlos Dehault Delassus, Lieutenant Governor, to Jonathan Owsley, for twelve hundred arpents of land, conditioned, that said Owsley shall build a saw and grist mill, dated 3d December, 1799; a plat of survey, certified 1st October, 1805.

Testimony taken. February 14, 1806. William Dillon, sworn, says that said land was settled in November, 1800; the same was, prior to and on the 20th December, 1803, actually inhabited and cultivated by the above claimant.

December 5, 1807. William Johnson, sworn, says said claimant had a slave.

December 1, 1808. Ezekiel Able, sworn, says that Jonathan Owsley inhabited and cultivated the land claimed in 1800, and until he died, and it has been inhabited and cultivated since by his representatives; commenced the building of a grist and saw mill in 1801, and completed them in 1802, when they went into operation, and have continued in operation ever since.

February 14, 1806: Present, Lucas, Penrose, and Donaldson, commissioners. The Board grant Mary Owsley and her heirs seven hundred and fifty arpents of land, as per the act of Congress in that case made and provided.

May 3, 1810: Present, Lucas, Penrose, and Bates. It is the opinion of a majority of the Board that this claim ought not to be confirmed; Penrose, commissioner, voting for a confirmation thereof, and the said majority declares that, if this claim had not exceeded eight hundred arpents, they would have voted for a confirmation.

JAMES MAXWELL, assignee of Ecuyer Jean Réné Guiho Sieur de Kerlezand, claiming five hundred arpents of land, situate on the Saline, district of St. Genevieve; produces a concession from Charles D. Delassus, dated 15th January, 1800, with a written certificate of reference of Morales, Intendant to the fiscal, and assessor, for his opinion, certified by Pedro P. Dalaur, notary public, under the date of the 22d October, 1802, who gives his opinion that the same may be granted, by his certificate, under his hand, dated 23d October, same year, followed by an order of survey from Morales, and a promise that, upon producing a plat of survey, a title in form will be granted, dated 25th October, same year.

Testimony taken. June 28, 1806. Israel Dodge, sworn, says that, when Kerlezand obtained the aforesaid concession, his family consisted of himself, wife, five children, and six slaves.

June 28, 1806: Present, Penrose and Donaldson, commissioners. The Board reject this claim, and observe that they are satisfied that the aforesaid concession was granted at the time it bears date.

May 3, 1810: Present, Lucas, Penrose, and Bates, commissioners. It is the opinion of the Board that this claim ought not to be confirmed.

JOHN LEWIS, claiming nine hundred and forty-seven arpents fifty-five perches of land, situate on the waters of Big river, district of St. Genevieve; produces a survey of the same, dated 22d January, and certified 27th February, 1806.

Testimony taken. June 25, 1806. William Reed, Jun., sworn, says that claimant arrived in the country in the year 1803, when he immediately proceeded to the improving of said land, cut house logs, and put up his cabin; that, in the beginning of 1804, he moved on it, raised a crop that year, and has actually inhabited and cultivated it to this day; that he had, on the 20th December, 1803, a wife and child.

December 5, 1807. Edward Johnson, sworn, says that said Lewis married a daughter of Joseph Reed, who was reputed to be a brother of old William Reed.

May 3, 1810: Present, Lucas, Penrose, and Bates. It is the opinion of the Board that this claim ought not to be granted.

JOHN MORGAN, Jun., claiming seven hundred and forty-eight arpents sixty-eight perches of land, situate on Bois Bruly, district of St. Genevieve; produces a plat of survey, certified 28th February, 1806.

Testimony taken. June 26, 1806. Camille Lassus, sworn, says that he was present when claimant obtained permission to settle from the commandant.

James McClean, sworn, says that claimant settled the said tract of land in 1800, and has actually cultivated the same to this day; that he had built on the same a cabin, wherein he lived until the year 1802; that the same being carried away by the water in that year, he moved to his father's, where he lived on the 20th December, 1803; that, in the spring of 1806, he put up a new cabin, where he moved, and is now actually inhabiting; was, on the 20th December, 1803, of the age of twenty-one years and upwards, and claims no other land, in his own name, in the territory.

May 3, 1810: Present, Lucas, Penrose, and Bates. It is the opinion of the Board that this claim ought not to be granted.

ELIAS AUSTIN ELLIOTT, assignee of Jacob Job, assignee of Joseph Reed, claiming seven hundred and twenty five arpents of land, situate in Bellevue settlement; produces a conveyance from Joseph Reed, Sen. to Jacob Job, dated April 7, 1805; also a deed of conveyance from said Job to claimant, dated 23d October, 1805.

Testimony taken. December 5, 1807. William Humphrey, sworn, says that he was present, in 1798 or 1799, at Mr. Deluziere's, commandant of New Bourbon, when said Deluziere gave permission to old William Reed to settle in his district for himself, and family, and connexions; and that he always understood that the above Joseph Reed was a brother of said William.

John Lewis, sworn, says that Joseph Reed came on the tract claimed in November, 1803; cut house logs and built a cabin; moved thereon some time before Christmas of the same year; raised a crop in 1804, and it has been inhabited and cultivated by or through them ever since; and that the said Joseph Reed had a wife and one child in 1803.

May 3, 1810: Present, Lucas, Penrose, and Bates. It is the opinion of the Board that this claim ought not to be granted.

ARCHIBALD MORGAN, claiming seven hundred and forty-eight arpents sixty-eight perches of land, situate on the Mississippi, district of St. Genevieve; produces a plat of survey, certified 27th February, 1806.

Testimony taken. June 26, 1806. Camille Lassus, sworn, says that he knows of permission to settle having been granted the said claimant.

James McClean, sworn, says that claimant settled said tract in the year 1802; built a house on the same, and did, prior to and on the 20th December, 1803, actually cultivate the same, living then at one Thomas Donohoe's; and further, that he was of the age of twenty-one years and upwards.

May 3, 1810: Present, Lucas, Penrose, and Bates, commissioners. It is the opinion of the Board that this claim ought not to be granted.

JOSEPH DONNAHOE, claiming four hundred arpents of land, situate on the Mississippi, district of St. Genevieve; produces to the Board a plat of survey of three hundred and ninety-nine arpents of land, dated 28th March, 1799; a concession from Zenon Trudeau, Lieutenant Governor, dated November 13, 1797.

Testimony taken. December 5, 1807. James Callaway, sworn, says that lie, the witness, went with claimant in 1798 or 1799 to cut logs, and that, in the spring following, they were collected together.

Frederick Woolfort, sworn, says that, in the year of the high May fresh, about nine years ago, he, the witness, passed by said tract, saw the logs collected, foundation laid, and cabbages growing, but no fence round them.

May 4, 1810: Present, Lucas, Penrose, and Bates. It is the opinion of the Board that this claim ought not to be granted.

FRANCIS CLARK, son of Henry, claiming two hundred and thirty arpents of land, situate on Bois Bruly creek, district of St. Genevieve; produces to the Board a notice to the recorder, dated 3d of December, 1807.

Testimony taken. December 5, 1807. Mary Fitzgibbon, sworn, says that she came to claimant's house in 1803; on said tract she saw a crop growing thereon; that claimant has inhabited and cultivated the same to this day, and had then a wife.

May 4, 1810: Present, Lucas, Penrose, and Bates, commissioners. It is the opinion of the Board that this claim ought not to be granted.

BENJAMIN COX, Jun. claiming seven hundred and forty-nine arpents fifty-two perches of land, situate on Cape Cinquehomme, district of St. Genevieve; produces a plat of survey of the same, certified 26th February, 1806.

Testimony taken. June 25, 1806. Camille Lassus, sworn, says that the claimant had obtained permission to settle on vacant lands.

William Middleton, sworn, says that claimant settled the said tract of land in the fall of 1803; made hay, sowed turnips, and planted peach stones; and further, that he did, prior to and on the 20th December, in that year, actually inhabit and cultivate the same, and was a single man, and of twenty-one years and upwards.

June 25, 1806: Present, Penrose and Donaldson, commissioners. The Board grant said claimant one hundred arpents of land, situate as aforesaid, provided so much be found vacant there.

May 4th, 1810: Present, Lucas, Penrose, and Bates, commissioners. It is the opinion of the Board that this claim ought not to be granted.

BENJAMIN COX, Sen., claiming eight hundred and forty-seven arpents fifty-two perches of land, situate on Cape Cinquehomme, district of St. Genevieve; produces to the Board a plat of survey, certified 26th February, 1806.

Testimony taken. June 26, 1806. William Middleton, sworn, says that he was present when permission was granted by the commandant to claimant to settle on vacant land; that he, the witness, settled said tract of land for claimant in 1802; made a garden on it; that, in 1804, a crop was raised by claimant, who has actually inhabited and cultivated the same to this day; and further, that he had, on the 20th December, 1803, a wife and child.

June 26, 1806: Present, Lucas, Penrose, and Donaldson. The Board reject this claim, for want of actual inhabitation and cultivation on 20th December, 1803.

May 4, 1810: Present, Lucas, Penrose, and Bates, commissioners. It is the opinion of the Board that this claim ought not to be granted.

JOHN PATTERSON, claiming seven hundred and eighty arpents of land, situate on the Mississippi, district of St. Genevieve; produces a plat of survey, certified 27th February, 1806.

Testimony taken. June 25, 1806. Alexander M'Connohoe, sworn, says that one Spencer Adams settled the said tract of land, and raised a house on the same in the year 1803; that claimant having purchased his improvement in the year 1805, he raised a crop on the same in the year 1805, and has actually cultivated it to this day; that he had, 20th December, 1803, two children, then living in the United States, and claims no other land in his own name in the territory.

Testimony taken. December 5, 1807. John Smith, sworn, says that the first improvement made on the place claimed was by one Archibald Comster that said Comster; did, in 1801, clear about eight or ten acres of land, and that, about 1802, a certain Adams came and raised a crop on said place, and lived with said Comster, in the house; that said Comster built in 1801; then said Adams went to the upper end of the farm in 1803, and put up a few logs, but did not finish the house, merely having put it up three logs high, and never did any thing on the place after.

May 4, 1810: Present, Lucas, Penrose, and Bates, commissioners. It is the opinion of the Board that this claim ought not to be granted.

WILLIAM JAMES, claiming six hundred arpents of land, situate on the river Aux Vase, district of St. Genevieve; produces a concession for the same from Zenon Trudeau, Lieutenant Governor, dated 20th February, 1798.

Testimony taken. December 5, 1807. Thomas Madden, duly sworn, says that said tract has been neither inhabited nor cultivated, but had the concession either in 1798 or 1799, for the purpose of surveying the same.

May 4, 1810: Present, Lucas, Penrose, and Bates, commissioners. It is the opinion of the Board that this claim ought not to be granted.

WILLIAM MISSELL, assignee of Roswell P. Johnson, assignee of Francis Vallee, claiming eight hundred arpents of land, situate on the river St. François, about three miles from the Mississippi, district of Arkansas; produces to the Board a concession from Francisco Caso y Luengo, dated 26th January, 1803, a transfer from Valliere to Johnson, dated 12th January, 1805, from Johnson to claimant, dated 22d September, 1805.

July 16, 1811: Present, Lucas, Penrose, and Bates, commissioners. It is the opinion of the Board that this claim ought not to be confirmed.

WILLIAM MISSELL, assignee of Henry Cassedy, claiming eight hundred arpents of land, situate on the Mississippi, at the mouth of the river St. François, district of Arkansas; produces to the Board a plat of survey, dated 11th February, 1803; a transfer, dated 29th November, 1804.

July 16, 1811: Present, Lucas, Penrose, and Bates, commissioners. It is the opinion of the Board that this claim ought not to be confirmed.

BENJAMIN FOOY, claiming eight hundred arpents of land, situate on the Mississippi, opposite Wolf river, district of Arkansas; produces to the Board a concession from Juan Ventura Morales, Intendant ad interim, dated 9th September, 1803; certified to be registered by Gilbert Leonard, and Aximiren, a plat of survey, dated 6th September, 1802, certified 3d May, 1803.

The following remark was made by Frederick Bates, commissioner, at Camp Esperance, June 27th, 1808:

Valuable improvements of various kinds, under the personal observation of the deputation while holding the session at Camp Esperance.

July 16th, 1811: Present, Lucas, Penrose, and Bates, commissioners. It is the opinion of the Board that this claim ought not to be confirmed.

BENJAMIN FOOY, assignee of John Hogan, claiming three hundred and twenty arpents of land, situate on the Mississippi, district of Arkansas, produces to the Board a concession from Augustin Grandé, late commandant, dated 16th September, 1802, and a concession from said Grandé, approved by Charles D. Delassus, Lieutenant Governor, dated 19th September, 1802; a plat of survey, dated 17th September, 1802; a transfer from Hogan to claimant, dated 7th January, 1805.

Testimony taken, at Camp Esperance, June 27, 1808. Isaac Fooy, duly sworn, says that this tract lies adjoining the tract cultivated by Henry Fooy, son of the claimant, and under the management and direction of the said Henry, and contiguous to his cultivated fields.

July 16, 1811: Present, Lucas, Penrose, and Bates, commissioners. It is the opinion of the Board that this claim ought not to be confirmed.

BENJAMIN FOOY, claiming six hundred and forty arpents of land, situate twelve miles northwestwardly from Fort Esperance, at the Wappenoche bayou, or the drain; produces to the Board a concession from Augustin Grandé, late commandant, dated 17th September, 1802; a second concession from said Grandé, approved by Delassus, Lieutenant Governor, dated 20th September, 1802; a plat of survey, dated 14th September, 1802.

July 16, 1811: Present, Lucas, Penrose, and Bates, commissioners. It is the opinion of the Board that this claim ought not to be confirmed.

BENJAMIN FOOY, assignee of John W. Hunt, claiming three hundred and twenty arpents of land, situate on the bayou Wappenoche, or the drain; produces to the Board a concession from Augustin Grandé, late commandant, dated 14th September, 1802; a second concession from the same, approved by C. D. Delassus, Lieutenant Governor, dated 18th September, 1802; a plat of survey, dated 16th September, 1802; a transfer from Hunt to claimant, dated 9th January, 1805.

July 16, 1811: Present, Lucas, Penrose, and Bates, commissioners. It is the opinion of the Board that this claim ought not to be confirmed.

ISAAC FOOY, claiming three hundred and twenty arpents of land, on the Mississippi, district of Arkansas, produces a concession from Augustin Grandé, late commandant, dated 1st October, 1802; a second concession from same, approved by Charles D. Delassus, Lieutenant Governor, 1st October, 1802.

Testimony taken, at Camp Esperance, June 27, 1808. John Henry Fooy, sworn, says that these premises were improved in the year 1800 or 1801, at which time there was a small cultivation of corn, and a cabin on this tract, since which it has not been cultivated.

July 16, 1811: Present, Lucas, Penrose, and Bates, commissioners. It is the opinion of the Board that this claim ought not to be confirmed.

JOHN GRACE, claiming three hundred and twenty arpents of land, situate on the bayou Wappenoche, district of Arkansas; produces to the Board a concession from Augustin Grandé, late commandant, dated 29th September, 1802; a second concession from said Grandé, approved by C. D. Delassus, Intendant Governor, dated 2d October, 1802; a plat of survey, dated 13th September, 1802.

Testimony taken, at Camp Esperance, June 27, 1808. John Henry Fooy, duly sworn, says that claimant deadened trees on this tract in 1802 or 1803, and made a large bark camp; no improvement since.

July 16, 1811: Present, Lucas, Penrose, and Bates, commissioners. It is the opinion of the Board that this claim ought not to be confirmed.

EZEKIEL BASSETT, claiming four hundred arpents of land, situate on the Mississippi, district of Arkansas; produces to the Board a concession from Francis y Luengo, late commandant of Arkansas, dated 6th February, 1803; appears to have been erased; a plat of survey, dated 1st February, 1804.

Testimony taken, at Camp Esperance, June 27, 1808. Phœbe Patterson, duly sworn, says that claimant settled on this tract in the year 1803; cleared a field without enclosing or cultivating it in the following year, 1804; cultivated a field of corn; a single man.

July 16, 1811: Present, Lucas, Penrose, and Bates, commissioners. It is the opinion of the Board that this claim ought not to be confirmed.

AUGUSTIN GRANDE, claiming nine hundred and ninety arpents of land, situate on bayou Wappenoche, district of Arkansas; produces to the Board a survey dated 15th January, 1806.

July 16, 1811: Present, Lucas, Penrose, and Bates, commissioners. It is the opinion of the Board that this claim ought not to be confirmed.

WILLIAM BASSETT, Jun., claiming six hundred and forty arpents of land, situate on bayou, a branch of Glaize; produces to the Board a concession from Francis y Luengo, late commandant of Arkansas, dated 20th March, 1803; a plat of survey, dated 11th February, 1803.

July 16, 1811: Present, Lucas, Penrose, and Bates, commissioners. It is the opinion of the Board that this claim ought not to be confirmed.

NATHANIEL BASSETT, claiming six hundred and forty arpents of land, situate on a branch of bayou Glaize, district of Arkansas; produces to the Board a concession from Francis y Luengo, late commandant of Arkansas, dated 20th March, 1803; a plat of survey, dated 12th April, 1803.

July 16, 1811: Present, Lucas, Penrose, and Bates, commissioners. It is the opinion of the Board that this claim ought not to be confirmed.

NOAH WALL, claiming six hundred and forty arpents of land, situate on Mississippi swamp, district of Arkansas; produces to the Board a concession from Francis y Luengo, late commandant of Arkansas, dated 23d March, 1803; a plat of survey, dated 10th April, 1803.

July 16, 1811: Present, Lucas, Penrose, and Bates, commissioners. It is the opinion of the Board that this claim ought not to be confirmed.

ANTHONY PENA, claiming three hundred and twenty arpents of land, situate on Alligator lake, district of Arkansas; produces to the Board a concession from Augustin Grandé, late commandant of Camp Esperance, dated 10th December, 1802; a second concession from said Grandé, approved by Charles D. Delassus, Lieutenant Governor, dated 10th December, 1802; a plat of survey, dated 13th December, 1802.

Testimony taken, at Camp Esperance, June 27, 1808. Augustin Grandé, duly sworn, says that this land was granted to claimant for services rendered the Spanish Government while witness was commandant of Camp Esperance.

****

July 16th, 1811: Present, Lucas, Penrose, and Bates, commissioners. It is the opinion of the Board that this claim ought not to be confirmed.

WILLIAM BASSETT, Sen., claiming two hundred and forty arpents of land, situate on the river Arkansas, district of Arkansas; produces to the Board a concession from Charles Villemont, late commandant of Arkansas, dated 12th July, 1800.
July 19th, 1811: Present, Lucas, Penrose, and Bates, commissioners. It is the opinion of the Board that this claim ought not to be confirmed.

AUGUSTIN GONZALES, claiming three hundred and twenty arpents of land, situate on Alligator lake, district of Arkansas; produces to the Board a concession from Augustin Grandé, late commandant of Camp Esperance, dated 10th December, 1802; a second concession from same, approved by Charles D. Delassus, Lieutenant Governor, dated 10th December, 1802; a plat of survey, dated 13th December, 1802.
Testimony taken, at Camp Esperance, June 27th, 1808. Augustin Grandé, duly sworn, says that this tract was granted during the command of witness at Camp Esperance to the claimant, for services rendered the Spanish Government.
July 19th, 1811: Present, Lucas, Penrose, and Bates, commissioners. It is the opinion of the Board that this claim ought not to be confirmed.

JEAN FRANCOIS ALMENDROS, claiming three hundred and twenty arpents of land, situate on Alligator lake, district of Arkansas, produces to the Board a concession from Augustin Grandé, late commandant at Camp Esperance, dated 10th December, 1802; a second concession from same, approved by Charles D. Delassus, Lieutenant Governor, dated 10th December, 1802; a plat of survey, dated 15th December, 1802.
Testimony taken, at Camp Esperance, June 27th, 1808. Augustin Grandé, duly sworn, says that this tract was granted during the command of witness at Camp Esperance to the claimant, for services rendered the Spanish Government.
July 19th, 1811: Present, Lucas, Penrose, and Bates, commissioners. It is the opinion of the Board that this claim ought not to be confirmed.

JOSEPH DOMINGUES, claiming three hundred and twenty arpents of land, situate on Alligator lake, district of Arkansas, produces to the Board a concession from Augustin Grandé, late commandant at Camp Esperance, dated 10th December, 1802; a second concession from same, approved by Charles D. Delassus, Lieutenant Governor, dated 10th December, 1802, surveyed 13th December, 1802.
Testimony taken, at Camp Esperance, June 27, 1808. Augustin Grandé, duly sworn, says that this tract was granted during the command of witness at Camp Esperance, to claimant, for services rendered the Spanish Government.
July 19, 1811: Present, Lucas, Penrose, and Bates, commissioners. It is the opinion of the Board that this claim ought not to be confirmed.

JEAN ANDRE ESCRIVANO, claiming three hundred and twenty arpents of land, situate on Alligator lake, district of Arkansas; produces to the Board a concession from Augustin Grandé, late commandant of Camp Esperance, dated 10th December, 1802; a second concession from same, approved by Charles D. Delassus, Lieutenant Governor, dated 10th December, 1802; a plat of survey, dated 13th December, 1802.
Testimony taken, at Camp Esperance, June 27, 1808. Augustin Grandé, duly sworn, says that this tract was granted during the command of witness at Camp Esperance, to the claimant, for services rendered the Spanish Government.
July 19, 1811: Present, Lucas, Penrose, and Bates, commissioners. It is the opinion of the Board that this claim ought not to be confirmed.

FRANCIS TROSON, claiming three hundred and twenty arpents of land, situate on Alligator lake, district of Arkansas; produces to the Board a concession from Augustin Grandé, late commandant of Camp Esperance, dated 10th December, 1802; a second concession from same, approved by Charles D. Delassus, Lieutenant Governor, dated 10th December, 1802; a plat of survey, dated 13th December, 1802.
Testimony taken, at Camp Esperance, June 27, 1808. Augustin Grandé, duly sworn, says that this tract was granted during the command of witness at Camp Esperance, to the claimant, for services rendered the Spanish Government.
July 19, 1811: Present, Lucas, Penrose, and Bates, commissioners. It is the opinion of the Board that this claim ought not to be confirmed.

JUSTO MARTIN, claiming three hundred and twenty arpents of land, situate on Alligator lake, district of Arkasnas; produces to the Board a concession from Augustin Grandé, late commandant of Camp Esperance, dated 10th December, 1802; a second concession from same, approved by Charles D. Delassus, Lieutenant Governor, dated 10th December, 1802; a plat of survey, dated 13th December, 1802.
Testimony taken, at Camp Esperance, June 27, 1808. Augustin Grandé, duly sworn, says that this tract was granted during the command of witness at Camp Esperance, to the claimant, for services rendered the Spanish Government.
July 19, 1811: Present, Lucas, Penrose, and Bates, commissioners. It is the opinion of the Board that this claim ought not to be confirmed.

JOHN RODRIGUEZ, claiming three hundred and twenty arpents of land, situate on Alligator lake, district of Arkansas; produces to the Board a concession from Augustin Grandé, late commandant of Camp Esperance, dated 10th December, 1802; a second concession from same, approved by Charles D. Delassus, Lieutenant Governor, dated 10th December, 1802; a plat of survey, dated 13th December, 1802.
Testimony taken, at Camp Esperance, June 27, 1808. Augustin Grandé, duly sworn, says that this tract was granted during the command of witness at Camp Esperance, to the claimant, for services rendered the Spanish Government.
July 19, 1811: Present, Lucas, Penrose, and Bates, commissioners. It is the opinion of the Board that this claim ought not to be confirmed.

Widow ELIZABETH JONES, claiming three hundred and twenty arpents of land, situate on Alligator lake, district of Arkansas; produces to the Board a concession from Augustin Grandé, late commandant of Camp Esperance, dated 31st August, 1802; a second concession from same, approved by Charles Dehault Delassus, Lieutenant Governor, dated 3d September, 1802; a plat of survey, dated 3d September, 1802.

July 19, 1811: Present, Lucas, Penrose, and Bates, commissioners. It is the opinion of the Board that this claim ought not to be confirmed.

MONTFORD PENNYMAN, claiming three hundred and twenty arpents of land, situate on bayou Wappenoche, district of Arkansas; produces to the Board a concession from Augustin Grandé, late commandant of Camp Esperance, dated 30th September, 1802; a second concession from same, approved by Charles D. Delassus, Lieutenant Governor, dated 30th September, 1802; a plat of survey, dated 30th September, 1802.

July 19, 1811: Present, Lucas, Penrose, and Bates, commissioners. It is the opinion of the Board that this claim ought not to be confirmed.

ABRAHAM RAMER, claiming nine hundred and fifty arpents of land, situate near the Mississippi, district of Arkansas; produces to the Board a notice to the Recorder; a plat of survey, dated 2d March, 1805.

Testimony taken, at Camp Esperance, June 27, 1808. Phœbe Patterson, duly sworn, says that these premises were improved in the year 1802; a house was then built, and a field of three or four acres cultivated in corn; this tract has been constantly inhabited and cultivated from the first improvement to the present time; claimant had a wife and two children in 1803.

July 19, 1811: Present, Lucas, Penrose, and Bates, commissioners. It is the opinion of the Board that this claim ought not to be granted.

SOLOMON BODWELL, claiming four hundred and forty arpents of land, situate near the river. St. François, district of Arkansas; produces to the Board a concession from Francisco Caso y Luengo, late commandant of Arkansas, dated 27th February, 1803.

Testimony taken, at Camp Esperance, June 27, 1808. William Russell, duly sworn, says claimant was a subject of His Catholic Majesty, and resided in Louisiana, in the year 1799, *certainly,* and witness thinks as early as the preceding year, and understood at that time that said Bodwell believed himself entitled to lands by virtue of that residence.

July 19, 1811: Present, Lucas, Penrose, and Bates, commissioners. It is the opinion of the Board that this claim ought not to be granted.

SYLVANUS PHILLIPS, claiming eight hundred arpents of land, near the river St. François, district of Arkansas; produce to the Board a concession from Francisco Caso y Luengo, late commandant of said district, dated 8th February, 1803.

Testimony taken, at Camp Esperance, June 27, 1808. William Bassett, duly sworn, says that claimant inhabited and cultivated this land in the year 1802, and constantly to the present time; at least twenty acres now in cultivation.

July 19, 1811: Present, Lucas, Penrose, and Bates, commissioners. It is the opinion of the Board that this claim ought not to be granted.

PETER EDWARDS, claiming four hundred arpents of land, situate on Eel river, nine miles above the mouth of the river St. François, district of Arkansas; produces to the Board a concession from Francisco Casso y Luengo, late commandant of said district, dated 8th February, 1803.

Testimony taken, at Camp Esperance, June 27, 1808. Sylvanus Phillips, duly sworn, says that these premises were cultivated and inhabited in the year 1796, and two or three of the following years; since which, it has remained unoccupied and uncultivated, except that, in 1804, a few peach stones were planted; and that claimant was a resident in Louisiana in the year 1803.

July 19, 1811: Present, Lucas, Penrose, and Bates, commissioners. It is the opinion of the Board that this claim ought not to be confirmed.

SYLVANUS PHILLIPS, assignee of Henry Curter, claiming four hundred arpents of land, situate and adjoining Francis Valliere, nine miles from the river Mississippi, district of Arkansas; produces to the Board a concession from Francisco Caso y Luengo, late commandant of Arkansas, dated 26th February 1803; an unauthenticated transfer, dated 6th June, 1804.

Testimony taken, at Camp Esperance, June 27, 1808. William Bassett, duly sworn, says that Curter was a resident of Louisiana in the year 1800, and is still in the country.

July 19, 1811: Present, Lucas, Penrose, and Bates, commissioners. It is the opinion of the Board that this claim ought not to be confirmed.

JOSEPH STILLWELL, claiming three hundred and twenty arpents of land, situate near the village of Arkansas, district of Arkansas; produces to the Board a concession from Francisco Caso y Luengo, late commandant of Arkansas, dated 8th December, 1802; a plat of survey, dated 26th May, 1806.

July 19, 1811: Present, Lucas, Penrose, and Bates, commissioners. It is the opinion of the Board that this claim ought not to be confirmed.

JOHN STILLWELL, claiming six hundred and forty arpents of land, situate six or nine miles from the river St. François and the Mississippi; produces to the Board a concession from Francisco Caso y Luengo, late commandant of Arkansas, dated 12th December, 1803.

Testimony taken, at Camp Esperance, June 28, 1808. Sylvanus Philips, duly sworn, says that John Stillwell, claimant, has been an inhabitant of Louisiana, and resident in the district of Arkansas, since the year 1798 to the present time.

July 19, 1811: Present, Lucas, Penrose, and Bates, commissioners. It is the opinion of the Board that this claim ought not to be confirmed.

HAROLD STILLWELL, claiming three hundred and twenty arpents of land, situate six or nine miles from the St. François and Mississippi, on waters of Lick creek; produces to the Board a concession from Francisco Caso y Luengo, late commandant of Arkansas, dated 16th December, 1802.

Testimony taken, at Camp Esperance, June 28, 1808. Sylvanus Phillips, duly sworn, says that claimant has been an inhabitant of Louisiana, and resident in the district of Arkansas, since the year 1798 to the present time.

July 19, 1811: Present, Lucas Penrose and Bates, commissioners. It is the opinion of the Board that this claim ought not to be confirmed.

ALEXANDER PETER, alias Alexis Picard, claiming eight hundred and forty acres of land, on river St. François, district of New Madrid; produces to the Board a notice to the Recorder.

Testimony taken, at Camp Esperance, June 28, 1808. Baptiste Grimard, duly sworn, says that premises have been constantly inhabited and cultivated from 1802 to the present time; a wife and two children in 1803; about ten or twelve arpents now in cultivation; witness lives in New Madrid, is an inhabitant of that village, and a voyager.

July 19, 1811: Present, Lucas, Penrose, and Bates, commissioners. It is the opinion of the Board that this claim ought not to be granted.

JAMES GOSSIOT, claiming two hundred and forty arpents of land, situate on Marechal's Hill, district of Arkansas; produces to the Board a concession from Francisco Caso y Luengo, late commandant of Arkansas, dated 3d January, 1803; a plat of survey, dated 20th March, 1806.

July 19, 1811: Present, Lucas, Penrose, and Bates, commissioners. It is the opinion of the Board that this claim ought not to be confirmed.

WILLIAM PATTERSON, claiming three hundred and twenty arpents of land, situate on Caney creek, district of Arkansas; produces to the Board a concession from Francisco Caso y Luengo, late commandant of Arkansas, dated 9th December, 1802; a plat of survey, dated March 10, 1802.

Testimony taken, at Camp Esperance, June 28, 1808. William Patterson, duly sworn, says that he, witness, saw these premises in 1802 or 1803, and saw a small cabin thereon, and a small clearing, probably intended for a plantation; several persons were then on the land, but did not appear to be residents; there was afterwards a regular inhabitation, and an enlargement of the cultivation, but at what particular time witness has forgotten.

July 19, 1811: Present, Lucas, Penrose, and Bates, commissioners. It is the opinion of the Board that this claim ought not to be confirmed.

SYLVANUS PHILLIPS, claiming two hundred and forty arpents of land, (not located,) in the district of Arkansas; produces to the Board a concession from Charles Villemont, late commandant of Arkansas, dated 27th September, 1800.

Testimony taken, at Camp Esperance, June 28, 1808. Joseph Stillman, duly sworn, says that claimant has been regularly an inhabitant of Louisiana, resident in the district of Arkansas, since the year 1798 to the present time.

July 19, 1811: Present, Lucas, Penrose, and Bates, commissioners. It is the opinion of the Board that this claim ought not to be confirmed.

JOHN BAPTISTE PLACIDE, alias PLACIE, claiming four hundred and eighty arpents of land, situate on river Arkansas, district of Arkansas; produces to the Board two certificates of Ignace de Leno, late commandant of Arkansas, (unauthenticated;) a plat of survey, dated 17th February, 1806.

Testimony taken, at Camp Esperance, July 4, 1808. Francis Vaugine, duly sworn, says that these premises have been constantly cultivated, without interruption, for thirteen years past; during the time of cultivation, this tract has always been inhabited; when crop has been secured, claimant has generally resided on another plantation.

Michel Petersee, sworn, says that there are about forty acres in cultivation; on this tract are two small houses.

July 22, 1811: Present, Lucas, Penrose, and Bates, commissioners. It is the opinion of the Board that this claim ought not to be granted.

JOSEPH BOUGY, Jun., claiming eight hundred arpents of land, situate on Arkansas swamp, district of Arkansas; produces to the Board a concession from Francisco Caso y Luengo, late commandant of Arkansas, dated 6th November, 1802; a plat of survey for eight hundred and twelve arpents, dated 19th March, 1806.

July 22, 1811: Present, Lucas, Penrose, and Bates, commissioners. It is the opinion of the Board that this claim ought not to be confirmed.

SAMUEL TREAT, assignee of Joseph Michel, assignee of Joseph Tessier, claiming four hundred and eighty arpents of land, district of Arkansas; produces to the Board a petition and recommendation for a concession from Charles Villemont, late commandant of Arkansas, dated March 17, 1799; a plat of survey, dated 9th April, 1806.

Testimony taken, at Arkansas village, July 5, 1808. William Glass, duly sworn, says that he, witness, cultivated and inhabited this tract in the years 1805 and 1806, and that, from the appearance of the improvements on this tract, he verily believes that they must have commenced before the year 1803; the peach trees appeared to be six or seven years old, and the house was then falling to decay from age.

Christopher Kepler, duly sworn, says that these premises were cultivated in corn eleven years ago; Tessier then lived on this land, and witness knows positively that this tract was inhabited and cultivated during the year 1803, till 20th December, and believes that such inhabitation and cultivation have been continued to this time.

July 22, 1811: Present, Lucas, Penrose, and Bates, commissioners. It is the opinion of the Board that this claim ought not to be confirmed.

SAMUEL TREAT, assignee of Francis Michel, assignee of Joseph Tessier, claiming eight hundred arpents of land, situate on river Caches, district of Arkansas; produces to the Board a petition and recommendation for a concession from Francisco Caso y Luengo, late commandant of Arkansas, dated 20th August, 1802; a plat of survey, dated 9th April, 1806; a transfer from Tessier to Michel, dated 1st July, 1806; a transfer from Michel to Treat, 16th March, 1807, for nine hundred and eighty acres of land.

July 22, 1811: Present, Lucas, Penrose, and Bates, commissioners. It is the opinion of the Board that this claim ought not to be confirmed.

JOHN BAPTISTE DECHASSIN, claiming six hundred and thirty arpents of land, situate on the Big bay, four and a half miles from Arkansas, district of Arkansas; produces to the Board a petition and recommendation for a concession from Charles de Villemont, late commandant of Arkansas, dated 2d April, 1798; a plat of survey dated 7th March, 1806, certified by Antoine Soulard, May 18, 1807.

Testimony taken, at Arkansas village, July 5, 1808. William H. Glass, duly sworn, says ten or twelve acres are now in cultivation; says, further, that there are indications on this tract of former improvements, to wit, the ruins of walls which appear to have been formed some years ago, a part of a dwelling-house; the fields have also vestiges of former cultivation.

Andrew Fagot, duly sworn, says that, in the year 1798, and in every succeeding year until the United States took possession, the hostile and disorderly conduct of the neighboring Indians was such as to render the cultivation of the soil unsafe, except in the immediate vicinity and under the protection of the post. Don Carlos de Villemont told the people desirous of settling themselves in the country that it was improper for them to do so, as his protection could not then be extended to them; the same interruptions, and the same advices, given in the time of Luengo, as during the command of his predecessor; witness believes claimant to be the oldest man in the settlement, where he has resided many years.

Joseph Stillwell, duly sworn, says (not specially in relation to this claim, but as regards the country generally) that, in the year 1798, and until the United States took possession of this post, the inhabitants, from time to time, suffered much and vexatious embarrassment from the marauding, disorderly, and violent inroads of the Indians; the property of the people was frequently stolen, and they were as often under apprehension of personal injury; witness remained in his house on his plantation, but he believes many persons were deterred from encountering similar hazards; a son of the witness has been in those times driven from the field where he was at work, by having a gun presented at him.

July 22, 1811: Present, Lucas, Penrose, and Bates, commissioners. It is the opinion of the Board that this claim ought not to be confirmed.

PETER LEFEVRE, assignee of Baptiste Soucier, claiming six hundred arpents of land, situate on White river, (Big island,) district of Arkansas; produces to the Board a petition and recommendation for a concession from Francisco Caso y Luengo, late commandant of Arkansas, dated 30th August, 1802; a plat of survey, dated 28th February, 1806; (a copy) a transfer, dated 15th September, 1804.

Testimony taken, at Arkansas, July 5, 1808. David Haker, duly sworn, says that premises were settled three years ago, four or five houses were then built, and six or seven acres planted in corn; since which, this land has been constantly inhabited and cultivated at this time.

July 22, 1811: Present, Lucas, Penrose, and Bates, commissioners. It is the opinion of the Board that this claim ought not to be confirmed.

LOUIS LEFEVRE, devisees of, claiming two hundred and fifty-seven arpents of land, situate on bayou La Prairie, district of Aakansas; produces to the Board a concession or order of survey from the Baron de Carondelet, Governor General, dated 8th February, 1792, a plat of survey, dated 17th February, 1806, also the last will and testament of said Louis Lefevre.

Testimony taken, at Arkansas village, district of Arkansas, July 6, 1808. Francis Vaugine, duly sworn, says that the premises were inhabited and cultivated in the year 1807; the testator died in the year 1795, and none of the present claimants are yet of the age of twenty-one years.

July 22, 1811: Present, Lucas, Penrose, and Bates, commissioners. It is the opinion of the Board that this claim ought not to be confirmed.

CHARLES DROUOT, claiming two hundred and forty-nine arpents of land, situate on bayou La Prairie, district of Arkansas; produces to the Board a petition and recommendation for a concession from Charles de Villemont, late commandant of Arkansas, dated May 9, 1799, for two hundred and forty arpents of land; a plat of survey, dated 18th February, 1806.

Testimony taken, at Arkansas village, July 6, 1808. John Larkin, duly sworn, says that a small house was built nine years ago, and inhabited one year, no cultivation at that time.

July 22, 1811: Present, Lucas, Penrose, and Bates, commissioners. It is the opinion of the Board that this claim ought not to be confirmed.

PETER RANDALL, assignee of John Moore, claiming two hundred and fifty-eight arpents of land, situate two miles from the village Arkansas, district of Arkansas; produces to the Board a plat of survey, dated 17th February, 1806, transfer, dated 5th September, 1804.

Testimony taken, at Arkansas village, July 6, 1808. Francis Vaugine, duly sworn, says that in the year 1801 claimant built a house and blacksmith's shop; a small plantation of corn and tobacco in the following year.

Christopher Coupman, duly sworn, says that witness assisted to build a house on this land eight years ago; a small field cleared, enclosed, and cultivated, and the house inhabited for the two following years; it was last year in corn.

July 22, 1811: Present, Lucas, Penrose, and Bates, commissioners. It is the opinion of the Board that this claim ought not to be granted.

CHRISTOPHER KEPLER, claiming two hundred and sixty-eight arpents of land, situate on the west side of the Great Prairie, district of Arkansas; produces a copy of survey, made 13th March, 1806.

Testimony taken, at Arkansas village, July 6, 1808. Christian Pringle, duly sworn, says that premises have been cultivated and inhabited six or seven acres, from the year 1801 or 1802 till the last year, and cultivated this year; about nine or ten acres now in cultivation, a wife and one child in 1803.

July 23, 1811: Present, Lucas, Penrose, and Bates, commissioners. It is the opinion of the Board that this claim ought not to be granted.

JOSEPH MICHEL, assignee of Francis Michel, assignee of Andrew Fagot, claiming eight hundred arpents of land, situate on a bay of White river, thirty-six miles from Arkansas, district of Arkansas; produces to the Board a concession from Francisco Caso y Luengo, late commandant of Arkansas, dated 6th November, 1802; a plat of survey, dated 5th April, 1806; a transfer from Fagot to Francis Michel, dated 2d July, 1806, from said Francis to claimant, dated 6th July, 1808.

Testimony taken, at Arkansas village, July 7, 1808. John Delaplace, duly sworn, says these premises were improved, about fourteen years ago, potatoes, corn, and other vegetables, cultivated, and a house built same year; cultivation suspended in consequence of Indian interruptions; peach trees were planted, improvements again resumed six years ago, and cultivation continued constantly to this time.

July 23, 1811: Present, Lucas, Penrose, and Bates, commissioners. It is the opinion of the Board that this claim ought not to be confirmed.

LOUIS GOTIOT, claiming six hundred and twenty-six arpents of land, situate between the Bay and Arkansas village; produces to the Board a plat of survey, of the same date, 24th February, 1806.

Testimony taken, at Arkansas village, July 7, 1808. Michel Petercel, duly sworn, says that these premises were cultivated seven years ago, and inhabited, and constantly to the present time; eight acres now in cultivation; claimant had a wife and four children in 1803.

July 23, 1811: Present, Lucas, Penrose, and Bates, commissioners. It is the opinion of the Board that this claim ought not to be granted.

JOSEPH MICHEL, assignee of Francis Michel, who was assignee of Peter Lefevre, assignee of Albert Berdu, claiming eight hundred arpents of land, situate on a bay of White river, district of Arkansas; produces to the Board a concession from Francisco Caso y Luengo, late commandant, dated 22d November, 1802; a plat of survey, dated 5th April, 1806; a transfer from Berdu to Lefevre, dated 24th April, 1804; from Lefevre to Francis Michel, dated 12th May, 1806; from said Francis to claimant, dated 6th July, 1808: said transfer on file.

Testimony taken, at Arkansas village, July 7, 1808. Peter Lefevre, Junior, duly sworn, says that premises were constantly inhabited and cultivated since the year 1800, inclusively, to the present time; some small buildings on this land; about ten acres now in cultivation.

July 23, 1811: Present, Lucas, Penrose, and Bates, commissioners. It is the opinion of the Board that this claim ought not to be granted.

JEAN BAPTISTE DEPLACIE, claiming seven hundred and fifty arpents of land, situate on river Caches, district of Arkansas; produces to the Board a notice to the recorder.

Testimony taken, at Arkansas village, July 7, 1808. Andrew Fagot, duly sworn, says that premises were cultivated and inhabited in 1795, '96, and '97; a house was then built, and about twenty arpents enclosed.

July 23, 1811: Present, Lucas, Penrose, and Bates, commissioners. It is the opinion of the Board that this claim ought not to be granted.

MARIA CLOSSEIN, widow of Peter Clossein, claiming seven hundred and fifty arpents of land, situate at the Bute Marechal, two leagues from the village of Arkansas, district of Arkansas; produces to the Board a notice to the recorder.

Testimony taken, at Arkansas village, July 7, 1808. John Jordilas, duly sworn, says that these premises were cultivated more than twelve years ago, when this tract was also inhabited; four acres were then enclosed, after two or three years habitation and cultivation; the Indian troubles caused it to be abandoned; the late Peter Clossein had a wife and two children.

July 23, 1811: Present, Lucas, Penrose, and Bates, commissioners. It is the opinion of the Board that this claim ought not to be granted.

LOUIS P. LEVY, claiming seven hundred and fifty arpents of land, situate on Arkansas river, forty leagues above the village, adjoining Michel Bonne; produces to the Board a notice to the recorder.

Testimony taken, at Arkansas village, July 7, 1808. Maurice Fortnay, duly sworn, says that the premises were cultivated and inhabited about five years ago; a dwelling house was then built; had a wife and one child.

July 23, 1811: Present, Lucas, Penrose, and Bates, commissioners. It is the opinion of the Board that this claim ought not to be granted.

JOSEPH MICHEL, assignee of Francis Michel, assignee of Peter Lefevre, assignee of Louis Soulegney, claiming four hundred arpents of land, situate in the district of Arkansas; produces to the Board a petition and recommendation for a concession from Francisco Caso y Luengo, late commandant, dated 8th December, 1802; a plat of survey, dated 9th April, 1806; a transfer from Soulegney to Lefevre, dated 30th April, 1804; from Lefevre to Francis Michel, dated 12th May, 1806; from said Francis to claimant, dated 6th July, 1808: said transfer on file.

Testimony taken, at Arkansas village, July 7, 1808. Peter Lefevre, Jun., duly sworn, says that four years ago witness saw a cabin, and some wood cut on this land, which appeared to have been done at least four or five years previously; this tract appeared to have been formerly cultivated.

July 23, 1811: Present, Lucas, Penrose, and Bates, commissioners. It is the opinion of the Board that this claim ought not to be confirmed.

JOSEPH MICHEL, assignee of Francis Michel, assignee of Peter Lefevre, assignee of Raphael Bennett, claiming four hundred arpents of land, situate in the district of Arkansas; produces a petition and recommendation for a concession from Francisco Caso y Luengo, late commandant, dated 6th December, 1802; a transfer from Bennett to Lefevre, dated 1st June, 1804; a plat of survey dated 10th April, 1806; a transfer from Lefevre to Francis Michel, dated 12th May, 1806; a transfer from said Francis to claimant, dated 6th July, 1808: said transfer on file.

Testimony taken, at Arkansas village, July 7, 1808. Peter Lefevre, Jun., duly sworn, says that improvements appeared to have been made on this land at an early time; he knows not when.

July 23, 1811: Present, Lucas, Penrose, and Bates, commissioners. It is the opinion of the Board that this claim ought not to be confirmed.

. JOSEPH MICHEL, assignee of Francis Michel, assignee of Peter Lefevre, assignee of Louis Pertius, claiming four hundred arpents of land, situate in the district of Arkansas; produces to the Board a petition and recommendation for a concession from Francisco Caso y Luengo, late commandant, dated 6th December, 1802; a plat of survey dated 10th April, 1806; a transfer from Pertius to Lefevre, dated 20th April, 1804; a transfer from Lefevre to Francis Michel, dated 12th May, 1806; a transfer from said Francis to claimant, dated 6th July, 1808: said transfer on file.

Testimony taken, at Arkansas village, July 7, 1808. Peter Lefevre, duly sworn, says that he saw trees cut in November, 1804.

July 23, 1811: Present, Lucas, Penrose, and Bates, commissioners. It is the opinion of the Board that this claim ought not to be confirmed.

JOSEPH MICHEL, assignee of Francis Michel, assignee of Peter Lefevre, assignee of Peter Pertius, claiming four hundred arpents of land, situate in the district of Arkansas; produces to the Board a petition and recommendation for a concession from Francisco Caso y Luengo, late commandant, dated 25th November, 1802; a plat of survey dated 10th April, 1806; a transfer from Pertius to Lefevre, dated 17th April, 1804; a transfer from Lefevre to Francis Michel, dated 12th May, 1806; a transfer from said Francis to claimant, dated 6th July, 1808: said transfer on file.

Testimony taken, at Arkansas village, July 7, 1808. Peter Lefevre, duly sworn, says that in December, 1804, saw a kind of a house, from which he conjectured this land had been cultivated.

July 23, 1811: Present, Lucas, Penrose, and Bates, commissioners. It is the opinion of the Board that this claim ought not to be confirmed.

JOSEPH MICHEL, assignee of Francis Michel, assignee of Peter Lefevre, assignee of Louis Berthelemay, claiming four hundred arpents of land, situate in the district of Arkansas; produces to the Board a petition and recommendation for a concession from Francisco Caso y Luengo, late commandant, dated 8th December, 1802; plat of survey, dated 9th April, 1806; a transfer from Berthelemay to Lefevre, dated 11th May, 1804; a transfer from Lefevre to Francis Michel, dated 12th May, 1806; a transfer from said Francis to claimant, dated 6th July, 1808: said transfer on file.
July 23, 1811: Present, Lucas, Penrose, and Bates, commissioners. It is the opinion of the Board that this claim ought not to be confirmed.

JOSEPH MICHEL, assignee of Francis Michel, assignee of Peter Lefevre, assignee of Louis Lariviere, claiming four hundred arpents of land, situate in the district of Arkansas; produces to the Board a petition and recommendation for a concession from Francisco Caso y Luengo, late commandant, dated 12th December, 1802; a plat of survey, dated 9th April, 1806; a transfer from Lariviere to Lefevre, dated 28th April, 1804; a transfer from Lefevre to Francis Michel, dated 12th May, 1806; a transfer from said Francis to claimant, dated 6th July, 1808: said transfer on file.
July 23, 1811: Present, Lucas, Penrose, and Bates, commissioners. It is the opinion of the Board that this claim ought not to be confirmed.

JOSEPH MICHEL, assignee of Francis Michel, assignee of Peter Lefevre, assignee of Joseph Belletto, claiming four hundred arpents of land, situate in the district of Arkansas; produces to the Board a petition and recommendation for a concession from Francisco Caso y Luengo, late commandant, dated 18th December, 1802; a plat of survey dated 9th April, 1806; a transfer from Belletto to Lefevre, dated 1st June, 1804; a transfer from Lefevre to Francis Michel, dated 12th May, 1806; a transfer from said Francis to claimant, dated July 6, 1808: said transfer on file.
July 23, 1811: Present, Lucas, Penrose, and Bates, commissioners. It is the opinion of the Board that this claim ought not to be confirmed.

JOSEPH MICHEL, assignee of Francis Michel, assignee of Peter Lefevre, assignee of Francis Peltier, claiming four hundred arpents of land, situate in the district of Arkansas; produces to the Board a petition and recommendation for a concession from Francisco Caso y Luengo, late commandant, dated 18th December, 1802; a plat of survey, dated 9th April, 1806; a transfer from Peltier to Lefevre, dated 1st May, 1804; a transfer from Lefevre to Francis Michel, dated 12th May, 1806; a transfer from said Francis to claimant, dated July 6, 1808: said transfer on file.
July 23: Present, Lucas, Penrose, and Bates, commissioners. It is the opinion of the Board that this claim ought not to be confirmed.

JOSEPH MICHEL, assignee of Francis Michel, assignee of Peter Lefevre, assignee of Antoine Trudell, claiming four hundred arpents of land, situate in the district of Arkansas; produces to the Board a petition and recommendation for a concession from Francisco Casso y Luengo, late commandant, dated 12th December, 1802; a plat of survey, dated 8th April, 1806; a transfer from Trudell to Lefevre, dated 23d April, 1804; a transfer from Lefevre to Francis Michel, dated 12th May, 1806; a transfer from said Francis to claimant, dated July 6, 1808: said transfer on file.
July 23, 1811: Present, Lucas, Penrose, and Bates, commissioners. It is the opinion of the Board that this claim ought not to be confirmed.

JOSEPH MICHEL, assignee of Francis Michel, assignee of Peter Lefevre, assignee of Antoine Jeanot; claiming four hundred arpents of land, situate in the district of Arkansas; produces to the Board a petition and recommendation for a concession from Francisco Caso y Luengo, late commandant, dated 20th December, 1802; a plat of survey, dated April 8, 1806; a transfer from Jeanot to Lefevre, dated 18th May, 1804; a transfer from Francis Michel to claimant, dated July 6, 1808; a transfer from Lefevre to Francis Michel, dated May 12, 1806: said transfer to Joseph Michel, on file.
July 23, 1811: Present, Lucas, Penrose, and Bates, commissioners. It is the opinion of the Board that this claim ought not to be confirmed.

JOSEPH MICHEL, assignee of Francis Michel, assignee of Peter Lefevre, assignee of Michel Bonne, claiming four hundred arpents of land, situate in the district of Arkansas; produces to the Board a petition and recommendation for a concession from Francisco Casso y Luengo, late commandant, dated 8th December, 1802; a plat of survey, dated 9th April, 1806; a transfer from Bonne to Lefevre, dated 10th October, 1804; from Lefevre to Francis Michel, dated 12th May, 1806; from said Francis to claimant, dated July 6, 1808: said transfer is on file.
July 23, 1811: Present, Lucas, Penrose, and Bates, commissioners. It is the opinion of the Board that this claim ought not to be confirmed.

JOSEPH SOUMANDE, claiming seven hundred and fifty arpents of land, situate on the north side of White river, district of Arkansas; produces to the Board a notice to the recorder, and a plat of survey, dated 6th April, 1806.
July 23, 1811: Present, Lucas, Penrose, and Bates, commissioners. It is the opinion of the Board that this claim ought not to be granted.

JOSEPH POUILLOT, claiming seven hundred and fifty arpents of land, situate on the north side of White river district of Arkansas; produces to the Board a plat of survey, dated April 6, 1806.
July 23, 1811: Present, Lucas, Penrose, and Bates, commissioners. It is the opinion of the Board that this claim ought not to be granted.

FRANCIS LAROZIE, claiming seven hundred and fifty arpents of land, situate near Prairie des Turcs, district of Arkansas; produces to the Board a plat of survey, dated 7th April, 1806.
July 23, 1811: Present, Lucas, Penrose, and Bates, commissioners. It is the opinion of the Board that this claim ought not to be granted.

MICHEL AQUITAN, claiming one thousand arpents of land, situate near the river Caches, district of Arkansas; produces to the Board a notice to the recorder, dated 1st June, 1808.

LAND GRANTS IN MISSOURI TERRITORY - 1805 - 1812

57

****

Testimony taken, at Arkansas village, July 7, 1808. John Deplace, being duly sworn, says that about thirteen years ago, in the time (during command) of Villemont, improvement commenced; house then built; cultivated during six successive years: after which the improvements were suspended, owing to the disorderly and hostile conduct of the Indians. Three years ago the cultivation and residence were resumed, and continued to this time. Claimant had a wife and ten children.

July 23, 1811: Present, Lucas, Penrose, and Bates, commissioners. It is the opinion of the Board that this claim ought not to be granted.

JACOB BRIGHT, assignee of Anselmy Bellette, claiming two hundred and seventy-six arpents of land, situate on the bayou of the Prairie, district of Arkansas; produces to the Board a petition and recommendation for a concession from Francisco Caso y Luengo, late commandant, dated 27th February, 1803, for two hundred and forty arpents; a plat of survey, dated 17th February, 1806; a transfer, dated 22d May, 1805.

July 23, 1811: Present, Lucas, Penrose, and Bates, commissioners. It is the opinion of the Board that this claim ought not to be confirmed.

MOSES PRICE, assignee of John Moore, claiming three hundred and twenty arpents of land, situate adjoining the claim of William Winter and Lefevre; produces to the Board a petition and recommendation for a concession from Charles de Villemont, late commandant, dated 4th June, 1798, for three hundred and twenty arpents; a plat of survey of one hundred and fifty-four arpents, dated 16th February, 1806; a transfer from Moore to claimant, dated 7th August, 1807.

July 23, 1811: Present, Lucas, Penrose, and Bates, commissioners. It is the opinion of the Board that this claim ought not to be confirmed.

PETER BURRELL, claiming two hundred and fifty-one arpents of land, situate adjoining land of Bonzy Brinsback and Joseph Deruis ux, district of Arkansas; produces to the Board a petition and recommendation from Charles de Villemont, late commandant, dated 4th September, 1800; a plat of survey, dated 27th March, 1806: said petition for two hundred and forty arpents.

Testimony taken, at Arkansas village, July 8, 1808. Michel Petersel, duly sworn, says that these premises have not been inhabited or cultivated; timber has been cut; but a fear of the Indians has prevented the cultivation and improvements which were contemplated. Claimant purchased one acre and a quarter of land, about three miles in the nearest (impracticable) direction from the premises, on which small lot claimant resided with a large family.

July 23, 1811: Present, Lucas, Penrose, and Bates, commissioners. It is the opinion of the Board that this claim ought not to be confirmed.

RAPHAEL BRINSBACK, claiming four hundred arpents of land, district of Arkansas; produces to the Board a petition and recommendation for a concession from Charles de Villemont, late commandant, dated 9th August, 1800; a plat of survey, dated 27th March, 1806.

July 23, 1811: Present, Lucas, Penrose, and Bates, commissioners. It is the opinion of the Board that this claim ought not to be confirmed.

GARMAIN CHARBONNEAU, claiming three hundred and twenty arpents of land, situate one mile and a half from Arkansas village, district of Arkansas; produces to the Board a petition and recommendation for a concession from Francisco Caso y Luengo, late commandant, dated 17th February, 1803; a plat of survey, dated 27th March, 1806.

July 23, 1811: Present, Lucas, Penrose, and Bates, commissioners. It is the opinion of the Board that this claim ought not to be confirmed.

JOHN S. BAIRD, claiming eight hundred arpents of land, situate on Turk bay, White river, district of Arkansas; produces to the Board a petition and recommendation for a concession from Francisco Caso y Luengo, late commandant, dated 30th December, 1802.

July 23, 1811: Present, Lucas, Penrose, and Bates, commissioners. It is the opinion of the Board that this claim ought not to be confirmed.

LOUIS PLACIDE, claiming six hundred arpents of land, situate on the river Aux Grues, or Crane river, to lake in bluff, adjoining land of Charles Bougy, district of Arkansas; produces to the Board a petition and recommendation for a concession from Francisco Caso y Luengo, late commandant, dated 6th November, 1802.

July 25, 1811: Present, Lucas, Penrose, and Bates, commissioners. It is the opinion of the Board that this claim ought not to be confirmed.

BENJAMIN LAFFERTY, assignee of Henry Hatton, claiming two hundred and fifty acres of land, situate opposite the upper end of the Devil's island, in the Mississippi, district of Cape Girardeau; produces to the Board a transfer from said Hatton to claimant, dated the 6th March, 1807.

Testimony taken, by Frederick Bates, commissioner, at Cape Girardeau, June 4, 1808, by authority from the Board.

Stephen Byrd, duly sworn, says that in the year 1803 Hatton chopped a few trees on this tract, and marked his name on others, saying that the commandant had permitted him to look for a mill-seat, and this was the one he had chosen; afterwards, in the spring of the present year, witness was on the premises, when he saw a cabin built, and about ten acres nearly cleared.

November 26, 1810: Present, Lucas, Penrose, and Bates, commissioners. It is the opinion of the Board that this claim ought not to be granted.

JOHN CLEMENT, claiming two hundred arpents of land, situate in Tywappety prairie, St. Charles, district of New Madrid; produces to the Board a permission to settle, from Henry Peyroux, commandant, dated 22d May, 1801.

Testimony taken, as aforesaid, at New Madrid, June 16, 1808. Jacob Myers, duly sworn, says that a cabin was built in 1800, and land cultivated about two years; since abandoned; claimant above the age of twenty-one years.

December 5, 1810: Present, Lucas, Penrose, and Bates, commissioners. It is the opinion of the Board that this claim ought not to be granted.

THOMAS W. WATERS & Co., assignees of Henry Lawson, assignee of Stephen Jones, assignee of John Kennedy, claiming five hundred arpents of land, situate on Tywappety, lake Le Bœuf, district of New Madrid; produces to the Board a certified copy of transfer from John Kennedy to Stephen Jones, dated 5th March, 1802; a transfer from Stephen Jones to Henry Lawson and Zadock McNew, dated 6th August, 1805; a transfer from Lawson to Thomas W. Waters & Co., dated 19th October, 1805.

Testimony taken, as aforesaid, at New Madrid, June 16, 1808. William Smith, duly sworn, says that claimant inhabited and cultivated in spring of 1801; built a cabin, cleared four or five acres of land, and constantly afterwards, until the present year; twenty acres now in cultivation; a wife and ten children in 1803.

December 5, 1801: Present, Lucas, Penrose, and Bates, commissioners. It is the opinion of the Board that this claim ought not to be granted.

PETER PORIER, claiming one hundred and thirty arpents of land, situate near Big Lake, Little Prairie, district of New Madrid; produces to the Board a permission to settle, from François Lesieur, No. 1219; a plat of survey, dated 23d February, 1806.

Testimony taken, as aforesaid, at New Madrid, June 17, 1808. Jacob Waggoner, duly sworn, says that premises were cultivated and inhabited in the year 1803, and constantly to this day; about five acres now in cultivation; wife and two children in 1803.

December 19, 1810: Present, Lucas, Penrose, and Bates, commissioners. It is the opinion of the Board that this claim ought not to be granted.

JOSEPH LAPLANTE, claiming two hundred and seventy arpents of land, situate near the Mississippi, district of New Madrid; produces to the Board a special permission to settle, from Henry Peyroux, commandant, dated 15th March, 1802; a plat of survey, dated 27th February, 1806, and signed M. Ameroux.

Testimony taken, as aforesaid, at New Madrid, June 17, 1808. Henry Godair, duly sworn, says that premises were cultivated from 1802, inclusive, till last year; four or five arpents then in cultivation; a wife and six or seven children in 1803.

December 19, 1810: Present, Lucas, Penrose, and Bates, commissioners. It is the opinion of the Board that this claim ought not to be granted.

JOHN BAPTISTE AIME, claiming nine hundred arpents of land, situate near the Mississippi, district of New Madrid; produces to the Board a notice to the recorder, and a plat of survey, dated 28th February, 1806.

Testimony taken, as aforesaid, at New Madrid, June 17, 1808. John B. Olive, duly sworn, says that premises have been inhabited and cultivated from either the year 1801 or 1802, to the present time; from eight to ten acres in cultivation in 1803.

December, 19, 1810: Present, Lucas, Penrose, and Bates, commissioners. It is the opinion of the Board that this claim ought not to be granted.

ANDREW BURNS, claiming one thousand and fifty arpents of land, near the Brushy Prairie, district of New Madrid; produces to the Board a notice to the recorder.

Testimony taken, as aforesaid, at New Madrid, June 18, 1808. William Cox, duly sworn, says that premises were inhabited and cultivated from the 1st of March, 1803; cleared about four acres in that year, and continued to inhabit and cultivate to this time; a wife and five children in 1803; eight or ten acres in cultivation.

December 19, 1810: Present, Lucas, Penrose, and Bates, commissioners. It is the opinion of the Board that this claim ought not to be granted.

REESE SHELBY, claiming seven hundred and fifty arpents of land, situate on the Mississippi, opposite the Iron Banks, district of New Madrid; produces to the Board a survey of the same, dated 10th February, 1806.

Testimony taken, as aforesaid, at New Madrid, June 18, 1808. William Cox, duly sworn, says that premises were inhabited and cultivated in the year 1803, and constantly to the present time, except in the year 1805; about eight or ten acres now in cultivation; no family; above the age of twenty-one years.

January 4, 1811: Present, Lucas, Penrose, and Bates, commissioners. It is the opinion of the Board that this claim ought not to be granted.

LOUIS SOJOURNER, claiming nine hundred arpents of land, situate on Brushy Prairie, district of New Madrid; produces to the Board a notice to the recorder.

Testimony taken, as aforesaid, at New Madrid, June 18, 1808. Jacob Myers, duly sworn, says that premises were cultivated and inhabited in 1802, and constantly to the present time; about fifteen or twenty acres now in cultivation; a wife and one child, and one slave in 1803.

January 4, 1811: Present, Lucas, Penrose, and Bates, commissioners. It is the opinion of the Board that this claim ought not to be granted.

DANIEL SEXTON, claiming three hundred and fifty arpents of land, situate on Caney creek, district of Cape Girardeau; produces to the Board a notice to the recorder.

Testimony taken, as aforesaid, at New Madrid, June 18, 1808. William Smith, duly sworn, says that claimant cultivated this tract in 1803, in which year he cleared, enclosed, and cultivated about three acres, and built two cabins; a wife and two children, and two slaves in 1803.

January 8, 1811: Present, Lucas, Penrose, and Bates, commissioners. It is the opinion of the Board that this claim ought not to be granted.

CHARLES CHARTERS, assignee of John Johnson, claiming seven hundred and fifty arpents of land, situate on bayou de Bœuf, district of New Madrid; produces to the Board a notice to the recorder.

Testimony taken, as aforesaid, at New Madrid, June 18, 1808. William Smith, duly sworn, says that in the year 1804 or 1805, claimant cultivated and improved this land, cleared a few acres of ground, and sunk a well.

January 8, 1811: Present, Lucas, Penrose, and Bates, commissioners. It is the opinion of the Board that this claim ought not to be granted.

BARTHELEMY TARDIVEAU, claiming two hundred and forty arpents of land, situate on bayou St. John and St. Thomas; produces to the Board a concession from the Baron de Carondelet, Governor General, dated 28th November, 1793; a plat of survey, dated 22d February, 1806, and signed Michel Ameroux.

Testimony taken, as aforesaid, at New Madrid, June 18, 1808. P. A. Laforge, duly sworn, says that timber has been cut on the premises for the purpose of building a mill, which witness understood was the only condition of the grant; said land is so subject to be overflowed as to be unfit for cultivation, and could only have been peti-tioned for the use above stated.

January 8, 1811: Present, Lucas, Penrose, and Bates, commissioners. It is the opinion of the Board that this claim ought not to be confirmed.

BARTHELEMY TARDIVEAU, claiming four hundred arpents of land, situate on bayou St. Thomas; produces to the Board a plat of survey, dated 28th February, 1806; for permission to settle, see list, No. 1369, on file.

Testimony taken, at New Madrid, as aforesaid, June 18, 1808. P. A. Laforge, duly sworn, says that premises were granted to claimant for the purpose of getting out timber for a mill, and to supply afterwards a mill for sawing logs; land being low, swampy, and unfit for cultivation.

January 8, 1811: Present, Lucas, Penrose, and Bates, commissioners. It is the opinion of the Board that this claim ought not to be granted.

JOSEPH MICHEL, assignee of Louis Tirard, claiming two hundred arpents of land, situate on lake Gayoso, dis-trict of New Madrid; produces to the Board a permission to settle, from François Lesieur, No. 1206; a plat of sur-vey, dated 8th January, 1806; a certified copy of transfer from said Tirard to claimant, dated 18th August, 1804.

Testimony taken, as aforesaid, at New Madrid, June 18, 1808. Francis Trenchard, duly sworn, says that premises were inhabited and cultivated in 1802, and constantly to this day; a wife and two children in 1803.

January 17, 1811: Present, Lucas, Penrose, and Bates, commissioners. It is the opinion of the Board that this claim ought not to be granted.

JOSEPH DUTAILLES, claiming seven hundred and forty-eight arpents sixty-eight perches of land, situate on river St. Francis, district of New Madrid, (on Big Island;) produces to the Board a notice to the recorder.

Testimony taken, as aforesaid, at New Madrid, June 19, 1808. Joseph Legrand, duly sworn, says that pre-mises were inhabited and cultivated in the beginning of 1803, and constantly to this time; seven or eight arpents now in cultivation; above twenty-one in 1803.

January 17, 1811: Present, Lucas, Penrose, and Bates, commissioners. It is the opinion of the Board that this claim ought not to be granted.

IGNACE BELAN, claiming eight hundred arpents of land, situate on fork of river St. Francis, district of New Madrid; produces to the Board a notice to the recorder.

Testimony taken, as aforesaid, at New Madrid, June 19th, 1808. Joseph Legrand, duly sworn, says that pre-mises were inhabited and cultivated in 1801, and constantly to this time between twenty and twenty-five acres; now in cultivation; a wife and child in 1803.

January 17, 1811: Present, Lucas, Penrose, and Bates, commissioners. It is the opinion of the Board that this claim ought not to be granted.

JOSEPH LAPOINTE, claiming seven hundred and forty-eight arpents sixty-eight perches of land, situate on Big Island, of river St. Francis, district of New Madrid; produces to the Board a notice to the recorder.

Testimony taken, as aforesaid, at New Madrid, June 19, 1808. Joseph Legrand, duly sworn, says that premises have been constantly inhabited and cultivated since the beginning of 1803 to this time; ten acres now in cultivation; above twenty-one years of age in 1803.

January 17, 1811: Present, Lucas, Penrose, and Bates, commissioners. It is the opinion of the Board that this claim ought not to be granted.

JOHN BAPTISTE MILLET, claiming seven hundred and forty-eight arpents sixty-eight perches of land, situate on Big Island of river St. Francis, district of New Madrid; produces to the Board a notice to the recorder.

Testimony taken, as aforesaid, at New Madrid, June 19th, 1808. Joseph Legrand, duly sworn, says that pre-mises have been constantly inhabited and cultivated from 1802; to this time about twenty-one years of age in 1803; five or six arpents in cultivation.

January 17, 1811: Present, Lucas, Penrose, and Bates, commissioners. It is the opinion of the Board that this claim ought not to be granted.

JOSEPH MILLET, claiming seven hundred and forty-eight arpents and sixty-eight perches of land, on Big Island of river St. Francis, district of New Madrid; produces to the Board a notice to the recorder.

Testimony taken, as aforesaid, at New Madrid, June 19th, 1808. Joseph Legrand, duly sworn, says that pre-mises were cultivated and inhabited early in 1803, and constantly to this time; four or five arpents now in cultiva-tion; above the age of twenty-one years in 1803.

January 17, 1811: Present, Lucas, Penrose, and Bates, commissioners. It is the opinion of the Board that this claim ought not to be granted.

JOSEPH BADEAU, claiming seven hundred and forty-eight arpents sixty-eight perches of land, situate on Big Island of river St. Francis, district of New Madrid; produces to the Board a notice to the recorder.

Testimony taken, as aforesaid, at New Madrid, June 19th, 1808. Joseph Legrand, duly sworn, says that pre-mises have been constantly inhabited and cultivated from 1802 to this day; six or seven arpents now in cultivation; above the age of twenty-one years in 1803.

January 17, 1811: Present, Lucas, Penrose, and Bates, commissioners. It is the opinion of the Board that this claim ought not to be granted.

PETER POWER, claiming eight hundred arpents of land, situate on Big Island of river St. Francis, district of New Madrid; produces to the Board a notice to the recorder.

Testimony taken, as aforesaid, at New Madrid, June 19th, 1808. Joseph Legrand, duly sworn, says that pre-mises have been constantly inhabited and cultivated from 1801 to the last year; widow now resides; twelve arpents now in cultivation; a wife and child in 1803.

January 17, 1811: Present, Lucas, Penrose, and Bates, commissioners. It is the opinion of the Board that this claim ought not to be granted.

STEPHEN L. HUILIER, claiming seven hundred and fifty arpents of land, situate on Big Island of river St. Francis, district of New Madrid; produces to the Board a notice to the recorder.

Testimony taken, as aforesaid, at New Madrid, June 19, 1808. Joseph Legrand, duly sworn, says that premises have been inhabited and cultivated, constantly from 1812 till this time; eight or nine arpents in cultivation; single man above the age of twenty-one in 1803.

January 17, 1811: Present, Lucas, Penrose, and Bates, commissioners. It is the opinion of the Board that this claim ought not to be granted.

ANDREW GODAIR, Jun., claiming nine hundred arpents of land, situate on Big Island of river St. Francis, district of New Madrid; produces to the Board a notice to the recorder.

Testimony taken, as aforesaid, at New Madrid, June 19, 1808. Joseph Legrand, duly sworn, says that premises were constantly inhabited and cultivated, from 1803 to this day; eight or nine arpents now in cultivation; a wife and child in 1803.

January 17, 1811. Present: Lucas, Penrose, and Bates, commissioners. It is the opinion of the Board that this claim ought not to be granted.

CHARLES GAIL, claiming seven hundred and fifty arpents of land, situate on Big Island of St. Francis, district of New Madrid; produces to the Board a notice to the recorder.

Testimony taken, as aforesaid, at New Madrid, June 19, 1808. Joseph Legrand, duly sworn, says that premises were inhabited and cultivated constantly to this day; twelve or fourteen acres now in cultivation; a wife and two children in 1803.

January 17, 1811: Present, Lucas, Penrose, and Bates, commissioners. It is the opinion of the Board that this claim ought not to be granted.

ANTHONY JANIS, claiming one thousand arpents of land, situate on Black water, fork of White river, district of New Madrid; produces to the Board a notice to the recorder.

Testimony taken, as aforesaid, at New Madrid, June 19, 1808. Joseph Legrand, duly sworn, says that premises have been inhabited and cultivated from 1801 to this time, constantly; a wife and six children in 1803; about thirty arpents now in cultivation.

January 17, 1811: Present, Lucas, Penrose, and Bates, commissioners. It is the opinion of the Board that this claim ought not to be granted.

NICHOLAS JANIS, claiming seven hundred and fifty arpents of land, situate on Black water, fork of White river, district of New Madrid; produces to the Board a notice to the recorder.

Testimony taken, as aforesaid, at New Madrid, June 19, 1808. Joseph Legrand, duly sworn, says that premises have been constantly inhabited and cultivated from beginning of 1803 to this day; five or six arpents now in cultivation; above the age of twenty-one years in 1803.

January 17, 1811: Present, Lucas, Penrose, and Bates, commissioners. It is the opinion of the Board that this claim ought not to be granted.

FRANCIS JANIS, claiming seven hundred and fifty arpents of land, situate on Black water, fork of White river, district of New Madrid; produces to the Board a notice to the recorder.

Testimony taken, as aforesaid, at New Madrid, June 19, 1808. Joseph Legrand, duly sworn, says that premises have been constantly inhabited and cultivated from the year 1802 to this day; five or six arpents now in cultivation; above the age of twenty-one years in 1803.

January 17, 1811: Present, Lucas, Penrose, and Bates, commissioners. It is the opinion of the Board that this claim ought not to be granted.

JOHN BAPTISTE JANIS, claiming seven hundred and fifty arpents of land, situate on Black water, fork of White river, district of New Madrid; produces to the Board a notice to the recorder.

Testimony taken, at New Madrid, as aforesaid, June 19, 1808. Joseph Legrand, duly sworn, says that premises were inhabited and cultivated in 1803, and constantly to the present time; eight or nine arpents now in cultivation; about the age of twenty-one years in 1803.

January 17, 1811: Present, Lucas, Penrose, and Bates, commissioners. It is the opinion of the Board that this claim ought not to be granted.

JOSEPH GUIGNOLET, claiming seven hundred and fifty arpents of land, situate on Black water, fork of White river, district of New Madrid; produces to the Board a notice to the recorder.

Testimony taken, as aforesaid, at New Madrid, June 19, 1808. Joseph Legrand, duly sworn, says that premises were inhabited and cultivated in 1802, and constantly to this day; fifteen or sixteen arpents now in cultivation; a wife and child in 1803.

January 17, 1811: Present, Lucas, Penrose, and Bates, commissioners. It is the opinion of the Board that this claim ought not to be granted.

LOUIS BABY, claiming three hundred arpents of land, situate on river Gayoso, district of New Madrid; produces to the Board a permission to settle No. 1209, from François Lesieur.

Testimony taken, as aforesaid, at New Madrid, June 18, 1808. Jacob Waggoner, duly sworn, says premises were improved in the fall of 1802; a cabin built in that year; in the following year 1803 inhabited and cultivated the premises and constantly to this time; about five acres in cultivation in 1803; above the age of twenty-one years in 1803.

January 25, 1811: Present, Lucas, Penrose, and Bates, commissioners. It is the opinion of the Board that this claim ought not to be granted.

ALEXANDER SAMSON, claiming three hundred arpents of land, in two surveys, the one of one hundred and twenty arpents, adjoining the village of Little Prairie, and the other of one hundred and eighty arpents on Gayoso, district of New Madrid, surveys dated 10th February, 1806; produces to the Board a permission to settle from François Lesieur for three hundred arpents, No. 1213.

Testimony taken, as aforesaid, at New Madrid, June 20, 1808. Francis Trenchard, duly sworn, says that premises were inhabited and cultivated in the year 1801, (the tract of one hundred and twenty,) and constantly till the year 1803; said tract cultivated by administration on the death of claimant till the present time; the tract of one hundred and eighty arpents was cultivated in 1803, (not inhabited,) and constantly to this time; claimant and wife died in 1803, leaving seven orphan children.

January 25, 1811: Present, Lucas, Penrose, and Bates, commissioners. It is the opinion of the Board that this claim ought not to be granted.

HARDY SOJOURNER, assignee of John Baptiste Barseloux, who was assignee of Anthony Trudell, claiming two hundred arpents of land, situate seven and a quarter miles northwest course from New Madrid; produces to the Board a transfer from said Trudell to said Barseloux, dated 18th September, 1801; a transfer from Barseloux to claimant, dated 27th March, 1804; a plat of survey of the same, dated 10th February, 1806; produces also an order of survey from Henry Peyroux, commandant, dated 4th October, 1800.

Testimony taken, as aforesaid, at New Madrid, June 20, 1808. Jacob Myers, duly sworn, says that premises were cultivated in the year 1802, and inhabited in 1803 and a part of the year 1804, and constantly cultivated until 1807; seven or eight acres in cultivation last year.

January 25, 1811: Present, Lucas, Penrose, and Bates, commissioners. It is the opinion of the Board that this claim ought not to be confirmed.

JOSEPH HUNOT, claiming eight hundred arpents of land, situate on Portage of river St. Francis, district of New Madrid; produces to the Board a permission to settle from François Lesieur, dated 20th June, 1802.

Testimony taken, as aforesaid, at New Madrid, June 20, 1808. Francis Trenchard, duly sworn, says that premises were inhabited and cultivated in the year 1802, and constantly to this time; seven or eight acres now in cultivation; a wife and three children and an orphan child in the year 1803.

January 31, 1811: Present, Lucas, Penrose, and Bates, commissioners. It is the opinion of the Board that this claim ought not to be granted.

CHRISTOPHER WINSOR, claiming seven hundred and fifty arpents of land, situate on the waters of river St. Francis, district of New Madrid; produces to the Board a notice to the recorder.

Testimony taken, as aforesaid, at New Madrid, June 20, 1808. William Cox, duly sworn, says that claimant put stock on this tract in 1803, and cultivated and inhabited that and the following year, since which he has planted fruit trees, and has continued to reside on the premises in the winter and spring of every following year; a housekeeper only.

January 31, 1811: Present, Lucas, Penrose, and Bates, commissioners. It is the opinion of the Board that this claim ought not to be granted.

PIERRE ANTOINE LAFORGE, assignee of John Baptiste Olive, assignee of Daniel Barton, assignee of Peter Higgins, claiming two hundred and forty arpents of land, situate on lake St. Mary, district of New Madrid; produces to the Board a petition and recommendation for a concession from Henry Peyroux, commandant, to Peter Higgins, dated 5th September, 1800; a certified abstract of the public sale of said premises, as the property of said Higgins, to Daniel Barton, dated 5th March, 1801; a certified abstract of the public sale of the said premises, as the property of Daniel Barton, to John Baptiste Olive, dated 4th September, 1804; and a certified copy of a transfer from said Olive to claimant, dated 29th September, 1804.

Testimony taken, as aforesaid, at New Madrid, June 20, 1808. Edward Robertson, duly sworn, says the premises were improved in the fall of 1799, cultivated and inhabited in 1800, and constantly till the last of the year 1806; twenty-four acres then in cultivation; a single man, about twenty-one years.

March 8, 1811: Present, Lucas, Penrose, and Bates, commissioners. It is the opinion of the Board that this claim ought not to be granted.

JOSEPH MICHEL, assignee of Simon Sublet and Samuel Masters, assignees of John Baptiste Barseloux, for two hundred arpents; and Joseph Michel, assignee of said Barseloux, for twenty arpents; claiming two hundred and twenty arpents of land, situate on lake St. Mary, district of New Madrid; produces to the Board a certified copy of a petition and recommendation for a concession from Henry Peyroux, commandant, dated September 27, 1800; a plat of survey, dated 7th November, 1796, signed Joseph Story; a conveyance from said Barseloux to claimant for about twenty arpents, dated 21st February, 1804; a conveyance from Simon Sublet and Samuel Masters to claimant, dated 18th February, 1806, for the remaining two hundred arpents; an assignment from Barseloux to claimant of a debt due from said Sublet and Masters, being the consideration money for said two hundred arpents, dated 21st February, 1804.

Testimony taken, as aforesaid, at New Madrid, June 20, 1808. Peter Dumay, duly sworn, says that premises were constantly inhabited and cultivated since the year 1798; thirty arpents now in cultivation; a wife and two children in 1803.

April 3, 1811: Present, Lucas, Penrose, and Bates, commissioners. It is the opinion of the Board that this claim ought not to be granted.

JOHN ROBERTS, Jun. claiming seven hundred and fifty arpents of land, situate on bayou St. John, district of New Madrid; produces to the Board a plat of survey, dated 10th February, 1806.

Testimony taken, as aforesaid, at New Madrid, June 21, 1808. William Coxe, duly sworn, says that premises were cultivated and inhabited in 1803, and constantly to this time; about seven acres now in cultivation; a wife in 1803.

April 3, 1811: Present, Lucas, Penrose, and Bates, commissioners. It is the opinion of the Board that this claim ought not to be granted.

RICHARD MASTERS, assignee of Benjamin Patterson, claiming four hundred arpents of land, situate on lake St. Mary, district of New Madrid; produces to the Board a petition and recommendation for a concession from Henry Peyroux, commandant, dated 3d September, 1800; a plat of survey, dated 3d July, 1797; a certified copy of transfer from Patterson to claimant, dated 18th January, 1802.

Testimony taken, as aforesaid, at New Madrid, June 21, 1808. Edward Patterson, duly sworn, says that premises were inhabited and cultivated in 1800, and constantly till last year; about sixteen or eighteen acres then in cultivation.

Luke Devore, sworn, says that Patterson had a wife and four children in 1803.

April 3, 1811: Present, Lucas, Penrose, and Bates, commissioners. It is the opinion of the Board that this claim ought not to be granted.

WILLIAM ZANES, assignee of William Masters, assignee of Peter O'Neal, *alias* Peter Neal, claiming seven hundred and fifty arpents of land, on lake St. Mary, district of New Madrid; produces, as a permission to settle, list No. 1369, (said list on file;) a plat of survey, dated 10th February, 1806; a certified copy of transfer of two

62   LAND GRANTS IN MISSOURI TERRITORY - 1805 - 1812

****

hundred arpents from Peter O'Neal to William Masters, dated 17th December, 1803; a certified copy of transfer from Masters to claimant, dated 5th September, 1804.

Testimony taken, as aforesaid, at New Madrid, June 21, 1808. William Coxe, duly sworn, says that premises were inhabited and cultivated in 1801, and constantly to the present time; about twelve or fourteen acres in cultivation; a single man, above the age of twenty-one years.

April 5, 1811: Present, Lucas, Penrose, and Bates, commissioners. It is the opinion of the Board that this claim ought not to be granted.

EDWARD ROBERTSON, claiming one thousand one hundred arpents of land, situate on waters of St. Francis, district of New Madrid; produces to the Board a notice to the recorder.

Testimony taken, as aforesaid, at New Madrid, June 21, 1808. Jacob Friend, duly sworn, says that premises were inhabited and cultivated in 1802, and constantly to the present time; thirty or forty acres are now cultivated; a wife, four children, and five slaves, in 1803.

April 5, 1811: Present, Lucas, Penrose, and Bates, commissioners. It is the opinion of the Board that this claim ought not to be granted.

THOMAS Y. HORSLEY, claiming one thousand arpents of land, on the Mississippi, below Little Prairie, district of New Madrid; produces to the Board a notice to the recorder.

Testimony taken, as aforesaid, at New Madrid, June 21, 1808. Luke Devore, duly sworn, says that premises were improved in 1801, and cultivated and inhabited in 1802, and constantly to the present time; about twelve acres now in cultivation; a wife and two children in 1803.

April 10, 1811: Present, Lucas, Penrose, and Bates, commissioners. It is the opinion of the Board that this claim ought not to be granted.

ELIAS WHEAT, claiming seven hundred and fifty arpents of land, situate on lake St. Mary, district of New Madrid; produces a notice to the recorder.

Testimony taken, as aforesaid, at New Madrid, June 21, 1808. William Coxe, duly sworn, says that premises were inhabited and cultivated in 1803, and constantly till the fall of 1807; about five or six acres in cultivation last year; a single man in 1803; about the age of twenty-one years.

April 10, 1811: Present, Lucas, Penrose and Bates, commissioners. It is the opinion of the Board that this claim ought not to be granted.

HENRY PEYROUX, assignee of Hugh McDonald Chisholm, claiming eighty-one arpents of land, situate on lake St. Mary, district of New Madrid; produces to the Board a petition, dated 2d July, 1797, with a recommendation from Charles Dehault Delassus, commandant, dated 4th July, 1797; a plat of survey, dated 25th April, 1797, survey stated to be made by order of Charles Dehault Delassus, commandant; a certified copy of transfer from Chisholm to claimant, dated 10th September, 1801.

Testimony taken, as aforesaid, at New Madrid, June 21, 1808. John Lamb, duly sworn, says that premises were improved and settled in 1797, and inhabited and cultivated to the present time, with the exception of a few occasional interruptions.

April 12, 1811: Present, Lucas, Penrose, and Bates, commissioners. It is the opinion of the Board that this claim ought not to be confirmed.

JACOB MYERS, claiming one thousand arpents of land, situate on the waters of lake St. Francis, district of New Madrid; produces to the Board a notice to the recorder.

Testimony taken, as aforesaid, at New Madrid, June 21, 1808. Thomas Y. Horsley, duly sworn, says that premises were inhabited and cultivated in the year 1801, and constantly to the present time; ten or fifteen arpents now in cultivation; a wife and three children in 1803.

April 12, 1811: Present, Lucas, Penrose, and Bates, commissioners. It is the opinion of the Board that this claim ought not to be granted.

JOHN BLOCK, claiming seven hundred and fifty arpents of land, situate near lake St. Ann, district of New Madrid; produces to the Board a plat of survey, dated 10th February, 1806.

Testimony taken, as aforesaid, at New Madrid, June 21, 1808. Thomas Y. Horsley, duly sworn, says that premises were inhabited and cultivated in 1802, and constantly to the last of 1807; about eight or nine acres last year in cultivation; a wife and child in 1803.

July 8, 1811: Present, Lucas, Penrose, and Bates, commissioners. It is the opinion of the Board that this claim ought not to be granted.

ELEAZER PATTERSON, claiming eight hundred and fifty arpents of land, situate on bayou of Big Lake, district of New Madrid; produces to the Board a notice to the recorder.

Testimony taken, at New Madrid, June 21, 1808. Jacob Waggoner, duly sworn, says that premises were improved in 1802, cultivated and inhabited in 1803, and constantly to the present time; three acres now in cultivation; a wife in 1803.

July 8, 1811: Present, Lucas, Penrose, and Bates, commissioners. It is the opinion of the Board that this claim ought not to be granted.

HEIRS AND REPRESENTATIVES OF RICHARD JONES WATERS, deceased, who was assignee of John Culbertson, assignee of Absalom Hichlin, claiming two hundred arpents of land, situate on river Pemiscon, district of New Madrid; produces to the Board a notice to the recorder.

Testimony taken, at New Madrid, June 21, 1808. Jacob Waggoner, duly sworn, says that premises were improved in 1801, and about an acre cleared in the following year, and constantly cultivated to the present day; not inhabited; three or four acres now in cultivation; a single man, over the age of twenty-one years, in 1803.

July 8, 1811: Present, Lucas, Penrose, and Bates, commissioners. It is the opinion of the Board that this claim ought not to be granted.

THOMAS W. CAULK, Junior, claiming seven hundred and fifty arpents of land, situate on lake St. Mary, district of New Madrid; produces to the Board a plat of survey, dated 10th February, 1806.

Testimony taken, at New Madrid, June 22, 1808. William Coxe, duly sworn, says premises were cultivated and inhabited in 1802, and constantly until the end of the last year; about seven acres last year in cultivation; a single man, above the age of twenty-one, in 1803.

July 8, 1811: Present, Lucas, Penrose, and Bates, commissioners. It is the opinion of the Board that this claim ought not to be granted.

TOUSSAINT GODAIR, Junior, claiming eight hundred arpents of land, situate on Big Portage, of river St. Francis; produces to the Board a notice to the recorder.

Testimony taken, at New Madrid, June 22, 1808. Joseph Serezo, duly sworn, says that premises were cultivated and inhabited in 1801, and constantly to the present time; about twenty arpents now in cultivation by claimant; a wife in 1803 and five children.

July 8, 1811: Present, Lucas, Penrose, and Bates, commissioners. It is the opinion of the Board that this claim ought not to be granted.

JOSEPH GRAVIER, claiming nine hundred arpents of land, situate on river St. Francis, district of New Madrid; produces to the Board a notice to the recorder.

Testimony taken, at New Madrid, June 22, 1808. Joseph Serezo, duly sworn, says that premises were inhabited and cultivated in 1801, and constantly to the present time; twenty arpents now in cultivation by claimant; a wife and one child in 1803.

July 8, 1811: Present, Lucas, Penrose, and Bates, commissioners. It is the opinion of the Board that this claim ought not to be granted.

PETER LAUSSON, claiming seven hundred and fifty arpents of land, situate on river St. Francis, district of New Madrid; produces to the Board a notice to the recorder.

Testimony taken, at New Madrid, June 22, 1808. Joseph Serezo, duly sworn, says that premises were inhabited and cultivated in 1802, and constantly to the present time; twenty-five arpents now in cultivation by claimant; a wife and five slaves in 1803.

July 8, 1811: Present, Lucas, Penrose, and Bates, commissioners. It is the opinion of the Board that this claim ought not to be granted.

IGNACE CHATTIGNY, claiming eight hundred arpents of land, situate on river St. Francis, district of New Madrid; produces to the Board a notice to the recorder.

Testimony taken, at New Madrid, June 22, 1808. Joseph Serezo, duly sworn, says that premises were inhabited and cultivated in 1801, and constantly to the present day; thirty arpents in cultivation by claimant; a wife and two children in 1803.

July 8, 1811: Present, Lucas, Penrose, and Bates, commissioners. It is the opinion of the Board that this claim ought not to be granted.

JOHN FRANCIS CHATTIGNY, claiming seven hundred and fifty arpents of land, situate on river St. Francis, district of New Madrid; produces to the Board a notice to the recorder.

Testimony taken, at New Madrid, June 22, 1808. Joseph Serezo, duly sworn, says that premises were inhabited and cultivated in 1801, and constantly to the present time; twenty arpents now in cultivation by claimant; a wife and child in 1803.

July 8, 1811: Present, Lucas, Penrose, and Bates, commissioners. It is the opinion of the Board that this claim ought not to be granted.

FRANCIS CANTELMY, claiming seven hundred and fifty arpents of land, situate on river St. Francis, district of New Madrid; produces to the Board a notice to the recorder.

Testimony taken, at New Madrid, June 22, 1808. Joseph Serezo, duly sworn, says that premises were inhabited and cultivated in 1801, and constantly to this time; twenty-five arpents now in cultivation; a wife and two children in 1803.

July 8, 1811: Present, Lucas, Penrose, and Bates, commissioners. It is the opinion of the Board that this claim ought not to be granted.

ALEXIS PICARD, claiming one thousand arpents of land, situate on river St. Francis, district of New Madrid; produces to the Board a notice to the recorder.

Testimony taken, at New Madrid, June 22, 1808. Joseph Serezo, duly sworn, says that premises were cultivated and inhabited in 1801, and constantly to the present time; thirty arpents now in cultivation; a wife and four children in 1803.

July 8, 1811: Present, Lucas, Penrose, and Bates, commissioners. It is the opinion of the Board that this claim ought not to be granted.

JOHN BAPTISTE GIRARD, claiming seven hundred and fifty arpents of land, situate on river St. Francis, district of New Madrid; produces to the Board a notice to the recorder.

Testimony taken, at New Madrid, June 22, 1808. Joseph Serezo, duly sworn, says that premises were cultivated and inhabited in 1801, and constantly to the present time; twenty-five arpents under fence; a wife and five children in 1803.

July 8, 1811: Present, Lucas, Penrose, and Bates, commissioners. It is the opinion of the Board that this claim ought not to be granted.

JOHN DOMINIQUE, claiming seven hundred and fifty arpents of land, situate on river St. Francis, district of New Madrid, produces to the Board a notice to the recorder.

Testimony taken, at New Madrid, June 22, 1808. Joseph Serezo, duly sworn, says that premises were inhabited and cultivated in 1802, and constantly to this time; twenty arpents now in cultivation; a single man, above the age of twenty-one years, in 1803.

July 8, 1811: Present, Lucas, Penrose, and Bates, commissioners. It is the opinion of the Board that this claim ought not to be granted.

PETER SAFFRAY, claiming six hundred and forty acres of land, situate on river St. Francis, district of New Madrid; produces to the Board a notice to the recorder.

Testimony taken, at New Madrid, June 22, 1808. Joseph Serezo, duly sworn, says that premises were inhabited and cultivated, from the year 1795 till 1804, by claimant, and afterwards, to the present time, by his heirs; a wife and two children in 1803; thirty arpents now in cultivation.

July 8, 1811: Present, Lucas, Penrose, and Bates, commissioners. It is the opinion of the Board that this claim ought not to be granted.

JOSEPH EATUE, claiming seven hundred and fifty arpents of land, situate on the portage of the bayou, district of New Madrid; produces to the Board a plat of survey, dated 10th February, 1806.

Testimony taken, at New Madrid, June 22, 1808. Toussaint Goder, duly sworn, says that premises were inhabited and cultivated, from 1802 till 1804, by claimant, and afterwards, to the present time, by his heirs; a single man, above the age of twenty-one years, in 1803.

July 8, 1811: Present, Lucas, Penrose, and Bates, commissioners. It is the opinion of the Board that this claim ought not to be granted.

PATRICK ESTES, claiming one thousand and fifty arpents of land, situate on the river St. Francis, district of ———; produces a plat of survey, certified 15th January, 1806.

Testimony taken. December 5, 1807. William Murphy, duly sworn, says that he applied to Commandant Deluziere, in 1801, for permission to settle for the persons who came with him to the country; that said commandant told him they might go and settle, and that claimant is one of the persons who came with him; that claimant built a cabin and moved there in 1802; cultivated a garden in 1803, but was not resident on the place in the month of December, that year; that claimant moved back to the same in the winter of 1805, raised a crop in 1806, and moved away again from the same in the winter of 1806, in consequence of his cabin being burnt.

May 29, 1810: Present, Lucas, Penrose, and Bates, commissioners. It is the opinion of the Board that this claim ought not to be granted.

BENJAMIN STROTHER, claiming six hundred arpents of land, situate on Cedar creek, district of St. Genevieve; produces a special permission to settle from Charles D. Delassus, Lieutenant Governor, dated 11th December, 1799; and a survey of the same taken 20th January, and certified 28th May, 1800.

Testimony taken. August 29, 1806. Present, Lucas and Penrose. William Bates, duly sworn, says that claimant began the building of a mill on said tract in the beginning of 1804; that the same was not completed until the beginning of 1805; and that claimant has actually inhabited and cultivated the same to this day, and was the head of a family.

May 29, 1810: Present, Lucas, Penrose, and Bates, commissioners. It is the opinion of the Board that this claim ought not to be confirmed.

JAMES MAXWELL, vicar general of the late province of Louisiana, claiming four leagues square, situate at the fork of Black river, in the district of St. Genevieve; produces a concession from Charles D. Delassus, dated November 3, 1799, and a survey of one hundred and twelve thousand eight hundred and ninety-six arpents, dated and certified the 9th day of February, 1806; he also produces an affidavit of Pierre Delassus Deluziere, stating that he was present, in the beginning of 1800, at a conversation which took place between the aforesaid claimant and Charles D. Delassus, then Lieutenant Governor, when the latter inquired of said claimant, where he intended to settle his large concession? Does not recollect the answer; that, a few days after, being at claimant's house, he saw, held, and read the aforesaid concession; a commission of vicar general of the province over the English and American settlers, signed Eng. de Llaguno, dated St. Lorenzo, 22d November, 1794; a letter from the bishop of Orleans, dated May 1, 1799, requesting his attention, as vicar general, to the whole of the clergy of the province, and informing him that he had recommended him to the King; a letter of instructions, founded upon a Spanish supreme consular state at Madrid, directed to claimant, through Lopez Armisto, secretary of the province, wherein the policy of Government towards emigrants is explained, instructing the Governor to grant them lands, and showing a desire that they might be converted to the Roman catholic religion.

Remark and decision of the Board. June 28, 1806; Present, Penrose and Donaldson, commissioners. The consideration on which this grant was founded being an obligation, on the part of claimant, to bring from Ireland Roman Catholic emigrants, and form a settlement of the same; the claimant alleged as a reason for not having complied with the said obligation, the then existing wars, and the subsequent prohibition of emigration from Ireland. The Board reject this claim, and are satisfied that it was granted at the time it bears date.

May 29, 1810: Present, Lucas, Penrose, and Bates, commissioners. On the motion of John B. C. Lucas, commissioner, as follows, to wit: Whereas it appears in the minutes of the former Board that the said Board have remarked that they are satisfied that the said concession was granted at the time the same bears date; and inasmuch as it does not appear that any suggestion of fraud and antedate was made either by the agent of the United States, or any of the members of the Board; which being the case, shows that no question did exist before said Board as to fraud or antedate, to which this decision, by way of remark, can apply; and whereas any decision without question is in itself preposterous, and might be considered as officious: therefore

Resolved, That this remark and decision be rescinded.

A question being taken on the motion it was negatived; and, on a question being taken on the claim, it is the unanimous opinion of the Board that this claim ought not to be confirmed.

JAMES MAXWELL, claiming three hundred arpents of land, situate on river Gaborie, district of St. Genevieve; produces a concession from Charles D. Delassus, dated September 19, 1799; and a survey of two hundred and ninety-nine arpents, certified, 26th February, 1806.

June 28, 1806. Present, Penrose and Donaldson, commissioners. The Board reject this claim, and observe that they believe the concession was granted at the time it bears date.

May 29, 1810: Present, Lucas, Penrose, and Bates, commissioners. It is the opinion of the Board that this claim ought not to be confirmed.

JAMES MAXWELL, claiming three thousand arpents of land, situate on the Mississippi, at the mouth of the river St. Laurent; produces a concession from Charles D. Delassus, Lieutenant Governor, dated September 10, 1799; a survey of the same, certified, 11th March, 1800; claimant produces also an original document of certain proceedings had before the Intendant General, the Assessor General, and an opinion of said Assessor General, and a confirmation of the same, by the Intendant Lopez Angulo, dated New Orleans, 8th July, 1800, reducing the claim of Peyroux to one league square; relating to a claim of land, set up by Henry Peyroux, and sundry inhabitants claiming land adjoining the said Peyroux, the said Maxwell declaring that he is one of said inhabitants, whose claim interferes with Peyroux, as appears by the testimony of Joseph Pratt.

Testimony taken. December 7, 1807. Camille Delassus, duly sworn, says that there was a house built by claimant on the tract, but does not remember in what time; believes that the house was large, and about forty or forty-five feet square, which has been burnt.

Joseph Pratt, duly sworn, says that he knows the land claimed; in 1801 he went with a public surveyor, by order of the commandant of St. Genevieve, for the purpose of ascertaining the distance from the mouth of the river St. Laurent to a place commonly called the Grand Glaize, which was the spot where the claim of Mr. Maxwell was intended to be located upon; that said land adjoined the claim of Peyroux.

June 28, 1806: Present, Penrose and Donaldson, commissioners. The Board reject this claim and observe that the said concession was granted at the time it bears date.

May 31, 1810: Present, Lucas, Penrose, and Bates, commissioners. The Board declare that from the testimony of Joseph Pratt, they are not satisfied that the survey has been made at the time it bears date; furthermore, John B. C. Lucas, commissioner, declares that he does not concur with the opinion of the former Board, to wit, that the said former Board is satisfied that the concession, or order of survey in the present case, was issued at the time it bears date, the said commissioner wishing at the same time to be understood that he does intend to say that it is antedated, leaving it to stand on such merits as it may possess.

Clement B. Penrose, commissioner, declares that, from the testimony above mentioned, he now has his doubts as to the date of the concession.

It is the opinion of the Board that this claim ought not to be confirmed.

JAMES MAXWELL, assignee of Bernard Pratte, claiming seven thousand and fifty-six arpents of land, situate on the river St. Francis, district of St. Genevieve; produces a concession from Charles D. Delassus, for the same, (not duly registered,) dated October 19, 1799; a survey of the same, certified 19th February, 1806, no condition inserted in said concession; also a deed of conveyance from said Pratte to claimant, dated May 8, 1806, and duly acknowledged the 9th of May, same year. The Board required further proof of the date of said concession, which were not adduced, May 5, 1806: Present, Penrose and Donaldson, commissioners.

May 31, 1810: Present, Lucas, Penrose, and Bates, commissioners. It is the opinion of the Board that this claim ought not to be confirmed.

JAMES MAXWELL, assignee of Bernard Pratte, who was assignee of Henry Diell, claiming five thousand arpents of land, situate on the river St. Francis, district of St. Genevieve; produces a concession from Charles D. Delassus, for the same, (not duly registered,) dated December 29, 1799; a survey of the same, certified February 19, 1806; a deed of transfer of the same, dated 14th November, 1805; also a deed of conveyance from said Pratte to claimant, dated May 8, 1806, and duly acknowledged, 9th May, same year; no condition expressed in said concession. May 5, 1806: Present, Penrose and Donaldson, commissioners. The Board require further proof of date of said concession, which were not adduced.

May 31, 1810: Present, Lucas, Penrose, and Bates, commissioners. It is the opinion of the Board that this claim ought not to be confirmed.

THOMAS RUSS, claiming one thousand one hundred and forty-six arpents forty-one perches of land, situate near the Mine à Breton, district of St. Genevieve; produces a survey of the same, certified 28th February, 1806; a certificate under the hand of John Fithial, commandant of Washitaw, that said Russ has been regularly admitted a subject of the King of Spain, dated May 3, 1786.

Testimony taken. December 7, 1807. Baptiste Valle, senior, duly sworn, says that he saw claimant inhabiting and cultivating land in the village of Mine à Breton, from the year 1792 until the year 1798, at which time the witness ceased to do business at that mine.

Testimony taken. June 28, 1806. Amable Parteny, duly sworn, says that claimant settled said tract of land in the year 1799, enclosed a park of about four acres, and has actually cultivated the same to this day; and further, that he knows that the commandant was at the mine in the year 1799, when he permitted claimant to settle on public lands, and that said claimant had, on the 20th day of December, 1803, a wife and five children.

June 2, 1810: Present, Lucas, Penrose, and Bates, commissioners. It is the opinion of the Board that this claim ought not to be granted.

RAPHAEL ST. JEMS, BATISTE BEQUET, VITAL ST. JEMS, AND BARTHOLOMEW ST. JEMS, claiming one thousand six hundred arpents of land, situate on the north fork of the river Saline; produces a concession from Zenon Trudeau, Lieutenant Governor, dated 1st February, 1798; a plat and certificate of survey for the same, by Thomas Maddon, dated 16th February, 1806.

Testimony taken. December 7, 1807. John Mary Legrand, duly sworn, says that he knows the tract claimed; that, in 1805, the same was inhabited and cultivated for the use of the claimant; that he knows that claimant laid a claim to that piece of land five or six years ago.

The paper purporting to be a plat and certificate of survey, signed by Thomas Maddon, is not authenticated by the proper surveyor.

June 1, 1810: Present, Lucas, Penrose, and Bates, commissioners. It is the opinion of the Board that this claim ought not to be confirmed.

WILLIAM GIROUARD, representatives of, claiming forty arpents of land, situate on the river Gaborie, called the fork, district of St. Genevieve; produces a concession from Zenon Trudeau, Lieutenant Governor, dated December 1, 1797; a plat and certificate of survey of the same, dated 18th January, 1798, signed A. Soulard, for thirty-two arpents of land; said tract is contiguous, and adjoining to the tract of eighty-six arpents thirty-five perches, claimed by claimant.

June 1, 1810: Present, Lucas, Penrose, and Bates, commissioners. It is the opinion of the Board that this claim ought not to be confirmed.

ADAM JOHNSTON, claiming two hundred and ninety arpents of land, situate on the river St. Francis, district of ———; produces a notice to the recorder, dated December 3, 1807.

Testimony taken. December 7, 1807. Camille Delassus, duly sworn, says that some time before 1803, claimant obtained permission from Peter Deluziere, commandant of New Bourbon, to settle on vacant lands.

William Johnston, duly sworn, says that in August, 1803, claimant went on said tract, and marked some trees, and cut down some bushes; that in 1804, claimant built a house, moved on the place since, and lives thereon at this present time; that claimant's family consisted, in 1803, of a wife and one child, and two slaves.

June 1, 1810: Present, Lucas, Penrose, and Bates, commissioners. It is the opinion of the Board that this claim ought not to be granted.

****

JOHN MATTHEWS, claiming one thousand and seventy arpents of land, situate on the north fork of the river St. Francis, district of St. Genevieve; produces a certificate of survey of one thousand and ten arpents and eighty perches of land, dated 13th February, 1806.

Testimony taken. February 15, 1806. John Callaway, duly sworn, says that claimant settled said land in the year 1802, and raised a crop on the same; that, in the month of September, 1803, after gathering the crop of that year, he went to Carolina for his family, leaving one James Campbell to take charge of his establishment, on which he had left a stock of cattle; that the said Campbell attended to the same during his absence; and that he returned with his family in January, 1804, and has to this day actually inhabited and cultivated the same; he had then a wife and three children.

Testimony taken. December 7, 1807. Camille Delassus, duly sworn, says that in 1802 claimant had permission from P. Deluziere, commandant of New Bourbon, to settle on vacant land.

February 15, 1806: Present, Lucas and Donaldson, commissioners. The Board reject this claim, and think it a case of equity.

June 4, 1810: Present, Lucas, Penrose, and Bates, commissioners. It is the opinion of the Board that this claim ought not to be granted.

HENRY DIELLE, claiming four hundred arpents of land, situate on the south side of the river Saline, district of St. Genevieve; produces a concession from Zenon Trudeau, Lieutenant Governor, dated February 15, 1798.

Testimony taken. December 7, 1807. Camille Delassus, duly sworn, says that in 1798 claimant showed him (witness) a concession, which is the same as the one above stated.

June 4, 1810: Present, Lucas, Penrose, and Bates, commissioners. It is the opinion of the Board that this claim ought not to be granted.

AARON ELLIOTT, assignee of James Maxwell, claiming seven arpents of land in *superficie*, situate near the village of St. Genevieve, district of St. Genevieve; produces a concession from Francis Vallé, commandant of St. Genevieve, dated 26th April, 1798; and a deed of conveyance from said Maxwell to claimant, dated 1st November, 1806.

Testimony taken. December 7, 1807. James Maxwell, duly sworn, says that in 1801 he began to get work done on said tract by digging for a well; believes that he went fifty or sixty feet deep, forty of which were a rock; that he grubbed and cleared part of the same, and had pickets hauled for fencing it.

Remark and opinion of the Board. June 4, 1810: Present, Lucas, Penrose, and Bates, commissioners. In the concession in this claim it is stated that Francis Vallé, commandant of St. Genevieve, was authorized, by an official letter from Zenon Trudeau, Lieutenant Governor, said to be dated the 10th February, 1795, to give the same; which official letter does not appear on record, nor is it produced.

It is the opinion of the Board that this claim ought not to be confirmed.

LOUIS GUIYARD, claiming sixteen hundred arpents of land, situate on the Mississippi, district of St. Louis, fifty-one miles north of the town of St. Louis; produces to the Board a concession for the same from Don Carlos Dehault Delassus, Lieutenant Governor, dated 9th November, 1799; a plat of survey of the same, dated 5th February, 1804, certified 8th March, same year.

June 4, 1810: Present, Lucas, Penrose, and Bates, commissioners. It is the opinion of the Board that this claim ought not to be confirmed.

CHARLES LARDOISE, claiming one thousand six hundred arpents of land, situate on waters of river Mississippi, district of St. Louis, seventy-two miles north of the town of St. Louis; produces to the Board a concession from Don Carlos Dehault Delassus, Lieutenant Governor, dated 9th November, 1799; a plat of survey, dated 19th February, 1804, certified 8th March, 1804.

June 4, 1810: Present, Lucas, Penrose, and Bates, commissioners. It is the opinion of the Board that this claim ought not to be confirmed.

ELIJAH BENTON, claiming six hundred and forty acres of land, situate on the west side of Big river, district of St. Genevieve; produces to the Board a plat of survey, dated 12th February, 1806, and certified by Antoine Soulard, 27th November, 1806.

Testimony taken. February 23, 1808. John Jones, duly sworn, says that claimant built a cabin on said tract of land in the fall of 1804, raised a crop in 1805, and has inhabited and cultivated the same to this day; further says that claimant had a wife and eleven children in the fall of 1804. (Claimant acknowledges that he never had any permission to settle.)

Testimony taken. November 25, 1808. Francis Wideman, duly sworn, says that in 1799 Francis Vallé, commandant of St. Genevieve, gave him, (witness,) with his family and connexions, as many as he could induce to come to the country, permission to settle, provided they would settle on the frontier, fifteen miles in front of the settlements; that he then wrote to his connexions to come to the country; that claimant came to the country in consequence of this letter, and that he is a brother-in-law to witness.

June 4, 1810: Present, Lucas, Penrose, and Bates, commissioners. It is the opinion of the Board that this claim ought not to be granted.

BAZIL GEARD, by his agent, Rufus Easton, claiming one league square of land, situate in the district of St. Charles, on the west bank of the Mississippi river, nearly opposite the village of Prairie du Chien; produces to the Board a notice of said claim, dated 23d June, 1807; a concession from Don Carlos Delassus, Lieutenant Governor of Upper Louisiana, dated 20th November, 1800, by which it appears that said Lieutenant Governor, Don Carlos D. Delassus, grants to him such quantity of land as he (claimant) demands in his petition, dated 15th October, 1800, to wit, such quantity as has heretofore been granted to faithful subjects according to law and usages, and also a plat representing said claim, dated 3d May, 1807.

Testimony taken. Nicholas Boloin, duly sworn, says that, seven years ago, he was on the place claimed; that there was then on the place a small cabin, and a piece of ground enclosed with a brush fence, about ten acres; that a hired man of claimant's was then residing on the place, and that there was corn and other things growing on the land at the same time; that he has known claimant as a trader living at Prairie du Chien twenty-six years.

Pierre Dorien, Sen., sworn, says that in 1796 claimant had a plantation on this side of the Mississippi, on a bayou, nearly opposite to Prairie du Chien, which was generally reputed to be the plantation of claimant; that claimant had on the place a house for his farmer, and also had stock on the place; saw a crop of corn growing at some time; in the following year, deponent was also on said place, which was then cultivated and inhabited by

****

said farmer; that claimant has lived at Prairie du Chien, as a trader, since 1799; that claimant has an Indian woman and children; does not know the number, but knows that he (claimant) raised them as his own.

Robert Dickson, sworn, says that said land was inhabited and cultivated by some of claimant's people ten years ago, and ever since, for his use, and that there was a house and barn on said land; that claimant had at least fifty acres in cultivation eight years ago, and ever since; that claimant has never been disturbed in his possession by the Indians around him; that he has heard several Indians say that the land belonged to claimant; that claimant resides a part of his time on the land claimed; says that the original petition to the Lieutenant Governor was written by him (deponent) at the time it bears date.

June 5, 1810: Present, Lucas, Penrose, and Bates, commissioners. It is the opinion of the Board that this claim ought not to be confirmed.

JACOB DONNER, assignee of John A. Sturgus and Jacob Horine, claiming sixteen hundred arpents of land, on Platen creek, district of St. Louis; produces a concession from Zenon Trudeau, to said John Sturgus for fifteen by twenty-five arpents, dated August 21, 1796; a survey of sixteen hundred arpents, dated 20th March, 1797, certified October 5, 1798; a transfer from said John Sturgus to the said Donner, and Jacob Horine, of said tract of land, dated October 15, 1802, and another transfer from said Horine to claimant, dated November 20 1800.

Testimony taken. June 21, 1806. St. James Bauvais, sworn, says that the said tract of land was settled about eight years ago, by the said John Sturgus, who had then two or three houses on it, and about forty or fifty acres under cultivation; that a mill had been built on said land, which said mill was afterwards carried away by the high freshes, and has since been rebuilt, and further, that the same was, prior to and on the 1st day of October, actually inhabited and cultivated, and has been so to this day.

June 21, 1806: Present, Penrose and Donaldson, commissioners. The Board reject this claim for want of a duly registered warrant of survey.

Remark and opinion of the Board. June 5, 1810: Present, Lucas, Penrose, and Bates, commissioners. The concession in this claim is for thirty by fifty arpents, and conditioned to build a mill. It is the opinion of a majority of the Board that this claim ought not to be confirmed. Clement B. Penrose voting for a confirmation of fifteen hundred arpents, the said majority declare that they would have voted for a confirmation had not this claim exceeded eight hundred arpents.

JAMES DUNN, assignee of Bohrer, claiming six hundred and forty arpents of land, situate in the district of St. Louis, on Big river; produces to the Board a notice of said claim to the recorder, a concession from Don Zenon Trudeau, Lieutenant Governor, to David Bohrer, for four hundred arpents of land, dated February 5, 1797; a plot of survey of six hundred and forty acres, made by J. T. Mitchel, deputy surveyor, for George Cunningham, dated 8th March, 1806.

Testimony taken. June 10, 1808. Sally Adams, sworn, says that when she came to this country in May, 1799, David Bohrer was then living in the country, has seen him frequently since, and believes him to be a resident.

Frederick Connor, sworn, says that in September, 1803, he, witness, cut logs for a cabin and partly built it, and deadened some trees on the land described in the plat of survey, then sold his work to David Bohrer, who said he bought it for the purpose of laying his concession on it.

Remark and opinion of the Board. June 5, 1810: Present, Lucas, Penrose, and Bates, commissioners. The concession in this claim is for four hundred arpents, and has several erasures in the material parts of the petition in different colored ink. It is the opinion of the Board that this claim ought not to be confirmed.

FRANCIS WIDEMAN, claiming four hundred arpents of land, on the Negro fork of the Merrimack, district of St. Louis; produces to the Board a notice to the recorder, and plat of survey, dated 9th April, 1808.

Testimony taken. June 20, 1808. Jonathan Heldebrand, sworn, says that in June or July, 1803, he was on the place claimed, and then saw claimant's wife living on the land, that the same was inhabited and cultivated that year and continued to be so for three years.

Mark Wideman, sworn, says that claimant raised a crop on the land claimed in 1801; inhabited and cultivated it the next year, and ever since; that claimant built a mill thereon in the year 1803.

November 25, 1808. On application of the claimant and cause shown, the Board open this claim for further testimony.

Joseph Gerrard, sworn, says that he was present about nine or ten years ago at St. Genevieve, when Francis Valle, commandant, gave claimant and his brothers, neighbors, and honest citizens, permission to settle.

June 5, 1810: Present, Lucas, Penrose, and Bates, commissioners. It is the opinion of the Board that this claim ought not to be granted.

WILLIAM EASTEP, claiming eight hundred and forty arpents of land, situate on the waters of the Merrimack, district of St. Louis; produces a survey of the same, dated 26th February, 1806.

Testimony taken. July 5, 1806. Francis Wideman, sworn, says that claimant settled the said tract of land in 1802, and raised a crop on the same; that he moved out of it towards the latter end of that year, and returned with his family in 1804, and further, that he had, on the 20th December, 1803, a wife and child.

June 5, 1810: Present, Lucas, Penrose, and Bates, commissioners. It is the opinion of the Board that this claim ought not to be granted.

ISAAC HERRINGTON, claiming six hundred and forty acres of land, on Connor's creek, district of St. Louis; produces to the Board a notice of said claim to the recorder, dated 15th June, 1808.

Testimony taken. June 20, 1808. Jonathan Heldebrand, sworn, says that claimant built a house on the place claimed in 1804, and marked the initials of his name on a tree and also the date; that claimant came to live with him (the witness) in the fall of 1802, and resided with him nearly two years; says that claimant had a wife and child in 1808.

Francis Wideman, sworn, says that he assisted in raising a cabin on the place claimed, for claimant in July or August, 1803, that he saw claimant in this country nine years ago, has seen him frequently since and believes him to be a resident from that time to this.

June 5, 1808: Present, Lucas, Penrose, and Bates, commissioners. It is the opinion of the Board that this claim ought not to be granted.

JAMES JAMES, claiming four hundred and seventy-four arpents of land, situate on Cold water, district of St. Louis; produces a survey of the same, certified 25th February, 1806.

Testimony taken. August 23, 1806. John S. Seely, sworn, says that claimant settled the said tract of land in 1804, built a house on the same, and has actually inhabited and cultivated it to this day.

June 5, 1810: Present, Lucas, Penrose, and Bates, commissioners. It is the opinion of the Board that this claim ought not to be granted.

BENJAMIN JAMES, claiming six hundred and ninety arpents of land, situate at Cold water, district of St. Louis; produces a certificate of permission to settle from James Mackay, dated 10th December, 1805, and a certificate of survey, dated February 12, 1806.

Testimony taken. February 21, 1806. Ebenezer Hodges, sworn, says that claimant put up a cabin on said land in the spring of 1803; that in 1804 he kept a school and actually inhabited the said tract of land; and further, that he did actually cultivate the same in the year 1805, and has inhabited and cultivated it to this day.

June 5, 1810: Present, Lucas, Penrose, and Bates, commissioners. It is the opinion of the Board that this claim ought not to be granted.

MORRIS JAMES, claiming four hundred arpents of land, situate on the river Missouri, district of St. Louis; produces to the Board a concession from Don Zenon Trudeau, Lieutenant Governor, dated 1st September, 1797, a plat and certificate of survey, dated 5th January, 1803.

Testimony taken. June 24, 1808. Guy Seelye, sworn, says that about July or August, 1803, claimant resided on his brother's place, adjoining his claim; cut hay on his own land, and cut and hauled logs in July or August, 1803; had a corn crib built; and some time during the winter following built a cabin and went to reside in it; made a garden in 1804, on the place; and has inhabited and cultivated the same ever since.

June 5, 1810: Present, Lucas, Penrose, and Bates, commissioners. It is the opinion of the Board that this claim ought not to be granted.

JOHN SULLENS, assignee of Robert Young, assignee of John Moreland, claiming three hundred arpents of land, situate on the river Aux Bœuf, district of St. Louis; produces a concession from Zenon Trudeau, dated 11th January, 1798; a survey of the same, certified the 10th December, 1805, together with a deed of transfer from said Moreland to said Robert Young, dated 29th May, 1799, and another deed from said Young to claimant, dated 2d February, 1805.

Testimony taken. August 19, 1806. Thomas Gibson, sworn, says that one Greenstreet settled said tract of land, built two very good cabins, and has raised a crop of corn this year.

James Greenstreet, sworn, says that he settled the said tract of land in 1805; cleared a small piece of land, sowed grass, and planted about four hundred peach stones; and that the same has been actually inhabited and cultivated to this day.

June 5, 1810: Present, Lucas, Penrose, and Bates, commissioners. It is the opinion of the Board that this claim ought not to be confirmed.

JOHN SULLENS, claiming five hundred arpents of land, situate on Fifi's creek, district of St. Louis.

Testimony taken. September 15, 1806. James Mackay, sworn, says that he did in 1801 permit the claimant to settle on vacant lands.

Samuel Adams, sworn, says that he knew claimant on said tract of land in 1802; that he did cut rails, house logs, and raised a crop on the same, and remained there for about eighteen months; that in 1803 the said tract of land was actually cultivated by claimant's brother, and for his (the claimant's) use; that his family being sick, and he poor and newly arrived in the country, he could not live on the same; that he moved on one tract the property of one Brown, and has never returned to said tract; had, on the 20th December, 1803, a wife and six children.

June 5, 1810: Present, Lucas, Penrose, and Bates, commissioners. It is the opinion of the Board that this claim ought not to be granted.

JOHN BUSHBY, assignee of Gabriel Marlow, claiming nine hundred arpents of land, on the north side of the river Missouri, on the waters of the river Tuque, district of St. Charles; produces to the Board a notice of said claim to the recorder without date; an assignment from said Marlow to claimant, dated 9th November, 1807.

Testimony taken. June 25, 1808. Joseph Chartran, ancient syndic of Choret village, sworn, says that while he was syndic of said village he gave permission to Gabriel Marlow to settle on said land; in pursuance of his permission said Marlow settled on said land in 1801, and inhabited the same that year; inhabited and cultivated the same in 1802, when he sold the same to claimant; said land has been inhabited and cultivated for the claimant's use ever since.

June 5, 1810: Present, Lucas, Penrose, and Bates, commissioners. It is the opinion of the Board that this claim ought not to be granted.

ELISHA BAKER, claiming one thousand four hundred and twenty-six arpents eighty-nine perches of land, situate on Bellevue settlement, district of St. Genevieve; produces to the Board a survey of the same, dated 15th February, and certified to be received for record by Antoine Soulard the 27th February, 1806; a written permission to settle on said land by Joseph Decelle, ancient syndic at the Mine à Breton, district aforesaid, dated 7th November, 1803.

Testimony taken. June 26, 1806. Walter Crow, sworn, says that he did, about October, 1803, go with claimant to examine a spot whereon claimant might form a settlement; that having found the above, he began the settlement of the same in the fall of that year; built a cabin on the same; that he hired that fall a man, who went on said land, cleared a spot, and planted fruit trees, such as peach, &c.; and further, that his two sons did actually inhabit it on the 20th December, 1803, for the use of the claimant; that in January, 1804, he moved the rest of his family on the same; raised a crop that year, and has actually inhabited and cultivated it to this day; had, on the 20th December, 1803, a wife and eleven children and a slave; was present when claimant obtained permission to settle on vacant lands.

June 6, 1810: Present, Lucas, Penrose, and Bates, commissioners. It is the opinion of the Board that this claim ought not to be granted.

WILLIAM BOYDSTON, claiming five hundred and eight arpents fifty-two perches of land, situate on Bellevue settlement, district of St. Genevieve; produces to the Board a survey of the same, dated the 15th February, and certified to be received for record by Antoine Soulard the 27th February, 1806; a written permission to settle on said land by Joseph Decelle, ancient syndic at the Mine à Breton, district aforesaid, dated 7th November, 1803.

Testimony taken. June 27, 1803. Elisha Baker, sworn, says that in November, 1803, claimant settled on the land claimed; built a cabin and planted corn in 1804; raised a crop, and has continued to inhabit and cultivate the same ever since; had a wife and four children in 1803.

****

June 6, 1810: Present, Lucas, Penrose, and Bates, commissioners. It is the opinion of a majority of the Board that this claim ought not to be granted; Frederick Bates, commissioner, voting for the granting of four hundred arpents of land.

ABRAHAM RICKMAN, claiming nine hundred and eighteen arpents thirty perches of land, situate on Bellevue settlement, district of St. Genevieve, produces to the Board a written permission to settle on said land by Joseph Decelle, ancient syndic at the Mine à Breton, district aforesaid, dated 7th November, 1803; a survey, dated 7th and certified 27th February, 1806.

Testimony taken. June 26, 1806. Thomas Baker, sworn, says that claimant settled said tract of land in the year 1803; built a house on the same, and did prior to and on the 20th December actually inhabit it; that in 1804 he raised a crop, and has actually inhabited and cultivated it to this day.

Elisha Baker, sworn, says that he was present when Decelle, the syndic of that settlement, granted claimant leave to settle on vacant lands; and that he had, on the 20th December, 1803, a wife, child, and a slave.

June 26, 1806: Present, Penrose and Donaldson, commissioners. The Board reject this claim for want of actual cultivation on the 20th December, 1803.

June 6, 1810: Present, Lucas, Penrose, and Bates, commissioners. It is the opinion of a majority of the Board that this claim ought not to be granted; Frederick Bates, commissioner, voting for the granting of two hundred and seventy arpents.

JOHN RICKMAN, claiming six hundred and ninety-three arpents seventy perches of land, situate on Bellevue settlement, district of St. Genevieve, produces to the Board a written permission on said land by Joseph Decelle, ancient syndic at the Mine à Breton, district aforesaid, dated 7th November, 1803; a survey of the same, dated 25th and certified 27th February, 1806.

Testimony taken. June 27, 1806. Elisha Baker, sworn, says that claimant had obtained from commandant a permission to settle, which he, the witness, saw, and further, that he, the said claimant, proceeded to the improving the said land in 1803; raised a crop in 1804; and has actually inhabited and cultivated the same to this day; that he had, 20th December, 1803, a wife.

June 6, 1810. Present, Lucas, Penrose, and Bates, commissioners. It is the opinion of the Board that this claim ought not to be granted.

THOMAS BAKER, claiming five hundred and sixty-two arpents sixty-three perches of land, situate on Bellevue settlement, district of St. Genevieve, produces to the Board a written permission to settle on said land, by Joseph Decelle, ancient syndic at the Mine à Breton, district aforesaid, dated 7th November, 1803; a survey of the same, dated 15th and certified 27th February, 1806.

Testimony taken. June 27, 1806. Benjamin Crow, sworn, says that claimant began the improving of said land in 1803, raised a crop in 1804, and, being then a single man of the age of twenty-one years or upwards, he lived with his father; that he, the witness, was present when claimant obtained permission from the commandant to settle vacant lands.

June 6, 1810: Present, Lucas, Penrose, and Bates, commissioners. It is the opinion of the Board that this claim ought not to be granted.

JOHN JANES, Jun., claiming six hundred and eighty-six arpents thirty perches of land, situate on Bellevue settlement, district of St. Genevieve; produces a survey of the same, dated the 18th and certified 28th February, 1806.

Testimony taken. June 26, 1806. Elisha Baker, sworn, says that claimant did, in 1804, clear about four acres of land on said tract, and raised a crop of turnips and timothy.

June 6, 1810: Present, Lucas, Penrose, and Bates, commissioners. It is the opinion of the Board that this claim ought not to be granted.

JOHN JANES, Sen., claiming six hundred and ten arpents eighty-two perches of land, situate on Big river, district of St. Genevieve; produces a survey of the same, dated 17th and certified 27th February, 1806.

Testimony taken. June 25, 1806. Elisha Baker, sworn, says that one Boydston improved said tract of land in November, 1803; that in the beginning of 1804 he gave the same up to claimant, who moved on it, and has actually inhabited and cultivated it to this day, and has now on the same a very good improvement. Claimant had, 20th December, 1803, a wife and nine children, has been in the country upwards of thirteen years, and claims no other land in his own name in the Territory.

June 6, 1810: Present, Lucas, Penrose, and Bates, commissioners. It is the opinion of the Board that this claim ought not to be granted.

WILLIAM JANES, claiming six hundred and twenty arpents twenty-seven perches of land, district of St. Genevieve, Bellevue settlement; produces to the Board a plat of survey dated 20th February, 1806, and certified to be received for record 27th February, 1806, by Antoine Soulard.

Testimony taken. June 27, 1808. Elisha Baker, sworn, says that in 1805 claimant had a cabin on the land, and has inhabited and cultivated the same ever since; raised a crop in 1805.

June 6, 1810: Present, Lucas, Penrose, and Bates, commissioners. It is the opinion of the Board that this claim ought not to be granted.

ELIJAH BAKER, claiming two hundred acres of land on Clear Water creek, district of St. Genevieve; produces to the Board a notice of said claim to the recorder, dated 27th June, 1808; also, a written permission to settle on said land, by Joseph Decelle, ancient syndic at the Mine à Breton, district aforesaid, dated 7th November, 1803.

Testimony taken. June 27, 1806. Elisha Baker, father of claimant, sworn, says that he knew of no person in the country, except himself, that can prove what was done on said land in 1803, the same being situated four miles from his house, in the pinery, and a retired situation; that claimant has occasionally cultivated said land since his improvement in the fall of 1803, when he cleared some ground, raised a crop on said land in 1804, and ever since, except the present year.

June 6, 1810: Present, Lucas, Penrose, and Bates, commissioners. It is the opinion of the Board that this claim ought not to be granted.

JOHN BALL, assignee of Levin Cropper, claiming four hundred arpents of land, situate at the Grand Glaize, district of St. Louis; produces a special permission to settle, from Zenon Trudeau, dated 10th February, 1798, and a survey of the same, dated 5th March, 1798, certified 2d April, 1799, together with a deed of transfer of the same, dated the 2d February, 1800.

****

Testimony taken. August 7, 1806. Joseph Conway, sworn, says that claimant settled the said tract in the spring of 1803, sowed about two acres of the same in corn, which was afterwards destroyed; that his stock lived on it a part of the year; that in 1804 he planted a nursery; claims no other land in his own name in the Territory.

Testimony taken. July 29, 1808. John Kinkead, sworn, says that claimant cleared a piece of ground on the land claimed in the spring of 1803; helped him to plough some land, about two acres; planted corn on the same; afterwards went to plough the corn, and found that the cattle had destroyed it; had rails made and hauled round the cleared ground, but did not put them up, in consequence of the corn being destroyed; claimant was a single man, and did not reside on the place, but lived in the neighborhood, about three or four miles off; in 1803 planted some apple trees, which deponent then saw growing; witness says that he came into this country six or seven years ago, and found claimant then living in the Territory.

June 6, 1810: Present, Lucas, Penrose, and Bates, commissioners. It is the opinion of the Board that this claim ought not to be confirmed.

ADAM MARTIN, claiming six hundred arpents of land, situate on Missouri, district of St. Charles; produces a concession from Zenon Trudeau, mostly destroyed, and dated 16th February, 1797; a further acknowledgment, by Charles D. Delassus, that a concession had been granted for the same, dated 10th September, 1802; together with a survey taken 20th October, 1803, certified 20th March, 1804.

Testimony taken. September 7, 1808. Kinkead Caldwell, sworn, says that he saw a man by the name of Price gathering corn on the tract claimed, in October, 1803; Price then told him that claimant had employed him to make the improvement, and since told him that claimant has paid him, said Price, two cows and calves for the same; says that the place claimed is a frontier situation, and the Indians were troublesome at that time.

Phœbe Wallace, sworn, says that claimant, on the 20th December, 1803, had a wife and nine children, eight of them living with him; that claimant has another claim for two hundred arpents of land, at Marie des Liards, which he bought of one Jacob Luntz.

June 6, 1808: Present, Lucas, Penrose, and Bates, commissioners. It is the opinion of the Board that this claim ought not to be confirmed.

LOUIS MARTIN, claiming three hundred arpents of land, situate on the south side of the Missouri, district of St. Louis; produces a special permission to settle, from Charles D. Delassus, dated the 8th February, 1801; and a survey of the same, dated 25th June, and certified 10th December, 1805.

Testimony taken. August 23, 1806. Thomas R. Musick, sworn, says that claimant has been in the country about seven or eight years, and that he began the settling of said tract in the year 1804.

Testimony taken. September 7, 1808. Kinkead Caldwell, sworn, says that he (the witness) came to this country eight years ago this fall; then found claimant residing here, has frequently seen him since, and believes that he has continued to be a resident ever since; that claimant began his settlement on said land in the fall of 1805, and has inhabited and cultivated the same ever since.

June 6, 1810: Present, Lucas, Penrose, and Bates, commissioners. It is the opinion of the Board that this claim ought not to be granted.

AUGUSTE CHOUTEAU, assignee of Toussaint Cerre, claiming an island in the Mississippi, commonly called the Parssa island, about eighteen miles from St. Louis, and six above the mouth of the Missouri; produces to the Board a concession from Don Carlos Dehault Delassus, Lieutenant Governor, for the same, to Toussaint Cerre, dated 15th January, 1800, a certified copy of a deed of conveyance from Toussaint Cerre to claimant, dated 28th December, 1803.

June 7, 1807: Present, Penrose and Bates, commissioners. It is the opinion of the Board that this claim ought not to be confirmed.

AUGUSTE CHOUTEAU, assignee of Pierre Janin, curate of St. Louis, claiming four thousand arpents of land, situate in the district of St. Louis, near the Mississippi; produces to the Board a concession from Don Carlos Dehault Delassus, Lieutenant Governor, to said Janin, for the same, dated 8th May, 1800; a plat and certificate of survey, dated 14th February, 1804, and certified the 5th March, same year; a certified copy of a deed of conveyance, from said Janin, dated 3d November, 1804.

June 7, 1810: Present, Penrose and Bates, commissioners. It is the opinion of the Board this claim ought not to be confirmed.

AUGUSTE CHOUTEAU, claiming one thousand two hundred and eighty-one arpents of land, situate on Beaver pond, district of St. Louis; produces a concession from Charles D. Delassus, dated 5th January, 1800, and a survey of the same, dated March 5, and certified April 10, 1801; the aforesaid concession granted for the purpose of procuring fuel for a distillery established by claimant, and which could not be kept in operation without fuel; he further produces a permission from Charles D. Delassus, to build the said distillery, the same being then considered by Government as an establishment of public utility and benefit; said permission dated January 3, 1800.

Testimony taken. July 26, 1806. Gabriel Dodie, sworn, says that claimant having purchased the said tract of land, built a house on the same in the year 1800.

Myers Michael, sworn, says that claimant had a distillery built prior to October, 1800.

A. Soulard, sworn, says that to his knowledge claimant did procure from the aforesaid tract of land the fuel necessary for the said distillery.

Testimony taken. September 14, 1808. David Delauney, sworn, says that he wrote the petition for permission to build a distillery, dated 5th November, 1799; that the same was written at the time the permission bears date, to wit, January 3, 1800.

June 8, 1810. Present, Lucas, Penrose, and Bates, commissioners. It is the opinion of the Board that this claim ought not to be confirmed.

EDWARD HEMPSTEAD, assignee of Mackay Wherry, sheriff of the district of St. Charles, who sold the same as the property of John B. Gates; produces to the Board a notice of said claim to the recorder, without date, but which is endorsed as having been received for record, June 30, 1808; said claim being for a lot in the town of St. Charles; produces, also, a deed of conveyance for the same from said sheriff, to claimant, dated 29th June, 1808.

Testimony taken. September 15, 1808. St. Paul Lacroix, sworn, says that he has been fourteen years in the country, that when he first came, he found said lot inhabited and cultivated, and has since been inhabited and cultivated to this day; in 1803, the same was inhabited and cultivated by Toussaint Soulair; was then the head of a family; that the boundaries of said lot, as stated in the deed of conveyance from said sheriff to claimant, are correct.

LAND GRANTS IN MISSOURI TERRITORY - 1805 - 1812

71

****

June 8, 1810: Present, Lucas, Penrose, and Bates, commissioners. It is the opinion of the Board that this claim ought not to be granted.

AUGUSTE CHOUTEAU, assignee of Joseph Marie and wife, claiming a lot of ground in the village of St. Charles, one hundred and twenty feet front, by one hundred and fifty in depth, French measure; produces to the Board a deed of conveyance for the same from said Marie and wife to claimant, dated 18th September, 1805.

Testimony taken. September 15, 1808. St. Paul Lacroix, sworn, says that he has been fourteen years in the country; that when he first came, he found said lot inhabited and cultivated, and has since been inhabited and cultivated to this day; that in 1803, said lot was inhabited and cultivated by Joseph Marie, and that the boundaries of said lot, as stated in the deed of conveyance from said Marie and wife to claimant, is correct.

June 8, 1810: Present, Lucas, Penrose, and Bates, commissioners. It is the opinion of the Board that this claim ought not to be granted.

ABRAHAM ARMSTRONG, claiming six hundred and forty acres of land, in the district of St. Genevieve; produces to the Board a notice to the recorder, together with a plat and certificate of survey, dated February 15, 1806.

Testimony taken. September 16, 1808. Benjamin Walker, sworn, says that in November, 1803, he (witness) planted about twelve hundred peach stones on the tract claimed; that in 1804, he inhabited and cultivated the same about seven months, then sold his right to claimant, who has inhabited and cultivated the same until last year, since when witness has not seen the place; witness says that, in 1803, he had a wife and two children; had no permission to settle, but went to live on Congress land.

June 8, 1810: Present, Lucas, Penrose, and Bates, commissioners. It is the opinion of the Board that this claim ought not to be granted.

GEORGE HORN, claiming three hundred arpents of land, situate on the Mississippi and Merrimack rivers, district of St. Louis; produces to the Board a notice of said claim to the recorder, dated 30th June, 1808.

Testimony taken. September 20, 1808. Philip Fine, sworn, says that Captain Stoddart, American commandant, gave claimant permission to settle in 1804, and that claimant did inhabit and cultivate the same in 1804, and until this day.

June 9, 1810: Present, Lucas, Penrose, and Bates, commissioners. It is the opinion of the Board that this claim ought not to be granted.

EDWARD BUTLER and PHILIP ROBERTS, representatives of Anne Skinner, claiming six hundred and forty arpents of land, on the waters of Grand Glaize, district of St. Louis; produces to the Board a notice of said claim to the recorder, dated June 20, 1808.

Testimony taken. September 20, 1808. James Stewart, sworn, says that, in the year 1802, he saw Anne Skinner, Edward Butler, and Philip Roberts, living together on the land claimed, and raised a crop that year; the year following Anne Skinner and Edward Butler raised a crop on the same; says that Anne Skinner was the reputed mother of Edward Butler and Philip Roberts, and that Philip Roberts had a wife and three children in 1803.

June 9, 1810: Present, Lucas, Penrose, and Bates, commissioners. It is the opinion of the Board that this claim ought not to be granted.

JOHN CHANDLER, claiming six hundred arpents of land, situate on the Missouri river, district of St. Louis; produces to the Board a concession from Charles Dehault Delassus, Lieutenant Governor, for a tract of land of six hundred arpents to be taken where the same might be found vacant, dated 17th June, 1803, and reciting a concession from Zenon Trudeau, Lieutenant Governor, dated 11th December, 1797, which is also produced; also a plat and certificate of survey dated the 20th February, 1804, and certified 26th February, same year.

Testimony taken. September 20, 1808. Richard Caulk, sworn, says that he (witness) came to the country in the month of January, 1798; that claimant accompanied him part of the way, and arrived in the country shortly after him, (witness.)

June 9, 1810: Present, Lucas, Penrose, and Bates, commissioners. It is the opinion of the Board that this claim ought not to be confirmed.

LAURENCE LONG, the heirs of, claiming six hundred arpents of land, situate in Creve Cœur settlement, district of St. Louis; produces to the Board an order of survey for the same from Zenon Trudeau, Lieutenant Governor, to Laurence Long, dated the 15th June, 1797; a plat and certificate of survey, dated 5th May, 1798, and certified 17th July, same year.

Testimony taken. September 21, 1810. John Ward, sworn, says a cabin was built on said tract in 1797, and inhabited about six weeks by Oliver Caldwell; that families inhabited the cabin for two different winters by permission from Laurence Long, to wit, the winters of 1798 and 1800 or 1801.

June 12, 1810: Present, Lucas, Penrose, and Bates, commissioners. It is the opinion of the Board that this claim ought not to be confirmed.

Concession without date; the date above is the date of the petition.

LAURENCE LONG, the heirs of, claiming four hundred arpents of land, situate adjoining John Ward's claim, Creve Cœur settlement, district of St. Louis; produces to the Board a concession from Zenon Trudeau, Lieutenant Governor, to Laurence Long, for the said land, formerly granted to Robert Baldridge, and surveyed for him, dated 15th March, 1798; a plat and certificate of survey of the same, in the name of Robert Baldridge, dated 20th February, 1798, and certified 30th March, 1798.

Testimony taken, September 21, 1808. John Ward, sworn, says that Laurence Long made sugar on the land in 1799, and one year since.

June 12, 1810: Present, Lucas, Penrose, and Bates, commissioners. It is the opinion of the Board that this claim ought not to be confirmed.

RICHARD CAULK, claiming four thousand arpents of land, situate on the river Calumet, district of St. Charles; produces a concession from Charles D. Delassus, dated 5th December, 1799; and a survey of the same taken 17th December, 1804, and certified 30th October, 1805.

Testimony taken. July 22, 1806. James Mackay, sworn, says that the aforesaid Thomas Caulk was, for some years, syndic of the Bon Homme settlement, in which capacity he received no compensation; and that he, the witness, verily believes that the aforesaid concession was granted him as a compensation for the same.

July 23, 1806: Full Board. The Board require further proof.

June 12, 1810: Present: Lucas, Penrose, and Bates, commissioners.

Remarks and opinion of the Board. The Board believe that there is a mistake made in the taking of the testimony of James Mackay in this claim; that the name of Thomas Caulk, in said testimony, was intended for Richard Caulk. It is the opinion of the Board that this claim ought not to be confirmed.

JOHN WATKINS, claiming seven thousand and fifty-six arpents of land, situate on the river Merrimack, district of St. Louis; produces to the Board a duly registered concession from Zenon Trudeau, dated 24th July, 1797; and a survey of the same, taken the 18th, and certified the 27th February, 1806.

Testimony taken. September 17, 1806. Antoine Soulard, sworn, says that when claimant left this place for New Orleans, he, the witness, received from him, among other papers left to his charge, the aforesaid concession; that he does not know whether it was granted at the time it bears date, but that he has seen, among the official papers of Zenon Trudeau, an order from the Baron de Carondelet to said Zenon Trudeau, to grant said claimant a league square.

September 17, 1806: Present, Lucas and Donaldson, commissioners. The Board reject this claim, and are satisfied that the same was granted at the time it bears date.

June 12, 1810: Present, Lucas, Penrose, and Bates, commissioners. It is the opinion of the Board that this claim ought not to be confirmed. Clement B. Penrose and Frederick Bates, commissioners, declare that the opinion of the former Board, as to the date of the concession in this claim, must be an error, as the said concession bears no date. John B. C. Lucas declares that he does not concur with the opinion of the former Board, so far as it appears by their minutes that they are satisfied that the concession was granted at the time it bears date.

JACQUES ST. VRAIN and ANTOINE SOULARD, claiming about three thousand two hundred and fifty arpents of land, situate at the Point of Missouri and Mississippi, district of St. Louis; produces to the Board a concession from Zenon Trudeau, dated 20th February, 1799, and a survey of three thousand six hundred and seventy-five arpents, dated 5th November, 1801, and certified 29th December, 1802; granted for a *vacherie*, and for cutting wood.

Testimony taken. August 23, 1806. Louis Labeaume, sworn, says that, in the month of January, 1799, Antoine Soulard, one of the above claimants, submitted to him a draught of a petition for the aforesaid concession, in order to have the same corrected, in case of any faults of language; that, in the same year, Jacques St. Vrain, one of the said claimants, kept a large stock of cattle, amounting to sixty or eighty heads, on said land, and that he saw a quantity of logs cut.

Manuel Lisa, sworn, says that, in the month of October, 1799, he went on said land, having first obtained leave from claimants to cut rails; that he remained there about two months, during which time he constantly saw St. Vrain's cattle on the same, and got milk from one of his cows.

Jacques Clamorgan, sworn, says that Anthony Soulard, having applied to him concerning a suitable situation for a *vacherie*, he, the witness, pointed out to him the aforesaid spot.

Auguste Chouteau, sworn, says that Anthony Soulard, having inherited from the estate of his mother-in-law a large stock of cattle, valued, as per inventory of said estate, at eight hundred and eighty-four dollars and fifty cents, he sent the same to the said tract of land.

August 23, 1806: Present, Penrose and Donaldson, commissioners. The Board are satisfied that the conditions of the grant have been complied with, and that the same was granted at the time it bears date.

June 13, 1810: Present, Lucas, Penrose, and Bates, commissioners. It is the opinion of the Board that this claim ought not to be confirmed. John B. C. Lucas, commissioner, declares that he does not concur in opinion with the former Board, in the present case, respecting the compliance with the condition specified in the concession, nor respecting the satisfaction which the said former Board expresses, that the concession was issued at the time it bears date. The said commissioner declares, at the same time, that he does not intend any thing contrary to the opinion of the said former Board, as before adverted to, but forbears giving any opinion on the said points, and leaves the whole to rest on such written and parole evidence as has been adduced in support thereof.

ANTOINE SOULARD, for the representatives of Gabriel Zenon Soulard, deceased, and in the name of and for James Gaston Soulard, claiming one thousand six hundred arpents of land, situate sixty-two miles north of St. Louis; produces to the Board a concession from Don Carlos Dehault Delassus, Lieutenant Governor, to said Gabriel Zenon Soulard and James Gaston Soulard, dated 20th October, 1799; a plat and certificate of survey of the same, dated 13th February, 1804, and certified 8th March of the same year.

Testimony taken. September 22, 1808. Jacques St. Vrain, sworn, says that, in six or eight months after the time his brother, Don Carlos Dehault Delassus, took command here, he knows of a concession having been given by him to the two sons of Antoine Soulard.

June 14, 1810: Present, Lucas, Penrose, and Bates, commissioners. It is the opinion of the Board that this claim ought not to be confirmed. The concession was granted for services rendered by Antoine Soulard, and for the purpose of educating his two sons for His Catholic Majesty's service.

ANTOINE SOULARD, claiming two hundred and fifty arpents of land, situate on the Missouri, district of St. Charles; produces a concession from Zenon Trudeau, granting said land for sugar-making, dated 6th January, 1799; a survey of the same, taken 7th February, and certified 23d August, 1803.

Testimony taken. September 17, 1806. Gregorie Sarpee, sworn, says that in 1799 a sugar camp was established on said land, and sugar made.

September 17, 1806: Present, Lucas and Donaldson, commissioners. The Board reject this claim, and are satisfied that the said concession was granted at the time it bears date.

June 14, 1810: Present, Lucas, Penrose, and Bates, commissioners. It is the opinion of the Board that this claim ought not to be confirmed. John B. C. Lucas, commissioner, declares, that he does not concur in opinion with the former Board in the present case, respecting the date of the concession; forbearing, at the same time, to give an opinion contrary to the same, and leaves it to rest upon such merit as it may offer in point of authenticity or date.

JESSE RICHARDSON, assignee of James Mackay, assignee of David Cole, claiming four hundred and thirty arpents of land, situate in the district of St. Charles; produces to the Board a concession from Zenon Trudeau, Lieutenant Governor, to David Cole, for the same, dated 23d January, 1798; a plat and certificate of survey, dated 15th February, 1805, and certified 10th December, 1805; a certified copy of a deed of transfer from David Cole to James Mackay, dated 14th July, 1799; a deed of transfer from James Mackay to claimant, dated 10th September, 1803.

June 14, 1810: Present, Lucas, Penrose, and Bates, commissioners. It is the opinion of the Board that this claim ought not to be confirmed.

EDWARD HEMPSTEAD, assignee of Antoine Marechal and Mary Catharine Tibeau, his wife, for himself and the heirs of François Moreau, deceased, claiming three hundred arpents of land, situate near the village of St. Ferdinand, district of St. Louis; produces to the Board an order of survey for the same, from Don Zenon Trudeau, Lieutenant Governor, to Antoine Marechal and François Moreau, dated 20th November, 1796; also, a deed of conveyance from Antoine Marechal and Mary Catherine Tibeau, his wife, to Edward Hempstead, one of the claimants, for their part of said claim, dated 7th February, 1805.

Testimony taken. September 29, 1808. Antoine Soulard, sworn, says that he knew Antoine Marechal and François Moreau; that they resided in the village of St. Ferdinand from the year 1796 to 1803; and were heads of families, and were farmers.

June 14, 1810: Present, Lucas, Penrose, and Bates, commissioners. It is the opinion of the Board that this claim ought not to be confirmed.

JACOB HORINE, claiming eight hundred arpents of land, situate in Rich Woods settlement, district of St. Genevieve; produces to the Board a concession from Charles Dehault Delassus, dated January 5, 1800; a survey of the same, dated November 1, 1803, and certified 15th January, 1804.

Testimony taken. July 5, 1806. Francis Wideman, sworn, says that claimant settled the said tract of land in 1804, and raised a crop on the same; and further, that he had a wife on the 20th day of December, 1803.

June 15, 1810: Present, Lucas, Penrose, and Bates, commissioners. It is the opinion of the Board that this claim ought not to be confirmed. The former Board required further proof. July 6, 1806.

MICHAEL HORINE, claiming one thousand two hundred and ninety-one arpents and fifteen perches of land, situate in Rich Woods settlement, district of St. Genevieve; produces to the Board a survey of the same, dated 11th and certified 27th February, 1806.

Testimony taken. July 5, 1806. Michael Butdrer, sworn, says that he was present when claimant obtained from the commandant permission to settle on vacant land.

Francis Wideman, sworn, says that claimant settled the said tract of land in the year 1804, and has actually inhabited and cultivated the same to this day, and had a wife and six children.

June 15, 1810: Present, Lucas, Penrose, and Bates, commissioners. It is the opinion of the Board that this claim ought not to be granted.

PETER DERBEGNY, claiming six thousand arpents of land, situate in the district of St. Charles; produces to the Board a notice of said claim to the recorder, dated 6th May, 1808; a concession from Charles Dehault Delassus, Lieutenant Governor, for the same to claimant, dated 20th September, 1799; a plat and certificate of survey of the same, dated January 15, 1801, and certified 5th March, same year.

Testimony taken. October 4, 1808. Antoine Soulard, sworn, says that claimant came to Louisiana with him (witness) in February, 1794, and was then the head of a family; and has resided in Louisiana ever since, except during the time of a mission to the city of Washington, as agent for the people of Orleans Territory.

June 15, 1810: Present, Lucas, Penrose, and Bates, commissioners. It is the opinion of the Board that this claim ought not to be confirmed.

SALMON RUGGLES, claiming four hundred and sixty-one and three quarter acres of land, situate on Bellevue settlement, district of St. Genevieve; produces to the Board two plats and certificates of survey, the one for four hundred and sixty-one and three-quarter acres, on the waters of Big river; the other for three hundred and five acres, situate on Flat creek, dated February 6, 1806; and both certified to be received for record 25th February, 1806.

Testimony taken. October 6, 1808. Gideon W. Treat, sworn, says that claimant settled on the tract of four hundred and sixty-one and three-quarter acres in the fall of 1802, and raised a crop in 1803, and has inhabited and cultivated the same ever since; in 1803 had a wife.

Moses Austin, sworn, says that in the fall of 1802 he (witness) applied to Don François Valle, commandant of St. Genevieve district, for permission for claimant to settle on vacant lands, which was then granted by said commandant.

June 15, 1810: Present, Lucas, Penrose, and Bates, commissioners. It is the opinion of a majority of the Board that this claim ought not to be granted; Frederick Bates, commissioner, voting for the granting of two hundred arpents.

SALMON RUGGLES, claiming three hundred and five acres of land, situate on Flat creek, district of St. ———; produces to the Board a plat and certificate of survey, dated February 6, 1806, and certified to be received for record, 25th February, 1806.

Testimony taken. October 6, 1808. Moses Austen, sworn, says that, in the fall of 1802, he (witness) applied to Don François Valle, commandant of St. Genevieve district, for permission for claimant to settle on vacant lands, which was then granted by said commandant.

June 15, 1810: Present, Lucas, Penrose, and Bates, commissioners. It is the opinion of the Board that this claim ought not to be granted.

DAVID STRICKLAND, claiming one thousand two hundred and forty-seven arpents of land, situate on Mine à Breton, district of St. Genevieve; produces to the Board a survey of the same, dated 25th, and certified 28th February, 1806.

Testimony taken. August 29, 1806. William Bates, sworn, says that said claimant settled the said tract of land in 1804, raised a crop on the same that year, and has actually inhabited and cultivated it to this day.

Testimony taken. October 7, 1808. Joseph Decelle, ancient syndic of the Mine à Breton settlement, sworn, says that claimant applied to him (witness) for permission to settle on vacant lands in 1803; witness told him he could not give a permission, as he (claimant) had a concession for land in Bois Bruile; that claimant then asked permission for his son John to settle on the land claimed, which he then gave him. On a written permission being produced to witness, appearing to be a permission to David Strickland to settle, dated 5th December, 1803, witness says it is the same paper; but that since that time it has been cut, and a part taken off, wherein he had revoked the permission given by him to David Strickland, and given one to his son, John Strickland, in consequence of David Strickland having a concession.

June 5, 1810: Present, Lucas, Penrose, and Bates, commissioners. It is the opinion of the Board that this claim ought not to be granted.

MARIE PHILIP LADUC, assignee of Albert Tison, claiming eight hundred arpents of land, situate on the ————, district of St. Charles; produces to the Board a concession from Charles D. Delassus, dated August 5, 1799; a certificate of survey of the same, dated 5th March, 1804; and a deed of transfer from said Albert Tison to claimant, dated 22d November, 1805.

Testimony taken. May 6, 1806. James St. Vreen, sworn, says that he knows positively that the above concession was granted at the time it bears date; that he saw the same in the possession of Albert Tison prior to October, 1800.

May 6, 1806: Present, Penrose and Donaldson, commissioners. The Board are satisfied that the above concession is not antedated; they, however, reject the same for want of actual habitation and cultivation prior to and on the 1st of October, 1800. Concession not duly registered.

June 16, 1810: Present, Lucas, Penrose, and Bates, commissioners. It is the opinion of the Board that this claim ought not to be confirmed. John B. C. Lucas, commissioner, declares that he does not concur in opinion with the former Board, in the present case, respecting the date of the concession, forbearing at the same time to give an opinion contrary to the same, and leaves it to rest upon such merit as it may offer in point of authenticity or date.

MARIE PHILIP LADUC, assignee of Joseph Laduc, claiming eight hundred arpents of land, situate on the Missouri, district of St. Charles; produces to the Board a concession from Don Carlos Dehault Delassus, Lieutenant Governor, for the same, to Joseph Laduc, dated 18th January, 1800; a plat and certificate of survey, dated 24th February, 1804, and certified 5th March, 1804; and also an assignment of the same from Joseph Laduc to claimant, dated 18th February, 1806.

June 16, 1810: Present, Lucas, Penrose, and Bates, commissioners. It is the opinion of the Board that this claim ought not to be confirmed.

PASCAL DETCHEMENDY, claiming one thousand two hundred and fifty-one arpents of land, situate on the river Au Vase, district of St. Genevieve; produces a concession from Zenon Trudeau, dated February 20, 1798; a survey of the same, dated 25th and certified 28th February, 1798.

Testimony taken. June 21, 1806. John Geubourd, sworn, says that he saw the land in the year 1799, when claimant had about twenty arpents of the same under cultivation; a house built and outhouses; and that it was, prior to and on the 1st of October, 1800, actually inhabited and cultivated, and has been so to this day; claimant had then a wife and two children.

June 16, 1810: Present, Lucas, Penrose, and Bates, commissioners. It is the opinion of a majority of the Board that this claim ought not to be confirmed; Clement B. Penrose, commissioner, voting for the confirmation of one thousand two hundred and fifty-one arpents of land, the said majority declare that if this claim had not exceeded eight hundred arpents they would have voted for a confirmation.

JEAN PIERRE CABANNE, claiming two thousand arpents of land, to be taken on any vacant land; produces to the Board a notice of said claim to the recorder, dated 31st May, 1808, in which he states his concession to have been lost; produces to the Board a registry of the same in book No. 2, marked B, page 44, lodged in the Recorder's Office.

Testimony taken. October 7, 1808. Claimant, sworn, says that he has not the concession in his hands at present; does not know where it is, and believes it to be lost.

Antoine Soulard, sworn, says that, about the year 1800, he had the concession of claimant in his possession, and then recorded it in the registry, as before stated, in book No. 2, marked B, page 44.

June 18, 1810: Present, Lucas, Penrose, and Bates, commissioners. It is the opinion of the Board that this claim ought not to be confirmed. The Board, on examining the registry referred to in the claim, to wit, book No. 2, marked B, find several concessions, of subsequent dates to the one referred to in page 44, in the pages of the book preceding that number, and, particularly in page 43, one dated 31st March, 1803; and also on examining the said alleged registry, book No. 1, page 27, the Board find a concession dated 21st November, 1803.

MARGARET LACHAISE, claiming a lot of land in the town of St. Louis, being a vacancy between Nicholas Lecompte and Jacques Clamorgan; produces to the Board an order from Don Carlos Dehault Delassus, Lieutenant Governor, to Antoine Soulard, to ascertain the lines of Nicholas Lecompte, that he may survey the vacancy conceded to claimant in 1802, dated 21st November, 1803.

June 18, 1810: Present, Lucas, Penrose, and Bates, commissioners. It is the opinion of the Board that this claim ought not to be confirmed.

JOHN PYATT, claiming four hundred and sixty-two arpents of land, situate on the Negro fork of the river Merrimack, district of St. Louis; produces to the Board a survey of the same, dated the 21st January, and certified 17th February, 1806.

Testimony taken. August 20, 1806. James Richardson, sworn, says that he knew the above claimant on the said tract of land about fifteen years ago; that he raised two crops on the same; that, in the year 1790, he was driven away by Indians; that he remained out until the year 1800, when he went back on said land; that, in 1801, he planted a crop of corn, and was again driven away; that some of the farmers were killed by the Indians in 1803; that, although not residing on said land, he still continued the cultivation of the same, and raised four crops; that, in the year 1805, he went again on said land, and has actually inhabited and cultivated it to this day.

June 18, 1810: Present, Lucas, Penrose, and Bates, commissioners. It is the opinion of the Board that this claim ought not to be granted.

PASCAL DETCHEMENDY, claiming one thousand six hundred arpents of land, situate on the river establishment, district of St. Genevieve; produces to the Board a concession for the same from Zenon Trudeau, Lieutenant Governor, dated 30th November, 1797; a plat of survey of the same, dated 2d May, 1798, and certified 1st November, 1799.

June 19, 1810: Present, Lucas, Penrose, and Bates, commissioners. It is the opinion of the Board that this claim ought not to be confirmed.

PASCAL DETCHEMENDY, assignee of Francis Poillevre, claiming sixteen hundred arpents of land, situate on the river establishment, district of St. Genevieve; produces to the Board a concession for the same from Charles Dehault Delassus, Lieutenant Governor, dated the 30th January, 1800, to the said Poillevre; a plat of survey of the same, dated 3d May, and certified 10th May, 1800; produces, also, an act of sale of the aforesaid property, passed before the commandant, dated 28th April, 1802, to claimant.

June 19, 1810: Present, Lucas, Penrose, and Bates, commissioners. It is the opinion of the Board that this claim ought not to be confirmed.

JAMES BURNS, assignee of Reuben Middleton, claiming six hundred and forty acres of land, situate on Bois Bruile, district of St. Genevieve; produces to the Board a notice to the recorder, dated 27th June, 1808.

Testimony taken. October 13, 1808. John Smith, Sen., sworn, says that, in the fall of the year 1804, Reuben Middleton cleared a small piece of ground on the land claimed, raised some turnips, and moved on the place and inhabited and cultivated the same in 1805; and further, that said land has been inhabited and cultivated ever since.

June 19, 1810: Present, Lucas, Penrose, and Bates, commissioners. It is the opinion of the Board that this claim ought not to be granted.

STEPHEN HANCOCK, claiming four hundred arpents of land, situate on the Missouri, district of St. Charles; produces to the Board, as a special permission to settle, a concession from Charles D. Delassus, dated September 21, 1799; and a certificate of survey of the same, dated September 17, 1802.

June 19, 1810: Present, Lucas, Penrose, and Bates, commissioners. It is the opinion of the Board that this claim ought not to be granted.

EZEKIEL ROGERS, claiming six hundred arpents of land, situate on river Dubois, district of St. Louis; produces to the Board a concession from Charles D. Delassus for the same, dated December 17, 1801; certificate of survey, dated March 1st, 1804; the above concession bearing date subsequent to 10th October, 1800.

The above claimant requested that the following circumstance may be entered on the minutes, to wit, that he holds no other title or claim to lands in his own name; and that he did, prior to and on the 1st day of October, 1800, reside upon and cultivate another tract of purchased lands.

June 19, 1810: Present, Lucas, Penrose, and Bates, commissioners. It is the opinion of the Board that this claim ought not to be confirmed.

JONATHAN HELDERBRAN, assignee of Jesse Cain, assignee of Robert Owens, assignee of John Megar, claiming two hundred arpents of land, situate on the Negro fork of the river Merrimack, district of St. Louis; produces to the Board a notice to the recorder, dated June 20, 1808; produces no assignments or transfers that the Board thought they could receive as such.

Testimony taken. October 13, 1808. William Bellew, sworn, says that, about thirty years ago, John Helderbran made an improvement on the land claimed, and inhabited and cultivated the same for five years, and then sold to John Megar, who, by his tenant, David Helderbran, cultivated the same one year more.

June 19, 1810: Present, Lucas, Penrose, and Bates, commissioners. It is the opinion of the Board that this claim ought not to be granted.

PIERRE CHOUTEAU, as the legal representative of Joseph Alvarez Hortez, deceased, claiming four thousand eight hundred and fifty arpents of land, situate in the district of St. Louis; produces to the Board a notice of said claim to the recorder; a concession for four thousand six hundred arpents, more or less, from Don Carlos Dehault Delassus, Lieutenant Governor, to Joseph Alvarez Hortez, dated 26th January, 1800; a plat and certificate of survey of four thousand eight hundred and fifty arpents, dated 15th March, 1803, and certified 17th June, same year.

Testimony taken. October 17, 1808. Hyacinthe St. Cyr, sworn, says that, six years ago, Joseph Alvarez Hortez had house logs cut, and a cabin put up, on the tract claimed, and that the same has been inhabited ever since by or for said Hortez, and was cultivated in 1804, and ever since.

Testimony taken. October 19, 1808. Auguste Chouteau sworn and questioned to that effect, says that Joseph Hortez, deceased, was in Louisiana at the taking possession of the country by the Spaniards, since which he was always employed by the Spanish Government; and in the various offices the duties of which he at various times discharged, the said Hortez possessed the confidence of the superior officers; witness believes that the civil services of said Hortez were never rewarded; as a compensation for the various militia services which he had at different time rendered, he was offered, as witness believes, rank in the army, but declined, and solicited and accepted the lands now claimed as a preferable recompense. The deceased was a Spaniard by birth, but reared in this country a numerous family of children, ten in number.

Antoine Soulard, sworn, says that the concession presented in this case was written or draughted by him, the witness, and completed by the Lieutenant Governor, at the time it bears date; that the lands mentioned therein were given as a compensation for said Hortez's services, rendered the Government in different capacities.

June 19, 1810: Present, Lucas, Penrose, and Bates, commissioners. It is the opinion of the Board that this claim ought not be confirmed.

Frederick Bates, commissioner, declares that, if this claim had not exceeded eight hundred arpents, he would have voted for a confirmation.

NEWTON HOWELL, claiming three hundred and fifty arpents of land, situate below the mouth of Femme Osage river, district of St. Charles; produces to the Board a notice to the recorder; and a concession for the same from Don Carlos Dehault Delassus, Lieutenant Governor, to claimant, dated 25th May, 1801; claimant was not of age at the time the grant was given.

Testimony taken. October 19, 1808. William Stewart, sworn, says that, in 1804, he, (witness,) by permission from claimant, had a camp on the tract claimed, and made sugar; and that sugar has been made on the same by and for claimant ever since.

James Mackay, sworn, says that, in the fall of 1803, he run a line between claimant and Arend Rutgers; and that he saw claimant, with several other persons, working on the place at the same time.

June 19, 1810: Present, Lucas, Penrose, and Bates, commissioners. It is the opinion of the Board that this claim ought not to be confirmed.

THOMAS HOWELL, claiming seven hundred and fifty acres of land, situate on waters of Darden, district of St. Charles; produces to the Board a survey of the same, dated 9th January, and certified 3d February, 1806.

Testimony taken. October 19, 1808. James Mackay, former commandant of St. Andre and St. Charles, sworn, says that he gave claimant permission to settle prior to 1803.

William Stewart, sworn, says claimant raised a crop on the tract claimed in 1803, but resided with his father, about one-half mile from the tract; claimant has had a stock on the same ever since, and cultivated it ever since; inhabited it since 1804, when he married.

June 19, 1810: Present, Lucas, Penrose, and Bates, commissioners. It is the opinion of the Board that this claim ought not to be granted.

ROBERT YOUNG, assignee of Asa Musick, who was assignee of John Day, claiming two hundred and forty arpents of land, situate south side of river Missouri, district of St. Louis; produces to the Board a concession from Zenon Trudeau, for the same, to John Day, dated March 2d, 1798; and a survey of the same, taken 10th February, and certified 20th May, 1800; a deed of transfer from John Day to Musick, dated 17th August, 1805, and another deed of transfer, from said Musick to claimant, dated 26th November, 1805.

Testimony taken. July 26, 1806. James Mackay, sworn, says that in the year 1800 a house was built on the said tract of land.

Testimony taken. September 6, 1806. Alexander Graham, sworn, says that the said tract of land was settled in the year 1799, by one M'Coy, who built a cabin, and wintered on the same; that one William Hughs lived on it in the year 1800; and further, that the aforesaid Asa Musick did, in 1804, actually cultivate the same, and raised a crop on it.

June 20, 1810: Present, Lucas, Penrose, and Bates, commissioners. It is the opinion of the Board that this claim ought not to be confirmed.

JOHN A. STURGES, Sen., assignee of Titus Strickland, claiming three hundred arpents of land, situate on river Platin, district of St. Louis; produces to the Board a special permission to settle, from Zenon Trudeau, dated 11th January, 1798; a survey of the same, taken March 18th, 1798, certified 7th October, 1799; and a deed of transfer of the same, dated July 11th, 1803.

Testimony taken. June 25, 1806. Humphrey Gibson, sworn, says that James Sturges, Jun., settled the said tract of land in the year 1803, and raised a crop on the same; and that it was on the 20th December, 1803, actually inhabited by claimant, who had then a wife and two children.

Testimony taken. October 19, 1808. Jacob Horine, sworn, says that he was acquainted with John A. Sturges, under the Spanish Government, and knows that said Sturges was a syndic for the upper part of St. Genevieve district.

June 20, 1810: Present, Lucas, Penrose, and Bates, commissioners. It is the opinion of the Board that this claim ought not to be confirmed.

JAMES STURGES, Jun., assignee of Jacob Strickland, claiming four hundred arpents of land, situate adjoining Titus Strickland, river Platin, district of St. Louis; produces to the Board a special permission to settle, from Zenon Trudeau, dated 9th January, 1798; a survey of the same taken 18th March, and certified 5th April, 1800; and a deed of transfer of the same, dated July 18th, 1803.

Testimony taken. June 25, 1806. Humphrey Gibson, sworn, says that he saw claimant on said land in 1803, and that the same was actually cultivated by John A. Sturges, Sen., and inhabited by claimant prior to and on the 20th December, 1803; who had then a wife and a child.

June 20, 1810: Present, Lucas, Penrose, and Bates, commissioners. It is the opinion of the Board that this claim ought not to be confirmed.

MICHAEL HORINE, heirs of, by their agent, Jacob Horine, claiming eight hundred and ninety-eight arpents of land, situate on Platin creek, district of St. Genevieve; as assignee of Abner Wood produces to the Board a notice to the recorder, and an assignment from Abner Wood, to said Horine, dated August 15th, 1805.

Testimony taken. October 19, 1806. John A. Sturges, sworn, says that Abner Wood inhabited and cultivated said land, 1804.

June 20, 1810: Present, Lucas, Penrose, and Bates, commissioners. It is the opinion of the Board that this claim ought not to be granted.

JOSIAH PARK, assignee of John Murphee, claiming five hundred and fifty arpents of land, situate on Fee Fee creek, district of St. Louis; produces to the Board a concession for the same from Don Carlos Dehault Delassus, Lieutenant Governor, to John Murphee, dated 25th November, 1799; also a plat and certificate of survey, dated 20th, and certified 24th February, 1806; a deed of conveyance from said Murphee and wife, to claimant, dated 27th June, 1805; also an official letter from Zenon Trudeau, Lieutenant Governor, to James Mackay, in which it is stated that as soon as said Murphee shall choose a spot, it shall be granted to him, dated 10th September, 1799.

Testimony taken. October 19, 1808. James Mackay, sworn, says that the official letter stated above was received by him near the time it bears date.

June 20, 1810: Present, Lucas, Penrose, and Bates, commissioners. It is the opinion of the Board that this claim ought not to be confirmed.

PHŒBE WHITESIDES, widow of John G. Whitesides, by David Musick, her agent, claiming six hundred arpents of land, district of St. Louis; produces to the Board a notice to the recorder.

Testimony taken. October 19, 1808. James Mackay, sworn, says that he had a concession in his hands granted to John G. Whitesides, for six hundred arpents of land, by Don Zenon Trudeau, Lieutenant Governor, some time in the year 1798; witness now believes the same to be lost.

June 20, 1810: Present, Lucas, Penrose, and Bates, commissioners. It is the opinion of the Board that this claim ought not to be granted.

JAMES STEWART, assignee of John Baptiste Rouillier, dit Bouche, claiming three hundred and twenty arpents of land, situate on Black water creek, south of the Merrimack, district of St. Louis; produces to the Board a notice of said claim to the recorder, dated 30th December, 1807; also a concession from Zenon Trudeau, Lieutenant Governor, to John Baptiste Rouillier, dit Bouche, for the same, dated 24th October, 1797; an assignment of the same from said Bouche to claimant, dated 15th June, 1803.

Testimony taken. October 20, 1808. John Wilson, sworn, says that claimant built a cabin on the tract claimed in the fall of 1802; then moved in it, and has inhabited and cultivated the same ever since.

June 20, 1810: Present, Lucas, Penrose, and Bates, commissioners. It is the opinion of the Board that this claim ought not to be confirmed.

JOHN HENSLEY, claiming seven hundred and twenty-seven arpents of land, situate on the Grand Glaize creek, of the river Merrimack, district of St. Louis; produces to the Board a notice of said claim to the recorder, dated 27th June, 1808; a plat and certificate of survey, dated 24th February, 1806; certified to be received for record, 27th same month, same year.

****

Testimony taken. October 20, 1808. James Mackay, former commandant of St. Andre, and St. Charles, sworn, says that he gave claimant permission to settle, prior to 1803.

William Hensley, sworn, says that claimant cut house logs on the place in 1803, and made hay; built a cabin in 1804; and inhabited and cultivated it that year, but has never resided on the same since then; in 1803, claimant was a single man.

June 20, 1810: Present, Lucas, Penrose, and Bates, commissioners. It is the opinion of the Board that this claim ought not to be granted.

DANIEL GRIFFITH, claiming six hundred arpents of land, situate district of St. Charles; produces to the Board a notice to the recorder, dated 13th April, 1808; also a concession for the same, from Don Carlos Dehault Delassus, to claimant, dated 18th April, 1801.

June 20, 1810: Present, Lucas, Penrose, and Bates, commissioners. It is the opinion of the Board that this claim ought not to be confirmed.

JOHN L. PETTIT, claiming seven hundred and fifty arpents of land, situate on a fork of river St. Francis, district of St. Genevieve; produces to the Board a certificate of a permission to settle, by Peter Delassus Deluziere, dated January 9, 1806; and a survey of the same, dated February 13, 1806.

Testimony taken. May 5, 1806. William Johnson, sworn, says that Benjamin Pettit settled the said land in 1803, for the use of the claimant, who had then gone down the river on a trading voyage; that said Benjamin Pettit is father to claimant; and that in the years 1803 and 1804, turnips were raised on said land, by the said Benjamin Pettit; witness never knew claimant.

Thomas Ruig, sworn, says that he knew claimant in the country in 1801; that he had then the appearance of a person of twenty-one years of age or upwards, and that he never saw him afterwards.

June 20, 1810: Present, Lucas, Penrose, and Bates, commissioners. It is the opinion of the Board that this claim ought not to be granted.

MARGARET BYRD, widow of Micajah Byrd, claiming one thousand one hundred and forty acres of land, situate on the waters of Little Rock creek, district of St. Louis; produces to the Board a plat of survey, dated 22d February, 1806, received for record 27th same month, same year.

Testimony taken. October 20, 1806. John Wilson, sworn, says that claimant went to live on the tract claimed in 1805; and has inhabited and cultivated the same ever since.

June 20, 1801: Present, Lucas, Penrose, and Bates, commissioners. It is the opinion of the Board that this claim ought not to be granted.

JOHN CONNOR, assignee of Isaac Vanmetre, claiming six hundred and forty arpents of land, situate on river Joachim, district of St. Louis; produces to the Board a permission to settle, granted by Francis Valle to said Isaac Vanmetre, dated March 24, 1801; and a certificate of survey of six hundred and ninety arpents, dated 1st February, 1806; a deed of transfer of said land, executed by the above named Isaac Vanmetre, to claimant, duly acknowledged, dated September 25, 1803.

Testimony taken. February 3, 1806. Walter Jewett, sworn, says that the above mentioned tract of land was inhabited and cultivated by Isaac Vanmetre in 1802, and until the 25th day of November, 1803, when he sold the same to claimant, and afterwards continued on it, as tenant to the said claimant, until November, 1804; and that the said tract of land has been actually cultivated and inhabited ever since.

June 21, 1810: Present, Lucas, Penrose, and Bates, commissioners. It is the opinion of the Board that this claim ought not to be granted.

MICHEL PLACIT, claiming one hundred and forty-three arpents of land, situate on the river establishment, district of St. Genevieve; produces to the Board a concession from Don Carlos Dehault Delassus, Lieutenant Governor, for the same, dated 10th January, 1800; a plat of survey, dated 25th February, 1800, certified 17th May, same year.

Testimony taken. October 21, 1808. John Baptiste Valle, sworn, says that claimant has made sugar on the tract claimed every year since 1799.

June 21, 1810: Present, Lucas, Penrose, and Bates, commissioners. It is the opinion of the Board that this claim ought not to be granted.

MICHEL PLACIT, assignee of William Guouard, assignee of John Hays, claiming thirty-five arpents of land, situate on the Mississippi river, district of St. Genevieve; produces to the Board a certified copy of a public sale of the property of said Hays to William Guouard, dated 19th November, 1797; a certified copy of a deed of transfer from said Guouard and wife to claimant, dated 22d December, 1801.

Testimony taken. October 21, 1808. John Baptiste Valle, Sen., sworn, says that in 1794, or 1795, one Joseph Decelle lived on the tract claimed, and continued to inhabit and cultivate the same three years, then sold to John Hays, who inhabited it a short time, when it was sold to William Guouard, and that the same has been inhabited and cultivated ever since.

June 21, 1810: Present, Lucas, Penrose, and Bates, commissioners. It is the opinion of the Board that this claim ought not to be granted.

DAVID HELDEBRAND, claiming nine hundred and sixty arpents of land, situate on the river Merrimack, district of St. Louis; produces to the Board a plat of survey, dated 24th February, 1806, certified to be received for record 27th same month, same year; for permission to settle, see Mackay's list sworn to and on file.

Testimony taken. October 21, 1808. William Bellew, sworn, says that claimant raised a crop on the tract claimed in 1803, and cut house logs, but lived on the opposite side of the river; inhabited and cultivated the tract claimed in 1804, and ever since.

June 21, 1810: Present, Lucas, Penrose, and Bates, commissioners. It is the opinion of the Board that this claim ought not to be granted.

NICHOLAS JARROT, assignee of Amable Roy, claiming eight hundred arpents of land, situate in the district of St. Charles; produces to the Board a plat and certificate of survey, dated 24th February, 1806. Certified to be received for record 28th February, 1806; a deed of conveyance from said Roy to claimant, dated 12th March, 1807.

Testimony taken. October 22, 1807. Joseph Roy, sworn, says that he was present when François Cruzat, Lieutenant Governor, gave Amable Roy permission to settle on the tract claimed; that Amable Roy settled on the tract claimed about twenty-two years ago, and inhabited and cultivated the same for three years, when it was abandoned in consequence of the Indians being troublesome; says that Amable Roy was never married.

June 21, 1810: Present, Lucas, Penrose, and Bates, commissioners. It is the opinion of the Board that this claim ought not to be granted.

REUBEN BAKER, claiming six hundred and forty acres of land, situate district of St. Genevieve; produces to the Board a survey of the same, dated 10th February, 1806; certified to be received for record 27th February, 1806.
Testimony taken. October 22, 1807. Christopher Barnhart, sworn, says that claimant inhabited said tract in February, 1801, and occasionally inhabited it that year; never saw any crop on the place.
June 21, 1810: Present, Lucas, Penrose, and Bates, commissioners. It is the opinion of the Board that this claim ought not to be granted.

JACOB COLLINS, claiming eight hundred and ninety arpents of land, situate on the Negro fork of the river Merrimack, district of St. Louis; produces to the Board a notice of claim to the recorder, dated 25th June, 1808; a plat of survey, dated 21st June, 1808, signed John Stuart, surveyor.
Testimony taken. October 22, 1808. John Wideman, sworn, says that claimant built a cabin on the place in 1802, and raised a crop; one Charles Pruett cultivated the same in 1803, but does not know for whom; that three years ago, claimant inhabited and cultivated the same and ever since; that claimant was one of the families that came to the country with him, the witness.
John Pruett, sworn, says that claimant, in 1803, had a wife and one child.
June 21, 1810: Present, Lucas, Penrose, and Bates, commissioners. It is the opinion of the Board that this claim ought not to be granted.

HUGH McCULLOCK, claiming nine hundred and one and a half arpents of land, situate on the river Merrimack, district of St. Louis; produces to the Board a survey of the same, dated February 12, 1806.
Testimony taken. July 5, 1806. Francis Wideman, sworn, says that he knew said claimant on said land in October, 1803; that he had then his family on the same, and was then engaged in cutting hay; and further that he raised a crop in 1804; and has actually inhabited and cultivated the same to this day; had, 20th December, 1803, a wife and child.
June 21, 1810: Present, Lucas, Penrose, and Bates, commissioners. It is the opinion of the Board that this claim ought not to be granted.

CLEMENT HAYDEN, assignee of John Greenwalt, claiming six hundred arpents of land, situate on the river Bois Bruile, district of St. Genevieve; produces to the Board a concession for the same from Zenon Trudeau, to said John Greenwalt, dated March 10, 1798; a certificate of survey of five hundred and ninety-five arpents, dated May 2, 1800; and a deed of transfer of said land, executed by the said John Greenwalt to the said claimant, dated October 21, 1803.
Testimony taken. February 4, 1806. Thomas Madden, sworn, says that the said Clement Hayden, has no claims to lands in his own name in this territory, to the best of his knowledge.
June 21, 1810: Present, Lucas, Penrose, and Bates, commissioners. It is the opinion of the Board that this claim ought not to be confirmed.

MARK BROOKS, assignee of William Strother, assignee of William Lowry, assignee of John O'Connor, claiming three hundred arpents of land, situate on Bois Bruile, district of St. Genevieve; produces a special permission to settle from Zenon Trudeau to said Connor, dated March 1, 1799; a survey of two hundred and ninety-nine arpents and twenty-eight perches, dated 1st June, and certified 5th November, 1800; a certificate of public sale of said land in favor of William Lowry, dated 18th December, 1803; a deed of transfer of the same from said Lowry to William Strother, dated 9th December, 1803; and another deed of transfer from said William Strother to claimant, dated 20th December, 1805.
Testimony taken. June 26, 1806. Alexander McConohee, sworn, says that the said tract of land was settled in the winter of 1800, by the said O'Connor, who cut house logs and made rails; that provisions being very scarce, he could not proceed any further with said settlement, being then a single man; that he was some short time after this killed by a person of the name of Stone, and that claimant having purchased the same in the fall of 1805, moved on it, and has actually inhabited and cultivated it to this day.
June 21, 1810: Present, Lucas, Penrose, and Bates, commissioners. It is the opinion of the Board that this claim ought not to be confirmed.

BENJAMIN CALDWELL, by his proxy, Robert Reynolds, claiming four hundred acres of land, situate on the river Saint Francis, district of Cape Girardeau; produces to the Board a notice of said claim to the recorder, dated February 8th, 1808.
Testimony taken. October 24, 1808. Daniel Thorn, sworn, says that he saw claimant inhabiting and cultivating the land claimed about six years ago; again saw him on the place about four years ago, when he was still inhabiting and cultivating the same, and had then a wife and two children.
June 22, 1810: Present, Lucas, Penrose, and Bates, commissioners. It is the opinion of the Board that this claim ought not to be granted.

JAMES CALDWELL, by his proxy, Robert Reynolds, claiming four hundred acres of land, situate on the river St. Francis, district of Cape Girardeau; produces to the Board a notice to the recorder, dated February 8th, 1808.
Testimony taken. October 24, 1808: Daniel Thorn, sworn, says that he saw claimant inhabiting and cultivating the tract in 1802, 1803, and 1804, and in 1803 had a wife and three children.
June 22, 1810: Present, Lucas, Penrose, and Bates, commissioners. It is the opinion of the Board that this claim ought not to be granted.

HENRY CLARK, eldest son of Francis Clark, claiming four hundred arpents of land, situate on Bois Bruile, district of Saint Genevieve; produces to the Board a concession for the same from Zenon Trudeau, Lieutenant Governor, to claimant, dated 2d February, 1798; a plat of survey dated 14th February, 1800, and certified 5th November, 1800; claimant is now under age.
June 22, 1810: Present, Lucas, Penrose, and Bates, commissioners. It is the opinion of the Board that this claim ought not to be confirmed.

JAMES VARNUM and RUFUS EASTON, claiming four hundred acres of land, situate between Joachim and Platen creeks, district of St. Louis; produces to the Board a notice to the recorder, an assignment for one half equal part and moiety of this tract, from said Varnum to Easton.

****

Testimony taken. September 19, 1806. Frederick Connor, sworn, says that in the year 1802 claimant built a distillery on said land; that, in 1803, claimant carried on the business of a distiller, and did, prior to and on the 20th day of December, 1803, actually inhabit said land; that the same was actually cultivated and a crop raised in the year 1804, that he (the witness) did, at the request of claimant, apply to Francis Valle, the commandant of St. Genevieve, for a permission to settle; that the said Francis Vallee permitted him, verbally, to settle on vacant lands; and further that the said claimant was, on the 20th of December, 1803, of the age of twenty-one years and upwards.

Same, sworn, 24th October, 1808. Says that James Varnum raised a still-house on the tract claimed, in 1801, put it into operation, and continued to inhabit and distil on the same until 1804; then raised a crop.

June 22, 1810: Present, Lucas, Penrose, and Bates, commissioners. It is the opinion of the Board that this claim ought not to be granted.

MARY EAGERS, claiming three hundred arpents of land, situate on Bois Bruile, district of St. Genevieve; produces to the Board a survey of the same, dated 11th and certified 27th February, 1806.

Testimony taken. June 26, 1806. John Hawkins, sworn, says that he was employed by claimant to survey the said tract of land, which was always considered as George Eager's property; that he went off in debt; when his wife took possession of the same, and rented it to a person who has actually inhabited and cultivated it to this day.

June 22, 1810: Present, Lucas, Penrose, and Bates, commissioners. It is the opinion of the Board that this claim ought not to be granted.

CHRISTIAN FENDER, claiming six hundred arpents of land, situate on Bois Bruile Bottom, district of St. Genevieve; produces to the Board a notice to the recorder, dated 7th December, 1807; a plat of survey in the name of William Girty, for six hundred and forty acres, dated February 12th, 1806, certified to be received for record 27th February, 1806.

Testimony taken. October 24, 1808. Alexander McCoushoe, sworn, says that claimant inhabited and cultivated the tract claimed in 1806, and ever since.

John Smith, Sen., sworn, says that claimant inhabited and cultivated in 1805, and ever since.

June 22, 1810: Present, Lucas, Penrose, and Bates, commissioners. It is the opinion of the Board that this claim ought not to be granted.

ISRAEL DODGE, assignee of Hypolite Bollon, claiming six hundred and eighty-two acres of land, situate on Bois Bruile, district of St. Genevieve; produces to the Board a plat of survey, dated 15th February, 1806, certified to be received for record, 27th February, 1806; also the sale of a concession, provided it shall be found in the archives of the post of St. Genevieve, for eighteen acres in front by forty in depth, sale dated 25th April, 1805.

Testimony taken. October 24, 1808. Alexander McConohow, sworn, says that, ten years ago, he rented from Hypolite Bollon a sugar camp on the tract claimed, and worked it for four or five years.

Joseph Tucker, sworn, says that, in 1799, he saw said Bollon in a camp on the tract claimed.

June 22, 1810: Present, Lucas, Penrose, and Bates, commissioners. It is the opinion of the Board that this claim ought not to be granted.

JOHN SUTTON FARROW, claiming three hundred and fifty arpents of land, situate on the river Dubois, district of St. Louis; produces to the Board a notice to the recorder, dated 28th June, 1808; a concession from Charles Dehault Delassus, Lieutenant Governor, dated 15th January, 1800; a plat of survey, dated 8th February, 1804, certified 1st March, 1804.

Claimant's father being present, says that claimant was not of age in 1800.

June 25, 1810: Present, Lucas, Penrose, and Bates, commissioners. It is the opinion of the Board that this claim ought not to be confirmed.

CALVIN ADAMS, assignee of Patrick Lee, assignee of Joseph Moutard, claiming one thousand three hundred and forty arpents of land, situate on Mill creek, district of St. Louis; produces to the Board a survey of the same, dated 16th November, 1805; a deed of transfer, executed before commandant, by Joseph Moutard, to said Patrick Lee, dated 7th November, 1800, and another deed of transfer, executed also before the commandant, by said Patrick Lee to claimant, dated 22d August, 1803.

Testimony taken. September 9, 1808. Auguste Chouteau, sworn, says that the aforesaid Joseph Moutard had no family; that the said tract of land was settled about twelve years ago, by one Cotard, for said Moutard; that the same was actually inhabited and cultivated until the year 1800; that it was well improved; said Moutard had on the same a house and out houses.

October 25, 1808. David Musick produces a deed of conveyance from said Adams and wife to him, dated 22d January, 1808; said deed on file.

June 25, 1810: Present, Lucas, Penrose, and Bates, commissioners. It is the opinion of the Board that this claim ought not to be granted. On comparing the plats of survey, this land appears to be within the tract claimed as the common of St. Louis.

CALVIN ADAMS, assignee of John Dowlin, assignee of John Gilmore, claiming seven hundred and forty-eight acres sixty-eight perches of land, situate on little Rock creek, district of St. Louis; produces to the Board a conveyance from John Gilmore to John Dowlin, dated 25th January, 1806; a conveyance from John Dowlin to claimant, dated 28th January, 1806; a plat of survey, dated 12th February, 1806, certified 22d February, 1806.

Testimony taken. October 25, 1808. William Savage, sworn, says that John Gilmore built a cabin on the tract claimed and moved in it in November, 1803, and inhabited and cultivated it in 1804 and 1805.

David Musick produces, as before, the same deed.

June 25, 1810: Present, Lucas, Penrose, and Bates, commissioners. It is the opinion of the Board that this claim ought not to be granted.

JULIAN PAPIN BENITO, claiming a lot of land to run from the lines of a lot of ground claimed by Benito Vasques, assignee of Alexis Marie, in the town of St. Louis, to the river; produces to the Board an order of survey from Don Carlos Dehault Delassus, Lieutenant Governor, dated 14th April, 1803, in which he declares that it may be surveyed, provided it does not injure the public road or the neighbors.

June 26, 1810: Present, Lucas, Penrose, and Bates, commissioners. It is the opinion of the Board that this claim ought not to be confirmed. This space has been termed the bank of the Mississippi; the lots between the main street and the Mississippi being one hundred and fifty feet only, as appears by the plat of the town St. Louis,

****

recorded by Pierre Chouteau and others, on behalf of the inhabitants of said town, as also in all the old concessions given for said lots; and it appears from said plat, that a nearly similar space of ground exists between the Mississippi and all the other lots that are situated between the Mississippi and main street.

CHARLES GRATIOT, assignee of John Ball, claiming two hundred and forty arpents of land, situate on the river Des Peres, district of St. Louis; produces a concession from Zenon Trudeau, dated 18th December, 1797; a survey of the same, dated 15th March, certified 5th June, 1799; together with a deed of transfer of the same, dated 11th November, 1803.

Testimony taken. September 20, 1806. Antoine Soulard, sworn, says that he surveyed the said tract of land in the year 1799; at which time the said John Ball had a house built on said land, and a field of about five or six arpents fenced.

John E. Allen, sworn, says, that the said Ball built his house in the year 1798.

James Mackay, sworn, says, that about seven years ago he saw a house and well on said land, and that the said John Ball claimed no other land in his own name in the territory.

June 26, 1810: Present, Lucas, Penrose, and Bates, commissioners. It is the opinion of the Board that this claim ought not to be confirmed.

CHARLES GRATIOT, claiming five hundred arpents of land adjoining the foregoing tract, conceded as an augmentation of wood for the use of claimant's saw mill on an adjoining tract; produces to the Board a concession from Charles D. Delassus, dated 18th January, 1800; a survey of the same, dated 20th November, 1802, certified 5th January, 1803.

September 20, 1806. The Board required further proof.

Testimony taken. September 20, 1806. Antoine Soulard, sworn, says that he cannot say when the said concession was granted, but sees nothing that contradicts the date thereof.

June 26, 1810: Present, Lucas, Penrose, and Bates, commissioners. It is the opinion of the Board that this claim ought not to be confirmed.

SAMUEL PRUITT, claiming nine hundred and six arpents of land, situate on the river Merrimack, district of St. Louis; produces to the Board a survey of the same, dated 21st, and certified 26th February, 1806.

Testimony taken. August 29, 1806. George Sip, sworn, says that one Joseph Horn moved on said tract of land in the beginning of 1803; that he raised a crop on the same and actually inhabited it until the 1st day of October, 1803, when claimant, having purchased the same, with one half of the crop on it, moved thereon, and has actually inhabited and cultivated it to this day; that he did that year plant trees; had, on the 20th day of December, a wife and four children, and has now about nine or ten acres under cultivation.

June 26, 1810: Present, Lucas, Penrose, and Bates, commissioners. It is the opinion of the Board that this claim ought not to be granted.

Testimony taken. October 26, 1808. In the above claim omitted Joseph Kiver, who being sworn, says that he, witness, was present when claimant paid Joseph Horn the consideration money for the purchase of the above claim.

See Joseph Horn's permission to settle, on Mackay's list.

DAVID BOYLE, claiming one thousand two hundred and twenty arpents of land, situate on Sandy creek, district of St. Louis.

Testimony taken. September 9, 1806. George Smirl, Jun., sworn, says that he saw claimant on a tract of land lying on Sandy creek; that, in October, 1803, he had a house, garden, and above thirty arpents of the same under fence, and that he did, prior to and on the 20th December, 1803, actually inhabit and cultivate the same, and had then a wife and six children.

Claimant produces the deposition of Richard Glover, taken before Benjamin Johnston, a Justice of the Peace, 22d September, 1805, as a proof of permission to settle.

June 26, 1810: Present, Lucas, Penrose, and Bates, commissioners. It is the opinion of the Board that this claim ought not to be granted.

ABRAHAM HELTEREBRAN, claiming eight-hundred and fifty arpents of land, situate on Negro fork of river Merrimack, district of St. Louis; produces to the Board a notice of claim, dated 27th June, 1808.

Testimony taken. 27th October, 1808. Christian Twalt Helterbran, sworn, says that claimant settled said land in February, 1804, and inhabited and cultivated the same ever since.

June 28, 1810: Present, Lucas, Penrose, and Bates, commissioners. It is the opinion of the Board that this claim ought not to be granted.

JOHN SINCLAIR, claiming one thousand two hundred and eighty arpents of land, situate on river St. Francis, district of St. Genevieve; produces to the Board a survey of the same, dated 20th and certified 26th February, 1806.

Testimony taken. June 25, 1806. Edward Johnston, sworn, says that he was present when claimant obtained permission to settle on vacant lands.

William Crawford, sworn, says that about the 15th December, 1803, he saw claimant on the said tract of land; that he was then actually inhabiting the same, and had with him his family, which then consisted of a wife and twelve children; that a crop had been raised on said land, but gathered prior to claimant's moving on it.

Testimony taken. October 27, 1808. Robert Burns, sworn, says that claimant went on said land five years ago, and has inhabited and cultivated the same ever since.

June 28, 1810: Present, Lucas, Penrose, and Bates, commissioners. It is the opinion of the Board that this claim ought not to be granted.

WILLIAM NASH, assignee of James Rankin, assignee of Charles Bruire, claiming eight hundred arpents of land, situate opposite Cedar island, district of St. Charles; produces to the Board a notice to the recorder; also a concession from Don Carlos Dehault Delassus, dated 5th November, 1800, also a plat and certificate of survey, dated February, 1804, and certified to be received for record 28th February, 1806; an alteration appearing to have been made in the original petition to the Lieutenant Governor.

Testimony taken. October 27, 1806. Louis Lebeaume, sworn, says he wrote said petition, and that the real date thereof is 3d of November, 1800; and that the same was actually written at the time it bears date.

June 28, 1810: Present, Lucas, Penrose, and Bates, commissioners. It is the opinion of the Board that this claim ought not to be confirmed.

WILLIAM RUSSELL, assignee of George Pursely, claiming one thousand one hundred arpents of land, situate on the waters of Point Labadie creek, district of St. Louis; produces to the Board a notice to the recorder, and a deed of transfer from George Pursely to claimant, dated 2d September, 1807.

Testimony taken. October 28, 1808. Aaron Colvin, sworn, says that George Pursely, seven years-ago, built a cabin on the tract claimed, and commenced clearing some ground, but never fenced it; he knows nothing else being done on the land by or for him, said Pursely.

Ambrose Bowles says that George Pursely was living on the tract claimed in April, 1803; had a garden fenced in and some things growing in it, when he was driven off by the Indians. For permission to settle see Mac-kay's list.

June 28, 1810: Present, Lucas, Penrose, and Bates, commissioners. It is the opinion of the Board that this claim ought not to be granted.

WILLIAM RUSSELL, assignee of George McFall, claiming nine hundred and fifty arpents of land, situate on the waters of Point Labadie creek, district of St. Louis; produces to the Board a notice to the recorder, dated June 27, 1808.

Testimony taken. October 28, 1807. Ambrose Bowles, sworn, says that this is the same tract claimed above by claimant as assignee of Pursely.

June 28, 1810: Present, Lucas, Penrose, and Bates, commissioners. It is the opinion of the Board that this claim ought not to be granted.

JAMES McCOURTNEY, widow and children of, to wit, Sally the wife, Susannah, Phœbe, Hannah, John,.Polly, Peggy, and James, the children claiming five hundred arpents of land, situate on Creve Cœur, district of St. Louis; claiming by their agent, John Johns.

Testimony taken. October 28, 1808. Alexander McCourtney, sworn, says that James McCourtney raised a crop on the land claimed in 1803; moved on the same in the spring of 1804; and it has been inhabited and cultivated ever since by himself and family; in 1803 James McCourtney had a wife and six children. For permission to settle see Mackay's list.

June 29, 1810: Present, Lucas, Penrose, and Bates, commissioners. It is the opinion of the Board that this claim ought not to be granted.

JAMES RANKIN, claiming eight hundred arpents of land, situate in district of St. Louis; produces to the Board a concession from Don Carlos Dehault Delassus Lieutenant Governor, dated 29th September, 1802; a plat of survey, dated 28th March, 1803, certified 17th June, 1803.

Testimony taken. October 28, 1808. Louis Labeaume, sworn, says that about September, 1802, he interpreted for claimant, who applied to the Lieutenant Governor for a piece of land, and Lieutenant Governor told him to go and choose a piece of land, and he would grant it to him.

Antoine Soulard, sworn, says that he wrote the decree to the concession of claimant, and believes it was written at the time it bears date, as Mr. Rankin came to the country about that time, and he (witness) advised him to get a concession.

June 29, 1810: Present, Lucas, Penrose, and Bates, commissioners. It is the opinion of the Board that this claim ought not to be confirmed.

JOSEPH BRAZEAU, claiming eight hundred arpents of land, situate on the river Mississippi, district of St. Charles; produces to the Board a concession from Don Carlos Dehault Delassus, Lieutenant Governor, for the same, dated 23d May, 1800; a plat of survey, dated 5th February, 1804, certified 8th March, 1804.

Testimony taken. October 28, 1808. David Delauney, sworn, says that he wrote the decree to the above concession, and it was written at the time it bears date.

June 29, 1810: Present, Lucas, Penrose, and Bates, commissioners. It is the opinion of the Board that this claim ought not to be confirmed.

LOUIS BRAZEAU, claiming eight hundred arpents of land, situate on the river Mississippi, district of St. Charles; produces to the Board a concession for the same from Don Carlos Dehault Delassus, Lieutenant Governor, dated 21st May, 1800, a plat of survey, dated 5th February, certified 8th March, 1804.

Testimony taken. October 28, 1808. David Delauney, sworn, says that he wrote the decree to the above concession, and that it was written at the time it bears date.

June 29, 1810: Present, Lucas, Penrose, and Bates, commissioners. It is the opinion of the Board that this claim ought not to be confirmed.

RICHARD APPLEGATE, claiming six hundred and forty acres of land, situate on Flat creek, district of St. Genevieve; produces to the Board a notice of claim to the recorder, dated 15th June, 1808, a plat of survey, dated 27th December, 1805, certified to be received for record, 26th February, 1806.

Testimony taken. November 2, 1808. Joseph Applegate, sworn, says that he was present in 1799 when Don Francisco Valle, commandant of St. Genevieve, gave claimant permission to settle.

Frederick Connor, sworn, says that in 1801 claimant settled and inhabited on Thomas Applegate's claim, but cultivated on the tract claimed, and has continued to cultivate the same until 1806, when he died; claimant was a single man in 1803.

June 29, 1810. Present, Lucas, Penrose, and Bates, commissioners. It is the opinion of the Board that this claim ought not to be granted.

ANTHONY and JOSEPH VILLARS, claiming six thousand arpents of land, situate on waters of Big river, district of St. Genevieve: produces to the Board a concession from Charles D. Delassus, dated October 11, 1799, and a plat of survey of the same without any date.

Testimony taken. June 21, 1808. John B. Valle, senior, sworn, says that he is guardian to claimants; that he advised them in 1799, to apply for the above concession, but never saw the same; and that they were under age when they obtained the same. The Board require further proof.

Testimony taken. November 3, 1808. Auguste Chouteau, sworn, says that Mr. Villars, father of the above claimants, was for thirty years a captain in the Spanish service; was also civil commandant at St. Genevieve and Arkansas, and for many years.

June 29, 1810: Present, Lucas, Penrose, and Bates, commissioners. It is the opinion of the Board that this claim ought not to be confirmed.

ROBERT RAMSEY, claiming three hundred and fifty arpents of land, situate in the district of St. Louis; produces to the Board a concession from Don Carlos Dehault Delassus, Lieutenant Governor, dated 10th December, 1799; a plat of survey, dated 7th March, 1803, and certified 27th February, 1804.

Testimony taken. November 4, 1808. Mordecai Bell, sworn, says that he (witness) built a cabin on the place claimed in 1802, then gave up his improvement to claimant, who got a concession for the same; in 1803, Thomas Gibson inhabited said land for claimant.

June 29, 1810: Present, Lucas, Penrose, and Bates, commissioners. It is the opinion of the Board that this claim ought not to be confirmed.

JULIAN DUBUQUE, assignee of François Cayolle, claiming seven thousand and fifty-six arpents of land, situate opposite Prairie du Chien; produces to the Board a concession from Don Carlos Dehault Delassus, Lieutenant Governor, to said Cayolle, dated 13th August, 1799, for the land between the mouth of a river Jaune and another river which empties in the Mississippi about one league lower down said Mississippi, so as the said tract make a quantity equal to a league square, but to include both rivers; a deed of conveyance from said Cayolle to said Dubuque, dated 7th May, 1805.

Testimony taken. November 12, 1808. Alexander Bellisime, sworn, says that about eight or nine years ago he saw a house on the premises, erected and inhabited by François Cayolle; that there was a garden of about one half arpent; the year following the said house was also inhabited by said Cayolle, and the garden cultivated; that the house was a large one.

Antoine Perrault, sworn, says that said tract has been continually cultivated, and the house occasionally inhabited, for nine years past.

July 2, 1810: Present, Lucas, Penrose, and Bates, commissioners. It is the opinion of the Board that this claim ought not to be confirmed.

JOHN JOHNS, claiming eight hundred and forty-nine arpents twelve perches of land, situate on the north side of the Richland creek; produces to the Board a plat of survey dated 12th January, 1806, and certified to be received for record by Antoine Soulard, surveyor general, 27th February, 1806.

Testimony taken. November 11, 1808. William Bellew, sworn, says that he was present about twenty or twenty-one years ago, when Fernando de Leyba, Lieutenant Governor, gave permission to Thomas Jones, father of the claimant, to settle at the spring; that said Jones went immediately to said land, built a cabin, and resided therein one winter; that Indians drove him off the next spring; said Jones never returned thereon, but died some years after; said Jones settled at the spring on the land now claimed.

Jesse Benton, sworn, says that claimant married and moved on said tract of land in 1804, resided thereon, and raised a crop; and that the same has been actually inhabited and cultivated ever since, by John Horine, he (the witness) believes for himself.

July 2, 1810: Present, Lucas, Penrose, and Bates, commissioners. It is the opinion of the Board that this claim ought not to be granted.

JESSE BENTON, claiming seven hundred and forty-seven arpents eighty-four perches, situate in the district of St. Genevieve, on the west branch of the Big river; produces to the Board a plat of survey dated 12th February, 1806, and certified 27th February, 1806.

Testimony taken. November 11, 1808. John Jones, sworn, says that claimant settled on the tract claimed in 1804; built a cabin that year and raised a crop, and has continued to inhabit and cultivate the same ever since; had, when he settled, a wife and three children.

July 2, 1810: Present, Lucas, Penrose, and Bates, commissioners. It is the opinion of the Board that this claim ought not to be granted.

KINKAID CALDWELL, claiming seven hundred arpents of land, situate in the district of St. Louis; produces to the Board a concession from Charles D. Delassus, dated 17th November, 1799, a survey of seven hundred and ten arpents, dated 17th October, 1803, certified 1st March, 1804.

Testimony taken. September 6, 1806. William Clark, sworn, says that about the month of October, 1804, he was on said land; that claimant was then actually settled on the same, and had formed a camp; that he saw a large patch of turnips growing on it, and took some, which he ate.

July 9, 1810: Present, Lucas, Penrose, and Bates, commissioners. It is the opinion of the Board that this claim ought not to be confirmed. September 6, 1806. The Board required further proof. Present, full Board:

ROBERT BUCHANNON, claiming five hundred arpents of land, situate on the waters of Creve Cœur, district of St. Louis; produces to the Board a special permission to settle, from Charles D. Delassus, dated 10th October, 1799; a survey of the same, dated 18th October, 1799, and certified 27th February, 1804.

Testimony taken. August 19, 1806. Robert Ramsey, sworn, says that claimant did, towards the latter end of October, 1803, cut house logs for the building of a house, which he completed in August, 1804; that he did raise a crop, and has actually inhabited and cultivated the same to this day; and, further, that he had, on the 20th December, 1803, a wife and six children, and claims no other land in his own name in the Territory; has been in the country upwards of six years.

July 9, 1810: Present, Lucas, Penrose, and Bates, commissioners. It is the opinion of the Board that this claim ought not to be confirmed.

MACKAY WHERRY, claiming one thousand six hundred arpents of land, situate in the district of St. Charles, unlocated, by virtue of a concession, said to be lost; produces to the Board a notice of claim, dated 24th June, 1808.

Testimony taken. November 18, 1808. Pierre Provenche, sworn, says that about the spring or summer of 1801, when he (witness) resided with Charles Dehault Delassus, Lieutenant Governor, he saw a concession from said Delassus to Mackay Wherry, and had the same in his possession, for one thousand six hundred arpents of land, lying in the district of St. Charles, on the river Darden or river Cuivre; claimant at that time resided in this country with his family.

Antoine Soulard, sworn, says that about the year 1800 he had a concession in his hands, for the purpose of making a survey, from Charles Dehault Delassus, Lieutenant Governor, to claimant, for six or eight hundred arpents of land; that he (witness) gave the said concession to some of the deputy surveyors; since when he has not seen it, nor does he know what has become of it.

July 9, 1810: Present, Lucas, Penrose, and Bates, commissioners. It is the opinion of the Board that this claim ought not to be confirmed.

****

Dehault Delassus, Lieutenant Governor, to Pierre Primo, for eight hundred arpents, dated 9th August, 1800; a plat of survey of said eight hundred arpents, dated 8th March, 1804, and certified same day; an assignment from said Primo to claimant for six hundred arpents, dated 5th December, 1803.

Testimony taken. November 23, 1808. David Delauney, sworn, says that he wrote the decree to the petition, in this claim, and that it was written at the time, or within a few days of the time, that it bears date; that Pierre Primo has resided in this country since 1799.

July 9, 1810: Present, Lucas, Penrose, and Bates, commissioners. It is the opinion of the Board that this claim ought not to be confirmed.

MANUEL LISA, assignee of Baptiste Riviere, claiming four hundred arpents of land, situate in the district of St. Louis; produces a concession from Zenon Trudeau, dated October 17, 1796; and a survey and plat of the same, dated February 25, 1806; a deed of transfer of the same, dated August 3, 1804: produces, also, a certificate from Antoine Soulard, stating that the land claimed is not vacant, and that Baptiste Riviere must obtain a new order of survey from the Lieutenant Governor, before it can be surveyed, dated 3d January, 1803; produces, also, an order of survey from Charles Dehault Delassus, Lieutenant Governor, dated 8th January, 1803.

Testimony taken. November 28, 1808. Antoine Soulard, sworn, says that he knows the concession from Zenon Trudeau, Lieutenant Governor, was given about the time it bears date; and that he had said concession in his hands to survey some time before his certificate was given, and that said certificate was given at the time it bears date.

May 8, 1806: Present, Penrose and Donaldson, commissioners. The Board reject this claim, and remark, that, from the antiquity of the instrument, from its appearance, and from the signature of Zenon Trudeau, they are satisfied that this is a *bona fide* claim, and that said concession is neither fraudulent nor antedated.

July 10, 1810: Present, Lucas, Penrose, and Bates, commissioners. It is the opinion of the Board that this claim ought not to be confirmed. The Board refer, as it respects the registry, to the remark in the claim of Jean P. Cabanne, book No. 4, page 386, [original record.]

MANUEL LISA, assignee of Philip Baccane, claiming four hundred and eighty arpents of land, situate in the district of St. Louis; produces to the Board a concession from Zenon Trudeau, dated December 14, 1796; and a certificate and survey, dated February 25, 1806; a deed of transfer of the same, dated August 3, 1804.

May 8, 1806: Present, Penrose and Donaldson, commissioners. The Board reject this claim.

The above remarks apply to this case.

July 10, 1810: Present, Lucas, Penrose, and Bates, commissioners. It is the opinion of the Board that this claim ought not to be confirmed.

RUFUS EASTON, assignee of George Bowers, who was the representative of William Crow, claiming seven hundred and forty-eight arpents and sixty-eight perches of land, situate on river Merrimack, district of St. Louis; produces to the Board a notice of claim to the recorder; and a deed of conveyance from said Bowers to claimant, dated 22d December, 1804.

Testimony taken. November 26, 1808. Jesse Raynor, sworn, says that William Crow lived with his wife and family on the place claimed near the Merrimack, twenty-three or twenty-four years ago; saw some fence at the same time; and that they lived about six months on the place; that George Bowers married the widow of Crow.

July 10, 1810: Present, Lucas, Penrose, and Bates, commissioners. It is the opinion of the Board that this claim ought not to be granted.

SYLVESTER LABADIE, claiming seven thousand and fifty-six arpents of land, situate on river Cuivre, district of St. Charles; produces to the Board a concession from Charles Dehault Delassus, dated 18th November, 1799; a survey and plat, dated 15th February, and certified 8th March, 1804. This concession bears no condition whatever.

Testimony taken. May 6, 1806. Charles Gratiot, sworn, says that claimant is a native of the country, and of the age of about twenty-eight years; that his father was, in many instances, and more particularly prior to the appointment of Peter Couteau, Sen. to the Indian department, employed by Government in the transacting of public business, such as Indian affairs, &c.; and further, that he (the witness) understood from claimant, about three or four years ago, that he had obtained a concession of a league square.

The Board required further proof.

July 10, 1810: Present, Lucas, Penrose, and Bates, commissioners. It is the opinion of the Board that this claim ought not to be confirmed.

ANDRE L. ANDREVILLE, claiming four thousand arpents of land, situate in the district of St. Charles.

Testimony taken. November 29, 1808. David Delauney, sworn, says that he thinks he wrote the decree to the petition in this claim, and that it was written at the time, or within a few days of the time, it bears date.

Witness being asked by the agent of the United States whether he remembers the time when he wrote the decree in this concession, answers that he does not; and on being questioned by agent of claimant whether he wrote a decree to any concession that was not written at the time, or within a few days of the time, that they bear date, answers that, to the best of his recollection, all decrees to concessions which were written by him were written at the time, or within a few days of the time, that they bear date.

Charles Gratiot, sworn, says that André L. Andreville, the claimant, has resided in this country for above twenty years past; that he was a tavern keeper and merchant, and now resides in the town of St. Louis.

July 10, 1810: Present, Lucas, Penrose, and Bates, commissioners. It is the opinion of the Board that this claim ought not to be confirmed.

BERNARD PRATTE, assignee of Elizabeth Due, assignee of Joseph Beauchemin, claiming eight hundred arpents of land, being the one-half of sixteen hundred arpents which was granted by Carlos Dehault Delassus, Lieutenant Governor, to Joseph Beauchemin, by concession bearing date the 30th January, 1800, situate on Peruque creek, district of St. Charles; produces to the Board the record of said concession, and a certified copy of a deed of transfer from Joseph Beauchemin to Mademoiselle Due for the said moiety, dated 5th April, 1804; also, a deed of transfer from the said Babet or Elizabeth Due to claimant, dated 10th April, 1807.

Testimony taken. November 29, 1808. Antoine Cheney, sworn, says that about eight years ago Joseph Beauchemin began to inhabit and cultivate a tract of land in the district of St. Charles, on Peruque creek and the Mississippi, and has continued to inhabit and cultivate the same to the present time.

Claimant produces also a plat of survey of the same by Mackay, certified 10th February, 1804.

July 10, 1810: Present, Lucas, Penrose, and Bates, commissioners. It is the opinion of a majority of the Board that this claim ought not to be confirmed; Clement B. Penrose, commissioner, voting for the confirmation of eight hundred arpents. Said majority declare that, if the concession upon which the above claim is founded had not exceeded eight hundred arpents, they would have voted for a confirmation.

CHARLES GRATIOT, claiming seven thousand and fifty-six arpents of land, situate on river Ohaha; produces to the Board a concession from Don Carlos Dehault Delassus, Lieutenant Governor, for the same, dated 6th January, 1801, stating that claimant should not be compelled to survey said land until there should be neighbors near said land.

July 11, 1810: Present, Penrose and Bates, commissioners. It is the opinion of the Board that this claim ought not to be confirmed.

JOHN MANN, claiming six hundred and forty acres of land, lying on both sides of the river St. François, district of St. Genevieve; produces to the Board a notice of claim, dated 25th June, 1808.

Testimony taken. November 30, 1808. John Callaway, sworn, says that claimant, in the winter of 1802, '3, moved on the place claimed, and inhabited and cultivated the same in 1803; in the fall of said year, sold it to Ezekiel Able; that the widow Pettit moved on the same that fall, as a tenant of said Able, and that said land has been inhabited and cultivated ever since; claimant, in 1803, had a wife and one slave.

July 12, 1810: Present, Lucas, Penrose, and Bates, commissioners. It is the opinion of the Board that this claim ought not to be granted.

WILLIAM DILLON, claiming six hundred and forty arpents of land, situate on the west side of the river St. François, opposite a concession claimed by James Dodson; produces to the Board a notice of claim.

Testimony taken. November 30, 1808. Samuel Campbell, sworn, says that in September, 1803, claimant built a cabin on the tract claimed, moved in it, and continued to reside in it that winter.

July 12, 1810: Present, Lucas, Penrose, and Bates, commissioners. It is the opinion of the Board that this claim ought not to be granted.

WILLIAM CRAWFORD, claiming one thousand one hundred and ninety arpents of land, situate on the river St. Francis, district of St. Genevieve; produces a survey, dated the 8th and certified 13th February, 1806.

Testimony taken. June 25, 1806. John Mathews, sworn, says that he saw claimant on said land about the latter end of July, 1803, that he had then a large field, and had raised a crop; and that he did, prior to and on the 20th December, 1803, actually inhabit and cultivate the same, and had then four children.

Benjamin Petit, sworn, says that he had, on the 20th December, 1803, nine slaves.

Camille Lassus, sworn, says that he was present when claimant obtained permission to settle vacant lands.

June 25, 1806: Present, Penrose and Donaldson, commissioners. The Board grant to the said claimant four hundred and eighty arpents of land, situate as aforesaid, provided so much be found vacant there.

July 12, 1810: Present, Lucas, Penrose, and Bates, commissioners. It is the opinion of the Board that this claim ought not to be granted.

JOSEPH BELCOUR, claiming four hundred arpents of land, situate on district of St. Genevieve, by a concession (as is alleged in his notice) from Don Carlos Dehault Delassus, Lieutenant Governor, dated 18th March, 1800.

Testimony taken. December 1, 1808. Archibald Huddleston, sworn, says that, about nine or ten years ago, he saw claimant working on the place claimed, at two different times, near a cabin, in which he saw claimant's clothes; that the said land was cultivated for the four following years.

July 12, 1810: Present, Lucas, Penrose, and Bates, commissioners. It is the opinion of the Board that this claim ought not to be confirmed.

JESSE CAIN, claiming one mile square of land, situate on river Merrimack, district of St. Louis, it being the place where John Romine lately resided, notice of claim recorded book C, page 517, of the Recorder's Office.

Rufus Easton, being present as claimant's agent, abandons all pretensions of claim to this tract.

July 12, 1810: Present, Lucas, Penrose, and Bates, commissioners. It is the opinion of the Board that this claim ought not to be granted.

PETER BORDEAUX, by his agent, William Russell, claiming seven hundred and fifty arpents of land, situate on district of St. Charles, adjoining the waters of Charette creek; produces to the Board a notice of claim.

Testimony taken. December 15, 1808. John Baptiste Luzon, sworn, says that about seven years ago, claimant inhabited and cultivated in the village of Charette, and ever since; claimant, in 1803, had a wife and four children.

July 12, 1810: Present, Lucas, Penrose, and Bates, commissioners. It is the opinion of the Board that this claim ought not to be granted.

DANIEL LITTLEJOHN, by his agent, William Russell, claiming one thousand two hundred arpents of land, situate in district of St. Charles, waters of Lick branch; produces to the Board a notice to the recorder.

Testimony taken. December 15, 1807. John Crow, sworn, says that claimant built a cabin, and cleared some land in 1804 on the tract claimed, and sowed turnip seed; moved from it same year.

July 12, 1810: Present, Lucas, Penrose, and Bates, commissioners. It is the opinion of the Board that this claim ought not to be granted.

WILLIAM RAMSEY, assignee of John Guion, claiming seven hundred and fifty arpents of land, situate in district of St. Charles, above Sandy creek; produces to the Board a notice of claim.

Testimony taken. December 15, 1807. George Ayrl, sworn, says that John Guion and John Ramsay, built a cabin on the place claimed, in 1801, and inhabited and cultivated it; moved off in the fall of same year; two crops have been raised on the place since by William Ewing and one McHugh.

June 12, 1810: Present, Lucas, Penrose, and Bates, commissioners. It is the opinion of the Board that this claim ought not to be granted.

JOHN LITTEN, by Edward Hempstead, his agent, claiming six hundred and forty acres of land, situate on Sandy creek, district of St. Louis; produces to the Board a notice of claim to the recorder; produces, also, a plat of survey for six hundred and forty acres, dated February 10, 1806.

****

Testimony taken. December 16, 1808. David Byles, sworn, says that claimant inhabited and cultivated the land claimed in 1803 and 1804; claimant was a single man in 1803.

July 12, 1810: Present, Lucas, Penrose, and Bates, commissioners. It is the opinion of the Board that this claim ought not to be granted.

WILLIAM RAMSAY, claiming six hundred and fifty arpents of land, situate on the river Teuque, south side of the Missouri, district of St. Charles; produces to the Board, as a special permission to settle, a concession from Charles D. Delassus, dated November 7, 1799; and a certificate of survey of said land, dated March 28, 1804.

Testimony taken. January 29, 1806. Stephen Jackson, sworn, says that he knew claimant early in the fall of 1803; that he did clear the said land in the spring of 1804; that his family was then on said land; and that he has from that time to this actually inhabited and cultivated the same.

Benjamin Rodgers, sworn, says that he has known claimant from the time he first arrived in this country, which was towards the latter end of October, 1799.

Testimony taken. January 17, 1809. George Ayers, sworn, says that in 1803, a short time before Christmas, claimant built a cabin on the land claimed, and inhabited it; in February following, 1804, he planted apple trees and garden roots; and has inhabited and cultivated said land to this day.

July 14, 1810: Present, Lucas, Penrose, and Bates, commissioners. It is the opinion of a majority of the Board that this claim ought not to be confirmed. Clement B. Penrose, commissioner, voting for the confirmation thereof.

PIERRE CHOUTEAU, claiming a tract of land, situate about twenty arpents above the town of St. Charles, commencing two arpents below a small creek on the Missouri, from thence, up the river, to the first land claimed, and forty arpents back; produces to the Board a concession for the same, from Don Carlos Dehault Delassus, Lieutenant Governor, dated 26th November, 1800; this tract including a tract of ten arpents front, by ten arpents depth, at the mouth of said creek, formerly granted by François Cruzat, Lieutenant Governor, to Augustus Chouteau by concession bearing date 2d April, 1787; and registered in book of registry, No. 4, folio 17, which concession is also produced by claimant; said land granted for the purpose of building a mill within a year and a day, otherwise to be re-united to the domain.

Testimony taken. January 25, 1809. Noel Mongrain, sworn, says that about twenty years ago, claimant commenced the building of a mill-dam upon land, about fifteen arpents above St. Charles; that deponent was himself employed by the claimant during part of the summer; that he assisted in hauling large pieces of timber for constructing a mill; witness recollects that a great deal of clay was hauled for the making of the dam; that, in the spring following, said dam was swept away by a large flood.

Auguste Chouteau, being present, declares, that he gave all his right (to the one hundred arpents claimed by concession given to him,) to his brother, the claimant.

July 13, 1810: Present, Lucas, Penrose, and Bates, commissioners. It is the opinion of the Board that this claim ought not to be confirmed.

JAMES RICHARDSON, claiming four hundred arpents of land, situate on river Maline, district of St. Louis; produces to the Board a concession from Don Carlos Dehault Delassus, Lieutenant Governor, for the same, dated 16th December, 1799; a plat of survey, taken 20th February, 1806.

Testimony taken. January 30, 1809. David Musick, sworn, says that, about nine or ten years ago, claimant built a still-house on the land claimed, and distilled in it about three years, and fenced in about one and a half acres of ground.

July 14, 1810: Present, Lucas, Penrose, and Bates, commissioners. It is the opinion of the Board that this claim ought not to be confirmed.

WILLIAM MASSEY, claiming four hundred and ninety arpents of land, situate on Point Labadie, district of St. Louis; produces to the Board a concession for the same from Charles D. Delassus, Lieutenant Governor, dated 9th September, 1799; and a survey of five hundred and ten arpents, taken 5th March, and certified 20th May, 1800.

Testimony taken. September 17, 1806: Present, Lucas and Donaldson. Antoine Soulard, sworn, says that he knows of nothing that can contradict the date of said concession. The Board reject this claim; are satisfied that the same was granted at the time it bears date.

Testimony taken. January 31, 1809. Jesse Richardson, sworn, says that, nine years ago, August last, claimant came to the country, and has continued to reside here ever since, except the time he returned to Kentucky for his family.

July 14, 1810: Present, Lucas, Penrose, and Bates, commissioners. It is the opinion of the Board that this claim ought not to be granted.

JOHN McKINNEY, claiming six hundred and fifty arpents of land, by virtue of a concession granted by Charles D. Delassus, Lieutenant Governor, dated 20th June, 1800; said land situate on the river Osage, on the north bank of the river Missouri; produces a concession from Charles Dehault Delassus, Lieutenant Governor, bearing date 20th June, 1800, for six hundred and fifty arpents of land, situate on the south side of the river Missouri; also, a plat of survey of the same quantity, on the north side of the Missouri, dated 12th November, 1803, and certified by Antoine Soulard, surveyor particular; said land appears, from the survey, to be situated about two miles below the river Teuque.

Testimony taken. March 29, 1809. James Mackay, sworn, says that he surveyed the aforesaid land, as deputy surveyor; at which time he saw a cabin erected on the same, which claimant told the witness was the cabin of him, said claimant.

Testimony taken. July 16, 1810. William Spencer, sworn, says that, in the fall of the year 1803, he (witness) was on the land claimed, and then saw a good cabin built on the same, some land fenced in, and a few peach and apple trees growing within the said enclosure; that, in the spring of 1804, he went with claimant to assist him to clear away the weeds from around the peach and apple trees, and trim the same; that he has seen the place every year since, and that there were gradual improvements making thereon until 1806, when he saw the daughter and son-in-law of claimant on said land; that the same has been inhabited and cultivated by the claimant ever since, and that at present there is upwards of fifty acres in cultivation.

July 16, 1810: Present, Lucas, Penrose, and Bates, commissioners. It is the opinion of the Board that this claim ought not to be confirmed.

ROBERT MCKINNEY, claiming seven hundred and eighty arpents of land, situate on the river Missouri, in the district of St. Charles; produces to the Board a concession for the same, from Don Carlos Dehault Delassus, Lieutenant Governor, dated 15th June, 1800; a plat of survey, dated 6th November, 1803, and certified 27th December, same year.

Testimony taken. July 16, 1810. John McKinney, sworn, says that he is not personally interested in this claim; that, about the 20th of October, 1804, he (witness) assisted in building a cabin on the land claimed for claimant, and fenced some land in, and sowed wheat therein, and planted apple and peach trees; that, in the year 1805, he sowed some garden seed, and planted corn on said land, which he did for the claimant; further saith that, on the 20th December, 1803, claimant resided in Kentucky.

July 16, 1810: Present, Lucas, Penrose, and Bates, commissioners. It is the opinion of the Board that this claim ought not to be confirmed.

HYACINTH ST. CYR, Jun. claiming four hundred arpents of land, situate in the district of St. Louis; produces to the Board a concession for the same, from Charles D. Delassus, Lieutenant Governor, dated 1st January, 1800; a survey, taken 29th December, 1801, and certified 5th January, 1802.

Testimony taken. September 17, 1806. Antoine Soulard, sworn, says that he knows of nothing contradicting the date of the aforesaid concession, but to the best of his knowledge believes that it was granted at the time it bears date; that Colonel Howard did acknowledge before him, that Hyacinth St. Cyr, the father of claimant, had met with losses for the service of the Government; that said St. Cyr, he well knew, could not be reimbursed for said losses, but that he, the said Colonel Howard, would recommend him to Zenon Trudeau.

Louis Lebeaume, sworn, says that he knows of Zenon Trudeau having promised Hyacinth St. Cyr, the father of claimant, that, in consequence of the losses he had met with, in the fulfilling of his contract with Government for the building of fortifications, he would grant his children lands, as the only compensation he could make him for his losses.

September 17, 1806: Present, Lucas and Donaldson. The Board reject this claim; and are satisfied that the same was granted at the time it bears date.

Testimony taken. January 31, 1809. Hyacinth St. Cyr, Sen., sworn, says that claimant is at present in his twenty-third year, was born in the country, and has always resided in the country, except for six years that he was sent to Canada for his education.

July 16, 1810: Present, Lucas, Penrose, and Bates, commissioners. It is the opinion of the Board that this claim ought not to be confirmed.

LEON N. ST. CYR, claiming four hundred and nine arpents of land, situate in the district of St. Louis; produces to the Board a concession from Charles D. Delassus, Lieutenant Governor, for the same, dated 1st January, 1800; a survey of the same, taken 3d January, and certified 2d March, 1802.

Antoine Soulard's testimony in the foregoing claim applies to this claim; also, same opinion and decision of former Board, as in preceding claim of Hyacinth St. Cyr, Jun.

Testimony taken. January 31, 1809. Hyacinth St. Cyr, Sen. sworn, says that claimant is seventeen or eighteen years of age at this time; was born in the country, and has always resided in it.

July 16, 1810: Present, Lucas, Penrose, and Bates, commissioners. It is the opinion of the Board that this claim ought not to be granted.

ABSALOM KINNERSON, claiming six hundred and forty arpents of land, situate on Bois Bruile, district of St. Genevieve; produces to the Board a notice to the recorder, dated 29th June, 1808; produces, also, a certificate of permission to settle, sworn to by Camille Delassus, as commandant ad interim; said permission on file.

Testimony taken. January 31, 1809. John Smith, sworn, says that claimant came to the country in 1800, and has resided in it ever since; in 1803 claimant had a wife and nine children; claimant never settled on the tract claimed until about eighteen months ago.

July 16, 1810: Present, Lucas, Penrose, and Bates, commissioners. It is the opinion of the Board that this claim ought not to be granted.

MATTHEW RAMEY, claiming one thousand and fifty-six arpents of land, situate on the river Des Peres, district of St. Louis; produces to the Board a plat of survey, dated 21st November, 1805, and certified 27th February, 1806. For permission to settle, see Mackay's list.

Testimony taken. January 31, 1809. John McDonald, sworn, says that in the latter end of 1803, just before or about Christmas, claimant cut house logs, built a camp, and resided on the land, and occasionally worked on the same until 1808, in which year he built a cabin, and raised a crop; died on the land in October, 1808.

July 16, 1810: Present, Lucas, Penrose, and Bates, commissioners. It is the opinion of the Board that this claim ought not to be granted.

CLAIBOURNE RHODES, assignee of David Rowland, claiming four hundred arpents of land, situate on river Cuivre, district of St. Charles; produces to the Board a notice of claim to the recorder; a conveyance from Daniel Rowland to claimant, dated 4th March, 1801.

Testimony taken. January 31, 1809. James Mackay, sworn, says that he saw, held, and read a concession from Zenon Trudeau, Lieutenant Governor, to Daniel Rowland, for four hundred arpents of land, witness believes dated in 1798; said concession called for land situate on river Cuivre, district of St. Charles.

Claimant, sworn, says that Daniel Rowland told him that he had a concession in 1801; says that he never saw it, neither does he know where it is to be found.

Jacob Hostetter, sworn, says that Daniel Rowland inhabited and cultivated on the land claimed in 1800; said Rowland had then a wife and one child.

July 16, 1810: Present, Lucas, Penrose, and Bates, commissioners. It is the opinion of the Board that this claim ought not to be confirmed.

THOMAS WITHERINGTON, claiming five hundred arpents of land, situate on Charette river, district of St. Charles, produces to the Board a concession from Don Carlos Dehault Delassus, Lieutenant Governor, dated 7th November, 1799; a plat of survey, dated 10th November, 1803, certified 5th April, 1804.

Testimony taken. January 31, 1809. John Witherington, son of claimant, sworn, says that, in 1804, claimant went to the place claimed, and laid the foundation of a house, put up two or three logs, and deadened some trees.

July 16, 1810: Present, Lucas, Penrose, and Bates, commissioners. It is the opinion of the Board that this claim ought not to be confirmed.

****

ARTHUR BURNS, Jun., claiming six hundred and forty acres of land, as assignee of Edmund Chandler, situate on river Sandy, district of St. Charles; produces to the Board a notice to the recorder, and a deed of conveyance from said Chandler to claimant, dated 30th December, 1805. For permission to settle see Mackay's list.

Testimony taken. February 3, 1809. Claibourne Rhodes, sworn, says that Edmund Chandler fenced in a piece of ground on the land claimed, (but resided in the neighborhood with witness;) planted watermelons and potatoes on the same in 1803; in 1804, claimant ploughed a piece of land and planted corn, which was never gathered in; said Chandler was a single man in 1803.

July 16, 1810. Present, Lucas, Penrose, and Bates, commissioners. It is the opinion of the Board that this claim ought not to be granted.

PAUL WHITLEY, assignee of Joshua Tansy, claiming three hundred arpents of land, situate on Grand Glaize, district of St. Louis; produces to the Board a concession from Charles D. Delassus, to one Joshua Tansy, dated 1st November, 1799, together with a certificate of survey of said three hundred arpents, dated February 29, 1804; a deed of transfer from Joshua Tansey to claimant, dated February 2, 1804.

Testimony taken. January 25, 1806. Abraham Johnston, sworn, says that claimant did, some time in the spring of 1803, engage a man to work on shares on said land; that accordingly he went on said land, put up a cabin, and after remaining a few months went away and broke his contract; that some part of said land was then fenced up, but that the same was not actually inhabited and cultivated prior to the 20th December, 1803.

Testimony taken. February 11, 1809. Samuel Gilbert, sworn, says that he (witness) has made sugar on the place claimed, for Paul Whitley, for five years past.

January 25, 1806: Present, Lucas and Penrose, and James Lowry Donaldson, commissioners. The Board reject this claim, the said land not being inhabited and cultivated on the 20th December, 1803; they observe, however, that the claimant, in the year 1803, cultivated his mother's plantation; that she had been abandoned by her husband; they further observe that he paid a valuable consideration for said land, and received a deed for the same executed before the commandant; he employed a man to cultivate, on shares, the said land; that the man so employed built a house, cut rails, &c.; was actually inhabiting, and was preparing for the cultivating of said land in the month of April, 1803, but afterwards run away and broke his contract.

July 17, 1810: Present, Penrose and Bates, commissioners. It is the opinion of the Board that this claim ought not to be confirmed.

JACOB MILLER, claiming three hundred and fifty arpents of land, situate on White waters, district of Cape Girardeau; produces to the Board a certificate of permission to settle, list B, on which said claimant is No 32; and a plat of survey, signed B. Cousin, and signed by Antoine Soulard, as received for record.

Testimony taken. Joseph Neyswanger, sworn, says that claimant settled in the year 1804; cleared five or six acres; built a cabin; in the same or following year, claimant sold the improvement and removed to another tract which he had purchased; which latter has an enclosure and cultivation of about ten acres; a cabin and a stable; inhabitation and cultivation to the present day; claimant has a wife and one child.

July 17, 1810: Present, Penrose and Bates, commissioners. It is the opinion of the Board that this claim ought not to be granted.

DANIEL BOLLINGER, son of John, claiming seven hundred and one arpents eighty-nine perches of land, situate on White waters, district of Cape Girardeau; produces to the Board a special permission to settle, list A, on which claimant is No. 104; and a plat of survey certified to be received for record 27th February, 1806, by Antoine Soulard, Surveyor General.

Testimony taken. May 1, 1806. Adam Stotler, sworn, says that claimant proceeded to the settling of said land in the fall of 1803; cut house logs, and began to put up his cabin, which having completed in the spring of 1804, he moved on said land, and has actually inhabited and cultivated it to this day; that he was of the age of twenty-one years and upwards on the 20th December, 1803; and claims no other land in his own name in the country.

July 17, 1810: Present, Penrose and Bates, commissioners. It is the opinion of the Board that this claim ought not to be granted.

GILBERT HECTOR, claiming one hundred and sixteen arpents twenty-five perches of land, situate on the waters of Hubble's creek, district of Cape Girardeau; produces to the Board a special permission to settle, list A, on which claimant is 141; and a plat of survey, dated 3d February, 1806, certified 13th February, same year.

July 17: Present, Penrose and Bates, commissioners. It is the opinion of the Board that this claim ought not to be granted.

JAMES WHITESIDES, assignee of James Williams, claiming four hundred and forty acres of land, situate near Flouresont village, district of St. Louis; produces to the Board a notice to the recorder, dated 16th June, 1808, also a deed of conveyance from said Williams to claimant, dated 12th September, 1805.

Testimony taken. March 28, 1809. William Patterson, sworn, says that, about the year 1797 or 1798, he saw a cabin which was called Williams's cabin, and that it was situated about three hundred yards northeast of Edmond Hodges's house; he also passed said cabin two or three times a week in 1797 and 1798, since when it was removed away; that he, deponent, never saw any person inhabiting it, nor any cultivation near it.

Thomas Hooper, sworn, says that he knew the above named Williams had a claim to land, but does not know where it was situated.

July 23, 1810: Present, Penrose and Bates, commissioners. It is the opinion of the Board that this claim ought not to be granted.

JAMES RICHARDSON, assignee of Hyacinth St. Cyr, claiming nine hundred and nineteen arpents of land, situate on lake Creve Cœur, district of St. Louis; produces to the Board a concession for the same, from Zenon Trudeau, Lieutenant Governor, to said St. Cyr, dated 1st February, 1798; a plat of survey, dated 3d February, 1798, and certified 5th April, 1798; produces also a certified extract of a public sale of the property of Francis St. Cyr, dated 11th July, (that is, sale made,) certified 29th November, 1805; alleged by claimant that the word "Francis" is a clerical error; whereupon the records of the district were brought before the Board and examined, when it appeared from the original documents that the extract has been erroneously made, and that the word Hyacinth should have been written in the place of Francis.

****

Testimony taken. March 30, 1809. Hyacinth St. Cyr, original claimant, sworn, says that he built a cabin of twenty feet square, which cabin was never inhabited; built also a sugar camp on the premises, and made sugar for five or six successive years.

July 23, 1810: Present, Penrose and Bates, commissioners. It is the opinion of the Board that this claim ought not to be confirmed.

THERESA BAROIS, VEUVE LAMEY, AND FRANÇOISE BRAZEAU, VEUVE DE BAPTISTE CHARLEVILLE, claiming sixteen hundred arpents of land, situate on river Des Peres; produces to the Board the record of a concession from Zenon Trudeau, Lieutenant Governor, dated 28th January, 1797; a plat of survey of the same, dated 15th December, 1800, and certified 25th December, same year.

Testimony taken. March 30, 1809. Joseph Charleville, the son, sworn, says that about twelve years ago, witness and a negro went on this tract of land, and built a house, and that about three years ago the premises were cultivated for claimant and constantly to the present time.

July 23, 1810: Present, Penrose and Bates, commissioners. It is the opinion of the Board that this claim ought not to be confirmed.

ANTONIO PRIEUR, claiming under a concession from Charles D. Delassus, for eight hundred arpents of land, dated 1st June, 1801; together with a certificate of survey of the same, dated February 15th, 1804.

The Board inform the claimant that they cannot act on the said claim; but must submit the same to the consideration of Congress.

December 11, 1805: Present, Lucas, Penrose, and Donaldson, commissioners.

July 25, 1810: Present, Lucas, Penrose, and Bates, commissioners. It is the opinion of the Board that this claim ought not to be confirmed.

PIERRE DUMONT, a native of Illinois, and who has no other claim by virtue of any concession ever granted him before; produces a concession from Charles D. Delassus, Lieutenant Governor, for sixteen hundred arpents of land, dated January 19, 1800; certificate of survey of the same, dated March 8, 1804.

July 25, 1810: Present, Lucas, Penrose, and Bates, commissioners. It is the opinion of the Board that this claim ought not to be confirmed.

FRANCIS HOWELL, claiming four hundred arpents of land; produces, as a special permission to settle, a concession from Zenon Trudeau, to one Alexander Andrews, (of whom he, claimant, is assignee,) dated November 10th, 1797; and a certificate of survey of said land, dated December 9, 1799; a deed of transfer of said land, passed before Mackay, executed by said Alexander Andrews to claimant, dated January 19th, 1800.

Testimony taken. January 31, 1806. James Flaugherty, sworn, says that claimant did, some time in 1800, proceed on the establishment of said land, and did, prior to and on the 20th December, 1803, actually inhabit and cultivate the said tract of land.

January 31, 1806: Present, Lucas, Penrose, and Donaldson, commissioners. The Board grants to Francis Howel, the above claimant, four hundred arpents of land, provided so much be found vacant.

July 31, 1810: Present, Lucas, Penrose, and Bates, commissioners. It is the opinion of the Board that this claim ought not to be confirmed. This tract has been granted to Francis Howell, as original claimant.

JOHN SCOTT, assignee of Thomas Johnston, claiming five hundred arpents of land; produces to the Board a concession for the same from Don Carlos Debault Delassus, Lieutenant Governor, to Thomas Johnston, dated 20th October, 1799; also, a survey of the same, dated 30th December, 1799, and certified 11th January, 1799; a deed of transfer from the said Johnston to claimant, dated 11th July, 1800.

Testimony taken. February 11, 1806. James Baldridge, sworn, says that the said land was, prior to and on the 20th December, 1803, actually inhabited and cultivated by the above claimant, who was then the head of a family.

February 11, 1806: Present, Lucas, Penrose, and Donaldson, commissioners. The Board grant to John Scott five hundred arpents of land, situate as aforesaid, as per the above concession.

July 31, 1810: Present, Lucas, Penrose, and Bates, commissioners. It is the opinion of the Board that this claim ought not to be confirmed.

EDWARD YOUNG, claiming one thousand two hundred and six arpents of land, situate on Creve Cœur, district of St. Louis; produces to the Board a certificate of a permission to settle, dated December 10, 1805, and a certificate of survey of said land, dated February 12, 1806.

Testimony taken. 12th February, 1806. John Johnes, sworn, says that the improving of said land never began till 1804, and that claimant has actually cultivated and inhabited the same to this day.

July 31, 1810: Present, Lucas, Penrose, and Bates, commissioners. It is the opinion of the Board that this claim ought not to be granted.

DANIEL BALDRIDGE, claiming eight hundred and fifty arpents of land, situate on the river Peruque, district of St. Charles; produces to the Board a certificate of a permission to settle, granted by Mackay, dated 9th December, 1805, and a certificate of survey of the said land, dated 11th February, 1806.

Testimony taken. February 12, 1806. Daniel Kiethley, sworn, says that claimant proceeded to the establishment of said land in 1803; began the building of a cabin, which was completed in 1804, when he married, moved on said land, and raised a crop thereon, and has actually inhabited and cultivated the same to this day.

July 31, 1810: Present, Lucas, Penrose, and Bates, commissioners. It is the opinion of the Board that this claim ought not to be granted.

WILLIAM SPENCE, claiming two hundred and fifty arpents of land, situate on the river Teuque; produces a special permission to settle; a concession from Charles D. Delassus, Lieutenant Governor, dated January 15, 1800; and a certificate of survey of the same, dated 28th May, 1804.

Testimony taken. February 14, 1806. David Bryan, sworn, says that claimant did, some time in 1803, cut logs for a cabin, and cleared about two arpents of the said land.

July 31, 1810: Present, Lucas, Penrose, and Bates, commissioners. It is the opinion of the Board that this claim ought not to be confirmed.

NATHAN BOON, claiming four hundred and twenty arpents of land, situate on Femme Osage; produces to the Board a concession from Charles D. Delassus, dated December 10, 1799, and a certificate of survey, dated March 28, 1805.

July 31, 1810: Present, Lucas, Penrose, and Bates, commissioners. It is the opinion of the Board that this claim ought not to be confirmed.

MATTHEW LOGAN, claiming eight hundred and fifty arpents of land, situate on the waters of river St. Francis; produces to the Board a certificate of a permission to settle, signed Peter D. Deluziere, dated December 13, 1805, and a certificate of survey of the same, dated 13th February, 1806.

Testimony taken, February 15, 1806. John Callaway, sworn, says that claimant did in 1803 cut logs for the building of a cabin; and that in April, 1804, he put up the same; he had, on the 20th December, 1803, a wife and one child.

July 31, 1810: Present, Lucas, Penrose, and Bates, commissioners. It is the opinion of the Board that this claim ought not to be granted.

WILLIAM NORTH, claiming eight hundred and forty arpents of land, situate on Big river; produces to the Board a certificate of survey of said land, dated February 18, 1806.

Testimony taken. February 20, 1806. Ezekiel Eastus, sworn, says that claimant did, prior to and on the 20th December, 1803, actually inhabit and cultivate the said land.

February 20, 1806: Present, Lucas, Penrose, and Donaldson, commissioners. The Board grant the above claimant eight hundred and fifty arpents of land, provided so much be found vacant there.

July 31, 1810: Present, Lucas, Penrose, and Bates, commissioners. It is the opinion of the Board that this claim ought not to be granted.

JOHN STARNETTER, claiming seven hundred and fifty arpents of land, situate on the waters of Grand river, district of St. Genevieve; produces to the Board a certificate of survey, dated 18th February, 1806.

Testimony taken. February 21, 1806. Robert Estes, sworn, says that claimant settled the land claimed in 1802, at which time he actually inhabited the same; that, in the spring of 1803, being obliged to go abroad on business, and having on said land a large stock, he left a person to cultivate and take charge of the same, during his absence; that he returned on the same in 1804, and has actually cultivated and inhabited the same to this day.

February 21, 1806: Present, Lucas and Penrose, commissioners. The Board conceiving that claimant had no other residence than the said tract of land, and that, when absent, his whole stock was left thereon, consider the same as actual habitation, and therefore grant him seven hundred and fifty arpents of land, situate as aforesaid, provided so much be found vacant there.

July 31, 1810: Present, Lucas, Penrose, and Bates, commissioners. It is the opinion of the Board that this claim ought not to be granted.

JACOB MOSTELLER, claiming seven hundred and fifty arpents of land, situate on Hazel run, waters of Terre Blue, district of St. Genevieve; produces to the Board a certificate of survey of the same, dated February 19, 1806.

Testimony taken. February 21, 1806. Robert Estes, sworn, says that claimant did, prior to and on the 20th December, 1803, actually inhabit and cultivate the said tract of land; is a hatter by trade, and carries on the same on said tract of land; and that he was then of the age of twenty-one years and upwards.

February 21, 1806: Present, Lucas and Penrose, commissioners. The Board grant said claimant seven hundred and fifty arpents of land, situate as aforesaid, provided so much be found vacant there.

July 31, 1810: Present, Lucas, Penrose, and Bates, commissioners. It is the opinion of the Board that this claim ought not to be granted.

ALEXANDER McCOURTNEY, claiming six hundred arpents of land, situate on the Missouri, district of St. Louis; produces to the Board a concession from Charles D. Delassus, Lieutenant Governor, dated November 26, 1799; a certificate of survey of the same, dated 1st March, 1804. The claimant holds no other claims to land, in his own name, in the Territory.

July 31, 1810: Present, Lucas, Penrose, and Bates, commissioners. It is the opinion of the Board that this claim ought not to be confirmed.

JAMES MEEK, claiming five hundred arpents of land, situate on Charette creek, district of St. Charles; produces to the Board a concession from Charles D. Delassus, Lieutenant Governor, dated 6th June, 1803, and a certificate of survey, dated February 28, 1806.

Testimony taken. April 2, 1806. David Kinkead, sworn, says that the said tract of land was settled by one James Clay in 1802; that the same was neither actually inhabited nor cultivated in 1803; and that, in 1804, claimant bought it from said James Clay, and raised a crop thereon in that year; he claims no other land, in his own name, in the Territory.

August 9, 1810: Present, Lucas, Penrose, and Bates, commissioners. It is the opinion of the Board that this claim ought not to be granted.

ADAM McCORD, claiming eight hundred and fifty arpents of land, situate on Charette creek, district of St. Charles; produces to the Board a certificate of survey, dated 28th February, 1803.

Testimony taken. April 2, 1806. William Ramsay, sworn, says that he went on said land in the fall of 1803, built a house, and made a garden; and that he did, in the beginning of 1804, proceed to the improving of the same; raised a crop that year, and actually inhabited and cultivated it to this day.

August 9, 1810: Present, Lucas, Penrose, and Bates, commissioners. It is the opinion of the Board that this claim ought not to be granted.

CLAIBOURNE THOMAS, claiming (as assignee of Charles Gill) seven hundred and fifty-six arpents of land, situate on Sandy creek, district of St. Louis; produces to the Board a certificate of survey, dated February 7, 1806; and a deed of transfer from said Charles Gill and Mary, his wife, to claimant, dated 4th July, 1804.

Testimony taken. April 4, 1806. William Moss, sworn, says that the said Charles Gill did, prior to and on the 20th December, 1803, actually inhabit and cultivate the said tract of land.

April 4, 1806: Present, Lucas and Penrose, commissioners. The Board grant the said claimant, assignee as aforesaid, eight hundred and fifty arpents of land, situate as aforesaid, provided so much be found vacant there.

August 9, 1810: Present, Lucas, Penrose, and Bates, commissioners. It is the opinion of the Board that this claim ought not to be granted.

WILLIAM DRENNON, claiming nine hundred and forty arpents of land, situate on the waters of the Grand Glaize, district of St. Louis; produces to the Board a certificate of survey, dated February 22, 1806.

Testimony taken. April 7, 1806. James Gray, sworn, says that claimant did, prior to and on the 20th December, 1803, actually inhabit and cultivate the said tract of land, and had then a wife and four children.

April 7, 1806: Present, Lucas and Penrose, commissioners. The Board grant the said claimant one thousand and fifty arpents of land, situate as aforesaid, provided so much be found vacant there.

August 9, 1810: Present, Lucas, Penrose, and Bates, commissioners. It is the opinion of the Board that this claim ought not to be granted.

ALEXANDER MCKINNEY, claiming five hundred and fifty arpents of land, situate on the Femme Osage, district of St. Charles; produces to the Board a concession from Charles D. Delassus, Lieutenant Governor, dated June 20, 1800; and a certificate of survey, dated December 27, 1803.

Testimony taken. April 14, 1806. Kinkead Caldwell, sworn, says that he saw the claimant's name on Mackay's list.

David Bryan, sworn, says that claimant improved said tract of land, and raised crops on the same.

August 9, 1810: Present, Lucas, Penrose, and Bates, commissioners. It is the opinion of the Board that this claim ought not to be confirmed.

JOHN MARSHALL, claiming seven hundred and twenty arpents of land, situate on Femme Osage, district of St. Charles; produces to the Board a concession, signed and dated as in the last claim, with a certificate of survey, also dated as aforesaid.

August 9, 1810: Present, Lucas, Penrose, and Bates, commissioners. It is the opinion of the Board that this claim ought not to be confirmed.

PETER SMITH, claiming five hundred arpents of land, situate on Femme Osage, district of St. Charles; produces to the Board a concession for the same from Charles D. Delassus, Lieutenant Governor, dated 24th June, 1800; with a certificate of survey, dated December 27, 1803.

Testimony taken. April 14, 1806. David Bryan, sworn, says that claimant did improve the said land in 1804, and cut house logs; and that he, the witness, raised a small crop of corn on the same.

August 9, 1810: Present, Lucas, Penrose, and Bates, commissioners. It is the opinion of the Board that this claim ought not to be confirmed.

FRANCIS WYATT, claiming eight hundred arpents of land, situate on Femme Osage, district of St. Charles; produces to the Board a concession from Charles D. Delassus, Lieutenant Governor, dated June 20, 1800; a certificate of survey, dated December 27, 1803.

Testimony taken. April 14, 1806. David Bryan, sworn, says that he saw a cabin on said land in 1803; also saw claimant, early in the fall of that year, come on the same.

August 9, 1810: Present, Lucas, Penrose, and Bates, commissioners. It is the opinion of the Board that this claim ought not to be confirmed.

JAMES MONTGOMERY, claiming three hundred arpents of land, situate on Femme Osage, district of St. Charles; produces to the Board a special permission to settle from Charles D. Delassus, Lieutenant Governor, dated 17th June, 1800, and a certificate of survey, dated December 27, 1803.

August 9, 1810: Present, Lucas, Penrose, and Bates, commissioners. It is the opinion of the Board that this claim ought not to be confirmed.

SAMUEL MEEK, claiming five hundred arpents of land, situate on Femme Osage, district of St. Charles; produces a special permission to settle from Charles D. Delassus, Lieutenant Governor, dated 10th June, 1803; and a certificate of survey, dated February 27, 1804.

Testimony taken. April 14, 1806. David Bryan, sworn, says that one William Lynn did, some time in 1802, proceed to the improving of said tract, and cleared about seven arpents of the same, and raised a crop; that afterwards, to wit, in 1803, he sold his improvement to claimant, who put up fences in that year; and further, that he, the witness, did raise flax on the same in the year 1804.

August 9, 1810: Present, Lucas, Penrose, and Bates, commissioners. It is the opinion of the Board that this claim ought not to be granted.

JAMES MILLS, representatives of, claiming one hundred and seventy-five arpents forty-seven perches of land, situate on Hubble's creek, district of Cape Girardeau; produces to the Board a plat of survey, signed B. Cousin, and certified to be received for record, 27th February, 1806, by Antoine Soulard, Surveyor General.

Testimony taken. April 15, 1805. James Earle, sworn, says that one Moses Hurley did, some time in the year 1798, settle said tract of land, and actually inhabited and cultivated the same until the year 1801; then he sold the same to the said James Mills, who moved on it, and raised a crop thereon that year; that he had obtained a verbal permission from the commandant Lorimier to settle on the same, and was about obtaining a concession or order of survey for said land when he died in the year 1802.

Testimony taken. June 4, 1808. (By Frederick Bates, commissioner at Cape Girardeau.)

John McCarty, sworn, says that this land was settled and cultivated in the year 1799; a cabin (a very good one) built, and the inhabitation and cultivation continued ever since, to the present time; ten or twelve acres now in cultivation at this time.

April 15, 1805: Present, Lucas and Donaldson, commissioners. The Board are satisfied that the said claimants are entitled by the act of inhabitation and cultivation to the said tract of land, but are obliged to reject it for want of a warrant or order of survey.

August 9, 1810: Present, Lucas, Penrose, and Bates, commissioners. It is the opinion of the Board that this claim ought not to be granted.

DAVID DELAUNEY, claiming eight hundred arpents of land, situate on the waters of the river Renaud, district of St. Charles; produces to the Board a concession from Charles D. Delassus, without any condition expressed in the same, dated January 8, 1800, and a survey of the same, taken 3d January, and certified 15th April, 1804.

Testimony taken. May 2, 1806. Antoine Soulard, being sworn true answers to give, &c.

Question. Were you the surveyor of Upper Louisiana under the Spanish Government?

Answer. Yes.

Question. Was it any part of the duties imposed on you by the Spanish laws and the functions of your office, to obey the orders of the Lieutenant Governor of the province, without any regard to their legality or illegality?

Answer. Yes; the Lieutenant Governor was accountable for it.

Question. From whom did you derive your appointment?

Answer. From the Governor General of Lower Louisiana, Baron De Carondelet.

Question. Is that your hand-writing? (showing him the aforesaid concession.)

Answer. I believe it is.

Question. Do you recollect when that was written, and is it your belief that it was written at the time it bears date?

Here the witness refused to answer; whereupon, he was asked by the Board whether he meant to give similar answers to the questions in all similar cases, and answered, yes.

August 18, 1810: Present, Penrose and Bates, commissioners. It is the opinion of the Board that this claim ought not to be confirmed.

DAVID DELAUNEY, claiming seven thousand and fifty-six arpents of land, situate in the district of St. Charles; produces to the Board a concession from Charles D. Delassus, Lieutenant Governor, without any condition expressed therein, dated May 9, 1800, and a survey of the same, dated December 25, 1803, and certified 20th January, 1804.

Testimony taken. May 2, 1806. Antoine Soulard, sworn, the same questions as in the foregoing claim were put to the deponent, to which he gave the same answers. Further proof required.

James St. Vrain was in the above two claims, sworn, who said that the above two concessions were granted at the time they bear date; that Charles D. Delassus (his, the witness's brother) informed him that he had been instructed by Gayoso, to grant lands to such respectable French emigrants as should come to this country; that claimant arrived at St. Genevieve, towards the latter end of 1799; that he, the witness, being then there with Delassus, the then Lieutenant Governor, this last informed him (the witness) that he wished much to have claimant at St. Louis, and requested of him (the witness) that he would endeavor to persuade him (claimant) to go to that place; informing him, at the same time, that he had it in his power to do much for him, and that he would reward him in lands, having received orders to that effect.

August 18, 1810: Present, Penrose and Bates, commissioners. It is the opinion of the Board that this claim ought not to be confirmed.

FRANCIS SOUCIER, claiming eight thousand eight hundred arpents of land, situate on the Mississippi, district of St. Charles; produces a concession from Charles D. Delassus, without any condition expressed in the same, dated September 18, 1799, and a survey of one thousand arpents, dated January 30, 1804, and certified 15th February, 1804; and another survey of one thousand arpents, dated May 1, 1805.

Testimony taken. May 2, 1806. Anthony Soulard, sworn. The same questions being put to him, he gave the same answers.

It was further proved to the satisfaction of the Board, that claimant is father of a family composed of himself, wife, and about fifteen children; was commandant of the Portage des Sioux for about eight years, for which he received no other compensation than the perquisites of office, which were trifling, and seldom paid; and, further, that he claims no other land in his own name in the Territory but a farm of four hundred arpents, now under cultivation. Further proof required.

August 18, 1810: Present, Penrose and Bates, commissioners. It is the opinion of the Board that this claim ought not to be confirmed.

PETER CHOUTEAU, assignee of Charles Tayon, Jun., claiming ten thousand arpents of land, situate on the river Renud, district of St. Charles; produces to the Board a concession from Charles Dehault Delassus, Lieutenant Governor, without any condition inserted in the same, dated October 15, 1799; a survey of the same, dated February 6, 1804, and certified on the 25th of the same month and year; and a deed of transfer of the same from the said Tayon to Peter Chouteau, dated January 3, 1804.

In this case the Board required that the age of claimant at the time of obtaining the concession should be proved, which was refused.

May 3, 1806. It appeared from the testimony of Antoine Soulard and Auguste Chouteau, that Mr. Charles Tayon had rendered services to the Spanish Government from the year 1770; that he was second in command at the siege of St. Joseph, which he contributed to take; that afterwards, from his merit, he received a commission of second lieutenant; that he was commandant of St. Charles from the year 1792 to the year 1804, during which time he rendered many services to Government, in operations against the Indians, training the militia, and protecting the district; that he never received any compensation, except eleven dollars a month as lieutenant, and his fees of office, which were trifling and seldom paid, exclusive of the lands claimed by him and family; that he spent a great part of his own property in his public employment, and appeared to have devoted himself to the interests of the province. The Board was satisfied that Mr. Charles Tayon, the father of the original proprietor, Francis Tayon, Jun., was an active and meritorious officer.

May 3, 1806: Present, Lucas, Penrose, and Donaldson, commissioners. The Board reject this claim, and is of opinion that, although it appears that the decree is antedated, yet, from testimony and circumstances, it hath not been antedated for fraudulent design, but merely to make the date of the above correspond with the date of the petition; and further, they are satisfied that the said decree or order of survey was issued before the 1st of October, 1800.

August 18, 1810: Present, Penrose and Bates, commissioners. It is the opinion of the Board that this claim ought not to be confirmed.

PETER CHOUTEAU, assignee of Elisha Herrington, assignee of Charles Tayon, Jun., claiming five hundred and ten arpents of land, situate on the river Dardenne, district of St. Charles; produces to the Board a concession from Zenon Trudeau, dated January 28, 1798; a survey of the same, dated the 8th and certified the 15th January, 1800; a deed of transfer of the same from the said Charles Tayon, Jun., to the said Elisha Herrington, dated 15th September, 1802; and a transfer from the said Elisha Herrington to the claimant, dated January 10, 1804. The age of the said Charles Tayon, Jun., at the time of obtaining said concession, was required to be proved, which was refused.

The Board applies here the aforesaid remarks on the testimony of Antoine Soulard and Auguste Chouteau.

August 18, 1810: Present, Penrose and Bates, commissioners. It is the opinion of the Board that this claim ought not to be confirmed.

FRANCIS BEATY, claiming five hundred and forty-eight arpents of land, situate on the river St. Francis, district of St. Genevieve; produces to the Board a certificate of survey of the same, dated February 26, 1806.

Testimony taken. August 5, 1806. Benjamin Pettit, sworn, says that claimant settled the said tract of land in the year 1802; and did, prior to and on the 20th December, 1803, actually inhabit and cultivate the same; had then a wife and three children.

William Johnston, sworn, says that Camille Delassus informed him that, when commandant, by interim, of New Bourbon, he had permitted claimant to settle on said tract of land.

May 5, 1806: Present, Penrose and Donaldson, commissioners. The Board grant the said claimant three hundred and fifty arpents of land, situate as aforesaid.

August 18, 1810: Present, Penrose and Bates, commissioners. It is the opinion of the Board that this claim ought not to be granted.

PETER CHOUTEAU, Sen., claiming seven thousand and fifty-six arpents of land, situate on the river St. Augustin, district of St. Charles; produces to the Board a concession from Zenon Trudeau, dated January 8, 1798, and a survey of the same, taken the 17th and certified the 29th December, 1803.

Testimony taken. May 5, 1806. Auguste Chouteau, sworn, says that he understood, about the time the above concession bears date, from his brother, the above claimant, that he had received such a concession; that he knew of his obtaining many concessions.

August 18, 1810: Present, Penrose and Bates, commissioners. It is the opinion of the Board that this claim ought not to be confirmed.

May 5, 1806: Present, Penrose and Donaldson, commissioners. The Board reject this claim, and are satisfied that it was granted at the time it bears date.

PETER CHOUTEAU, Jun., claiming an island in the river Missouri, called Lasso's island; produces to the Board a concession from Charles Dehault Delassus, Lieutenant Governor, dated January 18, 1800, and bearing no terms or conditions whatever.

Testimony taken. May 5, 1806. Marie P. Leduc, sworn, says that claimant was, at the time of obtaining said concession, about fifteen or sixteen years of age, and was born in this country.

James St. Vrain, sworn, says that he, the witness, arrived in this country in the year 1793; that, from the intimacy between him and Zenon Trudeau, and, after him, Charles Dehault Delassus, the brother to the witness, he was in the habit of frequently visiting these two commandants; that he heard them repeatedly say that they had received orders from their Government to grant to claimant's father and children lands; that he saw those orders; that he could not say positively that he saw any concession granted to any of claimant's family, prior to October, 1800; that he had heard Peter Chouteau, Sen., claimant's father, say that he had obtained a number of concessions for him and his children, and that, prior to October, 1800, he knows of claimant having obtained a concession for said island, but does not say positively when; knows of many important services rendered by Peter Chouteau, claimant's father, to Government, and believes he never received any other compensation for the same but such concessions as might be granted to him or his children.

August 18, 1810: Present, Penrose and Bates, commissioners. It is the opinion of the Board that this claim ought not to be confirmed.

WIDOW DUBREUIL, claiming seven thousand and fifty-six arpents of land, situate in the district of St. Charles; produces to the Board a concession from Charles Dehault Delassus, dated 6th November, 1799, and a survey and plat of the same, taken February 14th, and certified 5th March, 1804.

Testimony taken. May 6, 1806. James St. Vrain, sworn, says that he applied, at the request of claimant, to the Lieutenant Governor for the said concession; that the same was, to his certain knowledge, granted prior to October, 1800; that claimant is the mother of ten children, one of the oldest inhabitants in the country, and claims no other land in her own name in the Territory; and further, that he verily believes that her late husband never obtained a concession for lands in this country.

May 6, 1806: Present, Penrose and Donaldson. The Board are satisfied, from the above testimony, that the above concession is not antedated.

August 18, 1810: Present, Penrose and Bates, commissioners. It is the opinion of the Board that this claim ought not to be confirmed.

ANTOINE SAUGRAIN, claiming twenty thousand arpents of land, situate in the district of St. Charles; produces to the Board a concession from Zenon Trudeau to claimant, dated November 9, 1797; a survey of four thousand and six arpents, situate on the waters of the Missouri, dated December 27, 1803, and certified January 28, 1804; and another survey of three thousand arpents, situate on the waters of the Mississippi, dated January 7, and certified February 15, 1804.

Claimant produces a letter from Zenon Trudeau to him, inviting him to the country, dated September 12, 1797.

May 10, 1806: Present, Clement B. Penrose, commissioner. The Board reject this claim, and observe that they are satisfied that the above concession was granted at the time it bears date, and is *bona fide*, but not duly, registered. Approved the above proceedings.

August 18, 1810: Present, Penrose and Bates, commissioners. It is the opinion of the Board that this claim ought not to be confirmed.

ISRAEL DODGE, claiming one thousand arpents of land, situate in the district of St. Genevieve; produces to the Board a concession from Zenon Trudeau, dated February 1, 1798, and a survey of the same, taken 10th and cerfied 27th February, 1798.

Testimony taken. May 10, 1806. Camille Lassus, sworn, says that claimant built a very large house on said land about twelve months ago, to the raising whereof he, the witness, assisted him, the said claimant; that he had then a field under fence, saw some fruit trees on the same, and knows that claimant had, prior to that time, raised a crop of turnips and potatoes on the said land.

August 18, 1810: Present, Penrose and Bates, commissioners. It is the opinion of the Board that this claim ought not to be confirmed.

JOHN MULANPHY, assignee of Joseph Lacroix, claiming six hundred arpents of land, situate at the Prairie du Bœuf, district of St. Louis; produces a concession for the same to one Francis St. Cyr from Charles D. Delassus, dated 1st day of ————, 1800, and a certificate of survey of the same, dated 9th January, 1802; a certificate of public sale, by order of commandant, dated 28th April, 1805; and a deed of transfer of the same from the said Joseph Lacroix to claimant, dated 31st May, 1805.

Testimony taken. May 12, 1806. Pascal Cerré, sworn, says that he never heard of a concession for the aforesaid tract of land until about three or four years ago, when the same was surveyed; and that it never was inhabited or cultivated.

August 18, 1810: Present, Penrose and Bates, commissioners. It is the opinion of the Board that this claim ought not to be confirmed.

JAMES ST. VRAIN, assignee of Jean Baptiste Ambroise Doval, dit Degroseillier, claiming five thousand and fifty-six arpents; and JEAN BAPTISTE AMBROISE DOVAL, dit Degroseillier, claiming two thousand arpents of land; making, together, a tract of seven thousand and fifty-six arpents of land, situate in the district of St. Charles; produce a concession from Charles D. Delassus, Lieutenant Governor, for the same, dated November 19, 1799, and a survey of the same, taken 15th February, and certified 20th March, 1804; a deed of transfer of the same, dated 15th July, 1803.

Testimony taken. May 23, 1806. Charles Sanguinett, sworn, says, that when Zenon Trudeau was commandant, the said Doval informed him that he had the promise of a concession for an island adjoining the witness's land; and that some time afterwards, and upwards of six years ago, he informed him he had received a concession from Charles D. Delassus; that he (the witness) and the said Doval are neighbors, on terms of intimacy, and are in the habit of communicating on their private concerns.

August 18, 1810: Present, Penrose and Bates, commissioners. It is the opinion of the Board that this claim ought not to be confirmed.

DANIEL CLARK, claiming five thousand arpents of land, situate at a point of the river Lutre, district of St. Charles; produces a grant for the same from the Baron de Carondelet, dated July 27, 1797; a certificate from Antoine Soulard that the land prayed for and granted as above is not vacant, dated 17th December, 1799; and a new warrant of survey from Charles D. Delassus, in consequence of the above certificate, dated 5th January, 1800; a survey of said five thousand arpents, taken 5th March, and certified 1st May, 1801.

June 16, 1806: Present, Lucas, Penrose, and Donaldson, commissioners. This claim being unsupported by actual inhabitation and cultivation, the Board reject the same, and observe that the above concession is neither antedated nor fraudulent, and that the said last warrant of survey is duly registered.

August 18, 1810: Present, Penrose and Bates, commissioners. The concession in this claim from Don Carlos Dehault Delassus, Lieutenant Governor, is not duly registered, as stated. It is the opinion of the Board that this claim ought not to be confirmed.

DANIEL CLARK, assignee of Auguste Chouteau, claiming seven thousand and fifty-six arpents of land, situate at the river Aux Vases, district of St. Charles; produces to the Board a concession, from Zenon Trudeau, dated 25th January, 1798; a survey of the same, dated 17th March, and certified 1st May, 1801; and a deed of transfer of the same, dated 8th September, 1804.

Testimony taken. June 16, 1806. Auguste Chouteau, sworn, says that he is no wise interested in the said tract of land, and that he received the above concession at the time it bears date.

June 16, 1806: Present, Lucas, Penrose, and Donaldson, commissioners. This claim being unsupported by actual inhabitation and cultivation, the Board reject the same, and observe that the aforesaid concession is not duly registered, but that the same is neither antedated nor fraudulent.

August 18, 1810: Present, Penrose and Bates, commissioners. It is the opinion of the Board that this claim ought not to be confirmed.

DANIEL CLARK, assignee of Baptiste Champlain, claiming sixteen hundred arpents of land, situate on the waters of the river Cuivre, district of St. Charles; produces to the Board a concession from Charles D. Delassus, dated October 28, 1799; a survey of the same, dated 19th February and certified 8th March, 1804.

June 16: Present, Lucas, Penrose, and Donaldson, commissioners. The Board reject this claim; they are satisfied that the said concession is neither antedated nor fraudulent, but that the same is not duly registered.

August 18, 1810: Present, Penrose and Bates, commissioners. It is the opinion of the Board that this claim ought not to be confirmed.

DANIEL CLARK, assignee of Louis Charboneau, claiming sixteen hundred arpents of land, situate as aforesaid; produces a concession from Charles D. Delassus, dated January 19, 1800; a survey of the same, taken 19th February, and certified 8th March, 1804; and a deed of transfer of the same, dated 12th September, 1804.

June 16, 1806: Present, Lucas, Penrose, and Donaldson. The Board reject this claim, and require further proof of the date of the aforesaid concession, the same not being duly registered.

August 18, 1810: Present, Penrose, and Bates, commissioners. It is the opinion of the Board that this claim ought not to be confirmed.

DANIEL CLARK, assignee of Francis La Riviere, claiming sixteen hundred arpents of land, situate as aforesaid; produces to the Board a concession from Charles D. Delassus, dated 28th October, 1799, and not duly registered; a survey of the same, taken 19th February, certified 8th March, 1804; and a deed of transfer of the same, dated 13th September, 1804.

June 16, 1806. The Board reject this claim, and call for further proof of the date of said concession: Lucas, Penrose, and Donaldson, commissioners, being present.

August 18, 1810: Present, Penrose and Bates, commissioners. It is the opinion of the Board that this claim ought not to be confirmed.

DANIEL CLARK, assignee of Vincent Guitard, claiming eight hundred arpents of land, situate on the Mississippi river, district of St. Louis; produces to the Board a concession, not duly registered, from Charles D. Delassus, dated November 8, 1799; a survey of the same, taken 5th February, and certified 8th March, 1804; and a deed of transfer of the same, dated 8th September, 1804.

June 16, 1806: Present, Lucas, Penrose, and Donaldson, commissioners. The Board reject this claim, and are satisfied that the above concession is neither antedated nor fraudulent.

August 18, 1810: Present, Penrose and Bates, commissioners. It is the opinion of the Board that this claim ought not to be confirmed.

DANIEL CLARK, assignee of Augustin Gamache, claiming sixteen hundred arpents of land, situate on the river Merrimack, district of St. Louis; produces to the Board a concession, not duly registered, from Charles D. Delassus dated 18th December, 1799; a survey of the same, taken 17th January, and certified 29th same month, 1804; and a deed of transfer of the same, dated September 11, 1804.

June 16, 1806: Present, Lucas, Penrose, and Donaldson, commissioners. The Board reject this claim, and require further proof of the date of the above concession. The Board remark, as to the above last five preceding claims of Daniel Clark, that a letter of Daniel Clark was produced to the Board, which proved, to their satisfaction, that Mr. Delassus, the former commandant, had been employed by Mr. Clark to purchase lands for him in this country, and these claims were purchased by Mr. Delassus, for the account of Clark, by private contract, between Mr. Delassus and the five original grantees; that the purchase money of the same was paid by Mr. Auguste Chouteau, on account of Daniel Clark, upon orders drawn on him by Mr. Delassus.

August 18, 1810: Present, Penrose and Bates, commissioners. It is the opinion of the Board that this claim ought not to be confirmed.

ANTOINE DIEL, assignee of Stephen Pagget, claiming one hundred and fifty arpents of land, situate on river Aux Vases, district of St. Genevieve; produces to the Board a concession from Zenon Trudeau, dated September 1, 1797; and a certificate of survey, dated September 1, 1799; transfer 23d February, 1806.

Testimony taken. June 20, 1806. St. James Beauvais, sworn, says that the said Stephen Pagget settled the said tract of land for sugar making; built a furnace and put up kettles; about ten years ago built a house on the same, and lived thereon, when engaged in sugar making.

June 20, 1806: Present, Penrose and Donaldson, commissioners. The Board reject this claim for want of actual inhabitation and cultivation, prior to and on the 1st day of October, 1800, and of a duly registered warrant of survey.

August 18, 1810: Present, Penrose and Bates, commissioners. It is the opinion of the Board that this claim ought not to be confirmed.

WIDOW LALUMANDIERE, representatives of, claiming two hundred and forty arpents of land; situate at the river Aux Vases, district of St. Genevieve; produces to the Board a concession from Zenon Trudeau, dated February 1, 1798; and a survey of the same, dated 1st and certified 15th March, 1798.

Testimony taken. June 20, 1806. St. James Beauvais, sworn, says that the said Lalumandiere settled said tract of land about seven or eight years ago; built a cabin thereon, erected sugar works, and was in the habit of yearly inhabiting the same, when engaged in sugar making; that is to say, from January to March.

June 20, 1806: Present, Penrose and Donaldson, commissioners. The Board reject this claim for want of a duly registered warrant of survey, and also for want of actual inhabitation and cultivation, prior to and on the 1st of October, 1800.

August 18, 1810: Present, Penrose and Bates, commissioners. It is the opinion of the Board that this claim ought not to be confirmed.

PIERRE AUBUCHON, claiming two by forty arpents of land, situate on Lower Prairie, district of St. Genevieve; produces to the Board a concession from Zenon Trudeau, (not duly registered) dated November 13, 1797; a survey of the same, taken February 24, and certified April 17, 1798.

Testimony taken. June 20, 1806. St. James Beauvais, sworn, says that claimant did, about five or six years ago, make a park on said land, and fenced in the same.

June 20, 1806: Present, Penrose and Donaldson, commissioners. The Board reject this claim, the same being unsupported by actual inhabitation and cultivation, and observe that the said concession is neither antedated nor fraudulent.

August 18, 1810: Present, Penrose and Bates, commissioners. It is the opinion of the Board that this claim ought not to be confirmed.

FRANCIS MOREAU, representatives of, assignee of Francis Poillevre, claiming one thousand six hundred arpents of land, situate on waters of the river Merrimack, district of St. Genevieve; produces to the Board a duly registered concession from Zenon Trudeau, dated October 5, 1793; a survey of the same, dated 15th March, and certified 10th May, 1803; and a deed of transfer of the same, executed before Francis Valle, the commandant, dated 16th February, 1803.

August 18, 1810: Present, Penrose and Bates, commissioners. It is the opinion of the Board that this claim ought not to be confirmed.

FRANCIS JANIS, claiming thirty arpents of land, situate on the river Aux Vases, district of St. Genevieve; produces to the Board a petition to Zenon Trudeau for the same, stating his intention to establish a sugar camp, and the concession granted, in consequence of the said petition by Zenon Trudeau, dated 25th April, 1798; a survey of the same, dated 13th, and certified 30th May, 1799.

Testimony taken. June 20, 1806. Joseph Pratte, sworn, says that claimant put up sugar works on said land about seven years ago, built a house on the same, and has actually inhabited the same every year, when engaged in sugar making.

June 20, 1806: Present, Penrose and Donaldson, commissioners. The Board reject this claim for want of actual inhabitation and cultivation, prior to and on the 1st October, 1800, and of a duly registered warrant of survey; they observe that the above concession is neither antedated nor fraudulent.

August 18, 1810: Present, Penrose and Bates, commissioners. It is the opinion of the Board that this claim ought not to be confirmed.

BENJAMIN LACHANCE, claiming four hundred arpents of land, situate on the waters of Grand river, district of St. Genevieve; produces to the Board a concession from Charles D. Delassus, (not duly registered) dated May 8, 1800, and a survey of the same, taken 18th February, and certified 3d March, 1804.

June 20, 1806: Present, Penrose and Donaldson, commissioners. This claim being unsupported by actual inhabitation and cultivation, the Board reject the same; and observe that claimant was, at the time of obtaining said concession, under age; and claims no other land in his own name in the Territory. They require further proof of the date of said concession.

August 18, 1810: Present, Penrose and Bates, commissioners. It is the opinion of the Board that this claim ought not to be confirmed.

BAPTISTE JANIS, claiming four hundred arpents of land, situate on the river establishment, district of St. Genevieve; produces to the Board a certified copy of a permission to settle from Charles D. Delassus, dated November 15, 1800, and a survey of three hundred and eighty-three arpents taken 22d and certified 27th February, 1806.

Testimony taken. June 23, 1806. Jacques Guibourd, sworn, says that the aforesaid claimant built a cabin on the land claimed in 1800; cleared about five or six acres of the same; raised a crop on the same in 1802, and that the same was actually inhabited and cultivated for claimant's use, by his slaves, prior to and on the 20th December, 1803; and that claimant went yearly on the same with his family, at the time of harvest; had on the 20th December, 1803, a wife and eight children and five slaves.

August 23, 1810: Present, Lucas and Penrose, commissioners. It is the opinion of the Board that this claim ought not to be granted.

ROWLAND BOYD, claiming seven hundred and forty-eight arpents and sixty-eight perches of land, situate on the waters of the Saline, district of St. Genevieve; produces to the Board a survey of the same, taken 19th December, 1805, certified 26th February, 1806.

Testimony taken. June 23, 1806. Amos Rowark, sworn, says that one Boyce settled the said tract of land in the year 1801, and remained thereon until the spring of 1803, that the same was prior to and on the 20th December, 1803, actually inhabited and cultivated by claimant, who had then a wife and six children.

Joseph Tucker, sworn, says that the aforesaid Boyce had obtained a permission to settle from commandant; that having sold the same to one John Duval, he applied anew to commandant for a new permission to settle on vacant lands, which was granted him, and that the said John Duval sold his said permission to claimant.

June 23, 1806: Present, Penrose and Donaldson, commissioners. The Board being satisfied that claimant had a permission to settle, grant him five hundred arpents of land, situate as aforesaid, provided so much be found vacant there, and order a new survey of the same.

August 23, 1810: Present, Lucas and Penrose, commissioners. It is the opinion of the Board that this claim ought not to be granted.

THOMAS MADDON, claiming one thousand five hundred arpents of land, situate on the river Aux Vases, district of St. Genevieve; produces to the Board a concession from Zenon Trudeau, dated January 29, 1799; and a survey of the same, taken September 23, 1805, and certified 27th February, 1806.

Testimony taken. June 23, 1806. Joseph Westover, sworn, says that he did, in August, 1803, begin the building of a mill on the said tract of land; that some time prior to that, to wit, on Ash Wednesday in the year 1800, having gone on the said land to seek for a mill seat he was fired at by a party of Indians; that in consequence thereof claimant, who had intended to proceed to the building the said mill, gave up the idea of so doing for some time; that, in 1803, he did build the said mill; that he had on said land a cabin, in which the men engaged in the building as aforesaid, then lived; that the said mill was completed in 1804, when he began the cultivating of said land, and that the same has been actually inhabited and cultivated to this day. Claimant was at the time of obtaining said concession the head of a family.

June 23, 1806: Present, Penrose and Donaldson, commissioners. The Board reject this claim and observe that the aforesaid concession is neither antedated nor fraudulent; but that the same is not duly registered.

August 23, 1810: Present, Lucas, Penrose, and Bates, commissioners. It is the opinion of the Board that this claim ought not to be confirmed.

THOMAS MADDON, Jun., claiming eight hundred arpents of land, situate on the river Joachim, district of St. Genevieve; produces to the Board a concession from Charles D. Delassus, dated 30th December, 1799; a survey taken July 20, 1802, and certified 6th September, 1803.

June 23, 1806: Present, Penrose and Donaldson, commissioners. This claim being unsupported by actual inhabitation and cultivation, the Board reject the same, and require further proof of the date of said concession.

August 23, 1810: Present, Lucas and Penrose, commissioners. It is the opinion of the Board that this claim ought not to be granted.

THOMAS MADDON, Sen., claiming six thousand arpents of land, situate in the district of St. Genevieve; produces to the Board a concession for the same, from Charles D. Delassus, dated January 15, 1800; a certificate of survey of two thousand arpents, dated 14th December, 1805; and a further warrant of survey for four thousand arpents in consequence of the said claimant not having found more than two thousand arpents, in compliance with the aforesaid concession, the said warrant dated 15th March, 1800; and another certificate of survey of four thousand arpents, dated December 1, 1803.

June 23, 1806: Present, Penrose and Donaldson, commissioners. The Board reject this claim and call for further proof of the date of said concession; they observe, that the said claimant had, at the time of obtaining the said concession, a wife and seven children, and seven slaves; a surveyor of the said district, in which capacity he acted from the year 1797 until the change of Government.

August 23, 1810: Present, Lucas and Penrose, commissioners. It is the opinion of the Board that this claim ought not to be confirmed.

RICHARD MADDON, claiming eight hundred arpents of land, situate on the north branch of the Saline, district of St. Genevieve; produces to the Board a concession from Zenon Trudeau, to said claimant, for eight hundred arpents of land, dated April 18, 1798; and a survey of the same, taken 12th and certified 27th February, 1806.

June 23, 1806: Present, Penrose and Donaldson, commissioners. The Board reject this claim, and observe that claimant was, at the time of obtaining said concession, under age; that said concession was granted at the time it bears date; that the same is not duly registered.

August 23, 1810: Present, Lucas and Penrose, commissioners. It is the opinion of the Board that this claim ought not to be confirmed. John B. C. Lucas, commissioner, declares that he does not concur in opinion with the former Board, in the present case, respecting the satisfaction which the said former Board expresses, that the concession was issued at the time it bears date; the said commissioner declaring, at the same time, that he does not contend any thing contrary to the opinion of the said former Board as before adverted to, but forbears giving any opinion on the said points, and leaves the whole to rest upon such written and parole evidence as has been adduced in support thereof.

THOMAS MADDON, Jun., claiming eight hundred arpents of land, situate as aforesaid; produces to the Board a concession from Zenon Trudeau, dated as aforesaid, and a survey of the same taken and certified as aforesaid.

June 23, 1806: Present, Penrose and Donaldson, commissioners. The Board reject this claim, and remark as in the foregoing claim of Richard Maddon.

August 23, 1810: Present, Lucas and Penrose, commissioners. It is the opinion of the Board that this claim ought not to be confirmed. John B. C. Lucas, commissioner, remarks as in the foregoing claim of Richard Maddon.

****

JAMES MADDON, claiming eight hundred arpents of land, situate as aforesaid; produces to the Board a concession from Zenon Trudeau, dated as aforesaid, and a survey of the same taken and certified as aforesaid.

June 23, 1806: Present, Penrose and Donaldson, commissioners. The Board reject this claim, and remark as in the two foregoing claims of Richard and Thomas Maddon.

August 23, 1810: Present, Lucas and Penrose, commissioners. It is the opinion of the Board that this claim ought not to be confirmed. John B. C. Lucas, commissioner, remarks as in the two foregoing claims of Richard and Thomas Maddon.

ALBERT TISON, assignee of Andrew Chartrand, claiming eight hundred arpents of land, situate on the waters of the river Cuivre, district of St. Charles; produces to the Board a concession from Charles D. Delassus, for eight hundred arpents, dated 18th June, 1800; a survey and plat of the same, taken 13th February, and certified 20th March, 1804; and a deed of transfer of the same, dated 3d January, 1804.

May 8, 1806: Present, Penrose and Donaldson, commissioners. The Board require further proof. Witness on the part of the United States absent. The Board reject this claim, and observe that the concession or warrant of survey is not duly registered.

August 27, 1810: Present, Lucas, Penrose, and Bates, commissioners. It is the opinion of the Board that this claim ought not to be confirmed.

ALBERT TISON, assignee of Gabriel Constant, claiming eight hundred arpents of land, situate on the waters of the river Cuivre; produces to the Board a concession from Charles D. Delassus to said Constant, for eight hundred arpents, dated 24th March, 1800; a survey plat and certificate, dated as aforesaid; and a deed of transfer, dated 5th January, 1804.

The Board require further proofs.

Witness on the part of the United States.

Gabriel Constant, sworn, says that he never applied for the aforesaid concession; that claimant offered him one, but cannot tell when.

May 8, 1806: Present, Penrose and Donaldson, commissioners. The Board reject this claim; the said concession is not duly registered.

August 27, 1810: Present, Lucas, Penrose, and Bates, commissioners. It is the opinion of the Board that this claim ought not to be confirmed.

ALBERT TISON, assignee of Joseph Denoyer, claiming eight hundred arpents of land, situate as aforesaid; produces to the Board a concession from Charles D. Delassus to said Denoyer, for eight hundred arpents, dated January 15, 1800; a survey plat and certificate of the same, dated as aforesaid, and a transfer of the same, dated as aforesaid.

The Board require further proofs.

Witness on the part of the United States.

Joseph Denoyer, sworn, says that he never applied for a concession, and that about two years ago he had one offered to him by claimant.

May 8, 1806: Present, Penrose and Donaldson, commissioners. The Board reject this claim with the above remark.

August 27, 1810: Present, Lucas, Penrose, and Bates, commissioners. It is the opinion of the Board that this claim ought not to be confirmed.

ALBERT TISON, assignee of Gabriel Hunot, claiming eight hundred arpents of land, situate as aforesaid; produces to the Board a concession from Charles D. Delassus, to said Hunot, for eight hundred arpents of land, dated 9th May, 1800; survey plat and certificate as aforesaid, and a transfer of the same, dated December 3, 1803.

The Board require further proof.

Witness as aforesaid.

Gabriel Hunot, sworn, says that he never applied for a concession; that claimant offered him one, but cannot tell when.

May 8, 1806: Present, Penrose and Donaldson, commissioners. The Board reject this claim. Remark as above.

August 27, 1810: Present, Lucas, Penrose, and Bates, commissioners. It is the opinion of the Board that this claim ought not to be confirmed.

ALBERT TISON, assignee of Antoine Denoyer, claiming eight hundred arpents of land, situate as aforesaid; produces to the Board a concession from Charles D. Delassus, to said Denoyer, for eight hundred arpents, dated 7th February, 1800; a survey, plat, and certificate of the same, dated as aforesaid; and a deed of transfer, dated 5th January, 1804.

The Board require further proof. Witness as aforesaid.

Antoine Denoyer, sworn, says that he is now about twenty-one years of age; that he never applied for a concession; and that, about three years ago, claimant offered him one.

May 8, 1806: Present, Penrose and Donaldson, commissioners. The Board reject this claim. Remark as aforesaid.

August 27, 1810: Present, Lucas, Penrose, and Bates, commissioners. It is the opinion of the Board that this claim ought not to be confirmed.

ALBERT TISON, assignee of Augustin Langlois, claiming eight hundred arpents of land, situate as aforesaid; produces to the Board a concession from Charles D. Delassus to the said Langlois, for eight hundred arpents, dated 4th June, 1800; with a survey, plat, certificate, and deed of transfer of the same, dated as aforesaid.

The Board require further proof. Witness as aforesaid.

Augustin Langlois, sworn, says that he never applied for a concession; and that, about three or four years ago, claimant offered him one.

May 8, 1806: Present, Penrose and Donaldson, commissioners. The Board reject this claim. Remark as aforesaid.

August 27, 1810: Present, Lucas, Penrose, and Bates, commissioners. It is the opinion of the Board that this claim ought not to be confirmed.

ALBERT TISON, assignee of Louis Denoyer, claiming eight hundred arpents of land, situate as aforesaid; produces to the Board a concession from Charles D. Delassus to the said Louis Denoyer, for eight hundred arpents, dated 15th January, 1800; a survey, plat, certificate, and transfer of the same, dated as aforesaid.

The Board require further proof. Witness as aforesaid:

Louis Denoyer, sworn, says that he never applied for a concession; and that claimant, about three years ago, offered him one.

May 8, 1806: Present, Penrose and Donaldson, commissioners. The Board reject this claim. Remark as aforesaid.

August 27, 1810: Present, Lucas, Penrose, and Bates, commissioners. It is the opinion of the Board that this claim ought not to be confirmed.

ALBERT TISON, assignee of Francis Denoyer, claiming eight hundred arpents of land, situate as aforesaid; produces to the Board a concession from Charles D. Delassus to the said Francis Denoyer, dated as aforesaid, for eight hundred arpents; a survey, plat, certificate, and transfer of the same, dated as aforesaid.

The Board reject this claim. Remark as aforesaid.

August 27, 1810: Present, Lucas, Penrose, and Bates, commissioners. It is the opinion of the Board that this claim ought not to be confirmed.

ALBERT TISON, assignee of Charles B. Thibeault, claiming eight hundred arpents of land, situate as aforesaid: produces to the Board a concession from Charles D. Delassus to said Thibeault, for eight hundred arpents, dated December 7, 1799; survey plat, and certificate of the same, dated as aforesaid; and a deed of transfer of the same, January 10, 1804.

The Board require further proof.

May 8, 1806: Present, Penrose and Donaldson, commissioners. The Board reject this claim. Remark as aforesaid.

August 27, 1810: Present, Lucas, Penrose, and Bates, commissioners. It is the opinion of the Board that this claim ought not to be confirmed.

The nine foregoing claims are surveyed in one connected plat, forming an oblong, and each of the same figure. The petitions and transfers appear to be written in the same hand-writing. The decrees also appear to be all written in one hand-writing, and the appearance and texture of the paper are the same.

JOB WESTOVER, claiming three hundred and forty arpents of land, situate on river Aux Vases, district of St· Genevieve; produces to the Board a concession from Zenon Trudeau, dated January 10, 1798; a survey of three hundred and twenty-five arpents, taken 8th and certified 30th May, 1799.

June 23, 1806: Present, Penrose and Donaldson, commissioners. This claim being unsupported by actual inhabitation and cultivation, the Board reject the same. They observe that the said concession was granted at the time it bears date, and that the same is not duly registered.

August 27, 1810: Present, Lucas, Penrose, and Bates, commissioners. It is the opinion of the Board that this claim ought not to be confirmed. John B. C. Lucas, commissioner, declares that he does not concur in opinion with the former Board in the present case, respecting the satisfaction which the said former Board expresses, hat the concession was issued at the time it bears date.

JAMES FINLEY, claiming one thousand arpents of land, situate on Grand river, district of St. Genevieve; produces to the Board a concession from Zenon Trudeau, dated March 18, 1798; and a survey of eight hundred arpents, taken February 16, and certified 3d March, 1804.

June 23, 1806: Present, Penrose and Donaldson, commissioners. This claim being unsupported by actual inhabitation and cultivation, the Board reject the same, and observe that the aforesaid concession was granted at the time it bears date, and that claimant claims no other land in the Territory in his own name.

August 27, 1810: Present, Lucas, Penrose, and Bates, commissioners. It is the opinion of the Board that this claim ought not to be confirmed. John B. C. Lucas, commissioner, declares that he does not concur in opinion with the former Board in the present case, respecting the satisfaction which the said former Board expresses, that the concession was issued at the time it bears date.

JOSEPHUS TUCKER, claiming eight hundred and forty-six arpents of land, situate in the district of St. Genevieve; produces to the Board a survey of the same, taken 17th and certified on the 26th February, 1806.

Testimony taken. June 24, 1806. Tunis Quick, sworn, says that claimant settled in the beginning of 1803 on said land, and did, prior to and on the 20th December, 1803, actually inhabit and cultivate the same, and had then a wife.

Henry Dodge, sworn, says that he was present when claimant obtained from the commandant permission to settle.

June 24, 1806: Present, Penrose and Donaldson, commissioners. The Board grant to said claimant two hundred and fifty arpents of land, situate as aforesaid, provided so much be found vacant there.

August 27, 1810: Present, Lucas, Penrose, and Bates, commissioners. It is the opinion of the Board that this claim ought not to be granted.

SOLOMON MORGAN, claiming seven hundred and forty-eight arpents and sixty-eight perches of land, situate on the Mississippi, district of St. Genevieve; produces to the Board a survey of the same, taken the 10th and certified the 26th February, 1806.

Testimony taken. June 24, 1806. Camille Lassus, sworn, says that he was present when claimant obtained from commandant permission to settle on vacant land.

John Hawkins, sworn, says that claimant settled the said tract of land in the year 1802, and did, prior to and on the 20th December, 1803, actually inhabit and cultivate the same, and was then of the age of twenty-one years and upwards.

June 24, 1806: Present, Penrose and Donaldson, commissioners. The Board grant to said claimant two hundred arpents of land, situate as aforesaid, provided so much be found vacant there.

August 27, 1810: Present, Lucas, Penrose, and Bates, commissioners. It is the opinion of the Board that this claim ought not to be granted.

JONATHAN PRESTON, claiming one thousand one hundred and forty-four arpents and sixty-six perches of land, situate on Cape Cinqhomme, district of St. Genevieve; produces to the Board a survey of the same, taken the 17th and certified the 26th February, 1806.

****

Testimony taken. June 24, 1806. Camille Delassus, sworn, says that he was present when claimant obtained permission to settle on vacant lands from the commandant.

Elizabeth Quick, sworn, says that claimant did, prior to and on the 20th December, 1803, actually inhabit and cultivate the said tract of land; and had then a wife and six children.

June 24, 1806: Present, Penrose and Donaldson, commissioners. The Board grant said claimant five hundred arpents of land, provided so much be found vacant there, (situate as aforesaid.)

August 27, 1810: Present, Lucas, Penrose, and Bates, commissioners. It is the opinion of the Board that this claim ought not to be granted.

PETER VIRIAT, assignee of Nicholas Lachance, Jun., claiming four hundred arpents of land, situate on the river St. Francis, district of St. Genevieve; produces to the Board a concession from Charles D. Delassus, dated April 29, 1800; a survey of the same, taken 13th and certified 21st February, 1806; a deed of transfer of the same, dated 21st September, 1804, and executed by the said Nicholas Lachance and Judith his wife.

August 27, 1810: Present, Lucas, Penrose, and Bates, commissioners. It is the opinion of the Board that this claim ought not to be granted.

TITUS STRICKLAND, assignee of Joseph Lachance, and Louis La Croix, claiming one hundred and fifty arpents of land, situate on the Saline, district of St. Genevieve; produces to the Board a concession from Zenon Trudeau, granted for sugar making, dated February 1, 1798; and a survey of the same, dated January 8, and certified March 4, 1800.

Testimony taken. June 25, 1806. James Campbell, sworn, says that he (the witness) did, in the year 1805, make sugar on said land; that it had then the appearance of being worked as a sugar plantation five or six years preceding that period.

John Smith, sworn, says that he did, in the year 1803, see Titus Strickland, the above claimant, on said land, and that he was then engaged in making sugar.

August 27, 1810: Present, Lucas, Penrose, and Bates, commissioners. It is the opinion of the Board that this claim ought not to be confirmed.

MICHEL LACHANCE, claiming seventy-two arpents of land, situate on the waters of the river St. Francis, district of St. Genevieve; produces to the Board a concession from Charles D. Delassus, dated January 24, 1800; a survey of the same, certified 1st October, 1805.

June 25, 1806: Present, Penrose and Donaldson, commissioners. This claim being unsupported by actual inhabitation and cultivation, the Board reject the same; and are satisfied that it was granted at the time said concession bears date.

August 28, 1810: Present, Lucas, Penrose, and Bates, commissioners. It is the opinion of the Board that this claim ought not to be granted.

JOHN MANNING, claiming one thousand one hundred and thirty-eight arpents and thirty-four perches of land, situate on the Mississippi, district of St. Genevieve; produces to the Board a certificate of survey, dated February 26, 1806.

Testimony taken. June 25, 1806. Camille Delassus, sworn, says that he was present when claimant obtained from the commandant permission to settle on the public lands.

Robert Hinckson, sworn, says that claimant settled the said tract of land in the summer of 1803, and did, prior to and on the 20th December, in that year, actually inhabit and cultivate the said tract of land; and had then a wife and six children.

June 25, 1806: Present, Penrose and Donaldson, commissioners. The Board grant the aforesaid claimant five hundred arpents of land, provided so much be found vacant there.

August 28, 1810: Present, Lucas, Penrose, and Bates, commissioners. It is the opinion of the Board that this claim ought not to be granted.

THOMAS JONES, claiming seven hundred and fifteen arpents of land, situate on Big river, district of St. Genevieve; produces to the Board a survey of the same, taken 15th January, and certified 25th February, 1806.

Testimony taken. June 25, 1806. Abraham Baker, sworn, says that he, witness, settled the said tract of land in the year 1798, lived thereon until the next year, when he sold the same to one Thomas Alley, who did, prior to and on the 20th December, 1803, actually cultivate it; that the same has been actually cultivated to this day; that the said Thomas Alley was, on the 20th December, 1803, a single man, and is now supposed to be dead. Claimant claims no other land in his own name in the Territory.

August 28, 1810: Present, Lucas, Penrose, and Bates, commissioners. It is the opinion of the Board that this claim ought not to be granted.

JOHN CORDER, claiming four hundred and seventy-three arpents and ninety-five perches of land, situate on Bellevue, district of St. Genevieve; produces to the Board a survey of the same, taken 13th and certified 27th February, 1806.

Testimony taken. June 25, 1806. Elisha Baker, sworn, says that he saw claimant on said tract of land between the 10th and 15th days of November, 1803; that he moved on the same in 1804, and raised a crop; was, 20th December, 1803, of age, and a single man.

August 28, 1810: Present, Lucas, Penrose, and Bates, commissioners. It is the opinion of the Board that this claim ought not to be granted.

DAVID YARBOROUGH, claiming three hundred and forty-three arpents and sixty-three perches of land, situate on the Mississippi, district of St. Genevieve; produces to the Board a survey of the same, taken the 12th, and certified the 26th February, 1806.

Testimony taken. June 25, 1806. John Smith, sworn, says that some time about the fall of 1802, claimant, together with one James Hunter, called on him, the witness, and inquired of him whether the aforesaid tract of land was claimed by any one, to which he answered in the negative; that some time towards the latter end of that year, he saw claimant cutting house logs; that, in the following spring, he saw him cultivating the said tract; that *he* raised a crop on the same for the said James Hunter, he, the said James, having purchased the said tract, as witness was informed, from said claimant; that the said Hunter had, on the 20th December, 1803, a wife and four children, and gave said Yarborough a horse in payment for said tract.

August 28, 1810: Present, Lucas, Penrose, and Bates, commissioners. It is the opinion of the Board that this claim ought not to be granted.

JAMES HEWITT, assignee of Antoine Dejarlais, assignee of Louis Aubuchon, claiming eight hundred arpents of land, situate at Bellevue, district of St. Genevieve; produces to the Board a concession from Charles D. Delassus, to said Louis Aubuchon, dated 10th January, 1800; a survey of said land, dated 18th, and certified 27th February, 1806; a deed of transfer, executed by said Aubuchon to Antoine Dejarlias, dated 22d November, 1804; and another deed of transfer to claimant, dated 18th February, 1805.
Testimony taken. June 25, 1806. William Reed, sworn, says that, in the spring of 1805, claimant came to his house; that he settled the said tract of land, built a house, and raised a crop on the same that year, and has actually inhabited and cultivated it to this day; that he had then a wife, four children, and a slave.
June 25, 1806: Present, Penrose and Donaldson, commissioners. The Board reject this claim; and observe, that claimant purchased said concession for five hundred dollars, and has actually paid four hundred and ten of the same.
August 28, 1810: Present, Lucas, Penrose, and Bates, commissioners. It is the opinion of the Board that this claim ought not to be granted.

NICHOLAS LAPLANTE and VINCENT LAFOIS, claiming two hundred and twenty-four arpents of land, situate on the waters of the river establishment, district of St. Genevieve; produces to the Board a concession from Zenon Trudeau, dated November 13, 1797; and a survey of two hundred and twenty-four arpents, dated 15th December 1797, and certified 17th May, 1798.
Testimony taken. June 25, 1806. Joseph Pratte, sworn, says that he was on the said tract of land about six years ago, when the same was settled as a sugar camp, and that it has been actually inhabited to this day, at the time of sugar making, and been worked for that purpose every year.
June 25, 1806: Present, Penrose and Donaldson, commissioners. The Board reject this claim; and observe, that the said concession is not duly registered.
August 28, 1810: Present, Lucas, Penrose, and Bates, commissioners. It is the opinion of the Board that this claim ought not to be confirmed.

JAMES HUTCHINS, claiming eight hundred and forty-five arpents seventy-eight perches of land, situate on the Mississippi, district of St. Genevieve; produces to the Board a survey of the same, dated January 22, and certified February 26, 1806.
Testimony taken. June 26, 1806. Camille Lassus, sworn, says that he was present when claimant obtained from the commandant permission to settle on vacant lands.
Robert Hinckson, sworn, says that claimant settled the said tract of land in 1803; built a house on the same; that in January, 1804, he moved on it, raised a crop, and has actually inhabited and cultivated the same to this day; had, 20th December, 1803, a wife and four children.
September 1, 1810: Present, Lucas, Penrose, and Bates, commissioners. It is the opinion of the Board that this claim ought not to be granted.

THOMAS RARDIN, assignee of James Maxwell, claiming one thousand arpents of land, situate on the waters of the Mississippi, district of St. Genevieve; produces a special permission to settle from Zenon Trudeau, dated May 29, 1798; and a survey of the same dated November 20, 1799, and certified January 10, 1800.
Testimony taken. June 26, 1806. Titus Strickland, sworn, says that claimant settled the said tract of land in 1802; built a house in the beginning of 1803, and did, prior to and on the 20th December, 1803, actually inhabit and cultivate the same; and had then a wife and four children and four slaves.
June 26, 1806: Present, Penrose and Donaldson, commissioners. The Board grant to the said claimant four hundred and eighty arpents of land situate as aforesaid, provided so much be found vacant there.
September 1, 1810: Present, Lucas, Penrose, and Bates, commissioners. It is the opinion of the Board that this claim ought not to be confirmed.

WILLIAM HINCKSON, claiming one thousand and thirty-seven arpents of land, situate on Obrazeau creek, district of St. Genevieve; produces to the Board a survey of the same, dated January 13, and certified February 26, 1805.
Testimony taken. June 26, 1806. Camille Lassus, sworn, says that he was present when permission was granted claimant to settle on vacant lands.
George Hamilton, sworn, says that the claimant settled the aforesaid tract of land in the spring of 1803; and did, prior to and on the 20th December, 1803, actually inhabit and cultivate the same, and had then a wife, three children, and two slaves.
June 26, 1806: Present, Penrose and Donaldson, commissioners. The Board grant said claimant three hundred and ninety arpents of land, situate as aforesaid, provided so much be found vacant there.
September 1, 1810: Present, Lucas, Penrose, and Bates, commissioners. It is the opinion of the Board that this claim ought not to be granted.

ELI STRICKLAND, claiming seven hundred and seventy-five arpents of land, situate on the river Platen, district of St. Genevieve; produces to the Board a survey of the same dated 25th, and certified 27th February, 1806.
Testimony taken. June 26, 1806. Thomas Rardin, sworn, says that he was on the said tract of land in 1803, when he saw a field of about nine or ten acres planted in corn and cotton.
Robert Smith, sworn, says that in the fall of 1803, he went on said tract of land, when claimant actually inhabited the same, and had gathered a crop of corn and cotton; that he had then a wife and three children.
Camille Lassus, sworn, says that to his knowledge claimant had obtained permission to settle on vacant land.
June 26, 1806. The Board grant three hundred and fifty arpents of land, situate as aforesaid, provided so much be found vacant there.
September 1, 1810: Present, Lucas, Penrose, and Bates, commissioners. It is the opinion of the Board that this claim ought not to be granted.

CHARLES DUNCASTER, claiming nine hundred and ninety-seven arpents eighty-five perches of land, situate on Obrazeau creek, district of St. Genevieve; produces to the Board a survey of the same, dated 25th January, and 26th February, 1806.
Testimony taken. June 26, 1806. Camille Lassus, sworn, says that he was present when claimant obtained from the commandant permission to settle on vacant lands.

Henry Riley, sworn, says that claimant did, prior to and on the 30th December, 1803, actually inhabit and cultivate the same, and had then a wife and three children.

June 26, 1806: Present, Penrose and Donaldson, commissioners. The Board grant said claimant three hundred and fifty arpents of land, situate as aforesaid, provided so much be found vacant there.

September 1, 1810: Present, Lucas, Penrose, and Bates, commissioners. It is the opinion of the Board that this claim ought not to be granted.

BENJAMIN HARRISON, claiming seven hundred and forty-eight arpents sixty-eight perches of land, situate on Obrazeau creek, district of St. Genevieve; produces to the Board a survey of the same, dated 15th January, and certified 26th February, 1806.

Testimony taken. June 26, 1806. William Johnston, sworn, says that he saw a written permission to settle granted said claimant by the commandant; that he, the said claimant, settled the said tract of land, in the spring, and did, prior to and on the 20th December, 1803, actually inhabit and cultivate the same, and was then a single man, of the age of twenty-one years and upwards; had one slave.

June 26, 1806: Present, Penrose and Donaldson, commissioners. The Board grant said claimant one hundred and twenty arpents of land situate as aforesaid, provided so much be found vacant there.

September 1, 1810: Present, Lucas, Penrose, and Bates, commissioners. It is the opinion of the Board that this claim ought not to be granted.

JOHN EARS, claiming nine hundred and sixty arpents of land, situate on Big river, district of St. Genevieve; produces to the Board a survey of the same, dated January 4, and certified February 27, 1806.

Testimony taken. June 26, 1806. Joseph Gerrard, sworn, says that claimant cut two sets of cabin logs, and planted apple trees.

September 1, 1810: Present, Lucas, Penrose, and Bates, commissioners. It is the opinion of the Board that this claim ought not to be granted.

WILLIAM ASHBROOK, claiming six hundred and seventy-three arpents and forty-one and a half perches of land, situate on Bellevue, district of St. Genevieve; produces to the Board a survey of the same, dated 22d and certified 27th February, 1806.

Testimony taken. June 26, 1806. Walter Crow, sworn, says that claimant settled said tract of land in February, 1804, when he moved on it with his family, and has actually inhabited and cultivated the same to this day.

Elisha Baker, sworn, says that he was present when claimant obtained from the commandant permission to settle on vacant lands, and that he had, 20th December, 1803, a wife and child.

September 1, 1810: Present, Lucas, Penrose, and Bates, commissioners. It is the opinion of the Board that this claim ought not to be granted.

JOHN PAUL, claiming one thousand forty-eight arpents and fifteen perches of land, situate on Bellevue, district of St. Genevieve; produces to the Board a certificate of permission to settle; a survey of the same, dated 22d and certified 27th February, 1806.

Testimony taken. June 26, 1806. William Ashbrook, sworn, says that claimant settled said tract of land, in March, 1804; that he has been an inhabitant of the country for many years past, and had, on the 20th December, 1803, a wife and four children.

September 1, 1810: Present, Lucas, Penrose, and Bates, commissioners. It is the opinion of the Board that this claim ought not to be granted. Claimant produced permission to settle, on file.

LEMUEL WAKELY, claiming nine hundred and fifty-nine arpents of land, situate on Bellevue, district of St. Genevieve; produces to the Board a survey of the same, dated 21st and certified 27th February, 1806.

Testimony taken. June 26, 1806. Elisha Baker, sworn, says that claimant settled said tract of land in 1804, and has actually inhabited and cultivated the same to this day; that he had obtained from the commandant permission to settle on vacant lands; and had, on the 20th December, 1803, a wife and two children.

MILES GOFORTH, claiming one thousand two hundred and ninety-five arpents and thirty-four perches of land, situate on Bellevue, district of St. Genevieve; produces to the Board a survey of the same, dated 3d and certified 27th February, 1806.

Testimony taken. June 26, 1806. Benjamin Crow, sworn, says that he was present when claimant obtained from the commandant leave to settle on vacant lands; that, in 1803, when claimant was about proceeding to the improving and settling the said land, he was prevented from so doing by the bursting of a gun, which was near carrying off both arms of said claimant; that at that period he had already applied to him (the witness) to move him on the same; that he settled in the beginning of 1804, raised a crop that year, and has actually inhabited and cultivated the same; and further, that the said claimant, who was a soldier in the revolutionary war, had, on the 20th December, 1803, a wife and nine children.

September 1, 1810: Present, Lucas, Penrose, and Bates, commissioners. It is the opinion of the Board that this claim ought not to be granted.

JOSEPH MCMARTREE, claiming one thousand one hundred and ninety-seven arpents and ninety perches of land, situate on Bellevue, district of St. Genevieve; produces to the Board a survey of the same, dated 18th and certified 27th February, 1806.

Testimony taken. June 26, 1806. Benjamin Crow, sworn, says that claimant settled the said tract of land in 1803, raised a crop in 1804, and has actually inhabited and cultivated the same to this day; and further, that he had, on the 20th December, 1803, a wife and seven children.

September 1, 1810: Present, Lucas, Penrose, and Bates, commissioners. It is the opinion of the Board that this claim ought not to be granted.

JAMES BROWN, claiming seven hundred and forty-eight arpents and sixty-eight perches of land, situate on Bellevue, district of St. Genevieve; produces to the Board a survey of the same, dated 8th and certified 27th February, 1806.

Testimony taken. June 26, 1806. Elisha Baker, sworn, says that he (the witness) was on the said tract of land early in the year of 1804; that the same was then actually inhabited, and bore the marks of its having been cultivated the year before; and further, that it has been actually inhabited and cultivated to this day; had, on the 20th December, 1803, a wife and child.

September 1, 1803: Present, Lucas, Penrose, and Bates, commissioners. It is the opinion of the Board that this claim ought not to be granted.

JOHN OTTERY, claiming seven hundred and sixty-six arpents of land, situate on Bellevue, district of St. Genevieve; produces to the Board a survey of the same, taken 3d and certified 5th January, 1806.

Testimony taken. June 26, 1806. Benjamin Crow, sworn, says that he did, in the fall of 1803, go with claimant to look for a spot on which he might settle himself; that, having fixed on the aforesaid, he moved on the same, built a house, and actually inhabited it on the 20th December in that year; that he raised a crop in 1804, and has actually inhabited and cultivated the same to this day; and had, on the 20th December, 1803, a wife and two children.

September 1, 1810: Present, Lucas, Penrose, and Bates, commissioners. It is the opinion of the Board that this claim ought not to be granted.

CURTIS MORRIS, claiming seven hundred and forty-six arpents and seventy-five perches of land, situate on Bellevue, district of St. Genevieve; produces to the Board a survey of the same, taken 22d January, and certified 27th February, 1806.

Testimony taken. June 26, 1806. Benjamin Crow, sworn, says that claimant improved the said tract of land in 1804, built a house on the same, raised a crop in 1805, and had, on the 20th December, 1803, a wife.

Claimant produced to the Board a certificate of permission to settle, on file.

September 1, 1810: Present, Lucas, Penrose, and Bates, commissioners. It is the opinion of the Board that this claim ought not to be granted.

JOSEPH BEAR, claiming five hundred and ninety-three arpents of land, situate on river Platen, district of St. Genevieve; produces to the Board a survey of the same, dated 10th and certified 20th February 1806.

Testimony taken. June 26, 1806. Benjamin Crow, sworn, says that claimant did, prior to and on the 20th of December, 1803, actually inhabit and cultivate the said tract of land, and was then a single man, and of the age of twenty-one years and upwards.

September 1, 1810: Present, Lucas, Penrose, and Bates, commissioners. It is the opinion of the Board that this claim ought not to be granted.

DAVID CRIPS, claiming eight hundred and ninety-three arpents of land, situate on the Bois Bruile, district of St. Genevieve; produces to the Board a certificate of a permission to settle from Peter D. Deluziere, dated December 14th, 1805, and a survey of the same, dated 20th and certified 26th February, 1806.

Testimony taken. June 28, 1806. Thomas Allen, sworn, says that claimant settled the said tract of land in July, 1804, and has actually inhabited and cultivated the same to this day.

Jonathan Preston, sworn, says that claimant had, on the 20th December, 1803, a wife and six children.

September 1, 1810: Present, Lucas, Penrose, and Bates, commissioners. It is the opinion of the Board that this claim ought not to be granted.

HENRY GRASS, claiming seven hundred and sixty-eight arpents of land, situate on the waters of the river Saline, district of St. Genevieve; produces to the Board a certificate of a permission to settle, from Peter D. Deluziere, dated January 28th, 1806, and a survey of the same, dated 30th December, 1806, and certified 5th February, 1806.

Testimony taken. June 28, 1806. Amos Rowark, sworn, says that he, the witness, was on the said tract of land some time in 1803, when one David Tarborough lived there: that he had a garden on the same, out of which the witness was supplied with some greens and sallad.

Thomas Donohoe, sworn, says that claimant was living on said land, which had been improved before in November, 1803, and that he had, on the 20th December, 1803, when he actually inhabited and cultivated the same, a wife and child.

September 1, 1810: Present, Lucas, Penrose, and Bates, commissioners. It is the opinion of the Board that this claim ought not to be granted.

JAMES THOMPSON, claiming four hundred arpents of land, situate in district of St. Genevieve; produces to the Board a concession from Zenon Trudeau, dated February 15th, 1798, together with a survey of the same.

Testimony taken. June 28, 1806. Thomas Thompson, sworn, says that claimant did, in the year 1800, put up sugar works on said land and made sugar on the same, during which time he actually inhabited it, and raised a crop in 1805.

September 1, 1810: Present, Lucas, Penrose, and Bates, commissioners. It is the opinion of the Board that this claim ought not to be confirmed.

JAMES MAXWELL, assignee of Arthur O'Neal, claiming eight hundred arpents of land, situate on the river Gaborie; produces to the Board a concession for the same from Zenon Trudeau, to the said O'Neal, dated March 5th, 1798; a survey of four hundred and thirty-two arpents September 25th, 1803, and certified January 15th, 1804; and another survey of three hundred and sixty-seven arpents and fifty perches, taken January 26th, 1804, and certified 15th February, 1804, and a deed of transfer of the same, dated 1st March, 1799.

June 28th, 1806: Present, Penrose and Donaldson, commissioners. The Board reject this claim, and are of opinion that the said concession was granted at the time it bears date.

September 1st, 1810: Present, Lucas, Penrose, and Bates, commissioners. It is the opinion of the Board that this claim ought not to be confirmed. John B. C. Lucas, commissioner, declares that he does not concur in opinion with the former Board, in the present case, respecting the satisfaction which the said former Board expresses, that the concession was issued at the time it bears date.

DOMITILLE DAHAULT, claiming four thousand arpents of land, situate on the waters of the river St. Francis, district of St. Genevieve; produces to the Board a concession for the same, from Charles Dehault Delassus, Lieutenant Governor, dated September 17th, 1799; a survey of the same, taken 20th December, 1800, and certified 15th May, 1801.

September 1, 1810: Present, Lucas, Penrose, and Bates, commissioners. It is the opinion of the Board that this claim ought not to be confirmed.

PIERRE DELASSUS DELUZIERE, claiming eight hundred and ten arpents of land, situate in the district of St. Genevieve; produces to the Board a concession from Zenon Trudeau, dated November 25, 1798; a survey of three hundred and ten arpents, taken December 25, 1798, and certified 14th January, 1799; and another survey of five hundred arpents, taken 25th November, 1799, and certified 15th March, 1800.

Testimony taken. June 28, 1806. Israel Dodge, sworn, says that, in the year 1798, claimant built a cabin on the aforesaid tract of three hundred and ten arpents; that the same was, for five or six years, constantly inhabited by a free negro woman, but does not know whether she lived on the same as a tenant to claimant.

September 1, 1810: Present, Lucas, Penrose, and Bates, commissioners. It is the opinion of the Board that this claim ought not to be confirmed.

PIERRE DELASSUS DELUZIERE, claiming one thousand arpents of land, situate on the river establishment, district of St. Genevieve; produces to the Board a concession for the same from Zenon Trudeau, dated 25th January, 1798; a survey of the same, taken January 27th, and certified the 30th, 1798.

Testimony taken. June 28, 1806. Israel Dodge, sworn, says that a cabin was built on said land about the year 1799, and afterwards destroyed by fire.

September 1, 1810: Present, Lucas, Penrose, and Bates, commissioners. It is the opinion of the Board that this claim ought not to be confirmed.

ANNA SKINNER, assignee of John Atkins, claiming five hundred and ninety-five arpents of land, situate on the Joachim, district of St. Genevieve; produces to the Board a survey of the same, taken December 28, 1805, and certified February 26, 1806.

Testimony taken. June 28, 1806. Philip Roberts, sworn, says that the said John Atkins settled the said tract of land in 1803; built a house on the same; cleared lands which he did fence in; that he remained thereon for about six months; that one Isaac Vanmetre did move on it in 1804, as a tenant to said Atkins; that in 1805, the aforesaid claimant having purchased the aforesaid tract, one Edward Butler went on it for her use, and actually cultivated the same; and further, that the said John Atkins had, on the 20th December, 1803, a wife and six children.

September 1, 1810: Present, Lucas, Penrose, and Bates, commissioners. It is the opinion of the Board that this claim ought not to be granted.

JOSIAH McCLANNAHAN, assignee of the representatives of Gabriel Cerré, deceased, claiming three hundred arpents of land, situate in the district of St. Louis; produces to the Board a concession from Charles Dehault Delassus, dated January 5, 1800; a survey of the same, dated 27th and certified the 28th February, 1806; together with the act of public sale aforesaid.

Testimony taken. June 28, 1806. Anthony Soulard, sworn, says that he wrote the decree of the Lieutenant Governor to the said concession; that he does not know whether it was granted at the time it bears date; that it was granted for the building of a bridge, which was completed by said Gabriel Cerré about five years ago.

July 7, 1806: Present, Penrose and Donaldson, commissioners. The Board reject this claim; they are satisfied that the said concession was granted at the time it bears date.

September 1, 1810: Present, Lucas, Penrose, and Bates, commissioners. It is the opinion of a majority of the Board that this claim ought not to be confirmed; Clement B. Penrose, commissioner, voting for the confirmation of three hundred arpents of land.

JOSIAH McCLANNAHAN, assignee of Louis Debreuil, claiming eight hundred arpents of land, situate at the river Cuivre, district of St. Charles; produces to the Board a concession from Charles D. Delassus, Lieutenant Governor, dated November 14, 1799; a survey of the same, dated 19th February, and certified 20th March, 1804; and a deed of transfer of the same, dated April 1, 1805.

Testimony taken. July 7, 1806. Albert Tison, sworn, says that he saw the aforesaid concession in the spring of 1800; that Louis Debreuil was, at the time of obtaining the same, about nineteen years of age; is a native of the country, and claims no other land in his own name in the Territory.

July 7, 1806: Present, Penrose and Donaldson, commissioners. The Board reject this claim, and are satisfied it was granted at the time it bears date.

September 6, 1810: Present, Lucas, Penrose, and Bates, commissioners. It is the opinion of the Board that this claim ought not to be confirmed. John B. C. Lucas, commissioner, declares that he does not concur in opinion with the former Board in the present case respecting the satisfaction which the said former Board expresses, that the concession was issued at the time it bears date.

WINSLOW TURNER, claiming nine hundred and ninety-eight arpents of land, situate on the waters of the river Cuivre, district of St. Charles; produces a survey of the same, dated 4th February, 1806; and a certificate of a permission to settle, by William McConnel, syndic of said settlement under the Spanish Government.

Testimony taken. July 12, 1806. Joseph Cottle, sworn, says that claimant settled said tract of land, in September, 1803, built a house on the same, planted peachstones and sowed appleseeds; that he did also clear four or five acres of land, and fenced in the same; and that he did, in the beginning of 1804, move his family on the same, and has actually inhabited and cultivated it to this day; and had, on the 20th December, 1803, a wife and five children.

September 6, 1810: Present, Lucas, Penrose, and Bates, commissioners. It is the opinion of the Board that this claim ought not to be granted.

GEORGE SPENCER, claiming six hundred arpents of land, situate on bay du Roy, district of St. Charles; produces to the Board a concession from Charles D. Delassus, Lieutenant Governor, dated February 17, 1800; and a survey of the same, taken 3d December, 1803, and certified 20th January, 1804.

Claimant confesses that the above concession is antedated.

September 6, 1810: Present, Lucas, Penrose, and Bates, commissioners. It is the opinion of the Board that this claim ought not to be confirmed.

JOHN BOLI, assignee of Jesse Keyne, assignee of Charles Gill, assignee of François Poillievre, claiming one hundred and sixty arpents of land, situate on the river Merrimack, district of St. Louis; produces to the Board a concession duly registered, from Don Zenon Trudeau, to said Francis Poillievre for eight by forty arpents on each side of said river Merrimack, dated September 17, 1795; and a survey of the same dated and certified February 27, 1806; a deed of transfer from said François Poillievre to Charles Gill, dated December 31, 1795; one from said Gill to Jesse Keyne, dated November 4, 1799; and another from said Jesse Keyne to claimant, dated 27th June, 1798.

Testimony taken. July 17, 1806. Jacques Clamorgan, sworn, says that the said tract of land was settled and improved by one Catalan, that the said Catalan built a house on the same; and that it has been actually inhabited and cultivated to this day; and witness believes that it was actually inhabited and cultivated on the 1st day of October, 1800.

July 17, 1806: Present, Lucas and Penrose, commissioners. The Board confirm to claimant, assignee as aforesaid, one hundred and sixty arpents of land, situate as aforesaid, as per the aforesaid concession.

September 6, 1810: Present, Lucas, Penrose, and Bates, commissioners. It is the opinion of a majority of the Board that this claim ought not to be confirmed. Frederick Bates, commissioner, voting for the confirmation of one hundred and sixty arpents of land.

JOHN BOLI, claiming two hundred and sixty arpents of land, situate on the waters of the Merrimack; produces to the Board a survey of the same, dated 27th December, 1806.

Testimony taken. July 17, 1806. Jacques Clamorgan, sworn, says that claimant applied to Zenon Trudeau for permission to settle, and establish the said tract of land; that the same was granted to him provisionally, to wit, that said settlement should not prejudice the witness, who had an establishment adjoining the said tract; that about eight or ten years ago he saw a cabin on said tract; that claimant had then a garden on the same; that claimant has made sugar on the same every year; and further, that the Indians, who at that time were very troublesome, did at several times drive the inhabitants of that settlement away from their homes, and destroy their improvements.

September 6, 1810: Present, Lucas, Penrose, and Bates, commissioners. It is the opinion of the Board that this claim ought not to be granted.

GEORGE PERCELY, assignee of Francis Kissler, claiming one thousand and fifty-six arpents of land, situate on the river Peruque, district of St. Charles; produces to the Board a survey of the same, taken 7th December, 1805, and certified 2d January, 1806; and a deed of transfer of the same, dated November 6, 1803.

Testimony taken. July 19, 1806. Auguste Gillis, sworn, says that the said tract of land was settled in the beginning of the fall of 1803, by one James Swift, who built a cabin on the same; that Swift acknowledged before him (the witness) that he had sold his labor to one Francis Kissler; that the said Swift remained on the same until the winter of that year, when the said Kissler moved on it, and remained about one month and a half, when he was, by sickness, obliged to move to St. Charles, where he was put in the hands of a physician, and thereby unable to proceed any further with the cultivation of said land.

September 8, 1810: Present, Lucas, Penrose, and Bates, commissioners. It is the opinion of the Board that this claim ought not to be granted.

JAMES MACKAY, assignee of John Bishop, claiming three hundred and fifty arpents of land, situate on the Missouri, district of St. Louis; produces to the Board a concession from Charles D. Delassus, Lieutenant Governor, dated 14th November, 1799; and a survey of the same, dated 1st December, 1802, and certified 23d August, 1803; a deed of sale, dated 2d February, 1801.

Testimony taken. July 23, 1806. John Tayor, sworn, says that he (the witness) did, in 1804, build a house on said tract of land, made a field, and raised a crop; and that the same has been actually cultivated to this day.

September 8, 1810: Present, Lucas, Penrose, and Bates, commissioners. It is the opinion of the Board that this claim ought not to be confirmed.

JAMES MACKAY, assignee of Francis Duquett, assignee of Joseph Pichet, assignee of Hyacinth St. Cyr, claiming two and one-third arpents of land, being part of a square situate in village of St. Charles, now the property of the widow Boyer; produces to the Board a bill of sale, dated 30th November, 1804.

July 23, 1806: Present, Lucas, Penrose, and Donaldson, commissioners. The Board reject this claim, for want of a duly registered warrant of survey.

Testimony in the above claim omitted, July 23, 1806.

Jacques Clamorgan, sworn, says that, about ten years ago, Hyacinth St. Cyr owned the said lot; he built a horse-mill on the same; that he had then a house on it.

September 8, 1810: Present, Lucas, Penrose, and Bates, commissioners. It is the opinion of the Board that this claim ought not to be granted.

NATHANIEL WARREN, alias WARING, claiming seven hundred and fifty arpents of land, situate in the district of St. Charles; produces to the Board a survey, dated 21st February, 1806.

Testimony taken. July 26, 1806. John Wedden, sworn, says that the said tract was actually inhabited and cultivated by claimant in 1802, but not since.

September 8, 1810: Present, Lucas, Penrose, and Bates, commissioners. It is the opinion of the Board that this claim ought not to be granted.

CHARLES TAYON, assignee of Jean Baptiste Beland, claiming one hundred and sixty arpents of land, situate on the river Dardenne, district of St. Charles; produces to the Board a concession from Zenon Trudeau, dated 17th March, 1796; and a survey of the same, dated 1st December, 1799, and certified 8th January, 1800; and a deed of transfer, dated 20th June, 1804.

Testimony taken. July 30, 1806. John Lafleur, sworn, says that the said John Baptiste Beland was, at the time of obtaining the concession, the head of a family.

September 10, 1810: Present, Lucas, Penrose, and Bates, commissioners. It is the opinion of the Board that this claim ought not to be confirmed.

JOHN SAPPINGTON, claiming eight hundred arpents of land, as assignee of Pierre Diddier, situate on river Au Gravoix; produces to the Board a concession from Zenon Trudeau, dated March 20, 1796; a confirmation of the above concession from Charles D. Delassus, Lieutenant Governor, upon representation by the said Diddier that the same was lost, dated July 21, 1803; and a survey of the same, dated September 15, 1802, and certified 17th June, 1803; together with a deed of transfer of the same, dated 25th May, 1806.

Testimony taken. July 31, 1806. Gregoire Sarpee, sworn, says that the said Diddier did, in the spring of 1803, dig a well on said land; that he was, at the time of obtaining said concession, the head of a family, that the above claimant settled the same in the fall of that year, to wit, 1805, and has about ten acres of it in corn, and actually inhabits it.

Antoine Soulard, sworn, says that he has seen a concession from Zenon Trudeau for the aforesaid land; that he drew the additional one by Delassus; and further, that the facts therein stated are, to his recollection, perfectly true.

July 31, 1806: Present, Lucas, commissioner. The Board reject this claim, for want of actual inhabitation and cultivation prior to and on the 1st day of October, 1800, and also of a duly registered warrant of survey.

September 10, 1810: Present, Lucas, Penrose, and Bates, commissioners. It is the opinion of the Board that this claim ought not to be confirmed.

DANIEL RICHARDSON, assignee of John Caldwell, claiming four hundred and sixty arpents of land, situate on the Missouri, district of St. Louis; produces to the Board a survey of the same, dated 22d and certified 26th February, 1806.

Testimony taken. August 7, 1806. James Stevens, sworn, says that, in March, 1803, claimant did cut a few poles of said land, and was preparing to build and cultivate, but was prevented by the Indians.

September 10, 1803: Present, Lucas, Penrose, and Bates, commissioners. It is the opinion of the Board that this claim ought not to be granted.

JAMES MORRISON, assignee of Charles Dennis, claiming seven hundred and fifty arpents of land, situate on the river Dardenne, district of St. Charles; produces to the Board a survey of the same, dated the 22d, and certified 26th February, 1806; a deed of transfer, dated April 9, 1805.

Testimony taken. August 7, 1806. Joseph Voisin, sworn, says that the said Dennis did, some time in July, 1803, begin the building of a house, and planted fruit trees.

September 10, 1810: Present, Lucas, Penrose, and Bates, commissioners. It is the opinion of the Board that this claim ought not to be granted.

JOHN PHILLIPS, claiming seven hundred and fifty arpents of land, situate on river Aux Bœuf, district of St. Louis; produces to the Board a survey of the same, dated 26th December, 1805, and certified 25th February, 1806.

Testimony taken. August 18, 1805. James Pritchet, sworn, says that claimant did, prior to and on the 20th December, 1803, actually inhabit and cultivate the said tract of land.

Thomas Gibson, sworn, says that claimant moved on said land in the fall of 1803, and built a house on the same, into which he moved; that, in the spring of 1804, he saw trees growing on the same.

Charles Phillips, sworn, says that he was present when claimant obtained permission to settle on vacant lands; and that he was, on the 20th December, 1803, of the age of twenty-one years and upwards.

August 18, 1806: Present, Lucas and Penrose, commissioners. The Board grant said claimant one hundred arpents of land, situate as aforesaid, provided so much be found vacant there.

September 14, 1810: Present, Lucas, Penrose, and Bates, commissioners. It is the opinion of the Board that this claim ought not to be granted.

JONATHAN VINEYARD, claiming five hundred arpents of land, situate on the river Brois Bruile, district of St. Genevieve; produces to the Board a survey of the same, taken 27th December, 1805; and certified 27th January, 1806.

Testimony taken. August 19, 1806. James Cowan, sworn, says that claimant settled the said tract of land in September, 1804, and planted peach stones; that he saw the same growing the spring following; that he came from Georgia, and did not arrive in the country till that time; and further, that he has actually inhabited and cultivated the same to this day; had, when he arrived, a wife and two children.

September 14, 1810: Present, Lucas, Penrose, and Bates, commissioners. It is the opinion of the Board that this claim ought not to be granted.

JACQUES CLAMORGAN, assignee of Regis Loisel, claiming one hundred and fifty-one thousand one hundred and sixty-two arpents and eighty-five perches of land, situate on the Missouri; produces to the Board a concession for the same from Charles Dehault Delassus, Lieutenant Governor, dated 25th March, 1800, and a figurative plan of the same, dated 20th November, 1805.

Testimony taken. August 22, 1806. Antoine Tiebeau, sworn, says that the said land is situate upon the Missouri; that, in the year 1802, he, the witness, went up the said river with the said Regis Loisel, who built a four bastion fort of cedar, the whole at his own expense, and without any assistance from Government; that the year following, to wit, in 1803, they again went up together, when the said Loisel ascended, with witness, about sixty-five leagues higher up, and made a garden and large field; and further, that he, the witness, never heard of said Loisel having a concession for the same.

Auguste Chouteau, sworn, says that the aforesaid fort was built (begun) in 1800.

August 22, 1806: Present, Lucas, Penrose, and Donaldson, commissioners. The Board reject this claim, and require further proof.

September 14, 1810: Present, Lucas, Penrose, and Bates, commissioners. It is the opinion of the Board that this claim ought not to be confirmed.

JACQUES CLAMORGAN, claiming eight thousand arpents of land, situate on the river Merrimack, district of St. Louis; produces to the Board a concession from Zenon Trudeau, dated 20th September, 1796, granted for the purpose of procuring wood for claimant's salt-works, and a survey of the same, certified the 28th February, 1806.

Testimony taken. August 22, 1806. Joseph Brazeau, sworn, says that about ten years ago, when claimant was preparing to descend the river to New Orleans, he obtained a concession for eight thousand arpents of land, situate on the Merrimack, near his works.

September 14, 1810: Present, Lucas, Penrose, and Bates, commissioners. It is the opinion of the Board that this claim ought not to be confirmed.

IRA NASH, claiming sixteen hundred arpents of land, situate on the Missouri, district of St. Charles; produces to the Board a concession from Charles Dehault Delassus, dated 18th January, 1800, and a survey of the same, taken 20th January, and certified 15th February, 1804.

Testimony taken. August 23, 1806. Louis Lebaume, sworn, says that he knew claimant when employed at the public works, under the engineer of the province.

Antoine Soulard, sworn, says that he knew claimant when in the employment of Government; that in the year 1802 he went down to New Orleans; that claimant went with him, but does not know the object of his voyage; that when he returned he brought with him some papers under seal, and directed to the then Lieutenant Governor, but did not know the contents of the same; and further, that he does not know when the aforesaid concession was granted.

Claimant admits that he received the said concession on his return from New Orleans.

August 23, 1806: Present, Penrose and Donaldson, commissioners. The Board reject this claim, and observe that, from the above testimony, it appears evident that the aforesaid concession is antedated; and further, that the said claimant has a grant made him by the Board of two hundred and fifty arpents of land.

September 22, 1810: Present, Lucas, Penrose, and Bates, commissioners. It is the opinion of the Board that this claim ought not to be confirmed.

JAMES MITCHELL, claiming six hundred and forty-four arpents of land, situate on the Missouri, district of St. Charles; produces to the Board a survey of the same, dated 20th February, 1806.

Testimony taken. August 27, 1806. James Piper, sworn, says that claimant began his settlement in October, 1803, cleared some land, and cut house logs; that in 1804 he raised a crop of corn on the same, fenced in what he had cleared, and claims no other land in his own name in the Territory. For permission to settle, see Mackay's list.

September 22, 1810: Present, Lucas, Penrose, and Bates, commissioners. It is the opinion of the Board that this claim ought not to be granted.

JOHN BELL, assignee of Leonard Farrow, assignee of Matthew Wishant, claiming four hundred and fifty arpents of land, situate on the Missouri, district of St. Charles; produces to the Board a special permission to settle from Charles Dehault Delassus, Lieutenant Governor, dated 5th December, 1799; a survey of the same, taken 3d November, 1803, and certified the 15th February, 1804, together with a deed of transfer from Matthew Wishant to Leonard Farrow, dated 4th February, 1802, and another deed of transfer from the said Farrow to claimant, dated 2d February, 1803.

Testimony taken. August 29, 1806. David Durst, sworn, says that claimant did, in the beginning of 1804, build a house on said tract of land, and made a small improvement thereon; and further, that the same has been actually cultivated to this day by claimant, who had, on the 20th December, 1803, a wife and child.

September 22, 1810: Present, Lucas, Penrose, and Bates, commissioners. It is the opinion of the Board that this claim ought not to be confirmed.

THOMAS GILMORE, claiming four hundred arpents of land, situate on the Dardenne, district of St. Charles; produces to the Board a special permission to settle from Charles Dehault Delassus, Lieutenant Governor, dated 18th March, 1802, and a survey of the same, taken the 2d and certified the 28th February, 1806.

Testimony taken. August 29, 1806. George S. Spencer, sworn, says that claimant settled the said tract of land in 1804; that he had begun, and was going on with the building of a cabin, when the same was surveyed in by an older grant; and further, that he had, on the 20th December, 1803, a wife and child.

September 22, 1810: Present, Lucas, Penrose, and Bates, commissioners. It is the opinion of the Board that this claim ought not to be granted.

GEORGE BUCHANNON, claiming four hundred arpents of land, situate on the Dardenne, district of St. Charles; produces to the Board a special permission to settle from Zenon Trudeau, dated 24th February, 1798; a survey of the same, taken 29th December, 1799, and certified 10th January, 1800.

Testimony taken. August 29, 1806. David Durst, sworn, says that claimant settled on said tract of land, built a cabin, and cleared a few acres of the same, in 1801; that he remained thereon but six months; was of the age of twenty-one years and upwards, and claims no other land in his own name in the Territory, and is one of the followers of Colonel Daniel Boon.

September 22, 1810: Present, Lucas, Penrose, and Bates, commissioners. It is the opinion of the Board that this claim ought not to be confirmed.

DAVID MATTHEWS, assignee of William Tardy and Alexander McCourtney, which said Alexander McCourtney was assignee of William Tardy, assignee of Peter Vaughan; produces to the Board a concession from Zenon Trudeau to the said Peter Vaughan, dated 5th December, 1797, and a survey of the same, dated 5th February, and certified 17th May, 1800, together with a deed of transfer from the said Peter Vaughan to the said William Tardy for four hundred arpents of land, situate on the Missouri, district of St. Louis, dated 2d February, 1800; a deed of transfer from said Tardy to Alexander McCourtney for two hundred arpents of the same, dated 2d March, 1800; a deed of transfer from said McCourtney to claimant for the said two hundred arpents, dated 9th January, 1804; and lastly, by another deed of transfer from the said William Tardy to claimant for the remaining two hundred arpents, dated 2d March, 1802.

Testimony taken. August 30, 1806. William Massey, sworn, says that one James Massey settled the said tract of land, with the leave of James Mackay the commandant; that he raised a crop on the same in 1802, and remained on it until the fall of that year.

September 22, 1810: Present, Lucas, Penrose, and Bates, commissioners. It is the opinion of the Board that this claim ought not to be confirmed.

JOHN E. ALLEN, assignee of Antoine Dejarlais, assignee of Pierre Dodié, claiming six hundred arpents of land, situate in the district of St. Charles; produces to the Board a concession from Charles D. Delassus, Lieutenant Governor, dated 5th November, 1799, and granted to said Pierre Dodié; a survey of the same certified 28th February, 1806, together with a deed of transfer of the same, dated 5th October, 1804; and another deed of transfer from said Dejarlais to claimant, dated 25th December, 1804.

Testimony taken. August 30, 1806. David Delauney, sworn, says that he believes the aforesaid concession to be his own hand-writing; that he never did write any concession but what they did bear date with the time they were granted; that the said Dodié lived in the country and was a farmer; does not recollect when he saw said concession; that he was not in the habit of antedating; and further, that the said Pierre Dodié was at the time of obtaining said concession of the age of twenty-one years and upwards.

August 30, 1806: Present, Lucas, Penrose, and Donaldson, commissioners. The Board reject the claim, and require further proof.

September 22, 1810: Present, Lucas, Penrose, and Bates, commissioners. It is the opinion of the Board that this claim ought not to be confirmed.

LOUIS LEBEAUME, in his own name and his children's, claiming four thousand two hundred arpents of land, situate in the district of St. Charles; produces to the Board a concession from Charles D. Delassus, Lieutenant Governor, for eight hundred arpents of land, to said claimant's children, being four in number, and the residue to claimant, said concession dated 10th February, 1800; and a survey of the same, dated 25th December, 1803, and certified 20th January, 1804.

Testimony taken. September, 1806. James St. Vrain, sworn, says that he saw the concession aforesaid, in the year 1800, and was present when the same was handed to claimant by David Delauney.

Albert Tison, sworn, says that in 1800 the said Louis Debeaume loaded a pirogue with provisions and farming utensils; that having armed the same he took with him a negro slave and two Canadians and the witness; that they proceeded as far as the Portage des Sioux, when hearing of some white men having been killed by Indians, they were obliged to return and give up the intention he had then of settling the said tract of land.

Antoine Soulard, sworn, says that he wrote the decree of the Lieutenant Governor for said land, and verily believes it was granted at the time it bears date.

September 3, 1806: Present, Lucas and Donaldson, commissioners. The Board reject this claim, and are satisfied that the same was granted at the time it bears date.

September 22, 1810: Present, Lucas, Penrose, and Bates, commissioners. It is the opinion of the Board that this claim ought not to be confirmed.

WILLIAM HEBERT, dit Lacompte, assignee of Louis Barada, claiming one hundred and twenty arpents of land, situate at the Barriere des Noyers; produces to the Board a concession from Zenon Trudeau, dated 7th September, 1797; and a survey of the same, taken 25th January, 1798, together with a deed of transfer of the same, dated 11th December, 1805.

September 9, 1806: Present, Lucas and Donaldson, commissioners. This claim being unsupported by actual inhabitation and cultivation, the Board reject the same, and remark that they are satisfied it was granted at the time it bears date.

September 22, 1810: Present, Lucas, Penrose, and Bates, commissioners. It is the opinion of the Board that this claim ought not to be confirmed.

JAMES SMIRL, assignee of John Brindley, assignee of Hardy Ware, claiming seven hundred and forty arpents of land, situate on the river Merrimack, district of St. Genevieve; surveyed by Joseph Mitchell. (Papers not produced.)

Testimony taken. July 16, 1806. William Drennen, sworn, says that one Hardy Ware settled the said tract of land in the year 1799, and built a house on the same, and did, prior to and on the 1st October, 1800, actually inhabit and cultivate it; that Zenon Trudeau, the Lieutenant Governor, told him, in the presence of witness, to go and settle on vacant lands, and that he would give him a concession for such tract as he might make choice of; that he had, on the said 1st day of October, a wife and two children; and further, that the same has been actually cultivated from that time to this day.

James Stewart, sworn, says that he knew the said Hardy Ware, on the said tract of land in the year 1802; that he moved on it in February, 1803, and returned again between the 20th and 25th days of December in that year; and has actually inhabited and cultivated the same to April, 1806.

September 22, 1810: Present, Lucas, Penrose, and Bates, commissioners. It is the opinion of the Board that this claim ought not to be granted.

JAMES STEWART, claiming seven hundred and fifty arpents of land, situate on Black water, district of St. Louis; produces to the Board a survey of the same, dated 10th February, 1806.

Testimony taken. July 16, 1806. George Smirl, Jun., sworn, says that claimant settled the said tract of land in the year 1802, and did, prior to and on the 20th December, 1803, actually inhabit and cultivate the same; and had then a wife and five children.

September 22, 1810: Present, Lucas, Penrose, and Bates, commissioners. It is the opinion of the Board that this claim ought not to be granted.

IRA NASH, assignee of William Burch, claiming nine hundred and fifty-four arpents of land, situate in district of St. Louis; produces to the Board a plat and certificate of survey, dated 28th February, 1806, and a deed of transfer of the same, dated the 27th March, 1805.

Testimony taken. September 6, 1806. James Haff, sworn, says that said William Burch settled the said tract of land in 1798; that he began the building of a house, which was destroyed by fire before it was finished; that in the fall of that same year he cut a new set of house logs in order to re-build; that he afterwards settled near the river; that the said settlement has been confirmed to one Basey; that he was present when the said Burch, and one Thomas Smith (said Smith being, as he said, the owner of said land,) traded for four hundred arpents of land; that said Smith never settled the same.

September 22, 1810: Present, Lucas, Penrose, and Bates, commissioners. It is the opinion of the Board that this claim ought not to be granted.

WILLIAM NASH, assignee of Antoine Dejarlais, assignee of Albert Tison, assignee of Jacques St. Vrain, assignee of Joseph Deputy, claiming eight hundred arpents of land, situate on the Missouri, district of St. Charles; produces to the Board a concession from Charles D. Delassus, Lieutenant Governor, dated 5th March, 1800, and a survey of the same, taken in February, 1804, and certified 28th February, 1806, together with a deed of transfer of the same, dated November 5, 1803.

Testimony taken. September 16, 1806. David Delauney, sworn, says, that he believes, he wrote the aforesaid decree or concession; that he was in the habit of writing several of them, but cannot positively say when the aforesaid was written.

September 22, 1810: Present, Lucas, Penrose, and Bates, commissioners. It is the opinion of the Board that this claim ought not to be confirmed.

September 16, 1806. The Board require further proof.

IRA NASH, assignee of Albert Tison, assignee of Louis Collins, claiming eight hundred arpents of land, situate in the district of St. Charles; produces to the Board a concession from Charles D. Delassus, Lieutenant Governor, dated 7th March, 1800, together with a survey of the same, dated in February, 1804, and certified 28th February, 1806, together with a deed of transfer of the same, dated 5th November, 1803.

David Delauney's testimony in the foregoing case applies to this also.

September 16, 1806. The Board require further proof.

September 22, 1810: Present, Lucas, Penrose, and Bates, commissioners. It is the opinion of the Board that this claim ought not to be granted.

CHARLES D. DELASSUS, assignee of Auguste Chouteau, assignee of Louis Dupree, claiming eight hundred arpents of land, situate in the district of St. Charles; produces to the Board a concession from Charles D. Delassus, Lieutenant Governor, dated 6th March, 1799; and a survey of the same taken 19th February, and certified 4th

March, 1804; together with a deed of transfer from Louis Dupree to Auguste Chouteau, dated 22d June, 1802; and another deed of transfer from said Auguste Chouteau to claimant, dated 8th August, 1805.
September 17, 1806. The Board require further proof.
September 22, 1810: Present, Lucas, Penrose, and Bates, commissioners. It is the opinion of the Board that this claim ought not to be confirmed.

CHARLES D. DELASSUS, assignee of Auguste Chouteau, assignee of Peter Gamelin, claiming eight hundred arpents of land, situate in the district of St. Charles; produces to the Board a concession from Charles D. Delassus, Lieutenant Governor, dated 18th December, 1799; and a survey taken and certified as aforesaid; together with a deed of transfer from said Gamelin to Auguste Chouteau, dated 11th March, 1802; and another deed of transfer from Auguste Chouteau to claimant, dated 7th August, 1805.
September 17, 1806. The Board require further proof.
September 22, 1810: Present, Lucas, Penrose, and Bates, commissioners. It is the opinion of the Board that this claim ought not to be confirmed.

CHARLES D. DELASSUS, assignee of Auguste Chouteau, assignee of John Baptiste Challefloux, claiming six hundred arpents of land, situate on the Mississippi, district of St. Charles; produces to the Board a concession from Charles D. Delassus, Lieutenant Governor, dated 28th October, 1799; and a survey of the same taken 5th February, and certified 8th March, 1804; a transfer from Challefloux to Auguste Chouteau, dated 12th February, 1804; and another deed of transfer from Auguste Chouteau to claimant, dated 8th August, 1805.
September 22, 1810: Present, Lucas, Penrose, and Bates, commissioners. It is the opinion of the Board that this claim ought not to be confirmed.
September 17, 1806. The Board require further proof.

JOHN A. SEITZ, assignee of Antoine Saugrain, claiming eight hundred arpents of land, situate on the Portage des Scioux, district of St. Charles; produces to the Board a concession from Charles D. Delassus, Lieutenant Governor, dated 27th September, 1799, and a survey of the same dated 30th January, and certified 14th February, 1804; together with a deed of transfer of the same, dated 18th October, 1803.
September 22, 1810: Present, Lucas, Penrose, and Bates, commissioners. It is the opinion of the Board that this claim ought not to be confirmed.
September 17, 1806. The Board require further proof.

GEORGE SMIRL, Sen., claiming three hundred and twenty arpents of land, situate on Little Rock, district of St. Louis; produces to the Board a survey of the same, dated 11th January, 1806.
Testimony taken. September 17, 1806. Hardy Ware, sworn, says that one William Drennen settled the said tract of land in 1801; raised two crops on the same, to wit, in that year and the year 1802; that, in 1803, he planted a crop of corn, prior to the selling of the same to said claimant; that he moved out of said land prior to the winter of that year, and witness cannot say whether he gathered the said crop of corn; and further that he had, prior to and on the 20th December, 1803, a wife and four children.
September 22, 1810: Present, Lucas, Penrose, and Bates, commissioners. It is the opinion of the Board that this claim ought not to be granted.

GREGOIRE SARPY, assignee of John Baptiste Lamarche, claiming eight hundred arpents of land, situate on the Missouri; bounded on each side by one Chartrand and François Janis, in the rear by Emilian Forty; produces to the Board a concession from Zenon Trudeau, dated 18th November, 1798; and a survey of the same taken on the river Merrimack, in consequence of the aforesaid tract having previously been surveyed by another person; the said survey without date.
Testimony taken. September 19, 1806. Toussaint Cerré, sworn, says that the said claimant actually inhabited the said tract of land, as surveyed on the Merrimack about seven or eight years ago.
September 22, 1810: Present, Lucas, Penrose, and Bates, commissioners. It is the opinion of the Board that this claim ought not to be confirmed.

PALAGIE LABADIE, widow of Sylvester Labadie, claiming one hundred and sixty arpents of land, situate on the river Dardenne, district of St. Charles; produces to the Board a concession from Zenon Trudeau, dated 7th March, 1798; and a survey of the same, taken 10th December, 1799, and certified the 8th of January, 1800; together with a deed of transfer of the same, executed by Louise Longueville, the wife of Eliaame Remard, and acting as his attorney, dated 20th April, 1802.
September 22, 1810: Present, Lucas, Penrose, and Bates, commissioners. It is the opinion of the Board that this claim ought not to be confirmed.

ANTOINE SMITH, claiming one thousand two hundred arpents of land, situate on the King's bayou; produces to the Board a concession from Charles D. Delassus, Lieutenant Governor, dated 2d November, 1799; and a survey of the same, taken the 31st December, 1803, and certified 20th January, 1804.
September 22, 1810: Present, Lucas, Penrose, and Bates, commissioners. It is the opinion of the Board that this claim ought not to be confirmed.
September 20, 1806. The Board require further proof.

MACKAY WHERRY, claiming four hundred arpents of land, situate on the river Cuivre, district of St. Charles; produces to the Board a concession from Zenon Trudeau, dated 1st March, 1798; and a survey of the same, taken 18th December, 1803, and certified 20th January, 1804.
Testimony taken. September 20, 1806. James Mackay, sworn, says that he knows of claimant claiming no other land, in his own name, in the Territory.
September 28, 1810: Present, Lucas and Penrose, commissioners. It is the opinion of the Board that this claim ought not to be confirmed.

ISRAEL DODGE, claiming thirty arpents of land, situate on the waters of the Saline, district of St. Genevieve; produces to the Board a concession from Zenon Trudeau, dated 25th January, 1798, granting the same for a sugar plantation.
Testimony taken. Jacob Wise, sworn, says that he, the witness, saw a sugar camp on said tract, in the year 1798, in February; that he was then in partnership with claimant in the making of sugar.
Camille Lassus, sworn, says that, to his knowledge, claimant made sugar for two years successively on said land.

108   LAND GRANTS IN MISSOURI TERRITORY - 1805 - 1812

****

September 28, 1810: Present, Lucas and Penrose, commissioners. It is the opinion of the Board that this claim ought not to be confirmed.

ISRAEL DODGE, assignee of John Greenwalt, claiming —— arpents of land, situate on the waters of Bois Bruile, district of St. Genevieve; produces to the Board a deed of transfer, executed by the said John Greenwalt, dated 27th October, 1804.

Testimony taken. Camille Lassus, sworn, says that the said Greenwalt had obtained a permission to settle from Pierre Deluziere.

Thomas Maddon, sworn, says that the said Greenwalt had a concession for said land; that he, the witness, surveyed the same by virtue of said concession; that the same was bought by one Hayden, but believes never cultivated.

September 28, 1810: Present, Lucas, Penrose, and Bates, commissioners. It is the opinion of the Board that this claim ought not to be granted.

ETIENNE GOUVREAU, representatives of, claiming eight hundred arpents of land, situate on the Saline, district of St. Genevieve, and said to be granted for pasture land and sugar making; produce to the Board a concession from Zenon Trudeau, dated February 1, 1798.

Testimony taken. Henry Dielle, sworn, says that claimant made a sugar camp on said land in the year 1799; that he made sugar on it, and actually inhabited it when engaged in sugar making.

September 28, 1810: Present, Lucas, Penrose, and Bates, commissioners. It is the opinion of the Board that this claim ought not to be confirmed.

ETIENNE PARENT, claiming four hundred arpents of land, situate on the Saline creek, district of St. Genevieve; produces to the Board a concession from Zenon Trudeau, for the same, said to be granted for pasturage and sugar making, dated 1st February, 1798, and recorded in book C, page 459 of the Recorder's Office.

September 28, 1810: Present, Lucas, Penrose, and Bates, commissioners. It is the opinion of the Board that this claim ought not to be confirmed.

CAMILLE DELASSUS, assignee of Andrew Chavallier, claiming four hundred arpents of land; produces to the Board an unlocated concession from Charles D. Delassus, Lieutenant Governor, dated 18th October, 1799, and a deed of transfer, dated the 19th May, 1804.

June, 1806: Present, Lucas, Penrose, and Donaldson, commissioners. The Board require further proof of the date of said concession, and of the age of said Andrew Chavallier. Rejected.

September 28, 1810: Present, Lucas, Penrose, and Bates, commissioners. It is the opinion of the Board that this claim ought not to be confirmed.

PIERRE DELASSUS DELUZIERE, claiming one hundred arpents of land, situate on the Saline, district of St. Genevieve; produces to the Board a concession from Zenon Trudeau, dated the 20th January, 1798; and granting the same for sugar making.

Testimony taken. June, 1806. Israel Dodge, sworn, says that a sugar camp was established on said land in the year 1799.

September 28, 1810: Present, Lucas, Penrose, and Bates, commissioners. It is the opinion of the Board that this claim ought not to be confirmed.

JAMES MACKAY, assignee of Louis Boisse, assignee of John Scarlet, claiming two hundred arpents of land, being part of a tract of four hundred arpents; John Waters claiming the remainder, situate on the Missouri, district of St. Louis; bounded by Peter Chouteau, and one Janis; produces to the Board a permission to settle from Zenon Trudeau, dated 28th November, 1796; and a deed of transfer from Scarlet and Waters, dated 14th June, 1797; and another deed of transfer from Boisse to claimant, 23d March, 1805.

Testimony taken. July 23, 1806. Antoine Janis, sworn, says that the said Scarlet and Waters did, about nine years ago, build a house on said land; cut some wood which they employed in manufacturing, but cannot tell what; that they lived on it about six months.

September 28, 1810: Present, Lucas and Bates, commissioners. It is the opinion of the Board that this claim ought not to be granted.

PASCAL L. CERRE, claiming a league square of land surveyed in two parts or halves, one on the Big Spring of the river Merrimack, so as to include said spring; and the other at the fall of the forks of the Gasconade, and those of the Merrimack, called the Muddy; produces to the Board a concession from Charles D. Delassus, Lieutenant Governor, dated 8th November, 1799.

Testimony taken. September 15, 1806. Antoine Soulard, sworn, says that he wrote the aforesaid concession or decree of the Lieutenant Governor, but does not recollect if it was issued at the time it bears date; that a letter was addressed to Gabriel Cerre, the father of claimant, by the Governor General, Gayoso de Lemos, dated April 25, 1798, wherein he acknowledges the many services he has rendered to Government, and his claims to the generosity of the same; the Lieutenant Governor, on seeing said letter, inquired of him in what manner he might reward him; that the said Cerre replied that he was already advanced in years and not in want of lands, having already a sufficiency of the same, but recommended his son, the claimant, who had not then received any grant for lands, to the bounty of Government; and further, that the said claimant was, in the year 1798, the head of a family.

September 28, 1810: Present, Lucas and Bates, commissioners. It is the opinion of the Board that this claim ought not to be confirmed.

JAMES MACKAY, assignee of George Crump, claiming four hundred and fifty arpents of land, situate on the river Giugras, district of St. Louis; produces to the Board a concession from Charles D. Delassus, Lieutenant Governor, dated 9th May, 1800; and a deed of transfer of the same, 30th January, 1802.

Testimony taken. September 15, 1806. Hyacinth St. Cyr, sworn, says that about three years ago he saw a house on said land, but could not tell whether it was inhabited; saw no marks of cultivation.

September 28, 1810: Present, Lucas and Bates, commissioners. It is the opinion of the Board that this claim ought not to be confirmed.

JAMES MACKAY, assignee of Antoine Gautier, claiming ten arpents in front, situate on Marais Tomps Clare, by such quantity as may be found between the aforesaid Marais Tomps Clar and the crooked pond; produces to the Board a concession from Zenon Trudeau, dated 29th November, 1796 and a deed of transfer of the same, dated 1st July, 1804.

September 28, 1810: Present, Lucas and Bates, commissioners. It is the opinion of the Board that this claim ought not to be confirmed.

JAMES MACKAY, assignee of John McMillen, claiming six hundred and fifty arpents of land, situate on Feefee's creek, district of St. Louis; produces to the Board a concession from Charles D. Delassus, Lieutenant Governor, dated 21st September, 1799; and a deed of transfer of the same, dated 1st July, 1804.
September 17, 1806. The Board require further proof.
September 28, 1810: Present, Lucas and Bates, commissioners. It is the opinion of the Board that this claim ought not to be confirmed.

JOHN HAYS, assignee of Gabriel Nichol, assignee of Joseph Chevalier, claiming four hundred acres of land, situate on the Mississippi, district of Cape Girardeau; produces a concession from Don Carlos Dehault Delassus, Lieutenant Governor, for four hundred arpents of land, to Joseph Chevalier, dated 18th October, 1799; a plat of survey, dated 5th February, 1806, certified to be received for record 28th February, 1806, by Antoine Soulard, Surveyor General; a transfer from said Chevalier to said Nichol, dated 21st January, 1805, and a transfer from Nichol to claimant, dated 20th February, 1805.
October 6, 1810: Present, Penrose and Bates, commissioners. It is the opinion of the Board that this claim ought not to be confirmed.

ALEXANDER SOMMERVILLE, claiming seven hundred and fifty arpents of land, situate on river Pemiscon, district of New Madrid; produces to the Board a plat of survey by Michel Amaroux, deputy surveyor, New Madrid district, dated 24th February, 1806.
Testimony taken, at New Madrid, by Frederick Bates, commissioner. June 17, 1808. Jacob Waggoner, sworn, says that premises were improved in 1802, or previously, at which time witness saw a camp and some clearing on this tract; cultivated in 1803, but not inhabited; very little has since been done; claimant has no family in the country. For permission to settle, see list No. 1369, on which claimant will be found No. 230, for three hundred arpents.
October 6, 1810: Present, Lucas, Penrose, and Bates, commissioners. It is the opinion of the Board that this claim ought not to be granted.

THOMAS CLARK, Jun., claiming two hundred arpents of land, situate on the Mississippi, district of New Madrid; produces to the Board a notice to the recorder.
Testimony taken, at New Madrid, by Frederick Bates, commissioner, by authority from the Board, June 27, 1808. Stephen Jones, sworn, says that premises were never inhabited; cultivated in 1802; a cabin built.
October 6, 1810: Present, Lucas, Penrose, and Bates, commissioners. It is the opinion of the Board that this claim ought not to be granted.

JONATHAN HURLEY, claiming one thousand arpents of land, situate on head waters of the bayou St. Thomas; produces to the Board a certificate of survey, dated February 27, 1806.
Testimony taken. March 21, 1806. Jacob Myers, sworn, says that claimant did, prior to and on the 20th December, 1803, actually inhabit and cultivate the said tract of land, and had then a wife and six children.
March 21, 1806: Present, Lucas and Donaldson, commissioners. The Board grant the said claimant one thousand one hundred and fifty arpents of land, situate as aforesaid, provided so much be found vacant there.
October 6, 1810: Present, Penrose and Bates, commissioners. It is the opinion of the Board that this claim ought not to be granted.

JAMES DOUGLASS, claiming one thousand and fifty arpents of land, situate on bayou St. John; produces to the Board a certificate of survey of said land, dated February 27, 1806.
Testimony taken. March 21, 1806. Jacob Myers, sworn, says that claimant did, prior to and on the 20th December, 1803, actually inhabit and cultivate said tract of land, and had then a wife and four children.
March 21, 1806: Present, Lucas and Donaldson, commissioners. The Board grant said claimant one thousand and fifty arpents of land, situate as aforesaid, provided so much be found vacant there.
October 6, 1810: Present, Penrose and Bates, commissioners. It is the opinion of the Board that this claim ought not to be granted.

JAMES FOSTER, claiming eight hundred and seventy arpents of land, situate on the waters of Joachim, district of St. Louis; produces to the Board a plat of survey, signed William Russel, January 4, 1806; certified to be received for record, 25th February, same year, by Antoine Soulard, Surveyor General.
Testimony taken. July 7, 1809. Humphrey Gibson, sworn, says that claimant and other persons came to this country with witness, about the year 1801; witness then went to François Valle, commandant of St. Genevieve, and obtained permission for himself and company to settle on vacant lands.
James Gray, sworn, says that claimant raised a crop of corn on this land in 1803; but then lived with his father-in-law, adjoining this tract; built a house on said land, and cultivated it in 1804; inhabited and cultivated in 1805, and ever since.
October 9, 1810: Present, Lucas and Penrose, commissioners. It is the opinion of the Board that this claim ought not to be granted.

AMOS COX, claiming eleven hundred and fifty arpents of land, situate on Cypress swamp, district of New Madrid; produces to the Board a certificate of survey, dated February 27, 1806.
Testimony taken. March 12, 1806. Jacob Myers, sworn, says that claimant did, prior to and on the 20th day of December, 1803, actually inhabit and cultivate the said tract of land, and had then a wife and six children.
March 12, 1806: Present, Lucas and Donaldson, commissioners. The Board grant the said claimant eleven hundred and fifty arpents of land, situate as aforesaid, provided so much be found vacant there.
October 9, 1810: Present, Lucas and Penrose, commissioners. It is the opinion of the Board that this claim ought not to be granted.

HUGH BURNETT, claiming seven hundred and fifty arpents of land, situate upon the waters of bayou St. John, district of New Madrid; produces to the Board a certificate of survey of the same, dated the 28th February, 1806.
Testimony taken. March 20, 1806. George Wilson, sworn, says that the said Hugh Burnett did, prior to and on the 20th December, 1803, actually inhabit and cultivate the said tract of land, and was then of the age of twenty-one years and upwards.

****

March 20, 1806: Present, Lucas and Donaldson, commissioners. The Board grant the said claimant seven hundred and fifty arpents of land, situate as aforesaid, provided so much be found vacant there.

October 9, 1810: Present, Lucas and Penrose, commissioners. It is the opinion of the Board that this claim ought not to be granted.

MARGARET TASH, claiming three hundred arpents of land, situate on Tywappety, district of New Madrid; produces to the Board a notice to the recorder.

Testimony taken, by authority from the Board, at New Madrid, June 17, 1808, by Frederick Bates, commissioner. William Smith, sworn, says that premises were inhabited and cultivated in the year 1803, and constantly to the present time; about five acres now in cultivation; the widow (claimant) had three children in 1803.

October 9, 1810: Present, Lucas and Penrose, commissioners. It is the opinion of the Board that this claim ought not to be granted.

MARTIN TASH, claiming two hundred arpents of land, situate on Tywappety, district of New Madrid; produces to the Board a notice to the recorder.

Testimony taken, as aforesaid, at New Madrid, June 17, 1808, by Frederick Bates, commissioner. William Smith, sworn, says that premises were inhabited and cultivated in 1803, and constantly to the present time; about six or seven acres now in cultivation; believed to be twenty-two years of age, in 1803.

October 9, 1810: Present, Lucas and Penrose, commissioners. It is the opinion of the Board that this claim ought not to be granted.

SAMUEL PARKER, claiming two hundred arpents of land, situate on lake St. Mary, district of New Madrid; produces to the Board a plat and certificate of survey, dated February 2, 1798.

Testimony taken. March 11, 1806. George Wilson, sworn, says that, to the best of his knowledge, a warrant of survey was granted claimant for said land, and that claimant did, prior to and on the 1st October, 1800, actually inhabit and cultivate the same.

Testimony taken, by authority from the Board, at New Madrid, June 17, 1808, by Frederick Bates, commissioner. Joseph Story, sworn, says that, by order of Colonel Charles D. Delassus, late commandant, witness surveyed premises for claimant.

Isadore Scarlet, sworn, says that premises were inhabited and cultivated in the year 1798, and constantly during the three following years; a part of this tract sold to Thomas Coxe; has been constantly inhabited and cultivated; claimant had a wife and four children when he first made the settlement.

March 11, 1806: Present, Penrose and Donaldson, commissioners. The Board confirm to said claimant two hundred arpents of land, situate as aforesaid.

October 9, 1810: Present, Lucas and Penrose, commissioners. It is the opinion of the Board that this claim ought not to be granted.

WILLIAM SMITH, claiming four hundred arpents of land, situate five miles from the head of Tywappety Bottom; produces to the Board a notice to the recorder.

Testimony taken, by authority from the Board, at New Madrid, June 17, 1808, by Frederick Bates, commissioner. Stephen Jones, sworn, says that claimant built a cabin in the fall of 1803, and sowed some turnips; in the spring of next year put a tenant on this tract and raised a crop, also in the year 1805, since which time it has been vacant; three or four acres in cultivation in 1805.

Charles Lucas, sworn, says that claimant had a wife and seven children in 1803.

October 9, 1810: Present, Lucas and Penrose, commissioners. It is the opinion of the Board that this claim ought not to be granted.

GEORGE SMITH, claiming from three hundred to four hundred arpents of land, situate adjoining the fields of St. Ferdinand, (claiming as assignee of Peter Payan;) produces to the Board a special permission to settle, from Charles D. Delassus, dated 18th December, 1802; and a survey of four hundred and seventy-three arpents, taken 25th November, same year, and certified 5th January, 1803; and a deed of transfer of the same, dated February 14, 1805.

Testimony taken. September 15, 1806. John Ellis, sworn, says that the said Peter Payan settled the said tract of land in 1800, and did, prior to and on the 20th December, 1803, actually inhabit and cultivate the same; and had then a wife.

September 15, 1806: Present, Lucas and Donaldson, commissioners. The Board grant the said claimant assignee as aforesaid, two hundred arpents of land, situate as aforesaid, provided so much be found vacant there.

October 10, 1810: Present, Lucas, Penrose, and Bates, commissioners. It is the opinion of the Board that this claim ought not to be granted.

ANDREW RAMSAY, assignee of John Ramsay, assignee of Jesse Scruggs, who re-assigned to said John Ramsay, original claimant, claiming two hundred and forty arpents of land, situate on river Charles, district of Cape Girardeau; produces to the Board a concession from Zenon Trudeau, Lieutenant Governor, to John Ramsay for the same, dated 14th September, 1797; a plat of survey, certified 1st May, 1798, and dated 25th April, 1798; an assignment from John Ramsay to Jesse Scruggs, dated 24th October, 1807; a re-assignment from said Jesse Scruggs to John Ramsay, dated 25th April, 1808.

The following acknowledgment and testimony were taken, by authority of the Board at Cape Girardeau, June 1st, 1808, by Frederick Bates, commissioner.

John Ramsay personally appears, and acknowledges that he has conveyed to Andrew Ramsay all his right and title to these premises.

James Earl, sworn, says that there is no improvement, but that he saw claimant making sugar on this tract, and keeping stock in 1799.

December 26, 1810: Present, Lucas, Penrose, and Bates, commissioners. It is the opinion of the Board that this claim ought not to be confirmed.

JONATHAN FOREMAN, claiming seven hundred and sixty arpents and eighty perches of land; produces to the Board a certificate of survey of the same, dated January 10, 1800; and another survey of two hundred and thirty-four arpents, same date.

Testimony taken. April 14, 1806. James Earl, sworn, says that claimant did, prior to and on the 1st day of October, 1800, actually inhabit and cultivate the said tract of land.

Bartholomew Cousin, sworn, says that he has seen a concession for the said tract of land to claimant, granted by Zenon Trudeau, dated 5th January, 1798.

Testimony taken, by authority of the Board, at Cape Girardeau, May 31, 1808, by Frederick Bates, commissioner. William Daugherty, sworn, says that the first crop raised on this land was in 1799; a house built, and inhabited; and said premises have been ever since constantly inhabited and cultivated; about one hundred acres in cultivation; apple and peach orchard.

B. Cousin states, that Jonathan Foreman left, as said Foreman informed him, the original concession in pledge in or near Natchez.

April 14, 1806. Present, Lucas and Donaldson, commissioners. The Board confirm to the said claimant seven hundred and fifty arpents of land, being the said tract actually inhabited and cultivated by him prior to and on the 1st October, 1800; and postpone the decision on the second survey.

November 26, 1810: Present, Lucas, Penrose, and Bates, commissioners. It is the opinion of the Board that this claim ought not to be confirmed, because the allegation of the loss of the concession is not made on oath.

JOHN P. AIDENGER, assignee of James Earl, assignee of Jeremiah Conoway, claiming three hundred arpents of land, situate on White waters, district of Cape Girardeau; produces to the Board, as a special permission to settle, list B, on which Jeremiah Conoway is No. 10; a transfer from said Conoway to said Earl, dated 27th January, 1807; a transfer from said Earl to claimant, dated 21st April, 1808.

Testimony taken, by authority of the Board, at Cape Girardeau, June 1, 1808, by Frederick Bates, commissioner. James Ramsey, sworn, says that said land was first improved in 1802, by building a cabin; cleared, enclosed, and cultivated, about two and a half acres in corn in 1803; those of his family who cultivated the land inhabited it in the latter year.

November 26, 1810: Present, Lucas, Penrose, and Bates, commissioners. It is the opinion of a majority of the Board that this claim ought not to be granted; Frederick Bates, commissioner, voting for a confirmation thereof.

MATTHEW HUBBLE, assignee of Thomas Lewis, claiming three hundred and fifty arpents of land, situate on waters of Crooked creek, district of Cape Girardeau; produces to the Board, as a special permission to settle, list B, on which Thomas Lewis is No. 9; a deed of transfer from said Lewis to claimant, dated 23d January, 1807.

Testimony taken, as aforesaid, at Cape Girardeau, June 3, 1808, by Frederick Bates, commissioner. Robert Crump, sworn, says that six acres were cultivated in 1804; two cabins.

Abraham Byrd, affirmed, says that in the latter part of the year 1808, he saw a turnip field enclosed with poles, brush, and logs, and turnips growing therein; inhabited and cultivated at this time; ten acres now in cultivation; believes there was a cabin before the 20th December, 1803.

November 26, 1810: Present, Lucas, Penrose, and Bates, commissioners. It is the opinion of the Board that this claim ought not to be granted.

JACOB GREATER, heirs of, claiming eight hundred arpents of land, situate on White waters, district of Cape Girardeau; produces to the Board an affidavit of permission to settle, signed B. Cousin, and dated June 3, 1808.

Testimony taken, as aforesaid, at Cape Girardeau, June 3, 1808, by Frederick Bates, commissioner. John Byrd, Esq., sworn, says that this land was settled in the fall of 1803; a cabin then built and inhabited; a few acres cleared, enclosed, and cultivated, the following year; premises inhabited and cultivated constantly to the present time; between fifteen and twenty acres now in cultivation.

November 26, 1810: Present, Lucas, Penrose, and Bates, commissioners. It is the opinion of a majority of the Board that this claim ought not to be granted. Frederick Bates, commissioner, voting for the granting of five hundred and fifty arpents.

JAMES COX, claiming two hundred and forty arpents of land, situate on Gibany creek, district of Cape Girardeau; produces to the Board an affidavit of permission to settle, to John Cox, on vacant lands, dated June 3, 1808.

November 26, 1810: Present, Lucas, Penrose, and Bates, commissioners. It is the opinion of the Board that this claim ought not to be granted.

ROBERT McCOY, claiming three hundred and twenty arpents of land, situate in the district of Cape Girardeau; produces to the Board a concession from Juan Ventura Morales, Intendant General, dated May, 1802.

December 3, 1810: Present, Lucas, Penrose, and Bates, commissioners. It is the opinion of the Board that this claim ought not to be confirmed.

JAMES RILEY, claiming two hundred arpents of land, situate on Big prairie, district of New Madrid; produces to the Board a permission to settle, from Henry Peyroux, commandant of New Madrid district, dated 30th March, 1802; a plat of survey of the same, dated 10th February, 1806, certified 24th February, 1806.

Testimony taken, by authority from the Board, at New Madrid, June 13, 1808, by Frederick Bates, commissioner. Moses Hurley, sworn, says that in the year 1803 premises were partially improved, a house was built and inhabited towards the closing of that year; and witness thinks peach stones planted; about sixteen acres now in cultivation, and enclosed; fruit trees and other improvements; a dwelling house, smoke house, &c. In 1803, claimant had a wife and five children.

December 3, 1810: Present, Lucas, Penrose, and Bates, commissioners. It is the opinion of a majority of the Board that this claim ought not to be granted. Frederick Bates, commissioner, voting for a confirmation thereof.

JOHN TUCKER, assignee of William Doss, claiming one hundred and ninety-seven and one-third arpents of land, situate on Big swamp, district of New Madrid; produces to the Board a certified list of permission to settle, No. 1369, on which William Doss is No. 196, for two hundred arpents; a certified copy of a deed of conveyance from Doss to claimant, dated 13th November, 1802, certified 3d December, 1805; and a plat of survey, signed Joseph Story.

Testimony taken, as aforesaid, at New Madrid, June 15, 1808, by Frederick Bates, commissioner. Jacob Myers, sworn, says that Doss lived on premises, in a cabin, in the year 1800; sowed turnips; premises constantly inhabited and cultivated to this day; fifteen acres at least in cultivation at present; claimant had one child in 1803.

December 3, 1810: Present, Lucas, Penrose, and Bates, commissioners. It is the opinion of the Board that this claim ought not to be granted.

ABNER MASTERS, claiming two hundred arpents of land, situate in prairie St. Charles, district of New Madrid; produces to the Board a list, No. 1369, on which claimant is No. 155, as permission to settle; a plat of survey,

****

dated 11th January, 1806; certified 28th February, 1806, by Antoine Soulard, Surveyor General of the Territory of Louisiana.

 Testimony taken, as aforesaid, at New Madrid, June 15th, 1808, by Frederick Bates, commissioner. George Hacker, sworn, says that claimant has cut hay on the premises every year since 1802; in 1803 he split rails; claimant inhabits and cultivates the present year.

 December 4, 1810: Present, Lucas, Penrose, and Bates, commissioners. It is the opinion of the Board that this claim ought not to be granted.

 Robert Cummins, claiming three hundred arpents of land, situate on a fork of the river Pemiscon, district of New Madrid; produces to the Board a permission to settle, signed François Lesieur, commandant of the post, and dated 10th September, 1802; a plat of survey, signed Michel Ameroux, deputy surveyor district of New Madrid, and dated 24th February, 1806.

 Testimony taken, as aforesaid, at New Madrid, June 15, 1808, by Frederick Bates, commissioner. Jacob Waggoner, sworn, says premises were improved and cultivated in 1803; cultivated the following year, and constantly to this time; premises have now a house, and out-houses, peach and apple orchard; Cummins had a wife and three children in the year 1803.

 December 4, 1810: Present, Lucas, Penrose, and Bates, commissioners. It is the opinion of the Board that this claim ought not to be granted.

 James Connoway, claiming two hundred arpents of land, situate on the river Pemiscon, district of New Madrid; produces to the Board a permission to settle, from François Lesieur, commandant of the post, dated 28th July, 1802; a plat of survey, signed Michel Ameroux, deputy surveyor of district of New Madrid, and dated 24th February, 1806.

 Testimony taken, as aforesaid, at New Madrid, June 15, 1808, by Frederick Bates, commissioner. Jacob Waggoner, sworn, says that premises were cultivated, and a crop raised on it in the years 1803 and 1804, but never inhabited; claimant has no family, but is upwards of twenty-one years of age.

 December 4, 1810: Present, Lucas, Penrose, and Bates, commissioners. It is the opinion of the Board that this claim ought not to be granted.

 Nancy Ferguson, claiming three hundred arpents of land, situate in Tywappety, district of New Madrid; produces to the Board a certified list of permission to settle, formerly given, No. 1369, on which claimant is No. 298.

 Testimony taken, as aforesaid, at New Madrid, June 15, 1808, by Frederick Bates, commissioner. George Hacker, sworn, says that premises were improved in 1803, by splitting rails and clearing about an acre of ground; no crops raised till the present year; no inhabitation.

 December 5, 1810: Present, Lucas, Penrose, and Bates, commissioners. It is the opinion of the Board that this claim ought not to be granted.

 Absalom Hacker, claiming two hundred arpents of land, situate in Tywappety, district of New Madrid; produces to the Board a certified permission to settle, formerly given, No. 1369, on which claimant is No. 297.

 Testimony taken. June 15, 1808. George Hacker, sworn, says that premises were cultivated in the year 1802, and constantly to the present time; between three and four acres in cultivation; thinks he was twenty-one years of age in April, 1803.

 December 5, 1810: Present, Lucas, Penrose, and Bates, commissioners. It is the opinion of the Board that this claim ought not to be granted.

 Samuel Kenyon, claiming two hundred arpents of land, situate south end of prairie St. Charles, district of New Madrid; produces to the Board a certified permission to settle, formerly given, on which claimant is No. 272, on list No. 1369.

 Testimony taken. June 16, 1808. Jesse Masters, sworn, says that claimant built a cabin in the year 1802, and lived in it in 1802.

 William Masters, sworn, says that Lemuel Masters lived on and cultivated this tract in the year 1803, and till the 20th December.

 December 5, 1810: Present, Lucas, Penrose, and Bates, commissioners. It is the opinion of the Board that this claim ought not to be granted.

 Joseph Smith, claiming two hundred arpents of land, situate in prairie St. Charles, district of New Madrid; produces to the Board an order of survey from Henry Peyroux, commandant of New Madrid, dated 22d May, 1801.

 Testimony taken. June 16, 1808. Edward Matthews, sworn, says that a part of this claim was cultivated in 1801, and constantly till 1807; two or three acres now in cultivation.

 December 5, 1810: Present, Lucas, Penrose, and Bates, commissioners. It is the opinion of the Board that this claim ought not to be granted.

 Daniel Stringer, claiming one thousand and twenty arpents of land, situate on the Mississippi, district of New Madrid; produces to the Board a survey of the same, taken 2d and certified 28th February, 1806.

 Testimony taken. August 26, 1806. William Smith, sworn, says that he has seen in the possession of claimant a permission granted him by Henry Peyroux.

 Daniel Mullens, sworn, says that claimant did, prior to and on the 20th December, 1803, actually inhabit and cultivate the said tract of land, and had then a wife, three children, and one slave.

 June 16, 1808. Thomas Clark, sworn, says that premises were settled in the fall of 1802, and in the following year, and constantly to the present time premises have been inhabited and cultivated; about eighteen or twenty acres now in cultivation; claimant had in 1803 a wife and one slave.

 December 12, 1810: Present, Lucas, Penrose, and Bates, commissioners. It is the opinion of the Board that this claim ought not to be granted.

 Agnew Massey, claiming three hundred arpents of land, situate in Tywappety, district of New Madrid; produces to the Board a certified list of permission to settle, formerly given, No. 1369, on which claimant is No. 248.

 Testimony taken. June 16, 1808. Edward Matthews, sworn, says that, in the spring of 1802, claimant built a cabin, and inhabited, cleared, enclosed, and cultivated a few acres; he left the premises in the fall of that year, since which time it has neither been inhabited nor cultivated; claimant had a wife and one child.

 December 12, 1810: Present, Lucas, Penrose, and Bates, commissioners. It is the opinion of the Board that this claim ought not to be granted.

****

PETER LEWIS, claiming two hundred and forty arpents of land, situate on river Pemiscon, district of New Madrid; produces to the Board a certificate of permission to settle from François Lesieur, commandant, dated in 1801.

Testimony taken. June 16, 1808. Jacob Myers, sworn, says that premises were cultivated and inhabited by claimant constantly from 1801 till some time in the year 1804, first year included, and afterwards by other persons, uninterruptedly, to this time; a single man, upwards of twenty-one years of age; eight or ten acres now in cultivation.

The permission to settle, said to to be produced in this claim, cannot now be found on record or on file.

December 12, 1810: Present, Lucas, Penrose, and Bates, commissioners. It is the opinion of the Board that this claim ought not to be granted.

JACOB WAGGONER, claiming two hundred arpents of land, situate on river Pemiscon, district of New Madrid; produces to the Board a certified list of permission to settle, formerly given, No. 1369, on which claimant is No. 231.

Testimony taken. June 16, 1808. William Conaway, sworn, says that premises were settled, inhabited, cleared, and cultivated, and enclosed near three acres of land; inhabitation and cultivation continued constantly to this day; about seven acres now in cultivation; a wife and one child in the year 1803.

December 13, 1810: Present, Lucas, Penrose, and Bates, commissioners. It is the opinion of the Board that this claim ought not to be granted.

NICOLAS REVIELLE, claiming two hundred arpents of land, situate about twelve miles below the mouth of the Ohio, on the Mississippi; produces to the Board a notice to the recorder; also, as a special permission to settle, list A, on which claimant is No. 115.

Testimony taken. June 17, 1808. Stephen Jones, sworn, says that premises were improved in 1802, at which time a few acres were cleared, enclosed, and cultivated in potatoes and fruit trees; in the following year, 1803, claimant inhabited and cultivated, and constantly to the present time; about ten acres in corn, and fifteen acres under fence; a good cabin; a single man, about twenty-one years of age.

The permission produced in this claim has been produced in another claim of the claimant.

December 13, 1810: Present, Lucas, Penrose, and Bates, commissioners. It is the opinion of the Board that this claim ought not to be granted.

WILLIAM COX, claiming one thousand arpents of land, situate on the waters of the bayou St. John; produces to the Board a certificate of a permission to settle from Henry Peyroux, in May, 1802; and a certificate of survey, dated February 27, 1806.

Testimony taken. March 21, 1806. Jacob Myers, sworn, says that claimant did, prior to and on the 20th December, 1803, actually inhabit and cultivate the said tract of land, and had then a wife and three children.

June 17, 1808. John Friend, sworn, says he settled in 1802, raised grain on said tract in that year, (six or seven acres,) built a house, and inhabited it; premises have been constantly inhabited and cultivated to this day; about thirty acres now in cultivation; in 1803, claimant had a wife and two or three children.

The permission stated to be produced cannot now be found.

March 21, 1806: Present, Lucas and Penrose, commissioners. The Board grant the said William Cox one thousand arpents of land, situate as aforesaid, provided so much be found vacant there.

December 13, 1810: Present, Lucas, Penrose, and Bates, commissioners. It is the opinion of the Board that this claim ought not to be granted.

EDWARD ROBERTSON, assignee of Emsley Jones, claiming three hundred arpents of land, situate on the Mississippi, district of New Madrid; produces to the Board a certified list of permission to settle, formerly given, No. 1369, on which said Jones is No. 131.

Testimony taken. March 21, 1806. Jacob Myers, sworn, says that the said Emsley Jones actually inhabited and cultivated the said tract of land in 1802; that, some time in that year, the most part of his family being sick, and attributing the same to the situation of said land, he moved out of it, and settled on another tract, about nine or ten miles distant from the former, where he did, prior to and on the 20th of December, 1803, actually inhabit and cultivate.

July 7, 1809. John Friend, sworn, says that the premises were cultivated and inhabited in 1801, and premises have been constantly inhabited and cultivated to this day; about sixteen acres now in cultivation; a wife and three children in 1803.

December 13, 1810: Present, Lucas, Penrose, and Bates, commissioners. It is the opinion of the Board that this claim ought not to be granted.

PHILIP SHACKLER, claiming seven hundred and fifty arpents of land, situate on lake St. Mary, district of New Madrid; produces to the Board a certificate of survey, dated February 28, 1806, and a certificate of a permission to settle from Henry Peyroux, in 1802.

Testimony taken. March 21, 1806. Jacob Myers, sworn, says that claimant did, prior to and on the 20th December, 1803, actually inhabit and cultivate the said tract of land, and was then of the age of twenty-one years and upwards.

The permission stated to be produced in this claim is not found.

December 14, 1810: Present, Lucas, Penrose, and Bates, commissioners. It is the opinion of the Board that this claim ought not to be granted.

JAMES SMITH, claiming seven hundred and fifty arpents of land, situate on the Mississippi, Tywappety, district of New Madrid; produces to the Board an order of survey from Robert McCoy, commandant, for three hundred arpents, dated 10th October, 1799, and No. 1207.

Testimony taken. June 17, 1808. William Smith, sworn, says that premises were improved in the fall of 1803, cultivated and inhabited in that and the following year, about seven acres now prepared for cultivation, a wife and one child in 1803.

The order of survey stated to be produced, as permission to settle, has been produced in another claim of James Smith, by John Frazer and others.

December 14, 1810: Present, Lucas, Penrose, and Bates, commissioners. It is the opinion of the Board that this claim ought not to be granted.

JOSEPH MICHEL, assignee of Benjamin Douglas, claiming two hundred arpents of land, situate on the river Pemiscon, district of New Madrid; produces to the Board a plat of survey, signed Michel Ameroux, and dated 24th February, 1806; a conveyance from said Douglas to claimant, dated 16th September, 1805.

Testimony taken. June 17th, 1808. George Ruddell, sworn, says that premises were cultivated in the years 1802, 1803, and 1804; lived on the land in a camp in 1803, believes on the 20th December; no cabin; about three acres; no family; above twenty-one years of age.

December 14, 1810: Present, Lucas, Penrose, and Bates, commissioners. It is the opinion of the Board that this claim ought not to be granted.

Joseph Michel, claiming eight hundred arpents of land, situate on river Pemiscon, district of New Madrid; produces to the Board a certificate of permission to settle, from François Lesieur, dated October 22, 1802, and a certificate of survey, dated February 28, 1806.

Testimony taken: March 20, 1806. George Ruddell, sworn, says that claimant did, prior to and on the 20th December, 1803, actually inhabit and cultivate the said tract of land, having his negroes at work, and living thereon; during which time, claimant lived within the said district of New Madrid; he has no claim to lands in his own name in this Territory.

Testimony taken. June 17, 1808. George Ruddell, sworn, says that in 1803 claimant put a negro on this tract for the purpose of improving, also a stock of cattle, also a white tenant; premises have been constantly inhabited and cultivated, to this day; eight or ten acres now in cultivation.

P. A. Laforge, sworn, says that claimant had two children, wife, and fifteen negroes in the year 1803.

December 19, 1810: Present, Lucas, Penrose, and Bates, commissioners. It is the opinion of the Board that this claim ought not to be granted.

Francis Michel, claiming four hundred arpents of land, situate on river Pemiscon, district of New Madrid; produces to the Board a permission to settle from Francis Lesieur, dated October 28, 1803, and a certificate of survey, dated February 28, 1806.

Testimony taken. March 20, 1808. George Ruddell, sworn, says that the said tract of land was, prior to and on the 20th December, 1803, actually inhabited and cultivated, for the use of the claimant, and by his negroes.

March 20, 1806: Present, Lucas, Penrose, and Bates, commissioners. The Board reject this claim, the claimant not having himself actually inhabited and cultivated the said tract prior to and on the 20th December, 1803, and think it a case of equity.

Louis St. Aubin, claiming one hundred and twenty arpents of land, situate on Little Prairie, district of New Madrid; produces to the Board a certificate of permission to settle from Francis Lesieur, of the 2d January, 1802, certified A. Laforge, June 2, 1804, and a certificate of survey by Joseph Story, without date.

Testimony taken. March 20, 1806. George Ruddell, sworn, says that claimant did, prior to and on the 1st October, 1800, actually inhabit and cultivate the said tract of land, and was then the head of a family.

Testimony taken. June 17, 1808. Jacob Waggoner, sworn, says that premises were inhabited and cultivated in the year 1801; buildings on the lot adjoining; the said tract, or this tract, certainly joins the lots of the village, if not those of this claimant; seven or eight acres in cultivation; a wife and five children in 1803.

March 20, 1806: Present, Lucas and Donaldson, commissioners. The Board confirm to said claimant one hundred and twenty arpents of land, situate as aforesaid.

December 21, 1810: Present, Lucas, Penrose, and Bates, commissioners. It is the opinion of the Board that this claim ought not to be granted.

Francis Maisonville, claiming one thousand arpents of land, situate on the portage of the river St. Francis; produces to the Board a certificate of survey, dated February 26, 1806.

Testimony taken. March 20, 1806. George Wilson, sworn, says that claimant did, prior to and on the 20th December, 1803, actually inhabit and cultivate the said land, and had then a wife and three children.

June 17, 1808. Henry Godair, sworn, says that premises were inhabited and cultivated from 1802 to the present day; a wife and child in 1803; eighteen arpents now in cultivation.

March 20, 1806: Present, Lucas and Penrose, commissioners. The Board grant the said claimant one thousand arpents of land, situate as aforesaid, provided so much be found vacant there.

December 21, 1810: Present, Lucas, Penrose, and Bates, commissioners. It is the opinion of the Board that this claim ought not to be granted.

Pierre Latour, the heirs of, claiming one thousand one hundred and fifty arpents of land, situate on the portage of the river St. Francis; produces to the Board a certificate of survey of the same, dated February 28, 1806.

Testimony taken. March 20, 1806. George Wilson, sworn, says that claimant did, prior to and on the 20th December, 1803, actually inhabit and cultivate the said tract of land, and had then a wife and six children.

June 17, 1808. Francis Trenchard, sworn, says that premises were inhabited and cultivated in 1803, and constantly till about six months ago, when he died; had a wife and seven children in 1803.

March 20, 1806: Present, Lucas and Penrose, commissioners. The Board grant said claimant, one thousand one hundred and fifty arpents of land, situate as aforesaid, provided so much be found vacant there.

December 21, 1810: Present, Lucas, Penrose, and Bates, commissioners. It is the opinion of the Board that this claim ought not to be granted.

Joseph Labussiere, claiming seven hundred and fifty arpents of land, situate on the portage of the river St. Francis, district of New Madrid; produces to the Board a certificate of survey, dated February 28, 1806.

Testimony taken. March 20, 1806. George Wilson, sworn, says that claimant did, prior to and on the 20th December, 1803, actually inhabit and cultivate the said tract of land; and was then of the age of twenty-one years and upwards.

March 20, 1806: Present, Lucas and Penrose, commissioners. The Board grant to the said claimant seven hundred and fifty arpents of land, situate as aforesaid, provided so much be found vacant there.

December 21, 1810: Present, Lucas, Penrose, and Bates, commissioners. It is the opinion of the Board that this claim ought not to be granted.

Ignace Huno, claiming seven hundred and fifty arpents of land, situate at portage of the river St. Francis; produces to the Board a survey of said land, dated February 28, 1806.

Testimony taken. March 18, 1806. George Wilson, sworn, says that the said claimant did, prior to and on the 20th December, 1803, actually inhabit and cultivate the said tract of land, and was then of the age of twenty-one years and upwards.

March 18, 1806: Present, Lucas and Donaldson, commissioners. The Board grant the said claimant seven hundred and fifty arpents of land, situate as aforesaid, provided so much be found vacant there.

****

December 21, 1810: Present, Lucas, Penrose, and Bates, commissioners. It is the opinion of the Board that this claim ought not to be granted.

ANTOINE GAMELIN, claiming seven hundred and fifty arpents of land, situate at the portage of the river St. Francis; produces to the Board a certificate of survey of the same, dated 27th February, 1806.
Testimony taken. March 18, 1806. George Wilson, sworn, says that claimant did, prior to and on the 20th December, 1803, actually inhabit and cultivate the said tract of land, and was then of the age of twenty-one years and upwards.
March 18, 1806: Present, Lucas, Penrose, and Bates, commissioners. The Board grant to said claimant seven hundred and fifty arpents of land, situate as aforesaid, provided so much be found vacant there.
December 21, 1810: Present, Lucas, Penrose, and Bates, commissioners. It is the opinion of the Board that this claim ought not to be granted.

MADELINE DUBOIS, widow of Louis Dubois, claiming nine hundred arpents of land, situate at the portage of the river St. Francis; produces to the Board a certificate of survey of the same, dated February 28, 1806.
Testimony taken. March 18, 1806. George Wilson, sworn, says that the said Louis Dubois did, prior to and on the 20th December, 1803, actually inhabit and cultivate the said tract of land, and had then a wife and one child.
June 17, 1808. Henry Trenchard, sworn, says that premises were inhabited and cultivated from the year 1802, inclusive, to this day, for the use of claimant; four or five arpents now in cultivation; a wife and three children and an orphan child in 1803.
March 18, 1806: Present, Penrose and Donaldson, commissioners. The Board grant the said claimant nine hundred arpents of land, situate as aforesaid, provided so much be found vacant there.
December 21, 1810: Present, Lucas, Penrose, and Bates, commissioners. It is the opinion of the Board that this claim ought not to be granted.

PETER LOVEL, assignee of Joseph Charpentier, claiming two hundred and forty arpents of land, situate on lake Isidore, district of New Madrid; produces to the Board a petition and recommendation for a concession signed Henry Peyroux, dated September 24, 1800, and a certificate of survey of said land, dated December 10, 1797.
Testimony taken. March 15, 1806. Richard J. Waters, sworn, says that claimant did, prior to and on the 1st October, 1800, actually inhabit and cultivate the said tract of land.
June 17, 1808. Pierre Antoine Laforge, sworn, says that premises have been constantly inhabited and cultivated from the year 1797 to this time; about forty arpents now in cultivation; a wife and two children in 1803.
March 15, 1806: Present, Penrose and Donaldson, commissioners. The Board confirm to the said claimant two hundred and forty arpents of land, situate as aforesaid, as per the said petition and recommendation thereunto annexed.
December 21, 1810: Present, Lucas, Penrose, and Bates, commissioners. It is the opinion of the Board that this claim ought not to be confirmed.

CHARLES GUILBAULT, claiming one hundred and twenty arpents of land, situate back of Little Prairie, district of New Madrid; produces to the Board a concession from Henry Peyroux, dated 15th April, 1801, and a plat of survey.
Testimony taken. June 17 1808. Francis Lesieur, sworn, says that premises were inhabited and cultivated since 1800, inclusively, to this day; eleven or twelve acres now in cultivation; a wife and four children in 1803.
December 22, 1810: Present, Lucas, Penrose, and Bates, commissioners. It is the opinion of the Board that this claim ought not to be granted.

CHARLES GUILBAULT, claiming one hundred and thirty arpents of land, situate on the Mississippi, district of New Madrid; produces to the Board a petition and recommendation from Henry Peyroux for a concession, dated April 15, 1801, and a certificate of survey of the same, dated February 27, 1806.
Testimony taken. March 18, 1806. Robert McCoy, sworn, says that claimant did, prior to and on the 1st day of October, 1800, actually inhabit and cultivate the same.
March 18, 1806: Present, Penrose and Donaldson, commissioners. The Board confirm to said claimant one hundred and thirty arpents of land, as per the said petition and recommendation for a concession.
December 22, 1810: Present, Lucas, Penrose, and Bates, commissioners. It is the opinion of the Board that this claim ought not to be granted.

JOSEPH SEREZO, claiming nine hundred arpents of land, situate at the portage of the river St. Francis; produces to the Board a certificate of survey of the same, dated 28th February, 1806.
Testimony taken. March 20, 1806. George Wilson, sworn, says that claimant did prior to and on the 20th December, 1803, actually inhabit and cultivate the said tract of land, and had a wife and three children.
June 7, 1808. Hyacinth Gayon, sworn, says that premises were cultivated and inhabited in 1801 or 1802, and constantly to the present time; about four or five arpents in cultivation, and an orchard of peach trees; a wife and child in 1803.
March 20, 1806: Present, Lucas and Penrose. The Board grant to said claimant one thousand arpents of land, situate as aforesaid, provided so much be found vacant there.
December 22, 1810: Present, Lucas, Penrose, and Bates commissioners. It is the opinion of the Board that this claim ought not to be granted.

LOUIS ROY, claiming nine hundred and fifty arpents of land, situate on bayou of portage of the river St. Francis; produces to the Board a certificate of survey, dated February 28, 1806.
Testimony taken. March 20, 1806. George Wilson, sworn, says that claimant did, prior to and on the 20th December, 1803, actually inhabit and cultivate the said tract of land, and had then a wife and two children.
June 17, 1808. Hyacinth Gayon, sworn, says that premises were inhabited and cultivated since 1801 or 1802, and constantly to this time; seven or eight arpents now in cultivation; a wife and two children in 1803.
March 20, 1806: Present, Lucas and Penrose, commissioners. The Board grant to the said claimant nine hundred and fifty arpents of land, situate as aforesaid, provided so much be found vacant there.
December 22, 1810: Present, Lucas, Penrose, and Bates, commissioners. It is the opinion of the Board that this claim ought not to be granted.

****

MICHAEL BONNEAU, claiming seven hundred and fifty arpents of land, situate at the portage of the river St. Francis; produces to the Board a certificate of survey, dated February 28, 1806.

Testimony taken. March 20, 1806. George Wilson, sworn, says that claimant did, prior to and on the 20th December, 1803, actually inhabit and cultivate the said land; and was of the age of twenty-one years and upwards.

June 17, 1808. Hyacinth Gayon, sworn, says that the premises were inhabited and cultivated in 1802, and constantly to this day; a small orchard, three or four arpents in cultivation.

Joseph Michel, sworn, says that claimant in 1803 was between twenty-two and twenty-three years of age.

March 20, 1806: Present, Lucas and Donaldson, commissioners. The Board grants the said claimant seven hundred and fifty arpents of land, situate as aforesaid, provided so much be found vacant there.

December 22, 1810: Present, Lucas, Penrose, and Bates, commissioners. It is the opinion of the Board that this claim ought not to be granted.

JOHN WILEY, claiming one thousand one hundred and fifty arpents of land, situate on lake St. Mary's, district of New Madrid; produces to the Board a certificate of survey of seven hundred and fifty-four arpents, dated February 27, 1806; and another certificate of survey of same date, for three hundred and ninety-six arpents.

Testimony taken. March 15, 1806. Edward Robertson, sworn, says that claimant did, prior to and on the 20th December, 1803, actually inhabit and cultivate one of said tracts, to wit, seven hundred and fifty-four arpents, and had then a wife and six children.

June 18, 1808. William Cox, sworn, says that premises were inhabited and cultivated from February, or March, 1803, and constantly till this day; about twelve acres now in cultivation; a wife and six children in the year 1803.

March 15, 1806: Present, Penrose and Donaldson, commissioners. The Board grant said claimant one thousand one hundred and fifty arpents of land, including the said tract of seven hundred and fifty-four arpents, as aforesaid, the whole to form but one survey, provided so much be found vacant there; and reject the above survey of three hundred and ninety-six arpents as aforesaid.

December 22, 1810: Present, Lucas, Penrose, and Bates, commissioners. It is the opinion of the Board that this claim ought not to be granted.

FRANCIS LESIEUR, claiming one hundred and sixty arpents of land, situate on Little Prairie, district of New Madrid; produces to the Board a plat of survey of the same, dated 2d March, 1801, on Joseph Story's surveyor's registry.

Testimony taken. June 18, 1808. George Ruddell, sworn, says that premises were inhabited and cultivated in 1797, and constantly till the present time; between thirty and forty acres now in cultivation; a wife and three children, and one slave in 1803.

January 4, 1811: Present, Lucas, Penrose, and Bates, commissioners. It is the opinion of the Board that this claim ought not to be granted.

FRANCIS LESIEUR, claiming four arpents of land, situate on Little Prairie, district of New Madrid; produces to the Board a concession from Henry Peyroux, dated 19th February, 1801.

Testimony taken. June 18, 1808. George Ruddell, sworn, says that this lot has been constantly inhabited and cultivated since the year 1797; a mill built in 1800, which has constantly wrought, and is the only mill of the settlement.

January 4, 1811: Present, Lucas, Penrose, and Bates, commissioners. It is the opinion of the Board that this claim ought not to be confirmed.

FRANCIS LESIEUR, claiming two hundred and forty arpents of land, situate on Grand Cotes river, Mississippi; produces, as a special permission to settle, a recommendation from Henry Peyroux, dated February 23, 1801; and a certificate of survey of the same.

Testimony taken. June 18, 1808. George Ruddell, sworn, says that premises were improved in 1802, and inhabited and cultivated in the following year, and constantly to the present time; twenty-five acres now in cultivation; good orchard and buildings; a wife, five children, and three negroes in 1803.

March 24, 1806: Present, Lucas and Donaldson, commissioners. The Board reject this claim, the claimant having two tracts of land confirmed to him under separate claims; they observe, however, that the whole of his claim does not exceed eight hundred arpents; that he was, when under the Spanish Government, commandant of the post Little Prairie, and had a numerous family; they further observe, that it was given in evidence, that the said claimant did, prior to and on the 20th December, 1803, actually inhabit and cultivate the said tract of land.

January 4, 1811: Present, Lucas, Penrose, and Bates, commissioners. It is the opinion of the Board that this claim ought not to be confirmed.

THOMAS HARRIS, claiming seven hundred and fifty arpents of land, situate on the waters of the river St. Francis; produces to the Board a certificate of a permission to settle, from Francis Lesieur, and a certificate of survey, dated February 27, 1806.

Testimony taken. March 21, 1806. George Ruddell, sworn, says that claimant did, prior to and on the 20th December, 1803, actually inhabit and cultivate the said tract of land; and was then of the age of twenty-one years and upwards.

June 18, 1808. Jacob Waggoner, sworn, says that premises were cultivated and improved in the year 1803, and constantly to the present time; seven or eight acres now in cultivation; single man in 1803, above the age of twenty-one years.

August 21, 1806: Present, Lucas and Donaldson, commissioners. The Board grant said claimant seven hundred and fifty arpents of land, situate as aforesaid, provided so much be found vacant there.

January 8, 1811: Present, Lucas, Penrose, and Bates, commissioners. It is the opinion of the Board that this claim ought not to be granted.

CHARLES LOGNON, claiming two hundred arpents of land in two separate surveys, to wit, one tract of one hundred and twenty arpents, situate on the Little Prairie, and eighty arpents, situate on lake Gayoso; produces to the Board a certificate of a permission to settle on said two hundred arpents from François Lesieur, dated October 15, 1802; and a certificate of survey of one hundred and twenty arpents, dated February 10, 1801; and another plot of survey of eighty arpents, certified February 27, 1806.

Testimony taken. March 12, 1806. George Ruddell, sworn, says that the said claimant did, prior to and on the 20th December, 1803, actually inhabit and cultivate the said tract of twenty arpents, situate on the Little Prairie.

June 18, 1808. George Ruddell, sworn, says that these two tracts of land, making together the number of arpents claimed, have been improved, to, wit, the tract of one hundred and twenty arpents in 1802, and constantly inhabited and cultivated to this time, residing on this tract; claimant has constantly cultivated the other also till the last year, when the purchaser removed to it, and now inhabits it; about seven acres now in cultivation; wife and two children in 1803.

March 12, 1806: Present, Lucas and Donaldson, commissioners. The Board grant the said claimant one hundred and twenty arpents of land, situate as aforesaid, as per the said survey.

January 8, 1811: Present, Lucas, Penrose, and Bates, commissioners. It is the opinion of the Board that this claim ought not to be granted.

STEPHEN ROSS, assignee of Joseph Story, claiming three hundred arpents of land, situate on bayou St. Henry; produces to the Board a certificate of a permission to settle, from Henry Peyroux, in 1799; and a certificate of survey of the same; a deed of transfer of said land, from said Story to claimant, dated June 10, 1804.

Testimony taken. March 21, 1806. Edward Robertson, sworn, says that said Story settled said tract of land in the year 1799; and did, prior to and on the 1st day of October, actually inhabit and cultivate the same.

June 18, 1808. Andrew Scott, sworn, says that premises were improved partially in the year 1802, and a cabin built, and about one thousand rails made; claimant inhabited and cultivated, in 1804, about forty acres, and constantly till the present time.

Peter Lyon, sworn, says that fifty or sixty acres are now in cultivation; orchard of fruit trees.

Edward Robertson, sworn, says that premises were improved, some work done, in 1801; cultivated and inhabited in 1802, and till the present time; about sixty acres now in cultivation.

March 21, 1806. Present, Lucas and Penrose, commissioners. The Board confirm to the said claimant, assignee as aforesaid, three hundred arpents of land, as per said certificate of permission to settle.

January 14, 1811: Present, Lucas, Penrose, and Bates, commissioners. It is the opinion of the Board that this claim ought not to be granted.

ANTHONY BONNEAU, claiming seven hundred and fifty arpents of land, situate on the portage of the river St. Francis; produces to the Board a certificate of survey, dated February 28, 1806.

Testimony taken. March 20, 1806. George Wilson, sworn, says that claimant did, prior to and on the 20th December, 1803, actually inhabit and cultivate the said tract of land; and was then of the age of twenty-one years and upwards.

June 18, 1808. Joseph Legrand, sworn, says that premises were inhabited and cultivated constantly from the year 1802 to this day; six arpents now in cultivation; a single man above twenty-one years old.

March 20, 1806: Present, Lucas and Donaldson, commissioners. The Board grant the said claimant seven hundred and fifty arpents of land, situate as aforesaid, provided so much be found vacant there.

January 14, 1811: Present, Lucas, Penrose, and Bates, commissioners, It is the opinion of the Board that this claim ought not to be granted.

CHARLES BONNEAU, claiming seven hundred and fifty arpents of land, situate on the portage of the river St. Francis; produces to the Board a certificate of survey, dated 28th February, 1806.

Testimony taken. March 20, 1806. George Wilson, sworn, says that claimant did, prior to and on the 20th December, 1803, actually inhabit and cultivate the said tract of land; and was then of the age of twenty-one years and upwards.

June 18, 1808. Joseph Legrand, sworn, says that premises were inhabited and cultivated from 1802 until this day constantly; seven or eight arpents now in cultivation; a single man above twenty-one years of age.

March 20, 1806: Present, Lucas and Donaldson, commissioners. The Board grant the said claimant seven hundred and fifty arpents of land, situate as aforesaid, provided so much be found vacant there.

January 14, 1811: Present, Lucas, Penrose, and Bates, commissioners. It is the opinion of the Board that this claim ought not to be granted.

PETER DUMAY, claiming three hundred arpents of land, situate on Tywappety, adjoining Charles Findley, district of New Madrid; produces to the Board a notice to the recorder. For permission to settle, see list No. 1396.

Testimony taken. June 18, 1808. Stephen Jones, sworn, says that premises were inhabited and cultivated in 1803, (having been partially improved in 1802,) since which time, it has been constantly cultivated but not inhabited; six acres now in cultivation; two children in 1803.

January 14, 1811: Present, Lucas, Penrose, and Bates, commissioners. It is the opinion of the Board that this claim ought not to be granted.

ANTHONY GAXON, claiming two hundred arpents of land, situate on Tywappety, district of New Madrid; produces to the Board a notice to the recorder. For permission to settle see list No. 1369.

Testimony taken. June 18, 1808. Stephen Jones, sworn, says that premises were improved in 1803; a cabin built, and land cultivated, but not inhabited; constantly cultivated to this time; about five acres now in cultivation.

January 14, 1811: Present, Lucas, Penrose, and Bates, commissioners. It is the opinion of the Board that this claim ought not to be granted.

EUSTACE DELISLE, claiming seven hundred and fifty arpents of land, situate at the portage of the river St. Francis; produces to the Board a certificate of survey, dated February 28, 1806.

Testimony taken. March 17, 1806. George Wilson, sworn, says that claimant did, prior to and on the 20th day of December, 1803, actually inhabit and cultivate the said tract of land, and was then of the age of twenty-one years and upwards.

Joseph Legrand, sworn, says that premises were inhabited, and cultivated in the beginning of 1803, and constantly to this time; ten acres now in cultivation; a single man above the age of twenty-one years in 1803.

March 17, 1806: Present, Penrose and Donaldson, commissioners. The Board grant said claimant seven hundred and fifty arpents of land, situate as aforesaid, provided so much be found vacant there.

January 17, 1811: Present, Lucas, Penrose, and Bates, commissioners. It is the opinion of the Board that this claim ought not to be granted.

ETIENNE ST. MARY, Jun., claiming seven hundred and fifty arpents of land, situate at the portage of the river St. Francis; produces to the Board a certificate of survey of the same, dated 27th February, 1806.

****

Testimony taken. March 20, 1806. George Wilson, sworn, says that claimant did, prior to and on the 20th December, 1803, actually inhabit and cultivate the said tract of land, and was then of the age of twenty-one years and upwards.

June 19, 1808. Joseph Legrand, sworn, says that premises were inhabited and cultivated in 1802, and constantly to the present time; about five or six arpents now in cultivation; above the age of twenty-one years in the year 1803.

March 20, 1806: Present, Lucas and Penrose, commissioners. The Board grant said claimant seven hundred and fifty arpents of land, situate as aforesaid, provided so much be found vacant there.

January 17, 1811: Present, Lucas, Penrose, and Bates, commissioners. It is the opinion of the Board that this claim ought not to be granted.

JOHN BAPTISTE OLIVE, assignee of John Benoist, claiming seven hundred and fifty arpents of land, situate at the portage of the river St. Francis; produces to the Board a certificate of survey of the same, dated February 28, 1806.

Testimony taken. March 20, 1806. George Wilson, sworn, says that claimant did, prior to and on the 20th December, 1803, actually inhabit and cultivate the said tract of land, and was then of the age of twenty-one years and upwards.

June 18, 1808. Joseph Legrand, sworn, says that premises were cultivated and inhabited from 1802 to this time; about five arpents now in cultivation; a single man, in the year 1803, above the age of twenty-one years.

March 20, 1806: Present, Lucas and Donaldson, commissioners. The Board grant the said claimant seven hundred and fifty arpents of land, situate as aforesaid, provided so much be found vacant there.

January 22, 1811: Present, Lucas, Penrose, and Bates, commissioners. It is the opinion of the Board that this claim ought not to be granted.

FRANCIS B. CORVAISSER, assignee of Isaac Thompson, claiming one hundred and ninety-eight arpents of land, situate on the bayou St. Thomas; produces to the Board a petition, with a recommendation from Henry Peyroux for a concession, dated September 24, 1800; and a certificate of survey, dated February 27, 1795: a deed of transfer of said land from said Isaac Thompson to claimant, dated July 3, 1802.

Testimony taken. March 20, 1806. George Wilson, sworn, says that the said Isaac Thompson did, prior to and on the 1st October, 1800, actually inhabit and cultivate the said tract of land.

June 18, 1808. Joseph Legrand, sworn, says that the said premises were inhabited and cultivated from 1802 to this time; about five arpents now in cultivation; a single man, above the age of twenty-one years, in 1803.

March 20, 1806: Present, Lucas and Donaldson, commissioners. The Board confirm to the said claimant, assignee as aforesaid, two hundred and forty arpents of land, as per the said recommendation.

January 22, 1811: Present, Lucas, Penrose, and Bates, commissioners. It is the opinion of the Board that this claim ought not to be granted.

JOHN COLLINS, claiming seven hundred and fifty arpents of land, situate on the waters of the Pemiscon, district of New Madrid. For permission to settle, see François Lesieur's list on file.

Testimony taken. June 20, 1808. Jacob Waggoner, sworn, says that premises were improved in 1803; in the following year, inhabited and cultivated, and constantly to the present time; about five acres now in cultivation; claimant above the age of twenty-one years in 1800.

January 25, 1811: Present, Lucas, Penrose, and Bates, commissioners. It is the opinion of the Board that this claim ought not to be granted.

MARTIN COONTZ, claiming eleven hundred arpents of land, situate on bayou St. John, district of New Madrid; produces to the Board a certificate of survey, dated February 27, 1806.

Testimony taken. March 15, 1806. Edward Roberts, sworn, says that claimant did, prior to and on the 20th December, 1803, actually inhabit and cultivate the said tract of land, and had a wife and five children.

June 20, 1808. William Cox, sworn, says that, in March, 1803, claimant improved, and constantly inhabited and cultivated to this time; about eight or nine acres now in cultivation; a wife and five children in 1803.

March 15, 1806: Present, Penrose and Donaldson, commissioners. The Board grant the said claimant eleven hundred arpents of land, situate as aforesaid, provided so much be found vacant there.

January 31, 1811: Present, Lucas, Penrose, and Bates, commissioners. It is the opinion of the Board that this claim ought not to be granted.

JOHN LINK, claiming nine hundred arpents of land, situate on lake St. Mary, district of New Madrid; produces to the Board a certificate of survey, dated February 27, 1806.

Testimony taken. March 15, 1806. Edward Robinson, sworn, says that claimant did, prior to and on the 20th December, 1803, actually inhabit and cultivate the said tract of land, and had a wife and one child.

June 20, 1808. William Cox, sworn, says that premises were inhabited and cultivated in 1803, and constantly to the present time; eleven or twelve acres now in cultivation; a wife and two children, and one orphan, in 1803.

March 15, 1806: Present, Penrose and Donaldson, commissioners. The Board grant the said claimant nine hundred arpents of land, situate as aforesaid, provided so much be found vacant there.

January 31, 1811: Present, Lucas, Penrose, and Bates, commissioners. It is the opinion of the Board that this claim ought not to be granted.

PETER NEWKIRK, claiming seven hundred and fifty arpents of land, situate on lake St. Mary's, district of New Madrid; produces to the Board a certificate of survey of said land, dated February 27, 1806.

Testimony taken. March 15, 1806. Edward Robinson, sworn, says that claimant did, prior to and on the 20th day of December, 1803, actually inhabit and cultivate said tract of land, and was then of the age of twenty-one years and upwards.

June 20, 1808. William Coxe, sworn, says that premises were improved in 1803; a cabin built in which claimant occasionally resided, in 1804; claimant cultivated and resided permanently and constantly to the present time; about six acres now in cultivation; above the age of twenty-one years.

March 15, 1806: Present, Penrose and Donaldson, commissioners. The Board grant the said claimant seven hundred and fifty arpents of land, situate as aforesaid, provided so much be found vacant there.

January 31, 1811: Present, Lucas, Penrose, and Bates, commissioners. It is the opinion of the Board that this claim ought not to be granted.

DAVID TROTTER, claiming two hundred arpents of land, situate on the bayou St. Thomas, district of New Madrid; produces to the Board a special permission to settle, or warrant of survey for the same, from Henry Peyroux, dated 16th December, 1801; and a certificate of survey of the same, dated 22d February, 1806.

Testimony taken. June 20, 1808. William Cox, sworn, says that claimant built a cabin in 1802; cultivated and inhabited in the following year, and constantly to this time; twelve acres in cultivation; two slaves; a single man above the age of twenty-one years.

March 4, 1806: Present, Lucas, Penrose, and Donaldson, commissioners. The above claimant having two tracts of land under the same permission or warrant of survey, the one of which is actually inhabited and cultivated, and the other neither inhabited nor cultivated. The Board reject this claim.

January 31, 1811: Present, Lucas, Penrose, and Bates, commissioners. It is the opinion of the Board that this claim ought not to be granted.

JOB SELF, claiming one thousand two hundred arpents of land, situate on the bayou St. John, district of New Madrid; produces to the Board a certificate of survey of the same, dated February 27, 1806.

Testimony taken. March 14, 1806. George Wilson, sworn, says that claimant did, prior to and on the 20th December, 1803, actually inhabit and cultivate the said tract of land, and had then a wife and seven children.

June 20, 1808. William Coxe, sworn, says that premises were inhabited and cultivated in the year 1803, and constantly to the present time; a wife and seven children in 1803; eight or nine acres now in cultivation.

March 14, 1806: Present, Penrose and Donaldson, commissioners. The Board grant said claimant twelve hundred arpents of land, situate as aforesaid, provided so much be found vacant there.

January 31, 1811: Present, Lucas, Penrose, and Bates, commissioners. It is the opinion of the Board that this claim ought not to be granted.

MARY DUPUIS, widow of Isidore Dupuis, claiming nine hundred and fifty arpents of land, situate on Lime Kiln creek, district of New Madrid; produces to the Board a certificate of survey of the same, dated February 28, 1806.

Testimony taken. March 20, 1806. Jacob Myers, sworn, says that claimant did, prior to and on the 20th December, 1803, actually inhabit and cultivate the said tract of land, and had four children.

June 20, 1808. Jacob Friend, sworn, says that premises were inhabited and cultivated in the year 1802, and constantly till the fall of 1804; about six acres in cultivation in that fall; the widow had three children in 1803.

March 20, 1806: Present, Lucas and Penrose, commissioners. The Board grant widow Mary Dupuis nine hundred and fifty arpents of land, situate as aforesaid, provided so much be found vacant there.

January 31, 1811: Present, Lucas, Penrose, and Bates, commissioners. It is the opinion of the Board that this claim ought not to be granted.

FRANCIS MILLETT, claiming seven hundred and fifty arpents of land, situate on highest waters of lake St. Mary; produces to the Board a certificate of survey, dated February 28, 1806.

Testimony taken. March 20, 1806. Jacob Myers, sworn, says that claimant did, prior to and on the 20th December, 1803, actually inhabit and cultivate the said tract of land, and was then of the age of twenty-one years and upwards.

June 20, 1808. Jacob Friend, sworn, says that premises were settled and improved in the fall of 1802; and, in the following year, inhabited and cultivated, and constantly to the last of the year 1806; about eight acres now in cultivation; a wife and two children in the year 1803.

March 20, 1806: Present, Lucas and Penrose, commissioners. The Board grant said claimant seven hundred and fifty arpents of land, situate as aforesaid, provided so much be found vacant there.

January 31, 1811: Present, Lucas, Penrose, and Bates, commissioners. It is the opinion of the Board that this claim ought not to be granted.

MOSES VANCES, claiming seven hundred and fifty arpents of land, situate on the waters of the bayou of St. John; produces to the Board a certificate of survey of the same, dated February 28, 1806.

Testimony taken. March 20, 1806. Jacob Myers, sworn, says that claimant did, prior to and on the 20th December, 1803, actually inhabit and cultivate the said tract of land, and was then of the age of twenty-one years and upwards.

March 20, 1806: Present, Lucas and Penrose, commissioners. The Board grant the said claimant seven hundred and fifty arpents of land, situate as aforesaid, provided so much be found vacant there.

April 3, 1811: Present, Lucas, Penrose, and Bates, commissioners. It is the opinion of the Board that this claim ought not to be granted.

PIERRE ANTOINE LAFORGE, claiming one thousand one hundred and forty arpents of land, situate on the bayou St. Thomas, district of New Madrid; produces to the Board a certificate of survey, dated February 28, 1806.

Testimony taken. March 18, 1806. Edward Robertson, sworn, says that the said tract of land was, prior to and on the 20th December, 1803, actually inhabited and cultivated by the negroes of claimant for his use; he had then a wife and three children.

June 20, 1808. Jacob Friend, sworn, says that premises were inhabited and cultivated in the year 1802, and constantly to the last of the year 1807; about twelve or fourteen acres in cultivation last year.

John B. Olive, sworn, says that claimant had a wife, three children, and six slaves, in 1803.

March 18, 1806: Present, Penrose and Donaldson. The Board reject this claim, for want of actual inhabitation and cultivation by claimant himself; they observe that he holds no other claim in his own name in this Territory, and this a case of equity.

April 3, 1811: Present, Lucas, Penrose, and Bates, commissioners. It is the opinion of the Board that this claim ought not to be granted.

PIERRE FRANÇOIS LAFORGE, claiming seven hundred and fifty arpents of land, situate on bayou St. Thomas, district of New Madrid; produces to the Board a certificate of survey, dated February 28, 1806.

Testimony taken. March 18, 1806. Edward Robertson, sworn, says that claimant did, prior to and on the 20th December, 1803, actually inhabit and cultivate the said tract of land, and was then of the age of twenty-one years and upwards.

June 20, 1808. Jacob Friend, sworn, says that premises were inhabited and cultivated in 1803, and constantly to the present time; twenty or twenty-two acres in cultivation.

John B. Olive, sworn, says that claimant was above the age of twenty-one years in 1803.

March 18, 1806: Present, Penrose and Donaldson, commissioners. The Board grant said claimant seven hundred and fifty arpents of land, situate as aforesaid, provided so much be found vacant there.

April 3, 1811: Present, Lucas, Penrose, and Bates, commissioners. It is the opinion of the Board that this claim ought not to be granted.

JOHN LAVALLE, claiming one thousand and ninety arpents of land, situate on Marais des Peches, district of New Madrid; produces to the Board a certificate of survey of said land, dated February 27, 1806.

Testimony taken. March 18, 1806. Edward Robertson, sworn, says that claimant did, prior to and on the 20th December, 1803, actually inhabit and cultivate the said tract of land by his negroes.

June 20, 1808. Edward Robertson, sworn, says that premises were inhabited and cultivated in the spring of 1803, and constantly till the present time except one year, to wit, 1806; about eight or ten acres now in cultivation; a wife and three children, and three slaves in 1803.

March 18, 1806: Present, Penrose and Donaldson, commissioners. The Board reject this case for want of actual inhabitation and cultivation by claimant himself; they observe that claimant has no other claims to lands in his own name in this Territory, and think it a case of equity.

April 3, 1811: Present, Lucas, Penrose, and Bates, commissioners. It is the opinion of the Board that this claim ought not to be granted.

AUGUSTE DELAREBOUDIERE, claiming seven hundred and fifty arpents of land, situate on lake St. Mary's, district of New Madrid; produces to the Board a certificate of a permission to settle from Henry Peyroux, dated in the year 1803, and a certificate of survey, dated February 14, 1806.

Testimony taken. March 22, 1806. Edward Robertson, sworn, says that claimant did, prior to and on the 20th December, 1803, actually inhabit and cultivate the said tract of land, and was then of the age of twenty-one years and upwards.

March 22, 1806: Present, Penrose and Donaldson, commissioners. The Board grant said claimant seven hundred and fifty arpents of land, situate as aforesaid, provided so much be found vacant there.

April 3, 1811: Present, Lucas, Penrose, and Bates, commissioners. The permission stated to be produced is not found. It is the opinion of the Board that this claim ought not to be granted.

CHARLES CASTONGET, claiming seven hundred and fifty arpents of land, situate on lake St. Mary's, district of New Madrid; produces to the Board a certificate of survey of the same, dated February 28, 1806.

Testimony taken. March 20, 1806. Jacob Myers, sworn, says that claimant did, prior to and on the 20th December 1803, actually inhabit and cultivate the said tract of land, and was then of the age of twenty-one years and upwards.

June 20, 1808. Jacob Friend, sworn, says that premises were inhabited and cultivated in 1803, and constantly to the present time; single man, above twenty-one years of age; fourteen acres now in cultivation.

March 20, 1806: Present, Lucas and Penrose, commissioners. The Board grant the above claimant seven hundred and fifty arpents of land, situate as aforesaid, provided so much be found vacant there.

April 3, 1811: Present, Lucas, Penrose, and Bates, commissioners. It is the opinion of the Board that this claim ought not to be granted.

JOHN BAPTISTE THIBEAULT, claiming seven hundred and fifty arpents of land, situate on Marais des Peches, district of New Madrid; produces to the Board a certificate of survey of the same, dated February 28, 1806.

Testimony taken. March 20, 1806. Jacob Myers, sworn, says that claimant did, prior to and on the 20th December, 1803, actually inhabit and cultivate the said tract of land, and was then of the age of twenty-one years and upwards.

June 20, 1808. Jacob Friend, sworn, says that premises were inhabited and cultivated in the fall of 1804, at which time eight or perhaps seven acres in cultivation; above the age of twenty-one years.

March 20, 1806: Present, Lucas and Penrose, commissioners. The Board grant the said claimant seven hundred and fifty arpents of land, situate as aforesaid, provided so much be found vacant there.

April 3, 1811: Present, Lucas, Penrose, and Bates, commissioners. It is the opinion of the Board that this claim ought not to be granted.

JOSEPH MICHEL, assignee of John Robertson, claiming two hundred arpents of land, situate on lake Marais des Peches, district of New Madrid; produces to the Board, as a special permission to settle, a certificate of a petition, dated March 31, 1802, and a certificate of survey, dated February 2, 1806; a deed of transfer of said land, from Robertson to claimant, dated 2d May, 1805.

Testimony taken. March 20, 1806. Jacob Myers, sworn, says that said John Robertson did, prior to and on the 20th December, 1803, actually inhabit and cultivate the said tract of land.

June 20, 1808. William Coxe, sworn, says that premises were cultivated and inhabited in 1802, and constantly to this time; eight or nine acres now in cultivation; a wife in the year 1803.

March 20, 1806: Present, Lucas and Penrose, commissioners. The Board grant the said claimant, assignee as aforesaid, two hundred arpents of land, situate as aforesaid.

April 3, 1811: Present, Lucas, Penrose, and Bates, commissioners. It is the opinion of the Board that this claim ought not to be granted.

CHARLES CUROTTE, claiming one thousand arpents of land, situate on the waters of lake St. Mary's, district of New Madrid; produces to the Board a certificate of survey of the same, dated February 28, 1806.

Testimony taken. March 20, 1806. Jacob Myers, sworn, says that claimant did, prior to and on the 20th December, 1803, actually inhabit and cultivate the said tract of land, and had then a wife and three children.

June 20, 1808. Jacob Friend, sworn, says that premises were inhabited and cultivated in 1802, and constantly till the end of 1805; about eight or nine acres then in cultivation; a wife and four or five children.

March 20, 1806: Present, Lucas and Penrose, commissioners. The Board grant the said claimant one thousand arpents of land, situate as aforesaid, provided so much be found vacant there.

April 3, 1811: Present, Lucas, Penrose, and Bates, commissioners. It is the opinion of the Board that this claim ought not to be granted.

STEPHEN DUMAY, claiming seven hundred and fifty arpents of land, situate on the waters of the bayou St. John, district of New Madrid; produces to the Board a certificate of survey of the same, dated February 27, 1806.

Testimony taken. March 14, 1806. George Wilson, sworn, says that claimant did, prior to and on the 20th day of December, 1803, actually inhabit and cultivate the said tract of land, being then twenty-one years of age and upwards.

June 20, 1808. William Coxe, sworn, says that premises were inhabited and cultivated in the year 1802, and constantly to the present time; seven or eight acres now in cultivation; above the age of twenty-one years in 1803.

March 14, 1806: Present, Penrose and Donaldson, commissioners. The Board grant the said claimant seven hundred and fifty arpents of land, situate as aforesaid, provided so much be found vacant there.

****

April 3, 1811: Present, Lucas, Penrose, and Bates, commissioners. It is the opinion of the Board that this claim ought not to be granted.

JAMES DUNKIN, claiming seven hundred and fifty arpents of land, situate on lake St. Mary, district of New Madrid; produces to the Board a certificate of survey of the same, dated February 27, 1806.

Testimony taken. March 14, 1806. George Wilson, sworn, says that claimant did, prior to and on the 20th December, 1803, actually inhabit and cultivate the said land, being then of the age of twenty-one years and upwards.

June 21, 1808. William Coxe, sworn, says that a cabin was built, and ground cleared in 1802, cultivated and inhabited in 1803, and constantly till the end of 1806; above the age of twenty-one years in 1803; five acres now in cultivation.

March 14, 1806: Present, Penrose and Donaldson, commissioners. The Board grant said claimant seven hundred and fifty arpents of land, situate as aforesaid, provided so much be found vacant there.

April 3, 1811: Present, Lucas, Penrose, and Bates, commissioners. It is the opinion of the Board that this claim ought not to be granted.

JOHN HENTHORN, claiming seven hundred and fifty arpents of land, situate in the district of New Madrid; produces to the Board a certificate of survey of the same, dated February 27, 1806.

Testimony taken. March 14, 1806. Edward Robinson, sworn, says that claimant did, prior to and on the 20th December, 1803, actually inhabit and cultivate the said land, and was the head of a family.

June 21, 1808. Jacob Friend, sworn, says that premises were inhabited and cultivated in 1802, and constantly till the end of last year; about four or five acres in cultivation; a single man above the age of twenty-one years.

March 14, 1806: Present, Penrose and Donaldson, commissioners. The Board grant said claimant seven hundred and fifty arpents of land, situate as aforesaid, provided so much be found vacant there.

April 3, 1811: Present, Lucas, Penrose, and Bates, commissioners. It is the opinion of the Board that this claim ought not to be granted.

JOHN NEAL, claiming one thousand three hundred and fifty arpents of land, situate near the Mississippi, district of New Madrid; produces to the Board a certificate of survey, dated 27th February, 1806.

Testimony taken. March 15, 1806. George Wilson, sworn, says that claimant did, prior to and on the 20th December, 1803, actually inhabit and cultivate the said tract of land, and had then a wife and nine children.

March 15, 1806: Present, Penrose and Donaldson, commissioners. The Board grant the said claimant one thousand three hundred arpents of land, situate as aforesaid, provided so much be found vacant there.

April 5, 1811: Present, Lucas, Penrose, and Bates, commissioners. It is the opinion of the Board that this claim ought not to be granted.

JONAS FRIEND, claiming seven hundred and fifty arpents of land, situate in the district of New Madrid; produces to the Board a certificate of survey of the same, dated 10th February, 1806.

Testimony taken. April 18, 1806. John Friend, sworn, says that claimant settled said tract of land in 1801, and did, prior to and on the 20th December, 1803, actually inhabit and cultivate the said tract of land, and was then of the age of twenty-one years and upwards.

June 21, 1808. William Coxe, sworn, says that premises were inhabited and cultivated in 1802, and constantly till the present time, except the year 1805; eight acres now in cultivation; single man, above twenty-one years; supported a sister.

April 18, 1806: Present, Lucas and Donaldson, commissioners. The Board grant the said Jonas Friend seven hundred and fifty arpents of land, situate as aforesaid, provided so much be found vacant there.

April 5, 1811: Present, Lucas, Penrose, and Bates, commissioners. It is the opinion of the Board that this claim ought not to be granted.

WILLIAM ZANES, claiming one thousand and fifty arpents of land, situate on the waters of the lake St. Mary, district of New Madrid; produces to the Board a certificate of survey of the same, dated February 27, 1806.

Testimony taken. March 15, 1806. George Wilson, sworn, says that claimant did, prior to and on the 20th December, 1803, actually inhabit and cultivate the said tract of land, and had then a wife and four children.

June 21, 1808. William Coxe, sworn, says that premises were improved in 1802, inhabited and cultivated following year, and constantly to this time; six or seven acres now in cultivation; a wife and three children in 1803.

March 15, 1806: Present, Penrose and Donaldson. The Board grant the said claimant one thousand and fifty arpents of land, situate as aforesaid, provided so much be found vacant there.

April 5, 1811: Present, Lucas, Penrose, and Bates, commissioners. It is the opinion of the Board that this claim ought not to be granted.

JAMES SCOTT, claiming seven hundred and fifty arpents of land, situate on lake St. Mary, district of New Madrid; produces to the Board a certificate of survey of the same, dated February 27, 1806.

Testimony taken. March 15, 1806. Edward Robertson, sworn, says that claimant did, prior to and on the 20th December, 1803, actually inhabit and cultivate the said tract of land, and was then of the age of twenty-one years and upwards.

June 21, 1808. William Coxe, sworn, says that premises were improved in 1802, inhabited and cultivated in 1803, and constantly till 1805; a single man, above the age of twenty-one years.

March 15, 1806: Present, Penrose and Donaldson, commissioners. The Board grant said claimant seven hundred and fifty arpents of land, situate as aforesaid, provided so much be found vacant there.

April 5, 1811: Present, Lucas, Penrose, and Bates, commissioners. It is the opinion of the Board that this claim ought not to be granted.

PETER LOVEL, assignee of James Simpson, assignee of John Baptiste Gobeau, claiming two hundred and forty arpents of land, situate on lake St. Mary, district of New Madrid; produces to the Board a copy of a petition for a concession, dated December 20, 1802; and a plat and a certificate of survey of the same.

Testimony taken. March 15, 1806. Edward Robertson, sworn, says that claimant did, prior to and on the 1st October, 1800, actually inhabit and cultivate the said tract of land.

June 21, 1808. William Coxe, sworn, says that premises were cultivated and inhabited in 1801, and constantly to this time; about forty acres now in cultivation.

Thomas Horsley, sworn, says that Gobeau had, in 1803, a wife, two children, and two slaves.

March 15, 1806: Present, Penrose and Donaldson, commissioners. The Board confirm to said claimant eight hundred arpents of land, situate as aforesaid, provided so much be found vacant there.

April 10, 1811: Present, Lucas, Penrose, and Bates, commissioners. It is the opinion of the Board that this claim ought not to be granted.

JOSEPH VANDENBENDEN, claiming one hundred and twenty arpents of land, situate on bayou St. John, district of New Madrid; produces to the Board a certificate of permission to settle, from a Henry Peyroux, and a certificate of survey of the same.

Testimony [*taken.* March 18, 1806. Edward Robertson, sworn, says that claimant did, prior to and on the 1st day of October, 1800, actually inhabit and cultivate the said tract of land. For permission to settle, see list No. 1369.

June 21, 1808. William Coxe, sworn, says that premises were improved, cultivated, and inhabited in 1801, and constantly till 1805; about seven or eight acres in cultivation; above the age of twenty-one years in 1803.

March 18, 1806: Present, Penrose and Donaldson, commissioners. The Board confirm to the said claimant one hundred and twenty arpents of land, situate as aforesaid, as per the said certificate of permission to settle.

April 12, 1811: Present, Lucas, Penrose, and Bates, commissioners. It is the opinion of the Board that this claim ought not to be granted.

ELI SHELBY, claiming seven hundred and fifty arpents of land, situate on the waters of the bayou St. John, district of New Madrid; produces to the Board a certificate of survey of the same, dated February 27, 1803.

Testimony taken. March 14, 1806. George Wilson, sworn, says that claimant did, prior to and on the 20th day of December, 1803, actually inhabit and cultivate the said tract of land; and was then of the age of twenty-one years and upwards.

June 21, 1808. Luke Devoir, sworn, says that premises were inhabited and cultivated in 1803, and constantly till the spring of 1808, when he went to Orleans on business; eight or nine acres now in cultivation; above the age of twenty-one years in 1803.

March 14, 1806: Present, Penrose and Donaldson, commissioners. The Board grant the said claimant seven hundred and fifty arpents of land, situate as aforesaid, provided so much be found vacant there.

April 15, 1811: Present, Lucas, Penrose, and Bates, commissioners. It is the opinion of the Board that this claim ought not to be granted.

JOHN LAMB, assignee of James McMillen, claiming two hundred arpents of land, situate on lake St. Mary, district of New Madrid; produces to the Board a certificate from Peter A. Laforge, dated February 16, 1806, of his having had a concession; a certificate of survey of said land, dated January 2, 1798; and a deed of transfer from said McMillen to claimant, dated September 11, 1801.

Testimony taken. March 13, 1806. Robert McCoy, sworn, says that said McMillen did, prior to and on the 1st October, 1800, actually inhabit and cultivate the said land.

June 22, 1808. William Coxe, sworn, says that premises were cultivated and inhabited in the year 1800, and constantly to the present time; thirty acres now in cultivation; had a wife in 1803.

March 13, 1806: Present, Lucas and Donaldson, commissioners. The Board confirm to the claimant, assignee as aforesaid, two hundred arpents of land, situate as aforesaid, provided so much be found vacant there.

July 8, 1811: Present, Lucas, Penrose, and Bates, commissioners. It is the opinion of the Board that this claim ought not to be granted.

DAVID WENTZELL, assignee of Henry Masters, assignee of John Lathan, claiming three hundred arpents of land, situate on lake St. Mary, district of New Madrid; produces to the Board a copy of a warrant of survey from Henry Peyroux to one John Lathan, dated November 20, 1801, on Story's registry, and a certificate of survey of the same; a deed of transfer of said land from the said John Lathan to the said Henry Masters, dated January 15, 1804; and another deed of transfer from the said Henry Masters to claimant, dated January 25, 1806.

Testimony taken. March 12, 1806. Edward Robertson, sworn, says that the said John Lathan did actually cultivate and inhabit the said tract of land in the year 1801, and continued on the same until some time in the year 1803; and was not actually inhabiting and cultivating the same on the 20th day of December in that year.

June 22, 1808. William Coxe, sworn, says that premises were improved in 1801, cultivated and inhabited in 1802, and constantly to the present time; eight or nine acres now in cultivation; a wife and four children in 1803.

July 8, 1811: Present, Lucas, Penrose, and Bates, commissioners. It is the opinion of the Board that this claim ought not to be granted.

JOSEPH MICHEL, assignee of William Deakins, assignee of Jacob Myers, claiming two hundred arpents of land, situate on the highest waters of the lake St. Mary; produces to the Board a petition, with a recommendation from Henry Peyroux, for a concession, dated 24th September, 1800, and a certificate of survey of the same; a deed of transfer of said land from the William Deakins to claimant, dated 9th March, 1805.

Testimony taken. March 20, 1806. Edward Robertson, sworn, says that he was present when the sale of said land by Jacob Myers to said Deakins took place; and further, that he (the said Myers) did, prior to and on the 1st day of October, 1800, actually inhabit and cultivate the said tract of land.

June 22, 1808. Edward Robertson, sworn, says that premises were improved in 1799; cultivated and inhabited in 1800, and constantly till 1806; six acres then in cultivation; a wife and three children (Myers) in 1803.

March 20, 1806: Present, Lucas and Penrose, commissioners. The Board confirm to the said claimant, assignee as aforesaid, two hundred arpents of land, as per the said petition and recommendation for a concession.

July 9, 1811: Present, Lucas, Penrose, and Bates, commissioners. It is the opinion of the Board that this claim ought not to be granted.

JOSEPH MICHEL, assignee of William Deakins, assignee of Benjamin Myers, claiming two hundred arpents of land, situate on the highest waters of lake St. Mary, district of New Madrid; produces to the Board a petition and

****

recommendation from Henry Peyroux for a concession, dated 24th September, 1800, and a certificate of survey of the same; a deed of transfer of said land from the said William Deakins to claimant, dated March 9, 1805.

Testimony taken. March 20, 1806. Edward Robertson, sworn, says that he was present at the sale of the said land by Benjamin Myers to the said Deakins; and that he (the said Myers) did, prior to and on the 1st October, 1800, actually inhabit and cultivate the said tract of land.

June 22, 1808. Edward Robertson, sworn, says that premises were improved in 1799, cultivated and inhabited in 1800, and constantly till 1806; six or eight acres then in cultivation; a single man, above the age of twenty-one years in 1803.

March 20, 1806: Present, Lucas and Penrose, commissioners. The Board confirm to the said claimant, assignee as aforesaid, two hundred arpents of land, as per the said petition and recommendation for a concession.

July 9, 1811: Present, Lucas, Penrose, and Bates, commissioners. It is the opinion of the Board that this claim ought not to be granted.

JAMES ASHWORTH, assignee of the widow of Joseph Hunot, claiming two hundred arpents of land, situate on the portage of the bayou ———, district of New Madrid; produces to the Board a plat of survey, dated in Story's registry March 10, 1800; a decree of the commandant, authorizing the widow to sell the property, dated 8th January, 1804, a certified copy; transfer, dated 8th May, 1804. For permission to settle, see list No. 1369, on which Joseph Hunot is No. 60.

Testimony taken. June 22, 1808. Toussaint Godair, sworn, says that premises were inhabited from 1802 to this time; twelve acres now in cultivation; in 1803 Hunot had a wife and three children.

July 11, 1811: Present, Lucas, Penrose, and Bates, commissioners. It is the opinion of the Board that this claim ought not to be granted.

JONAS CARL, claiming one thousand and seventy-three arpents of land, situate on lake St. Anne, district of New Madrid; produces to the Board a certificate from Peter A. Laforge, dated November 22, 1805, that a permission had been granted him to settle on said land by Lavalle; and a certificate of survey of said tract, dated 22d February, 1806.

Testimony taken. March 4, 1806. George Wilson, sworn, says that claimant did, prior to and on the 20th December, 1803, actually inhabit and cultivate the said tract of land; and had then a wife and six children.

March 4, 1806: Present, Lucas, Penrose, and Donaldson, commissioners. The Board grant the said claimant one thousand one hundred and fifty arpents of land, situate as aforesaid, provided so much be found vacant there.

July 15, 1811: Present, Lucas, Penrose, and Bates, commissioners. It is the opinion of the Board that this claim ought not to be granted:

LOUIS COIGNARD, claiming four hundred and ten arpents of land, situate on the bayou St. Thomas, district of New Madrid; produces to the Board a certified copy of a concession from the Baron de Carondelet, granted in 1800, and certified by Henry Peyroux, 20th June, 1804; and a certificate of survey, dated March 13, 1800.

Testimony taken. March 13, 1806. Richard J. Waters, sworn, says that claimant did, prior to and on the 1st October, 1800, actually inhabit and cultivate the said tract of land.

June 22, 1808. Benjamin Patterson, sworn, says that premises were improved in 1798 and 1799, in which years they were cultivated and inhabited, and constantly for the three following years, as the property of the claimant.

M. P. Leduc, sworn, says claimant had, in 1803, a wife, two children, and one servant.

March 13, 1806: Present, Penrose and Donaldson, commissioners. The Board confirm to claimant four hundred and ten arpents of land, as per the said certificate of concession.

July 15, 1811: Present, Lucas, Penrose, and Bates, commissioners. It is the opinion of the Board that this claim ought not to be granted.

RICHARD JONES WATERS, assignee of Benjamin Patterson, claiming four hundred arpents of land, situate near St. Isidore, district of New Madrid; produces to the Board a recommendation for a concession, signed Henry Peyroux, dated September 24, 1800, and a certificate of survey of the said land, dated March 6, 1798; a deed of transfer of the same, from said Benjamin Patterson, dated February 8, 1806.

Testimony taken. March 10, 1806. George Wilson, sworn, says that the said land was actually settled and cultivated by the said Benjamin Patterson, in the year 1797, and that he did, prior to and on the 1st October, 1800, actually inhabit and cultivate the same.

March 10, 1806: Present, Penrose and Donaldson, commissioners. The Board confirm to Richard Jones Waters, assignee as aforesaid, four hundred arpents of land, as per the said recommendation and petition thereto annexed.

July 15, 1811: Present, Lucas, Penrose, and Bates, commissioners. It is the opinion of the Board that this claim ought not to be confirmed.

WILLIAM CLARK, claiming seven hundred and fifty arpents of land, situate on bayou St. John, district of New Madrid; produces to the Board a notice to the recorder.

Testimony taken. June 22, 1808. Thomas Y. Horsley, sworn, says that premises were cultivated and inhabited in the year 1802, and constantly to the present time; about six or seven acres now in cultivation; a single man; above the age of twenty-one years in 1803.

July 15, 1811: Present, Lucas, Penrose, and Bates, commissioners. It is the opinion of the Board that this claim ought not to be granted.

JESSE DEVOIR, claiming seven hundred and fifty arpents of land, situate near the waters of the bayou St. John, district of New Madrid; produces to the Board a notice to the recorder.

Testimony taken. June 22, 1808. Thomas Y. Horsley, sworn, says that premises were cultivated and inhabited in the year 1801, and constantly to this time; six acres now in cultivation; above the age of twenty-one years in 1803.

July 15, 1811: Present, Lucas, Penrose, and Bates, commissioners. It is the opinion of the Board that this claim ought not to be granted.

MATTHIAS BELSON, claiming nine hundred arpents of land, situate on the waters of the bayou St. John, district of New Madrid; produces to the Board a certificate of survey of the same, dated February 27, 1803.

Testimony taken. March 14, 1806. George Wilson, sworn, says that claimant did, prior to and on the 20th December, 1803, actually inhabit and cultivate the said tract of land, and had then a wife and three children.

June 22, 1808. Samuel Masters, sworn, says that premises were improved in 1803, and inhabited in that year; not since inhabited, but occasionally cultivated; four or five acres in cultivation in 1803; a wife and two children and an apprentice.

March 14, 1806: Present, Penrose and Donaldson, commissioners. The Board grant said claimant one thousand arpents of land, situate as aforesaid, provided so much be found vacant there.

July 15, 1811: Present, Lucas, Penrose, and Bates, commissioners. It is the opinion of the Board that this claim ought not to be granted.

JOHN BUTLER, Jun., claiming twelve hundred arpents of land, situate on bayou St. John, district of New Madrid; produces to the Board a notice to the recorder.

Testimony taken. June 22, 1808. Luke Devoir, sworn, says that premises were cultivated and inhabited in 1801, and constantly to the last of the year 1804, and then cultivated only to the present time; about eight acres now in cultivation; a wife and eight children in 1803.

July 16, 1811. Present, Lucas, Penrose, and Bates, commissioners. It is the opinion of the Board that this claim ought not to be granted.

JOSEPH VANDENBENDEN, assignee of Jean Vian, alias Viot, claiming three hundred arpents of land, situate on bayou St. John, district of New Madrid; produces to the Board a certificate from Henry Peyroux of his having had a concession for the same; a certificate of survey, dated February 27, 1806; and a deed of transfer of said land from the said John Vian, alias Viot, to one Joseph Vandenbenden, dated January 28, 1806.

Testimony taken. March 18, 1806. George Wilson, sworn, says that the said John Viot did, prior to and on the 1st October, 1800, actually inhabit and cultivate the said tract of land.

June 22, 1808. Samuel Masters, sworn, says that premises were cultivated some time previously to 1802, when witness first saw it; in that year it was inhabited and cultivated; not certain as to 1803, but in 1804 it was inhabited, and constantly to this time; twelve acres now in cultivation.

March 18, 1806: Present, Penrose and Donaldson, commissioners. The Board confirm to the said claimant, assignee as aforesaid, three hundred arpents of land, situate as aforesaid, as per the aforesaid certificate of a concession.

July 16, 1811: Present, Lucas, Penrose, and Bates, commissioners. It is the opinion of the Board that this claim ought not to be granted.

THOMAS THOMPSON, claiming one thousand arpents of land, situate in district of New Madrid, by virtue of a verbal permission to settle; produces to the Board a certificate of survey, dated February 27, 1806.

Testimony taken. March 11, 1806. George Ruddell, sworn, says that the said Thomas Thompson, did, prior to and on the 20th December, 1803, actually inhabit and cultivate the said tract of land, and had then a wife and three children.

June 22, 1808. Thomas Y. Horsley, sworn, says that premises were inhabited and cultivated in 1801, and constantly to this time; about nine or ten acres now in cultivation; a wife and three or four children.

March 11, 1806: Present, Penrose and Donaldson, commissioners. The Board grant Thomas Thompson one thousand arpents of land, situate as aforesaid, provided so much be found vacant there.

July 16, 1811: Present, Lucas, Penrose, and Bates, commissioners. It is the opinion of the Board that this claim ought not to be granted.

GABRIEL HUNOT, claiming seven hundred and fifty arpents of land, situate on waters of the Mississippi, district of New Madrid; produces to the Board a certificate of survey, dated February 27, 1806.

Testimony taken. March 14, 1806. George Wilson, sworn, says that claimant did, prior to and on the 20th December, 1803, actually inhabit and cultivate said tract of land, and was the head of a family.

July 30, 1808. Thomas Horsley, sworn, says that this tract was inhabited and cultivated for claimant in the year 1802, and constantly until the end of the last year; about six or eight acres in cultivation; above the age of twenty-one years in 1803.

March 14, 1806: Present, Penrose and Donaldson, commissioners. The Board grant the said claimant seven hundred and fifty arpents of land, situate as aforesaid, provided so much be found vacant there.

July 25, 1811: Present, Lucas, Penrose, and Bates, commissioners. It is the opinion of the Board that this claim ought not to be granted.

RICHARD JONES WATERS, assignee of George Wilson, claiming one hundred arpents of land, situate on bayou St. John, district of New Madrid; produces to the Board an order of survey to the children of George Wilson, from Henry Peyroux, commandant, dated 9th January, 1801; a plat of survey, dated 26th March, 1801, on Story's registry; a transfer from George Wilson to claimant, dated 25th November, 1807.

Testimony taken. July 30, 1808. Thomas Horsley, sworn, says that premises were inhabited and cultivated for claimant in 1800, and constantly until last fall; four or five acres in cultivation; a wife and five children in 1803.

July 25, 1811: Present, Lucas, Penrose, and Bates, commissioners. It is the opinion of the Board that this claim ought not to be granted.

RICHARD JONES WATERS and JOHN REED, assignees of Abraham Keeney, claiming nine hundred arpents of land, on waters of bayou St. Thomas, district of New Madrid; produces to the Board a plat of survey, dated 10th February, 1806; a transfer, dated 25th October, 1806.

Testimony taken. July 30, 1808. Benjamin Patterson, sworn, says that this tract was inhabited and cultivated in 1801, and constantly to the present time; fifteen acres now in cultivation; a wife and one child in 1803.

July 25, 1811: Present, Lucas, Penrose, and Bates, commissioners. It is the opinion of the Board that this claim ought not to be granted.

GEORGE JOHNSTON, claiming seven hundred and fifty-five arpents of land, situate near lake Ricardo, district of New Madrid; produces to the Board a certificate of survey, dated February 27, 1806.

Testimony taken. March 14, 1806. George Wilson, sworn, says that claimant did, prior to and on the 20th December, 1803, actually inhabit and cultivate the said tract of land, and was then of the age of twenty-one years and upwards.

Testimony taken. July 30, 1808. Thomas Horsley, sworn, says that this tract was cultivated and inhabited in 1802, and constantly to this time; sixteen or seventeen acres now in cultivation; a wife and one child in 1803.

March 14, 1806. Present, Penrose and Donaldson, commissioners. The Board grant the said claimant seven hundred and fifty arpents of land, situate as aforesaid, provided so much be found vacant there.

July 25, 1811: Present, Lucas, Penrose, and Bates, commissioners. It is the opinion of the Board that this claim ought not to be granted.

JOHN PATTERSON, claiming one thousand arpents of land, situate between the town of New Madrid and village of Little Prairie, district of New Madrid; produces to the Board a notice to the recorder.

Testimony taken. July 30, 1808. Luke Devoir, sworn, says that in 1802, this tract was inhabited and cultivated, and constantly to the present time; twelve acres now in cultivation; a wife and three children in 1803.

July 26, 1811: Present, Lucas, Penrose, and Bates, commissioners. It is the opinion of the Board that this claim ought not to be granted.

BENONI PATTERSON, the heirs and representatives of, claiming nine hundred and fifty arpents of land, situate between the town of New Madrid and Little Prairie, district of New Madrid; produces to the Board a notice to the recorder.

Testimony taken. July 30, 1808. Luke Devoir, sworn, says that in 1802 this tract was inhabited and cultivated, and constantly until March, 1807; fourteen acres then in cultivation; a wife and three children in 1803.

July 26, 1811: Present, Lucas, Penrose, and Bates, commissioners. It is the opinion of the Board that this claim ought not to be granted.

HIRAM PATTERSON, the heirs and representatives of, claiming seven hundred and fifty arpents of land, situate between the town of New Madrid and Little Prairie, district of New Madrid; produces to the Board a notice to the recorder.

Testimony taken. July 30, 1808. Luke Devoir, sworn, says that in 1802 this tract was inhabited and cultivated, and continued constantly until the month of March, 1807; sixteen acres then in cultivation; above the age of twenty-one years.

July 26, 1811: Present, Lucas, Penrose, and Bates, commissioners. It is the opinion of the Board that this claim ought not to be granted.

BENJAMIN PATTERSON, Sen., claiming one thousand one hundred arpents of land, situate between the town of New Madrid and Little Prairie, district of New Madrid; produces to the Board a notice to the recorder.

Testimony taken. July 30, 1808. Luke Devoir, sworn, says that in 1803 this tract was inhabited and cultivated, and constantly until this time; thirty-one or thirty-two acres now in cultivation; a wife and four children in 1803; besides which, he provides for and supports in his family four other children.

July 26, 1811: Present, Lucas, Penrose, and Bates, commissioners. It is the opinion of the Board that this claim ought not to be granted.

WHOLMAN BANKSON, claiming seven hundred and fifty arpents of land, situate on bayou St. John, district of New Madrid; produces to the Board a notice to the recorder.

Testimony taken. July 30, 1808. Benjamin Patterson, sworn, says that these premises have been constantly inhabited and cultivated from the year 1802, inclusive, until the present time; eight acres now in cultivation; a single man; above the age of twenty-one years in 1803.

July 26, 1811: Present, Lucas, Penrose, and Bates, commissioners. It is the opinion of the Board that this claim ought not to be granted.

ISAAC THOMPSON, claiming seven hundred and fifty arpents of land, situate on the portage of the river St. Francis; produces to the Board a certificate of survey of the same, dated 27th February, 1806.

Testimony taken. March 18, 1806. George Wilson, sworn, says that claimant did, prior to and on the 20th December, 1803, actually inhabit and cultivate the said tract of land, and had then a wife.

July 30, 1808. Thomas Y. Horsley, sworn, says that this tract was inhabited and cultivated in 1802, and constantly until the present time; six or eight acres now in cultivation; a wife and one slave in 1803.

July 26, 1811: Present, Lucas, Penrose, and Bates, commissioners. It is the opinion of the Board that this claim ought not to be granted.

March 18, 1806: Present, Penrose and Donaldson, commissioners. The Board grant the said claimant eight hundred and fifty arpents of land, situate as aforesaid, provided so much be found vacant there.

FRANCES GODFROY, widow of Louis Vandenbenden, claiming four hundred arpents of land, situate on lake St. Mary, and bayou St. Isidore, district of New Madrid; produces to the Board a recommendation for a concession annexed to a petition of the said Frances Godfroy, from Henry Peyroux, dated September 24, 1800; and a certificate of survey of said land, dated February 27, 1806.

Testimony taken. March 10, 1806. George Wilson, sworn, says that the said Frances Godfroy did actually inhabit and cultivate the said tract of land in 1797, and that the same was, prior to and on the 1st of October, 1800, actually inhabited and cultivated.

July 30, 1808. Benjamin Patterson, sworn, says that this tract was inhabited and cultivated in 1797; one crop raised, and abandoned; after which, in the year 1800, it was again inhabited and cultivated for the claimant's benefit, and constantly till this time; twenty or twenty-five acres now in cultivation.

March 10, 1806: Present, Penrose and Donaldson, commissioners. The Board confirm to said claimant four hundred arpents of land, as per the said recommendation and petition.

July 26, 1811: Present, Lucas, Penrose, and Bates, commissioners. It is the opinion of the Board that this claim ought not to be confirmed.

CLEMENT HADEN, claiming one thousand two hundred and fifty arpents of land, situate on Bois Bruile, district of St. Genevieve, by virtue of a permission to settle, granted in October, 1803, and certified December 14, 1805; a certificate of survey of said land, dated 3d February, 1806.

Testimony taken. February 4, 1806. Joseph Tucker, sworn, says that claimant arrived in this country in the fall of 1803; went back, and returned with his family in the beginning of 1804; that he then moved on said tract of land, and raised a crop on the same in that year, and has actually inhabited and cultivated it to this day; that the said tract of land was, prior to and on the 20th December, 1803, actually inhabited and cultivated by one

****

Luke Matenly; that the said Luke Matenly did, some time in January, 1804, acknowledge, before the witness, that he had sold his improvement right to the said claimant Haden.

February 4, 1806: Present, Lucas, Penrose, and Donaldson, commissioners. The Board grant claimant Haden, assignee of Luke Matenly, one thousand arpents of land, situate as aforesaid, provided so much be found vacant there.

August 14, 1811: Present, Penrose and Bates, commissioners. Permission stated to be produced not found on record. It is the opinion of the Board that this claim ought not to be granted.

DAVID EDWARDS, claiming nine hundred arpents of land, situate on the Dardenne, district of St. Charles; produces to the Board a certificate of permission to settle from James Mackay, dated 30th January, 1806; and a certificate of survey of the same, dated 7th February, 1806.

Testimony taken. February 21, 1806. George Price, sworn, says that claimant did, prior to and on the 20th December, 1803, actually inhabit and cultivate the said tract of land, and had then a wife.

February 21, 1806: Present, Lucas, Penrose, and Donaldson, commissioners. The Board grant the said claimant eight hundred arpents of land, provided so much be found vacant there.

August 14, 1811: Present, Penrose and Bates, commissioners. Permission stated to be produced not found on record. It is the opinion of the Board that this claim ought not to be granted.

JOHN A. HENTON, claiming seven hundred and eighty arpents of land, situate on Terre Blue, district of St. Genevieve; produces to the Board a certificate of survey of said land, dated 20th February, 1806.

Testimony taken. February 21, 1806. Jacob Mosteller, sworn, says that claimant did settle said tract of land, and actually inhabit the same, in 1802; that, in the fall of that year, he lost his wife; and that, having been taken sick on the same, and having no one to take care of him, he moved out, but raised a crop thereon in that year.

February 21, 1806: Present, Lucas, Penrose, and Donaldson, commissioners. The Board reject this claim, and think it a case of equity.

August 14, 1811: Present, Penrose and Bates, commissioners. It is the opinion of the Board that this claim ought not to be granted.

RICHARD JONES WATERS, assignee of Benjamin Harrison, assignee of George Ruddell, claiming two hundred arpents of land, situate in the district of New Madrid, on a lake adjoining a tract claimed by claimant, as assignee aforesaid; produces to the Board a recommendation from Henry Peyroux, dated December 1, 1800, and a plat of survey, annexed to the tract adjoining, as aforesaid, dated March 1, 1796; also, the assignment from the said Ruddell and Harrison.

Testimony taken. March 10, 1806. Robert McCoy, sworn, says that the family of George Ruddell, in the year 1796, consisted of himself, a wife, six children, and six negroes, whereby, agreeably to the Spanish laws and usages respecting the granting of lands, he was entitled to six hundred and twenty arpents of land; that, in the petition of the said Ruddell annexed to his concession, the quantity of six hundred arpents is prayed for, and the Baron de Carondelet grants "the four hundred arpents he solicits." It is the opinion of the Board that the Baron de Carondelet intended to have granted six hundred arpents instead of four hundred. They are satisfied that there was a mistake in the Intendant, and that his intention was to have granted the quantity prayed for; and it being proved that the same was actually inhabited and cultivated prior to and on the 1st October, 1800, they confirm to the said claimant, assignee as aforesaid, the said two hundred arpents, being the residue of the said tract of six hundred arpents.

March 10, 1806: Present at the decision of the foregoing claim, Penrose and Donaldson, commissioners.

August 9, 1811: Present, Penrose and Bates, commissioners. The petition and recommendation stated to be produced is not found on record. It is the opinion of the Board that this claim ought not to be confirmed.

ANDREW WOODS, claiming seven hundred and fifty arpents of land, situate in the district of New Madrid; produces to the Board a certificate of survey, dated February 15, 1806.

Testimony taken. March 11, 1806: George Wilson, sworn, says that the said tract of land was, prior to and on the 20th December, 1803, actually inhabited and cultivated for the use of the claimant.

March 11, 1806. Present, Penrose and Donaldson, commissioners. The Board reject this claim, the said land not being actually inhabited and cultivated by claimant himself.

August 14, 1811: Present, Penrose and Bates, commissioners. It is the opinion of the Board that this claim ought not to be granted.

JESSE PENDEGRASS, claiming four hundred arpents of land, situate near lake Ricardo, district of New Madrid; produces to the Board a certificate of a permission to settle from Henry Peyroux, dated September 9, 1801; and a certificate of survey, dated February 27, 1806.

Testimony taken. March 11, 1806. George Wilson, sworn, says that the said tract of land was, prior to and on the 20th December, 1803, actually inhabited and cultivated for the use of claimant.

March 11, 1806: Present, Penrose and Donaldson, commissioners. The Board reject this claim, the said land not being actually inhabited and cultivated by claimant himself, but for his use.

August 9, 1811: Present, Penrose and Bates, commissioners. It is the opinion of the Board that this claim ought not to be granted.

PATRICK CONNOR, claiming seven hundred and fifty arpents of land, situate on bayou St. John, district of New Madrid; produces to the Board a certificate of survey, dated February 27, 1806.

Testimony taken. March 13, 1806. George Wilson, sworn, says that claimant did, prior to and on the 20th December, 1803, actually inhabit and cultivate the said land.

March 13, 1806: Present, Penrose and Donaldson, commissioners. The Board, presuming a permission to settle, grant claimant seven hundred and fifty arpents of land, situate as aforesaid, provided so much be found vacant there.

August 14, 1811: Present, Penrose and Bates, commissioners. It is the opinion of the Board that this claim ought not to be granted.

JESSE DEMINT, claiming nine hundred arpents of land, situate on the bayou St. John, district of New Madrid; produces to the Board a certificate of survey of the same, dated February 27, 1806.

Testimony taken. March 14, 1806. George Wilson, sworn, says that claimant did, prior to and on the 20th December, 1803, actually inhabit and cultivate the said tract of land, and had a wife and one child.

****

March 14, 1806: Present, Penrose and Donaldson, commissioners. The Board grant claimant nine hundred arpents of land, situate as aforesaid, provided so much be found vacant there.

August 14, 1811: Present, Penrose and Bates, commissioners. It is the opinion of the Board that this claim ought not to be granted.

CONRAD CARPENTER, representatives of, claiming one thousand one hundred arpents of land, situate near the Mississippi, district of New Madrid; produces to the Board a certificate of survey of the said land, dated February 27, 1806.

Testimony taken. March 14, 1806. George Wilson, sworn, says that the said Conrad Carpenter did, prior to the 20th December, 1803, actually inhabit and cultivate the said tract of land, and that the same was, on that day and year, actually inhabited and cultivated by the above claimant; that the said Conrad Carpenter left a wife and seven children.

March 14, 1806: Present, Penrose and Donaldson, commissioners. The Board grant the aforesaid claimant one thousand one hundred arpents of land, situate as aforesaid, provided so much be found vacant there.

August 14, 1811: Present, Penrose and Bates, commissioners. It is the opinion of the Board that this claim ought not to be granted.

SAMUEL JONES, claiming seven hundred and fifty arpents of land, situate on bayou St. John, district of New Madrid; produces to the Board a certificate of survey, dated 27th February, 1806.

Testimony taken. March 14, 1806. George Wilson, sworn, says that claimant did, prior to and on the 20th December, 1803, actually inhabit and cultivate the said tract of land, and was then of the age of twenty-one years and upwards.

March 14, 1806: Present, Penrose and Donaldson, commissioners. The Board grant the said claimant seven hundred and fifty arpents of land, situate as aforesaid, provided so much be found vacant there.

August 14, 1811: Present, Penrose and Bates, commissioners. It is the opinion of the Board that this claim ought not to be granted.

JOSEPH STORY, assignee of Louis Lardoise, claiming two hundred arpents of land, situate on bayou de Bœuf, district of New Madrid; produces to the Board a certificate of permission to settle from Henry Peyroux, dated 12th February, 1806; a certificate of survey of the same; and a deed of transfer of said land from said Louis Lardoise to claimant, dated October 19, 1805.

Testimony taken. March 21, 1806. George Wilson, sworn, says that the said Louis Lardoise did, prior to and on the 1st day of October, 1800, actually inhabit and cultivate the said tract of land.

March 21, 1806: Present, Lucas and Penrose, commissioners. The Board confirm to the said claimant, assignee as aforesaid, two hundred arpents of land, situate as aforesaid, as per the said certificate of permission to settle.

August 14, 1811: Present, Penrose and Bates, commissioners. It is the opinion of the Board that this claim ought not to be granted.

SAMUEL DORSEY, assignee of Samuel Adams, claiming one thousand four hundred arpents of land, situate in Marais des Peches, district of New Madrid; produces to the Board a certificate of survey, dated February 26, 1806, and a deed of transfer of the same, dated 26th May, 1805.

Testimony taken. March 21, 1806. Edward Robertson, sworn, says that the said Samuel Adams did, prior to and on the 20th December, 1803, actually inhabit and cultivate the said tract of land, and had then eleven children.

March 21, 1806: Present, Lucas and Donaldson, commissioners. The Board grant the said claimant, assignee as aforesaid, one thousand three hundred arpents of land, situate as aforesaid, provided so much be found vacant there.

August 15, 1811: Present, Penrose and Bates, commissioners. It is the opinion of the Board that this claim · ought not to be granted.

EDWARD ROBERTSON, assignee of Daniel Barton, claiming ten arpents of land, situate in Big Prairie, district of New Madrid; produces to the Board a certificate of a warrant of survey from Henry Peyroux, dated April 12, 1802; a certificate of survey, dated 13th March, 1806; and a certificate of public sale of the said Barton's property, by Henry Peyroux, when the same was purchased by claimant, dated 4th September, 1804.

August 15, 1811: Present, Penrose and Bates, commissioners. It is the opinion of the Board that this claim ought not to be granted.

JOHN ROBERTSON, claiming three hundred and thirty arpents of land, situate on lake St. Mary, district of New Madrid; produces to the Board a certificate of survey, dated February 28, 1806.

Testimony taken. March 24, 1806. Jacob Myers, sworn, says that claimant did, prior to and on the 20th December, 1803, actually inhabit and cultivate the said tract of land, and was then of the age of twenty-one years and upwards.

March 24, 1806: Present, Lucas and Donaldson, commissioners. The Board grant the said claimant seven hundred and fifty arpents of land, situate as aforesaid, provided so much be found vacant there.

August 15, 1811: Present, Penrose and Bates, commissioners. It is the opinion of the Board that this claim ought not to be granted.

CHARLES ELLIS, claiming nine hundred and ninety-seven arpents eighty-five perches of land, situate on creek Capes and Comes, district of Cape Girardeau; produces to the Board a certificate of survey of the same, dated 26th February, 1806.

Testimony taken. April 21, 1806. Barney Burns, sworn, says that one John Fisher did, in the year 1801, build a cabin on said land, and cultivate the same; that one John Smith built another cabin on the said land in 1802, and actually inhabited and cultivated it; and that the said claimant rented it to a person who did, prior to and on the 20th December, 1803, actually inhabit and cultivate the same; and further, that he, the said claimant, did, in the year 1804, move on the said land, and has actually inhabited and cultivated the same to this day.

April 21, 1806: Present, Lucas and Donaldson, commissioners. The Board reject this case for want of actual inhabitation by claimant prior to and on 20th December, 1803, and think it a hard case.

August 15, 1811: Present, Penrose and Bates, commissioners. It is the opinion of the Board that this claim ought not to be granted.

CHRISTOPHER HARNESS, claiming seven hundred and forty-seven arpents of land, situate on St. Francis, district of Cape Girardeau; (for permission to settle see list sworn to by Laremer and cousins;) produces to the Board a certificate of survey of the same, dated February 19, 1806.

Testimony taken. May 25, 1806. Jesse Smith, sworn, says that the said claimant settled the said land in 1801; that year he went away, and returned on the same in the year 1803; raised a crop thereon in 1804; that he was, prior to and on the 20th December, 1803, of twenty-one years and upwards, and claims no other land in his own name in the Territory.

Robert E. Logan, sworn, says that claimant returned to the country about the beginning of 1803.

August 15, 1811: Present, Penrose and Bates, commissioners. It is the opinion of the Board that this claim ought not to be granted.

DAVID REESE, claiming two hundred and forty arpents of land, situate on a fork of the river St. Francis, district of Cape Girardeau; produces to the Board a certificate of survey, dated 19th February, 1806.

Testimony taken. May 5, 1806. Robert A. Logan, sworn, says that claimant settled the said tract of land by his agent, Charles Logan, in 1803; that he moved on the same in the fall of 1805, and has actually inhabited and cultivated the same to this day; was of the age of twenty-one years and upwards on the 20th December, 1803, and claims no other land in his own name in the Territory.

August 15, 1811: Present, Penrose and Bates, commissioners. It is the opinion of the Board that this claim ought not to be granted.

CHARLES LOGAN, claiming eight hundred arpents of land, situate on waters of the river St. Francis, district of Cape Girardeau; produces to the Board a certificate of survey of the same, dated January 30, 1806.

Testimony taken. May 5, 1806. Thomas Ring, sworn, says that he saw claimant, some time about Christmas in the year 1803, on said land; that he was then informed he had been on the same before; that he raised a crop on the same in 1804, and had a wife and three children.

David Logan, sworn, says that prior to the 20th December, 1803, he was at Charles Logan's, the above claimant; that the said Logan told him he had planted peach stones, and showed him the place; that the ground had the appearance of having been lately dug up; that, being on the same place early in the spring of 1804, he saw peach trees growing on the same spot shown him by claimant in the preceding year; that claimant had a wife, four children, and three negroes; and that he has actually inhabited and cultivated the same to this day. Permission to settle sworn to.

May 5, 1806: Present, Penrose and Donaldson, commissioners. The Board grant said claimant four hundred and sixty arpents of land, situate as aforesaid, provided so much be found vacant there.

August 15, 1811: Present, Penrose and Bates, commissioners. It is the opinion of the Board that this claim ought not to be granted.

RICHARD JONES WATERS, assignee of Dinah Martin Rees, claiming four hundred arpents of land, situate in the district of New Madrid; produces to the Board a recommendation from Henry Peyroux, in favor of the said Dinah, for a concession, dated September 24th, 1800, and a survey of said land; a deed of transfer of said four hundred arpents from the said Dinah Martin Rees to claimant, dated January 2, 1800.

Testimony taken. March 7, 1806. George Wilson, sworn, says that the said tract of land was, prior to and on the 1st day of October, 1800, actually inhabited and cultivated.

March 7, 1806: Present, Lucas and Donaldson, commissioners. The Board confirm to the claimant, assignee, &c. the said tract of four hundred arpents, as per the said recommendation.

August 16, 1811: Present, Penrose and Bates, commissioners. It is the opinion of the Board that this claim ought not to be confirmed.

SILVESTER LABADIE, representatives of, claiming eight arpents in front by forty in depth of land, situate on the Mississippi, district of St. Louis; produces to the Board a concession from Estevan Merot, dated 27th May, 1791, with a proviso that the same does not prejudice any one; and a certificate of survey of three hundred and twenty arpents, dated January 1, 1806, certified January 27, 1806; a concession from Manuel Perez, Lieutenant Governor, to Silvester Labadie, for eight arpents front by eight arpents in depth, back to the road leading from St. Louis to Oide Poke, prairie Catalon, dated 9th August, 1788.

Testimony taken. May 13, 1806. Gregorie Sarpee, sworn, says that the said Silvester Labadie, having obtained the aforesaid concession, proceeded to the improvement and cultivation of said land, but was prevented from so doing by the Lieutenant Governor, who, upon the remonstrance of the inhabitants of the village, ordered him, the said Silvester Labadie, to stop any further improvements on the said land until the Intendant below should be made acquainted with the circumstance of said claim, and have decreed otherwise.

August 16, 1811: Present, Penrose and Bates, commissioners. It is the opinion of the Board that this claim ought not to be confirmed.

THOMAS MADDON, assignee of Thomas Dodge, claiming eight by forty arpents of land, situate on the river Aux Vases, district of St. Genevieve; produces to the Board a concession from Zenon Trudeau, not duly registered, dated 1st June, 1797; a survey of two hundred and eighty-four arpents, taken 3d May, and certified 10th September, 1799; together with a deed of transfer of the same, executed before Peter D. Deluzier, dated October 13th, 1803.

Testimony taken. June 23, 1806. Israel Dodge, sworn, says that the said land was first settled by the inhabitants of New Bourbon; that, at the time of the inundation of the lower point, twenty acres of said land were under cultivation; that one Mr. Degaire, an inhabitant of the village, and one of those who cultivated the said land at that period, and who was then their syndic, gave said land to Thomas Dodge, who obtained a concession for the same; that he was under age at the time of obtaining the same, and claims no other land in his own name in the Territory; and further, that the above claimant, having purchased the said tract, did, in 1804, at a great expense, build a distillery on the same, which was afterwards destroyed.

June 23, 1806: Present, Penrose and Donaldson, commissioners. This claim being unsupported by actual inhabitation and cultivation, the Board reject the same.

August 17, 1811: Present, Penrose and Bates, commissioners. It is the opinion of the Board that this claim ought not to be confirmed.

THOMAS RINEY, assignee of Clement Heyden, claiming nine hundred arpents of land, situate in the district of St. Genevieve; produces to the Board a survey of the same, dated November 28th, 1805, and certified 3d February, 1806; a certificate from Peter Deluzier that he had permitted claimant to settle on vacant lands, dated 14th December, 1805.

Testimony taken. June 25, 1806. Sarah Tucker, sworn, says that the said Clement Heyden settled the said tract of land in the fall of 1803; fenced in a small tract, in which he sowed apple seeds and peach stones; and that he did, prior to and on the 20th December, 1803, actually inhabit and cultivate the same, and had a house on it; that he had, on the said 20th day of December, a wife and six children; and further, that the above claimant, having purchased the same, moved on it in 1804, and has actually inhabited and cultivated it to this day.

June 25, 1806: Present, Penrose and Donaldson, commissioners. The Board grant the said claimant, assignee as aforesaid, six hundred arpents of land, situate as aforesaid, provided so much be found vacant there.

August 17, 1811: Present, Penrose and Bates, commissioners. It is the opinion of the Board that this claim ought not to be granted.

JACQUE ST. VRAIN, claiming nine hundred arpents of land, situate on Cold Water, district of St. Louis; produces to the Board a concession from John V. Morales, dated New Orleans, 22d April, 1802, subjecting the said claimant to the 3d, 4th, 6th, 7th, and 9th articles of Morales's regulations; and a survey of the same, dated February 5, 1799.

Testimony taken. May 13, 1806. Marie P. Leduc, sworn, says that the above claimant had, in 1799, about sixty arpents of said land under fence, a great part of which was then cultivated, and that the same was, prior to and on the 1st October, 1800, actually inhabited and cultivated; and further, that the said claimant has now under fence upwards of one hundred and fifty arpents.

May 13, 1806: Present, Penrose, commissioner. The Board ascertain this claim to be a Spanish title completed. Approved, 13th May, 1806.

August 17, 1811: Present, Penrose and Bates, commissioners. The Board decline revising this claim. Originals not produced.

JACQUE ST. VRAIN, assignee of Daniel Quick, claiming five hundred and fifty arpents of land, and DANIEL QUICK, claiming two hundred and fifty arpents, situate in the district of St. Charles; produce to the Board a concession from Charles Dehault Delassus for eight hundred arpents of land to the said Daniel Quick, dated February 5, 1801; a certificate of survey of the same, dated March 5, 1804; and a deed of transfer, dated December 3, 1803.

May 28, 1806: Present, Penrose, commissioner. The Board cannot act on this claim. Approved, June 10, 1806.

August 17, 1811: Present, Penrose and Bates, commissioners. It is the opinion of the Board that this claim ought not to be confirmed.

JACQUE ST. VRAIN, assignee of Louis Lajoye, claiming five hundred and fifty arpents of land, situate in the district of St. Charles; produces to the Board a concession from Charles Dehault Delassus to the said Louis Lajoye, dated 19th February, 1800; together with a deed of transfer of the same, dated 17th December, 1803.

May 28, 1806: Present, Penrose, commissioner. The Board require further proof of the date of the above concession on behalf of the United States.

August 17, 1811: Present, Penrose and Bates, commissioners. It is the opinion of the Board that this claim ought not to be confirmed.

JACQUE ST. VRAIN, assignee of Francis Belonge, claiming five hundred and fifty arpents of land, and FRANCIS BELONGE, claiming two hundred and fifty arpents, situate in the district of St. Charles; produce to the Board a concession from Charles Dehault Delassus for eight hundred arpents, dated 20th December, 1799; a survey, dated 9th January, 1804; and a transfer of the same, dated December 13, 1803.

May 28, 1806: Present, Penrose, commissioner. The Board require further proof of the date of the above concession. Approved, June 10, 1806. The Board reject this claim.

August 17, 1811: Present, Penrose and Bates, commissioners. It is the opinion of the Board that this claim ought not to be confirmed.

JACQUE ST. VRAIN, assignee of Peter Roussell, claiming six hundred arpents, and PETER ROUSSELL, claiming two hundred arpents of land, situate on the river Cuivre, district of St. Charles; produce to the Board a concession from Charles D. Delassus to the said Roussell for eight hundred arpents, dated January 25, 1800; a survey, dated 20th February, certified 28th March, 1804; and a deed of transfer of the same, dated 5th January, 1804.

Present, Penrose, commissioner. The Board require further proof of the date of the above concession, on behalf of the United States. Approved, June 10.

Testimony taken. May 28, 1806. Peter Roussell, sworn, says that some time in March, 1804, as he believes, he received from Louis Lebeaume a concession for which he never had applied; that, some time in January or February of that same year, Lebeaume asked him if he wanted land, to which he replied he would take it if it was given him; that the said concession did not remain in his possession; and further, that in the said month of March he signed an assignment of six hundred arpents of the same to the above claimant, but received nothing for the same; that he has since sold the remaining two hundred arpents to another person; was, at the time of receiving said concession, twenty-five years of age, and had a wife and child; never cultivated the same, nor inhabited it; and that he claims no other land in his own name in this Territory.

August 17, 1811: Present, Penrose and Bates, commissioners. It is the opinion of the Board that this claim ought not to be confirmed.

JACQUE ST. VRAIN, assignee of Francis Paquette, claiming six hundred arpents, and FRANCIS PAQUETTE, claiming two hundred arpents of land, situate on river Cuivre, district of St. Charles; produce to the Board a concession from Charles D. Delassus for eight hundred arpents of land to the said Paquette, dated April 5, 1800; a survey of the same, dated February 20, and certified 28th March, 1804; and a deed of transfer of the same, dated 10th January, 1804.

May 28, 1806: Present, Penrose, commissioner. The Board require further proof of the date of the above concession.

The Board reject this claim. Approved, 10th June.

August 17, 1811: Present, Penrose and Bates, commissioners. It is the opinion of the Board that this claim ought not to be confirmed.

JACQUE ST. VRAIN, assignee of Joseph Hebert, claiming six hundred arpents; and JOSEPH HEBERT, claiming two hundred arpents of land, situate on river Cuivre, district of St. Charles; produce to the Board a concession from Charles D. Delassus to the said Hebert for eight hundred arpents, dated April 15, 1800; a survey of the same, dated 20th February, and certified 28th March, 1804; and a transfer, dated 10th January, 1804.

May 28, 1806: Present, Penrose, commissioner. The Board require further proof of the date of the above concession.

The Board reject this claim. Approved 10th June.

August 17, 1811: Present, Penrose and Bates, commissioners. It is the opinion of the Board that this claim ought not to be confirmed.

JACQUE ST. VRAIN, assignee of Benjamin Quick, claiming six hundred arpents of land, and BENJAMIN QUICK, claiming two hundred arpents, situate on river Cuivre, district of St. Charles; produce to the Board a concession from Charles D. Delassus to the said Quick for eight hundred arpents, dated 10th March, 1801; a survey of the same, dated 20th February, certified 28th March, 1804; and a transfer, dated December 6th, 1803.

August 17, 1811: Present, Penrose and Bates, commissioners. It is the opinion of the Board that this claim ought not to be confirmed.

JACQUE ST. VRAIN, assignee of Rivet, claiming six hundred arpents, and RIVET, claiming two hundred arpents of land, situate on river Cuivre, district of St. Charles; produce to the Board a concession from Charles D. Delassus to the said Rivet for eight hundred arpents, dated 28th February, 1800; survey taken 20th February, and certified 28th March, 1804; and a transfer of the same, dated 12th February, 1804.

May 28, 1806: Present, Penrose, commissioner. The Board require further proof of the date of the above concession. Rejected. Approved, 10th June.

August 17, 1811: Present, Penrose and Bates, commissioners. It is the opinion of the Board that this claim ought not to be confirmed.

JACQUE ST. VRAIN, assignee of Antoine Dejarlais, claiming six hundred arpents, and ANTOINE DEJARLAIS, claiming two hundred arpents of land, situate on river Cuivre, district of St. Charles; produce to the Board a concession from Charles D. Delassus to the said Dejarlais for eight hundred arpents, dated March 19, 1800; a survey of the same, taken 20th February, and certified 28th March, 1804; and a transfer of the same, dated 10th December, 1803.

May 28, 1806: Present, Penrose, commissioner. The Board require further proof of the date of the above concession. The Board reject this claim.

August 17, 1811: Present, Penrose and Bates, commissioners. It is the opinion of the Board that this claim ought not to be confirmed.

JACQUE ST. VRAIN, assignee of John Basye, claiming one thousand arpents of land, and JOHN BASYE, claiming six hundred arpents of land, situate on river Cuivre, district of St. Charles; produce to the Board a concession from Charles D. Delassus to the said Basye for sixteen hundred arpents of land, dated 8th January, 1801; a survey of the same, dated 10th February, and certified 20th March, 1804; transfer of the same, dated September 3, 1803.

August 17, 1811: Present, Penrose and Bates, commissioners. It is the opinion of the Board that this claim ought not to be confirmed.

JACQUE ST. VRAIN, assignee of Joseph Jamison, claiming six hundred arpents, and JOSEPH JAMISON, claiming two hundred arpents of land, situate on river Cuivre, district of St. Charles; produce to the Board a concession from Charles D. Delassus, dated February 9, 1802; a survey of the same, dated 10th February, 1804; and a deed of transfer of the same, dated December 5, 1803.

August 17, 1811: Present, Penrose and Bates, commissioners. It is the opinion of the Board that this claim ought not to be confirmed.

JACQUE ST. VRAIN, assignee of Baptiste Joseph Billot, claiming six hundred arpents, and BAPTISTE JOSEPH BILLOT, claiming two hundred arpents of land, situate on river Cuivre, district of St. Charles; produce to the Board a concession from Charles D. Delassus to said Billot for eight hundred arpents, dated 29th February, 1800; a survey taken 11th February, and certified 20th March, 1804; and a deed of transfer of the same, dated 10th January, 1804.

The Board require further proof of the date of the said concession on behalf of the United States.

Testimony taken. May 28, 1806. Baptiste Joseph Billot, sworn, says that about two years ago, understanding that Louis Lebeaume was dealing out concessions, he expressed a wish to have one, if possible to obtain it; that, some days after, one Albert Tison called on him (the witness) and tendered him a concession; that he then signed the petition for the same, and at the same time executed a deed of transfer of some part of it, for which he received an iron pot; and further, that he had then a wife and four children, and claims no other land in his own name in the Territory.

May 28, 1806: Present, Penrose, commissioner. The Board reject this claim. Approved, 10th June, 1806.

August 17, 1811: Present, Penrose and Bates, commissioners. It is the opinion of the Board that this claim ought not to be confirmed.

JACQUE ST. VRAIN, assignee of Baptiste Delisle, claiming six hundred arpents, and BAPTISTE DELISLE, claiming two hundred arpents of land, situate on river Cuivre, district of St. Charles; produce to the Board a concession from Charles D. Delassus to said Delisle for eight hundred arpents, dated April 25, 1800; a survey of the same, dated February 11, certified 20th March, 1804; and a deed of transfer, dated 17th December, 1804.

May 28, 1806: Present, Penrose, commissioner. The Board require further proof of the date of the said concession. The Board reject this claim. Approved, 10th June.

August 17, 1811: Present, Penrose and Bates, commissioners. It is the opinion of the Board that this claim ought not to be confirmed.

JACQUE ST. VRAIN, assignee of Baptiste Delisle, Jun., claiming six hundred arpents of land, and BAPTISTE DELISLE, Jun., claiming two hundred arpents, situate on river Cuivre, district of St. Charles; produce to the Board a concession from Charles D. Delassus to said Delisle for eight hundred arpents, dated October 9, 1799; a survey of the same, dated 11th February, and certified 20th March, 1804; and a deed of transfer of the same, dated January 5, 1804.

LAND GRANTS IN MISSOURI TERRITORY - 1805 - 1812   131

****

May 28, 1806: Present, Penrose, commissioner. The Board require further proof of the date of the said concession. The Board reject this claim. Approved, 10th June.

August 17, 1811: Present, Penrose and Bates, commissioners. It is the opinion of the Board that this claim ought not to be confirmed.

JACQUE ST. VRAIN, assignee of Paul Dejarlais, claiming six hundred arpents, and PAUL DEJARLAIS, claiming two hundred arpents of land, situate on river Cuivre, district of St. Charles; produce to the Board a concession from Charles D. Delassus to said Dejarlais for eight hundred arpents, dated July 11, 1800; a survey of the same, dated 11th February, and certified 20th March, 1804; and a deed of transfer of the same, dated 12th December, 1803.

June 28, 1806: Present, C. B. Penrose, commissioner. The Board require further proof of the date of said concession, on behalf of the United States. Approved, 10th June.

Testimony taken. May 28, 1806. Paul Dejarlais, sworn, says that some time in the spring of 1804 Lebeaume called upon him, and told him that if he wanted lands he might have some; to which he (the witness) replied, that if he was to pay nothing for the same he should like to have it; that accordingly, some time in June of that year, (as he believes) Lebaume gave him a concession for eight hundred arpents of land; that the Spanish officers had not then left the country; and that when the said concession was given him, he gave an assignment of six hundred arpents of the same, for which he did not receive any thing; and further, that he had then a wife and child, and claims no other land in his own name in the Territory.

August 17, 1811: Present, Penrose and Bates, commissioners. It is the opinion of the Board that this claim ought not to be confirmed.

FRANCIS BERTHEAUME, alias Francis Barume, claiming nine hundred and eighteen arpents and thirty perches of land, situate on Apple creek, district of Cape Girardeau; produces to the Board a survey of the same, dated 24th January, and certified 26th February, 1806.

Testimony taken. June 25, 1806. Camille Lassus, sworn, says that he was present when commandant did permit claimant to settle on vacant land.

Robert Hinckson, sworn, says that claimant cultivated the said tract of land in 1802, and did, prior to and on the 20th December, 1803, actually inhabit and cultivate the same; and had then three children and one slave.

June 25, 1806: Present, Penrose and Donaldson, commissioners. The Board grant the said claimant two hundred and seventy arpents of land, situate as aforesaid, provided so much be found vacant there.

August 19, 1811: Present, Penrose and Bates, commissioners. It is the opinion of the Board that this claim ought not to be granted.

JOSEPH BRAZEAU, claiming three hundred and forty-seven arpents of land, joining a former concession, and granted him as a compensation, beginning at the aforesaid tract granted him by Cruzat, district of ———; produces to the Board a concession from Charles D. Delassus, dated November 19, 1799; and a survey of the same, forming the whole of the above tract claimed by him, and dated the 28th May, and certified the 21st August, 1803.

July 19, 1806: Present, Lucas, Penrose, and Donaldson, commissioners. This claim being unsupported by actual inhabitation and cultivation, the Board reject the same. They remark that they are satisfied that the aforesaid concession was granted at the time it bears date; but that the same interferes with a tract of land claimed by the inhabitants of the town of St. Louis as a common.

August 19, 1811: Present, Penrose and Bates, commissioners. It is the opinion of the Board that this claim ought not to be confirmed.

AUGUSTE CHOUTEAU, assignee of widow Rontier, assignee of Joseph Mainville, claiming sixty arpents of land, situate in the Grand Prairie of St. Louis, district of St. Louis; produces to the Board a duly registered act of survey, signed St. Ange, and ratified by Peter Piernuss, dated 23d May, 1772.

July 25, 1806: Present, Lucas and Donaldson, commissioners. The Board ascertain this claim to be a French grant completed by Spanish regulations.

August 19, 1811: Present, Penrose and Bates, commissioners. It is the opinion of the Board that this claim ought not to be confirmed.

CHRISTOPHER CARPENTER, representative of John Carpenter, claiming seven hundred and forty-eight arpents sixty-eight perches of land, situate in the district of St. Louis; produces to the Board a survey of the same, dated 17th February, 1806.

Testimony taken. July 29, 1806. Joseph Sips, sworn, says that the said John Carpenter settled the said tract of land in the year 1802; that in 1803 he cleared a field of about four or five acres, and did, prior to and on the 20th December, 1803, actually inhabit and cultivate the same, and had no family but the above claimant.

August 19, 1811: Present, Penrose and Bates, commissioners. It is the opinion of the Board that this claim ought not to be granted.

LEWIS DICKSON, assignee of William Vanburhelow, claiming eleven hundred and forty-eight arpents of land, situate on Cape Cinqhomme, lower end of Bois Bruile, district of St. Genevieve; produces to the Board a certificate of survey of the same, dated December 14, 1805; a certificate from Pierre D. Deluzier, stating that prior to the year 1800 he had permitted claimant to settle on vacant lands, dated 10th December, 1806.

Testimony taken. July 29, 1806. Joshua Fisher, sworn, says that he, the witness, settled the said land in the year 1800; built a cabin, and fenced in about two acres, and lived thereon until March following, when, having sold to claimant, he moved out.

Levi Wiggins, sworn, says that he, the witness, did, in October, 1803, having first obtained claimant's leave to that effect, move on said land; cleared a few acres; planted apple seeds in a corner, which he fenced in; that his object was then the raising of stock, which he did until the spring of 1804; that since that period he has lived on the same, and has now a large stock on it as tenant of the above claimant.

July 29, 1806: Present, Lucas and Penrose, commissioners. The Board reject this claim for want of a duly registered warrant of survey.

August 19, 1811: Present, Penrose and Bates, commissioners. It is the opinion of the Board that this claim ought not to be granted.

JAMES NORRIS, claiming three hundred and fifty-one arpents of land, situate on Willow's swamp, district of Cape Girardeau; produces to the Board a certificate of permission to settle, dated 23d April, 1802; and a survey of said land, taken 17th, and certified 28th February, 1806.

Testimony taken. August 13, 1806. William Cox, sworn, says that the said claimant settled the said tract of land in the year 1802, and did, prior to and on the 20th December, 1803, actually inhabit and cultivate the same; and had then a wife, three children, and three slaves. The permission stated to be produced not found on record.

August 13, 1806: Present, Lucas, Penrose, and Donaldson, commissioners. The Board grant the said claimant four hundred and ten arpents of land, situate as aforesaid, provided so much be found vacant there.

August 19, 1811; Present, Penrose and Bates, commissioners. It is the opinion of the Board that this claim ought not to be granted.

JOHN DRAPER, claiming seven hundred and forty-seven arpents of land, situate on Dardenne, district of St. Charles; produces to the Board a survey of the same, dated February 12, 1806; and a certificate of permission to settle from James Mackay, dated 28th February, 1806.

Testimony taken. July 12, 1806. Zadock Woods, sworn, says that claimant settled said tract of land in 1802, built a house on the same, and enclosed a few arpents of the same; that he was by profession a well digger, and on the 20th December, 1803, of the age of twenty-one years and upwards.

Certificate of permission stated to be produced not found on record.

August 19, 1811: Present, Penrose and Bates, commissioners. It is the opinion of the Board that this claim ought not to be granted.

JEAN PERRY, claiming three thousand arpents of land, situate on river Aux Bœufs, district of St. Louis; produces to the Board a concession, dated July, 1798.

August 23, 1806: Present, Penrose and Donaldson, commissioners. This claim being unsupported by actual inhabitation and cultivation, the Board reject this claim, and observe, that, from a letter in the possession of claimant, now produced to them, they are satisfied that the said concession was granted at the time it bears date.

August 20, 1811: Present, Penrose and Bates, commissioners. It is the opinion of the Board that this claim ought not to be confirmed.

STEPHEN BYRD, assignee of Daniel Mullins, assignee of Jesse Bowden, claiming four hundred and twenty-eight arpents of land, situate on the waters of the Mississippi, district of New Madrid; produces to the Board a certified copy of a permission to settle, by Henry Peyroux, certified by Peter A. Laforge, civil commandant of New Madrid, under date of May 14, 1804; and a survey, dated 24th January, 1804, together with a deed of transfer of the same, from Jesse Bowden to said Daniel Mullins, dated 30th March, 1805; and another deed of transfer of the same from said Mullins to claimant, dated 12th July, 1805.

Testimony taken. August 25, 1806. William Smith, sworn, says that the said Bowden raised two crops on said land, having settled the same in 1801; that he did, prior to and on the 20th December, 1803, actually inhabit the same, and had then a wife and two children, and one slave; and that the same has been actually inhabited and cultivated to this day.

August 20, 1811: Present, Penrose and Bates, commissioners. It is the opinion of the Board that this claim ought not to be granted.

GEORGE STRINGER, claiming eight hundred and fifty arpents of land, situate in the district of New Madrid; produces to the Board a survey of the same, dated 10th February, 1806, and certified 28th same month.

August 25, 1806: Present, Lucas, commissioner. This claim being unsupported by inhabitation and cultivation, the Board reject the same.

August 20, 1811: Present, Penrose and Bates, commissioners. It is the opinion of the Board that this claim ought not to be granted.

MARTIN RUGGLES, claiming seven hundred and forty-eight arpents seventeen perches of land, situate in the district of St. Genevieve; produces to the Board two surveys, dated the 1st, and certified the 25th February, 1806.

Testimony taken. August 29, 1806. John McNeal, sworn, says that claimant settled one of the aforesaid tracts, to wit, that one of two hundred and three arpents fifty-five perches, in the spring of 1803; and did, prior to and on the 20th December, 1803, actually inhabit and cultivate the same, and was then of the age of twenty-one years and upwards.

August 29, 1806: Present, Lucas and Penrose, commissioners. The Board reject this claim for want of proof of permission to settle. They remark that, independent of the actual settlement of the aforesaid tract, claimant has, at a very great expense, built a very valuable saw-mill on the aforesaid tract of five hundred and forty-four arpents.

August 20, 1811: Present, Penrose and Bates, commissioners. One survey not found on record. It is the opinion of the Board that this claim ought not to be granted.

GUILLEAUME HEBERT, dit Lecompte, claiming one hundred and twenty feet by sixty or seventy feet depth, situate in the town of St. Louis, district of St. Louis, granted for stone quarrying; produces to the Board a concession from Charles D. Delassus, dated 5th September, 1799.

Testimony taken. September 9, 1806. Auguste Chouteau, sworn, says that he did, about seven or eight years ago, quarry stones on said lot by claimant's leave, and paid him five sous per load.

August 20, 1811: Present, Penrose and Bates, commissioners. The Board refer to their remarks made in the claim of Julian Papin Benito; this being similarly situated. It is the opinion of the Board that this claim ought not to be confirmed.

JOHN WATKINS, claiming eight hundred arpents of land, situate on the Missouri, district of St. Charles; produces to the Board a duly registered concession from Zenon Trudeau, dated 6th February, 1797; and a survey of the same, taken 14th November, 1803, and certified 15th April, 1804.

Testimony taken. September 17, 1806. Antoine Soulard, sworn, says that he wrote the aforesaid concession, and that the date of the same is perfectly correct.

September 22, 1808. Antoine Soulard, being re-examined concerning his testimony given in this case, 17th September, 1806, says, that by the term "perfectly correct," he meant that the concession was given at the time it bears date.

September 17, 1806: Present, Lucas and Donaldson, commissioners. The Board reject this claim, and are satisfied that the said concession was granted at the time it bears date:

August 20, 1811: Present, Penrose and Bates, commissioners. It is the opinion of the Board that this claim ought not to be confirmed.

JOHN BAPTISTE LAMARCHE, claiming six by forty arpents of land, situate on the Missouri, district of St. Louis, to be bounded on each side by one Chartrand and Francis Janis, and on the rear by Emilian Forty; produces to the Board a concession from Zenon Trudeau, dated 18th November, 1798; and a survey of said quantity, taken on the river Merrimack, in consequence of the aforesaid tract having been previously surveyed by another person; the said survey without date.

Testimony taken. September 29, 1806. Toussaint Cerre, sworn, says that the said claimant actually inhabited the said tract of land, as surveyed on the Merrimack, about seven or eight years ago.

August 20, 1811: Present, Penrose and Bates, commissioners. It is the opinion of the Board that this claim ought not to be confirmed.

HUGH BRANNON, claiming two hundred and fifty arpents of land, situate in the district of Cape Girardeau; produces to the Board a permission to settle, certified by Louis Lorimier, under the date of July 24, 1804.

Testimony taken. August 22, 1806. Daniel Thorn, sworn, says that the said land lies on a branch of the White waters, about a mile from John May's; that claimant settled the said tract of land in the year 1804, and has actually inhabited and cultivated the said land to this day; had, on the 20th December, 1803, a wife.

August 20, 1811: Present, Penrose and Bates, commissioners. Permission stated to be produced not found on record. It is the opinion of the Board that this claim ought not to be granted.

JACQUES CLAMORGAN, claiming five hundred and thirty-six thousand nine hundred and four arpents and twenty-nine perches of land, situate on the Mississippi, district of New Madrid; produces to the Board a concession from Charles D. Delassus, the then commandant of New Madrid, dated August 9, 1796, stating the same to be granted for establishing a ropewalk, and forming a Canadian establishment for the purpose of raising hemp, together with a survey of the same, taken the 30th January to the 12th February, and certified the 20th February, 1806.

The Board require further proof.

August 20, 1811: Present, Penrose and Bates, commissioners. It is the opinion of the Board that this claim ought not to be confirmed.

ROBERT SPENCER, assignee of the widow of Louis Hunot, claiming three hundred and twenty arpents of land, situate on the river Cuivre, district of St. Charles; produces to the Board a concession from Zenon Trudeau, Lieutenant Governor, dated 11th December, 1797, to Louis Hunot, and a certified copy of a deed of conveyance from said widow to claimant, dated 16th March, 1804.

On the objection of the agent, alleging fraud and antedate, the Board require further proof.

Testimony taken. August 8, 1807. Noel A. Prierer, sworn, says that he has been ten years and a half in the village of St. Charles, and that Lewis Hunot was then residing in said village, and was the head of a family at that time; and that he, the said Hunot, died five years ago, in this country; and that his widow and children are still residing in it.

George Geaty, sworn, says that in 1798 the said Hunot tried to engage him, the witness, to go and settle with him on the river Cuivre, the said Hunot alleging that he had a concession from Zenon Trudeau for land there, at what he called the Prairie des Butes, but that he refused to go, from his wife's objecting to the distance from the inhabitants.

August 21, 1811: Present, Penrose and Bates, commissioners. It is the opinion of the Board that this claim ought not to be confirmed.

JOHN BAPTISTE DUBAY, claiming seven hundred and forty-eight arpents and sixty-eight perches of land, situate on the south side of the river Missouri, opposite the town of St. Charles, district of St. Louis; produces to the Board a notice to the recorder, dated 7th September, 1807.

Testimony taken. September 11, 1807. Jacques Chovan, sworn, says that the claimant settled the above claim in 1803, that is to say, he inhabited said land, and that he saw a crop of corn growing on said land in 1803, and that claimant has continued to inhabit and cultivate the same ever since, and that in the year 1803 claimant was the head of a family, but does not know whether he had children; the claimant declares that he never had permission to settle.

August 21, 1811: Present, Penrose and Bates, commissioners. It is the opinion of the Board that this claim ought not to be granted.

FRANCIS VALLE, the representatives of, claiming seventy arpents of land, being an augmentation of a tract of twenty-five arpents square granted said Valle by Neon de Villiere in 1764, situate in the district of St. Genevieve; produces to the Board a concession from Zenon Trudeau, dated 9th March, 1798; a plat of survey, dated 15th March, 1798.

August 21, 1811: Present, Penrose and Bates, commissioners. It is the opinion of the Board that this claim ought not to be confirmed.

WILLIAM MONTGOMERY, claiming eight hundred arpents of land, situate on a run which empties itself into the river Platte, two miles from his habitation, district of St. Genevieve; produces to the Board a petition for said land, and a declaration from Francis Valle, commandant of St. Genevieve, directing him to apply to the Lieutenant Governor for the same, dated 12th September, 1803; and a plat and certificate of survey, dated January 13, 1806, for eight hundred acres of land, situate on Terre Blue creek, which empties into Big river.

Testimony taken. December 3, 1807. James Cunningham, sworn, says that the tract which he speaks of is the one situated on the Terre Blue; that claimant began to work in 1805, and that in 1806 there were two houses built on said land, and a saw-mill; the houses have been occupied, and the mill worked occasionally ever since.

August 21, 1811: Present, Penrose and Bates, commissioners. It is the opinion of the Board that this claim ought not to be granted.

WILLIAM FLYNN, Jun., claiming two hundred and forty arpents of land, situate on the Bois Bruile, district of St. Genevieve; produces to the Board a notice to the recorder, dated 3d December, 1807.

Testimony taken. December 3, 1807. William Flynn, Sen., sworn, says that in the year 1804, to the best of his knowledge, (recollection) he assisted his son, the claimant, to clear about one quarter of an acre of land, and enclosed the same, and also cultivated turnips thereon the same fall, but does not know whether the crop of turnips was taken off or gathered; does not know the age of his son exactly, but believes him to be about twenty-three or twenty-four years of age at this time; nor does he know whether his son had permission to settle.

August 21, 1811: Present, Penrose and Bates, commissioners. It is the opinion of the Board that this claim ought not to be granted.

EDWARD PERRY, by his agent Thomas Berry, claiming four hundred arpents of land, situate on the east side of Wild Horse creek, Missouri bottom, district of St. Louis; produces to the Board a notice to the recorder, of said claim, dated 16th April, 1808, and claiming also by virtue of a concession for the same, which is said to be lost.

Testimony taken. April 18, 1808. William Bellew, sworn, says that he was present when claimant obtained a concession from Don Zenon Trudeau, Lieutenant Governor of Upper Louisiana in 1797, for four hundred arpents of land, situate as aforesaid, and heard the same translated; that claimant was then above the age of twenty-one years; resided in this country but one year, to wit, in 1797, and then left the country; says that he (deponent) had the said concession in his possession, but gave it to some person to return to him, at this time unknown, without any written order from claimant; says that said land is situate on the east side of Wild Horse creek, adjoining the Missouri bottom; that claimant built a house on said place in 1797, had two or three acres in cultivation, and raised a crop of corn the same year, and that the same was cultivated the two following years, and crops of corn raised for claimant's use; that in the year 1801 the said tract of land was surveyed in by Captain James Mackay for his own use, and a tenant put thereon.

On application of Thomas Berry, agent for claimant, it is ordered by the Board, the Honorable Frederick Bates dissenting, that a *didimus* issue to any judge for the county of Clark, Indiana Territory, where it is alleged the claimant resides, to administer an oath to claimant, so that it may be certified to the Board whether the concession in this case be in his possession, or that the same be lost, or out of his power to obtain it.

September 26, 1808. In the above case, the *didimus* is returned as taken on the 15th July last, and duly certified, in substance, as follows: that claimant did lodge his concession in the hands of William Bellew; that the same is now mislaid or lost, and cannot be produced by claimant; and that he has never sold or transferred the same to any person whatever.

August 21, 1811: Present, Penrose and Bates, commissioners. It is the opinion of the Board that this claim ought not to be confirmed.

MARY NICOLLE LEBOIS, claiming two hundred and forty-four and a half arpents of land, situate in the commons of St. Louis; produces to the Board a concession from Don Carlos Dehault Delassus, Lieutenant Governor, for the same, dated 11th May, 1803; a plat and certificate of survey, dated 27th May, 1803, and certified 20th August same year.

August 21, 1811: Present, Penrose and Bates, commissioners. It is the opinion of the Board that this claim ought not to be confirmed.

ROBERT WILSON, claiming three hundred arpents of land, situate on the waters of Meadow creek, district of Cape Girardeau; produces to the Board a notice of claim to the recorder, dated 30th June, 1808.

Testimony taken. October 10, 1808. Lewis Lathan, sworn, says that claimant inhabited and cultivated the land claimed in 1806, and to this day.

August 21, 1811: Present, Penrose and Bates, commissioners. It is the opinion of the Board that this claim ought not to be granted.

JACOB KELLY, Jun., claiming three hundred arpents of land, situate on the east side of St. Francis' river, district of Cape Girardeau; produces to the board a notice to the recorder, dated 10th June, 1808.

Testimony taken. October 13, 1808. Isaac E. Kelly, sworn, says that claimant built a half faced cabin on the land claimed in 1801, and then exchanged said land with Jacob Kelly, Sen., who cut house logs on the same in January, 1804, and in March following built a cabin and moved on the same, and has inhabited and cultivated the same ever since.

August 21, 1811: Present, Penrose and Bates, commissioners. It is the opinion of the Board that this claim ought not to be granted.

CALVIN ADAMS, assignee of Auguste Charan, claiming two hundred and forty arpents of land, situate at Portage des Sioux, district of St. Charles; produces to the Board the record of a concession from Zenon Trudeau, Lieutenant Governor, to Auguste Charan, for the same, dated 21st April, 1797; also a transfer of the same from said Charan to claimant, dated 12th November, 1803.

Testimony taken. March 28, 1809. James Peper, sworn, says that Claibourn Rhodes ploughed and planted about one acre and a half of corn in 1798 on the tract claimed, but did not enclose it; sold his labor to one Crosby, who sold it to Louis Gor; has known the land claimed ever since, and nothing has been done on the same by Auguste Charan; Crosby raised two crops on the tract claimed in 1799 and 1800; also heard Rhodes say that he had sold the said land to Calvin Adams; did not know Adams to be in the country until a year or two after the sale to Crosby.

August 22, 1811: Present, Penrose and Bates, commissioners. It is the opinion of the Board that this claim ought not to be confirmed.

MERIWETHER LEWIS, assignee of Pierre Chouteau, assignee of Alexander Clark, claiming three hundred and eight arpents of land, situate at Portage des Sioux, district of St. Charles; produces to the Board a letter of office from Zenon Trudeau, Lieutenant Governor, to François Saucier, authorizing the establishment of Portage des Sioux, and of the inhabitants there, and appointing said François Saucier commandant there; said letter is dated 15th March, 1799; also an official letter from Don Carlos Dehault Delassus, Lieutenant Governor, to François Saucier, containing an extract of a letter from the Marquis de Casa Calvo to said Delassus, approving the conduct of Zenon Trudeau, Lieutenant Governor, in making said establishment of Portage des Sioux; also a general plat of survey, dated 15th February, 1804, and certified 2d March, 1804.

August 22, 1811. Present, Penrose and Bates, commissioners. It is the opinion of the Board that this claim ought not to be confirmed.

MERIWETHER LEWIS, assignee of Pierre Chouteau, assignee of Etienne Papin, assignee of Baptiste McDonald, claiming eighty arpents of land, situate at Portage des Sioux, district of St. Charles; produces to the Board the same papers as in the foregoing claim.

August 22, 1811: Present, Penrose and Bates, commissioners. It is the opinion of the Board that this claim ought not to be confirmed.

MERIWETHER LEWIS, assignee of Pierre Chouteau, assignee of Jacques Godfroy, claiming eighty arpents of land, situate at Portage des Sioux, district of St. Charles; produces to the Board the same papers as in the foregoing claims.

August 22, 1811: Present, Penrose and Bates, commissioners. It is the opinion of the Board that this claim ought not to be confirmed.

MERIWETHER LEWIS, assignee of James Peper, assignee of Joseph Challefour, claiming eighty arpents of land, situate at Portage des Sioux, district of St. Charles; produces to the Board the same papers as in the foregoing claims.

August 22, 1811: Present, Penrose and Bates, commissioners. It is the opinion of the Board that this claim ought not to be confirmed.

MERIWETHER LEWIS, assignee of Rufus Easton, assignee of David Eshborough, claiming eighty arpents of land, situate at Portage des Sioux, district of St. Charles; produces to the Board the same papers as in the foregoing claims.

August 22, 1811: Present, Penrose and Bates, commissioners. It is the opinion of the Board that this claim ought not to be confirmed.

JOHN McQUICK, claiming eighty arpents of land, situate at Portage des Sioux, district of St. Charles; produces to the Board the same papers as in the foregoing claims.

August 22, 1811: Present, Penrose and Bates, commissioners. It is the opinion of the Board that this claim ought not to be confirmed.

CHARLES EBER, claiming eighty arpents of land, situate at Portage des Sioux, district of St. Charles; produces to the Board the same papers as in the foregoing claims.

August 22, 1811: Present, Penrose and Bates, commissioners. It is the opinion of the Board that this claim ought not to be confirmed.

ESTEVAN PAPIN, claiming eighty arpents of land situate at Portage des Sioux, district of St. Charles; produces to the Board the same papers as in the foregoing claims.

August 22, 1811: Present, Penrose and Bates, commissioners. It is the opinion of the Board that this claim ought not to be confirmed.

CHARLES ROY, claiming eighty arpents of land, situate at Portage des Sioux, district of St. Charles; produces to the Board the same papers as in the foregoing claims.

August 22, 1811: Present, Penrose and Bates, commissioners. It is the opinion of the Board that this claim ought not to be confirmed.

MATTIE SONCIER, fils, claiming eighty arpents of land, situate at Portage des Sioux, district of St. Charles; produces to the Board the same papers as in the foregoing claims.

August 22, 1811: Present, Penrose and Bates, commissioners. It is the opinion of the Board that this claim ought not to be confirmed.

JOSEPH LOUIS GOE, claiming eighty arpents of land, situate at Portage des Sioux, district of St. Charles; produces to the Board the same papers as in the foregoing claims.

August 22, 1811: Present, Penrose and Bates, commissioners. It is the opinion of the Board that this claim ought not to be confirmed.

BAPTISTE PUGOT, claiming eighty arpents of land, situate at Portage des Sioux, district of St. Charles; produces to the Board the same papers as in the foregoing claims.

August 22, 1811: Present, Penrose and Bates, commissioners. It is the opinion of the Board that this claim ought not to be confirmed.

THOMAS WHITLEY, claiming eighty arpents of land, situate at Portage des Sioux, district of St. Charles; produces to the Board the same papers as in the foregoing claims.

August 22, 1811: Present, Penrose and Bates, commissioners. It is the opinion of the Board that this claim ought not to be confirmed.

BAPTISTE LACROIX, claiming forty arpents of land, situate at Portage des Sioux, district of St. Charles; produces to the Board the same papers as in the foregoing claims.

August 22, 1811: Present, Penrose and Bates, commissioners. It is the opinion of the Board that this claim ought not to be confirmed.

ESTEVAN PEPIN, claiming forty arpents of land, situate at Portage des Sioux, district of St. Charles; produces to the Board the same papers as in the foregoing claims.

August 22, 1811: Present, Penrose and Bates, commissioners. It is the opinion of the Board that this claim ought not to be confirmed.

PEDRO CLERMONT, claiming eighty arpents of land, situate at Portage des Sioux, district of St. Charles; produces to the Board the same papers as in the foregoing claims.

August 22, 1811: Present, Penrose and Bates, commissioners. It is the opinion of the Board that this claim ought not to be confirmed.

ANTOINE LEFAGE, claiming forty arpents of land, situate at Portage des Sioux, district of St. Charles; produces to the Board the same papers as in the foregoing claims.

August 22, 1811: Present, Penrose and Bates, commissioners. It is the opinion of the Board that this claim ought not to be confirmed.

FRANCISCO HONORE, claiming eighty arpents of land, situate at Portage des Sioux, district of St. Charles; produces to the Board the same papers as in the foregoing claims.

August 22, 1811: Present Penrose and Bates, commissioners. It is the opinion of the Board that this claim ought not to be confirmed.

ANTOINE VINCENT BOUIS, claiming two hundred and fifteen feet front of land running back to the Mississippi, in the town of St. Louis; produces to the Board a concession from Don Carlos Dehault Delassus, Lieutenant Governor for the same, dated 18th October, 1799, given for the purpose of quarrying stone, and shall leave the road open that ought to be along the river.

Testimony taken. November 19, 1808. Louis Brazeaux, sworn, says that about seventeen years ago he saw claimant getting stone from said lot; about seven years ago, and about five years ago, again saw him getting stone from the same. The Board refer to their remarks in the claim of Julian Papin Benito, this claim being similarly situated.

August 22, 1811: Present, Penrose and Bates, commissioners. It is the opinion of the Board that this claim ought not to be confirmed.

JESSE RAYNOR, claiming seven hundred and forty-eight arpents sixty-eight perches of land, situate on Sandy creek, district of St. Louis; produces to the Board a notice to the recorder, dated 27th May, 1808.

Testimony taken. November 26, 1808. William Jones, sworn, says that about twenty-three or twenty-four years ago Jesse Raynor had his stock on the land claimed, and built a cabin; and that said stock remained on the place one year.

Claimant declares that he has not resided in this territory since 1792.

August 24, 1811: Present, Penrose and Bates, commissioners. It is the opinion of the Board that this claim ought not to be granted.

BERNARD PRATTE, assignee of John Baptiste Trudeau, claiming seventy by seventy-two feet of land, a lot situate in the town of St. Louis, to be taken back of the lot which said Trudeau then occupied, and adjoining another lot of twenty feet front, sold by said Trudeau to claimant; produces to the Board a deed of transfer from said Trudeau to claimant, dated 29th July, 1808; and certified before Thomas F. Riddick, a Justice of the Peace, the 30th of June, 1808.

The Board refer to the papers of John Baptiste Trudeau, for a concession from Charles D. Delassus, dated 20th October, 1799.

The Board also refer to their remarks made in the claim of Julian Papin Benito; this claim being similarly situated.

August 24, 1811: Present, Penrose and Bates, commissioners. It is the opinion of the Board that this claim ought not to be confirmed.

ANTOINE SOULARD, claiming one thousand and forty-two arpents of land, situate on the Mississippi, district of St. Louis; produces to the Board a certified copy of a plat and certificate of survey of the same, certified at New Orleans, Ximens, 28th April, 1802, which survey is stated to be founded on an order from the Lieutenant Governor, Zenon Trudeau, dated 28th January, 1798; survey dated 15th March, 1798, certified by Antoine Soulard 2d April, same year; also produces a grant from Don Juan Ventura Morales, Intendant ad interim, for the same to claimant, granted on condition that he shall comply with the third, fourth, sixth, seventh, and ninth articles of the ordinancy of his Intendancy, dated 17th July, 1799; grant dated 28th April, 1802, and found in the abstract of all the concessions and patented grants of land appertaining to the district of Louisiana, recorded in the registers kept by the Spanish and French Governments, of the province of Louisiana, since the 2d July, 1756, and until the 3d of April, 1802, transmitted to this Board by the Secretary of the Treasury.

Testimony taken. November 30, 1808. Auguste Chouteau, sworn, says that, about 1798 or 1799, said tract was inhabited and cultivated, for claimant, and has continued so to be ever since, in 1801 had about twenty-five arpents of land in cultivation.

January 13, 1809. On the application of claimant to introduce further testimony, and Auguste Chouteau, formerly a witness in this claim, being present, and stating that he was probably mistaken in the quantity of land cultivated in 1801, the Board are of opinion that this claim be opened and claimant permitted to introduce further evidence.

George Dogget, sworn, says that in the year 1800 claimant had forty acres under fence, and that about thirty-five of which were under cultivation.

William Massey, sworn, says that in 1802 claimant had about forty acres in cultivation, and in 1803 had between fifty and sixty acres in cultivation.

August 24, 1811: Present, Penrose and Bates, commissioners. The Board declare that this claim is not a grant made and completed, prior to 1st of October, 1800.

NOEL MONGRAIN, claiming seven thousand and fifty-six arpents of land, situate on Little Saline creek, emptying into the Osage river; produces to the Board a notice of claim, and a certificate from Cheveux Blanc, Chief of the Great Osage nation, in which he declares that he has given to Noel Mongrain, his little brother, for the services that he has rendered him and his nation, one league square of land, situate as aforesaid, dated 20th June, 1797, and acknowledged before Bernard Pratte, one of the Judges of the Court of Common Pleas, for St. Louis district, by said Cheveux Blanc, through his interpreter, Jacques Sonde, 30th June, 1808.

Testimony taken. December 10, 1808. Jacques Sonde, sworn, says that Noel Mongrain was born in the Osage nation, of an Osage woman, the aunt of Cheveux Blanc; that Noel Mongrain has forbidden persons to hunt on the land claimed, and has had persons hunting on the same for ten years past; that the witness drew the instrument of writing from Cheveux Blanc to Noel Mongrain; that the other Indians said it was unnecessary for them to sign it as Cheveux Blanc had the right to give the land, and what he did would be well done; that said Mongrain, when he separated himself from the nation and came to live with the whites, renounced his claim to his part of the Osage country, in common with the other Indians; and that said land was given him for his part.

Pierre Chouteau, Indian agent, sworn, says that in the council which he had the 10th November last, in which a treaty was made between the United States and the Osage, about twelve hundred of the great and little Osage Indians were present, and Cheveux Blanc, the chief, expressly excepted in council from the cession they were then making the land claimed by Noel Mongrain on the little Saline, stating that the said land had been heretofore granted to him, and that all this nation consented to what was done by Cheveux Blanc.

August 24, 1811: Present, Penrose and Bates, commissioners. This claim being neither embraced by the law, usages, and customs of the Spanish Government, nor the acts of Congress, the Board decline giving any opinion thereon, and order that a copy of the written evidence accompany the report of this claim.

GEORGE CAVENDER, assignee of Norris Monday, assignee of Daniel Brent, claiming five hundred arpents of land, situate on Cape Girardeau district; produces to the Board a notice of claim, and an assignment from Norris Monday to George Cavender, proved the 10th June, 1808, by Jacob Kelly, one of the witnesses, before Christopher Hays, Judge.

Testimony taken. December 1, 1808. Elijah Welch, sworn, says that Daniel Brent built a house on the land claimed in 1803, and inhabited and cultivated it that year; left it some time during same year; that one Kelly moved in the cabin, and inhabited and cultivated it for two years.

August 24, 1811: Present, Penrose and Bates, commissioners. It is the opinion of the Board that this claim ought not to be granted.

JOSEPH MATHEWS, claiming two hundred arpents of land, situate on the bayou le Bœuf, district of New Madrid; produces to the Board a certificate of a permission to settle, from Henry Peyroux, dated 13th March, 1802.

Testimony taken. March 21, 1806. George Wilson, sworn, says that claimant did, prior to and on the 1st day of October, 1800, actually inhabit and cultivate the said tract of land.

March 21, 1806: Present, Lucas and Donaldson, commissioners. The Board confirm to the said claimant two hundred arpents of land, situate as aforesaid, as per said permission to settle, (certificate of permission.)

JACOB MYERS, claiming a lot of one arpent, in the district of Madrid, and village of New Madrid; produces to the Board a recommendation from Henry Peyroux, dated 22d May, 1801.

Testimony taken. March 22, 1806. Richard J. Waters, sworn, says that claimant did, prior to and on the 20th December, 1803, actually inhabit and cultivate the said lot.

March 22, 1806: Present, Penrose and Donaldson, commissioners. The Board grant the said Jacob Myers the town lot aforesaid, saving the right of Francis Hudson to the same, if any he has.

September 30, 1811: Present, Lucas, Penrose, and Bates, commissioners. It is the opinion of the Board that this claim ought not to be granted.

JACOB MYERS, assignee of Francis Hudson, claiming two arpents of land, situate in the village of New Madrid; produces to the Board a certificate of a permission to settle, from Henry Peyroux; and a deed of exchange of property, between the said claimant and the said Francis Hudson, dated September 1, 1801.

Testimony taken. March 22, 1806. George Wilson, sworn, says that said tract, or town lot, was, prior to and on the 1st day of October, 1800.

March 22, 1806; Present, Penrose and Donaldson, commissioners. The Board confirm to the said claimant, assignee as aforesaid, the said two arpents, or town lots, as per the said permission to settle, (certificate of permission to settle.)

September, 30, 1811: Present, Lucas, Penrose, and Bates, commissioners. It is the opinion of the Board that this claim ought not to be granted.

FRANCIS MOREAU, representatives of, claiming forty by eighty arpents of land, situate on the river settlement, district of St. Genevieve; produce to the Board a concession not duly registered, from Zenon Trudeau, dated November 16, 1797; and a survey of one thousand seven hundred and sixty arpents, taken November 16, 1799, and certified 16th February, 1800.

Testimony taken. June 20, 1806. St. James Beauvais, sworn, says that claimant did, about nine years ago, settle the said tract of land, built a house on the same, made a park on the same, and raised a crop in the year 1798; and that the said land was, prior to and on the 1st day of October, 1800, actually inhabited and cultivated, and is so to this day.

June 20, 1806: Present, Penrose and Donaldson, commissioners. The Board reject this claim for want of a duly registered warrant of survey.

September 30, 1811: Present, Lucas, Penrose, and Bates, commissioners. It is the opinion of a majority of the Board that this claim ought not to be confirmed; Clement B. Penrose, commissioner, voting for a confirmation. Said majority declares, that if this claim had not exceeded eight hundred arpents they would have voted for a confirmation.

THOMAS MADDON, claiming twenty-five by forty arpents of land, situate at New Bourbon, district of St. Genevieve; produces to the Board a concession from Zenon Trudeau, to one Israel Dodge, for the same, dated 20th September, 1793; and another concession from the said Zenon Trudeau to claimant for the said tract, in consequence of the said Israel Dodge having relinquished his right to the same, in favor of one Joseph Fenwick; and also, in consequence of the said Fenwick's relinquishment of the same to said claimant, the last aforesaid concession dated November 10, 1797; and a survey of one thousand and fifty arpents, taken April 23d, and certified May 23, 1798.

Job Westover, sworn, says that about nine years ago, he (the witness) went on said land with the claimant to mark the same; that claimant settled it the same year, built a house, and has actually inhabited and cultivated it from that date until the year 1804.

June 23, 1806: Present, Penrose and Donaldson, commissioners. The Board reject this claim, the said last concession to claimant not being duly registered; and observe, that the former one to Israel Dodge was duly registered.

September 30, 1811: Present, Lucas, Penrose, and Bates, commissioners. It is the opinion of a majority of the Board that this claim ought not to be confirmed; Clement B. Penrose, commissioner, voting for a confirmation thereof. Said majority declare, that if his claim had not exceeded eight hundred arpents, they would have voted for a confirmation.

JOHN SMITH, Sen., assignee of David Strickland, claiming three hundred arpents of land, situate on the Mississippi, district of St. Genevieve; produces to the Board a concession from Charles D. Delassus, dated December 20, 1799; a survey of the same, taken the 6th February, and certified the 3d March, 1804; and a certificate of public sale of the effects and property of the said David Strickland, dated December 18, 1803.

September 30, 1811, Present, Lucas, Penrose, and Bates, commissioners. Concession and survey stated to be produced; not found on record. It is the opinion of the Board that this claim ought not to be confirmed.

JOSEPH BECQUETTE, claiming one hundred and fifty arpents of land, situate on river Aux Vases, district of St. Genevieve; produces to the Board a concession from Zenon Trudeau, dated May 1, 1797; and a survey of seventy-one arpents taken and certified May 4, 1798.

Testimony taken. June 25, 1806. John Baptiste Taumier, being duly sworn, says that claimant settled the said tract of land for a sugar camp about ten years ago; and that the same has been attended to yearly for the purpose of making sugar; claimant having a cabin and sugar kettles on the same to this day; had, at the time of obtaining this concession, a wife and seven children.

September 30, 1811: Present, full Board. It is the opinion of the Board that this claim ought not to be granted.

THOMAS WITHERINGTON, claiming a lot, No 3, in the name of Solomon, village of Marais des Liards, district of St. Louis; produces to the Board a general letter of office from Zenon Trudeau, Lieutenant Governor, dated 2d November, 1794; said lot one hundred and fifty feet square.

Testimony taken. August 7, 1806. Robert Owen, sworn, says that, about ten years ago, a house was built on said lot by one Birot, who, about seven years ago, built another, which has been actually inhabited to this day as a school-house.

October 1, 1811: Present, Lucas, Penrose, and Bates, commissioners. It is the opinion of the Board that this claim ought not to be confirmed.

JOHN BAPTISTE VALLE, Sen., claiming forty by forty arpents of land, situate on the river establishment, district of St. Genevieve; produces to the Board a concession not duly registered from Zenon Trudeau, dated 6th March, 1798; and a survey of one thousand four hundred and seventy-five arpents, dated November 8, 1799, and certified 5th February, 1800.

Testimony taken. June 20, 1806. St. James Beauvais, sworn, says that claimant settled the said tract of land about nine years ago, built a house on the same, and cleared some land; and that the same was, prior to and on the 1st day of October, 1800, actually inhabited and cultivated for the use of said claimant, who has, at this day, about thirty acres under cultivation, and still keeps increasing it.

October 21, 1808. Michel Placit, dit Michau, sworn, says that said tract was inhabited and cultivated ten years ago, by or for claimant, and ever since.

June 20, 1806: Present, Penrose and Donaldson, commissioners. The Board reject this claim; the aforesaid concession not duly registered.

October 2; 1811: Present, Lucas, Penrose, and Bates, commissioners. It is the opinion of a majority of the Board that this claim ought not to be confirmed; Clement B. Penrose, commissioner, voting for a confirmation. Said majority declare, that if this claim had not exceeded eight hundred arpents, they would have voted for a confirmation.

JAMES MACKAY, claiming four thousand four hundred and sixty arpents of land, situate on Wild Horse creek, district of St. Louis; produces to the Board a concession from Zenon Trudeau, Lieutenant Governor, dated 23d December, 1797, conditioned for the building of a mill and establishing a farm; produces a plat of survey, dated 6th March, 1798, and certified 23d December, 1798.

Testimony taken. October 27, 1808. James Colvin, sworn, says that claimant, about eight or nine years ago, built a cabin, and commenced building the dam for a mill on the tract claimed; says there was some cultivation.

Aaron Colvin, sworn, says that, about eight or nine years ago, there was a crop raised on said land for claimant; and also there were crops raised on said land for claimant the two following years; about seven years ago, there was a field of about ten or eleven acres cleared, and rails cut to fence it; does not know whether it was enclosed or not, as witness left the neighborhood.

October 2, 1811: Present, Lucas, Penrose, and Bates, commissioners. It is the opinion of a majority of the Board that this claim ought not to be confirmed; Clement B. Penrose, commissioner, voting for a confirmation. Said majority declare, that if this claim had not exceeded eight hundred arpents, they would have voted for a confirmation.

MICHAEL BUTCHER, BARTHOLOMEW BUTCHER, BOSTON BUTCHER, and PETER BLOOM, claiming four hundred arpents of land, situate on waters of river St. François, district of St. Genevieve; produces to the Board a petition to the Intendant, together with a recommendation from Pierre D. Delassus Deluziere, commandant of New Bourbon, dated 15th December, 1802; a plat of survey, dated 23d February, 1806.

October 3, 1811: Present, Lucas, Penrose, and Bates, commissioners. It is the opinion of the Board that this claim ought not to be confirmed.

MICHAEL BUTCHER, BARTHOLOMEW BUTCHER, BOSTON BUTCHER, and PETER BLOOM, claiming one thousand two hundred arpents of land, situate on waters of Big river, district of St. Genevieve; produces to the Board a petition and recommendation from Pierre D. Delassus Deluziere, commandant of New Bourbon, dated 15th December, 1802; a plat of survey, dated 25th February, 1806, certified 28th February, 1806.

October 3, 1811: Present, Lucas, Penrose, and Bates, commissioners. It is the opinion of the Board that this claim ought not to be confirmed.

JOSEPH WALLER, assignee of Jonathan Bouis, claiming three hundred arpents of land, situate on the Mississippi, about four miles below Waller's ferry, district of Cape Girardeau; produces to the Board, as a permission to settle, list A, on which Jonathan Bouis is No. 21, for three hundred arpents; a transfer from Bouis to claimant, dated 8th December, 1806.

Testimony taken. June 6, 1808. Stephen Byrd, sworn, says that in 1806 saw a cabin, said to have been built by Bouis, as witness understood.

October 3, 1811: Present, Lucas, Penrose, and Bates, commissioners. It is the opinion of the Board that this claim ought not to be granted.

JOHN DANEY, claiming seven hundred and fifty arpents of land, situate on portage of the river St. François, district of New Madrid; produces to the Board a certificate of survey, dated February 28, 1806.

Testimony taken. March 17, 1806. George Wilson, sworn, says that claimant did, prior to and on the 20th December, 1803, actually inhabit and cultivate the said tract of land; and was then of the age of twenty-one years and upwards.

June 18, 1808. Joseph Legrand, sworn, says that premises were improved in 1803, since which time (the spring of that year) they have been constantly inhabited and cultivated; above twenty-one years in 1803; seven or eight acres in cultivation in 1803.

March 17, 1806: Present, Penrose and Donaldson, commissioners. The Board grant the said claimant seven hundred and fifty arpents of land, situate as aforesaid, provided so much be found vacant there.

October 3, 1810: Present, Lucas, Penrose, and Bates, commissioners. It is the opinion of the Board that this claim ought not to be confirmed.

LAND GRANTS IN MISSOURI TERRITORY - 1805 - 1812

139

****

HUGH McDONALD CHISHOLM, claiming seventy-five arpents of land, situate on lake St. Mary, district of New Madrid; produces to the Board a plat of survey, dated 22d January, 1796.

Testimony taken. June 20, 1808. Peter Dumay, sworn, says that premises were cultivated and inhabited in 1800, and constantly to the present time; eight acres now in cultivation; a wife, and four children, and two slaves in 1803.

October 3, 1811: Present, Lucas, Penrose, and Bates, commissioners. It is the opinion of the Board that this claim ought not to be confirmed.

JOHN BAPTISTE BARSELOUX, claiming a lot of one arpent of land, situate in the district of New Madrid, village of Little Prairie, No. 3 in square No. 1; produces to the Board an order of survey from Henry Peyroux, commandant, dated 27th February, 1801; a plat of survey of the same, dated January 3, 1806, signed Francis Lesieur.

The following testimony in this claim, and generally as to the lots in the village of Little Prairie, taken by authority from the Board, at New Madrid, June 22, 1808, by Frederick Bates, commissioner.

Pierre A. Laforge, sworn, says that these lots have been inhabited and cultivated at different times and in succession, from the year 1798 till 1803, at which time they were all inhabited.

July 9, 1811: Present, Lucas, Penrose, and Bates, commissioners. It is the opinion of the Board that this claim ought not to be confirmed.

JOHN BAPTISTE BARSELOUX, claiming lot No. 4 of square No. 1, of land situate in the district of New Madrid, village of Little Prairie; produces to the Board the same papers as above; testimony taken as above.

July 9, 1811: Present, Lucas, Penrose, and Bates, commissioners. It is the opinion of the Board that this claim ought not to be confirmed.

JOSEPH GENEREUX, claiming a lot of one arpent of land, situate in the district of New Madrid, village of Little Prairie, No. 5 of square No. 2; produces to the Board the same papers as in the foregoing claim, and the same testimony as aforesaid.

July 9, 1811: Present, Lucas, Penrose, and Bates, commissioners. It is the opinion of the Board that this claim ought not to be confirmed.

JOSEPH GENEREUX, claiming a lot of one arpent of land, situate in the district of New Madrid, village of Little Prairie, No. 6 of square No. 2; produces to the Board the same papers as in the foregoing claims, and the same testimony as aforesaid.

July 9, 1811: Present, Lucas, Penrose, and Bates, commissioners. It is the opinion of the Board that this claim ought not to be confirmed.

LEWIS ST. AUBIN, claiming a lot of one arpent of land, situate in the district of New Madrid, village of Little Prairie, No. 11 of square No. 3; produces to the Board the same papers as in the foregoing claims, and the same testimony as aforesaid.

July 9, 1811: Present, Lucas, Penrose, and Bates, commissioners. It is the opinion of the Board that this claim ought not to be confirmed.

LEWIS ST. AUBIN, claiming a lot of one arpent of land, situate in the district of New Madrid, village of Little Prairie, No. 12 of square No. 3; produces to the Board the same papers as in the foregoing claims, and the same testimony as aforesaid.

July 9, 1811: Present, Lucas, Penrose, and Bates, commissioners. It is the opinion of the Board that this claim ought not to be confirmed.

JOHN RUDDELL, claiming a lot of one arpent of land, situate in the district of New Madrid, village of Little Prairie, No. 15 of square No. 4; produces to the Board the same papers as in the foregoing claims, and the same testimony as aforesaid.

July 9, 1811: Present, Lucas, Penrose, and Bates, commissioners. It is the opinion of the Board that this claim ought not to be confirmed.

JOHN RUDDELL, claiming a lot of one arpent of land, situate in the district of New Madrid, village of Little Prairie, No. 16 of square No. 4; produces to the Board the same papers as in the foregoing claims, and the same testimony as aforesaid.

July 9, 1811: Present, Lucas, Penrose, and Bates, commissioners. It is the opinion of the Board that this claim ought not to be confirmed.

JOSEPH RIENDEAU, claiming a lot of one arpent of land, situate in the district of New Madrid, village of Little Prairie, No. 17 of square No. 5; produces to the Board the same papers as in the foregoing claims, and the same testimony as aforesaid.

July 9, 1811: Present, Lucas, Penrose, and Bates, commissioners. It is the opinion of the Board that this claim ought not to be confirmed.

JOSEPH RIENDEAU, claiming a lot of one arpent of land, situate in the district of New Madrid, village of Little Prairie, No. 18 of square No. 5; produces to the Board the same papers as in the foregoing claims, and the same testimony as aforesaid.

July 9, 1811: Present, Lucas, Penrose, and Bates, commissioners. It is the opinion of the Board that this claim ought not to be confirmed.

LOUIS ST. AUBIN, claiming a lot of one arpent of land, situate in the district of New Madrid, village of Little Prairie, No. 19 of square No. 5; produces to the Board the same papers as in the foregoing claims, and the same testimony as aforesaid.

July 9, 1811: Present, Lucas, Penrose, and Bates, commissioners. It is the opinion of the Board that this claim ought not to be confirmed.

LOUIS ST. AUBIN, claiming a lot of one arpent of land, situate in the district of New Madrid, village of Little Prairie, No. 20 of square No. 5; produces to the Board the same papers as in the foregoing claims, and the same testimony as aforesaid.

July 9, 1811: Present, Lucas, Penrose, and Bates, commissioners. It is the opinion of the Board that this claim ought not to be confirmed.

JOSEPH GENEREUX, claiming a lot of one arpent of land, situate in the district of New Madrid, village of Little Prairie, No. 21 of square No. 6; produces to the Board the same papers as in the foregoing claims, and the same testimony as aforesaid.

July 9, 1811: Present, Lucas, Penrose, and Bates, commissioners. It is the opinion of the Board that this claim ought not to be confirmed.

JOSEPH GENEREUX, claiming a lot of one arpent of land, situate in the district of New Madrid, village of Little Prairie, No. 22 of square No. 6: produces to the Board the same papers as in the foregoing claims, and the same testimony as aforesaid.
July 9, 1811: Present, Lucas, Penrose, and Bates, commissioners. It is the opinion of the Board that this claim ought not to be confirmed.

PIERRE PORIER, claiming a lot of one arpent of land, situate in the district of New Madrid, village of Little Prairie, No. 23 of square No. 6; produces to the Board the same papers as in the foregoing claims, and the same testimony.
July 9, 1811: Present, Lucas, Penrose, and Bates, commissioners. It is the opinion of the Board that this claim ought not to be confirmed.

PIERRE PORIER, claiming a lot of one arpent of land, situate in the district of New Madrid, village of Little Prairie, No 24 of square No. 6; produces to the Board.the same papers as in the foregoing claims; and the same testimony as aforesaid.
July 9, 1811: Present, Lucas, Penrose, and Bates, commissioners. It is the opinion of the Board that this claim ought not to be confirmed.

FRANCOIS LESIEUR, claiming a lot of one arpent of land, situate in the district of New Madrid, village of Little Prairie, No. 25 of square No. 7; produces to the Board the same papers as in the foregoing claims, and the same testimony as aforesaid.
July 9, 1811: Present, Lucas, Penrose, and Bates, commissioners. It is the opinion of the Board that this claim ought not to be confirmed.

FRANCOIS LESIEUR, claiming a lot of land, containing one arpent, situate in the district of New Madrid, village of Little Prairie, No. 26 of square No. 7; produces to the Board the same papers as in the foregoing claims, and the same testimony.
July 9, 1811: Present, Lucas, Penrose, and Bates, commissioners. It is the opinion of the Board that this claim ought not to be confirmed.

FRANCOIS LESIEUR, claiming a lot of one arpent of land, situate in the district of New Madrid, village of Little Prairie, No. 28 of square No. 7; produces to the Board the same papers as in the foregoing claims, and the same testimony as aforesaid.
July 9, 1811: Present, Lucas, Penrose, and Bates, commissioners. It is the opinion of the Board that this claim ought not to be confirmed.

AMABLE GUION, claiming a lot of one arpent of land, situate in the district of New Madrid, village of Little Prairie, No. 29 of square No. 8; produces to the Board the same papers as in the foregoing claims, and the same testimony.
July 9, 1811: Present, Lucas, Penrose, and Bates, commissioners. It is the opinion of the Board that this claim ought not to be granted.

AMABLE GUION, claiming a lot of one arpent of land, situate in the village of Little Prairie, district of New Madrid, No. 30 of square No. 8; produces to the Board the same papers as in the foregoing claims, and the same testimony as aforesaid.
July 9, 1811: Present, Lucas, Penrose, and Bates, commissioners. It is the opinion of the Board that this claim ought not to be confirmed.

LUC BELLEFEUILLE, claiming a lot of land of one arpent, situate in the district of New Madrid, village of Little Prairie, No. 31 of square No. 8; produces to the Board the same papers as in the foregoing claims, and the same testimony as aforesaid.
July 9, 1811: Present, Lucas, Penrose, and Bates, commissioners. It is the opinion of the Board that this claim ought not to be confirmed.

LUC BELLEFEUILLE, claiming a lot of one arpent of land, situate in the district of New Madrid, village of Little Prairie, No. 32 of square No. 8; produces to the Board the same papers as in the foregoing claims, and the same testimony.
July 9, 1811: Present, Lucas, Penrose, and Bates, commissioners. It is the opinion of the Board that this claim ought not to be confirmed.

Widow LACOURSE, claiming a lot of one arpent of land, situate in the district of New Madrid, village of Little Prairie, No. 33 of square No. 9; produces to the Board the same papers as in the foregoing claims, and the same testimony as aforesaid.
July 9, 1811: Present, Lucas, Penrose, and Bates, commissioners. It is the opinion of the Board that this claim ought not to be confirmed.

Widow LACOURSE, claiming a lot of one arpent of land, situate in the district of New Madrid, village of Little Prairie, No 34 of square No. 9; produces to the Board the same papers as in the foregoing claims, and the same testimony as aforesaid.
July 9, 1811: Present, Lucas, Penrose, and Bates, commissioners. It is the opinion of the Board that this claim ought not to be confirmed.

****

JEAN BAPTISTE BELLEFEUILLE, claiming a lot of one arpent of land, situate in the district of New Madrid, village of Little Prairie, No. 35 of square No. 9; produces to the Board the same papers as in the foregoing claims, and the same testimony as aforesaid.

July 9, 1811: Present, Lucas, Penrose, and Bates, commissioners. It is the opinion of the Board that this claim ought not to be confirmed.

JEAN BAPTISTE BELLEFEUILLE, claiming a lot of one arpent of land, situate in the district of New Madrid, village of Little Prairie, No. 36 of square No. 9; produces to the Board the same papers as in the foregoing claims, and the same testimony as aforesaid.

July 9, 1811: Present, Lucas, Penrose, and Bates, commissioners. It is the opinion of the Board that this claim ought not to be confirmed.

ELOY DEJARLAIS, claiming a lot of one arpent of land, situate in the district of New Madrid, village of Little Prairie, No. 37 of square No. 10; produces to the Board the same papers as in the foregoing claims, and the same testimony.

July 9, 1811: Present, Lucas, Penrose, and Bates, commissioners. It is the opinion of the Board that this claim ought not to be confirmed.

ELOY DEJARLAIS, claiming a lot of one arpent of land, situate in the district of New Madrid, village of Little Prairie, No. 38 of square No. 10; produces to the Board the same papers as in the foregoing claims, and the same testimony as aforesaid.

July 9, 1811: Present, Lucas, Penrose, and Bates, commissioners. It is the opinion of the Board that this claim ought not to be granted.

JOSEPH PAYNE, claiming a lot of one arpent of land, situate in the district of New Madrid, village of Little Prairie, No. 39 of square No. 10; produces to the Board the same papers as in the foregoing claims, and the same testimony as aforesaid.

July 9, 1811: Present, Lucas, Penrose, and Bates, commissioners. It is the opinion of the Board that this claim ought not to be confirmed.

JOSEPH PAYNE, claiming a lot of one arpent of land, situate in the district of New Madrid, village of Little Prairie, No. 40 of square No. 10; produces to the Board the same papers as in the foregoing claims, and the same testimony as aforesaid.

July 9, 1811: Present, Lucas, Penrose, and Bates, commissioners. It is the opinion of the Board that this claim ought not to be confirmed.

SIMON SUBLIL, claiming a lot of one arpent of land, situate in the district of New Madrid, village of Little Prairie, No. 41 of square No. 11; produces to the Board the same papers as in the foregoing claims, and the same testimony as aforesaid.

July 9, 1811: Present, Lucas, Penrose, and Bates, commissioners. It is the opinion of the Board that this claim ought not to be confirmed.

PIERRE NOBLESSE, claiming a lot of one arpent of land, situate in the district of New Madrid, village of Little Prairie, No. 43 of square No. 11; produces to the Board the same papers as in the foregoing claims, and the same testimony as aforesaid.

July 9, 1811: Present, Lucas, Penrose, and Bates, commissioners. It is the opinion of the Board that this claim ought not to be confirmed.

PIERRE NOBLESSE, claiming a lot of one arpent of land, situate in the district of New Madrid, village of Little Prairie, No. 44 of square No. 11; produces to the Board the same papers as in the foregoing claims, and the same testimony as aforesaid.

July 9, 1811: Present, Lucas, Penrose, and Bates, commissioners. It is the opinion of the Board that this claim ought not to be confirmed.

HIBERNOIS, claiming a lot of one arpent of land, situate in the district of New Madrid, village of Little Prairie, No. 45 of square No. 12; produces to the Board the same papers as in the foregoing claims, and the same testimony as aforesaid.

July 9, 1811: Present, Lucas, Penrose, and Bates, commissioners. It is the opinion of the Board that this claim ought not to be confirmed.

HIBERNOIS, claiming a lot of one arpent of land, situate in the district of New Madrid, village of Little Prairie, No. 46 of square No. 12; produces to the Board the same papers as in the foregoing claims, and the same testimony as aforesaid.

July 9, 1811: Present, Lucas, Penrose, and Bates, commissioners. It is the opinion of the Board that this claim ought not to be confirmed.

BAPTISTE PELLETIER, claiming a lot of one arpent of land, situate in the district of New Madrid, village of Little Prairie, No. 60 of square No. 16: produces to the Board the same papers as in the foregoing claims, and the same testimony as aforesaid.

July 9, 1811: Present, Lucas, Penrose, and Bates, commissioners. It is the opinion of the Board that this claim ought not to be confirmed.

EUSTACE PELTIER, claiming a lot of one arpent of land, situate in the district of New Madrid, village of Little Prairie, No. 62 of square No. 16; produces to the Board the same papers as in the foregoing claims, and the same testimony as aforesaid.

July 9, 1811: Present, Lucas, Penrose, and Bates, commissioners. It is the opinion of the Board that this claim ought not to be confirmed.

EUSTACE PELTIER, claiming a lot of one arpent of land, situate in the district of New Madrid, village of Little Prairie, No. 63 of square No. 16; produces to the Board the same papers as in the foregoing claims, and the same testimony as aforesaid.

July 9, 1811: Present, Lucas, Penrose, and Bates, commissioners. It is the opinion of the Board that this claim ought not to be confirmed.

FRANCOIS TRENCHARD, claiming a lot of one arpent of land, situate in the district of New Madrid, village of Little Prairie, No. 64 of square No. 17; produces to the Board the same papers as in the foregoing claims, and the same testimony as aforesaid.
July 9, 1811: Present, Lucas, Penrose, and Bates, commissioners. It is the opinion of the Board that this claim ought not to be confirmed.

FRANCOIS TRENCHARD, claiming a lot of one arpent of land, situate in the district of New Madrid, village of Little Prairie, No. 65 of square No. 17; produces to the Board the same papers as in the foregoing claims, and the same testimony as aforesaid.
July 9, 1811: Present, Lucas, Penrose, and Bates, commissioners. It is the opinion of the Board that this claim ought not to be confirmed.

CHARLES GUIBEAULT, claiming a lot of one arpent of land, situate in the district of New Madrid, village of Little Prairie, No. 74 of square No. 19; produces to the Board the same papers as in the foregoing claims, and the same testimony as aforesaid.
July 9, 1811: Present, Lucas, Penrose, and Bates, commissioners. It is the opinion of the Board that this claim ought not to be confirmed.

CHARLES GUIBEAULT, claiming a lot of one arpent of land, situate in the district of New Madrid, village of Little Prairie, No. 75 of square No. 19; produces to the Board the same papers as in the foregoing claims, and the same testimony as aforesaid.
July 9, 1811: Present, Lucas, Penrose, and Bates, commissioners. It is the opinion of the Board that this claim ought not to be confirmed.

JEAN VIAND, claiming a lot of one, arpent of land, situate in the district of New Madrid, village of Little Prairie, No. 78 of square No. 20; produces to the Board the same papers as in the foregoing claims, and the same testimony as aforesaid.
July 9, 1811: Present, Lucas, Penrose, and Bates, commissioners. It is the opinion of the. Board that this claim ought not to be confirmed.

JEAN VIAND, claiming a lot of one arpent of land, situate in the district of New Madrid, village of Little Prairie, No. 79 of square No. 20; produces to the Board the same papers as in the foregoing claims, and the same testimony as aforesaid.
July 9, 1811: Present, Lucas, Penrose, and Bates, commissioners. It is the opinion of the Board that this claim ought not to be granted.

RAPHAEL LESIEUR, claiming a lot of one arpent of land, situate in the district of New Madrid, village of Little Prairie, No. 80 of square No. 21; produces to the Board the same papers as in the foregoing claims, and the same testimony as aforesaid.
July 9, 1811: Present Lucas, Penrose, and Bates, commissioners. It is the opinion of the Board that this claim ought not to be confirmed.

RAPHAEL LESIEUR, claiming a lot of one arpent of land, situate in the district of New Madrid, village of Little Prairie, No. 81 of square 21; produces to the Board the same papers as in the foregoing claims, and the same testimony as aforesaid.
July 9, 1811: Present, Lucas, Penrose, and Bates, commissioners. It is the opinion of the Board that this claim ought not to be confirmed.

JOSEPH DORION, claiming a lot of one arpent of land, situate in the district of New Madrid, village of Little Prairie, No. 82 of square No. 20; produces to the Board the same papers as in the foregoing claims, and the same testimony as aforesaid.
July 9, 1811: Present, Lucas, Penrose, and Bates, commissioners. It is the opinion of the Board that this claim ought not to be confirmed.

JOSEPH DORION, claiming a lot of one arpent of land, situate in the district of New Madrid, village of Little Prairie, No. 83 of square No. 21; produces to the Board the same papers as in the foregoing claims, and the same testimony as aforesaid.
July 9, 1811: Present, Lucas, Penrose, and Bates, commissioners. It is the opinion of the Board that this claim ought not to be confirmed.

HYACINTH GAYON, claiming a lot of one arpent of land, situate in the district of New Madrid, village of Little Prairie, No. 86 of square No. 22; produces to the Board the same papers as in the foregoing claims, and the same testimony as aforesaid.
July 9, 1811: Present, Lucas, Penrose, and Bates, commissioners. It is the opinion of the Board that this claim ought not to be confirmed.

HYACINTH GAYON, claiming a lot of one arpent of land, situate in the district of New Madrid, village of Little Prairie, No. 87 of square No 22; produces to the Board the same papers as in the foregoing claims, and the same testimony as aforesaid.
July 9, 1811: Present, Lucas, Penrose, and Bates, commissioners. It is the opinion of the Board that this claim ought not to be confirmed.

JEAN MONTMENIE, claiming a lot of one arpent of land, situate in the district of New Madrid, village of Little Prairie, No. 92 of square No 24; produces to the Board the same papers as in the foregoing claims, and the same testimony as aforesaid.
July 9, 1811: Present, Lucas, Penrose, and Bates, commissioners. It is the opinion of the Board that this claim ought not to be confirmed.

JEAN MONTMENIE, claiming a lot of one arpent of land, situate in the district of New Madrid, village of Little Prairie, No. 93 of square No. 24; produces to the Board the same papers as in the foregoing claims, and the same testimony as aforesaid.

****

July 9, 1811: Present, Lucas, Penrose, and Bates, commissioners. It is the opinion of the Board that this claim ought not to be confirmed.

BAPTISTE CHARTIER, claiming a lot of one arpent of land, situate in the district of New Madrid, village of Little Prairie, No. 96 of square No. 25; produces to the Board same papers as in the foregoing claims, and the same testimony as aforesaid.
July 9, 1811: Present, Lucas, Penrose, and Bates, commissioners. It is the opinion of the Board that this claim ought not to be confirmed.

BAPTISTE CHARTIER, claiming a lot of one arpent of land, situate in the district of New Madrid, village of Little Prairie, No. 97 of square No. 25; produces to the Board the same papers as in the foregoing claims, and the same testimony as aforesaid.
July 9, 1811: Present, Lucas, Penrose, and Bates, commissioners. It is the opinion of the Board that this claim ought not to be confirmed.

GEORGE RODDEL, claiming a lot of one arpent of land, situate in the district of New Madrid, village of Little Prairie, No. 98 of square No. 25; produces to the Board the same papers as in the foregoing claims, and the same testimony as aforesaid.
July 9, 1811: Present, Lucas, Penrose, and Bates, commissioners. It is the opinion of the Board that this claim ought not to be confirmed.

FRANÇOIS LANGLOIS, claiming a lot of one arpent of land, situate in the district of New Madrid, village of Little Prairie, No. 101 of square No. 26; produces to the Board the same papers as in the foregoing claims, and the testimony as aforesaid.
July 9, 1811: Present, Lucas, Penrose, and Bates, commissioners. It is the opinion of the Board that this claim ought not to be confirmed.

GEORGE RODDEL, claiming a lot of one arpent of land, situate in the district of New Madrid, in the village of Little Prairie, No. 99 of square No. 25; produces to the Board the same papers as in the foregoing claims, and the same testimony as aforesaid.
July 9, 1811: Present, Lucas, Penrose, and Bates, commissioners. It is the opinion of the Board that this claim ought not to be confirmed.

FRANCIS LANGLOIS, claiming a lot of one arpent of land, situate in the district of New Madrid, village of Little Prairie, No. 101 of square No. 26; produces to the Board the same papers as in the foregoing claims, and the same testimony as aforesaid.
July 9, 1811: Present, Lucas, Penrose, and Bates, commissioners. It is the opinion of the Board that this claim ought not to be confirmed.

JOHN DERLAN, claiming a lot of one arpent of land, situate in the district of New Madrid, village of Little Prairie, No. 102 of square No. 26; produces to the Board the same papers as in the foregoing claims, and the same testimony as aforesaid.
July 9, 1811: Present, Lucas, Penrose, and Bates, commissioners. It is the opinion of the Board that this claim ought not to be confirmed.

JOHN DERLAN, claiming a lot of one arpent of land, situate in the district of New Madrid, village of Little Prairie, No. 103 of square No. 26; produces to the Board the same papers as in the foregoing claims, and the same testimony as aforesaid.
July 9, 1811: Present, Lucas, Penrose, and Bates, commissioners. It is the opinion of the Board that this claim ought not to be confirmed.

JEAN MONTMENIE, claiming a lot of one arpent of land, situate in the district of New Madrid, village of Little Prairie, No. 104 of square No. 27; produces to the Board the same papers as in the foregoing claims, and the same testimony as aforesaid.
July 9, 1811: Present, Lucas, Penrose, and Bates, commissioners. It is the opinion of the Board that this claim ought not to be confirmed.

JEAN MONTMENIE, claiming a lot of one arpent of land, situate in the district of New Madrid, village of Little Prairie, No. 105 of square No. 27; produces to the Board the same papers as in the foregoing claims, and the same testimony as aforesaid.
July 9, 1811: Present, Lucas, Penrose, and Bates, commissioners. It is the opinion of the Board that this claim ought not to be confirmed.

JOSEPH CLAUDE GONET, claiming a lot of one arpent of land, situate in the district of New Madrid, village of Little Prairie, No. 108 of square No. 28; produces to the Board the same papers as in the foregoing claims, and the same testimony as aforesaid.
July 9, 1811: Present, Lucas, Penrose, and Bates, commissioners. It is the opinion of the Board that this claim ought not to be confirmed.

JOSEPH CLAUDE GONET, claiming a lot of one arpent of land, situate in the district of New Madrid, village of Little Prairie, No. 109 of square No. 28; produces to the Board the same papers as in the foregoing claims, and the same testimony as aforesaid.
July 9, 1811: Present, Lucas, Penrose, and Bates, commissioners. It is the opinion of the Board that this claim ought not to be confirmed.

B. MARTIN, claiming one arpent front by thirty in depth of land, situate adjoining the town of St. Genevieve; produces to the Board a concession from Zenon Trudeau, Lieutenant Governor, for two thousand five hundred and twenty arpents of land, circumscribed by natural boundaries, granted as commons to sundry inhabitants of St. Genevieve, in which the claimant has conceded to him the quantity claimed; said concession dated 16th November, 1797.

Testimony taken. June 20, 1806. Walter Fenwick, sworn, says that the aforesaid tract of two thousand five hundred and twenty arpents had been surveyed about five or six years' ago; that he has been an inhabitant of the country for nine years, during which time the said tract has supplied the town of St. Genevieve with fire-wood.

August 16, 1811: Present, Penrose and Bates, commissioners. It is the opinion of the Board that this claim ought not to be confirmed.

JULIAN RATTLE, claiming two arpents front by thirty in depth of land, situate adjoining the town of St. Genevieve; produces to the Board the same concession as in the foregoing claims, and the same testimony as aforesaid.

August 16, 1811: Present, Penrose and Bates, commissioners. It is the opinion of the Board that this claim ought not to be confirmed.

JOSEPH PRATTE, claiming three arpents front by thirty in depth of land, situate adjoining the town of St. Genevieve, district of St. Genevieve; produces to the Board the same concession as in the foregoing claims, and the same testimony as aforesaid.

August 16, 1811: Present, Penrose and Bates, commissioners. It is the opinion of the Board that this claim ought not to be confirmed.

FRANCIS JANIS, claiming three arpents front by thirty in depth, adjoining the town of St. Genevieve, district of St. Genevieve; produces to the Board the same concession as in the foregoing claims, and the same testimony as aforesaid.

August 16, 1811: Present, Penrose and Bates, commissioners. It is the opinion of the Board that this claim ought not to be confirmed.

JOHN BAPTISTE PLACIE, claiming two arpents front by thirty in depth of land adjoining the town of St. Genevieve, district of St. Genevieve; produces to the Board the same concession as in the foregoing claims, and the same testimony as aforesaid.

August 16, 1811: Present, Penrose and Bates, commissioners. It is the opinion of the Board that this claim ought not to be confirmed.

AMABLE PARTINA, dit Mason, claiming one arpent front by thirty in depth of land, situate adjoining the town of St. Genevieve, district of St. Genevieve; produces to the Board the same concession as in the foregoing claims, and the same testimony as aforesaid.

August 16, 1811: Present, Penrose and Bates, commissioners. It is the opinion of the Board that this claim ought not to be confirmed.

ST. JAMES BEAUVAIS, claiming ten arpents front by thirty in depth of land, situate adjoining the town of St. Genevieve, district of St. Genevieve; produces to the Board the same concession as in the foregoing claims, and the same testimony as aforesaid.

August 16, 1811: Present, Penrose and Bates, commissioners. It is the opinion of the Board that this claim ought not to be confirmed.

LOUIS BOLDUC, claiming two arpents in front by thirty in depth of land, situate adjoining the town of St. Genevieve, district of St Genevieve; produces to the Board the same concession as in the foregoing claims, and the same testimony as aforesaid.

August 16, 1811: Present, Penrose and Bates, commissioners. It is the opinion of the Board that this claim ought not to be confirmed.

FRANCIS VALLE, claiming six arpents front by thirty in depth of land, situate adjoining the town of St. Genevieve, district of St. Genevieve; produces to the Board the same concession as in the foregoing claims, and the same testimony as aforesaid.

August 16, 1811: Present, Penrose and Bates, commissioners. It is the opinion of the Board that this claim ought not to be confirmed.

JOHN BAPTISTE JANIS; claiming two arpents front by thirty in depth of land, situate adjoining the town of St. Genevieve, district of St. Genevieve; produces to the Board the same concession as in the foregoing claims, and the same testimony as aforesaid.

August 16, 1811: Present, Penrose and Bates, commissioners. It is the opinion of the Board that this claim ought not to be confirmed.

VITAL BEAUVAIS, claiming three arpents front by thirty in depth of land, situate in the district of St. Genevieve, adjoining the town of St. Genevieve; produces to the Board the same concession as in the foregoing claims, and the same testimony as aforesaid.

August 16, 1811: Present, Penrose and Bates, commissioners. It is the opinion of the Board that this claim ought not to be confirmed.

FRANCIS MOREAU, claiming three arpents front by thirty in depth of land, situate adjoining the town of St. Genevieve, district of St. Genevieve; produces to the Board the same concession as in the foregoing claims, and same testimony as aforesaid.

August 16, 1811: Present, Penrose and Bates, commissioners. It is the opinion of the Board that this claim ought not to be confirmed.

FRANCIS SIMONEAU, claiming one arpent front by thirty in depth of land, situate adjoining the town of St. Genevieve, district of St. Genevieve; produces to the Board the same papers as in the foregoing claims, and the same testimony as aforesaid.

August 16, 1811: Present, Penrose and Bates, commissioners. It is the opinion of the Board that this claim ought not to be confirmed.

LACOMB, claiming one arpent front by thirty in depth of land, situate adjoining the town of St. Genevieve, district of St. Genevieve; produces to the Board the same concession as in the foregoing claims, and the same testimony as aforesaid.

August 16, 1811: Present, Penrose and Bates, commissioners. It is the opinion of the Board that this claim ought not to be confirmed.

FRANCIS LACROIX, claiming one arpent front by thirty in depth of land, adjoining the town of St. Genevieve, district of St. Genevieve; produces to the Board the same concession as in the foregoing claims, and the same testimony as aforesaid.

August 16, 1811: Present, Penrose and Bates, commissioners. It is the opinion of the Board that this claim ought not to be confirmed.

JEROME MATES, claiming one arpent front by thirty in depth of land, situate adjoining the town of St. Genevieve, district of St. Genevieve; produces to the Board the same concession as in the foregoing claims, and the same testimony as aforesaid.

August 16, 1811: Present, Penrose and Bates, commissioners. It is the opinion of the Board that this claim ought not to be confirmed.

RANGE, claiming one arpent in front by thirty in depth, adjoining the town of St. Genevieve, district of St. Genevieve; produces to the Board the same concession as in the foregoing claims, and the same testimony as aforesaid.

August 16, 1811: Present, Penrose and Bates, commissioners. It is the opinion of the Board that this claim ought not to be confirmed.

JOHN BAPTISTE LACROIX, claiming one arpent in front by thirty in depth of land, situate adjoining the town of St. Genevieve, district of St. Genevieve; produces to the Board the same concession as in the foregoing claims, and the same testimony as aforesaid.

August 16, 1811: Present, Penrose and Bates, commissioners. It is the opinion of the Board that this claim ought not to be confirmed.

INHABITANTS OF ST. GENEVIEVE, claiming two arpents front by thirty in depth of land, situate adjoining the town of St. Genevieve, district of St. Genevieve; produces to the Board the same concession as in the foregoing claims, and the same testimony as aforesaid.

August 16, 1811: Present, Penrose and Bates, commissioners. It is the opinion of the Board that this claim ought not to be confirmed.

WIDOW EMANUEL, claiming one arpent front by thirty in depth, adjoining the town of St. Genevieve, district of St. Genevieve; produces to the Board the same concession as in the foregoing claims, and the same testimony as aforesaid.

August 16, 1811: Present, Penrose and Bates, commissioners. It is the opinion of the Board that this claim ought not to be confirmed.

LOUIS GOVREAU, claiming two arpents front by thirty in depth, situate adjoining the town of St. Genevieve, district of St. Genevieve; produces to the Board the same concession as in the foregoing claims, and the same testimony as aforesaid.

August 16, 1811: Present, Penrose and Bates, commissioners. It is the opinion of the Board that this claim ought not to be confirmed.

DEGUIRE, Sen., claiming one arpent front by thirty in depth, situate adjoining the town of St. Genevieve, district of St. Genevieve; produces to the Board the same concession as in the foregoing claims, and the same testimony as aforesaid.

August 16, 1811: Present, Penrose and Bates, commissioners. It is the opinion of the Board that this claim ought not to be confirmed.

GRINON, claiming one arpent in front by thirty in depth, situate adjoining the town of St. Genevieve, district of St. Genevieve; produces to the Board the same concession as in the foregoing claims, and the same testimony as aforesaid.

August 16, 1811: Present, Penrose and Bates, commissioners. It is the opinion of the Board that this claim ought not to be confirmed.

HENRY GOVREAU, claiming one arpent front by thirty in depth of land, situate adjoining the town of St. Genevieve, district of St. Genevieve; produces to the Board the same concession as in the foregoing claims, and the same testimony as aforesaid.

August 16, 1811: Present, Penrose and Bates, commissioners. It is the opinion of the Board that this claim ought not to be confirmed.

HENRY DIELLE, claiming two arpents front by thirty in depth of land, situate adjoining the town of St. Genevieve, district of St. Genevieve; produces to the Board the same concession as in the foregoing claims, and the same testimony as aforesaid.

August 16, 1811: Present, Penrose and Bates, commissioners. It is the opinion of the Board that this claim ought not to be confirmed.

CHARLES VALLE, claiming two arpents front by thirty in depth of land, situate adjoining the town of St. Genevieve, district of St. Genevieve; produces to the Board the same concession as in the foregoing claims, and the same testimony as aforesaid.

August 16, 1811: Present, Penrose and Bates, commissioners. It is the opinion of the Board that this claim ought not to be confirmed.

LOUIS BOLDUC, claiming three arpents front by thirty in depth of land, situate adjoining the town of St. Genevieve, district of St. Genevieve; produces to the Board the same concession as in the foregoing claims, and the same testimony as aforesaid.

August 16, 1811: Present, Penrose and Bates, commissioners. It is the opinion of the Board that this claim ought not to be confirmed.

STEPHEN BOLDUC, claiming two arpents front by thirty in depth of land, situate adjoining the town of St. Genevieve, district of St. Genevieve; produces to the Board the same concession as in the foregoing claims, and the same testimony as aforesaid.

August 16, 1811: Present, Penrose and Bates, commissioners. It is the opinion of the Board that this claim ought not to be confirmed.

WIDOW BELLEMAR, claiming one arpent front by thirty in depth of land, situate adjoining the town of St. Genevieve, district of St. Genevieve; produces to the Board the same concession as in the foregoing claims, and the same testimony as aforesaid.
August 16, 1811: Present, Penrose and Bates, commissioners. It is the opinion of the Board that this claim ought not to be confirmed.

JOHN BAPTISTE BECQUETTE, claiming two arpents front by thirty in depth of land, situate adjoining the town of St. Genevieve, district of St. Genevieve; produces to the Board the same concession as in the foregoing claims, and the same testimony as aforesaid.
August 16, 1811: Present, Penrose and Bates, commissioners. It is the opinion of the Board that this claim ought not to be confirmed.

WIDOW BERMIER, claiming one arpent front by thirty in depth of land, situate adjoining the town of St. Genevieve, district of St. Genevieve; produces to the Board the same concession as in the foregoing claims, and the same testimony as aforesaid.
August 16, 1811: Present, Penrose and Bates, commissioners. It is the opinion of the Board that this claim ought not to be confirmed.

PAUL DEGUIRE, claiming one arpent front by thirty in depth of land, situate adjoining the town of St. Genevieve, district of St. Genevieve; produces to the Board the same concession as in the foregoing claims, and the same testimony as aforesaid.
August 16, 1811: Present, Penrose and Bates, commissioners. It is the opinion of the Board that this claim ought not to be confirmed.

TISSEROT, claiming one arpent front by thirty in depth of land, situate adjoining the town of St. Genevieve, district of St. Genevieve; produces to the Board the same concession as in the foregoing claims, and the same testimony as aforesaid.
August 16, 1811: Present, Penrose and Bates, commissioners. It is the opinion of the Board that this claim ought not to be confirmed.

GRASSARD, claiming three arpents front by thirty in depth of land, situate adjoining the town of St. Genevieve, district of St. Genevieve; produces to the Board the same concession as in the foregoing claims, and the same testimony as aforesaid.
August 16, 1811: Present, Penrose and Bates, commissioners. It is the opinion of the Board that this claim ought not to be confirmed.

TONNELIER, claiming one arpent front by thirty in depth of land, situate adjoining the town of St. Genevieve, district of St. Genevieve; produces to the Board the same concession as in the foregoing claims, and the same testimony as aforesaid.
August 16, 1811: Present, Penrose and Bates, commissioners. It is the opinion of the Board that this claim ought not to be confirmed.

JOSEPH LACHANCE, claiming one arpent front by thirty in depth of land, situate adjoining the town of St. Genevieve, district of St. Genevieve; produces to the Board the same concession as in the foregoing claims, and the same testimony as aforesaid.
August 16, 1811: Present, Penrose and Bates, commissioners. It is the opinion of the Board that this claim ought not to be confirmed.

JOHN BAPTISTE BECQUETTE, Jun., claiming two arpents front by thirty in depth of land, situate adjoining the town of St. Genevieve, district of St. Genevieve; produces to the Board the same concession as in the foregoing claims, and the same testimony as aforesaid.
August 16, 1811: Present, Penrose and Bates, commissioners. It is the opinion of the Board that this claim ought not to be confirmed.

ELREUNE GAOIOT, claiming one arpent front by thirty in depth of land, situate adjoining the town of St. Genevieve, district of St. Genevieve; produces to the Board the same concession as in the foregoing claims, and the same testimony as aforesaid.
August 16, 1811: Present, Penrose and Bates, commissioners. It is the opinion of the Board that this claim ought not to be confirmed.

PIERRE BELOTE, claiming one arpent front by thirty in depth of land, situate adjoining the town of St. Genevieve, district of St. Genevieve; produces to the Board the same concession as in the foregoing claims, and the same testimony as aforesaid.
August 16, 1811: Present, Penrose and Bates, commissioners. It is the opinion of the Board that this claim ought not to be confirmed.

WIDOW LAFLEUR, claiming three arpents front by thirty in depth of land, situate adjoining the town of St. Genevieve, district of St. Genevieve; produces to the Board the same concession as in the foregoing claims, and the same testimony as aforesaid.
August 16, 1811: Present, Penrose and Bates, commissioners. It is the opinion of the Board that this claim ought not to be confirmed.

ETIENNE PARENT, claiming two arpents front by thirty in depth of land, situate adjoining the town of St. Genevieve, district of St. Genevieve; produces to the Board the same concession as in the foregoing claims, and the same testimony as aforesaid.

August 16, 1811: Present, Penrose and Bates, commissioners. It is the opinion of the Board that this claim ought not to be confirmed.

CHEVALIER, claiming two arpents front by thirty in depth of land, situate adjoining the town of St. Genevieve, district of St. Genevieve; produces to the Board the same concession as in the foregoing claims, and the same testimony as aforesaid.
August 16, 1811: Present, Penrose and Bates, commissioners. It is the opinion of the Board that this claim ought not to be confirmed.

MICHEL LACHANCE, claiming one arpent front by thirty in depth of land, situate adjoining the town of St. Genevieve, district of St. Genevieve; produces to the Board the same concession as in the foregoing claims, and the same testimony as aforesaid.
August 16, 1811: Present, Penrose and Bates, commissioners. It is the opinion of the Board that this claim ought not to be confirmed.

FRANCIS BERMIER, claiming one arpent front by thirty in depth of land, situate adjoining the town of St. Genevieve, district of St. Genevieve; produces to the Board the same concession as in the foregoing claims, and the same testimony as aforesaid.
August 16, 1811: Present, Penrose and Bates, commissioners. It is the opinion of the Board that this claim ought not to be confirmed.

RICHELET LANGLIER, claiming one arpent front by thirty in depth of land, situate adjoining the town of St. Genevieve, district of St. Genevieve; produces to the Board the same concession as in the foregoing claim, and the same testimony as aforesaid.
August 16, 1811: Present, Penrose and Bates, commissioners. It is the opinion of the Board that this claim ought not to be confirmed.

JOSEPH PAPIN, claiming eight hundred arpents of land, on any vacant land; produces to the Board a concession from Charles Dehault Delassus, Lieutenant Governor, for the same, dated 27th January, 1800; granted for five thousand six hundred arpents.
June 18, 1810: Present, Lucas, Penrose, and Bates, commissioners. It is the opinion of the Board that this claim ought not to be confirmed.

ALEXANDER PAPIN, claiming eight hundred arpents of land, on any vacant land; produces to the Board the aforesaid concession.
June 18, 1810: Present, Lucas, Penrose, and Bates, commissioners. It is the opinion of the Board that this claim ought not to be confirmed.

HYPOLITE PAPIN, claiming eight hundred arpents of land, on any vacant land; produces to the Board the aforesaid concession.
June 18, 1810: Present, Lucas, Penrose, and Bates, commissioners. It is the opinion of the Board that this claim ought not to be confirmed.

PIERRE PAPIN, claiming eight hundred arpents of land, on any vacant land; produces to the Board the aforesaid concession.
June 18, 1810: Present, Lucas, Penrose, and Bates, commissioners. It is the opinion of the Board that this claim ought not to be confirmed.

SYLVESTER PAPIN, claiming eight hundred arpents of land, on any vacant land; produces to the Board the aforesaid concession.
June 18, 1810: Present, Lucas, Penrose, and Bates, commissioners. It is the opinion of the Board that this claim ought not to be confirmed.

DIDIER PAPIN, claiming eight hundred arpents of land, on any vacant land; produces to the Board the aforesaid concession.
June 18, 1810: Present, Lucas, Penrose, and Bates, commissioners. It is the opinion of the Board that this claim ought not to be confirmed.

THEODORE PAPIN, claiming eight hundred arpents of land, on any vacant land; produces to the Board the aforesaid concession.
June 18, 1810: Present, Lucas, Penrose, and Bates, commissioners. It is the opinion of the Board that this claim ought not to be confirmed.

CHARLES DEHAULT DELASSUS, claiming thirty thousand arpents of land, where the same may be found vacant; produces to the Board an official letter from the Baron de Carondelet to Dehault Delassus, father of claimant, stating that he had ordered Zenon Trudeau to grant to him a certain tract of land which he had requested, and also a plantation, sufficiently large for their cultivation and establishment, should be granted to his son-in-law and sons, dated 8th May, 1793; produces also to the Board a concession for the same, dated 10th February, 1798, from Zenon Trudeau, Lieutenant Governor.
June 18, 1810: Present, Lucas, Penrose, and Bates, commissioners. It is the opinion of the Board that this claim ought not to be confirmed.

ROBERT SLOAN, claiming seven hundred and forty-eight arpents sixty-eight perches of land, situate in Bellevue, district of St. Genevieve; produces to the Board a survey of the same, dated 20th and certified 27th February, 1806; also, a deposition of permission to settle, given April 3, by Joseph Decelle, syndic.
Testimony taken. June 26, 1806. William Ashbrook, sworn, says that claimant settled the said tract of land in the spring of 1804, raised a crop, and has actually inhabited and cultivated the same to this day; and had, on 20th December, 1803, a wife and ten children.
June 18, 1811: Present, Lucas, Penrose, and Bates, commissioners. It is the opinion of the Board that this claim ought not to be confirmed.

PASCAL DETCHEMENDY, assignee of Nicholas Lachance, claiming seventy-four arpents and forty poles of land, situate on the river Gaborie, district of St. Genevieve; produces to the Board a concession from Zenon Trudeau, dated 1st September, 1797; a survey, taken 2d October, and certified 1st November, 1797; and a transfer of the same, passed before Joseph Pratt, the then acting commandant, dated April 24, 1801.

June 21, 1806: Present, Penrose and Donaldson, commissioners. This claim being unsupported by actual inhabitation and cultivation, the Board reject the same, and observe that this tract is adjoining a tract claimed by said Detchemendy, as assignee of John Windle Engle; that a part of the land said to be cultivated in said claim forms a part of this tract; and that the said two lots or tracts are out lots, and intended merely for cultivation.

June 18, 1810: Present, Lucas, Penrose, and Bates, commissioners. It is the opinion of the Board that this claim ought not to be confirmed.

JAMES McDONALD, claiming three hundred and twenty arpents of land, situate at Marais des Liards, district of St. Louis; produces to the Board a notice of said claim, entered with the recorder 27th May, 1808; also, a copy of a plat of survey of one thousand six hundred arpents, said to be founded on a decree of the Lieutenant Governor, dated 8th December, 1796, made 25th March, 1797, for Louis Honoré, certified by Silas Bent, deputy surveyor general, dated 25th July, 1807, as copied from the records in his office; said McDonald claiming as assignee of Louis Honoré.

Testimony taken. May 30, 1808. James Richardson, sworn, says that he surveyed said land, by directions from Antoine Soulard, surveyor general, in the spring of 1797; that he had the concession on which said survey was made several times in his hands before that time; that said concession was granted by Don Zenon Trudeau, Lieutenant Governor, to Louis Honoré, (father,) for eight by forty arpents; to Francis, (son,) eight by forty arpents; to Baptiste, (son,) eight by forty arpents; to Michel, (son,) eight by forty arpents; to Noel, (son,) eight by forty arpents; making, in the whole, forty arpents square; that he actually saw conveyances, in 1799 and 1800, from Louis Honoré, (father,) Francis, (son,) Michel, (son,) and Noel, (son,) for eight by forty arpents of land each, situate as aforesaid, to James McDonald, and that it appeared to be witnessed; the said parties acknowledged to him (the witness) to have signed a conveyance of their said land to said McDonald, some time after.

Louis Lebeaume, sworn, says that claimant put into his hands, about the year 1800 or 1801, a concession from Zenon Trudeau, Lieutenant Governor, to Louis Honoré (father) and sons, for one thousand six hundred arpents of land, situate as aforesaid; that he took a conveyance from Baptiste Honoré, one of the sons, to claimant, for his part of the said concession; at the same time had in his possession conveyances purporting to be from Louis Honoré, (father,) and he thinks two of the sons, to claimant.

Claimant, sworn, says that, in going from the town of St. Louis, on horseback, to his house on said land, in 1805, having then in his saddle-bags, and with him, all the papers, to wit, the concession and conveyances, relating to said claim, his horse ran away with him, threw him, and went off with said bags; that, in search after them, some days after, he found said bags, with the bridle of his horse in them, but that they contained no papers, which were missing, together with some other articles; that he has never since had said papers in his possession, neither does he know where they are.

Claimant declares that he understood the Lieutenant Governor refused to have sales passed before him, and therefore did not apply.

James Richardson says that he knows of neither inhabitation nor cultivation on said land prior to the sale by said Honoré; does not know of Louis Honoré (father) having any other claim, but François, Baptiste, and Noel, had other claims; that claimant settled on said land in the fall of 1799, or spring of 1800, built a cabin, and has inhabited and cultivated the same to this day.

June 4, 1810: Present, Lucas, Penrose, and Bates, commissioners. It is the opinion of the Board that this claim ought not to be confirmed.

JAMES McDONALD, assignee of Francis Honoré, claiming three hundred and twenty arpents of land, situate at Marais des Liards, district of St. Louis; produces to the Board the same papers as in the aforesaid claims, and the same testimony as aforesaid.

June 4, 1810: Present, Lucas, Penrose, and Bates, commissioners. It is the opinion of the Board that this claim ought not to be confirmed.

JAMES McDONALD, assignee of Baptiste Honoré, claiming three hundred and twenty arpents of land, situate at Marais des Liards, district of St. Louis; produces to the Board the same papers as in the foregoing claims, and the same testimony as aforesaid.

June 4, 1810: Present, Lucas, Penrose, and Bates, commissioners. It is the opinion of the Board that this claim ought not to be confirmed.

JAMES McDONALD, assignee of Michel Honoré, claiming three hundred and twenty arpents of land, situate at Marais des Liards, district of St. Louis; produces to the Board the same papers as in the foregoing claims, and the same testimony as aforesaid.

June 4, 1810: Present, Lucas, Penrose, and Bates, commissioners. It is the opinion of the Board that this claim ought not to be confirmed.

JAMES McDONALD, assignee of Noel Honoré, claiming three hundred and twenty arpents of land, situate at Marais des Liards, district of St. Louis; produces to the Board the same papers as in the foregoing claims, and the same testimony as aforesaid.

June 4, 1810: Present, Lucas, Penrose, and Bates, commissioners. It is the opinion of the Board that this claim ought not to be confirmed.

FRANÇOIS DUNNEGANT, claiming one hundred and sixty arpents of land, situate at Fontaine des Biches, district of St. Louis; produces to the Board a notice of said claim to the recorder, dated May 14, 1808; and also a concession for the same to claimant from François Cruzat, Lieutenant Governor, dated 6th October, 1782, and registered folio 5, book No. 4, of the book of registry of concessions, for four arpents front by forty arpents deep, situate at Fontaine des Biches, distant about three leagues from St. Louis.

Testimony taken. September 13, 1808. Simon Coursant, sworn.

Question by claimant. Do you know the Fontaine des Biches, and where it is situated?

Answer. Yes, I know two of them; they are situate near river Aux Biches. The river Aux Biches is the last river emptying into the Missouri, on the south side towards its mouth, and is the same near which the United States' cantonment at present stands; says that he has not seen the river in twenty years, and it has emptied itself since then into the Missouri considerably lower down; that the springs are situated close to the end of the little rock, (upper one) on the Missouri, near Cold Water; says that what he calls Cold Water is a spring that empties itself out of the rocks, close to the banks of the Missouri, very high up, and falls into the Missouri; that the Fontaine Cold Water is not the Fontaine des Biches, and is near three miles distant above, and the Fontaine des Biches is on the right side of the river La Biche in the Missouri bottom, below the ridge of rocks; that the river which runs by St. Ferdinand, and empties into the Missouri, is what he calls La Biche; and that all the prairie and woods near was called Prairie les Biches, and woods of les Biches; that he knows of no cultivation ever having been done at said springs; that the people generally cut wood in the Missouri bottom, and made camps; but does not know who they were, or whether they were on the land claimed; says that as to danger from Indians, in that neighborhood there always has been until now.

Auguste Chouteau, sworn, says that on the right side of the Missouri, about a league above its mouth on the river, there is a chain of rocks, about a quarter of a mile long; about twenty arpents below said rocks a little river empties itself into the Missouri, called La Biche; and that about four arpents from the bank of the Missouri, and ten arpents on the right side of said river La Biche, there is a spring or springs called Fontaine des Biches, and that the same Fontaine des Biches, is now called Belle Fontaine; says that he knows of no settlement made by Dunnegant, the claimant, on the place claimed; that, about the year 1786, claimant was appointed commandant of St. Ferdinand, and continued so from that time until the American Government took place; that from 1782 until claimant was appointed commandant, the Indians were troublesome; and there were orders for the inhabitants of this country not to settle out of the towns.

Testimony taken. September 14, 1808. Pierre Chouteau, sworn, says that the spring called the Biche spring is situated a little below the river Aux Biches, which spring is so called because it is situated a little distance from the Glaize aux Biches, and river Aux Biches, and is the same which is now called Belle Fontaine, near the United States' cantonment, and the river called the Aux Biches is the same, now called Cold Water river; says that he has been acquainted with the situation of said spring for thirty-five years past; never heard of any other spring called Aux Biches; that he always knew the same by that name; says that he never knew of any improvement being made at or near said spring, except the improvement of land; that for the last twenty-five years he has not been in that part of the country until the cantonment was built, since when he has been there frequently; that the first time he saw said spring since twenty-five years, was when he went with General Wilkinson to choose a place for a cantonment, and then he saw land, mill, and improvement.

Baptiste Valle, sworn, says that the springs now called Cold Water, behind the United States' cantonment, ten arpents at most from the same, was formerly called Biche springs; never knew of any other springs being called by that name, nor saw any improvement at that place previous to the building of the camp; that twenty-five or twenty-six years past, he hunted there during two years, but has not been there since except last year.

Toussaint Parent, sworn, says that twenty-seven years past, and before he knew the Biche spring, situate about ten or twelve arpents from the Missouri, and about fifteen or twenty arpents from the mouth of the river Aux Biches, never knew of any other springs of that name; at that time there was neither cabin or improvement made at that place, nor has he seen any since.

William Davis, a witness on the part of Massey, sworn, says that François Dunnegant went with him, the witness, to the public sale of land of Ezekiel Lard, deceased, when the same was cried and sold to William Massey; that he did not hear said Dunnegant make any objection to the sale; says that he knows a spring near the Glaize aux Biches, which was near to William Patterson's survey, and about one and a half miles from the cantonment, called Biche spring; that he has been acquainted with the name of said spring about ten years.

The foregoing claim contested by said Dunnegant and William Massey, assignee of Ezekiel Lard.

June 8, 1810: Present, Lucas, Penrose, and Bates, commissioners. It is the opinion of the Board that this claim ought not to be confirmed.

WILLIAM MASSEY, assignee of Ezekiel Lard, claiming six hundred arpents of land, situate on the Missouri bottom, district of St. Louis; produces to the Board a concession for one thousand arpents of land, granted by Zenon Trudeau, Lieutenant Governor, to Ezekiel Lard, and dated 10th September, 1797; a plat and certificate of survey of one thousand arpents, dated 5th April, 1798, and certified 18th July, same year; a certified copy of an adjudication at public sale of the effects of Ezekiel Lard, dated 24th April, 1803, to claimant, for six hundred arpents of said land, and certified 23d January, 1806.

Testimony taken. September 13, 1808. Jacques St. Vrain, sworn, says that in 1797 or 1798, Ezekiel Lard erected a saw-mill and grist-mill, and cleared and cultivated a field on the tract claimed, about one and a half arpents from Belle Fontaine, near where the United States' cantonment now stands; that he saw the mill agoing in 1799, and that said tract has always been inhabited and cultivated from its first establishment to this day.

Pascal Cerre, sworn, says that in 1798, Ezekiel Lard went to live on the place claimed; cleared a field in the bottom, between the mouth of what is now called Cold Water creek and Belle Fontaine, and erected a saw-mill the following year; that said land has been inhabited and cultivated until the death of William Musick, which happened about three or four years ago, since which he does not know whether it was cultivated or not; that all the springs under the Bluff, between Cold Water creek and the plantation of witness on the Mississippi, went by the appellation of Lean Froid, since the year 1787; that he has known the land claimed for fifteen or sixteen years past, but knows of no improvement being made on the same, except what he has before stated; that he never heard until lately of a spring called La Biche; but that the St. Ferdinand Fields was called Prairie des Biches, and to the north-east of said Prairie there was a place called Glaize aux Biches; that Cold Water creek and St. Ferdinand creek is the same, which passes through St. Ferdinand and discharges itself into the Missouri near the present United States' cantonment.

Question. By the agent of Francis Dunnegant. Do you know any thing of Francis Dunnegant's circumstances as to property?

Answer. I know that since the year 1787 he has been reputed to be a poor man, but as to character one of the best amongst us.

John Graham, sworn, says that Ezekiel Lard made an improvement on the place claimed in 1797, and began to build a grist and saw-mill in 1798, cleared a field, raised corn, and finished his mills; said land has been inhabited and cultivated ever since.

Antoine Soulard, sworn, says that he knows of a concession being granted to Ezekiel Lard, for the purpose of building a saw-mill, at the time the concession bears date; that said Lard was put in possession of the same by deponent, as surveyor, and for which he, deponent, received his fees of survey; that Zenon Trudeau, Lieutenant Governor, supported said undertaking by lending to said Lard two hundred dollars, towards assisting him in building said mill; that the said sum of two hundred dollars was reimbursed to deponent, as attorney in fact for Zenon Trudeau; that at the time of making the survey of said land, there was no objection made to the survey, nor did he know, at that time, of François Dunnegant having a claim, nor does he know of any opposition being made by said Dunnegant to said Lard's claim; says that he never knew of Dunnegant having a claim to said land, until it was known that the American Government was to take possession of the country, and until after the death of Lard.

James Richardson, sworn, says that he has been in this country twenty-one years past; that sixteen years ago deponent was at the place now called Belle Fontaine, and saw no improvement at that time, or appearances of any; that the first improvement he knows of, was made by Ezekiel Lard; that said Lard supported himself and family by his milk and farm, having no other resources to this deponent's knowledge.

Nicholas Hebert, dit Lacompte, sworn, says that since forty-five years ago he has been frequently in the Missouri bottom, near the mouth on the right side; knows of a spring called Leanfroid, at the rocks on the Missouri; that the springs where the United States' cantonment at present is, he understood to be called the springs of the Point of the fort; that he has never known them to be called by the name of Fontaine des Biches; that the river which empties itself into the Missouri, at the said cantonment, was formerly called the river of Prairie les Biches; knows of a Grand Glaize about five or six miles below St. Ferdinand, called Glaize des Biches.

Additional testimony of James Richardson; says that he has heard some old inhabitant say that the spring in the village of St. Ferdinand was called Fontaine des Biches; and has heard others say that a spring at Guy Seylee, which is near the spring that tumbles into the Missouri, called Cold Water, was also called Fontaine des Biches.

June 8, 1810: Present, Lucas, Penrose, and Bates, commissioners. Statement omitted in the proper place, viz. WILLIAM MASSEY, claiming six hundred arpents of a tract of one thousand arpents; Morris James, claiming two hundred arpents of the same tract of one thousand arpents; recorded in book D, page 216, of the recorder's office. The representatives of Ezekiel Lard, claiming the remaining two hundred arpents.

It is the opinion of a majority of the Board that this claim ought not to be confirmed. Clement B. Penrose, commissioner, voted for the confirmation of one thousand arpents of land. The said majority declare, that if the concession on which the above claims are founded had not exceeded eight hundred arpents, they would have voted for a confirmation.

RODOLPH TILLIER, assignee of Benito Vasquez, Jun., claiming eight hundred arpents of land, situate in the district of St. Louis; produces to the Board a concession from Charles Dehault Delassus, Lieutenant Governor, to the said Benito Hypolite, Antoine Joseph, and Pierre Vasquez, the children of Benito Vasquez, Sen., for eight hundred arpents each, granted to them for the purpose of settling the said Benito Vasquez, Jun., and educating his four younger brothers, who then were minors, and as a compensation for services rendered the Spanish Government by their father, Benito Vasquez, said concession dated the 17th February, 1800; a survey of the aforesaid eight hundred arpents, dated the 27th February, 1806; and a deed of transfer of the same, executed by the aforesaid Benito Vasquez, Jun., dated 11th February, 1806.

Testimony taken. August 25, 1806. Hyacinth St. Cyr, sworn, says that Benito Vasquez, Sen., the father of the said Benito and brothers, told him, the witness, about five or six years ago, that he had received a concession for his children of eight hundred arpents each; that the aforesaid Benito Vasquez, Jun. was, at the time of claiming said concession, of the age of twenty-one years and upwards; that his father, who was a Spaniard by birth, was a confidential officer of Government; that he acted for some time as commandant, by interim, and witness believes never received any compensation for his services.

Charles Gratiot, sworn, says that the said Benito Vasquez, Sen., is by birth a Spaniard; that he was the first militia captain, and acted sometimes as commandant, by interim, and never received any pecuniary compensation for his services.

Testimony taken. May 22, 1808. Jacques Clamorgan, sworn, says that he knows that this land was given as compensation to Benito Vasquez, Jun., for services rendered to the Spanish Government by his father; that said Benito, the father, was a confidential person under said Government, and a Spaniard by birth.

August 25, 1806: Present, Lucas and Penrose, commissioners. The Board reject this claim; they are satisfied that the said concession was granted at the time it bears date. They remark, that the grant is expressly given to the children, as is said in the body of it, as a compensation for the public services of the father, and that they may locate and establish it in two or three vacant places of the domain, where it shall be convenient.

September 22, 1810: Present, Lucas and Bates, commissioners. It is the opinion of the Board that this claim ought not be confirmed. John B. C. Lucas, commissioner, declares that he does not concur in opinion with the former Board in the present case, respecting the satisfaction which the said former Board expresses, that the concession was granted at the time it bears date.

ANTOINE VASQUEZ, claiming eight hundred arpents of land, situate in the district of St. Louis; produces to the Board the same concession as in the foregoing claims, and same testimony as aforesaid.

August 25, 1806: Present, Lucas and Penrose, commissioners. The Board reject this claim, and remark as aforesaid.

September 22, 1810: Present, Lucas, Penrose, and Bates, commissioners. It is the opinion of the Board that this claim ought not to be confirmed. John B. C. Lucas, commissioner, declares as aforesaid.

HYPOLITE VASQUEZ, claiming eight hundred arpents of land, situate in the district of St. Louis; produces to the Board the same concession as in the foregoing claims, and same testimony as aforesaid.

August 25, 1806: Present, Lucas and Penrose, commissioners. The Board reject this claim, and remark as aforesaid.

September 22, 1810: Present, Lucas, Penrose, and Bates, commissioners. It is the opinion of the Board that this claim ought not to be confirmed. John B. C. Lucas, commissioner, declares as aforesaid.

JOSEPH VASQUEZ, claiming eight hundred arpents of land, situate in the district of St. Louis; produces to the Board the same concession as in the foregoing claims, and same testimony as aforesaid.

August 25, 1806: Present, Lucas and Penrose, commissioners. The Board reject this claim, and remark as aforesaid.

September 22, 1810: Present, Lucas, Penrose, and Bates, commissioners. It is the opinion of the Board that this claim ought not to be confirmed. John B. C. Lucas, commissioner, declares as aforesaid.

PIERRE VASQUEZ, claiming eight hundred arpents of land, situate in the district of St. Louis; produces to the Board the same concession as in the foregoing claims, and the same testimony as aforesaid.

August 25, 1806: Present, Lucas and Penrose, commissioners. The Board reject this claim, and remark as aforesaid.

September 22, 1810: Present, Lucas, Penrose, and Bates, commissioners. It is the opinion of the Board that this claim ought not to be confirmed. John B. C. Lucas, commissioner, declares as aforesaid.

GEORGE AYREY, claiming seven hundred and fifty arpents of land, situate in the district of St. Charles; produces to the Board a plat of survey, dated 24th and certified 26th February, 1806.

October 9, 1811: Present, Lucas, Penrose, and Bates, commissioners. It is the opinion of the Board that this claim ought not to be granted.

ADAM BROWN, assignee of Deodat Allen, assignee of Philip Fine, claiming two hundred arpents of land, situate in Marais des Liards, district of St. Louis; produces to the Board a concession from Zenon Trudeau, Lieutenant Governor, to Philip Fine, and Charles Seales, dated 26th November, 1795; a plat of survey, dated 15th February, 1797, and certified same day; a conveyance from Fine to Allen, dated 24th October, 1805; from Allen to Brown, dated 4th October, 1805.

October 9, 1811: Present, Lucas, Penrose, and Bates, commissioners. It is the opinion of the Board that this claim ought not to be confirmed.

FREDERICK CONNOR, assignee of John Atkins, claiming one thousand one hundred and twenty-five arpents of land, situate on river Joachim, district of St. Louis; produces to the Board a notice to the recorder; a conveyance from said Atkins to claimant, dated 17th May, 1805.

October 9, 1811: Present, Lucas, Penrose, and Bates, commissioners. It is the opinion of the Board that this claim ought not to be granted.

LOUIS LEBEAUME, assignee of Francis Arnow, claiming eight hundred arpents of land, situate sixty-five miles north of St. Louis, district of St. Charles; produces to the Board a concession from Charles D. Delassus, Lieutenant Governor, to said Arnow, dated 28th February, 1800; a plat of survey, dated 20th February, 1804, certified 28th March, same year; certificate from the recorder of St. Louis district that there is a deed of conveyance in his office from Arnow to claimant, dated 3d May, 1803; certificate dated 24th May, 1806.

October 9, 1811: Present, full Board. It is the opinion of the Board that this claim ought not to be confirmed.

WILLIAM ANDERSON, claiming seven hundred and forty-eight arpents and sixty-eight perches of land, situate on the forks of the Missouri and Mississippi, district of St. Charles; produces to the Board a notice to the recorder.

October 9, 1811: Present, full Board. It is the opinion of the Board that this claim ought not to be granted.

JOSEPH WALLER, assignee of Laferty David Allen, claiming seven hundred and forty-eight arpents and sixty-eight perches of land, situate in Double springs, district of Cape Girardeau; produces to the Board a notice to the recorder.

October 9, 1811: Full Board. It is the opinion of the Board that this claim ought not to be granted.

JOSEPH WALLER, assignee of Laferty David Allen, claiming two hundred and forty arpents of land, situate in Double springs, district of Cape Girardeau; produces to the Board a notice to the recorder.

October 9, 1811: Full Board. It is the opinion of the Board that this claim ought not to be granted.

DAVID ANDREWS, claiming three hundred and fifty arpents of land, situate in the district of New Madrid; produces to the Board an order of survey from Charles D. Delassus, commandant, dated 7th February, 1798.

October 9, 1811: Present, full Board. It is the opinion of the Board that this claim ought not to be confirmed.

ROBERT BARCLAY, claiming eight hundred arpents of land, situate on the river Aux Boeufs, district of St. Louis; produces to the Board a concession from Charles D. Delassus, Lieutenant Governor, dated 6th March, 1802; a plat of survey, dated 21st January, 1804, and certified 15th February, 1804.

October 9, 1811: Present, full Board. It is the opinion of the Board that this claim ought not to be confirmed.

JOHN MULLANPHY, assignee of Louis Boisse, claiming two hundred arpents of land, situate on river Cuivre, district of St. Charles; produces to the Board a notice to the recorder.

October 9, 1811: Present, full Board. It is the opinion of the Board that this claim ought not to be confirmed.

CLAIBOURNE RHODES, assignee of James Burns, claiming three hundred arpents of land, and JAMES BURNS, claiming three hundred arpents of land, situate forty-six miles west of St. Louis; produce to the Board a concession from Charles D. Delassus, dated 10th February, 1802; a plat of survey, dated 10th February, 1804, and certified 20th March, 1804; a conveyance from Burns to Rhodes, for three hundred arpents, dated 11th October, 1784.

October 9, 1811: Present, full Board. It is the opinion of the Board that this claim ought not to be confirmed.

AMOS STODDARD, assignee of James Rankin, assignee of Hypolite Bolon, claiming four hundred arpents of land, situate on the Missouri, district of St. Charles; produces to the Board a concession from Charles D. Delassus, Lieutenant Governor, dated 17th March, 1800; a plat of survey, dated 19th March, 1801, certified 1st May, 1801; a conveyance from Bolon to Rankin, dated 5th December, 1803; from Rankin to claimant, dated 25th February, 1805.

October 10, 1811: Present, full Board. It is the opinion of the Board that this claim ought not to be confirmed.

AMOS STODDARD, assignee of James Mackay, assignee of Mordecai Bell, claiming three hundred and fifty arpents of land, situate near the town of St. Louis, district of St. Louis; produces to the Board a plat of survey, dated 21st January, 1806, certified 27th January, 1806; conveyance from Bell to Mackay, dated 29th May, 1804; from Mackay to claimant, dated 26th September, 1805.

October 10, 1811: Present, full Board. It is the opinion of the Board that this claim ought not to be confirmed.

CALVIN ADAMS, assignee of Philip Riviere, assignee of Joseph Biancour, assignee of Louis Ried, claiming three arpents of land, adjoining the town of St. Louis; produces to the Board a conveyance from Ried to ——, dated 24th May, 1788; from Riviere to Adams, dated 3d December, 1805; a plat of survey, dated 27th February, 1806, certified 28th February, 1806.

October 10, 1811: Present, full Board. It is the opinion of the Board that this claim ought not to be confirmed.

NICHOLAS BOLVIN, claiming four hundred and forty-three arpents and thirty-six perches of land, situate on Apple creek, district of St. Genevieve; produces to the Board a plat of survey, dated 23d January, 1806, certified 28th February, 1806.

October 10, 1811: Present, full Board. It is the opinion of the Board that this claim ought not to be granted.

WILLIAM BRADLEY, claiming five hundred arpents of land, situate in the district of St. Louis; produces to the Board a concession from Charles D. Delassus, Lieutenant Governor, dated March, 1801; a plat of survey, dated 22d February, 1806, and certified 27th February, 1806.

October 10, 1811: Present, full Board. It is the opinion of the Board that this claim ought not to be confirmed.

THOMAS BULL, claiming one hundred and eighty arpents twenty-seven perches of land, situate on the waters of Hubble's creek, district of Cape Girardeau; produces to the Board a plat of survey, dated 3d February, 1806, and certified 13th February, 1806.

October 10, 1811: Present, full Board. It is the opinion of the Board that this claim ought not to be granted.

JACOB BARKS, claiming seven hundred and forty-eight arpents sixty-eight perches of land, situate in the district of Cape Girardeau; produces to the Board a notice of the recorder.

October 10, 1811: Present, full Board. It is the opinion of the Board that this claim ought not to be granted.

PIERRE BARRIBEAU, claiming a lot in the town of St. Louis; produces to the Board an order of survey from Zenon Trudeau, Lieutenant Governor, dated 19th October, 1794, and a grant and declaration that he has put claimant in possession, dated 20th October, 1794.

October 18, 1811: Present, full Board. It is the opinion of the Board that this claim ought not to be confirmed.

JOSEPH BRAZEAU, claiming seven hundred and fifty-six arpents of land, situate in the district of St. Charles, on the river Antonia; produces to the Board a concession from Zenon Trudeau, Lieutenant Governor, dated 18th December, 1797; a plat of survey, dated 19th December, 1803, and certified 29th December, same year.

October 18, 1811: Present, full Board. It is the opinion of the Board that this claim ought not to be confirmed.

JOHN BURK, claiming one thousand arpents of land, situate in the district of St. Genevieve; produces to the Board a concession from Charles D. Delassus, Lieutenant Governor, dated 20th November, 1799; a plat of survey, dated 1st January, 1806, and certified February, 1806.

October 18, 1811: Present, full Board. It is the opinion of the Board that this claim ought not to be confirmed.

DAVID BROWN, claiming six hundred arpents of land, situate in the district of St. Louis; produces to the Board a plat of survey stated to have been made in pursuance of a concession from Zenon Trudeau, Lieutenant Governor; survey dated 15th November, 1797, certified 5th March, 1798.

October 18, 1811: Present, full Board. It is the opinion of the Board that this claim ought not to be confirmed.

JAMES MORRISON, assignee of Joseph Beauchamp, claiming two hundred and forty arpents of land, situate on Dardennes, district of St. Charles; produces to the Board a concession from Zenon Trudeau, Lieutenant Governor, to said Beauchamp, dated 18th June, 1796; a plat of survey, dated 1st December, 1799, certified 8th January, 1800; a transfer from Beauchamp to claimant, dated 4th September, 1805.

October 18, 1811: Present, full Board. It is the opinion of the Board that this claim ought not to be confirmed.

JOSEPH LAPIERRE, claiming sixty-one arpents five perches of land, as assignee of Francis Bernard, situate on fields of St. Charles, district of St. Charles; produces to the Board a letter of office or order of survey from Zenon Trudeau, Lieutenant Governor, dated 22d February, 1797; a plat of survey, dated 5th March, 1797, and certified 10th March, 1797; a transfer from Bernard to Lapierre, dated February 9, 1804.

October 18, 1811: Present, full Board. It is the opinion of the Board that this claim ought not to be confirmed.

FRANCIS BOURASSAS, claiming eight hundred arpents of land, situate near Merrimack, district of St. Louis; produces to the Board a concession from Charles D. Delassus, Lieutenant Governor, dated 6th December, 1799; plat of survey, dated 17th January, 1804, and certified 29th January, 1804.

October 18, 1811: Present, full Board. It is the opinion of the Board that this claim ought not to be confirmed.

LOUIS LABEAUME, assignee of Louis Boure, claiming eight hundred arpents of land, situate on Salt river, district of St. Charles; produces to the Board a concession from Charles D. Delassus, Lieutenant Governor, dated 17th October, 1799; a certified extract of a sale from Boure to claimant, made 12th March, 1803; a plat of survey, dated 4th January, and certified 5th March, 1804.

October 18, 1811: Present, full Board. It is the opinion of the Board that this claim ought not to be confirmed.

LOUIS LABEAUME, assignee of Jean Baptiste Bravier, claiming six hundred arpents of land, and said BRAVIER, claiming two hundred arpents of land, situate sixty-five miles north of St. Louis, district of St. Charles; produce to the Board a concession from Charles D. Delassus, dated 11th April, 1800; a plat of survey, dated 20th February, 1804, and certified 28th March, 1804; a transfer from Bravier to claimant, dated 12th December, 1803.

October 18, 1811: Present, full Board. It is the opinion of the Board that this claim ought not to be confirmed.

****

LOUIS LABEAUME, assignee of Francis Bernard, claiming six hundred arpents, and said BERNARD, claiming two hundred arpents of land, situate sixty-five miles north of St. Louis, district of St. Charles; produce to the Board a concession from Charles D. Delassus, Lieutenant Governor, dated 16th January, 1800; a plat of survey, dated 20th February, 1804, and certified 28th March, 1804; a transfer from Bernard to claimant, dated 10th January, 1804.

October 18, 1811: Present, full Board. It is the opinion of the Board that this claim ought not to be confirmed.

LOUIS LABEAUME, assignee of Louis Boisse, claiming eight hundred arpents of land, situate sixty-five miles north of St. Louis, district of St. Charles; produces to the Board a concession from Charles D. Delassus, Lieutenant Governor, dated January 18, 1800; plat of survey, dated 20th February, 1804, certified 28th March, 1804; a certified extract of sale made by Boisse to claimant, dated 2d November, 1803.

October 18, 1811: Present, full Board. It is the opinion of the Board that this claim ought not to be confirmed.

LOUIS LABEAUME, assignee of Antoine Bezet, claiming eight hundred arpents of land, situate sixty-five miles north of St. Louis, district of St. Charles; produces to the Board a concession from Charles D. Delassus, Lieutenant Governor, dated 13th September, 1800; a plat of survey, dated 20th February, 1804, and certified 28th March, 1804; a certified extract of sale made by Bezet to claimant, dated 7th November, 1803.

October 18, 1811: Present, full Board. It is the opinion of the Board that this claim ought not to be confirmed.

LOUIS LABEAUME, claiming eight hundred arpents of land, as assignee of Louis Lamalice, situate sixty-five miles north of St. Louis, district of St. Charles; produces to the Board a concession from Charles D. Delassus, Lieutenant Governor, dated 18th November, 1799; a plat of survey, dated 20th February, 1804, and certified 28th March, 1804; a certified extract of a sale made by Lamalice to claimant, dated 7th November, 1803.

October 18, 1811: Present, full Board. It is the opinion of the Board that this claim ought not to be confirmed.

LOUIS LABEAUME, assignee of Francis Motier, claiming six hundred arpents, and said MOTIER, claiming two hundred arpents of land, situate sixty-five miles north of St. Louis, district of St. Charles; produce to the Board a concession from Charles D. Delassus, Lieutenant Governor, dated 18th April, 1800; a plat of survey, dated 20th February, and certified 28th March, 1804; a transfer from Motier to claimant, dated 20th February, 1804.

October 18, 1811: Present, full Board. It is the opinion of the Board that this claim ought not to be confirmed.

LOUIS LABEAUME, assignee of John Drouen, claiming eight hundred arpents of land, situate sixty-five miles north of St. Louis, district of St. Charles; produces to the Board a concession from Charles D. Delassus, Lieutenant Governor, dated 5th October, 1799; a plat of survey, dated 20th February, and certified 28th March, 1804; a certified extract of sale, made by Drouen to claimant, dated 3d September, 1803.

October 18, 1811: Present, full Board. It is the opinion of the Board that this claim ought not to be confirmed.

LOUIS LABEAUME, assignee of Francisco Marichal, claiming six hundred arpents, and said MARICHAL, claiming two hundred arpents of land, situate sixty-five miles north of St. Louis; produce to the Board a concession from Charles D. Delassus, Lieutenant Governor, dated 11th April, 1799; a plat of survey, dated 20th February, and certified 28th March, 1804; a transfer from Marichal to claimant, dated 5th December, 1803.

October 18, 1811: Present, full Board. It is the opinion of the Board that this claim ought not to be confirmed.

LOUIS LABEAUME, assignee of Joseph Hubert, claiming six hundred arpents, and said HUBERT, claiming two hundred arpents of land, situate sixty-five miles north of St. Louis, district of St. Charles; produces to the Board a concession from Charles Dehault Delassus, Lieutenant Governor, dated 16th March, 1800; a plat of survey, dated 20th February, and certified 28th March, 1804; a transfer from said Hubert to claimant, dated 12th December, 1803.

October 18, 1811: Present, full Board. It is the opinion of the Board that this claim ought not to be confirmed.

LOUIS LABEAUME, assignee of Jean Louis Marc, claiming six hundred arpents, and said MARC, claiming two hundred arpents of land, situate sixty-five miles north of St. Louis; produce to the Board a concession from Charles D. Delassus, Lieutenant Governor, dated 24th January, 1800; a plat of survey, dated 20th February, and certified 28th March, 1804; a transfer from said Marc to claimant, dated 9th January, 1804.

October 9, 1811: Present, full Board. It is the opinion of the Board that this claim ought not to be confirmed.

LOUIS LABEAUME, assignee of Baptiste Marley, claiming eight hundred arpents of land, situate sixty-five miles north of St. Louis, district of St. Charles; produces to the Board a concession from Charles D. Delassus, Lieutenant Governor, dated 17th December, 1799; a plat of survey, dated 20th February, and certified 28th March, 1804; a certified extract of sale, made by Marley to claimant, dated 31st October, 1803.

October 18, 1811: Present, full Board. It is the opinion of the Board that this claim ought not to be confirmed.

LOUIS LABEAUME, assignee of Baptiste Domine, claiming six hundred arpents, and said DOMINE, claiming two hundred arpents of land, situate sixty-five miles north of St. Louis, district of St. Charles; produce to the Board a concession from Charles D. Delassus, Lieutenant Governor, dated 28th October, 1799; a plat of survey, dated 20th February, and certified 28th March, 1804; a transfer from Domine to claimant, dated 14th December, 1803.

October 18, 1811: Present, full Board. It is the opinion of the Board that this claim ought not to be confirmed.

LOUIS LABEAUME, assignee of Louis Charleville, claiming eight hundred arpents of land, situate sixty-five miles north of St. Louis, district of St. Charles; produces to the Board a concession from Charles D. Delassus, Lieutenant Governor, dated 14th November, 1799; a plat of survey, dated 20th February, and certified 28th March, 1804; a certified extract of sale, made by Charleville to claimant, dated 7th October, 1803.

October 18, 1811: Present, full Board. It is the opinion of the Board that this claim ought not to be confirmed.

154

LAND GRANTS IN MISSOURI TERRITORY - 1805 - 1812

****

LOUIS LABEAUME, assignee of Joseph Charleville, claiming eight hundred arpents of land, situate sixty-five miles from St. Louis, (north;) produces to the Board a concession from Charles D. Delassus, Lieutenant Governor, dated 16th November, 1799; a plat of survey, dated 20th February, and certified 28th March, 1804; a certified extract of sale, made by said Charleville to claimant, dated 7th October, 1803.

October 18, 1811: Present, full Board. It is the opinion of the Board that this claim ought not to be confirmed.

LOUIS LABEAUME, assignee of Joseph Presse, claiming eight hundred arpents of land, situate sixty-five miles north of St. Louis, district of St. Charles; produces to the Board a concession from Charles D. Delassus, Lieutenant Governor, dated 10th December, 1799; a plat of survey, dated 20th February, and certified 28th March, 1804; a certified extract of sale, made by said Presse to claimant, dated 4th September, 1803.

October 18, 1811: Present, full Board. It is the opinion of the Board that this claim ought not to be confirmed.

LOUIS LABEAUME, assignee of Michel Valle, claiming six hundred arpents, and said VALLE, claiming two hundred arpents of land, situate sixty-five miles north of St. Louis, district of St. Charles; produce to the Board a concession from Charles D. Delassus, Lieutenant Governor, dated 16th March, 1800; a plat of survey, dated 20th February, and certified 28th March, 1804; a transfer from said Valle to claimant, dated 20th December, 1803.

October 18, 1811: Present, full Board. It is the opinion of the Board that this claim ought not to be confirmed.

LOUIS LABEAUME, assignee of Jean Baptiste Provenchee, claiming eight hundred arpents of land, situate sixty-five miles north of St. Louis, district of St. Charles; produces to the Board a concession from Charles D. Delassus, Lieutenant Governor, dated 15th January, 1800; a plat of survey, dated 20th February, and certified 28th March, 1804; a certified extract of sale, made by Provenchee to claimant, dated 7th November, 1803.

October 18, 1811: Present, full Board. It is the opinion of the Board that this claim ought not to be confirmed.

LOUIS LABEAUME, assignee of Augustin Lefevre, claiming six hundred arpents, and said LEFEVRE, claiming two hundred arpents of land, situate sixty-five miles north of St. Louis, district of St. Charles; produce to the Board a concession from Charles D. Delassus, Lieutenant Governor, dated 11th June, 1800; a plat of survey, dated 20th February, and certified 28th March, 1804; a transfer from Lefevre to claimant, dated 5th December, 1803.

October 18, 1811: Present, full Board. It is the opinion of the Board that this claim ought not to be confirmed.

LOUIS LABEAUME, assignee of Louis Varré, claiming eight hundred arpents of land, situate sixty-five miles north of St. Louis, district of St. Charles; produces to the Board a plat of survey, dated 20th February, and certified 28th March, 1804.

October 18, 1811: Present, full Board. It is the opinion of the Board that this claim ought not to be confirmed.

LOUIS LABEAUME, assignee of John Godino, claiming eight hundred arpents of land, situate sixty-five miles north of St. Louis, district of St. Charles; produces to the Board a plat of survey, dated 20th February, and certified 28th March, 1804.

October 18, 1811: Present, full Board. It is the opinion of the Board that this claim ought not to be confirmed.

JACQUE ST. VRAIN, assignee of St. James Beauvais, claiming eight hundred arpents of land, situate sixty-five miles north of St. Louis, district of St. Charles; produces to the Board a concession from Charles D. Delassus, Lieutenant Governor, dated 23d September, 1800; a plat of survey, dated 20th February, and certified 28th March, 1804; a certified extract of sale made by said Beauvais to claimant, dated 8th July, 1804.

October 18, 1811: Present, full Board. It is the opinion of the Board that this claim ought not to be confirmed.

JACQUE ST. VRAIN, assignee of William Clark, claiming eight hundred arpents of land, situate sixty-five miles north of St. Louis; produces to the Board a concession from Charles D. Delassus, Lieutenant Governor, dated 30th October, 1800; a plat of survey, dated 20th February, and certified 28th March, 1804; a certified extract of sale made by said Clark to claimant, dated 3d December, 1803.

October 18, 1811: Present, full Board. It is the opinion of the Board that this claim ought not to be confirmed.

JACQUE ST. VRAIN, assignee of James Hoff, claiming eight hundred arpents of land, situate sixty-five miles north of St. Louis, district of St. Charles; produces to the Board a concession from Charles D. Delassus, Lieutenant Governor, dated 15th November, 1800; a plat of survey, dated 20th February, and certified 28th March, 1804; a certified extract of sale made by said Hoff to claimant, dated 3d September, 1803.

October 18, 1811: Present, full Board. It is the opinion of the Board that this claim ought not to be confirmed.

JACQUE ST. VRAIN, assignee of John Baptiste Demoulin, claiming eight hundred arpents of land, situate sixty-five miles north of St. Louis, district of St. Charles; produces to the Board a concession from Zenon Trudeau, Lieutenant Governor, dated 7th November, 1800; a plat of survey, dated 20th February and certified 28th March, 1804; a certified extract of a sale made 12th May, 1803, by Demoulin to claimant.

October 18, 1811: Present, full Board. It is the opinion of the Board that this claim ought not to be confirmed.

JACQUE ST. VRAIN, assignee of Louis Grimard, dit Carpenter, claiming eight hundred arpents of land, situate sixty-five miles north of St. Louis, district of St. Charles; produces to the Board a concession from Charles D. Delassus, Lieutenant Governor, dated 17th November, 1799; a plat of survey, dated 20th February, and certified 28th March, 1804; a certified extract of sale made by said Grimard to claimant, dated 5th August, 1803.

October 18, 1811: Present, full Board. It is the opinion of the Board that this claim ought not to be confirmed.

JACQUE ST. VRAIN, assignee of Regis. Vasseur, claiming eight hundred arpents of land, situate sixty-five miles north of St. Louis, district of St. Charles; produces to the Board a concession from Charles D. Delassus, Lieutenant Governor, dated 23d September, 1799; a plat of survey, dated 20th February, and certified 28th March, 1804; a certified extract of sale made by said Vasseur to claimant, dated 5th August, 1803.
    October 18, 1811: Present, full Board. It is the opinion of the Board that this claim ought not to be confirmed.

JACQUE ST. VRAIN, assignee of John Baptiste De Quarry, claiming eight hundred arpents of land, situate sixty-five miles north of St. Louis, district of St. Charles; produces to the Board a concession from Charles D. Delassus, Lieutenant Governor, dated 8th March, 1802; a plat of survey, dated 20th February, and certified 28th March, 1804; a certified extract of sale made by said De Quarry to claimant, dated 4th June, 1803.
    October 18, 1811: Present, full Board. It is the opinion of the Board that this claim ought not to be confirmed.

JACQUE ST. VRAIN, assignee of Dominick Huge, claiming eight hundred arpents of land, situate sixty-five miles north of St. Louis, district of St. Charles; produces to the Board a concession from Charles D. Delassus, Lieutenant Governor, dated 14th October, 1799; a plat of survey, dated 20th February, and certified 28th March, 1804; a certified extract of sale made by said Huge to claimant, dated 4th May, 1803.
    October 18, 1811: Present, full Board. It is the opinion of the Board that this claim ought not to be confirmed.
    The foregoing twenty-eight claims are found in one connected plat.

LOUIS BARRADA, claiming a lot in St. Charles village, district of St. Charles, one hundred and thirty by three hundred feet of land; produces to the Board a notice to the recorder.
    October 18, 1811: Present, full Board. It is the opinion of the Board that this claim ought not to be granted.

ASHUR BADGLEY, claiming seven hundred and forty-eight arpents, and sixty-eight perches of land, situate in Merrimack, district of St. Louis; produces to the Board a notice to the recorder.
    October 18, 1811: Present, full Board. It is the opinion of the Board that this claim ought not to be granted.

JAMES BRYANT, claiming two hundred and forty-seven arpents of land, situate in Missouri, district of St. Charles; produces to the Board a concession from Charles D. Delassus, Lieutenant Governor, dated 21st September, 1799; a plat of survey, dated 20th May, 1801, certified 1802.
    October 11, 1811: Present, full Board. It is the opinion of the Board that this claim ought not to be granted.

RUFUS EASTON, assignee of George Bowers, claiming seven hundred and forty-eight arpents and sixty-eight perches of land, situate on Elk river, district of St. Louis; produces to the Board a notice to the recorder; a transfer from Bowers to claimant, dated 22d December, 1806.
    October 18, 1811: Present, full Board. It is the opinion of the Board that this claim ought not to be granted.

RUFUS EASTON, assignee of George Bowers, claiming seven hundred and forty-eight arpents and sixty-eight perches of land, situate in Grand Glaize, district of St. Louis; produces to the Board a notice to the recorder; a transfer from Bowers to claimant, dated 22d December, 1806.
    October 18, 1811: Present, full Board. It is the opinion of the Board that this claim ought not to be granted.

MADAME DERUISSEAUX, claiming seventy-three arpents of land, situate on river Arkansas, district of Arkansas; produces to the Board a plat of survey, dated 21st February, 1806, certified 18th May, 1807.
    October 18, 1811: Present, full Board. It is the opinion of the Board that this claim ought not to be granted.

GEORGE W. CARMICHAEL and THOMAS PETERKINS, assignees of Benjamin Allen, assignee of Levy Perry, claiming six hundred arpents of land, situate on the Mississippi, district of Arkansas; produce to the Board a petition to the commandant of Arkansas, and recommendation from said commandant, dated 25th February, 1803; a plat of survey, dated 30th January, 1804, signed Henry Cassady; a transfer from Perry to Allen, dated 15th March, 1804; a transfer from Allen to claimants, dated 8th June, 1804.
    October 18, 1811: Present, full Board. It is the opinion of the Board that this claim ought not to be granted.

THOMAS PETERKINS, assignee of Henry Cassady, claiming four hundred arpents of land on Mississippi, district of Arkansas; produces to the Board a certificate from Francisco Caso y Luengo, stating that Henry Cassady had a concession for the same, dated October, 1802; certificate, dated 7th October, 1804; a plat of survey dated 27th November, 1804, signed Henry Cassady; a conveyance from Cassady to claimant, dated January 1, 1805.
    October 18, 1811: Present, full Board. It is the opinion of the Board that this claim ought not to be granted.

ASHER BROWN, claiming eight hundred arpents of land, situate on the Mississippi, district of Arkansas; produces to the Board a notice to the recorder; a plat of survey, dated 27th February, 1803, signed Henry Cassady.
    October 18, 1811: Present, full Board. It is the opinion of the Board that this claim ought not to be granted.

JOHN BARNABAS, claiming seven hundred and forty-eight arpents and sixty-eight perches of land, situate on river Cuivre, district of St. Charles; produces to the Board a notice to the recorder.
    October 18, 1811: Present, full Board. It is the opinion of the Board that this claim ought not to be granted.

HENRY BURLEY, claiming two hundred and forty arpents of land, situate on river St. Francis, district of St. Genevieve; produces to the Board a notice to the recorder.
    October 18, 1811: Present, full Board. It is the opinion of the Board that this claim ought not to be granted.

EDWARD BRADLEY, claiming five hundred arpents of land, situate on the Missouri, district of St. Louis; produces to the Board a concession from Charles Dehault Delassus, Lieutenant Governor, dated 25th June, 1800.
    October 18, 1811: Present, full Board. It is the opinion of the Board that this claim ought not to be confirmed.

TIMOTHY BELLEW, claiming four hundred arpents of land, situate on Marais des Liards, district of St. Louis; produces to the Board a petition to Zenon Trudeau, Lieutenant Governor; a reference of the same to command-

****

ant of Marais des Liards, by Zenon Trudeau, dated 13th February 1798; and a certificate from said commandant, that the granting of the same will injure no one.
    October 18, 1811: Present, full Board. It is the opinion of the Board that this claim ought not to be confirmed.

    DANIEL M. BOON, claiming four hundred arpents of land, situate on river Loutre, district of St. Charles;
produces to the Board a concession from Charles Dehault Delassus, Lieutenant Governor, dated 18th March, 1802;
a plat of survey, dated 2d February, and certified 28th March, 1804.
    October 18, 1811: Present, full Board. It is the opinion of the Board that this claim ought not to be confirmed.

    FRANCIS BITTICK, claiming one thousand three hundred and fifty arpents of land, situate on Merrimack, district
of St. Louis; produces to the Board a notice to the recorder.
    October 18, 1811: Present, full Board. It is the opinion of the Board that this claim ought not to be granted.

    JACOB BRIGHT, assignee of John Baptiste Billette, claiming two hundred and seventy-six arpents of land, situ-
ate in the district of Arkansas; produces to the Board a petition and recommendation from Caso y Luengo,
commandant, dated 17th February, 1803; a plat of survey, dated 27th February, 1806, certified 18th May, 1807; a
transfer from Billette to claimant, dated 2d May, 1805.
    October 18, 1811: Present, full Board. It is the opinion of the Board that this claim ought not to be confirmed.

    JOHN BAPTISTE BILLETTE, claiming four hundred arpents of land, situate on bayou La Glaize, district of Ar-
kansas; produces to the Board a petition and recommendation from Caso y Luengo, commandant, dated 6th
March, 1803.
    October 18, 1811: Present, full Board. It is the opinion of the Board that this claim ought not to be confirmed.

    LOUIS BILLETTE, claiming four hundred arpents of land, situate on river Anguilles, district of Arkansas; pro-
duces to the Board a petition and recommendation from Caso y Luengo, commandant, dated 1st March, 1803.
    October 18, 1811: Present, full Board. It is the opinion of the Board that this claim ought not to be confirmed.

    DAVID LINN and ISRAEL LINN, assignees of Mills Barefield, claiming seven hundred and forty-eight arpents and
sixty-eight perches of land, situate in district of Arkansas; produces to the Board a petition and recommendation
from Caso y Luengo, commandant, dated 23d March, 1803; transfer from Barefield to claimant, dated March 2,
1807.
    October 18, 1811: Present, full Board. It is the opinion of the Board that this claim ought not to be confirmed.

    JOHN BAPTISTE BOURETTE, claiming four hundred arpents of land, situate on Salt river, district of St. Charles;
produces to the Board a concession from Charles Dehault Delassus, Lieutenant Governor, dated 10th January, 1801;
plat of survey, signed Fremo Delaurier.
    October 18, 1811: Present, full Board. It is the opinion of the Board that this claim ought not to be confirmed.

    JACQUE CLAMORGAN, assignee of Joseph Bochan, claiming eight hundred arpents of land, situate on river Tuque,
district of St. Charles; produces to the Board a conveyance from Bochan to claimant, dated 21st January, 1806.
    October 18, 1811: Present, full Board. It is the opinion of the Board that this claim ought not to be granted.

    THOMAS GWIN, assignee of William Davis, assignee of Antoine Barrada, alias Bardo, claiming eight hundred
arpents of land, situate on Mississippi, district of St. Charles; produces to the Board a concession from Zenon
Trudeau, Lieutenant Governor, dated 10th August, 1797; a plat of survey, dated 4th February, and certified 20th
March, 1804; a transfer from Barada to Davis, dated 10th February, 1808, from Davis to claimant, dated 1st March,
1807.
    October 18, 1811: Present, full Board. It is the opinion of the Board that this claim ought not to be confirmed.

    RUFUS EASTON and WILLIAM RUSSELL, assignees of Ludwell Bacon, claiming one thousand arpents of land,
situate on Big Maneto creek, district of St. Charles; produce to the Board a concession from Charles D. Delassus,
Lieutenant Governor, dated 14th December, 1802; a transfer from Bacon to claimants, dated 27th April, 1807.
    October 18, 1811: Present, full Board. It is the opinion of the Board that this claim ought not to be confirmed.

    RUFUS EASTON, assignee of Joseph Bombardier, assignee of John Bole and Madame Bourdoin, claiming two
lots in Carondelet village; produces to the Board a transfer from Bombardier to claimant, dated September 5, 1807.
    October 18, 1811: Present, full Board. It is the opinion of the Board that this claim ought not to be granted.

    RUFUS EASTON, assignee of Jacob Isam, assignee of Peter Bellew, claiming seven hundred and forty-eight
arpents and sixty-eight perches of land, situate in the district of Cape Girardeau; produces to the Board a transfer
from Bellew to Isam, dated 15th August, 1804.
    October 18, 1811: Present, full Board. It is the opinion of the Board that this claim ought not to be granted.

    ALBERT TISON, assignee of Louis Labeaume, assignee of Francis M. Benoit, claiming eight hundred arpents of
land, situate at Rich Woods, district of St. Genevieve; produces to the Board a concession from Charles D. Delassus, Lieutenant Governor, dated 14th August, 1800; a plat of survey, signed John Terry, certified by Antoine
Soulard, 15th March, 1808; a transfer from Benoit to Labeaume, dated 5th March, 1805; from Labeaume to
claimant, dated 19th September, 1807.
    October 18, 1811: Present, full Board. It is the opinion of the Board that this claim ought not to be confirmed.

    JAMES BURNS, Senior, claiming eight hundred and forty arpents of land, situate on Crooked creek, district of
Cape Girardeau; produces to the Board a notice to the recorder.
    October 18, 1811: Present, full Board. It is the opinion of the Board that this claim ought not to be granted.

    SARAH BULL, claiming two hundred and twenty arpents of land, situate in the district of New Madrid; produces
to the Board a notice to the recorder.
    October 18, 1811: Present, full Board. It is the opinion of the Board that this claim ought not to be granted.

    LEMUEL CHENEY, representatives of, assignees of Simon Brundog, claiming seven hundred and forty-eight
arpents and sixty-eight perches of land, situate in the district of Cape Girardeau; produce to the Board a notice
to the recorder.
    October 18, 1811: Present, full Board. It is the opinion of the Board that this claim ought not to be granted.

LAND GRANTS IN MISSOURI TERRITORY - 1805 - 1812

157

****

ABRAHAM BYRD, claiming seven hundred and twenty arpents of land, situate in the district of New Madrid; produces to the Board an order of survey from Delassus, commandant, dated 7th July, 1798.

October 18, 1811: Present, full Board. It is the opinion of the Board that this claim ought not to be confirmed.

ISIDORE SKERRITT, assignee of Adam Bointon, claiming three hundred and twenty arpents of land, situate at Camp Esperance, district of Arkansas; produces to the Board a plat of survey, signed B. Fooy, dated 2d October, 1802; a transfer from Bointon to claimant, dated 10th September, 1804.

October 18, 1811: Present, full Board. It is the opinion of the Board that this claim ought not to be granted.

FRANCIS COTTAR, claiming eight hundred arpents of land, situate on the river De Pere, district of St. Louis; produces to the Board a concession from Charles D. Delassus, Lieutenant Governor, dated 24th September, 1799; a plat of survey, dated 25th April, 1802, certified 21st August, 1803.

October 18, 1811: Present, full Board. It is the opinion of the Board that this claim ought not to be confirmed.

THOMAS CRISPIN, claiming two hundred arpents of land, situate in the district of New Madrid; produces to the Board an order of survey from Henry Peyroux, commandant, dated 7th June, 1801, and a plat of survey of the same, dated 2d February, 1806.

October 18, 1811: Present, full Board. It is the opinion of the Board that this claim ought not to be confirmed.

JOHN MULLANPHY, assignee of Helen Tayon, widow of Louis Chevalier, claiming forty arpents of land, situate at Little Prairie, adjoining the town of St. Louis, district of St. Louis; produces to the Board a transfer from widow Tayon to claimant, dated 21st August, 1805.

October 18, 1811: Present, full Board. It is the opinion of the Board that this claim ought not to be granted.

JOHN MULLANPHY, assignee of Helen Tayon, widow of Louis Chevalier, assignee of Labassiere, assignee of Dame Hebert, claiming forty arpents of land, situate at Grand Prairie, district of St. Louis; produces to the Board a transfer from Helen Tayon, widow, dated 21st August, 1805.

October 18, 1811: Present, full Board. It is the opinion of the Board that this claim ought not to be granted.

JAMES W. COCKRAN, claiming eight hundred arpents of land, situate forty miles north of St. Louis, district of St. Charles; produces to the Board a concession from Charles D. Delassus, Lieutenant Governor, dated 5th July, 1800; a plat of survey, dated 11th February, 1804, and certified 8th March, 1804.

October 18, 1811: Present, full Board. It is the opinion of the Board that this claim ought not to be confirmed.

JOHN BYRD, assignee of Joshua Crutchelow, claiming five hundred arpents of land, situate in the district of Cape Girardeau; produces to the Board a plat of survey, dated 30th December, 1805.

October 18, 1811: Present, full Board. It is the opinion of the Board that this claim ought not to be granted.

GABRIEL CERRE, claiming four hundred arpents of land, situate on the river Merrimack, district of St. Louis; produces to the Board a concession from Charles D. Delassus, Lieutenant Governor, dated 13th August, 1799.

October 18, 1811: Present, full Board. It is the opinion of the Board that this claim ought not to be confirmed.

URI CAMPBELL and WILLIAM G. CAMPBELL, assignees of William Campbell, claiming seven hundred and forty-eight arpents and sixty-eight perches of land, situate on river Castor, district of Cape Girardeau; produce to the Board a plat of survey, dated 15th February, 1806, and certified 26th February, 1806; a deed of gift from said Campbell to claimant, dated 23d July, 1804.

October 18, 1811: Present, full Board. It is the opinion of the Board that this claim ought not to be granted.

JOHN CALDWELL, claiming six hundred arpents of land, situate on Grand Glaize, district of St. Louis; produces to the Board a plat of survey, dated 6th January, 1806, certified 20th February, 1806.

October 18, 1811: Present, full Board. It is the opinion of the Board that this claim ought not to be granted.

JONATHAN HUBELE, Sen., claiming four hundred arpents of land, situate in the district of Cape Girardeau; produces to the Board list A, on which claimant is No. 12.

November 1, 1811: Present, full Board. It is the opinion of the Board that this claim ought not to be confirmed.

WIDOW JAMES MILLS, claiming two hundred and fifty arpents of land, situate in the district of Cape Girardeau; produces to the Board list A, on which claimant is No. 15.

November 1, 1811: Present, full Board. It is the opinion of the Board that this claim ought not to be confirmed.

JOHN THOMPSON, claiming four hundred arpents of land, situate in the district of Cape Girardeau; produces to the Board list A, on which claimant is No. 20.

November 1, 1811: Present, full Board. It is the opinion of the Board that this claim ought not to be confirmed.

ISAAC KELLY, claiming three hundred arpents of land, situate in the district of Cape Girardeau; produces to the Board list A, on which claimant is No. 25.

November 1, 1811: Present, full Board. It is the opinion of the Board that this claim ought not to be confirmed.

JOHN HENTHORN, claiming two hundred and fifty arpents of land, situate in the district of Cape Girardeau; produces to the Board list A, on which claimant is No. 43.

November 1, 1811: Present, full Board. It is the opinion of the Board that this claim ought not to be confirmed.

JAMES COX, claiming three hundred arpents of land, situate in the district of Cape Girardeau; produces to the Board list A, on which claimant is No. 47.

November 1, 1811: Present, full Board. It is the opinion of the Board that this claim ought not to be confirmed.

JOHN BURROWS, claiming three hundred arpents of land, situate in the district of Cape Girardeau; produces to the Board list A, on which claimant is No. 58.

November 1, 1811: Present, full Board. It is the opinion of the Board that this claim ought not to be confirmed.

LEMUEL HARTGROVE, claiming three hundred arpents of land, situate in the district of Cape Girardeau; produces to the Board list A, on which claimant is No. 59.

November 1, 1811: Present, full Board. It is the opinion of the Board that this claim ought not to be confirmed.

PETER FRANKS, claiming two hundred and fifty arpents of land; situate in the district of Cape Girardeau; produces to the Board list A, on which claimant is No. 63.

November 1, 1811: Present, full Board. It is the opinion of the Board that this claim ought not to be confirmed.

BARTON FRANKS, claiming two hundred and fifty arpents of land situate in the district of Cape Girardeau; produces to the Board list A, on which claimant is No. 64.

November 1, 1811: Present, full Board. It is the opinion of the Board that this claim ought not to be confirmed.

JACOB SHARADIN, claiming three hundred arpents of land, situate in the district of Cape Girardeau; produces to the Board list A, on which claimant is No. 65.

November 1, 1811: Present, full Board. It is the opinion of the Board that this claim ought not to be confirmed.

JOHN SHARADIN, claiming three hundred arpents of land, situate in the district of Cape Girardeau; produces to the Board list A, on which claimant is No. 66.

November 1, 1811: Present, full Board. It is the opinion of the Board that this claim ought not to be confirmed.

ROWLAND MEREDITH, claiming two hundred and fifty arpents of land, situate in the district of Cape Girardeau; produces to the Board list A, on which claimant is No. 74.

November 1, 1811: Present, full Board. It is the opinion of the Board that this claim ought not to be confirmed.

WASHINGTON ABERNATHIE, claiming three hundred arpents of land, situate in the district of Cape Girardeau; produces to the Board list A, on which claimant is No. 76.

November 1, 1811: Present, full Board. It is the opinion of the Board that this claim ought not to be confirmed.

HUGH CONNELLY, Jun., claiming three hundred arpents of land, situate in the district of Cape Girardeau; produces to the Board list A, on which claimant is No. 77.

November 1, 1811: Present, full Board. It is the opinion of the Board that this claim ought not to be confirmed.

JONATHAN FOREMAN, Jun., claiming three hundred arpents of land, situate in the district of Cape Girardeau; produces to the Board list A, on which claimant is No. 78.

November 1, 1811: Present, full Board. It is the opinion of the Board that this claim ought not to be confirmed.

MICHAEL QUINN, claiming four hundred arpents of land, situate in the district of Cape Girardeau; produces to the Board list A, on which claimant is No. 83.

November 1, 1811: Present, full Board. It is the opinion of the Board that this claim ought not to be confirmed.

JOSEPH MAGEE, claiming four hundred arpents of land, situate in the district of Cape Girardeau; produces to the Board list A, on which claimant is No. 84.

November 1, 1811: Present, full Board. It is the opinion of the Board that this claim ought not to be confirmed.

GEORGE CAVENDER, claiming five hundred arpents of land, situate in the district of Cape Girardeau; produces to the Board list A, on which claimant is No. 93.

November 1, 1811: Present, full Board. It is the opinion of the Board that this claim ought not to be confirmed.

DANIEL GROUNT, claiming three hundred arpents of land, situate in the district of Cape Girardeau; produces to the Board list A, on which claimant is No. 96.

November 1, 1811: Present, full Board. It is the opinion of the Board that this claim ought not to be confirmed.

FREDERICK BOLLINGER, son of Philip, claiming three hundred arpents of land, situate in the district of Cape Girardeau; produces to the Board list A, on which claimant is No. 101.

November 1, 1811: Present, full Board. It is the opinion of the Board that this claim ought not to be confirmed.

DAVID BOLLINGER, son of Matthias, claiming three hundred arpents of land, situate in the district of Cape Girardeau; produces to the Board list A, on which claimant is No. 102.

November 1, 1811: Present, Full Board. It is the opinion of the Board that this claim ought not to be confirmed.

JAMES JAMES, claiming two hundred and fifty arpents of land, situate in the district of Cape Girardeau; produces to the Board list A, on which claimant is No. 112.

November 1, 1811: Present, full Board. It is the opinion of the Board that this claim ought not to be confirmed.

LAND GRANTS IN MISSOURI TERRITORY - 1805 - 1812

159

****

JOHN HENRY SMITH, claiming two hundred arpents of land, situate in the district of Cape Girardeau; produces to the Board list A, on which claimant is No. 113.
November 1, 1811: Present, full Board. It is the opinion of the Board that this claim ought not to be confirmed.

THOMAS HERRING, claiming two hundred and fifty arpents of land, situate in the district of Cape Girardeau; produces to the Board list A, on which claimant is No. 114.
November 1, 1811: Present, full Board. It is the opinion of the Board that this claim ought not to be confirmed.

JAMES DOWTY, claiming one hundred arpents of land, situate in the district of Cape Girardeau; produces to the Board list A, on which claimant is No. 130.
November 1, 1811: Present, full Board. It is the opinion of the Board that this claim ought not to be confirmed.

WILLIAM STROTHER, claiming three hundred arpents of land, situate in the district of Cape Girardeau; produces to the Board list A, on which claimant is No. 133.
November 1, 1811: Present, full Board. It is the opinion of the Board that this claim ought not to be confirmed.

JAMES RANDALL, claiming one hundred arpents of land, situate in the district of Cape Girardeau; produces to the Board list A, on which claimant is No. 134.
November 1, 1811: Present, full Board. It is the opinion of the Board that this claim ought not to be confirmed.

SAMUEL RANDALL, claiming four hundred arpents of land, situate in the district of Cape Girardeau; produces to the Board list A, on which claimant is No. 135.
November 1, 1811: Present, full Board. It is the opinion of the Board that this claim ought not to be confirmed.

MEDAD RANDALL, claiming one hundred arpents of land, situate in the district of Cape Girardeau; produces to the Board list A, on which claimant is No. 137.
November 1, 1811: Present, full Board. It is the opinion of the Board that this claim ought not to be confirmed.

JOHN LOSLA, claiming two hundred arpents of land, situate in the district of Cape Girardeau; produces to the Board list A, on which claimant is No. 138.
November 1, 1811: Present, full Board. It is the opinion of the Board that this claim ought not to be confirmed.

SIMEON KENYON, claiming one hundred arpents of land, situate in the district of Cape Girardeau; produces to the Board list A, on which claimant is No. 143.
November 1, 1811: Present, full Board. It is the opinion of the Board that this claim ought not to be confirmed.

SAMUEL STROTHER, claiming one hundred and fifty arpents of land, situate in the district of Cape Girardeau; produces to the Board list A, on which claimant is No. 144.
November 1, 1811: Present, full Board. It is the opinion of the Board that this claim ought not to be confirmed.

WILLIAM SMITH, claiming four hundred arpents of land, situate in the district of Cape Girardeau; produces to the Board list A, on which claimant is No. 145.
November 1, 1811: Present, full Board. It is the opinion of the Board that this claim ought not to be confirmed.

JEREMIAH THOMAS, claiming three hundred arpents of land, situate in the district of Cape Girardeau; produces to the Board list A, on which claimant is No. 150.
November 1, 1811: Present, full Board. It is the opinion of the Board that this claim ought not to be confirmed.

WILLIAM DOUGHERTY, claiming four hundred arpents of land, situate in the district of Cape Girardeau; produces to the Board list A, on which claimant is No. 153.
November 1, 1811: Present, full Board. It is the opinion of the Board that this claim ought not to be confirmed.

WILLIAM MURPHY, claiming two hundred arpents of land, situate in the district of Cape Girardeau; produces to the Board list A, on which claimant is No. 154.
November 1, 1811: Present, full Board. It is the opinion of the Board that this claim ought not to be confirmed.

ADAM STOTLER, claiming two hundred arpents of land, situate in the district of Cape Girardeau; produces to the Board list A, on which claimant is No. 163. (List A is dated 30th January, 1803.)
November 1, 1811: Present, full Board. It is the opinion of the Board that this claim ought not to be confirmed.

JACOB ZANOR, claiming four hundred arpents of land, situate in the district of Cape Girardeau; produces to the Board list B, on which claimant is No. 5. (List B is dated 28th July, 1804.)
November 1, 1811: Present, full Board. It is the opinion of the Board that this claim ought not to be granted.

THOMAS MORRIS, claiming five hundred arpents of land, situate in the district of Cape Girardeau; produces to the Board list B, on which claimant is No. 6.
November 1, 1811: Present, full Board. It is the opinion of the Board that this claim ought not to be granted.

CURTIS WILBORN, claiming six hundred arpents of land, situate in the district of Cape Girardeau; produces to the Board list B, on which claimant is No. 10.
November 1, 1811: Present, full Board. It is the opinion of the Board that this claim ought not to be granted.

JAMES WILBORN, claiming three hundred arpents of land, situate in the district of Cape Girardeau; produces to the Board list B, on which claimant is No. 11.
November 1, 1811: Present, full Board. It is the opinion of the Board that this claim ought not to be granted.

JOHN BALDWIN, claiming four hundred arpents of land, situate in the district of Cape Girardeau; produces to the Board list B, on which claimant is No. 12.
November 1, 1811: Present, full Board. It is the opinion of the Board that this claim ought not to be granted.

WILLIAM SMITH, JUN., claiming three hundred arpents of and, situate in the district of Cape Girardeau; produces to the Board list B, on which claimant is No. 13.
November 1, 1811: Present, full Board. It is the opinion of the Board that this claim ought not to be granted.

JAMES MAY, claiming six hundred arpents of land, situate in the district of Cape Girardeau; produces to the Board list B, on which claimant is No. 14.
November 1, 1811: Present, full Board. It is the opinion of the Board that this claim ought not to be granted.

DANIEL KRYTZ claiming, five hundred arpents of land, situate in the district of Cape Girardeau; produces to the Board list B, on which claimant is No. 26.
November 1, 1811: Present, full Board. It is the opinion of the Board that this claim ought not to be granted.

ABRAHAM KRYTZ, claiming two hundred and fifty arpents of land, situate in the district of Cape Girardeau; produces to the Board list B, on which claimant is No. 27.
November 1, 1811: Present, full Board. It is the opinion of the Board that this claim ought not to be granted.

JOHN HANG, claiming three hundred arpents of land, situate in the district of Cape Girardeau; produces to the Board list B, on which claimant is No. 29.
November 1, 1811: Present, full Board. It is the opinion of the Board that this claim ought not to be granted.

JACOB BARKS, claiming two hundred and fifty arpents of land, situate in the district of Cape Girardeau; produces to the Board list B, on which claimant is No. 36.
November 1, 1811: Present, full Board. It is the opinion of the Board that this claim ought not to be granted.

JACOB CROFT, claiming two hundred and fifty arpents of land, situate in the district of Cape Girardeau; produces to the Board list B, on which claimant is No. 37.
November 1, 1811: Present, full Board. It is the opinion of the Board that this claim ought not to be granted.

ALEXANDER BULNER, or BURTON, claiming three hundred arpents of land, situate in the district of Cape Girardeau; produces to the Board list B, on which claimant is No. 38.
November 1, 1811: Present, full Board. It is the opinion of the Board that this claim ought not to be granted.

JOSEPH McCABE, claiming two hundred and fifty arpents of land, situate in the district of Cape Girardeau; produces to the Board list B, on which claimant is No. 40.
November 1, 1811: Present, full Board. It is the opinion of the Board that this claim ought not to be granted.

JOHN SHIELDS, claiming five hundred arpents of land, situate in the district of Cape Girardeau; produces to the Board list B, on which claimant is No. 43.
November 1, 1811: Present, full Board. It is the opinion of the Board that this claim ought not to be granted.

REZIN BAILEY, claiming two hundred and fifty arpents of land, situate in the district of Cape Girardeau; produces to the Board list B, on which claimant is No. 44.
November 1, 1811: Present, full Board. It is the opinion of the Board that this claim ought not to be granted.

MOSES BYRNES, claiming three hundred arpents of land, situate in the district of Cape Girardeau; produces to the Board list B, on which claimant is No. 45.
November 1, 1811: Present, full Board. It is the opinion of the Board that this claim ought not to be granted.

MORGAN BYRNES, Sen., claiming four hundred arpents of land, situate in the district of Cape Girardeau; produces to the Board list B, on which claimant is No. 46.
November 1, 1811: Present, full Board. It is the opinion of the Board that this claim ought not to be granted.

MORGAN BYRNES, Jun., claiming three hundred arpents of land, situate in the district of Cape Girardeau; produces to the Board list B, on which claimant is No. 47.
November 1, 1811: Present full Board. It is the opinion of the Board that this claim ought not to be granted.

JOSEPH BUAL, claiming four hundred arpents of land, situate in the district of Cape Girardeau; produces to the Board list B, on which claimant is No. 58.
November 1, 1811: Present, full Board. It is the opinion of the Board that this claim ought not to be granted. Stated in said permission to have come to the country in 1804.

GABRIEL CONSTANT, fils, claiming thirty-five arpents of land, situate on Belle Point, near Carondelet, district of St. Louis; produces to the Board a concession from Zenon Trudeau, Lieutenant Governor, dated 14th September, 1795; a report of survey, dated 15th April, 1796.
November 1, 1811: Present, full Board. It is the opinion of the Board that this claim ought not to be confirmed.

LOUIS KROW, claiming nine hundred arpents of land, situate on Charles's run, district of St. Charles; produces to the Board a plat of survey, dated 20th December, 1805, certified 20th February, 1806.
November 1, 1811: Present, full Board. It is the opinion of the Board that this claim ought not to be granted.

NICHOLAS COONTZ, claiming one hundred and twenty arpents of land, situate at Marais Croche, district of St. Charles; produces to the Board a concession from Zenon Trudeau, Lieutenant Governor, dated 1st September, 1796; a plat of survey, dated 1st September, 1796.

****

November 1, 1811: Present, full Board. It is the opinion of the Board that this claim ought not to be. confirmed.

Manuel Lisa, assignee of Francis Cailloux, alias Cayon, claiming five hundred arpents of land, situate on the river Matis, district of St. Louis; produces to the Board a concession from Charles D. Delassus, Lieutenant Governor, to Francis Cailloux, for one thousand six hundred arpents of land, dated 3d January, 1800; and three plats of survey, two of four hundred arpents each, and one of four hundred and sixty arpents, dated 25th February, 1806; Francis Cayon claims one thousand one hundred arpents of the above tract.
November 1, 1811: Present, full Board. It is the opinion of the Board that this claim ought not to be confirmed.

James Mackay, assignee of John Colgin, claiming one thousand two hundred arpents of land, situate in St. Andre, district of St. Louis; produces to the Board a concession from Zenon Trudeau, Lieutenant Governor, dated 15th December, 1798, to John Colgin.
November 2, 1811: Present, full Board. It is the opinion of the Board that this claim ought not to be confirmed.

Almond Cottle, claiming eight hundred and fifty-six arpents of land, situate at Peruque, district of St. Charles; produces to the Board a notice to the recorder.
November 2, 1811: Present, full Board. It is the opinion of the Board that this claim ought not to be granted.

Joseph Chartran, Jun., claiming nine hundred and fifty arpents of land, situate in Missouri, district of St. Charles; produces to the Board a notice to the recorder.
November 2, 1811: Present, full Board. It is the opinion of the Board that this claim ought not to be granted.

Catherine Crepau, claiming a lot in the town of St. Louis, one hundred feet, by one hundred and fifty feet; produces to the Board a concession from Zenon Trudeau, Lieutenant Governor, dated 11th May: the petition is dated 8th May, 1797.
November 2, 1811: Present, full Board. It is the opinion of the Board that this claim ought not to be confirmed.

Auguste Chouteau, claiming seven thousand and fifty-six arpents of land, situate on the river St. Augustin, district of St. Charles; produces to the Board a concession from Zenon Trudeau, Lieutenant Governor, dated 8th January, 1798; a plat of survey, dated 20th December, 1803, and certified 29th December, 1803.
November 2, 1811: Present, full Board. It is the opinion of the Board that this claim ought not to be confirmed.

Aristides Auguste Chouteau, claiming seven thousand and fifty-six arpents of land, situate on the river Ramsey, district of St. Charles; produces to the Board a concession from Zenon Trudeau, Lieutenant Governor, dated 8th September, 1798; a plat of survey, dated 29th December, 1803, and certified 20th January, 1804.
November 2, 1811: Present, full Board. It is the opinion of the Board that this claim ought not to be confirmed.

Paul Chouteau, claiming two thousand arpents of land, situate in the district of St. Charles, on the river Cuivre; produces to the Board a concession from Charles D. Delassus, Lieutenant Governor, dated 9th October, 1799; a plat of survey, dated 20th February, 1804, and certified 20th March, 1804.
November 2, 1811: Present, full Board. It is the opinion of the Board that this claim ought not to be confirmed.

Cerre Chouteau, claiming two thousand arpents of land, situate on the river Cuivre, district of St. Charles; produces to the Board a concession from Charles D. Delassus, Lieutenant Governor, dated 9th October, 1799; a plat of survey, dated 20th February, 1804, and certified 20th March, 1804.
November 2, 1811: Present, full Board. It is the opinion of the Board that this claim ought not to be confirmed.

Therese Crely, wife of Louis Tison Honoré, claiming three thousand five hundred and twenty-eight arpents of land, situate on the north side of the river Jeffreon, district of St. Charles; produces to the Board a concession from Charles D. Delassus, Lieutenant Governor, dated 6th April, 1803.
November 2, 1811: Present, full Board. It is the opinion of the Board that this claim ought not to be confirmed.

John Choisser, claiming seven hundred and forty-eight arpents and sixty-eight perches of land, situate in Hopefield, district of Arkansas; produces to the Board a notice to the recorder.
November 2, 1811: Present, full Board. It is the opinion of the Board that this claim ought not to be granted.

John Choisser, assignee of John W. Hunt, assignee of William Cotton, claiming seven hundred and forty-eight arpents and sixty-eight perches of land, situate in Hopefield, district of Arkansas; produces to the Board a notice to the recorder, and a transfer from said Hunt to claimant, dated 10th October, 1801.
November 2, 1811: Present, full Board. It is the opinion of the Board that this claim ought not to be granted.

Michael Crow, claiming three hundred and fifty arpents of land, situate on the waters of the river Cuivre, district of St. Charles; produces to the Board a concession from Charles D. Delassus, Lieutenant Governor, dated 10th October, 1799; a plat of survey, dated 25th December, 1803, and certified 20th January, 1804.
November 2, 1811: Present, full Board. It is the opinion of the Board that this claim ought not to be confirmed.

Francis Collard, claiming forty arpents of land, situate near the town of St. Louis, district of St. Louis; produces to the Board a concession from Zenon Trudeau, Lieutenant Governor, dated 3d November, 1796.
November 2, 1811: Present, full Board. It is the opinion of the Board that this claim ought not to be confirmed.

****

JOHN CAROTHERS, Sen., claiming four hundred and forty arpents of land, situate in the district of Cape Girardeau; produces to the Board a notice to the recorder.
November 2, 1811: Present, full Board. It is the opinion of the Board that this claim ought not to be granted.

JOHN CAROTHERS, claiming four hundred arpents of land, situate in the district of Cape Girardeau; produces to the Board a notice to the recorder.
November 2, 1811: Present, full Board. It is the opinion of the Board that this claim ought not to be granted.

FRANCIS DUQUETTE, assignee of Charles Cardinal, claiming sixty arpents of land, situate in the district of St. Charles; produces to the Board a transfer from Cardinal to claimant, dated 28th January, 1805.
November 2, 1811: Present, full Board. It is the opinion of the Board that this claim ought not to be granted.

JOHN BAPTISTE DORVAL, dit Degrosillier, assignee of Guillaume Hebert, dit Lacompte, assignee of John Baptiste Cambas, claiming a lot in St. Louis, district of St. Louis, one hundred and twenty by one hundred and fifty feet; produces to the Board a transfer from Lacompte to claimant, dated 15th July, 1793.
November 13, 1811: Present, full Board. It is the opinion of the Board that this claim ought not to be granted.

RUFUS EASTON, assignee of Francis Lacomb, assignee of Julian Chouquette, claiming two hundred and seventy arpents of land, situate on the river des Peres, district of St. Louis; produces to the Board a notice to the recorder, and a transfer from Lacomb to claimant, dated 23d January, 1808.
November 13, 1811: Present, full Board. It is the opinion of the Board that this claim ought not to be granted.

JOHN COONTZ and EDWARD HEMPSTEAD, claiming four hundred and fifty arpents of land, situate in the district of St. Charles; produce to the Board a concession from Charles D. Delassus, Lieutenant Governor, to John Coontz, dated 29th May, 1800; a transfer of one half of said tract to Edward Hempstead, dated June 18, 1808: said transfer unauthenticated.
November 13, 1811: Present, full Board. It is the opinion of the Board that this claim ought not to be confirmed.

EDWARD HEMPSTEAD and HENRY HIGHT, assignees of the sheriff of St. Charles district, who sold the same as the property of James Cooper, assignee of Antoine Marechal, assignee of John Cook, claiming a lot in the village of St. Charles; produces to the Board a transfer from Cook to Marechal, dated 26th September, 1803; from Marechal to Cook, dated 10th September, 1805; from sheriff to claimants, dated 14th July, 1807.
November 13, 1811: Present, full Board. It is the opinion of the Board that this claim ought not to be granted.

LOUIS LEMONDE, claiming a lot on St. Louis, one hundred and twenty by three hundred feet of land; produces to the Board a notice to the recorder.
November 13, 1811: Present, full Board. It is the opinion of the Board that this claim ought not to be granted.

ALEXANDER McNAIR, assignee of Bartholomew Courtmanche, claiming a lot of land in the village of St. Charles; produces to the Board a notice to the recorder.
November 13, 1811: Present, full Board. It is the opinion of the Board that this claim ought not to be granted.

JOHN McPHERSON, assignee of John Canor, heir of Hugh Canor, deceased, claiming eight hundred arpents of land, situate on Platin creek, district of St. Louis; produces to the Board a notice to the recorder.
November 13, 1811: Present, full Board. It is the opinion of the Board that this claim ought not to be granted.

HENRY PEYROUX, claiming a lot of one arpent of land in the village of New Madrid, as assignee of Hugh McDonald Chisholm; produces to the Board a transfer from Chisholm to claimant, dated 23d June, 1798.
November 13, 1811: Present, full Board. It is the opinion of the Board that this claim ought not to be granted.

HENRY PEYROUX, assignee of Hugh McDonald Chisholm, assignee of Charles Bonneau, claiming a lot of one arpent of land, situate in the village of New Madrid, district of New Madrid; produces to the Board a transfer from Chisholm to claimant, dated 23d June 1798.
November 13, 1811: Present, full Board. It is the opinion of the Board that this claim ought not to be granted.

HENRY PEYROUX, assignee of Hugh McDonald Chisholm, assignee of Peter Duroche, claiming a lot of one arpent of land, situate in the village of New Madrid, district of New Madrid; produces to the Board a transfer from Chisholm to claimant dated 23d July, 1798.
November 13, 1811: Present, full Board. It is the opinion of the Board that this claim ought not to be granted.

HENRY PEYROUX, assignee of Hugh McDonald Chisholm, claiming one hundred and twenty arpents of land, situate on bayou St. Mary, district of New Madrid; produces to the Board a petition and recommendation from Charles D. Delassus, commandant, dated 4th July, 1797; a transfer from Chisholm to claimant dated 10th September, 1801.
November 13, 1811: Present, full Board. It is the opinion of the Board that this claim ought not to be confirmed.

SAMUEL COX, claiming two hundred and forty arpents of land, situate in the district of Cape Girardeau; produces to the Board a permission to settle, sworn to by Louis Lorrimer, dated 3d June, 1808.
November 13, 1811: Present, full Board. It is the opinion of the Board that this claim ought not to be granted.

BARBARA CALDWELL, claiming four hundred arpents of land, situate on Lake St. Mary, district of New Madrid; produces to the Board a notice to the recorder.
November 13, 1811: Present, full Board. It is the opinion of the Board that this claim ought not to be granted.

THOMAS CHAFFIN, claiming three hundred and two arpents of land, situate on waters of river Saline, district of St. Genevieve; produces to the Board a concession from Charles D. Delassus, Lieutenant Governor, dated 20th December, 1799; a plat of survey, dated 15th May, 1801.
November 13, 1811: Present, full Board. It is the opinion of the Board that this claim ought not to be confirmed.

****

JOSEPH CLAVET, claiming seven hundred and forty-eight arpents and sixty-eight perches of land, situate in the district of New Madrid; produces to the Board a notice to the recorder.
November 13, 1811: Present, full Board. It is the opinion of the Board that this claim ought not to be granted

WILLIAM MUSICK, heirs and representatives of, assignee of Rufus Easton and John Coontz, assignee of William Clark, claiming eight hundred arpents of land, situate in the district of Saint Charles; produce to the Board a certificate from Antoine Soulard, that said William Clark had a concession granted him by Zenon Trudeau, Lieutenant Governor, for eight hundred arpents of land, at the point of the Missouri, which was afterwards annulled and permission given him to choose the same quantity of any vacant land of the King's domain, said certificate dated 28th May, 1804; a transfer from Clark to Easton and Coontz, dated 8th February, 1805; from Easton and Coontz to claimant, dated 25th April, 1805.
November 13, 1811: Present, full Board. It is the opinion of the Board that this claim ought not to be confirmed.

THOMAS CRUCE, claiming three hundred and eighty arpents of land, situate in the district of New Madrid; produces to the Board a permission to settle from Henry Peyroux, commandant, dated 12th January, 1802.
November 13, 1811: Present, full Board. It is the opinion of the Board that this claim ought not to be granted.

HENRY CANOUR, claiming two hundred and fifty arpents of land, situate in the district of New Madrid; produces to the Board a permission to settle, from Henry Peyroux, commandant, dated 12th January, 1802.
November 13, 1811: Present, full Board. It is the opinion of the Board that this claim ought not to be granted.

JAMES GUIBOUR DUBRIELLE, claiming four hundred and four arpents of land, situate on the river establishment, district of St. Genevieve; produces to the Board a concession from Zenon Trudeau, Lieutenant Governor, dated 4th June, 1797; a plat of survey, dated 27th December and certified 30th December, 1799.
November 13, 1811: Present, full Board. It is the opinion of the Board that this claim ought not to be confirmed.

RUFUS EASTON, assignee of Louis Boure, assignee of Gregorie Sarpy, administrator of John Baptiste Defaux, claiming one arpent in front by thirty in depth, situate three miles southwest of St. Louis, district of St. Louis; produces to the Board a concession from Zenon Trudeau, Lieutenant Governor, dated 1st October, 1797; a plat of survey, dated 25th January, 1798, certified 5th February, 1798; a transfer from Sarpy, administrator to Boure, dated 7th February, 1802; a transfer from Boure to claimant, dated 12th February, 1805.
November 13, 1811: Present, full Board. It is the opinion of the Board that this claim ought not to be confirmed.

LOUIS BOLDUC and PARFAIL DUFOUR, Sen., claiming eight hundred arpents of land, situate on Fourche Duclos, district of St. Genevieve; produces to the Board a concession from Charles D. Delassus, Lieutenant Governor, dated 25th April, 1803.
November 13, 1811: Present, full Board. It is the opinion of the Board that this claim ought not to be confirmed.

ANTOINE DUBRIELLE, claiming ten thousand arpents of land, situate on river Aux Bœufs, district of St. Charles; produces to the Board a concession from Charles D. Delassus, Lieutenant Governor, dated 19th December, 1799; a plat of survey of one thousand arpents, dated 24th February, 1806, signed Freeman Delaurier, deputy surveyor.
November 13, 1811: Present, full Board. It is the opinion of the Board that this claim ought not to be confirmed.

SUSANNA DOGGETT, claiming one thousand one hundred and forty-six arpents and forty-one perches of land, situate on Flat river, district of St. Genevieve; produces to the Board a notice to the recorder, and a plat of survey made for Jacob Doggett, dated January 16, 1806, and certified 27th February, 1806.
November 13, 1811: Present, full Board. It is the opinion of the Board that this claim ought not to be granted.

WILLIAM DAVIS, claiming three hundred and thirty-eight arpents and seven perches of land, situate on Bellevue, district of St. Genevieve; produces to the Board a notice to the recorder; a plat of survey, dated 28th February, 1806, and certified 27th February, 1806.
November 13, 1811: Present, full Board. It is the opinion of the Board that this claim ought not to be granted.

PAUL DEJARLAIS, claiming a lot of land in St. Ferdinand village, district of St. Louis; produces to the Board a concession from Francis Dunnegant, commandant of said village, dated 26th November, 1801.
November 13, 1811: Present, full Board. It is the opinion of the Board that this claim ought not to be confirmed.

PAUL DEJARLAIS, assignee of Joseph Lacroix, claiming a lot of land, situate in the village of St. Ferdinand, district of St. Louis; produces to the Board a transfer from Lacroix to claimant, dated 11th July, 1803.
November 13, 1811: Present, full Board. It is the opinion of the Board that this claim ought not to be granted.

BAPTISTE DUCHOUQUETTE, claiming four thousand arpents of land, situate opposite the mouth of Osage river, district of St. Charles; produces to the Board a concession from Charles D. Delassus, Lieutenant Governor, dated 30th December, 1800.
November 13, 1811: Present, full Board. It is the opinion of the Board that this claim ought not to be confirmed.

ALEXANDER GRIMEAU, claiming a lot in the town St. Louis, district of St. Louis, one hundred and fifty feet by one hundred and fifty feet, as assignee of Etienne Drouin, assignee of Paul Dupuis, assignee of Gregoire Sarpy, who bought the same at a public sale of the effects of Mr. Devolsey; produces to the Board a public sale of said lot to Gregoire Sarpy, dated 17th March, 1798; a transfer from Sarpy to Dupuis, dated 23d May, 1798; a transfer from Dupuis to Etienne Drouin, dated 23d August, 1798; and a transfer from Drouin to claimant, dated 14th October, 1799.
November 13, 1811: Present, full Board. It is the opinion of the Board that this claim ought not to be granted.

MORIS JAMES, assignee of Charles Dejarlais, claiming three hundred arpents of land, situate on the Missouri, district of St. Louis; produces to the Board a record of a concession from Charles D. Delassus, Lieutenant Governor, dated 26th August, 1799; a plat of survey, dated 5th December, 1803, certified 27th December, 1803; a transfer from Dejarlais to claimant, dated 3d June, 1803.

November 13, 1811: Present, full Board. It is the opinion of the Board that this claim ought not to be confirmed.

HENRY HIGHT, assignee of Charles Dejarlais, claiming four hundred and seventy acres of land, situate on the Missouri, district of St. Louis; produces to the Board a notice to the recorder, and a transfer from Dejarlais to claimant, dated 30th December, 1805.

November 13, 1811: Present, full Board. It is the opinion of the Board that this claim ought not to be granted.

JACQUES CLAMORGAN, assignee of François Dunnegant, claiming eight hundred arpents of land, situate on the Merrimack, district of St. Louis; produces to the Board a concession from Charles D. Delassus, Lieutenant Governor, dated 17th December, 1802, for eight hundred arpents on Grand Glaize; a petition and decree of Delassus, Lieutenant Governor, therein authorizing the said Dunnegant to locate the land claimed on any vacant land, dated 7th January, 1803; a plat of survey of seven hundred and fifty arpents, dated 28th February and certified 29th February, 1806, a transfer from Dunnegant to claimant, dated 1st July, 1805.

November 13, 1811: Present, full Board. It is the opinion of the Board that this claim ought not to be confirmed.

LOUIS DELISLE, Jun., claiming eight hundred arpents of land, situate on Bon Femme, district of St. Charles; produces to the Board a concession from Charles D. Delassus, Lieutenant Governor, dated 29th November, 1799; a plat of survey, dated 23d January and certified 15th February, 1804.

November 14, 1811: Present, full Board. It is the opinion of the Board that this claim ought not to be confirmed.

PETER DELASSUS DELUZIERE, claiming one thousand arpents of land, situate on the river establishment, district of St. Genevieve; produces to the Board the record of a concession from Zenon Trudeau, Lieutenant Governor, dated 25th January, 1798; a plat of survey, dated 25th and certified 30th January, 1798.

November 14, 1811: Present, full Board. It is the opinion of the Board that this claim ought not to be confirmed.

ISRAEL DODGE, claiming seven thousand and fifty-six arpents of land, situate in the district of St. Genevieve; produces to the Board the record of a concession, from Charles D. Delassus, Lieutenant Governor, dated 11th December, 1800.

November 14, 1811: Present, full Board. It is the opinion of the Board that this claim ought not to be confirmed

LOUIS LABEAUME, assignee of Louis Delisle, claiming two thousand five hundred arpents of land, situate in the district of St. Charles; produces to the Board the record of a concession from Charles D. Delassus, Lieutenant Governor, dated 6th December, 1799; a plat of survey, dated 14th February, and certified 14th March, 1804; a certified extract of a sale, made by Delisle to claimant, dated 7th October, 1803.

November 14, 1811: Present, full Board. It is the opinion of the Board that this claim ought not to be confirmed.

ANDRE LANDREVILLE, assignee of Louis Delaurier, claiming a lot of land in St. Louis, one hundred and twenty feet front, back to the Mississippi; produces to the Board the record of a transfer from Delaurier to claimant, dated 1st August, 1793.

November 14, 1811: Present, full Board. It is the opinion of the Board that this claim ought not to be granted.

LAMBERT LAJOY, assignee of Francis Desalle, dit Cayolle, claiming a lot in the village of Carondelet, district of St. Louis, one hundred and fifty feet by three hundred feet; produces to the Board the record of a concession from Zenon Trudeau, Lieutenant Governor, to Lambert Lajoy, dated 25th June, 1795; a declaration from Zenon Trudeau, Lieutenant Governor, that he had put claimant in possession of the lot claimed, dated 27th June, 1795.

November 14, 1811: Present, full Board. It is the opinion of the Board that this claim ought not to be confirmed.

JOSEPH PRESSE, assignee of Francis Delaurier, claiming two lots in the village of St. Ferdinand, district of St. Louis, one hundred and fifty feet by three hundred feet; produces to the Board a record of a transfer from Delaurier to claimant, dated 27th January, 1803.

November 14, 1811: Present, full Board. It is the opinion of the Board that this claim ought not to be confirmed.

RUFUS EASTON, assignee of George Bowers, assignee of James Donnelly, claiming seven hundred and forty-eight arpents and sixty-eight perches of land, situate on Joachim creek, district of St. Louis; produces to the Board a notice to the recorder, and record of a transfer from Bowers to claimant, dated 22d December, 1806.

November 14, 1811: Present, full Board. It is the opinion of the Board that this claim ought not to be granted.

WILLIAM CHRISTY, assignee of Robert Young, assignee of John Doghead, claiming five hundred and fifty arpents of land, situate in the district of St. Louis; produces to the Board the record of a concession from Charles D. Delassus, Lieutenant Governor, dated 20th September, 1799; a transfer from Doghead to Young, dated 20th July, 1802; a transfer from Young to claimant, dated 21st July, 1807.

November 14, 1811: Present, full Board. It is the opinion of the Board that this claim ought not to be confirmed.

JOSEPH AND FRANCIS DERUISSEAUX, claiming four hundred arpents of land, situate on Arkansas river, district of Arkansas; produces to the Board the record of a petition and recommendation for a concession thereon by Charles D. Villemont, commandant, dated 15th July, 1794; a plat of survey, dated 18th February, 1806, signed Godfrey Jones.

November 14, 1811: Present, full Board. It is the opinion of the Board that this claim ought not to be confirmed.

****

GEORGE DUNN, claiming seven hundred and forty-eight arpents and sixty-eight perches of land, situate on Mississippi and Missouri, district of St. Charles; produces to the Board a notice to the recorder.
November 14, 1811: Present, full Board. It is the opinion of the Board that this claim ought not to be granted.

JACOB DONNER, heirs of, claiming five hundred arpents of land, situate on Platin creek, district of St. Louis; produces to the Board the record of a concession from Charles D. Delassus, Lieutenant Governor, dated 20th January, 1800.
November 14, 1811: Present, full Board. It is the opinion of the Board that this claim ought not to be confirmed.

JOSHUA DELAPLANE, claiming six hundred arpents of land, situate on the waters of the Saline, district of St. Genevieve; produces to the Board a notice to the recorder.
November 14, 1811: Present, full Board. It is the opinion of the Board that this claim ought not to be granted.

BENJAMIN DELAPLANE, claiming six hundred arpents of land, situate on the waters of the Saline, district of St. Genevieve; produces to the Board a notice to the recorder.
November 14, 1811: Present, full Board. It is the opinion of the Board that this claim ought not to be granted.

CHARLES FREMON DELORIARE, assignee of Frederick Dickson, claiming eight hundred arpents of land, situate on Salt river, district of St. Charles; produces to the Board the record of a concession from Charles D. Delassus, Lieutenant Governor, dated 5th June, 1802; a plat of survey certified by Antoine Soulard, 15th November, 1807; a certified extract of sale made by Dickson to claimant, dated 30th June, 1803.
November 14, 1811: Present, full Board. It is the opinion of the Board that this claim ought not to be confirmed.

CHARLES FREMON DELORIARE, assignee of Louis Labeaume, assignee of Francis Duchouquette, claiming four hundred arpents of land, and said DUCHOUQUETTE, claiming four hundred arpents of land, situate on Salt river, district of St. Charles; produce to the Board the record of a concession from Charles D. Delassus, Lieutenant Governor, dated 14th October, 1799; a plat of survey, signed Fremon Deloriare, deputy surveyor, dated 27th September, 1805; a transfer from Duchouquette to Labeaume, dated 7th December, 1803; a transfer from Labeaume to claimant, dated 15th July, 1806.
November 14, 1811: Present, full Board. It is the opinion of the Board that this claim ought not to be confirmed.

CHARLES FREMON DELORIARE, assignee of Albert Tison, assignee of Pierre Lord, assignee of René Dodier, claiming eight hundred arpents of land, situate on Salt river, district of St. Charles; produces to the Board a record of a concession from Charles D. Delassus, Lieutenant Governor, dated 9th April, 1800; a plat of survey, signed Fremon Deloriare, deputy surveyor, dated 27th September, 1805; a transfer from Lord to Tison, without date; a transfer from Tison to claimant, dated 25th April, 1808; a transfer from Dodier to Lord, dated 25th February, 1805.
November 14, 1811: Present, full Board. It is the opinion of the Board that this claim ought not to be confirmed.

LOUIS LABEAUME, assignee of Margaret Becquette, widow of Dodier and others, heirs of Gabriel Dodier, claiming two arpents by forty, situate on prairie adjoining the town of St. Louis, district of St. Louis; produces to the Board a concession from St. Ange and Purnas, Lieutenant Governor, dated 23d May, 1772; a record of a conveyance from said widow Dodier and others, to claimant, dated 18th August, 1806. In the margin of the concession is written, "reuni au domain du roy pour les avoir abandonnée depuis long-temps. St. Louis, Juin 4, 1793."
November 14, 1811: Present, full Board. It is the opinion of the Board that this claim ought not to be confirmed.

LOUIS LABEAUME, assignee of Margaret Becquette, widow of Dodier and others, heirs of Frances M. Motier, widow Dodier, claiming three by forty arpents of land, situate on prairie adjoining the town of St. Louis, district of St. Louis; produces to the Board a concession from St. Ange and Purnas, Lieutenant Governor, dated 23d May, 1772; a record of transfer from said widow Dodier and others to claimant, dated 18th August, 1806. In the margin of the concession is written, "reuni au domain du roy pour les avoir abandonnée depuis long-temps. St. Louis, Juin 4, 1793."
November 14, 1811: Present, full Board. It is the opinion of the Board that this claim ought not to be confirmed.

JOHN MYERS, assignee of Jacques Guiberd, assignee of Pascal Detchemendy, claiming five hundred and twenty-six arpents of land, situate on river Aux Vases, district of St. Genevieve; produces to the Board a record of a relinquishment of claim from Detchemendy to Guiberd, dated 26th January, 1800; a transfer from Guiberd to claimant, dated 26th August, 1805.
November 14, 1811: Present, full Board. It is the opinion of the Board that this claim ought not to be confirmed.

WILLIAM MORRISON, assignee of Pascal Detchemendy, claiming seven thousand and fifty-six arpents of land, situate in the district of St. Genevieve; produces to the Board a record of a concession from Charles D. Delassus, Lieutenant Governor, dated 28th December, 1799; a transfer from Detchemendy to claimant, dated 29th December, 1806.
November 14, 1811: Present, full Board. It is the opinion of the Board that this claim ought not to be confirmed.

AMABLE PARTINAIS, assignee of Parfait Dufour, claiming a lot of land in the village of Mine à Breton, district of St. Genevieve; produces to the Board a record of transfer from Dufour to claimant, dated 4th February, 1806.
November 14, 1811: Present, full Board. It is the opinion of the Board that this claim ought not to be granted.

JEREMIAH ABLE, assignee of Joseph Doubleeye, claiming seven hundred and forty-eight arpents and sixty-eight perches of land, situate on river St. François, district of Cape Girardeau; produces to the Board a notice to the recorder.
November 14, 1811: Present, full Board. It is the opinion of the Board that this claim ought not to be granted.

JOSEPH DENNIS, claiming two hundred and fifty arpents of land, situate on Big Bend of the Mississippi, district of Cape Girardeau; produces to the Board a notice to the recorder.

November 14, 1811: Present, full Board. It is the opinion of the Board that this claim ought not to be granted.

JOSEPH DOUBLEGE, claiming seven hundred and forty-eight arpents and sixty-eight perches of land, situate in the district of St. Genevieve; produces to the Board a notice to the recorder.

November 14, 1811: Present, full Board. It is the opinion of the Board that this claim ought not to be granted.

PARFAIT DUFOUR, claiming eight hundred arpents of land, situate near St. Genevieve village, district of St. Genevieve; produces to the Board a notice to the recorder.

November 14, 1811: Present, full Board. It is the opinion of the Board that this claim ought not to be granted.

PETER MENARD, assignee of Peter Dumay, claiming one thousand arpents of land, situate near Old Cape, district of Cape Girardeau; produces to the Board the record of a concession from Charles D. Delassus, Lieutenant Governor, dated 23d January, 1800; a transfer from Dumay to claimant, dated 20th May, 1806.

November 14, 1811: Present, full Board. It is the opinion of the Board that this claim ought not to be confirmed.

JOHN SMITH T., assignee of Camille Delassus, claiming one hundred and twenty arpents of land, situate on Common fields, district of St. Genevieve; produces to the Board a notice to the recorder; record of a transfer, dated 5th February, 1805, from Camille Delassus to claimant.

November 14, 1811: Present, full Board. It is the opinion of the Board that this claim ought not to be granted.

MACKAY WHERRY, assignee of the sheriff of St. Louis district, who sold the same as the property of Gregoire Sarpy, assignee of John Baptiste Dauphin, claiming four hundred arpents of land, situate on river Feefee, district of St. Louis; produces to the Board a record of a concession from Zenon Trudeau, Lieutenant Governor, to John Baptiste Dauphin, dated 28th November, 1798; a deed from sheriff to claimant, dated 29th June, 1808.

November 14, 1811: Present, full Board. It is the opinion of the Board that this claim ought not to be confirmed.

JACQUE CLAMORGAN, claiming five hundred thousand arpents of land, situate on rivers Mississippi, Dardenne, and Cuivre, district of St. Charles; produces to the Board a concession from Zenon Trudeau, Lieutenant Governor, dated 3d March, 1797; also, four letters to claimant, from Zenon Trudeau, Juan Ventura Morales, and Baron de Carondelet.

November 14, 1811: Present, full Board. It is the opinion of the Board that this claim ought not to be confirmed.

JACQUE CLAMORGAN, claiming sixty arpents front on Mississippi, Dardennes, and Chorette rivers, back to the hills, about two hundred arpents, district of St. Charles; produces to the Board the same concession and papers as in the preceding claim.

November 14, 1811: Present, full Board. It is the opinion of the Board that this claim ought not to be confirmed.

JACQUE CLAMORGAN, claiming sixty arpents of land front on the Mississippi, commencing above the mouth of Cuivre river up the Mississippi and back to the hills; produces to the Board the same concession and papers as in the foregoing claims.

November 14, 1811: Present, full Board. It is the opinion of the Board that this claim ought not to be confirmed.

ISAAC DEWAN, claiming two hundred and fifty arpents of land, situate at Tywappety, district of New Madrid; produces to the Board the record of an order of survey from Henry Peyroux, commandant, dated 22d May, 1801.

November 14, 1811: Present, full Board. It is the opinion of the Board that this claim ought not to be confirmed.

CHARLES DEMOSS, claiming two hundred and fifty arpents of land, situate at Tywappety, district of New Madrid; produces to the Board the record of an order of survey from Henry Peyroux, commandant, dated 22d May, 1801.

November 14, 1811: Present, full Board. It is the opinion of the Board that this claim ought not to be confirmed.

WILLIAM DOSS, claiming two hundred arpents of land, situate at Tywappety, district of New Madrid; produces to the Board the record of an order of survey from Henry Peyroux, commandant, dated 22d May, 1801.

November 14, 1811: Present, full Board. It is the opinion of the Board that this claim ought not to be confirmed.

JAMES DOWTY, claiming two hundred and fifty arpents of land, situate in the district of New Madrid; produces to the Board an order of survey (the record of) from Charles Delassus, commandant, dated July 7, 1798.

November 14, 1811: Present, full Board. It is the opinion of the Board that this claim ought not to be confirmed.

JOHN HAGUE, assignee of Alexander Doudle, claiming three hundred acres of land, situate on Bois Bruile, district of St. Genevieve; produces to the Board a notice to the recorder.

November 14, 1811: Present, full Board. It is the opinion of the Board that this claim ought not to be granted.

JACQUE ST. VRAIN, assignee of Eusibus Hubbard, claiming eight hundred arpents of land, situate sixty miles northwest of St. Louis, district of St. Charles; produces to the Board a record of a concession from Charles D. Delassus, Lieutenant Governor, dated 7th January, 1803; a plat of survey, dated 7th January, 1804, certified 5th March, 1804.

****

November 14, 1811: Present, full Board. It is the opinion of the Board that this claim ought not to be confirmed.

JACQUE ST. VRAIN, assignee of Felix Hubbard, claiming eight hundred arpents of land, situate sixty miles northwest of St. Louis, district of St. Charles; produces to the Board a record of a concession from Charles D. Delassus, Lieutenant Governor, dated 20th November, 1800; a plat of survey, dated 17th January, 1804, certified 5th March, 1804.
November 14, 1811: Present, full Board. It is the opinion of the Board that this claim ought not to be confirmed.

JACQUE ST. VRAIN, assignee of T. Todd, claiming eight hundred arpents of land, situate sixty miles northwest of St. Louis, district of St. Charles; produces to the Board the record of a concession from Charles D. Delassus, Lieutenant Governor, dated 15th May, 1801; a plat of survey as aforesaid.
November 14, 1811: Present, full Board. It is the opinion of the Board that this claim ought not to be confirmed.

JACQUE ST. VRAIN, assignee of Jacob Eastwood, claiming eight hundred arpents of land, situate sixty miles northwest of St. Louis, district of St. Charles; produces to the Board a record of a concession from Charles D. Delassus, Lieutenant Governor, dated 8th February, 1801; and a plat of survey as aforesaid.
November 14, 1811: Present, full Board. It is the opinion of the Board that this claim ought not to be confirmed.

JACQUE ST. VRAIN, assignee of Daniel Hubbard, claiming eight hundred arpents of land, situate sixty miles northwest of St. Louis, district of St. Charles; produces to the Board a record of a concession from Charles D. Delassus, Lieutenant Governor, dated 20th November, 1800; a plat of survey as aforesaid.
November 14, 1811: Present, full Board. It is the opinion of the Board that this claim ought not to be confirmed.
The five foregoing claims are found in one connected plat.

WILLIAM BASSETT, assignee of Ebenezer Fulsom, claiming eighty-three arpents of land, situate on Mississippi, district of Arkansas; produces to the Board a plat of survey, dated 20th January, 1803, signed Cassady; a transfer from Fulsom to claimant, dated 2d November, 1805.
November 14, 1811: Present, full Board. It is the opinion of the Board that this claim ought not to be granted. .

JOSEPH FENWICK, claiming four hundred and seventy-eight and a half arpents of land, situate on the Mississippi, district of St. Genevieve; produces to the Board a record of a plat of survey, dated 16th January, 1806, certified 26th February, 1806.
November 14, 1811: Present, full Board. It is the opinion of the Board that this claim ought not to be granted.

WILLIAM HACKER, assignee of Elijah Ford, claiming two hundred arpents of land, situate on bayou Bœuf, district of New Madrid; produces to the Board a record of a petition and recommendation for a concession from Peyroux, commandant, dated 16th June, 1801; a plat of survey, signed Joseph Story; a transfer from Ford to claimant, dated 1st December, 1805.
November 14, 1811: Present, full Board. It is the opinion of the Board that this claim ought not to be confirmed.

JACQUE ST. VRAIN, assignee of Antoine Flandrin, claiming six thousand arpents of land, situate at Grand Glaize, district of St. Louis; produces to the Board a record of a concession from Charles D. Delassus, Lieutenant Governor, dated 15th January, 1800; a plat of survey, dated 20th June, 1806, signed Fremon Deloriare.
November 14, 1811: Present, full Board. It is the opinion of the Board that this claim ought not to be confirmed.

MICHEL FORTIN, claiming eight hundred arpents of land, situate on Merrimack, district of St. Louis; produces to the Board the record of a concession from Charles D. Delassus, Lieutenant Governor, dated 9th November, 1799; a plat of survey, dated 16th January, 1804, and certified 29th January, 1804.
November 14, 1811: Present, full Board. It is the opinion of the Board that this claim ought not to be confirmed.

WILLIAM FITZGIBBONS, claiming four hundred and twenty arpents and forty-six perches of land, situate on the Bois Bruile, district of St. Genevieve; produces to the Board a plat of survey, dated 12th February and certified 26th February, 1806.
November 14, 1811: Present, full Board. It is the opinion of the Board that this claim ought not to be granted.

WALTER FENWICK, claiming one thousand arpents of land, situate on the Merrimack, district of St. Genevieve; produces to the Board a record of a concession from Zenon Trudeau, Lieutenant Governor, dated 10th June, 1797; the record of a plat of survey, dated 27th September, 1799, and certified 10th January, 1800.
November 14, 1811: Present, full Board. It is the opinion of the Board that this claim ought not to be confirmed.

GEORGE WASHINGTON MORRISON, assignee of Asa Farrow, claiming six hundred arpents of land, situate in Missouri, district of St. Louis; produces to the Board the record of a concession from Zenon Trudeau, Lieutenant Governor, dated 5th August, 1797.
November 14, 1811: Present, full Board. It is the opinion of the Board that this claim ought not to be confirmed.

GEORGE WASHINGTON MORRISON, assignee of Ebenezer Farrow, claiming six hundred arpents of land, situate in Missouri, district of St. Louis; produces to the Board the record of a concession from Zenon Trudeau, Lieutenant Governor, dated 5th August, 1797.
November 14, 1811: Present, full Board. It is the opinion of the Board that this claim ought not to be confirmed.

EMILY FOSTIN, representative of Francis Fostin, claiming one hundred and five thousand eight hundred and forty arpents of land, situate on the river Saline, district of St. Louis; produces to the Board a record of a petition to Zenon Trudeau, Lieutenant Governor, and a declaration of Zenon Trudeau thereon that the King does not grant such large tracts, but that if the petitioner will moderate his demand to a suitable quantity it shall be granted, dated 30th January, 1799.

November 14, 1811: Present, full Board. It is the opinion of the Board that this claim ought not to be confirmed.

John Smith T., assignee of Joseph Fenwick, claiming twenty thousand arpents of land, situate on the river St. Francis, district of St. Genevieve; produces to the Board the record of a concession from Zenon Trudeau, Lieutenant Governor, dated 18th August, 1796.
November 14, 1811: Present, full Board. It is the opinion of the Board that this claim ought not to be confirmed.

Walter Fenwick, claiming a lot of land in the village of St. Genevieve, district of St. Genevieve; produces to the Board the record of a concession from Francis Valle, commandant, dated 22d December, 1800.
November 14, 1811: Present, full Board. It is the opinion of the Board that this claim ought not to be confirmed.

Walter Fenwick, claiming ten thousand arpents of land, situate on the river Mine La Mott, district of St. Genevieve; produces to the Board the record of a concession from Zenon Trudeau, Lieutenant Governor, dated the 23d August, 1796.
November 14, 1811: Present, full Board. It is the opinion of the Board that this claim ought not to be confirmed.

Thomas Fenwick, claiming five hundred arpents of land, situate on Apple creek, district of St. Genevieve; produces to the Board the record of a concession from Zenon Trudeau, Lieutenant Governor, dated 10th June, 1797.
November 14, 1811: Present, full Board. It is the opinion of the Board that this claim ought not to be confirmed.

Ezekiel Fenwick, claiming five hundred arpents of land, situate on Apple creek, district of St. Genevieve; produces to the Board the record of a concession from Zenon Trudeau, Lieutenant Governor, dated 10th June, 1797.
November 14, 1811: Present, full Board. It is the opinion of the Board that this claim ought not to be confirmed.

Martin Fenwick, claiming five hundred arpents of land, situate on Apple creek, district of St. Genevieve; produces to the Board the record of a concession from Zenon Trudeau, Lieutenant Governor, dated 10th June, 1797.
November 14, 1811: Present, full Board. It is the opinion of the Board that this claim ought not to be confirmed.

James Fenwick, claiming five hundred arpents of land, situate on Apple creek, district of St. Genevieve; produces to the Board the record of a concession from Zenon Trudeau, Lieutenant Governor, dated 10th June, 1797.
November 14, 1811: Present, full Board. It is the opinion of the Board that this claim ought not to be confirmed.

Leo Fenwick, claiming five hundred arpents of land, situate on Apple creek, district of St. Genevieve; produces to the Board the record of a concession from Zenon Trudeau, Lieutenant Governor, dated 10th June, 1797.
November 14, 1811: Present, full Board. It is the opinion of the Board that this claim ought not to be confirmed.

John Ferguson, claiming seven hundred and forty-eight arpents and sixty-eight perches of land, situate at the fork of the Mississippi and Missouri rivers, district of St. Charles; produces to the Board a notice to the recorder.
November 19, 1811: Present, full Board. It is the opinion of the Board that this claim ought not to be granted.

Silas Fletcher, claiming three hundred arpents of land, situate in Tywappety, district of New Madrid; produces to the Board the record of an order of survey from Henry Peyroux, commandant, dated 22d May, 1801.
November 19, 1811: Present, full Board. It is the opinion of the Board that this claim ought not to be confirmed.

Charles Findley, claiming three hundred and twenty-five arpents of land, situate in Tywappety, district of New Madrid; produces to the Board the record of an order of survey from Henry Peyroux, commandant, dated 22d May, 1801.
November 19, 1811: Present, full Board. It is the opinion of the Board that this claim ought not to be confirmed.

Elijah Ford, claiming two hundred arpents of land, situate in Tywappety, district of New Madrid; produces to the Board the record of an order of survey from Henry Peyroux, commandant, dated 22d May, 1801.
November 14, 1811: Present, full Board. It is the opinion of the Board that this claim ought not to be confirmed.

Esther, mulattaess, assignee of Louis Guirard, claiming a lot in the town of St. Louis, district of St. Louis; produces to the Board the record of a concession from Zenon Trudeau, Lieutenant Governor, dated 14th November, 1796; record of a transfer from Guitard to claimant, dated 23d August, 1798.
November 19, 1811: Present, full Board. It is the opinion of the Board that this claim ought not to be confirmed.

Benjamin Gardiner, heirs of, claiming seven hundred and fifty arpents of land, situate on the Missouri, district of St. Charles; produces to the Board the record of a plat of survey, dated 24th and certified 28th February, 1806.
November 19, 1811: Present, full Board. It is the opinion of the Board that this claim ought not to be granted.

Albert Tison, assignee of Antoine Gaguirie, claiming one thousand eight hundred arpents of land, situate on the Missouri, district of St. Charles; produces to the Board the record of a concession from Charles D. Delassus, Lieutenant Governor, dated 12th January, 1800; record of a plat of survey, dated February, 1804, certified 28th February, 1806; record of a transfer from Gaguirie to claimant, dated 11th January, 1805.

LAND GRANTS IN MISSOURI TERRITORY - 1805 - 1812
****

169

November 19, 1811: Present, full Board. It is the opinion of the Board that this claim ought not to be confirmed.

LAMBERT LAJOY, assignee of Joseph Guenard, claiming a lot in the village of Carondelet, district of St. Louis; produces to the Board the record of a transfer from Guenard to claimant, dated 8th June, 1799.
November 19, 1811: Present, full Board. It is the opinion of the Board that this claim ought not to be granted.

GABRIEL BILDERBACK and DANIEL McMILLEN, assignees of Aaron Graham, claiming eight hundred arpents of land, situate on Lake St. Mary, district of New Madrid; produce to the Board the record of a transfer from Graham to claimants, dated 20th June, 1805.
November 19, 1811: Present, full Board. It is the opinion of the Board that this claim ought not to be granted.

AUGUSTE CHOUTEAU, assignee of Etienne Guitard, claiming eight hundred arpents of land, situate on the Mississippi, district of St. Charles; produces to the Board the record of a concession from Charles D. Delassus, Lieutenant Governor, dated 9th November, 1799; the record of a plat of survey, dated 5th February, 1804, certified 8th March, 1804; the record of a transfer from Guitard to claimant, dated 17th December, 1804.
November 19, 1811: Present, full Board. It is the opinion of the Board that this claim ought not to be confirmed.

JOHN CAMPBELL, assignee of John Griger, claiming six hundred and five and a half arpents of land, situate on the Merrimack, district of St. Louis; produces to the Board the record of a plat of survey, signed William Russell, dated 6th July, 1807; the record of a transfer from Griger to claimant, dated 20th February, 1805.
November 20, 1811: Present, full Board. It is the opinion of the Board that this claim ought not to be granted.

JACQUE GUIBORD, claiming four arpents of land, situate in the village of St. Genevieve, district of St. Genevieve; produces to the Board the record of a concession from Francis Valle, commandant, dated 15th June, 1799.
November 20, 1811: Present, full Board. It is the opinion of the Board that this claim ought not to be confirmed.

ELISHA WINTERS, claiming one million arpents of land, situate on Arkansas river, district of Arkansas; produces to the Board the following concession, in the words and figures following, to wit:

El Baron de Carondelet, Caballero de la religion de San Juan, Mariscal de Campo de los reales exercitos, Gobernador General, Vice Patrono de las provincias de la Luisiana, Florida Occidental, e Inspector de sus tropas, &a.

Deseando promover la poblacion y agricultura por todos los medios que las circunstancias politicas de estos tiempos proporcionan, y atendiendo á las proposiciones hechas al Gobierno por Elisha Winters para formar un establecimiento en el puesto de Arkansas para el cultivo de trigo, lino, y cañamo: Concedo desele luego, para que pueda verificarse al dicho Elisha Winters mil arpanes de tierra quadrados; á Guillermo Winters, quinientos quadrados; á Gabriel Winters, quinientos quadrados; y á Samuel Price, Ricardo Price, Guillermo Huble, Juan Price, Guillermo Russell, Joseph Stillwell, y Walter Carr, quince arpanes de tierra de frente, á cada uno, con la respectiva profundidad de quaronta, con respeto á los buenos informes que se me handado de su excelente conducta y buenos principios, baxo la expresa condicion deque luego que se hubieren establecido con las diligencias de apeo que el comandante del puesto dispondra se practique; se provera á cada uno el correspondiente retulo en forma, y que el establecimiento se hade formar unido, y lo mas proximo que sea posible, no admitiendo con el mas familias Americanas, que las nombradas, y las que el Gobierno permitiere; bien que el comandante podra admitir los buenos colonos que se presenten, Españoles, Franceses, Alemanes, ú Olandeses, aunque de ningun modo se admitiran vagos; pues de la inobservancia de esta clausula, se hace cargo al comandante, siempre que en el termino de un año no esten ocupadas las tierras destinadas en esta documento á las familias nombradas, es nula esta concesion, que acumplira en todas sus partes el comandante del distrito, á quien se encarga la estricta observancia de todo, asi como el buen trato y humanidad propria del Gobierno Español.

Dado el presente en la Nueva Orleans, á viente y siete de Junio de mil setecientos noventa y siete.
EL BARON DE CARONDELET.
ANDRES LOPEZ ARMESTO.

A certificate of Charles Trudeau, recorder of the city of Orleans, dated 2d March, 1808, accompanied by a plat of survey of one million arpents, said to have been found deposited in his archives, under the date of the 12th October, 1798.

A plat of survey of one million arpents, certified by Henry Cassady, 10th November, 1805, stating that said tract was surveyed in 1798, and resurveyed in part by said Cassady in 1802.

June 18, 1808. The Board met, on application of a claimant: Present, John B. C. Lucas and Clement B. Penrose. In the case of Elisha Winters and William Winters, the first claiming one million arpents of land, the latter two hundred and fifty thousand arpents, Joshua G. Clarke, agent for said Elisha and William, on his affidavit filed, moves the Board for a *dedimus* to take the deposition of Don Charles de Villemont, now said to be residing in West Florida. Motion overruled.

July 19, 1811: Present, full Board. It is the opinion of the Board that this claim ought not to be confirmed.

WILLIAM WINTERS, claiming two hundred and fifty thousand arpents of land, situate on White river, district of Arkansas; produces to the Board the above concession, in the claim of Elisha Winters; and a plat of survey, dated 28th February, 1806, certified 28th April, 1806.

Testimony taken, by Frederick Bates, commissioner, at Camp Esperance, June 28, 1808. Joseph Stillwell, sworn, says that he has no interest in this claim; (sworn in chief,) says that, in 1798, witness was on this tract of land, in the month of April; had a cabin built; and in the course of that year enclosed fifteen or twenty acres of land, and cultivated a part thereof; claimant continued to inhabit and cultivate the first improvement, and to enlarge the same, till the year 1806.

Sylvanus Phillips, sworn, says that claimant arrived at Arkansas early in March, 1798, and very soon afterwards commenced his improvements on the tract of land now claimed; and witness repeats the same facts mentioned in the foregoing testimony of Joseph Stillwell.

William Bassett, sworn, says that William Winters was in possession of this tract when witness arrived in this country, in the year 1799; had a cabin, and perhaps more than one, in that year; a considerable plantation enclosed; the number of acres not known or not recollected by witness; several acres that year in cultivation; claimant inhabited and cultivated this tract constantly from the year 1799 till 1805 or 1806.

Testimony taken, as aforesaid, at Arkansas village, July 5, 1808. Andrew Fagot, sworn, says that claimant came to the Arkansas in 1798, bringing with him a stock of cattle, to wit, a stallion, a mare, some horned cattle, and sheep; in same year claimant took possession of the lands claimed; in the month of March, built a dwelling house and several out-houses; cleared, enclosed, and cultivated about thirty acres; remained inhabiting and cultivating for five or six of the following years.

Francis Vaugine, sworn, says that Wiliam Winters arrived at Arkansas in the year 1798 or 1799; in the fall of same year (as well as witness recollects) took possession of these lands; built a dwelling house and cabins for his slaves; he also erected a cotton gin; about forty-five or perhaps fifty acres cleared, enclosed, and cultivated, in the course of a few years, after the first establishment; continued to inhabit and cultivate the premises for four or five years.

Francis Vaugine, sworn, says that Winters arrived at Arkansas in the year 1798 or 1799, and left this country in April, 1806; during this intermediate time, premises were constantly inhabited and cultivated; when claimant left this part of the country, a tenant was left by him on these premises, to wit, his brother-in-law.

June 18, 1808: Present, Lucas and Penrose, commissioners.

In the case of Elisha Winters and William Winters, the first claiming one million of arpents of land, the latter two hundred and fifty thousand arpents. Joshua G. Clarke, agent for said Elisha and William, on his affidavit filed motions to the Board for a dedimus to take the deposition of Don Charles de Villemont, now said to be residing in West Florida; motion overruled.

July 19, 1811: Present, full Board. It is the opinion of the Board that this claim ought not to be confirmed.

GABRIEL WINTERS, claiming two hundred and fifty thousand arpents of land, situate on the fork of bayou Middle, district of Arkansas; produces to the Board the foregoing concession as in the claim of Elisha Winters; a certificate of Charles Trudeau, recorder of the city of New Orleans, dated 2d March, 1808, accompanied by plat of survey of two hundred and fifty thousand arpents, said to have been found deposited in his archives, under the date of the 12th October, 1798. A plat and certificate of survey of two hundred and fifty thousand arpents, signed Henry Cassady, dated 24th November, 1802, stated to be made in pursuance of an order from Charles Trudeau.

July 19, 1811: Present, full Board. It is the opinion of the Board that this claim ought not to be confirmed.

SAMUEL PRICE, claiming six hundred arpents of land, situate in the district of Arkansas; produces to the Board the same concession as produced in the claim of Elisha Winters.

July 19, 1811: Present, full Board. It is the opinion of the Board that this claim ought not to be confirmed.

RICHARD PRICE, claiming six hundred arpents of land, situate in the district of Arkansas; produces to the Board the same concession as produced in the claim of Elisha Winters.

July 19, 1811: Present, full Board. It is the opinion of the Board that this claim ought not to be confirmed-

WILLIAM HUBBLE, claiming six hundred arpents of land, situate in the district of Arkansas; produces to the Board the same concession as produced in the claim of Elisha Winters.

July 19, 1811: Present, full Board. It is the opinion of the Board that this claim ought not to be confirmed.

JOHN PRICE, claiming six hundred arpents of land, situate in the district of Arkansas; produces to the Board the same concession as produced in the claim of Elisha Winters.

July 19, 1811: Present, full Board. It is the opinion of the Board that this claim ought not to be confirmed.

WILLIAM RUSSELL, claiming six hundred arpents of land, situate in the district of Arkansas; produces to the Board the same concession as produced in the claim of Elisha Winters.

July 19, 1811: Present, full Board. It is the opinion of the Board that this claim ought not to be confirmed.

JOSEPH STILLWELL, claiming six hundred arpents of land, situate in the district of Arkansas; produces to the Board the same concession as produced in the claim of Elisha Winters.

July 19, 1811: Present, full Board. It is the opinion of the Board that this claim ought not to be confirmed.

WALTER CARR, claiming six hundred arpents of land, situate in the district of Arkansas; produces to the Board the same concession as produced in the claim of Elisha Winters.

July 19, 1811: Present, full Board. It is the opinion of the Board that this claim ought not to be confirmed.

CHARLES GRATIOT, Jr., claiming two thousand five hundred arpents of land, situate on the Merrimack, district of St. Louis; produces to the Board the record of a concession from Charles D. Delassus, Lieutenant Governor, dated 16th December, 1802.

November 20, 1811: Present, full Board. It is the opinion of the Board that this claim ought not to be confirmed.

JOHN GREEN, claiming four hundred arpents of land, situate on the river Cuivre, district of St. Charles; produces to the Board the record of a concession from Charles D. Delassus, Lieutenant Governor, dated 19th February, 1800, the record of a plat of survey, dated 25th December, 1803, certified 20th January, 1804.

November 20, 1811: Present, full Board. It is the opinion of the Board that this claim ought not to be confirmed.

ROBERT GREEN, claiming four hundred arpents of land, situate on the river Cuivre, district of St. Charles; produces to the Board the record of a concession from Charles D. Delassus, Lieutenant Governor, dated 19th February, 1800; the record of a plat of survey, dated 23d December, 1803, and certified 20th January, 1804.

November 20, 1811: Present, full Board. It is the opinion of the Board that this claim ought not to be confirmed.

JAMES GREEN, Jr., claiming eight hundred arpents of land, situate on the river Cuivre, district of St. Charles; produces to the Board the record of a concession from Charles D. Delassus, Lieutenant Governor, dated 17th December, 1799; the record of a plat of survey, dated 24th December, 1803, certified 20th January, 1804.

November 20, 1811: Present, full Board. It is the opinion of the Board that this claim ought not to be confirmed.

JADUTHAN KENDAL, assignee of Charles Gill, claiming four hundred arpents of land, situate in the district of St. Louis; produces to the Board the record of a petition to Zenon Trudeau, Lieutenant Governor, dated 14th August, 1797, and a declaration of Antoine Soulard, that the land is not vacant; a concession from Charles D. Delassus, Lieutenant Governor, annexed to the same, dated 24th November, 1803, ordering the same quantity to be surveyed on any vacant land; also the record of a transfer from Gill to claimant, dated 21st November, 1803.

LAND GRANTS IN MISSOURI TERRITORY - 1805 - 1812

****

171

November 20, 1811: Present, full Board. It is the opinion of the Board that this claim ought not to be confirmed.

JADUTHAN KENDAL, assignee of Charles Gill, claiming four hundred arpents of land, situate on Joachim creek, district of St. Louis; produces to the Board the record of a concession from Zenon Trudeau, Lieutenant Governor, dated 15th ——, 1799; record of a transfer from Gill to claimant, dated 9th August, 1804.
November 20, 1811: Present, full Board. It is the opinion of the Board that this claim ought not to be confirmed.

ROBERT MORRISON, assignee of John Gerlaud, claiming seven hundred and forty-eight arpents sixty-eight perches of land, situate on Apple creek, district of St. Genevieve; produces to the Board a notice to the recorder.
November 20, 1811: Present, full Board. It is the opinion of the Board that this claim ought not to be granted.

ROBERT MORRISON, assignee of Matthew Gerlaud, claiming seven hundred and forty-eight arpents and sixty-eight perches of land, situate on Apple creek, district of St. Genevieve; produces to the Board a notice to the recorder.
November 20, 1811: Present, full Board. It is the opinion of the Board that this claim ought not to be granted.

ROBERT MORRISON, assignee of Morris Oath, claiming seven hundred and forty-eight arpents sixty-eight perches of land, situate on Apple creek, district of St. Genevieve; produces to the Board a notice to the recorder.
November 20, 1811: Present, full Board. It is the opinion of the Board that this claim ought not to be granted.

ROBERT MORRISON, assignee of Anaud Dunks, claiming seven hundred and forty-eight arpents sixty-eight perches of land, situate on Apple creek, district of St. Genevieve; produces to the Board a notice to the recorder.
November 20, 1811: Present, full Board. It is the opinion of the Board that this claim ought not to be granted.

HENRY PEYROUX, assignee of Hugh McDonald Chisholm, assignee of John Simon Guerin, claiming a lot of one arpent of land, in the village of New Madrid; produces to the Board the record of a concession from the Baron de Carondelet, Governor General, dated 21st November, 1796; the record of a transfer from Guerin to Chisholm, dated 23d February, 1796.
November 20, 1811: Present, full Board. It is the opinion of the Board that this claim ought not to be granted.

HENRY PEYROUX, assignee of Charles Guilbault, claiming two lots in the village of New Madrid, district of New Madrid; produces to the Board a notice to the recorder, being part of square No. 122.
November 20, 1811: Present, full Board. It is the opinion of the Board that this claim ought not to be granted.

WILLIAM RUSSELL, assignee of Charles Gill, claiming nine hundred arpents of land, situate on Sandy creek, district of St. Louis; produces to the Board the record of a transfer from Gill to claimant, dated 2d January, 1806.
November 20, 1811: Present, full Board. It is the opinion of the Board that this claim ought not to be granted.

THOMAS TYLER, assignee of John Gerrard, claiming three hundred and twenty arpents of land, situate on the Grand Glaize, district of St. Louis; produces to the Board the record of a transfer from Gerrard to claimant, dated 4th October, 1789.
November 20, 1811: Present, full Board. It is the opinion of the Board that this claim ought not to be granted.

JOHN SMITH T., assignee of Alexis Griffar, claiming sixty arpents of land, situate on the common fields of St. Genevieve, district of St. Genevieve; produces to the Board the record of a transfer from Griffar to claimant, dated 20th January, 1805.
November 20, 1811: Present, full Board. It is the opinion of the Board that this claim ought not to be granted.

JAMES PIPER, assignee of Peter Lord, assignee of Francis Giguares, claiming eight hundred arpents of land, situate on the Missouri, district of St. Charles; produces to the Board the record of a concession from Charles D. Delassus, Lieutenant Governor, dated 14th May, 1800; the record of a transfer from Giguares to Lord, dated 4th December, 1804; the record of a transfer from Lord to claimant, dated 5th December, 1804.
November 20, 1811: Present, full Board. It is the opinion of the Board that this claim ought not to be confirmed.

JOSHUA DODSON, assignee of Purnell Howard, claiming four hundred arpents of land, situate on Smith's creek, district of St. Charles; produces to the Board the record of a concession from Charles D. Delassus, Lieutenant Governor, dated 25th November, 1799; the record of a plat of survey, dated 28th March, 1804; the record of a transfer from Howard to claimant, dated 30th March, 1804.
November 20, 1811: Present, full Board. It is the opinion of the Board that this claim ought not to be confirmed.

RUFUS EASTON, assignee of Peter Hostetter, claiming three hundred arpents of land, situate in the district of New Madrid; produces to the Board the record of a permission to settle from Henry Peyroux, commandant, dated 30th March, 1802; the record of a transfer from Hostetter to claimant, dated 25th July, 1804.
November 20, 1811: Present, full Board. It is the opinion of the Board that this claim ought not to be granted.

DURRITT HUBBARD, claiming eight hundred arpents of land, situate one hundred and thirty-one miles northwest of St. Louis, district of St. Charles; produces to the Board the record of a petition to Charles D. Delassus Lieutenant Governor, dated 29th November, 1800; and a concession thereto annexed from said Delassus, Lieutenant Governor; the record of a plat of survey, dated 2d January, 1804, certified 10th February, 1804.

November 20, 1811: Present, full Board. It is the opinion of the Board that this claim ought not to be confirmed.

GILBERT HODGES, claiming four hundred arpents of land, situate on the Missouri, district of St. Louis; produces to the Board the record of a concession from Zenon Trudeau, Lieutenant Governor, dated 2d March, 1798; the record of a plat of survey, dated 21st October, 1802, certified 17th December, 1802.

November 20, 1811: Present, full Board. It is the opinion of the Board that this claim ought not to be confirmed.

JAMES HUTCHINS, claiming eight hundred and forty-five arpents seventy-eight perches of land, situate on the Mississippi, district of St. Genevieve; produces to the Board the record of a plat of survey, dated 26th January, 1806, certified 26th February, 1806.

November 20, 1811: Present, full Board. It is the opinion of the Board that this claim ought not to be granted.

DAVID HORINE, claiming seven hundred and forty-seven arpents eighty-eight perches of land, situate on Rich Woods, district of St. Genevieve; produces to the Board the record of a plat of survey, dated 12th, and certified 27th February, 1806.

November 20, 1811: Present, full Board. It is the opinion of the Board that this claim ought not to be granted.

SAMUEL HOLMES, claiming eight hundred and forty arpents of land, situate on Peruque, district of St. Charles; produces to the Board the record of a plat of survey, dated 24th February, and certified 28th February, 1806.

November 20, 1811: Present, full Board. It is the opinion of the Board that this claim ought not to be granted.

JOHN HAYS, claiming four hundred arpents of land, situate on Hottentot creek, district of Cape Girardeau; produces to the Board the record of a plat of survey, dated 5th and certified 28th February, 1806.

November 20, 1811: Present, full Board. It is the opinion of the Board that this claim ought not to be granted.

PETER HARTLE, claiming three hundred and forty-five arpents of land, situate in the district of Cape Girardeau; produces to the Board the record of a plat of survey, dated 15th January, 1806.

November 20, 1811: Present, full Board. It is the opinion of the Board that this claim ought not to be granted.

EDWARD HAWTHORN, claiming seven hundred and forty-eight arpents and sixty-eight perches of land, situate on Castor river, district of Cape Girardeau; produces to the Board the record of a plat of survey, dated 18th, and certified 26th February, 1806.

November 20, 1811: Present, full Board. It is the opinion of the Board that this claim ought not to be granted.

ROBERT HARPER, claiming nine hundred and thirty-seven arpents and five perches of land, situate in the district of Cape Girardeau; produces to the Board the record of a plat of survey, dated 19th February, 1806, and certified February, 1806.

November 20, 1811: Present, full Board. It is the opinion of the Board that this claim ought not to be granted.

WILLIAM SPURGIN, assignee of Purnell Howard, claiming eight hundred and fifty arpents of land, situate in Femme Osage, district of St. Charles; produces to the Board the record of a plat of survey, dated 20th and certified 27th February, 1806; the record of a transfer from Howard to claimant, dated 26th November, 1805.

November 20, 1811: Present, full Board. It is the opinion of the Board that this claim ought not to be granted.

THOMAS HOWARD, claiming seven hundred and fifty arpents of land, situate in Camp Esperance, district of Arkansas; produces to the Board the record of a plat of survey, dated 8th January, 1806, certified April 28, 1806.

November 20, 1811: Present, full Board. It is the opinion of the Board that this claim ought not to be granted.

GEORGE WASHINGTON MORRISON, assignee of Andrew Harris, claiming six hundred arpents of land, situate in Grand Glaize, district of St. Louis; produces to the Board the record of a concession from Charles D. Delassus, Lieutenant Governor, dated 7th June, 1803; the record of a plat of survey, dated 20th February, 1804, signed Mackay.

November 20, 1811: Present, full Board. It is the opinion of the Board that this claim ought not to be confirmed.

JAMES MACKAY, assignee of John Long, assignee of John Henry, claiming nine hundred arpents of land, situate on river Bonne Femme, district of St. Charles; produces to the Board the record of a concession from Zenon Trudeau, Lieutenant Governor, dated 7th February, 1798; the record of a transfer from Henry to Long, dated June, 1801; the record of a transfer from Long to claimant, dated 8th February, 1805.

November 20, 1811: Present, full Board. It is the opinion of the Board that this claim ought not to be confirmed.

JAMES MACKAY, assignee of John Long, assignee of William Hartley, claiming six hundred and fifty arpents of land, situate in Missouri, district of St. Louis; produces to the Board the record of a concession from Charles D. Delassus, Lieutenant Governor, dated 14th January, 1800; the record of a transfer from Hartley to Long, dated 10th February, 1801; the record of a transfer from Long to claimant, dated 8th February, 1805.

November, 1811: Present, full Board. It is the opinion of the Board that this claim ought not to be confirmed.

JOHN HARVEY, claiming seven hundred and forty-eight arpents and sixty-eight perches of land, situate in the district of Cape Girardeau; produces to the Board a notice to the recorder.

November 20, 1811: Present, full Board. It is the opinion of the Board that this claim ought not to be granted.

PURNELL HOWARD, claiming seven hundred and forty-eight arpents and sixty-eight perches of land, situate in the forks of the Mississippi and Missouri, district of St. Charles; produces to the Board a notice to the recorder.

November 20, 1811: Present, full Board. It is the opinion of the Board that this claim ought not to be granted.

HENRY PEYROUX, assignee of Manuel Dias, assignee of Joseph Bernardo, assignee of Francis Hamelin, claiming one arpent, a lot, in the village of New Madrid, district of New Madrid; produces to the Board the record of a concession from Estevan Mirot, Governor General, dated 15th July, 1791; the record of a declaration of Portell, commandant, that Joseph Bernardo had proved to him that a deed was to have passed from said Hamelin to said Bernardo; in consequence, said commandant grants a mortgage on said property, dated 30th August, 1794; the record of a transfer from Bernardo to Dias, dated 15th August, 1795; the record of a permission from Dias to claimant, dated 16th June, 1800.

November 20, 1811: Present, full Board. It is the opinion of the Board that this claim ought not to be confirmed.

ELIJAH SMITH, assignee of Joseph Whitehouse, assignee of Manuel Lisa, assignee of Francis Chatulon, alias Godin, assignee of Hyacinth Hamelin, claiming a lot in the town of St. Louis, sixty feet by one hundred and twenty feet; produces to the Board the record of a transfer from Hamelin to Chatulon, dated 30th July, 1805; the record of a transfer from Lisa to Whitehouse, dated 6th November, 1806; the record of a transfer from Whitehouse to claimant, dated 20th October, 1807.

November 20, 1811: Present, full Board. It is the opinion of the Board that this claim ought not to be granted.

JEREMIAH ABLE, assignee of Ezekiel Able, assignee of Joseph Waller, assignee of Peter Franks, assignee of Benjamin Hartgrove, claiming seven hundred and forty-eight arpents and sixty-eight perches of land, situate in the district of Cape Girardeau; produces to the Board a notice to the recorder.

November 20, 1811: Present, full Board. It is the opinion of the Board that this claim ought not to be granted.

JOHN CULBERTSON, assignee of Absolom Hacker, claiming two hundred arpents of land, situate on the Pemiscon, district of New Madrid; produces to the Board a notice to the recorder.

November 20, 1811: Present, full Board. It is the opinion of the Board that this claim ought not to be granted.

JOHN HORINE, claiming six hundred arpents of land, situate in the district of St. Genevieve; produces to the Board a notice to the recorder.

November 20, 1811: Present, full Board. It is the opinion of the Board that this claim ought not to be granted.

JOHN HAGUE, claiming seven hundred and forty-eight arpents and sixty-eight perches of land, situate on Big river, district of St. Genevieve; produces to the Board a notice to the recorder.

November 20, 1811: Present, full Board. It is the opinion of the Board that this claim ought not to be granted.

JARRAD JAMES, claiming seven hundred and forty-eight arpents sixty-eight perches of land, situate in the district of St. Genevieve; produces to the Board the record of a plat of survey, dated 17th February, and certified 27th February, 1806.

November 20, 1811: Present, full Board. It is the opinion of the Board that this claim ought not to be granted.

LOUIS JONES, claiming four hundred and sixty-five arpents of land, situate in the district of St. Charles; produces to the Board the record of a plat of survey, dated 18th and certified 28th February, 1806.

November 20, 1811: Present, full Board. It is the opinion of the Board that this claim ought not to be granted.

JOHN NICHOLASSHUN, assignee of Malachi Jones, claiming seven hundred and ninety acres of land, situate in Tywappety, district of Cape Girardeau; produces to the Board the record of a permission to settle from Henry Peyroux, commandant, dated 12th January, 1802; the record of a plat of survey, dated 28th February, 1806, and certified 27th February, 1806; the record of a transfer from Jones to claimant, dated 4th October, 1803.

November 20, 1811: Present, full Board. It is the opinion of the Board that this claim ought not to be granted.

WILLIAM JAMISON, claiming eight hundred arpents of land, situate on the Mississippi, district of St. Charles; produces to the Board the record of a concession from Charles D. Delassus, Lieutenant Governor, dated 10th January, 1800; the record of a plat of survey, dated 4th January and certified 5th March, 1804.

November 20, 1811: Present, full Board. It is the opinion of the Board that this claim ought not to be confirmed.

ANTOINE JANIS, claiming one hundred and sixty arpents of land, situate in Dardennes, district of St. Charles; produces to the Board the record of a concession from Zenon Trudeau, Lieutenant Governor, dated 18th November, 1796; the record of a plat of survey, dated 15th December, 1799, and certified 8th January, 1800.

November 20, 1811: Present, full Board. It is the opinion of the Board that this claim ought not to be confirmed.

FRANCIS JANIS and BAPTISTE JANIS, assignee of Antoine Janis, assignee of Nicolas Janis, claiming a remnant of land, situate between the common field and river Gaborie, district of St. Genevieve; produces to the Board the record of a relinquishment of title from Nicolas Janis to Antoine Janis, dated 30th March, 1790; the record of a duly registered approval by Henry Peyroux, commandant, dated 3d April, 1790; the record of a transfer from Antoine Janis to Francis and Baptiste Janis, dated 21st August, 1801.

November 20, 1811: Present, full Board. It is the opinion of the Board that this claim ought not to be confirmed.

IRA COTTLE and DANIEL JOHNSTON, claiming seven hundred and forty-eight arpents sixty-eight perches of land, situate in Peruque, district of St. Charles; produces to the Board a notice to the recorder.

November 20, 1811: Present, full Board. It is the opinion of the Board that this claim ought not to be granted.

CHARLES FREMON DELORIARE, assignee of John Baptiste Jeffre, claiming eight hundred arpents of land, situate on Salt river, district of St. Charles; produces to the Board the record of a concession from Charles D. Delassus, Lieutenant Governor, dated 9th October, 1800; the record of a plat of survey, certified by A. Soulard, 15th November, 1807; the record of a certified extract of sale made by Jeffre to claimant, dated 10th May, 1805.

November 20, 1811: Present, full Board. It is the opinion of the Board that this claim ought not to be confirmed.

LOUIS LABEAUME, assignee of Peter Lord, assignee of Louis Zequares, claiming eight hundred arpents of land, situate in Rich Woods, district of St. Genevieve; produces to the Board the record of a concession from Charles D. Delassus, Lieutenant Governor, dated 13th June, 1800; the record of a plat of survey, certified by Soulard, 15th March, 1808; the record of a transfer from Zequares to Lord, dated 12th January, 1805; record of a transfer from Lord to claimant, dated 18th July, 1806.

November 20, 1811: Present, full Board. It is the opinion of the Board that this claim ought not to be confirmed.

THOMAS TYLER, assignee of Thomas Jones, claiming one thousand arpents of land, situate at Grand Glaize, district of St. Louis; produces to the Board a notice to the recorder, and the record of a transfer from Jones to claimant, dated 7th April, 1789.

November 20, 1811: Present, full Board. It is the opinion of the Board that this claim ought not to be granted.

JOSEPH TUCKER, assignee of Elensley Jones, claiming seven hundred and forty-eight arpents sixty-eight perches of land, situate in the district of St. Genevieve; produces to the Board a notice to the recorder.

November 20, 1811: Present, full Board. It is the opinion of the Board that this claim ought not to be granted.

MALACHI JONES, claiming two hundred and eighty arpents of land, situate in the district of New Madrid; produces to the Board the record of a permission to settle from Henry Peyroux, commandant, dated 12th January, 1802.

November 20, 1811: Present, full Board. It is the opinion of the Board that this claim ought not to be granted.

MALACHI JONES, Sen., claiming two hundred arpents of land, situate in the district of New Madrid; produces to the Board the record of a permission to settle from Henry Peyroux, commandant, dated 12th January, 1802.

November 20, 1811: Present, full Board. It is the opinion of the Board that this claim ought not to be granted.

CALEB JONES, claiming one hundred and eighty arpents of land, situate in the district of New Madrid; produces to the Board the record of a permission to settle from Henry Peyroux, commandant, dated 12th January, 1802.

November 20, 1811: Present, full Board. It is the opinion of the Board that this claim ought not to be granted.

PATRICK FILER, claiming three hundred arpents of land, situate in the district of New Madrid; produces to the Board the record of a permission to settle from Henry Peyroux, commandant, dated 12th January, 1802.

November 20, 1811: Present, full Board. It is the opinion of the Board that this claim ought not to be granted.

JAMES MACKAY, assignee of John Long, assignee of Andre Kincaid, claiming six hundred arpents of land, situate in the district of St. Charles, on river Teuque; produces to the Board the record of a concession from Charles D. Delassus, Lieutenant Governor, dated 28th January, 1800; the record of a transfer from Kincaid to Long, dated 4th February, 1802; record of a transfer from Long to claimant, dated 8th February, 1805.

November 20, 1811: Present, full Board. It is the opinion of the Board that this claim ought not to be confirmed.

PETER CHOUTEAU, heir of Paul Gregoire Kiercerau, claiming three by forty arpents of land, situate on the prairie adjoining the town of St. Louis, district of St. Louis; produces to the Board a concession from St. Ange and Purnas, Lieutenant Governor, dated 23d May, 1772. In the margin of the concession is written "reuni au domain du roy, pour les avoir abandonnée depuis long-temps. 4 Juin, 1793. Trudeau."

November 20, 1811: Present, full Board. It is the opinion of the Board that this claim ought not to be confirmed.

PETER CHOUTEAU, assignee of Mary Kiercerau, representative of Rene Kiercerau, claiming sixty arpents of land, situate on Prairie Lajoy, district of St. Louis; produces to the Board the record of a concession from St. Ange and Purnas, Lieutenant Governor, dated 23d May, 1772; in the margin of the concession is written "reuni au domain du roy, pour les avoir abandonnée depuis long-temps. 4 Juin, 1793. Trudeau;" record of transfer from Mary, widow of Antoine de Hêtre, to claimant, dated 19th May, 1808.

November 20, 1811: Present, full Board. It is the opinion of the Board that this claim ought not to be confirmed.

JOSEPH KEFFER, claiming one thousand arpents of land, situate on the Merrimack, district of St. Louis; produces to the Board a notice to the recorder.

November 20, 1811: Present, full Board. It is the opinion of the Board that this claim ought not to be granted.

JACQUE CHAUVIN, assignee of Charles Tayon, assignee of Paul Gregoire Kiercerau, claiming a lot in St. Louis, district of St. Louis, one hundred and twenty by one hundred and fifty feet; produces to the Board the record of a certificate of public sale from Charles Tayon, as guardian of the children of Kiercerau, dated 5th December, 1779.

November 20, 1811: Present, full Board. It is the opinion of the Board that this claim ought not to be granted.

ABSALOM KINNERSON, claiming six hundred and forty arpents of land, situate on Brois Bruile, district of St. Genevieve; produces to the Board a notice to the recorder.

November 20, 1811: Present, full Board. It is the opinion of the Board that this claim ought not to be granted.

LEVIN MASTERS, claiming two hundred arpents of land, situate in the district of New Madrid; produces to the Board the record of a permission from Henry Peyroux, commandant, dated 3d March, 1802.

November 23, 1811: Present, full Board. It is the opinion of the Board that this claim ought not to be granted.

JOHN BAPTISTE BELLAND, assignee, by public sale, of the estate of John P. Roy, alias Lapense, claiming forty arpents of land, situate in the district of St. Louis; produces to the Board the record of a receipt for purchase money from Prieur, administrator of the estate, dated July 6, 1804.

November 23, 1811: Present, full Board. It is the opinion of the Board that this claim ought not to be granted.

CALVIN ADAMS, assignee of Celeste Lalande, wife of Joseph Deplacie, attorney for John Baptiste Lalande, claiming a lot in the town of St. Louis, district of St. Louis; produces to the Board the record of a transfer from Celeste Lalande to claimant, dated 14th November, 1801.

November 23, 1811: Present, full Board. It is the opinion of the Board that this claim ought not to be granted.

AUGUSTE CHOUTEAU, assignee of Regis Loisel, claiming a lot one hundred and twenty feet front, running back to the Mississippi, situate in the town of St. Louis, district of St. Louis; produces to the Board the record of a certificate of public sale of the effects of Regis Loisel to claimant, dated 7th July, 1805.

November 23, 1811: Present, full Board. It is the opinion of the Board that this claim ought not to be granted.

PHILIP FINE, assignee of John Laiboud, claiming one hundred and fifty by two hundred and seventy feet of land, situate in the village à Robert, district of St. Louis; produces to the Board the record of a transfer from Laiboud to claimant, dated 5th February, 1795.

November 23, 1811: Present, full Board. It is the opinion of the Board that this claim ought not to be granted.

MARY LABASTIE, a free negro woman, assignee of Joseph Lewis, assignee of Louis Reed, assignee of Joseph Labuseure, assignee of William Biset, claiming two hundred and forty by three hundred feet of land, situate in the town of St. Louis, district of St. Louis; produces to the Board the record of a transfer from Labuseure to Reed, dated 2d June, 1781.

November 23, 1811: Present, full Board. It is the opinion of the Board that this claim ought not to be granted.

JAMES LEWIS, claiming nine hundred arpents of land, situate on river Cuivre, district of St. Charles; produces to the Board the record of a plat of survey, dated 3d and certified 14th February, 1806.

November 23, 1811: Present, full Board. It is the opinion of the Board that this claim ought not to be granted.

ANTOINE LAMARCHE, claiming seven hundred and fifty arpents of land, situate on Lamarche's creek, district of St. Charles; produces to the Board the record of a plat of survey, dated 20th December, 1805, and certified 27th February, 1806.

November 23, 1811: Present, full Board. It is the opinion of the Board that this claim ought not to be granted.

ABSALOM LINK, claiming five hundred and ten arpents of land, situate on White-oak run, district of St. Louis; produces to the Board the record of a plat of survey, dated 21st November, 1805, and certified 25th January, 1806.

November 23, 1811: Present, full Board. It is the opinion of the Board that this claim ought not to be granted.

JOHN LOGAN, heirs of, claiming four hundred and ninety-one arpents seventy-five and a half perches of land, situate in the district of St. Genevieve; produce to the Board the record of a plat of survey, dated 18th December, 1805, countersigned by Antoine Soulard.

November 23, 1811: Present, full Board. It is the opinion of the Board that this claim ought not to be granted.

JOHN LONG, claiming ten thousand arpents of land, situate on rivers Dubois and St. John, district of St. Louis; produces to the Board the record of a concession from Zenon Trudeau, Lieutenant Governor, dated 1st September, 1797; the record of a plat of survey, on river St. John, for five thousand arpents, dated 20th January and certified 27th February, 1806; the record of a plat of survey, on river Dubois, for five thousand and fifty arpents, dated 21st March, 1805, and certified 27th February, 1806.

November 23, 1811: Present, full Board. It is the opinion of the Board that this claim ought not to be confirmed.

FRANCIS BOUTHILLIER, assignee of Francis Lesieur, claiming three thousand arpents of land, situate on the Mississippi, district of St. Charles; produces to the Board the record of a concession from Charles D. Delassus, Lieutenant Governor, dated 14th January, 1802; the record of a plat of survey, dated 27th December, 1803, certified 20th January, 1804; the record of a transfer from Lesieur to claimant, dated 14th January, 1803.

November 23, 1811: Present, full Board. It is the opinion of the Board that this claim ought not to be confirmed.

EDWARD HEMPSTEAD, assignee of the sheriff of St. Charles district, who sold the same as the property of John Campbell and White Matlock, assignee of Louis Labeaume, assignee of Pierre Lord, claiming eight hundred arpents of land, on bay du Roy, district of St. Charles; produces to the Board the record of a concession from Charles D. Delassus, Lieutenant Governor, dated 9th December, 1799; the record of a plat of survey, dated 8th February, and certified 15th April, 1803; the record of a transfer from Labeaume to Campbell and Matlock, dated 20th April, 1805; the record of a transfer from the sheriff of St. Charles district to claimant, dated 29th June, 1808.

November 23, 1811: Present, full Board. It is the opinion of the Board that this claim ought not to be confirmed.

JOHN CAMPBELL, assignee of Philip Fine, assignee of Sylvester Labadie, claiming a lot in the town of St. Louis, district of St. Louis, one hundred and twenty by one hundred and fifty feet; produces to the Board the record of a plat of survey, dated and certified 27th February, 1806.

November 23, 1811: Present, full Board. It is the opinion of the Board that this claim ought not to be granted.

ST. PAUL LACROIX, claiming one thousand six hundred arpents of land, situate on the Mississippi, district of St. Charles; produces to the Board the record of a concession from Charles D. Delassus, Lieutenant Governor, dated 15th December, 1799; the record of a plat of survey, dated 1st January and certified 10th February, 1804.

November 23, 1811: Present, full Board. It is the opinion of the Board that this claim ought not to be confirmed.

ANDREW LALANDE, claiming one hundred and twenty arpents of land, situate on river Aux Vases, district of St. Genevieve; produces to the Board the record of a concession from Zenon Trudeau, Lieutenant Governor, dated 20th February, 1798; the record of a plat of survey, dated 5th May and certified 10th September, 1799.

November 23, 1811: Present full Board. It is the opinion of the Board that this claim ought not to be confirmed.

PELAGIE CHOUTEAU, veuve Labadie, claiming one hundred and twenty arpents of land, situate in Dardennes, district of St. Charles; produces to the Board the record of a concession from Charles D. Delassus, Lieutenant Governor, dated 8th December, 1802; the record of a plat of survey, dated 25th November, and certified 22d December, 1803.

November 25, 1811: Present, full Board. It is the opinion of the Board that this claim ought not to be confirmed.

WIDOW LECLERC, assignee of Charles Fremon Deloriare, claiming four hundred and two arpents of land, situate on the Mississippi, district of St. Genevieve; produces to the Board the record of a concession from Charles D. Delassus, Lieutenant Governor, dated 10th December, 1799; the record of a plat of survey, dated 21st and certified 26th February, 1806.

November 25, 1811: Present, full Board. It is the opinion of the Board that this claim ought not to be confirmed.

MARIE PHILIP LEDUC, assignee of Auguste Leclerc, claiming one hundred and twenty by three hundred feet, and AUGUSTE LECLERC, claiming one hundred and twenty by three hundred feet of land, in the town of St. Louis, district of St. Louis; produces to the Board a plat of survey and a concession thereon from Zenon Trudeau, Lieutenant Governor, dated 17th May, 1796; the record of a transfer from Elias Leclerc to Leduc, dated 14th August, 1802.

November 25, 1811: Present, full Board. It is the opinion of the Board that this claim ought not to be confirmed.

PETER LASHAWAY, claiming nine hundred arpents of land, situate on the Merrimack, district of St. Louis; produces to the Board the record of a plat of survey, dated 26th and certified 28th February, 1806.

November 25, 1811: Present, full Board. It is the opinion of the Board that this claim ought not to be granted.

JACQUE ST. VRAIN, assignee of ___ riel Lord, claiming three hundred and sixty arpents of land, situate on Spanish Ponds, district of St. Louis; produces to the Board the record of a concession from Charles D. Delassus, Lieutenant Governor, dated 12th July, 1800; the record of a plat of survey, dated 3d December, 1803, and certified 23d August, 1803.

November 25, 1811: Present, full Board. It is the opinion of the Board that this claim ought not to be confirmed.

WILLIAM LONG, claiming four hundred arpents of land, situate in the district of St. Louis; produces to the Board the record of a concession from Charles D. Delassus, Lieutenant Governor, dated 10th October, 1799.

November 25, 1811: Present, full Board. It is the opinion of the Board that this claim ought not to be confirmed.

DANIEL LITTLEJOHN, claiming twelve hundred arpents of land, situate on waters of Lick branch, district of St. Charles; produces a notice to the recorder.

November 25, 1811: Present, full Board. It is the opinion of the Board that this claim ought not to be granted.

FRANCIS LESIEUR, claiming four hundred arpents of land, situate on the portage des Sioux, district of St. Charles; produces to the Board the record of a concession from Zenon Trudeau, Lieutenant Governor, dated 13th April, 1799.

November 25, 1811: Present, full Board. It is the opinion of the Board that this claim ought not to be confirmed.

PIERRE CHOUTEAU, assignee of Joseph Laprisse, claiming sixty by two hundred and fifty feet of land, situate in the town of St. Louis, district of St. Louis; produces to the Board the record of a transfer from Laprisse to claimant, dated 12th May, 1808.

November 25, 1811: Present, full Board. It is the opinion of the Board that this claim ought not to be granted.

CHARLES FREMON DELORIARE, assignee of Joseph P. La Marche, claiming eight hundred arpents of land, situate on Salt river, district of St. Charles; produces to the Board the record of a concession from Charles D. Delassus, Lieutenant Governor, dated 10th February, 1800; the record of a plat of survey, dated 15th November, 1807, signed Soulard; record of a transfer from La Marche to claimant, dated 25th May, 1805.

November 25, 1811; Present, full Board. It is the opinion of the Board that this claim ought not to be confirmed.

SILVESTER LABADIE, claiming one hundred arpents of land, by such quantity as may be found opposite from the upper to the lower end of the island Bœuf, in the Missouri, district of St. Louis; produces to the Board the record of a concession from Charles D. Delassus, Lieutenant Governor, dated 19th December, 1800.
November 25, 1811: Present, full Board. It is the opinion of the Board that this claim ought not to be confirmed.

LEVIS LUCAS, claiming seven hundred and forty-eight arpents sixty-eight perches of land, situate on the forks of the Missouri and Mississippi, district of St. Charles; produces to the Board a notice to the recorder.
November 25, 1811: Present, full Board. It is the opinion of the Board that this claim ought not to be granted.

MANUEL LISA, assignee of John Baptiste Lorins, claiming a lot in St. Louis, district of St. Louis, three hundred feet in depth, front not stated; produces to the Board the record of a transfer from Lorins to claimant, dated 11th July, 1799.
November 25, 1811: Present, full Board. It is the opinion of the Board that this claim ought not to be granted.

WILLIAM LAUGHRY, claiming four hundred and fifty arpents of land, situate on Indian creek, district of St. Genevieve; produces to the Board the record of a concession from Charles D. Delassus, Lieutenant Governor, dated 19th March, 1802.
November 25, 1811: Present, full Board. It is the opinion of the Board that this claim ought not to be confirmed.

BAPTISTE LORINS, claiming four hundred and eighty arpents of land, situate on the Portage des Sioux, district of St. Charles; produces to the Board the record of a concession from Zenon Trudeau, Lieutenant Governor, dated 14th December, 1796.
November 25, 1811: Present, full Board. It is the opinion of the Board that this claim ought not to be confirmed.

HENRY LAUGHON, Sen., claiming seven hundred and forty-eight arpents sixty-eight perches of land, situate on the Mississippi, district of St. Charles; produces to the Board a notice to the recorder.
November 25, 1811: Present, full Board. It is the opinion of the Board that this claim ought not to be granted.

HENRY LAUGHON, Jun., claiming seven hundred and forty-eight arpents sixty-eight perches of land, situate on the Mississippi, district of St. Charles; produces to the Board a notice to the recorder.
November 25, 1811: Present, full Board. It is the opinion of the Board that this claim ought not to be granted.

LOUIS SELF, claiming five hundred arpents of land, situate on Big river, district of St. Genevieve; produces to the Board the record of a plat of survey, dated 21st June, 1808, signed John Steward.
November 25, 1811: Present, full Board. It is the opinion of the Board that this claim ought not to be granted.

CHARLES LOGAN, claiming seven hundred and forty-eight arpents sixty-eight perches of land, situate in the district of Cape Girardeau; produces to the Board a permission to settle; sworn to by Louis Lorrimer.
November 25, 1811. Present, full Board. It is the opinion of the Board that this claim ought not to be granted.

MILTON LEWIS, claiming three hundred and fifty-two arpents of land, situate on Dardennes, district of St. Charles; produces to the Board the record of a concession from Charles D. Delassus, Lieutenant Governor, dated 15th February, 1800; the record of a plat of survey, dated 9th February, 1804, and certified 20th March, 1804.
November 25, 1811: Present, full Board. It is the opinion of the Board that this claim ought not to be confirmed.

ADRIAN LANGLOIS claiming fifteen hundred arpents of land, situate in the district of St. Genevieve; produces to the Board a notice to the recorder. The concession stated in said record is not found on record.
November 25, 1811: Present, full Board. It is the opinion of the Board that this claim ought not to be confirmed.

ROBERT LANE, claiming three hundred arpents of land, situate on the Mississippi, district of Cape Girardeau; produces to the Board the record of an order of survey from Henry Peyroux, commandant, dated 22d May, 1811.
November 25, 1811: Present, full Board. It is the opinion of the Board that this claim ought not to be confirmed.

BENJAMIN LAUGHERTY, claiming two hundred arpents of land, situate on the Mississippi, district of Cape Girardeau; produces to the Board a record of an order of survey from Henry Peyroux, commandant, dated 22d May, 1801.
November 25, 1811: Present, full Board. It is the opinion of the Board that this claim ought not to be confirmed.

EDMUND HOGAN, assignee of Alexander Mellikin, claiming two hundred and forty arpents of land, situate on the Mississippi, district of Cape Girardeau; produces to the Board the record of a concession from Zenon Trudeau, Lieutenant Governor, dated 5th January, 1798; the record of a plat of survey dated 8th December, 1799, and certified 5th January, 1800.
November 25, 1811: Present, full Board. It is the opinion of the Board that this claim ought not to be confirmed.

JOURDAIN, assignee of John Francis Mishau, claiming one thousand two hundred arpents of land, situate on the Mississippi, district of St. Charles; produces to the Board the record of a concession from Charles D. Delassus, Lieutenant Governor, dated 2d March, 1802; the record of a plat of survey, dated 10th January, and certified 15th February, 1804.
November 25, 1811: Present, full Board. It is the opinion of the Board that this claim ought not to be confirmed.

John Mullanphy, assignee of Francis Motier, claiming two hundred arpents of land, situate in the district of St. Charles; produces to the Board a notice to the recorder.
November 25, 1811: Present, full Board. It is the opinion of the Board that this claim ought not to be granted.

Didier Marchand, claiming eight hundred arpents of land, situate on the Mississippi, district of St. Louis; produces to the Board the record of a concession from Charles D. Delassus, Lieutenant Governor, dated 8th September, 1802; the record of a plat of survey, dated 16th and certified 29th December, 1803.
November 25, 1811: Present, full Board. It is the opinion of the Board that this claim ought not to be confirmed.

Peter Martin, claiming eight hundred arpents of land, situate on the Mississippi, district of St. Louis; produces to the Board the record of a certificate from Antoine Soulard, stating that he had made a survey by virtue of a concession from Charles D. Delassus, Lieutenant Governor, dated 30th January, 1800, said certificate dated 12th October, 1805; a plat of survey, dated 19th February and certified 8th March, 1804.
November 25, 1811: Present, full Board. It is the opinion of the Board that this claim ought not to be confirmed.

Edward Matthews, claiming seven hundred and fifty arpents of land, situate in the district of New Madrid; produces to the Board the record of a plat of survey, dated 19th December, 1805, and certified 27th February, 1806.
November 25, 1811: Present, full Board. It is the opinion of the Board that this claim ought not to be granted.

John Byrd, assignee of Jacob Myers, and Kessiah Myers, claiming five hundred acres of land, situate in the district of Cape Girardeau; produces to the Board the record of a transfer from Jacob and Kessiah Myers, dated 12th April, 1802.
November 25, 1811: Present, full Board. It is the opinion of the Board that this claim ought not to be granted.

John Baptiste Belland, assignee of Jean Louis Marc, claiming eighty arpents of land, situate on the Missouri, district of St. Louis; produces to the Board the record of a transfer from Marc to claimant, dated 6th October, 1803.
November 25, 1811: Present, full Board. It is the opinion of the Board that this claim ought not to be granted.

John Baptiste Moreau, claiming two hundred and forty arpents of land, situate near the village of St. Genevieve, district of St. Genevieve; produces to the Board the record of a concession from Zenon Trudeau, Lieutenant Governor, dated 16th November, 1797; the record of a plat of survey, dated 9th December, 1797, and certified 1st January, 1798.
November 25, 1811: Present, full Board. It is the opinion of the Board that this claim ought not to be confirmed.

Widow Baptiste Marly, assignee of Hubert Tabeau, claiming a lot of land, in the town of St. Louis, district of St. Louis, one hundred and twenty by one hundred and fifty feet; produces to the Board the record of a transfer from Tabeau to Marly, dated 21st August, 1786.
November 25, 1811: Present, full Board. It is the opinion of the Board that this claim ought not to be granted.

Matthew Mullins, claiming seven hundred and forty-five arpents sixty-eight perches of land, situate on Bellevue, district of St. Genevieve; produces to the Board the record of a plat of survey, dated 5th January, and certified 25th February, 1806.
November 25, 1811: Present, full Board. It is the opinion of the Board that this claim ought not to be granted.

Charles McLane, claiming seven hundred and forty-five arpents sixty-eight perches of land, situate on Bellevue, district of St. Genevieve; produces to the Board the record of a plat of survey, dated 15th and certified 28th February, 1806.
November 25, 1811: Present, full Board. It is the opinion of the Board that this claim ought not to be granted.

James Michew, claiming six hundred arpents of land, situate in the district of St. Charles; produces to the Board the record of a plat of survey, dated 15th January and certified 28th February, 1806.
November 25, 1811: Present, full Board. It is the opinion of the Board that this claim ought not to be granted.

Charles McDermit, claiming seven hundred and forty-eight arpents sixty-eight perches of land, situate in the district of St. Genevieve; produces to the Board the record of a plat of survey, certified 18th February, 1806.
November 25, 1811: Present, full Board. It is the opinion of the Board that this claim ought not to be granted.

James Mitchell, claiming six hundred and forty arpents of land, situate on the Missouri, district of St. Charles, produces to the Board the record of a plat of survey, dated 20th and certified 25th February, 1806.
November 27, 1811: Present, full Board. It is the opinion of the Board that this claim ought not to be granted.

William Masters, claiming six hundred and fifty arpents of land, situate in the district of New Madrid; produces to the Board the record of a plat of survey, dated 8th and certified 28th February, 1806.
November 27, 1811: Present, full Board. It is the opinion of the Board that this claim ought not to be granted.

Abner Masters, claiming five hundred and fifty arpents of land, situate in the district of New Madrid; produces to the Board the record of a plat of survey, dated 8th and certified 28th February, 1806.
November 27, 1811: Present, full Board. It is the opinion of the Board that this claim ought not to be granted.

LAND GRANTS IN MISSOURI TERRITORY - 1805 - 1812

179

****

EDWARD HEMPSTEAD, assignee of the sheriff of St. Charles district, who sold the same as the property of John Campbell and White Matlock, assignees of Jacques St. Vrain, assignee of Baptiste Marion, claiming six hundred arpents, and said MARION claiming two hundred arpents of land, situate in the district of St. Charles; produce to the Board the record of a concession from Charles D. Delassus, Lieutenant Governor, dated 21st————, 1800; the record of a plat of survey dated 28th March, 1804, certified 9th January, 1806; the record of a transfer from Marion to St. Vrain, dated 10th January, 1804; the record of a transfer from St. Vrain to Campbell and Matlock, dated 29th August, 1805; the record of a transfer from sheriff to claimant, dated 29th June, 1800.

November 27, 1811: Present, full Board. It is the opinion of the Board that this claim ought not to be confirmed.

LOUIS LABEAUME, assignee of Charles Mainvill, claiming six hundred arpents of land, and said MAINVILL claiming two hundred arpents of land, situate on Salt river, district of St. Charles; produce to the Board the record of a concession from Charles D. Delassus, Lieutenant Governor, dated 18th November, 1799; the record of a plat of survey, dated the 4th January and certified 5th March, 1804; the record of a transfer from Mainvill to claimant, dated 9th December, 1803.

November 27, 1811: Present, full Board. It is the opinion of the Board that this claim ought not to be confirmed.

GEORGE WASHINGTON MORRISON, assignee of William Morrison, claiming seven hundred and fifty arpents of land, situate in the district of St. Charles; produces to the Board the record of a concession from Charles D. Delassus, Lieutenant Governor, dated 9th June, 1803.

November 27, 1811: Present, full Board. It is the opinion of the Board that this claim ought not to be confirmed.

GEORGE WASHINGTON MORRISON, assignee of William Morrison, claiming eight hundred arpents of land, situate in the district of St. Charles; produces to the Board the record of a concession from Charles D. Delassus, Lieutenant Governor, dated 15th January, 1803.

November 27, 1811: Present, full Board. It is the opinion of the Board that this claim ought not to be confirmed.

GEORGE WASHINGTON MORRISON, claiming four hundred arpents of land, situate on lake Creve Cœur, district of St. Louis; produces to the Board the record of a concession from Charles D. Delassus, Lieutenant Governor, dated 8th June, 1803.

November 27, 1811: Present, full Board. It is the opinion of the Board that this claim ought not to be confirmed.

RUFUS EASTON, assignee of Michael Masterson, claiming four hundred arpents of land, situate on the river Mattest, district of St. Louis; produces to the Board the record of a concession from Zenon Trudeau, Lieutenant Governor, dated 23d September, 1799; the record of a transfer from Masterson to claimant, dated 5th March, 1805.

November 27, 1811: Present, full Board. It is the opinion of the Board that this claim ought not to be confirmed.

DAVID MIRACLE, claiming four hundred arpents of land, situate on the Missouri, district of St. Charles; produces to the Board a notice to the recorder.

November 27, 1811: Present, full Board. It is the opinion of the Board that this claim ought not to be granted.

THOMAS MARES, claiming seven hundred and forty-eight arpents sixty-eight perches of land, situate on the river Merrimack, district of St. Louis; produces a notice to the recorder. Rufus Easton, produces the record of a transfer from Mares, dated 14th September, 1807, for one-half of this claim.

November 27, 1811: Present, full Board. It is the opinion of the Board that this claim ought not to be granted.

ANTOINE VINCENT BOUIS, assignee of Louis Boure, assignee of Joseph Mainville, claiming a lot of land in the town of St. Louis, district of St. Louis, one hundred and twenty by one hundred and fifty feet; produces to the Board the record of an exchange of property between Boure and claimant, dated 23d June, 1795.

November 27, 1811: Present, full Board. It is the opinion of the Board that this claim ought not to be granted.

ANTOINE VINCENT BOUIS, assignee of Francis Laberge, assignee of Joseph Morin, claiming forty arpents of land, situate on Barriere Desnoyer, district of St. Louis; produces to the Board the record of a transfer from Laberge to claimant, dated 23d March, 1805.

November 27, 1811: Present, full Board. It is the opinion of the Board that this claim ought not to be granted.

HENRY COOK, heir of McCormack, claiming one thousand arpents of land, situate on Mill creek, district of St. Louis; produces to the Board a notice to the recorder.

November 27, 1811: Present, full Board. It is the opinion of the Board that this claim ought not to be granted.

CHARLES FREMON DELORIARE, assignee of Joseph Marie, claiming eight hundred arpents of land, situate on Salt river, district of St. Charles; produces to the Board the record of a concession from Charles D. Delassus, Lieutenant Governor, dated January 10, 1801; the record of a certified extract of sale, made by Marie to claimant, dated 1st March, 1804.

November 27, 1811: Present, full Board. It is the opinion of the Board that this claim ought not to be confirmed.

RUFUS EASTON, assignee of Jacob Isam, assignee of David McMoultrie, claiming seven hundred and forty-eight arpents sixty-eight perches of land, situate on Byrd's creek, district of Cape Girardeau; produces to the Board the record of a transfer from McMoultrie to Isam, dated 25th July, 1804.

November 27, 1811: Present, full Board. It is the opinion of the Board that this claim ought not to be granted.

RUFUS EASTON, assignee of Jacob Isam, assignee of Jacob Myers, claiming seven hundred and forty-eight arpents sixty-eight perches of land, situate in the district of Cape Girardeau; produces to the Board the record of a transfer from Myers to Isam, dated 15th March, 1804.

****

November 27, 1811: Present full Board. It is the opinion of the Board that this claim ought not to be granted.

Louis Labeaume, assignee of Baptiste Pacquette, assignee of Joseph Morin, claiming one hundred and sixty arpents of land, situate on White Ox Prairie, district of St. Louis; produces to the Board the record of a concession from Zenon Trudeau, Lieutenant Governor, dated 9th September, 1797; the record of a plat of survey, certified 20th February, 1806; the record of a transfer from Morin to Pacquette, dated 8th May, 1804; the record of a transfer from Pacquette to claimant, dated 8th May, 1804.
November 27, 1811: Present, full Board. It is the opinion of the Board that this claim ought not to be confirmed.

Joseph Marie, claiming one thousand six hundred arpents of land, situate seventy-four miles north of St. Louis, district of St. Charles; produces to the Board the record of a concession from Charles D. Delassus, Lieutenant Governor, dated 3d January, 1800; the record of a plat of survey, dated 19th February and certified 8th March, 1804.
November 27, 1811: Present, full Board. It is the opinion of the Board that this claim ought not to be confirmed.

Manuel Gonzales Moro, claiming seven thousand and fifty-six arpents of land, situate on the river Cuivre, district of St. Charles; produces to the Board the record of a concession from Charles D. Delassus, Lieutenant Governor, dated 16th September, 1799.
November 27, 1811: Present, full Board. It is the opinion of the Board that this claim ought not to be confirmed.

James McCulloch, claiming seven hundred and forty-eight arpents sixty-eight perches, situate on Negro fcrk, district of St. Louis; produces to the Board a notice to the recorder.
November 27, 1811: Present, full Board. It is the opinion of the Board that this claim ought not to be granted.

Abraham Musick, claiming six hundred arpents of land, situate on Creve Cœur, district of St. Louis; produces to the Board a notice to the recorder.
November 27, 1811: Present, full Board. It is the opinion of the Board that this claim ought not to be granted.

John Myers, claiming five hundred arpents of land, situate on the waters of St. Ferdinand, district of St. Louis; produces to the Board the record of a concession from Charles D. Delassus, Lieutenant Governor, dated December 18, 1802.
November 27, 1811: Present, full Board. It is the opinion of the Board that this claim ought not to be confirmed.

Uel Musick, claiming three hundred and fifty arpents of land, situate on Feefee's creek, district of St. Louis; produces to the Board the record of a concession from Charles D. Delassus, Lieutenant Governor, dated 14th January, 1800.
November 27, 1811: Present, full Board. It is the opinion of the Board that this claim ought not to be confirmed.

Henry Peyroux, assignee of Peter Menard, assignee of Joseph Vandenbenden, claiming two arpents of land, lot No. 120, in the village of New Madrid; produces to the Board the record of a transfer from Adrian Langlois, agent of Peter Menard, to claimant, dated 2d May, 1804.
November 27, 1811: Present, full Board. It is the opinion of the Board that this claim ought not to be granted.

Henry Peyroux, assignee of Major, claiming one arpent of land, situate in the village of New Madrid, district of New Madrid; produces to the Board a notice to the recorder.
November 27, 1811: Present, full Board. It is the opinion of the Board that this claim ought not to be granted.

Charles Sanguinett, assignee of Hyacinth St. Cyr, assignee of John Baptiste Martigny, claiming four hundred and eighty arpents of land, situate on the Mississippi, district of St. Louis; produces to the Board a notice to the recorder.
November 27, 1811: Present, full Board. It is the opinion of the Board that this claim ought not to be confirmed.

William Murphy, claiming five hundred and fifty arpents of land, situate in the district of New Madrid; produces to the Board the record of an order of survey from Delassus, commandant, dated 7th July, 1798.
November 27, 1811: Present, full Board. It is the opinion of the Board that this claim ought not to be confirmed.

Peter Menard, assignee of Alexis Morris, claiming four hundred arpents of land, situate in the district of St. Genevieve; produces to the Board a notice to the recorder.
November 27, 1811: Present, full Board. It is the opinion of the Board that this claim ought not to be confirmed.

William Moss, claiming three hundred and fifty acres of land, situate in the district of St. Louis; produces to the Board a notice to the recorder.
November 27, 1811: Present, full Board. It is the opinion of the Board that this claim ought not to be granted.

George Hays, assignee of Norris Monday, claiming seven hundred and forty-eight arpents sixty-eight perches of land, situate in the district of Cape Girardeau; produces to the Board a notice to the recorder; the record of a transfer from Monday to claimant, dated 2d November, 1802.
November 27, 1811: Present, full Board. It is the opinion of the Board that this claim ought not to be granted.

JEREMIAH ABLE, assignee of Ezekiel Able, assignee of William Hared, claiming seven hundred and forty-eight arpents sixty-eight perches of land, situate in the district of Cape Girardeau; produces to the Board a notice to the recorder.

November 27, 1811: Present, full Board. It is the opinion of the Board that this claim ought not to be granted.

JEREMIAH ABLE, assignee of Ezekiel Able, claiming seven hundred and forty-eight arpents sixty-eight perches of land, situate in the district of Cape Girardeau; produces to the Board a notice to the recorder.

November 27, 1811: Present, full Board. It is the opinion of the Board that this claim ought not to be granted.

JACOB MYERS, claiming three hundred and fifty arpents of land, situate in the district of New Madrid; produces to the Board the record of an order of survey from Henry Peyroux, commandant, dated 22d May, 1801.

November 27, 1811: Present, full Board. It is the opinion of the Board that this claim ought not to be confirmed.

REESE MEREDITH, assignee of James Mettz, claiming one hundred and fifty acres of land, situate in the district of Cape Girardeau; produces to the Board a notice to the recorder; and an obligation from Mettz to claimant to convey him said land, dated 21st March, 1801.

November 27, 1811: Present, full Board. It is the opinion of the Board that this claim ought not to be granted.

WILLIAM MASTERS, claiming three hundred arpents of land, situate at Tywappety, district of New Madrid; produces to the Board the record of a permission to settle from Henry Peyroux, commandant, dated 12th January, 1802.

November 27, 1811: Present, full Board. It is the opinion of the Board that this claim ought not to be granted.

JOHN MASTERS, claiming three hundred arpents of land, situate at Tywappety, district of New Madrid; produces to the Board the record of a permission to settle from Henry Peyroux, commandant, dated 12th August, 1802.

November 27, 1811: Present, full Board. It is the opinion of the Board that this claim ought not to be granted.

JOHN MASTERS, Jun., claiming two hundred arpents of land, situate at Tywappety, district of New Madrid; produces to the Board the record of a permission to settle from Henry Peyroux, commandant, dated 12th August, 1802.

November 27, 1811: Present, full Board. It is the opinion of the Board that this claim ought not to be granted.

SAMUEL MASTERS, claiming three hundred and fifty arpents of land, situate at Tywappety, district of New Madrid; produces to the Board the record of a permission to settle from Henry Peyroux, commandant, dated 12th August, 1802.

November 27, 1811: Present, full Board. It is the opinion of the Board that this claim ought not to be granted.

ALEXANDER MELLEKIN, claiming three hundred and fifty arpents of land, situate at Tywappety, district of New Madrid; produces to the Board the record of a permission to settle from Henry Peyroux, commandant, dated 12th August, 1802.

November 27, 1811: Present, full Board. It is the opinion of the Board that this claim ought not to be granted.

MARY SMITH, claiming two hundred and fifty arpents of land, situate at Tywappety, district of New Madrid; produces to the Board the record of a permission to settle from Henry Peyroux, commandant, dated 12th August, 1802.

November 27, 1811: Present, full Board. It is the opinion of the Board that this claim ought not to be granted.

ROBERT OWENS, claiming one hundred and fifty by three hundred feet of land, situate in the village of Robert, district of St. Louis; produces to the Board the record of an acknowledgment from Zenon Trudeau, Lieutenant Governor, that he had given a concession for the said village, dated 23d December, 1795; a figurative plat of survey, duly registered, signed Maturin Bouvet, declaring that, by an order of survey from Zenon Trudeau, Lieutenant Governor, dated 7th October, 1794, he had surveyed said village.

November 27, 1811: Present, full Board. It is the opinion of the Board that this claim ought not to be confirmed.

DAVID HILDERBRAND, claiming one hundred and fifty feet by one hundred and fifty feet, lot No. 11, situate in the village of Robert, district of St. Louis; produces to the Board the same as in the foregoing.

November 27, 1811: Present, full Board. It is the opinion of the Board that this claim ought not to be confirmed.

JACOB, claiming one hundred and fifty by three hundred feet of land, situate as above; produces to the Board the same as aforesaid, the same being lot No. 10.

November 27, 1811: Present, full Board. It is the opinion of the Board that this claim ought not to be confirmed.

JOHN LAIBOR, claiming five hundred and fifty by one hundred and thirty-five feet, lot No. 12, situate as aforesaid; produces to the Board the same as the foregoing.

November 27, 1811: Present, full Board. It is the opinion of the Board that this claim ought not to be confirmed.

ST. GERMAIN, claiming one hundred and fifty by one hundred and fifty feet, lot No. 21, situate as aforesaid, and produces as aforesaid.

November 27, 1811: Present, full Board. It is the opinion of the Board that this claim ought not to be confirmed.

SOLOMON, claiming one hundred and fifty by one hundred and fifty feet of land, lot No. 20, situate as aforesaid, and produces as aforesaid.

November 27, 1811: Present, full Board.   It is the opinion of the Board that this claim ought not to be confirmed.

CALVE, claiming one hundred and fifty by one hundred and fifty feet of land, lot No. 28; produces to the Board the same as aforesaid, and situate as aforesaid.

November 27, 1811: Present, full Board.   It is the opinion of the Board that this claim ought not to be confirmed.

WILLIAM BELON, claiming one hundred and fifty by one hundred and fifty feet of land, lot No. 15, situate as aforesaid, and produces as aforesaid.

November 27, 1811: Present, full Board.   It is the opinion of the Board that this claim ought not to be confirmed.

THOMAS JONES, claiming one hundred and fifty by one hundred and fifty feet of land, lot No. 23, situate as aforesaid, and produces as aforesaid.

November 27, 1811: Present, full Board.   It is the opinion of the Board that this claim ought not to be confirmed.

PHILLIP FINE, claiming one hundred and fifty by one hundred and fifty feet of land, lot No. 6, situate as aforesaid, produces as aforesaid.

November 27, 1811: Present, full Board.   It is the opinion of the Board that this claim ought not to be confirmed.

JOHN LAIBOR, claiming one hundred and fifty by one hundred and fifty feet of land, lot No. 8, situate as aforesaid, produces as aforesaid.

November 27, 1811: Present, full Board.   It is the opinion of the Board that this claim ought not to be confirmed.

JOHN LAIBOR, claiming one hundred and fifty by one hundred and fifty feet of land, lot No 17, situate as aforesaid, produces as aforesaid.

November 27, 1811: Present, full Board.   It is the opinion of the Board that this claim ought not to be confirmed.

DAVID HILDERBRAND, claiming one hundred and fifty by one hundred and fifty feet of land, lot No. 9, situate as aforesaid, produces as aforesaid.

November 27, 1811: Present, full Board.   It is the opinion of the Board that this claim ought not to be confirmed.

ST. GERMAIN, claiming one hundred and fifty by one hundred and fifty feet of land, lot No 22, situate as aforesaid, produces as aforesaid.

November 27, 1811: Present, full Board.   It is the opinion of the Board that this claim ought not to be confirmed.

WILLIAM BELLEW, claiming one hundred and fifty by one hundred and fifty feet of land, lot No. 16, situate as aforesaid, produces as aforesaid.

November 27, 1811: Present, full Board.   It is the opinion of the Board that this claim ought not to be confirmed.

ISAAC HILDERBRAND, claiming one hundred and fifty by one hundred and fifty feet, lot No. 18, produces as aforesaid.

November 27, 1811: Present, full Board.   It is the opinion of the Board that this claim ought not to be confirmed.

THOMAS JONES, claiming one hundred fifty by one hundred and fifty feet, lot No. 24, produces as above.

November 27, 1811: Present, full Board.   It is the opinion of the Board that this claim ought not to be confirmed.

PHILIP FINE, claiming one hundred and fifty by one hundred and fifty feet, lot No. 7, produces as above.

November 27, 1811: Present, full Board.   It is the opinion of the Board that this claim ought not to be confirmed.

THOMAS L. NORRIS, claiming five hundred and ninety-five arpents of land, situate on the Mississippi, district of Cape Girardeau; produces the record of a plat of survey, dated 4th and certified 27th February, 1806.

November 27, 1811: Present, full Board.   It is the opinion of the Board that this claim ought not to be granted.

JAMES ROGERS, assignee of John Neighbour, claiming one hundred arpents of land, situate on Marais des Liards, district of St. Louis; produces a notice to the recorder.

November 27, 1811: Present, full Board.   It is the opinion of the Board that this claim ought not to be granted.

JACQUES ST. VRAIN, assignee of Francis Normando, claiming two thousand five hundred arpents of land, situate on river Loutre, district of St. Charles; produces the record of a concession from Delassus, Lieutenant Governor, dated the 20th November, 1799; the record of a plat of survey, signed Fremon Deloriare.

November 27, 1811: Present, full Board.   It is the opinion of the Board that this claim ought not to be confirmed.

JOSEPH FENWICK, claiming two arpents in front by forty arpents depth, situate near New Bourbon, district of St. Genevieve; produces the record of a general concession to the inhabitants of St. Genevieve and New Bourbon, from Zenon Trudeau, Lieutenant Governor, dated 15th February, 1798.

November 27, 1811: Present, full Board.   It is the opinion of the Board that this claim ought not to be confirmed.

****

ANDREW DEGUIRE, Sen., claiming forty arpents of land, situate as aforesaid; produces as aforesaid.
November 27, 1811: Present, full Board. It is the opinion of the Board that this claim ought not to be confirmed.

ETIENNE GOVREAU, claiming forty arpents of land, situate as aforesaid; produces as aforesaid.
November 27, 1811: Present, a full Board. It is the opinion of the Board that this claim ought not to be confirmed.

JOSEPH LEPERCH, claiming twenty arpents of land, situate as aforesaid; produces as aforesaid.
November 27, 1811: Present, a full Board. It is the opinion of the Board that this claim ought not to be confirmed.

LOUIS BOLDUC, claiming eighty arpents of land, situate as aforesaid; produces as aforesaid.
November 27, 1811: Present, a full Board. It is the opinion of the Board that this claim ought not to be confirmed.

LOUIS LACOMBE, claiming twenty arpents of land, situate as aforesaid; produces as aforesaid.
November 27, 1811: Present, a full Board. It is the opinion of the Board that this claim ought not to be confirmed.

NICHOLAS LACHANCE, père, claiming forty arpents of land, situate as aforesaid; produces as aforesaid.
November 27, 1811: Present, a full Board. It is the opinion of the Board that this claim ought not to be confirmed.

GABRIEL LACHANCE, claiming forty arpents of land, situate as aforesaid; produces as aforesaid.
November 27, 1811: Present, a full Board. It is the opinion of the Board that this claim ought not to be confirmed.

JOHN BAPTISTE MOREAU, claiming forty arpents of land, situate as aforesaid; produces as aforesaid.
November 27, 1811: Present, a full Board. It is the opinion of the Board that this claim ought not to be confirmed.

ETIENNE PARENT, claiming forty arpents of land, situate as aforesaid; produces as aforesaid.
November 27, 1811: Present, a full Board. It is the opinion of the Board that this claim ought not to be confirmed.

JOHN BAPTISTE MOREAU, claiming twenty arpents of land, situate as aforesaid; produces as aforesaid.
November 27, 1811: Present, a full Board. It is the opinion of the Board that this claim ought not to be confirmed.

MARIE ROMPRES, veuve BERMIU, claiming forty arpents of land, situate as aforesaid; produces as aforesaid.
November 27, 1811: Present, a full Board. It is the opinion of the Board that this claim ought not to be confirmed.

FRANCIS OBUCHON, claiming eighty arpents of land, situate as aforesaid; produces as aforesaid.
November 27, 1811: Present, a full Board. It is the opinion of the Board that this claim ought not to be confirmed.

LOUISA VALLE, veuve LECLERC, claiming one hundred and twenty arpents of land, situate as aforesaid; produces as aforesaid.
November 27, 1811: Present, a full Board. It is the opinion of the Board that this claim ought not to be confirmed.

STEPHEN BOLDUC, claiming forty arpents of land, situate as aforesaid; produces as aforesaid.
November 27, 1811: Present, a full Board. It is the opinion of the Board that this claim ought not to be confirmed.

HENRY DIELLE, claiming forty arpents of land, situate as aforesaid; produces as aforesaid.
November 27, 1811: Present, a full Board. It is the opinion of the Board that this claim ought not to be confirmed.

JOHN PRICE and WILLIAM PERRY, assignee of Jacob Neal, claiming two hundred arpents of land, situate on river Mine à Breton, district of St. Genevieve; produce the record of a concession from Delassus, Lieutenant Governor, dated 29th November, 1799.
November 27, 1811: Present, a full Board. It is the opinion of the Board that this claim ought not to be confirmed.

JOHN PRICE and WILLIAM PERRY, assignee of Samuel Neal, claiming two hundred arpents of land, situate as aforesaid; produce as aforesaid.
November 27, 1811: Present, a full Board. It is the opinion of the Board that this claim ought not to be confirmed.

JOHN HAWKINS, assignee of John Newman, claiming seven hundred and forty-eight arpents and sixty-eight perches of land, situate on south fork of Saline river, district of St. Genevieve; produces a record of a transcript from Newman to Hawkins, dated 5th October, 1805.
November 27, 1811: Present, a full Board. It is the opinion of the Board that this claim ought not to be granted.

GRIFFITH BROWN, assignee of Daniel McCoy, assignee of Thomas Overstreet, claiming seven hundred and forty-eight arpents and sixty-eight perches of land, situate in the district of St. Charles.
November 27, 1811: Present, a full Board. It is the opinion of the Board that this claim ought not to be granted.

JOHN McFERRAN, assignee of Andrew Kenney, assignee of Jacob Odum and James Bradshaw, claiming eight hundred arpents of land, situate on Odom's spring, district of St. Genevieve; produces a notice to the recorder.
November 27, 1811: Present, a full Board. It is the opinion of the Board that this claim ought not to be granted.

JOHN OGEUNE, claiming four hundred arpents of land, situate on Grand Marais, district of New Madrid; produces the record of an order of survey from Francis Lesieur, commandant, dated 3d May, 1802.
November 27, 1801: Present, a full Board. It is the opinion of the Board that this claim ought not to be confirmed.

JOHN MULLANPHY, assignee of John Orain, claiming two hundred arpents of land, situate on river Cuivre, district of St. Charles; produces a notice to the recorder.
November 27, 1811: Present, a full Board. It is the opinion of the Board that this claim ought not to be confirmed.

JOHN MULLANPHY, assignee of John Baptiste Provenche, claiming two hundred arpents of land, situate as aforesaid; produces a notice to the recorder.
November 27, 1811: Present, a full Board. It is the opinion of the Board that this claim ought not to be confirmed.

JOHN MULLANPHY, assignee of Louis Boisse, claiming two hundred arpents of land, situate as aforesaid; produces to the Board a notice to the recorder.
November 27, 1811: Present, a full Board. It is the opinion of the Board that this claim ought not to be confirmed.

JOHN MULLANPHY, assignee of Denoyer, claiming two hundred arpents of land, situate as aforesaid; produces a notice to the recorder.
November 27, 1811: Present, a full Board. It is the opinion of the Board that this claim ought not to be confirmed.

JOHN MULLANPHY, assignee of Francis Motier, claiming two hundred arpents of land, situate as aforesaid; produces a notice to the recorder.
November 27, 1811: Present, a full Board. It is the opinion of the Board that this claim ought not to be confirmed.

WILLIAM PALMER, claiming one thousand arpents of land, situate in Cape Grey, district of St. Charles; produces the record of a concession from Charles D. Delassus, Lieutenant Governor, dated the 8th February, 1802; record of a plat of survey, dated the 10th December, and certified the 29th December, 1803.
November 27, 1811: Present, a full Board. It is the opinion of the Board that this claim ought not to be confirmed.

GABRIEL HUNOT, père, claiming a lot of one arpent, in New Madrid village, corner of Dauphin and St. Eulalie streets; produces a certificate from Henry Peyroux, commandant, dated 21st March, 1804, stating that he had given permission to claimant, during his command of that post, to settle on said lot; that he had also, prior to the 24th September, 1800, forwarded claimant's petition, with the commandant's recommendation thereon, in order to obtain the decree of the Intendant General of the province; also a general plat of survey of the town of New Madrid, dated April, 1794.
December 2, 1811: Present, a full Board. It is the opinion of the Board that this claim ought not to be granted.

JOSEPH HUNOT, père, claiming a lot of one arpent, situate as aforesaid, and produces as aforesaid.
December 2, 1811: Present, a full Board. It is the opinion of the Board that this claim ought not to be granted.

JOHN BAPTISTE LANGLOIS, claiming a lot of one arpent, situate as aforesaid, and produces as aforesaid.
December 2, 1811: Present, a full Board. It is the opinion of the Board that this claim ought not to be granted.

ANDREW WILSON, claiming a lot of one arpent, situate as aforesaid, and produces as aforesaid.
December 2, 1811: Present, a full Board. It is the opinion of the Board that this claim ought not to be granted.

JOHN LAFERNAIT, claiming a lot of two arpents, situate as aforesaid, and produces as aforesaid.
December 2, 1811: Present, a full Board. It is the opinion of the Board that this claim ought not to be granted.

GABRIEL HUNOT, Jr., claiming a lot of one arpent, situate as aforesaid, and produces as aforesaid.
December 2, 1811: Present, a full Board. It is the opinion of the Board that this claim ought not to be granted.

MANUEL VIOLET, claiming a lot of one arpent, situate as aforesaid, and produces as aforesaid.
December 2, 1811: Present, a full Board. It is the opinion of the Board that this claim ought not to be granted.

FRANCIS LANGLOIS, claiming a lot of one arpent, situate as aforesaid, and produces as aforesaid.
December 2, 1811: Present, a full Board. It is the opinion of the Board that this claim ought not to be granted.

JOSEPH HUNOT, Jr., claiming a lot of one arpent, situate as aforesaid, and produces as aforesaid.
December 2, 1811: Present, a full Board. It is the opinion of the Board that this claim ought not to be granted.

JAMES SMITH, claiming a lot of one arpent, situate as aforesaid, and produces as aforesaid.
December 2, 1811: Present, a full Board. It is the opinion of the Board that this claim ought not to be granted.

****

PIERRE GARREAU, claiming a lot of one arpent, situate as aforesaid, and produces as aforesaid.
December 2, 1811: Present, a full Board. It is the opinion of the Board that this claim ought not to be granted.

ANDREW GODAIR, claiming a lot of one arpent, situate as aforesaid, and produces as aforesaid.
December 2, 1811: Present, a full Board. It is the opinion of the Board that this claim ought not to be granted.

PIERRE DISCORDIS, claiming a lot of one arpent, situate as aforesaid, and produces as aforesaid.
December 2, 1811: Present, a full Board. It is the opinion of the Board that this claim ought not to be granted

ALEXIS PICARD, claiming a lot of two arpents, situate as aforesaid, and produces as aforesaid.
December 2, 1811: Present, a full Board. It is the opinion of the Board that this claim ought not to be granted.

NICHOLAS ST. JEAN, claiming a lot of one arpent, situate as aforesaid, and produces as aforesaid.
December 2, 1811: Present, a full Board. It is the opinion of the Board that this claim ought not to be granted.

PIERRE GONET, claiming a lot of two arpents, situate as aforesaid, and produces as aforesaid.
December 2, 1811: Present, a full Board. It is the opinion of the Board that this claim ought not to be granted.

LOUIS COIGNARD, claiming a lot of two arpents, situate as aforesaid, and produces as aforesaid.
December 2, 1811: Present, a full Board. It is the opinion of the Board that this claim ought not to be granted.

PETER PERRON, claiming a lot of one arpent, situate as aforesaid, and produces as aforesaid.
December 2, 1811: Present, a full Board. It is the opinion of the Board that this claim ought not to be granted.

JOSEPH MONTAUVERT, claiming a lot of two arpents, situate as aforesaid, and produces as aforesaid.
December 2, 1811: Present, a full Board. It is the opinion of the Board that this claim ought not to be granted.

CHARLES CASTONGET, claiming a lot of one arpent, situate as aforesaid, and produces as aforesaid.
December 2, 1811: Present, a full Board. It is the opinion of the Board that this claim ought not to be granted.

ANTOINE VACHARD, claiming a lot of one arpent, situate as aforesaid, and produces as aforesaid.
December 2, 1811: Present, a full Board. It is the opinion of the Board that this claim ought not to be granted.

JOHN BAPTISTE CHARTIER, claiming a lot of two arpents, situate as aforesaid, and produces as aforesaid.
December 2, 1811: Present, a full Board. It is the opinion of the Board that this claim ought not to be granted.

JOSEPH CHARPENTIER, claiming a lot of two arpents, situate as aforesaid, and produces as aforesaid.
December 2, 1811: Present, a full Board. It is the opinion of the Board that this claim ought not to be granted.

TOUSSAINT GODAIR, claiming a lot of two arpents, situate as aforesaid, and produces as aforesaid.
December 2, 1811: Present, a full Board. It is the opinion of the Board that this claim ought not to be granted.

MATHIAS BELSON, claiming a lot of two arpents, situate as aforesaid, and produces as aforesaid.
December 2, 1811: Present, a full Board. It is the opinion of the Board that this claim ought not to be granted.

JOHN BAPTISTE GOBEAU, claiming a lot of two arpents, situate as aforesaid, and produces as aforesaid.
December 2, 1811: Present, a full Board. It is the opinion of the Board that this claim ought not to be granted.

BENJAMIN MYERS, claiming a lot of two arpents, situate as aforesaid, and produces as aforesaid.
December 2, 1811: Present, a full Board. It is the opinion of the Board that this claim ought not to be granted.

JACOB MYERS, claiming a lot of one arpent, situate as aforesaid, and produces as aforesaid.
December 2, 1811: Present, a full Board. It is the opinion of the Board that this claim ought not to be granted.

FRANCIS HUDSON, claiming a lot of two arpents, situate as aforesaid, and produces as aforesaid.
December 2, 1811: Present, a full Board. It is the opinion of the Board that this claim ought not to be granted.

PIERRE DUMAY, claiming a lot of two arpents, situate as aforesaid, and produces as aforesaid.
December 2, 1811: Present, a full Board. It is the opinion of the Board that this claim ought not to be granted.

JOHN BAPTISTE PERRON, claiming a lot of one arpent, situate as aforesaid, and produces as aforesaid.
December 2, 1811: Present, a full Board. It is the opinion of the Board that this claim ought not to be granted.

GIRARD DORLAC, claiming a lot of one arpent, situate as aforesaid, and produces as aforesaid.
December 2, 1811: Present, full Board. It is the opinion of the Board that this claim ought not to be granted.

JOSEPH STORY, claiming a lot of two arpents, situate as aforesaid, and produces as aforesaid.
December 2, 1811: Present, full Board. It is the opinion of the Board that this claim ought not to be granted.

THOMAS JOHNSON, claiming a lot of one arpent, situate as aforesaid, and produces as aforesaid.
December 2, 1811: Present, full Board. It is the opinion of the Board that this claim ought not to be granted.

LOUIS LARDOISE, claiming a lot of one arpent, situate as aforesaid, and produces as aforesaid.
December 2, 1811 Present, full Board. It is the opinion of the Board that this claim ought not to be granted.

RICHARD JONES WATERS, claiming eight arpents, situate as aforesaid, and produces as aforesaid.
December 2, 1811: Present, full Board. It is the opinion of the Board that this claim ought not to be granted.

FRANCIS RICHE DUPIN, claiming a lot of two arpents, situate as aforesaid, and produces as aforesaid.
December 2, 1811: Present, full Board. It is the opinion of the Board that this claim ought not to be granted.

NICHOLAS DAPRON, claiming a lot of one arpent, situate as aforesaid, and produces as aforesaid.
December 2, 1811: Present, full Board. It is the opinion of the Board that this claim ought not to be granted.

JOSEPH DUMAY, claiming a lot of one arpent, situate as aforesaid, and produces as aforesaid.
December 2, 1811: Present, full Board. It is the opinion of the Board that this claim ought not to be granted.

ETIENNE DUMAY, claiming a lot of one arpent, situate as aforesaid, and produces as aforesaid.
December 2, 1811: Present, full Board. It is the opinion of the Board that this claim ought not to be granted.

MICHEL BONTRONC, claiming a lot of two arpents, situate as aforesaid, and produces as aforesaid.
December 2, 1811: Present, full Board. It is the opinion of the Board that this claim ought not to be granted.

FRANCIS ST. MARIE, claiming a lot of two arpents, situate as aforesaid, and produces as aforesaid.
December 2, 1811: Present, full Board. It is the opinion of the Board that this claim ought not to be granted.

P. ST. MARIE, claiming a lot of one arpent, situate as aforesaid, and produces as aforesaid.
December 2, 1811: Present, full Board. It is the opinion of the Board that this claim ought not to be granted.

JOHN BAPTISTE ST. MARIE, claiming a lot of one arpent, situate as aforesaid, and produces as aforesaid.
December 2, 1811: Present, a full Board. It is the opinion of the Board that this claim ought not to be granted.

JOHN BAPTISTE OLIVE, claiming a lot of two arpents, situate as aforesaid, and produces as aforesaid.
December 2, 1811: Present, a full Board. It is the opinion of the Board that this claim ought not to be granted.

LUKE DEVORE, claiming a lot of two arpents, situate as aforesaid, and produces as aforesaid.
December 2, 1811: Present, a full Board. It is the opinion of the Board that this claim ought not to be granted.

SAMUEL MASTERS, claiming a lot of two arpents, situate as aforesaid, and produces as aforesaid.
December 2, 1811: Present, a full Board. It is the opinion of the Board that this claim ought not to be granted.

LEMUEL MASTERS, claiming a lot of two arpents, situate as aforesaid, and produces as aforesaid.
December 2, 1811: Present, a full Board. It is the opinion of the Board that this claim ought not to be granted.

ROBERT MASTERS, claiming a lot of two arpents, situate as aforesaid, and produces as aforesaid.
December 2, 1811: Present, a full Board. It is the opinion of the Board that this claim ought not to be granted.

LOUIS BABY, claiming a lot of two arpents, situate as aforesaid, and produces as aforesaid.
December 2, 1811: Present, a full Board. It is the opinion of the Board that this claim ought not to be granted.

AMBROSE SERAPHIN, claiming a lot of one arpent, situate as aforesaid, and produces as aforesaid.
December 2, 1811: Present, a full Board. It is the opinion of the Board that this claim ought not to be granted.

JOSEPH LAPLANTE, claiming a lot of one arpent, situate as aforesaid, and produces as aforesaid.
December 2, 1811: Present, a full Board. It is the opinion of the Board that this claim ought not to be granted.

JOHN BAPTISTE THIBEAUD, claiming a lot of one arpent, situate as aforesaid, and produces as aforesaid.
December 2, 1811: Present, a full Board. It is the opinion of the Board that this claim ought not to be granted.

G. GERMAIN, claiming a lot of two arpents, situate as aforesaid, and produces as aforesaid.
December 2, 1811: Present, a full Board. It is the opinion of the Board that this claim ought not to be granted.

JOHN BAPTISTE CHARTIER, claiming a lot of one arpent, situate as aforesaid, and produces as aforesaid.
December 2, 1811: Present, a full Board. It is the opinion of the Board that this claim ought not to be granted.

RICHARD MASTERS, claiming a lot of two arpents, situate as aforesaid, and produces as aforesaid.
December 2, 1811: Present, a full Board. It is the opinion of the Board that this claim ought not to be granted.

ALEXIS LALANDE, assignee, by public sale, of Francis Delin, assignee of the widow of Michel Rollete, assignee of Belle Peche, claiming a lot in St. Louis, one hundred and twenty by one hundred and fifty feet; produces a record of transfer from Rollete to Delin, dated 15th February, 1777; record of public sale of Delin's property to claimant, dated 30th November, 1788.
December 6, 1811: Present, a full Board. It is the opinion of the Board that this claim ought not to be granted.

WILLIAM NASH, assignee of Antoine Dejarlais, assignee of Louis Labeaume, assignee of Baptiste Presse, claiming eight hundred arpents of land, situate on the Missouri, district of St. Charles; produces record of a concession from Delassus, Lieutenant Governor, dated 29th December, 1800; record of plat of survey, dated February, 1804, and certified 28th February, 1806; record of transfer of six hundred arpents from Presse to Labeaume, dated 10th January, 1804; record of transfer from Labeaume to Dejarlais, dated 18th July, 1804; record of transfer of two hundred arpents from Presse to Dejarlais, dated 10th July, 1804; record of transfer of eight hundred arpents from Dejarlais to claimant, dated 1804.
December 6, 1811: Present, a full Board. It is the opinion of the Board that this claim ought not to be confirmed.

CHARLES PRUIT, heirs of, claiming one thousand one hundred and fifty arpents of land, situate on the Merrimack, district of St. Louis; produces a notice to the recorder.
December 6, 1811: Present, a full Board. It is the opinion of the Board that this claim ought not to be granted.

AMABLE PATNOTE, claiming seven hundred and forty-eight arpents sixty-eight perches of land, situate at Bellevue, district of St. Genevieve; produces a record of plat of survey, dated February 5, 1806, certified 28th February, 1806.
December 6, 1811: Present, a full Board. It is the opinion of the Board that this claim ought not to be granted.

THOMAS POWERS, claiming six hundred and fifty arpents of land, situate on the river St. John, district of St. Louis; produces the record of a petition, dated 31st January, 1800, and a concession annexed to the same, without a date, from Delassus, Lieutenant Governor, for six hundred and fifty arpents; record of a plat of survey, dated 22d February, 1806, and certified 27th February, 1806.

December 6, 1811: Present, a full Board. It is the opinion of the Board that this claim ought not to be confirmed.

ETIENNE PEPIN, claiming one thousand six hundred arpents of land, situate on the Dardenne, district of St. Charles; produces the record of a concession from Delassus, Lieutenant Governor, dated 18th October, 1800.

December 6, 1811: Present, a full Board. It is the opinion of the Board that this claim ought not to be confirmed.

ST. JAMES BEAUVAIS, assignee of Amable Partenais, claiming six hundred arpents of land, situate on the river Au Vase, district of St. Genevieve; produces record of a concession from Zenon Trudeau, Lieutenant Governor, dated 1st September, 1797; record of a plat of survey, dated 4th December, 1798, certified 1st December, 1798; record of a transfer from Partenais to claimant, dated 7th January, 1802.

December 6, 1811: Present, a full Board. It is the opinion of the Board that this claim ought not to be confirmed.

Widow CHARLEVILLE, assignee of Basil Prouly, claiming a lot in St. Louis, one hundred and twenty by one hundred and fifty feet; produces record of a transfer from Prouly to claimant, dated 30th May, 1799.

December 6, 1811: Present, a full Board. It is the opinion of the Board that this claim ought not to be granted.

JOHN CAMPBELL and WHITE MATLOCK, assignees of John Coontz and Joseph Perkins, claiming a lot in St. Louis, sixty by one hundred and fifty feet; produces record of a transfer from Coontz and Perkins to claimants, dated 14th January, 1805.

December 6, 1811: Present, a full Board. It is the opinion of the Board that this claim ought not to be granted.

LOUIS DUBREUIL, assignee of Baptiste Presse, claiming two lots in St. Ferdinand village, district of St. Louis, one hundred and fifty by three hundred feet; produces record of a transfer from Presse to claimant, dated 4th February, 1803.

December 6, 1811: Present, a full Board. It is the opinion of the Board that this claim ought not to be granted.

DANIEL PHILLIPS, claiming one thousand and ninety-seven arpents twenty-eight perches of land, situate at Prairie spring, district of St. Genevieve; produces record of a plat of survey, dated 25th and certified 28th February, 1806.

December 6, 1811: Present, a full Board. It is the opinion of the Board that this claim ought not to be granted.

Madame BERALD SARPY, assignee of Bernard Pratte, claiming eight hundred arpents of land, situate on the Merrimack, district of St. Louis; produces record of a concession from Zenon Trudeau, Lieutenant Governor, dated 24th May, 1799; and a certificate from the surveyor that the land is not vacant; a record of an order from Delassus, Lieutenant Governor, to survey the same on vacant lands, dated 6th May, 1803; record of a plat of survey, dated 4th January, and certified 15th April, 1804; record of a transfer from Pratte to claimant, dated 17th October, 1800.

December 6, 1811: Present, a full Board. It is the opinion of the Board that this claim ought not to be granted.

JOSEPH M. PAPIN, claiming eight by twenty-five arpents of land, situate in the commons of St. Louis; produces the record of a concession from Charles D. Delassus, Lieutenant Governor, dated 29th December, 1802.

December 6, 1811: Present, a full Board. It is the opinion of the Board that this claim ought not to be confirmed.

JOHN SMITH, assignee of John Price, claiming five hundred arpents of land, situate in New Bourbon, district of St. Genevieve; produces the record of a concession from Zenon Trudeau, Lieutenant Governor, dated 15th November, 1797; record of a plat of survey, dated 10th December, 1797, certified 8th February, 1798; record of a transfer from Price to claimant, dated 14th August, 1805.

December 6, 1811: Present, a full Board. It is the opinion of the Board that this claim ought not to be confirmed.

PETER PROVENCHERE, claiming ten thousand arpents of land, situate on Grand Calumet, district of St. Charles; produces the record of a concession from Delassus, Lieutenant Governor, dated 3d March, 1800; record of a plat of survey, dated 16th February, 1804, certified 5th March, 1804.

December 6, 1811: Present, a full Board. It is the opinion of the Board that this claim ought not to be confirmed.

WALTER FENWICK, assignee of Joseph Perez, claiming a lot in the village of St. Genevieve, two arpents; produces record of a concession from Francis Valle, commandant, dated 10th July, 1793.

December 6, 1811: Present, a full Board. It is the opinion of the Board that this claim ought not to be confirmed.

EDWARD HEMPSTEAD and CLAIBOURNE RHODES, assignees of Antoine Dejarlais, assignee of Andrew Peltier, claiming eight hundred arpents of land, situate in the district of St. Charles; produces the record of a concession not signed, dated 15th May, 1800; record of a transfer from Peltier to Dejarlais, dated 14th January, 1804; record of a transfer from Dejarlais to Rhodes without date; record of a transfer from Rhodes to Hempstead, for one-half of this tract, dated 25th June, 1808.

December 6, 1811: Present, a full Board. It is the opinion of the Board that this claim ought not to be confirmed.

BENJAMIN PETIT, Jun., claiming five hundred arpents of land, situate on the river St. Francis, district of St. Genevieve; produces a notice to the recorder.

December 6, 1811: Present, a full Board. It is the opinion of the Board that this claim ought not to be granted.

PIERRE AUGUSTE PRATTE, claiming six hundred arpents of land, situate on Big river, district of St. Genevieve; produces the record of a concession from Delassus, Lieutenant Governor, dated 5th September, 1799.

December 6, 1811: Present, a full Board. It is the opinion of the Board that this claim ought not to be confirmed.

JOSEPH PRATTE, claiming twenty thousand arpents of land, situate on the river St. Francis, district of St. Genevieve; produces the record of a concession from Zenon Trudeau, Lieutenant Governor, dated 17th Oct. 1797.
December 6, 1811: Present, a full Board. It is the opinion of the Board that this claim ought not to be confirmed.

HENRY PRATTE, claiming six hundred arpents of land, situate on Big river, district of St. Genevieve; produces the record of a concession from Delassus, Lieutenant Governor, dated 5th September, 1799.
December 6, 1811: Present, a full Board. It is the opinion of the Board that this claim ought not to be confirmed.

ANTOINE PRATTE, claiming five hundred arpents of land, situate as aforesaid; produces the record of a concession from Delassus, Lieutenant Governor, dated 5th September, 1799.
December 6, 1811: Present, a full Board. It is the opinion of the Board that this claim ought not to be confirmed.

HENRY PEYROUX, claiming two arpents, situate in the village of New Madrid; produces a notice to the recorder.
December 6, 1811: Present, a full Board. It is the opinion of the Board that this claim ought not to be granted.

HENRY PEYROUX, claiming four arpents of land, situate as aforesaid; produces a notice to the recorder.
December 6, 1811: Present, a full Board. It is the opinion of the Board that this claim ought not to be granted.

HENRY PEYROUX, claiming four arpents of land, situate as aforesaid; produces a notice to the recorder.
December 6, 1811: Present, a full Board. It is the opinion of the Board that this claim ought not to be granted.

HENRY PEYROUX, claiming forty arpents of land, situate as aforesaid; produces a notice to the recorder.
December 6, 1811: Present, a full Board. It is the opinion of the Board that this claim ought not to be granted.

HENRY PEYROUX, claiming one and a half arpents of land, situate as aforesaid; produces a notice to the recorder.
December 6, 1811: Present, a full Board. It is the opinion of the Board that this claim ought not to be granted.

HENRY PEYROUX, assignee of Francis Pasquin, claiming six arpents of land, situate in the district of New Madrid; produces a notice to the recorder.
December 6, 1811: Present, a full Board. It is the opinion of the Board that this claim ought not to be granted.

HENRY PEYROUX, assignee of Francis Pasquin, claiming five arpents of land, situate in the village of New Madrid; produces a notice to the recorder.
December 6, 1811: Present, a full Board. It is the opinion of the Board that this claim ought not to be granted.

PIERRE PALARDIE, claiming one thousand arpents of land, situate in the district of St. Charles; produces a notice to the recorder.
December 6, 1811: Present, a full Board. It is the opinion of the Board that this claim ought not to be granted.

SOLOMON PETTIT, claiming four hundred arpents of land, situate in the district of St. Charles; produces a record of a concession from Delassus, Lieutenant Governor, dated 4th January, 1803.
December 6, 1811: Present, a full Board. It is the opinion of the Board that this claim ought not to be confirmed.

JEREMIAH ABLE, assignee of Ezekiel Able, assignee of John Shields, assignee of William Page, claiming seven hundred and forty-eight arpents and sixty-eight perches of land, situate on White Waters, district of Cape Girardeau; produces a notice to the recorder.
December 6, 1811: Present, a full Board. It is the opinion of the Board that this claim ought not to be granted.

SAMUEL PARKER, heirs of, claiming three hundred arpents of land, situate in the district of Cape Girardeau; produces a notice to the recorder.
December 6, 1811: Present, a full Board. It is the opinion of the Board that this claim ought not to be granted.

PETER PERTUIS, claiming one hundred and twenty-one arpents of land, situate in the district of Arkansas; produces to the Board the record of a petition and recommendation from Carlos de Villemont, commandant, dated 3d February, 1799; record of a plat of survey, dated 13th April, 1806, signed Godfrey Jones.
December 6, 1811: Present, a full Board. It is the opinion of the Board that this claim ought not to be confirmed.

JOHN PRICE, claiming four thousand arpents of land, situate on Grand river, district of St. Genevieve; produces a record of a concession from Delassus, Lieutenant Governor, dated 6th March, 1800; record of a plat of survey, dated 15th December, 1802, certified 7th September, 1803.
December 6, 1811: Present, a full Board. It is the opinion of the Board that this claim ought not to be confirmed.

JAMES QUICK, claiming eight hundred and forty arpents of land, situate in the district of St. Genevieve; produces the record of a plat of survey, dated 15th and certified 26th February, 1806.
December 6, 1811: Present, a full Board. It is the opinion of the Board that this claim ought not to be granted.

STEPHEN QUIMBY, claiming seven hundred and forty acres of land, situate at Tywappety, district of New Madrid; produces the record of a petition and recommendation, not signed; record of a plat of survey, dated 3d of February and certified 27th February, 1806.
December 6, 1811: Present, a full Board. It is the opinion of the Board that this claim ought not to be confirmed.

****

LOUIS LABEAUME, assignee of Albert Tison, assignee of Jacque St. Vrain, assignee of Avon Quick, claiming eight hundred arpents of land, situate at Rich Woods, district of St. Genevieve; produces a record of a concession from Delassus, Lieutenant Governor, to Quick, dated 20th March, 1801; record of a certificate from Soulard, that the land petitioned for is not vacant; record of a plat of survey, dated 20th December, 1803; certificate of survey from Soulard, dated 15th March, 1808; record of transfer from St. Vrain to Tison, dated 3d November, 1804.

December 6, 1811: Present, a full Board. It is the opinion of the Board that this claim ought not to be confirmed.

DANIEL MULLEN, assignee of Alexander Roy, claiming two hundred arpents of land, situate in the district of New Madrid, on the river Pemiscon; produces the record of a concession from Francis Lesieur, commandant, dated 15th October, 1802; record of a plat of survey, dated 20th February and certified 26th February, 1806; record of a transfer from Roy to claimant, dated 24th September, 1804.

December 6, 1811: Present, a full Board. It is the opinion of the Board that this claim ought not to be confirmed.

WILLIAM RAMSAY, claiming seven hundred and forty-eight arpents and sixty-eight perches of land, situate in the district of St. Charles; produces the record of a plat of survey, dated 20th February, 1806, and certified February, 1806.

December 6, 1811: Present, a full Board. It is the opinion of the Board that this claim ought not to be granted.

MICHAEL RABER, claiming seven hundred and forty-eight arpents of land, situate on Big river, district of St. Genevieve; produces the record of a plat of survey, dated 24th February and certified 27th February, 1806.

December 6, 1811: Present, a full Board. It is the opinion of the Board that this claim ought not to be granted.

AMABLE ROY, claiming seven hundred and forty-eight arpents of land, situate on Sandy creek, district of St. Charles; produces a record of a plat of survey, dated 4th February and certified 28th February, 1806.

December 6, 1811: Present, a full Board. It is the opinion of the Board that this claim ought not to be granted.

JOHN RUSSELL, claiming five hundred arpents of land, situate on river Bœuf, district of St. Louis; produces a record of a concession from Delassus, Lieutenant Governor, dated 25th November, 1801; record of a plat of survey, dated 22d and certified 27th February, 1806.

December 6, 1811: Present, a full Board. It is the opinion of the Board that this claim ought not to be confirmed.

ENOS RANDALL, Jun., claiming eight hundred and thirty-six arpents and sixteen perches of land, situate on Randall's creek, district of Cape Girardeau; produces the record of a plat of survey, dated 2d February and certified 13th February, 1806.

December 6, 1811: Present, a full Board. It is the opinion of the Board that this claim ought not to be granted.

JAMES ROGERS, claiming seven hundred and sixty-six arpents of land, situate at Negro fork of the Merrimack, district of St. Louis; produces the record of a plat of survey, dated 29th January and certified 24th February, 1806.

December 6, 1811: Present, a full Board. It is the opinion of the Board that this claim ought not to be granted.

JOHN RAMSEY, claiming eight hundred and forty-eight arpents and eighty perches of land, situate in the district of St. Charles; produces the record of a plat of survey, certified 28th February, 1806.

December 6, 1811: Present, a full Board. It is the opinion of the Board that this claim ought not to be granted.

DANIEL RICHARDSON, claiming four hundred and sixty arpents of land, situate at Point Labadie, district of St. Louis; produces the record of a plat of survey, dated 22d and certified 26th February, 1806.

December 6, 1811: Present, a full Board. It is the opinion of the Board that this claim ought not to be granted.

JAMES MACKAY, assignee of Seneca Rollins, claiming four hundred arpents of land, situate in the district of St. Charles; produces the record of a concession from Charles D. Delassus, Lieutenant Governor, dated 22d December, 1802; the record of a transfer from Rollins to claimant, dated 1st May, 1804.

December 6, 1811: Present, a full Board. It is the opinion of the Board that this claim ought not to be confirmed.

JOHN SMITH T., assignee of Louis Robarge, claiming four hundred arpents of land, situate in Saline, district of St. Genevieve; produces the record of a concession from Zenon Trudeau, Lieutenant Governor, dated 15th February, 1798.

December 6, 1811: Present, a full Board. It is the opinion of the Board that this claim ought not to be confirmed.

ANTOINE V. BOUIS, assignee of Charles Rober and wife, assignee of Antoine Riviere, claiming sixty arpents of land, situate in Prairie Catalan, district of St. Louis; produces the record of a transfer from Antoine Riviere, Jun., to Robert, dated 11th February, 1797; record of a transfer from Robert and wife to claimant, dated 25th November, 1807.

December 6, 1811: Present, a full Board. It is the opinion of the Board that this claim ought not to be granted.

EDWARD HEMPSTEAD, assignee of John P. Gates, assignee of Joseph Robidou, claiming forty arpents of land, situate in the fields of St. Charles; produces the record of a transfer from the sheriff of St. Charles, who sold the same, as the property of John P. Gates, to claimant, dated 29th June, 1808.

December 6, 1811: Present, a full Board. It is the opinion of the Board that this claim ought not to be granted.

****

NICHOLAS JARROT, assignee of Joseph Roy, claiming eight hundred arpents of land, situate in the district of St. Charles; produces the record of a transfer from Roy to claimant, dated 2d March, 1807.

December 6, 1811: Present, a full Board. It is the opinion of the Board that this claim ought not to be granted.

JADUTHAN KENDAL, assignee of Michel Ragen, claiming four hundred arpents of land, situate on Plattin creek, district of St. Genevieve; produces a certificate from Charles D. Delassus, dated 9th August, 1804, stating that he had had the petition and recommendation from the commandant of St. Genevieve in his possession, and had lost the same, which prevented his making a decree thereon; the record of a transfer from Ragen to claimant, dated 8th July, 1803.

December 6, 1811: Present, a full Board. It is the opinion of the Board that this claim ought not to be confirmed.

LOUIS LABEAUME, assignee of Francis Lacombe, assignee of Joseph Roy, claiming six hundred arpents of land, situate at Bay du Roy, district of St. Charles; produces the record of a concession from Charles D. Delassus, Lieutenant Governor, dated 5th April, 1800; the record of a transfer from Roy to Lacombe, dated 15th July, 1804; the record of a transfer from Lacombe to claimant, dated 10th August, 1804.

December 6, 1811: Present, a full Board. It is the opinion of the Board that this claim ought not to be confirmed.

JOHN MULLANPHY, assignee of Manuel A. Rocque, assignee of Hyacinth St. Cyr, claiming six arpents and eighteen and four-ninth perches of land, situate near St. Ferdinand, district of St. Louis; produces the record of a certificate of survey, dated 10th April, 1797, which is declared to have been made in consequence of an order of survey from Zenon Trudeau, dated 16th March, 1797; the record of an act of public sale of the property of Hyacinth St. Cyr, dated 2d March, 1803; the record of a transfer from Rocque to claimant, dated 27th August, 1806.

December 6, 1811: Present, a full Board. It is the opinion of the Board that this claim ought not to be confirmed.

JOHN MULLANPHY, assignee of Manuel A. Rocque, claiming ten arpents of land, situate as aforesaid; produces the record of a concession from Charles D. Delassus, Lieutenant Governor, dated 5th April, 1801; the record of a transfer from Rocque to claimant, dated 27th August, 1806.

December 6, 1811: Present, a full Board. It is the opinion of the Board that this claim ought not to be confirmed.

JOHN MULLANPHY, assignee of Manuel A. Rocque, assignee of Pierre Devot, claiming one hundred and eighty by three hundred feet of land, situate as aforesaid in St. Ferdinand village; produces record of the public sale of the property of Pierre Devot, by which it appears that M. A. Rocque became purchaser of the said lot, dated 3d July, 1803; record of a transfer from Rocque to claimant, dated 27th August, 1806.

December 6, 1811: Present, a full Board. It is the opinion of the Board that this claim ought not to be granted.

JOHN MULLANPHY, assignee of Manuel A. Rocque, assignee of Joseph Laprise, claiming a lot in St. Ferdinand village, one hundred and fifty by one hundred and eighty-five feet; produces the record of a conveyance from Laprise to Rocque, dated 26th January, 1803; record of a transfer from Rocque to claimant, dated 27th August, 1806.

December 6, 1811: Present, a full Board. It is the opinion of the Board that this claim ought not to be granted.

JAMES MORRISON, assignee of Pierre Roy, claiming forty arpents of land, situate near the town of St. Louis; produces record of a transfer from Roy to claimant, dated 15th June, 1805.

December 6, 1811: Present, a full Board. It is the opinion of the Board that this claim ought not to be granted.

HENRY O'HARA, assignee of Louis Robert, claiming three hundred arpents of land, situate on Glaize à Baguette, district of St. Louis; produces the record of transfer from Robert to claimant, dated 17th March, 1785.

December 6, 1811: Present, a full Board. It is the opinion of the Board that this claim ought not to be granted.

MACKAY WHERRY, CATHARINE DODGE, and ALEXANDER MCNAIR, heirs and representatives of widow Camp, claiming one-half, and the legal representatives of ANTOINE REITHE, claiming the remainder of two thousand nine hundred and five arpents fifty-six perches forty feet and six inches of land, situate on river des Peres, district of St. Louis; produce a patent to Anna Oliva Camp and Antoine Reithe, conditioned for the compliance with the third, fourth, sixth, seventh, and ninth articles of instructions of the Intendancy, from Juan Ventura Morales, Intendant General, dated 19th June, 1802; a plat of survey, dated 31st December, 1797, signed A. Soulard. Said patent, found in the "abstract of all the concessions and patented grants of land appertaining to the district of Louisiana, recorded in the registers kept by the Spanish and French Governments of the provinces of Louisiana, since the 2d July, 1756, and until the 3d of April, 1802," transmitted to the Board by the Secretary of the Treasury.

December 9, 1811: Present, a full Board. The Board ascertain that this is not a title made and completed prior to the 1st October, 1800.

AREND RUTGERS, assignee of William Dunn, claiming seven thousand and fifty-six arpents of land, situate on river Cuivre and Femme Osage, district of St. Charles; produces the record of a concession from Delassus, Lieutenant Governor, dated 18th June, 1802; plat of survey of eight hundred arpents on Femme Osage, dated 17th November, 1803, certified 22d December, 1803; record of a plat of survey of six thousand two hundred and fifty-six arpents on river Cuivre, dated 3d December, 1803, certified 5th January, 1804.

December 9, 1811: Present, full Board. It is the opinion of the Board that this claim ought not to be confirmed.

JOHN ROURKE, claiming seven hundred and fifty-six arpents of land, situate on Dardennes, district of St. Charles; produces record of a plat of survey, dated 16th December, 1805, certified February, 1806.

December 9, 1811: Present, a full Board. It is the opinion of the Board that this claim ought not to be granted.

CHARLES REFIELD, claiming eight hundred and forty-five arpents of land, situate on Canny creek, district of Arkansas; produces the record of a petition and recommendation from Caso y Luengo, commandant, dated 28th January, 1803; record of a plat of survey, signed Henry Cassady.

December 9, 1811: Present, a full Board. It is the opinion of the Board that this claim ought not to be confirmed.

CHARLES REFIELD, Junior, claiming four hundred arpents of land, situate as above; produces record of a petition and recommendation from Caso y Luengo, commandant, dated 28th January, 1803; record of a plat of survey, dated 1st February, 1804, signed Henry Cassady.
December 9, 1811: Present, a full Board. It is the opinion of the Board that this claim ought not to be confirmed.

MOSES RUSSELL, claiming four hundred arpents of land, situate on Charette creek, district of St. Charles; produces record of a concession from Delassus, Lieutenant Governor, dated 14th February, 1803.
December 9, 1811: Present, a full Board. It is the opinion of the Board that this claim ought not to be confirmed.

JOSEPH RUSSELL, claiming five hundred arpents of land, situate in district of St. Charles; produces record of a concession from Delassus, Lieutenant Governor, dated 4th December, 1802.
December 9, 1811: Present, a full Board. It is the opinion of the Board that this claim ought not to be confirmed.

JAMES RUSSELL, claiming six hundred arpents of land, situate in district of St. Charles; produces record of a concession from Delassus, Lieutenant Governor, dated 14th December, 1802.
December 9, 1811: Present, a full Board. It is the opinion of the Board that this claim ought not to be confirmed.

ANTOINE RIVIERE, claiming fifty acres of land, situate adjoining town of St. Louis; produces notices to the recorder.
December 9, 1811: Present, a full Board. It is the opinion of the Board that this claim ought not to be granted.

PHILIP ROBERTS, claiming one thousand and fifty arpents of land, situate in the district of St. Louis; produces a notice to the recorder.
December 9, 1811: Present, a full Board. It is the opinion of the Board that this claim ought not to be granted.

DAVID REESE, claiming three hundred arpents of land, situate on St. Francis, district of Cape Girardeau; produces a notice to the recorder.
December 9, 1811: Present, a full Board. It is the opinion of the Board that this claim ought not to be granted.

PETER MENARD, assignee of Peter Dumay, assignee of Bartholomew Richard, claiming one thousand two hundred arpents of land, situate in the district of Cape Girardeau; produces the record of a concession from Zenon Trudeau, Lieutenant Governor, dated 29th September, 1798.
December 9, 1811: Present, a full Board. It is the opinion of the Board that this claim ought not to be confirmed.

PHILIP ROBERTS, claiming one thousand and ninety-seven arpents of land, situate on the Merrimack, district of St. Louis; produces a notice to the recorder.
December 9, 1811: Present, a full Board. It is the opinion of the Board that this claim ought not to be granted.

STEPHEN QUIMBY, claiming two hundred arpents of land, situate in the district of New Madrid; produces the record of an order of survey from Henry Peyroux, commandant, dated 22d May, 1801.
December 9, 1811: Present, a full Board. It is the opinion of the Board that this claim ought not to be confirmed.

JOSIAH QUIMBY, claiming two hundred arpents of land, situate in the district of New Madrid; produces the record of an order of survey from Henry Peyroux, commandant, dated 22d May, 1801.
December 9, 1811: Present, a full Board. It is the opinion of the Board that this claim ought not to be confirmed.

JOHN BAPTISTE RACINE, claiming three hundred arpents of land, situate on Big Prairie, district of New Madrid; produces the record of an order of survey from Robert McCoy, commandant, dated 10th October, 1799.
December 9, 1811: Present, a full Board. It is the opinion of the Board that this claim ought not to be confirmed.

ANDREW RAMSAY, claiming three hundred arpents of land, situate on Big Prairie, district of New Madrid; produces the record of an order of survey from Robert McCoy, commandant, dated 10th October, 1799.
December 9, 1811: Present, a full Board. It is the opinion of the Board that this claim ought not to be confirmed.

DANIEL RICHELET, claiming two hundred arpents of land, situate on Big Bayou, district of New Madrid; produces the record of an order of survey from Henry Peyroux, commandant, dated 7th April, 1801.
December 9, 1811: Present, a full Board. It is the opinion of the Board that this claim ought not to be confirmed.

MARTIN RODNEY, claiming four hundred and ninety arpents of land, situate in the district of New Madrid; produces the record of an order of survey from C. D. Delassus, commandant, dated 7th July, 1798.
December 9, 1811: Present, a full Board. It is the opinion of the Board that this claim ought not to be confirmed.

LAURENCE SYDENER, claiming seven hundred and fifty arpents of land, situate on the Missouri, district of St. Charles; produces the record of a concession from Delassus, Lieutenant Governor, dated 20th June, 1802; record of a plat of survey, dated 7th November, 1803, certified 27th December, 1803.

December 9, 1811: Present, a full Board. It is the opinion of the Board that this claim ought not to be confirmed.

PETER SOMMALT, claiming three hundred arpents of land, situate on Peruque, district of St. Charles; produces the record of a concession from Charles D. Delassus, Lieutenant Governor, dated 9th November, 1799; record of a plat of survey, dated 22d November, 1799, certified 11th January, 1800.

December 9, 1811: Present, a full Board. It is the opinion of the Board that this claim ought not to be confirmed.

AUGUSTE CHOUTEAU, assignee of Hyacinth St. Cyr, claiming a lot in St. Louis, one hundred and twenty by one hundred and fifty feet; produces the record of an extract of public sale of the property of said St. Cyr, dated 1801.

December 9, 1811: Present, a full Board. It is the opinion of the Board that this claim ought not to be granted.

WILLIAM JAMES, assignee of Robert Smith, claiming seven hundred and eighty-two arpents of land, situate on the river Aux Vases, district of St. Genevieve; produces the record of a concession from Zenon Trudeau, Lieutenant Governor, dated 17th November, 1797; the record of a plat of survey, dated 11th January and certified 2d March, 1798; record of a transfer from Smith to claimant, dated 9th March, 1798.

December 9, 1811: Present, a full Board. It is the opinion of the Board that this claim ought not to be confirmed.

DANIEL SEXTON, claiming three hundred arpents of land, situate on Caney creek, district of New Madrid; produces the record of a petition and recommendation for a concession from Peyroux, commandant, dated 12th April, 1802.

December 9, 1811: Present, a full Board. It is the opinion of the Board that this claim ought not to be confirmed.

LOUIS SELF, claiming two hundred and ninety-two arpents and forty-six perches of land, situate on Bellevue, district of St. Genevieve; produces the record of a plat of survey, dated 21st February and certified 28th February, 1806.

December 9, 1811: Present, a full Board. It is the opinion of the Board that this claim ought not to be granted.

DANIEL SEXTON, claiming six hundred and seventy-one acres of land, situate at Tywappety, district of Cape Girardeau; produces record of a plat of survey, dated 15th February and certified 28th February, 1806.

December 9, 1811: Present, a full Board. It is the opinion of the Board that this claim ought not to be granted.

MARY SMITH, claiming three hundred acres of land, situate as aforesaid; produces record of a plat of survey, dated 7th February and certified 27th February, 1806.

December 9, 1811: Present, a full Board. It is the opinion of the Board that this claim ought not to be granted.

JOHN NICHOLAS SHUN, claiming eight hundred and seventy-seven arpents thirty-six perches of land, situate on the Mississippi, district of St. Louis; produces record of a concession from Delassus, Lieutenant Governor, dated 11th November, 1801; record of a plat of survey, dated 9th January and certified 28th February, 1806.

December 9, 1811: Present, a full Board. It is the opinion of the Board that this claim ought not to be confirmed.

GEORGE SMIRL, assignee of James Smirl, assignee of William Drennon, assignee of Gabriel Dodie, claiming eight hundred and forty-seven acres of land, situate at Little Rock, district of St. Louis; produces record of a plat of survey, dated 13th January and certified 17th February, 1806; record of a transfer from Dodie to Drennon, dated 29th July, 1803; record of a transfer from Drennon to James Smirl, dated 7th May, 1804; record of transfer from James Smirl to claimant, dated 18th July, 1804.

December 9, 1811: Present, a full Board. It is the opinion of the Board that this claim ought not to be granted.

PIERRE CHOUTEAU, assignee of Etienne St. Pierre, claiming a tract of land, beginning at the foot of the hills below the mouth of the river Bergen, and ascending said river one league, including the Pointe Basse, opposite Mill Island, district of St. Charles; produces record of a transfer from Delassus, Lieutenant Governor, dated 8th October, 1799; record of a transfer from St. Pierre to claimant, dated 3d January, 1804.

December 9, 1811: Present, a full Board. It is the opinion of the Board that this claim ought not to be confirmed.

ANDREW SNODDY, claiming eight hundred arpents of land, situate in the district of St. Genevieve; produces record of a concession from Delassus, Lieutenant Governor, dated 28th May, 1800.

December 9, 1811: Present, a full Board. It is the opinion of the Board that this claim ought not to be confirmed.

JACQUE CLAMORGAN, assignee of Joseph Sumande, claiming sixty by one hundred and twenty feet of land or lot in St. Louis; produces record of a transfer from Sumande to claimant, dated 9th September, 1786.

December 9, 1811: Present, a full Board. It is the opinion of the Board that this claim ought not to be granted.

GREGOIRE SARFY, claiming six thousand arpents of land, situate on the river des Peres, district of St. Louis; produces record of a concession from Charles D. Delassus, Lieutenant Governor, dated 28th October, 1802; record of a plat of survey of four thousand and two arpents, dated 18th March, 1803; record of a plat of survey of one thousand four hundred arpents, dated 2d January, and certified 15th April, 1804.

December 9, 1811: Present, a full Board. It is the opinion of the Board that this claim ought not to be confirmed.

****

ANTOINE SAUGRAIN, assignee of Gregoire Sarpy, claiming a lot in St. Louis, sixty by three hundred feet; produces record of a transfer from Sarpy to claimant, dated 3d March, 1803.
December 9, 1811: Present, a full Board. It is the opinion of the Board that this claim ought not to be granted.

ANTOINE SAUGRAIN, assignee of Gregoire Sarpy, claiming a lot in St. Louis, sixty by three hundred feet; produces record of a transfer from Sarpy to claimant, dated 18th May, 1802.
December 9, 1811: Present, a full Board. It is the opinion of the Board that this claim ought not to be granted.

CHARLES SANGUINETT, claiming four thousand three hundred and forty arpents fifty-eight perches of land, situate at the point of Missouri and Mississippi, district of St. Charles; produces record of a concession for eight hundred arpents from Baron de Carondelet, Governor General, dated 6th April, 1797; record of a concession from Charles D. Delassus, Lieutenant Governor, for an augmentation of said land, described in certain bounds, dated 19th December, 1799; record of a plat of survey of four thousand three hundred and forty arpents fifty-eight perches of land, dated 30th January and certified 15th February, 1804.
December 9, 1811: Present, a full Board. It is the opinion of the Board that this claim ought not to be confirmed.

ELIJAH SMITH, claiming a league square of land, situate in the district of St. Genevieve; produces record of a concession from Zenon Trudeau, Lieutenant Governor, dated 18th May, 1797.
December 9, 1811: Present, a full Board. It is the opinion of the Board that this claim ought not to be confirmed.

HENRY C. SMITH, claiming four hundred arpents of land, situate at Cape Cinq-hommes, district of St. Genevieve; produces record of a concession from Delassus, Lieutenant Governor, dated 24th January, 1800; record of a plat of survey of two hundred arpents on the Mississippi, dated 2d February, and certified 10th March, 1800; record of a plat of survey of one hundred and forty-six arpents, dated 1st February, and certified 10th March, 1800.
December 9, 1811: Present, a full Board. It is the opinion of the Board that this claim ought not to be confirmed.

PETER CHOUTEAU, assignee of Matthew Soucier, claiming one thousand two hundred arpents of land, situate on the river Mississippi, district of St. Charles; produces record of a concession from Delassus, Lieutenant Governor, dated 28th November, 1800.
December 9, 1811: Present, a full Board. It is the opinion of the Board that this claim ought not to be confirmed.

PASCAL DITCHEMENDY, assignee of Jacque St. Vrain, claiming twenty-five by sixty arpents of land, situate on Mud river, district of St. Genevieve; produces a notice to the recorder.
December 9, 1811: Present, a full Board. It is the opinion of the Board that this claim ought not to be confirmed.

ALEXANDER McNAIR, assignee of the sheriff of St. Louis district, who sold the same as the property of Gregoire Sarpy, claiming forty arpents of land, situate on Barriere Desnoyers, district of St. Louis; produces the record of a transfer from sheriff to claimant, dated 9th June, 1808.
December 9, 1811: Present, a full Board. It is the opinion of the Board that this claim ought not to be granted.

HUGH STEPHENSON, heirs of, claiming four hundred arpents of land, situate on the Missouri, district of St. Louis; produce the record of an order of survey from Zenon Trudeau, Lieutenant Governor, dated 13th April, 1797; record of a plat of survey, dated 8th February and certified 20th May, 1800.
December 9, 1811: Present, a full Board. It is the opinion of the Board that this claim ought not to be confirmed.

JONATHAN SKINNER, claiming three hundred acres of land, situate on Grand Glaize, district of St. Louis; produces a notice to the recorder.
December 9, 1811: Present, a full Board. It is the opinion of the Board that this claim ought not to be granted.

JOHN STRICKLAND, claiming six hundred arpents of land, situate on Big river, district of St. Genevieve; produces a notice to the recorder.
December 9, 1811: Present, a full Board. It is the opinion of the Board that this claim ought not to be granted.

ABRAHAM SMITH, claiming six hundred arpents of land, situate in the district of St. Charles; produces a notice to the recorder.
December 9, 1811: Present, a full Board. It is the opinion of the Board that this claim ought not to be granted.

CHARLES SANGUINETT, claiming three thousand arpents of land, on an island in the Mississippi called Isle Cabaret, district of St. Louis; produces the record of a concession from Baron de Carondelet, Governor General, dated 6th April, 1797.
December 9, 1811: Present, a full Board. It is the opinion of the Board that this claim ought not to be confirmed.

JOSEPH SILVAIN, claiming two hundred and fifty arpents of land, situate in the district of Cape Girardeau; produces the record of a concession from Delassus, Lieutenant Governor, dated 15th December, 1799.
December 9, 1811: Present, a full Board. It is the opinion of the Board that this claim ought not to be confirmed.

JAMES SUMMERS, claiming two hundred and fifty acres of land, situate on White river, district of Cape Girardeau; produces a notice to the recorder.
December 9, 1811: Present, a full Board. It is the opinion of the Board that this claim ought not to be granted.

JOHN SHARADIN, claiming three hundred acres of land, situate as aforesaid; produces a notice to the recorder.
December 9, 1811: Present, a full Board. It is the opinion of the Board that this claim ought not to be granted.

RICHARD JONES WATERS, assignee of Russel Hewitt, assignee of John Tutham, assignee of Joseph Story, claiming ninety arpents of land, situate on bayou St. Thomas, district of New Madrid; produces a notice to the recorder.
December 9, 1811: Present, a full Board. It is the opinion of the Board that this claim ought not to be granted.

GEORGE ROBERT SPENCER, claiming eight hundred arpents of land, situate on the river Jacob, district of St. Charles; produces the record of a concession from Zenon Trudeau, Lieutenant Governor, dated 14th June, 1797; record of a plat of survey, dated 5th November, 1797, certified 5th March, 1798.
December 9, 1811: Present, a full Board. It is the opinion of the Board that this claim ought not to be confirmed.

DUBREUIL, claiming two hundred and seventeen by one hundred feet, lot No. 3, in the village of St. Ferdinand, district of St. Louis; produces a general plat of survey of the village of St. Ferdinand, dated 3d October, 1794; said to have been made in pursuance of an order of survey from Zenon Trudeau, Lieutenant Governor.
December 9, 1811: Present, a full Board. It is the opinion of the Board that this claim ought not to be confirmed.

LOUIS MARC, claiming three hundred by one hundred and fifty feet, lot No. 4; produces as above.
December 9, 1811: Present, a full Board. It is the opinion of the Board that this claim ought not to be confirmed.

GAGNE, claiming three hundred by one hundred and fifty feet, lot No. 5; produces as above.
December 9, 1811: Present, a full Board. It is the opinion of the Board that this claim ought not to be confirmed.

CRELY, claiming three hundred by three hundred feet, lot No. 6; produces as above.
December 9, 1811: Present, a full Board. It is the opinion of the Board that this claim ought not to be confirmed.

BAPTISTE DELISLE, claiming three hundred by three hundred feet, lot No. 23; produces as above.
December 9, 1811: Present, a full Board. It is the opinion of the Board that this claim ought not to be confirmed.

DELAURIERE, claiming one hundred and fifty by one hundred and fifty feet, lot No. 24; porduces as above.
December 9, 1811: Present, a full Board. It is the opinion of the Board that this claim ought not to be confirmed.

LOUIS MARIE, claiming one hundred and fifty by one hundred and fifty feet, lot No. 25; produces as aforesaid.
December 9, 1811: Present, a full Board. It is the opinion of the Board that this claim ought not to be confirmed.

BACCANE, claiming three hundred by one hundred and fifty feet, lot No. 26; produces as aforesaid.
December 9, 1811: Present, a full Board. It is the opinion of the Board that this claim ought not to be confirmed.

GAGNE, claiming one hundred and eighty-five by one hundred and fifty feet, lot No. 27; produces as above.
December 9, 1811: Present, a full Board. It is the opinion of the Board that this claim ought not to be confirmed.

MADAME LADOUCEUR, claiming one hundred and eighty-five by one hundred and fifty feet, lot No. 28; produces as above.
December 9, 1811: Present, a full Board. It is the opinion of the Board that this claim ought not to be confirmed.

DESJARDIN, claiming one hundred and eighty-five by one hundred and fifty feet, lot No. 29; produces as above.
December 9, 1811: Present, a full Board. It is the opinion of the Board that this claim ought not to be confirmed.

CALVE, claiming one hundred and eighty-five by one hundred and fifty feet, lot No. 30; produces as above.
December 9, 1811: Present, a full Board. It is the opinion of the Board that this claim ought not to be confirmed.

PANETON, claiming one hundred and eighty-five by one hundred and fifty feet, lot No. 31; produces as above.
December 9, 1811: Present, a full Board. It is the opinion of the Board that this claim ought not to be confirmed.

COUDRE, claiming one hundred and eighty-five by one hundred and fifty feet, lot No. 32; produces as above.
December 9, 1811: Present, a full Board. It is the opinion of the Board that this claim ought not to be confirmed.

FRANCIS MARÉCHAL, claiming one hundred and eighty-five by one hundred and fifty feet, lot No. 34; produces as above.
December 9, 1811: Present, a full Board. It is the opinion of the Board that this claim ought not to be confirmed.

BAPTISTE DESHOMET, claiming one hundred and eighty-five by one hundred and fifty feet, lot No. 33; produces as above.
December 9, 1811: Present, a full Board. It is the opinion of the Board that this claim ought not to be confirmed.

BACCANE, claiming one hundred and fifty by one hundred and fifty feet, lot No. 35; produces as above.
December 9, 1811: Present, a full Board. It is the opinion of the Board that this claim ought not to be confirmed.

****

LABROSSE, claiming one hundred and fifty by one hundred and fifty feet, lot No. 36; produces as above.
December 9, 1811: Present, a full Board. It is the opinion of the Board that this claim ought not to be confirmed.

ALEXIS PICARD, claiming three hundred by three hundred feet, lot No. 39; produces as aforesaid.
December 9, 1811: Present, a full Board. It is the opinion of the Board that this claim ought not to be confirmed.

L'HABITANT, claiming one hundred and fifty by one hundred and fifty feet, lot No. 60; produces as above.
December 9, 1811: Present, a full Board. It is the opinion of the Board that this claim ought not to be confirmed.

CADIEN, claiming one hundred and eighty-five by one hundred and fifty feet, lot No. 66; produces as above.
December 9, 1811: Present, a full Board. It is the opinion of the Board that this claim ought not to be confirmed.

RIVET, claiming three hundred and seventy by three hundred feet, lot No. 68; produces as above.
December 9, 1811: Present, a full Board. It is the opinion of the Board that this claim ought not to be confirmed.

FRANCIS DELAURIERE, claiming one hundred and fifty by one hundred and fifty feet, lot No. 105; produces as above.
December 9, 1811: Present, a full Board. It is the opinion of the Board that this claim ought not to be confirmed.

CLAMORGAN, claiming one hundred and fifty by one hundred and fifty feet, lot No. 101; produces as above.
December 9, 1811: Present, a full Board. It is the opinion of the Board that this claim ought not to be confirmed.

CLAMORGAN, claiming one hundred and fifty by one hundred and fifty feet, lot No. 102; produces as above.
December 9, 1811: Present, a full Board. It is the opinion of the Board that this claim ought not to be confirmed.

CLAMORGAN, claiming one hundred and fifty by one hundred and fifty feet, lot No. 103; produces as above.
December 9, 1811: Present, a full Board. It is the opinion of the Board that this claim ought not to be confirmed.

CLAMORGAN, claiming one hundred and fifty by one hundred and fifty feet, lot No. 104; produces as above.
December 9, 1811: Present, a full Board. It is the opinion of the Board that this claim ought not to be confirmed.

ANTOINE MARECHAL, claiming two arpents, lot A; produces as above.
December 9, 1811: Present, a full Board. It is the opinion of the Board that this claim ought not to be confirmed.

JACQUE TABEAU, claiming three hundred by one hundred and eighty feet, lot B, produces as above.
December 9, 1811: Present, a full Board. It is the opinion of the Board that this claim ought not to be confirmed.

CAPTAIN BEAUROSIER DUNNEGANT, claiming two hundred and fifty by one hundred and eighty feet, lot C; produces as above.
November 9, 1811: Present, a full Board. It is the opinion of the Board that this claim ought not to be confirmed.

ROBIDOUX, claiming one hundred and sixty by one hundred and eighty feet, lot D; produces as aforesaid.
December 9, 1811: Present, a full Board. It is the opinion of the Board that this claim ought not to be confirmed.

CALVE, claiming one hundred and twenty by one hundred and eighty feet, lot E; produces as above.
December 9, 1811: Present, a full Board. It is the opinion of the Board that this claim ought not to be confirmed.

LACHAISE, claiming one hundred and eight by one hundred and eighty feet, lot F; produces as above.
December 9, 1811: Present, a full Board. It is the opinion of the Board that this claim ought not to be confirmed.

LAMMARE, claiming one hundred and twenty by one hundred and eighty feet, lot G; produces as above.
December 9, 1811: Present, a full Board. It is the opinion of the Board that this claim ought not to be confirmed.

TRUDELL and MENARD, claiming two hundred and forty by one hundred and eighty feet, lot H; produces as above.
December 9, 1811: Present, a full Board. It is the opinion of the Board that this claim ought not to be confirmed.

MORO, claiming three hundred by one hundred and eighty feet, lot K; produces as above.
December 9, 1811: Present, a full Board. It is the opinion of the Board that this claim ought not to be confirmed.

NOEL BRUNETT, claiming three hundred by three hundred feet, lot No. 107; produces as above.
December 9, 1811: Present, a full Board. It is the opinion of the Board that this claim ought not to be confirmed.

MERCIER, claiming three hundred by three hundred feet, lot No. 106; produces as above.

****

December 9, 1811: Present, a full Board. It is the opinion of the Board that this claim ought not to be confirmed.

INHABITANTS OF ST. FERDINAND VILLAGE, claiming two hundred and seven by two hundred feet, lot No. 2, Terrien de l'Eglise; produce as above.
December 9, 1811: Present, a full Board. It is the opinion of the Board that this claim ought not to be confirmed.

INHABITANTS OF ST. FERDINAND VILLAGE, claiming five hundred by three hundred feet, grave-yard lot; produce as above.
December 9, 1811: Present, a full Board. It is the opinion of the Board that this claim ought not to be confirmed.

JOHN BAPTISTE BELLAND, assignee of Charles Tayon, Jun., assignee of Andrew Blondeau, claiming eighty arpents of land, and ANDREW BLONDEAU, claiming four hundred arpents of land, situate on river Peruque, district of St. Charles; produce the record of a transfer from Tayon to claimant, dated 7th July, 1804.
December 9, 1811: Present, a full Board. It is the opinion of the Board that this claim ought not to be confirmed.

JOSEPH TUCKER, claiming four hundred and sixty-nine acres of land, situate in the district of St. Genevieve; produces the record of a plat of survey, dated 18th December, 1805, certified 26th February, 1806.
December 10, 1811: Present, a full Board. It is the opinion of the Board that this claim ought not to be granted.

HENRY TUCKER, claiming nine hundred and forty-nine arpents of land, situate as aforesaid; produces the record of a plat of survey, dated 20th December, 1805, certified 27th February, 1806.
December 10, 1811: Present, a full Board. It is the opinion of the Board that this claim ought not to be granted.

WILLIAM THOMPSON, claiming seven hundred and ninety acres of land, situate in the district of Cape Girardeau; produces the record of a plat of survey, dated 14th February and certified 28th February, 1806.
December 10, 1811: Present, a full Board. It is the opinion of the Board that this claim ought not to be granted.

JAMES THOMPSON, claiming three hundred and ninety-six arpents of land, situate in the district of St. Genevieve; produces the record of a concession from Zenon Trudeau, Lieutenant Governor, dated 20th February, 1798; record of a plat of survey, dated 3d February and certified 5th March, 1800.
December 10, 1811: Present, a full Board. It is the opinion of the Board that this claim ought not to be confirmed.

EDWARD HEMPSTEAD, assignee of the sheriff of St. Charles district, who sold the same as the property of John Campbell and White Matlock, assignee of Jacque St. Vrain, assignée of Toussaint Tourville, claiming six hundred arpents, and said TOURVILLE claiming two hundred arpents of land, situate in the district of St. Charles; produces the record of a concession from Charles D. Delassus, Lieutenant Governor, dated 18th January, 1800; record of a plat of survey, dated 11th February, 1804, certified 9th January, 1806; record of a transfer from Tourville to St. Vrain, dated 12th February, 1800; record of a transfer from St. Vrain to Campbell and Matlock, dated 29th August, 1805; record of a transfer from the sheriff to claimant, dated 29th January, 1808.
December 10, 1811: Present, a full Board. It is the opinion of the Board that this claim ought not to be confirmed.

MARIE PHILIP LEDUC, assignee of Albert Tison, claiming seven thousand and fifty-six arpents of land, situate fifty-one miles north of St. Louis, district of St. Charles; produces the record of a concession from Charles D. Delassus, Lieutenant Governor, dated 17th December, 1800; record of a plat of survey, dated 15th February and certified 20th March, 1804; record of a transfer from Tison to claimant, dated 20th November, 1805.
December 10, 1811: Present, a full Board. It is the opinion of the Board that this claim ought not to be confirmed.

ANTOINE SAUGRIN, assignee of Francis Tayon, assignee of Joseph Tayon, claiming a lot in St. Louis, one hundred and twenty by one hundred and fifty feet; produces the record of a transfer from Francis Tayon to claimant, dated 9th July, 1805.
December 10, 1811: Present, a full Board. It is the opinion of the Board that this claim ought not to be granted.

CHARLES TAYON, Jun., claiming eight hundred arpents of land, situate on Missouri river, district of St. Charles; produces the record of a concession from Charles D. Delassus, Lieutenant Governor, dated 18th October, 1802; a record of a plat of survey, dated 13th February and certified 28th February, 1806.
December 10, 1811: Present, a full Board. It is the opinion of the Board that this claim ought not to be confirmed.

PETER CHOUTEAU, assignee of Joseph Tayon, claiming a lot of one hundred and twenty by one hundred and fifty feet in the town of St. Louis; produces the record of a transfer from Tayon to claimant, dated 14th July, 1799.
December 10, 1811: Present, a full Board. It is the opinion of the Board that this claim ought not to be granted.

PETER CHOUTEAU, assignee of Charles Tayon, claiming one thousand six hundred arpents of land, situate in the district of St. Louis; produces the record of a concession from. Delassus, Lieutenant Governor, dated 16th January, 1800; the record of a transfer from Tayon to claimant, dated 17th December, 1803.
December 10, 1811: Present, a full Board. It is the opinion of the Board that this claim ought not to be confirmed.

PETER CHOUTEAU, executor of Joseph Tayon, claiming forty arpents of land, situate on the prairie adjoining the town of St. Louis; produces a concession from St. Ange and Piernas, Lieutenant Governors, dated 23d May,

1772. In the margin of this concession is written " reuni au domain du roy, pour les avoir abandonné depuis long-temps. St. Louis, 4 Juin, 1793. Trudeau."

December 10, 1811: Present, a full Board. It is the opinion of the Board that this claim ought not to be confirmed.

CHARLES GRATIOT, assignee of Leve Thiel, claiming two hundred arpents of land, situate on the Merrimack, district of St. Louis; produces the record of a concession from Delassus, Lieutenant Governor, dated 15th December, 1799.

December 10, 1811: Present, a full Board. It is the opinion of the Board that this claim ought not to be confirmed.

LOUIS LABEAUME, assignee of John Baptiste Tison, claiming seven thousand and fifty-six arpents of land, situate on Salt river, district of St. Charles; produces the record of a concession from Delassus, Lieutenant Governor, dated 19th November, 1799; the record of a transfer from Tison to claimant, dated 20th May, 1803.

December 10, 1811: Present, full Board. It is the opinion of the Board that this claim ought not to be confirmed.

HENRY PEYROUX, assignee of Bartholomew Tardiveau & Co., claiming eight arpents of land, situate in the district of New Madrid; produces the record of a transfer from Tardiveau & Co. to claimant, dated 3d November, 1802.

December 10, 1811: Present, a full Board. It is the opinion of the Board that this claim ought not to be granted.

BAPTISTE TAUMIER, claiming six by forty arpents of land, situate on river Lafourche, district of St. Genevieve; produces the record of a concession from Zenon Trudeau, Lieutenant Governor, dated 13th November, 1797.

December 10, 1811: Present, a full Board. It is the opinion of the Board that this claim ought not to be confirmed.

LOUIS BUAT, and others, claiming a tract of land, situate between the two forks of river Gabourij, and adjoining the forty arpent lots near Prairie à Gautier, district of St. Genevieve; produce the record of a concession from Zenon Trudeau, Lieutenant Governor, dated 1st September, 1797.

December 10, 1811: Present, a full Board. It is the opinion of the Board that this claim ought not to be confirmed.

SOLOMON THORN, claiming six hundred arpents of land, situate in the district of New Madrid; produces a notice to the recorder.

December 10, 1811: Present, a full Board. It is the opinion of the Board that this claim ought not to be granted.

JOHN TAYLOR, claiming eight hundred arpents of land, situate in Arkansas district, river St. Francis; produces the record of a concession from Francisco Caso y Luengo, commandant, dated 6th January, 1803.

December 10, 1811: Present, a full Board. It is the opinion of the Board that this claim ought not to be confirmed.

HENRY GLASS, assignee of Joseph Mating, assignee of Francis Merryman, assignee of David Yarborough, claiming seven hundred and sixty-eight arpents of land, situate on river Saline, district of St. Genevieve; produces the record of a plat of survey, dated 30th December, 1805, certified 5th February, 1806; the record of a transfer from Yarborough to Merryman, dated 20th February, 1804; the record of a transfer from Merryman to Mating, dated 5th February, 1804; the record of a transfer from Mating to claimant, dated 19th August, 1804; the record of a certificate of permission to settle, dated 20th February, 1806, signed Pierre Delassus Deluziere.

December 10, 1811: Present, a full Board. It is the opinion of the Board that this claim ought not to be granted.

JESSE and ABIJAH HUNT, assignees of William Strother, assignee of Basil Valle, claiming three hundred arpents of land, situate in the district of St. Genevieve; produce the record of a concession from Delassus, Lieutenant Governor, dated 1st November, 1799; the record of a plat of survey, dated 28th December, 1799, certified 10th January, 1800; the record of a transfer from Strother to claimant, dated 4th June, 1806.

December 10, 1811: Present, a full Board. It is the opinion of the Board that this claim ought not to be confirmed.

JOHN BTE. VALLE, Jr., claiming seven hundred and thirty arpents of land, situate on the river establishment, district of St. Genevieve; produces the record of a concession from Delassus, Lieutenant Governor, dated 24th December, 1799; the record of a plat of survey, dated 14th January and certified 10th February, 1800.

December 10, 1811: Present, a full Board. It is the opinion of the Board that this claim ought not to be confirmed.

MARIE LOUISA VALLE VILLARS, claiming seven thousand and fifty-six arpents of land, situate on river Saline, district of St. Genevieve; produces the record of a copy of concession, certified by Diego Maxwell, 18th February; concession dated 17th September, 1796; the record of a plat of survey, dated 3d February, 1803, certified 3d January, 1804.

December 10, 1811: Present, a full Board. It is the opinion of the Board that this claim ought not to be confirmed.

JOHN CAMPBELL and WHITE MATLOCK, assignees of Benito Vasquez, claiming sixty arpents of land, situate on Grand Prairie, district of St. Louis; produce the record of a transfer from Benito to claimants, dated 30th March, 1805; the record of a plat of survey, dated and certified 28th February, 1806.

December 10, 1811: Present, a full Board. It is the opinion of the Board that this claim ought not to be granted.

JOHN CAMPBELL and WHITE MATLOCK, assignees of Benito Vasquez, claiming forty arpents of land, situate as aforesaid; produce the record of a transfer from Vasquez to claimants, dated 30th March, 1805; the record of a plat of survey, dated and certified 28th February, 1806.

December 10, 1811: Present, a full Board. It is the opinion of the Board that this claim ought not to be granted.

JOHN CAMPBELL and WHITE MATLOCK, assignees of Benito Vasquez, claiming a lot in St. Louis, three hundred by one hundred feet; produces the record of a transfer from Vasquez to claimants, dated 30th March, 1805; the record of a plat of survey, dated and certified 28th February, 1806.

December 10, 1811: Present, a full Board. It is the opinion of the Board that this claim ought not to be granted.

MARY VALLE, claiming one thousand six hundred and fifty-eight arpents of land, situate on the river Au Vase, district of St. Genevieve; produces the record of a concessson from Zenon Trudeau, Lieutenant Governor, dated 13th August, 1796; record of a plat of survey, dated 15th August, 1796, certified 1st September, 1797.

December 10, 1811: Present, a full Board. It is the opinion of the Board that this claim ought not to be confirmed.

JOHN BAPTISTE VALLE, claiming seven thousand and fifty-six arpents of land, situate at the river establishment, district of St. Genevieve; produces the record of a concession from Zenon Trudeau, Lieutenant Governor, dated 4th July, 1796; the record of a petition to the Governor General, and a recommendation thereon, dated 27th February, 1802, with a reference of Morales to Peter Derbigny, for a translation of the papers.

December 10, 1811: Present, a full Board. It is the opinion of the Board that this claim ought not to be confirmed.

ANTOINE V. BOUIS, assignee of Gabriel Hunot, assignee of Louis Bodoin, assignee of Joseph Hunot, assignee of Noel Viens, claiming a lot in the village of Carondelet, district of St. Louis, one hundred and fifty feet square; produces the record of a transfer, from Gabriel Hunot to claimant, dated 11th January, 1808.

December 10, 1811: Present, a full Board. It is the opinion of the Board that this claim ought not to be granted.

WILLIAM MORRISON, assignee of Charles Fremon Delauriare, assignee of Francis Valle, claiming a lot in St. Genevieve village of two arpents; produces the record of a transfer from Valle to Delauriare, dated 6th May, 1803; the record of a transfer from Delauriare to claimant, dated 22d January, 1807.

December 10, 1811: Present, a full Board. It is the opinion of the Board that this claim ought not to be granted.

BASIL VALLE, claiming a lot in St. Genevieve village of two arpents; produces the record of a concession from Antoine Doro, commandant, dated 11th September, 1785.

December 10, 1811: Present, a full Board. It is the opinion of the Board that this claim ought not to be confirmed.

WILLIAM USERY, claiming seven hundred and forty-eight arpents and sixty-eight perches of land, situate on the river St. Francis, district of New Madrid; produces a notice to the recorder.

December 10, 1811: Present, a full Board. It is the opinion of the Board that this claim ought not to be granted.

WILLIAM VANTICO, claiming seven hundred and forty-eight arpents and sixty-eight perches of land, situate on the Forks of Missouri and Mississippi, district of St. Charles; produces a notice to the recorder.

December 10, 1811: Present, a full Board. It is the opinion of the Board that this claim ought not to be granted.

FRANCIS VALLE, heirs and representatives of, claiming four hundred arpents of land, situate at Mineral de Fer, district of St. Genevieve; produce the record of a petition to the Intendant, and recommendation for a concession from Delassus, Lieutenant Governor, dated 29th September, 1808.

December 10, 1811: Present, a full Board. It is the opinion of the Board that this claim ought not to be confirmed.

MATHIAS VANDERHIDER, representatives of, claiming four hundred arpents of land, situate on Negro Fork of the Merrimack, district of St. Louis; produces the record of a concession from Zenon Trudeau, Lieutenant Governor, dated 16th March, 1797.

December 10, 1811: Present, a full Board. It is the opinion of the Board that this claim ought not to be confirmed.

LOUIS VACHARD, claiming nine hundred and fifty arpents of land, situate on the Mississippi, district of New Madrid; produces a notice to the recorder.

December 10, 1811: Present, a full Board. It is the opinion of the Board that this claim ought not to be granted.

JOHN COONTZ, assignee of Jeremiah Wray, claiming twenty-five by twenty toises of land, situate at the village of St. Charles, district of St. Charles; produces the record of a concession from Zenon Trudeau, Lieutenant Governor, dated 3d July, 1796; the record of a plat of survey, dated 5th July, 1796.

December 10, 1811: Present, a full Board. It is the opinion of the Board that this claim ought not to be confirmed.

RICHARD JONES WATERS, claiming two thousand arpents of land, situate on the bayou St. John and St. Thomas, district of New Madrid; produces the record of an order of survey from Henry Peyroux, commandant, dated 25th August, 1800; the record of a plat of survey, signed Joseph Story.

December 10, 1811: Present, a full Board. It is the opinion of the Board that this claim ought not to be confirmed.

RICHARD JONES WATERS, claiming sixteen arpents of land, situate on the bayou St. John, district of New Madrid; produces the record of a plat of survey, dated the 10th and certified 27th February, 1806.

December 10, 1811: Present, a full Board. It is the opinion of the Board that this claim ought not to be granted.

JOSEPH WALLACE, claiming seven hundred and fifty arpents of land, situate in the district of St. Charles; produces the record of a plat of survey, dated 30th and certified 27th February, 1806.

December 10, 1811: Present, a full Board. It is the opinion of the Board that this claim ought not to be granted.

JOHN WILLGATE, claiming seven hundred and forty-eight arpents sixty-eight perches of land, situate on White waters, district of Cape Girardeau; produces record of a plat of survey, signed B. Cousin, countersigned Antoine Soulard, without date.

December 10, 1811: Present, a full Board. It is the opinion of the Board that this claim ought not to be granted.

JOSEPH WEBKINS, claiming seven hundred and fifty arpents of land, situate in the district of Cape Girardeau; produces record of a plat of survey, dated 17th and certified 26th February, 1806.

December 10, 1811: Present, a full Board. It is the opinion of the Board that this claim ought not to be granted.

LOUIS TAYON, claiming eight hundred arpents of land, situate on Missouri, district of St. Charles; produces record of a concession from Delassus, Lieutenant Governor, dated 18th October, 1802; record of a plat of survey, dated 14th and certified 28th February, 1806.

December 10, 1811: Present, a full Board. It is the opinion of the Board that this claim ought not to be confirmed.

ALBERT TISON, assignee of Louis Labeaume, assignee of James Williams, claiming four hundred arpents of land, situate in the district of St. Louis; produces record of a concession from Delassus, Lieutenant Governor, dated 15th April, 1803; record of a transfer from Williams to Labeaume, dated 29th April, 1806.

December 10, 1811: Present, a full Board. It is the opinion of the Board that this claim ought not to be confirmed.

FREDERICK WOOLFORD, claiming seven hundred and forty-eight arpents sixty-eight perches of land, situate on the river St. Laurent, district of St. Genevieve; produces notice to the recorder.

December 10, 1811: Present, a full Board. It is the opinion of the Board that this claim ought not to be granted.

ANDREW WALKER, claiming eight hundred and fifty arpents of land, situate on river Dardennes, district of St. Charles; produces notice to the recorder; and a plat of survey, dated 25th September, 1806, not signed.

December 10, 1811: Present, a full Board. It is the opinion of the Board that this claim ought not to be granted.

AQUILLA WICKERHAM, claiming seven hundred and forty-eight arpents sixty-eight perches of land, situate on Negro fork, Merrimack, district of St. Louis; produces notice to the recorder.

December 10, 1811: Present, a full Board. It is the opinion of the Board that this claim ought not to be granted.

JACOB WICKERHAM, claiming seven hundred and forty-eight arpents sixty-eight perches of land, situate as aforesaid; produces notice to the recorder.

December 10, 1811: Present, a full Board. It is the opinion of the Board that this claim ought not to be granted.

JAMES WILLIAMS, claiming two hundred and forty arpents of land, situate in the district of New Madrid; produces notice to the recorder.

December 10, 1811: Present, a full Board. It is the opinion of the Board that this claim ought not to be granted.

EDWARD YOUNG, claiming eight hundred arpents of land, situate on Maneto Saline, district of St. Louis; produces the record of a concession from Charles D. Delassus, Lieutenant Governor, dated 15th January, 1800.

December 10, 1811: Present, a full Board. It is the opinion of the Board that this claim ought not to be confirmed.

ROWLAND BOYD, assignee of Joseph Boyer, assignee of Swanson Yarborough, claiming six hundred and forty arpents of land, situate on the south fork of Saline creek, district of St. Genevieve; produces a notice to the recorder.

December 10, 1811: Present, a full Board. It is the opinion of the Board that this claim ought not to be granted.

JEAN MARIE PAPIN, claiming two hundred and forty-three arpents of land, situate on river Gabouri, district of St. Genevieve; produces the record of a concession from Zenon Trudeau, Lieutenant Governor, dated 13th November, 1797; record of a plat of survey, dated 20th March, 1799, certified 1st November, 1799.

The following testimony in this claim was taken by John B. C. Lucas, commissioner, at St. Genevieve, 2d May, 1809, by authority from the Board:

Boston Butcher, duly sworn, deposes that the land claimed is situated two miles and a half from St. Genevieve, northwest of said place; that he was employed by claimant to make rails and fence on premises, which he did about the last part of September, 1803; that the enclosure he then made contained about one-half of an acre; that he, deponent, planted cherry trees for said claimant in the said enclosure in October or November of the aforesaid year; that the said land was cultivated the next following year for the use of claimant.

December 14, 1811: Present, a full Board. It is the opinion of the Board that this claim ought not to be confirmed.

JACQUE CLAMORGAN, claiming forty by eighty arpents of land, situate in Merrimack, district of St. Louis; produces a duly registered concession from Zenon Trudeau, Lieutenant Governor, dated 5th October, 1793, and a survey of the same, dated 28th and certified 29th February, 1806; produces also record of a declaration from Zenon Trudeau, Lieutenant Governor; that he had put claimant in possession of said land, with a figurative plat accompanying the same, dated 5th October, 1793.

Testimony taken, July 17, 1806. John Boli, being duly sworn, says that one James Head, who had lived on said land, moved out about ten years ago; that a person by the name of House afterwards moved on the same; raised two crops, and was afterwards, to wit, about six years ago, killed by the Indians; witness cannot tell for whose use he then cultivated the said land.

July 17, 1806: Present, John B. C. Lucas and Clement B. Penrose, commissioners. The Board reject this claim. They are satisfied that the said concession was granted at the time it bears date.

December 14, 1811: Present, a full Board. It is the opinion of the Board that this claim ought not to be confirmed.

ANTOINE VINCENT BOUIS, claiming one thousand arpents of land, situate on the river Missouri, district of St. Louis; produces a concession from Zenon Trudeau, Lieutenant Governor, dated 11th November, 1794.

Testimony taken, January 29, 1808. Jean Louis Marc, duly sworn, says that at least twelve years ago during the time that Don Zenon Trudeau was Lieutenant Governor of Upper Louisiana, he, the deponent, applied to him for a tract of land, situate between Emilian Yosti and Nicolas Lecompte; the Lieutenant Governor replied that he believed he had already granted the said land to Antoine Vincent Bouis; the deponent being informed by several other persons that the said land did belong to Antoine Vincent Bouis, he went to him and agreed with him to settle on said land for three or four years as the tenant of said Bouis; and that said Vincent Bouis was to let him have three or four arpents of land if he complied with his contract; and that the said Vincent Bouis verbally agreed to give the deponent ten or twelve head of cows, and from sixteen to twenty sows. This agreement took place in the fall, and in the spring following he, the deponent, went on said tract of land and built a small cabin, and made sugar; and that in the spring following he built a good cabin on the land between Yosti and Lecompte, on a place which he supposed would be vacant, and that in case he was on the land of Antoine Vincent Bouis he would get land from said Bouis, but should it be vacant, he would hold it in his own right; made and fenced in a field of about three arpents, and continued on it about twenty months. Further saith that Vincent Bouis never complied with his contract, but told him that his time was still going on; that said Vincent Bouis's stock was scattered about in the rushes, and could not collect them; that when the lines should be drawn, he would allow him the land according to contract; that during the time he was settled on said land, a man by the name of Shultz went and cut house-logs on said tract; and that the deponent gave notice of it to Antoine Vincent Bouis; and that the said Bouis applied to the Lieutenant Governor, Zenon Trudeau, and obtained an order forbidding the said Shultz from cutting logs on said land; further says that his house was in the road of the Indians to their hunting ground, and that his wife was frequently insulted by them; he therefore left the house and went near to St. Charles, expecting to return when there should be other settlers near the place which he had left; says that he went a voyage up the Missouri, and when he returned found trees marked on said land; says that at the time he made said settlement he considered himself as the tenant of Antoine Vincent Bouis; further saith that about seven or eight months after he had settled with his family in his large cabin, Joseph Williams came and settled near him; deponent says that while settled on said land he raised corn, tobacco, and garden stuff; had raised nothing when said Williams made his settlement, it not being planting time, but had fenced in his field.

Testimony taken, February 1, 1808. Louis Braseau, duly sworn, says that he saw Jean Louis Marc making sugar at the bottom of a hill near the road from St. Louis to St. Charles, about ten or eleven years ago; the said Jean Louis Marc told deponent at that time that he was working on the land of Antoine V. Bouis; deponent further saith that he knows that Jean Louis Marc was making sugar between the settlement of Emilian Yosti and Nicholas Lecompte, and that there was a cabin built on said place, in which said Jean Louis then lived.

November 1, 1809: Present, a full Board. It is the opinion of a majority of the Board that this claim ought not to be confirmed; Clement B. Penrose, commissioner, voting for the confirmation thereof.

SAMUEL DORSEY, claiming eight hundred arpents of land, situate on the Mississippi, district of Cape Girardeau; produces to the Board a concession for the same, from Don Carlos Dehault Delassus, Lieutenant Governor, dated 28th December, 1799; a plat of survey, dated 3d February, 1806; certified to be received for record 26th February same year, by Antoine Soulard, surveyor general.

July 12, 1809: Present, a full Board. This claim being now taken up, and a vote taken thereon, the Board are unanimously of opinion that it ought not to be confirmed.

MORRIS WILLIAMS, LEMON and JAMES HODGE, claiming seven hundred and twenty arpents of land, situate on Cape Labrouche creek, district of Cape Girardeau; produce to the Board a certificate of permission to settle from Louis Lorimier, commandant of Cape Girardeau district, dated June 7th, 1808, and sworn to before Robert Green.

The following testimony in the foregoing claim was taken by Frederick Bates, commissioner, at Cape Girardeau, June 7, 1808, by authority from the Board. Andrew Ramsay, Sen., duly sworn, says that the premises were settled in the year 1797, built a cabin, cleared, enclosed, and cultivated a field of two or three acres; premises cultivated two years in succession, and again in the year 1800 they were inhabited and cultivated.

Testimony as aforesaid, taken at New Madrid. June 13, 1809. Moses Hurley, sworn, says that in 1797 premises were settled; built a house and lived in it, and cleared, enclosed, and cultivated a field, and four crops raised in succession a part of this time, to wit, 1799; premises were occupied by witness as tenant for claimants. William Smith, duly sworn, says that in 1798 a crop was cultivated on premises, and two houses built; next year cleared six or eight acres; cultivation continued till the end of the year 1800, after which premises left vacant the cultivation for claimants.

March 19, 1810: Present, a full Board. It is the opinion of the Board that this claim ought not to be confirmed.

BARTHOLOMEW COUSIN, claiming eight thousand arpents of land, with allowance of three twentieths for roads, &c.; produces to the Board a concession from Don Carlos Dehault Delassus, Lieutenant Governor, for the same, dated 31st March, 1803; a plat of survey of one thousand arpents, situate on the river Mississippi, and Cape Lacruche creek, district of Cape Girardeau, dated 5th March, 1800, and certified 27th February, 1806; a plat of survey of one thousand one hundred and thirteen arpents and thirty-nine perches, situate on the Mississippi, district as aforesaid, dated 5th March, 1800, countersigned Antoine Soulard, surveyor general of Louisiana; a plat of survey of four thousand seven hundred arpents of an island in the Mississippi, district as aforesaid, dated 5th March, 1800, and certified 27th February, 1806; a plat of survey of three thousand three hundred and fifty arpents, situate on the forks of White Water creek, district as aforesaid, certified 27th February, 1806, by Antoine Soulard, surveyor general of the Territory of Louisiana; a plat of survey of one thousand and eighty-two arpents and forty-one perches, claimed partly as assignee of Baptiste Godair, to wit, for one hundred and seventy-five arpents, situate on the Big Swamp, district aforesaid, certified 27th February, 1806, by Antoine Soulard, surveyor general; a deed of transfer from John Baptiste Godair, for said one hundred seventy-five arpents, dated 28th July, 1804, the grant in this claim stated to be given as compensation for services rendered by claimant as interpreter and public writer, for which he is said never to have received any other compensation; produces also to the Board a petition from William Smith, to the commandant of Cape Girardeau, for the sale of certain property left by Benjamin Rose in August, 1799, together with the order of said commandant for the sale thereof, dated 7th May, 1802, a paper signed William Smith and Edward Hogan, dated 16th October, 1802, purporting to be a valuation and arbitration of labor done by Stephen Quimby on said survey, also Stephen Quimby's receipt for the amount of the award; also a paper purporting to be the conditions by which a certain Thomas Welburn rented premises of B. Cousin, and an order from Louis Lorimier to prevent Daniel Sexton from trespassing on the premises, dated 26th September, 1804; a petition of B. Cousin, and the decree of Don Carlos Dehault Delassus, Lieutenant Governor, for annulling the concession and warrant of survey of Benjamin Rose and Morris Williams, dated 12th December, 1803.

The following acknowledgment was made before Frederick Bates, commissioner, at Cape Girardeau, June 4, 1808. B. Cousin acknowledges that he surveyed this tract for B. Rose 12th April, 1799, by decree of Zenon Trudeau, Lieutenant Governor.

November 26, 1810: Present, full Board. It is the opinion of the Board that this claim ought not to be confirmed.

JAMES BRADY, assignee of Benjamin Rose, interfering with the above claim, claiming two hundred and forty arpents of land, situate on the Mississippi, district of Cape Girardeau; produces to the Board an affidavit of permission to settle, in favor of Benjamin Rose, from Louis Lorimier, commandant of Cape Girardeau district, dated 30th June, 1808; and a deed of transfer from said Rose to claimant, dated 25th April, 1808.

The following testimony taken June 3, 1808, at Cape Girardeau, by Frederick Bates, commissioner. Andrew Ramsay, Sen., duly sworn, says that Rose settled in 1798, built a cabin, cleared, enclosed, and cultivated a small lot; the premises were cultivated and inhabited the whole of the year 1803; about ten acres in cultivation. Solomon Thorn, duly sworn, says that Rose cleared, enclosed, and cultivated, in the year 1798, about three or four acres; left it with Smith and Ramsay, in the fall of that year, or spring of 1799, as tenants, to take care of his property, stock, &c.; the premises were cultivated in the year 1803, six or seven acres, as witness believes, for Rose.

Testimony taken, June 6, 1809. Andrew Ramsay, Sen., duly sworn, says that on the return of Rose to this country, he remonstrated with the commandant against the hardship of losing his lands on account of his absence. To which the commandant replied, you ought to have your lands. Witness then went with him to B. Cousin, the interfering claimant, who promised to supply him with lands elsewhere. Rose refused this offer.

The following testimony taken at New Madrid, June 15, 1808, by Frederick Bates, commissioner. William Smith, duly sworn, says that the premises were settled, inhabited, and cultivated, in the years 1799 and 1800; a house was built during this time, and between two and three acres cleared, enclosed, and cultivated. In the latter year, after laying by his crop, Rose went to Kentucky for his family. On his arrival in Kentucky, Rose wrote to witness, informing him that he had been arrested for debt, and could not immediately return, concluding with a request that witness should take care of his plantation until his affairs could be settled, when he intended to bring out his family. In compliance with this request, witness put one Franklin as a tenant on this land in the year 1801. On the removal of whom, in the same year, one Quimby was put on the premises by witness, as agent for Rose, who cultivated one or two crops.

November 26, 1810: Present, a full Board. It is the opinion of the Board that this claim ought not to be granted.

CHARLES FINDLEY, assignee of William Patterson, claiming four hundred and fifty arpents of land, situate on Tywappety, district of New Madrid; produces an order of survey from Henry Peyroux, commandant, dated 19th December, 1800; a certified copy of a lease and obligation to convey premises to claimant, dated 9th February, 1802.

Testimony taken, August 26, 1806. William Smith, being duly sworn, says that the said William Patterson, who was at the time of obtaining said warrant of survey, the head of a family, did, prior to and on the 1st day of October, 1800, actually inhabit and cultivate the said tract of land.

Testimony taken at New Madrid, June 15, 1808, by Frederick Bates, commissioner. William Smith, duly sworn, says premises were improved in the fall of 1800, at which time a cabin was built; in the following year the premises were cultivated and inhabited, and constantly to this time; about forty or fifty acres now in cultivation; Patterson had a wife and about seven children in 1803.

December 4, 1810: Present, a full Board. It is the opinion of the Board that this claim ought not to be confirmed.

CHARLES FINDLEY, assignee of Resa Bowie, claiming three hundred arpents of land, situate on the Mississippi, district of New Madrid; produces an order of survey from Henry Peyroux, commandant, dated 19th December, 1800; a power of attorney from said Bowie to Abraham Byrd to give a deed for said land, dated April the 6th, 1802; and a deed of transfer for the same, dated 4th December, 1805.

Testimony taken, August 26, 1806. William Smith, being duly sworn, says that, at the request of said Bowie, he applied to the commandant for a concession for said land, which was accordingly granted; that the said Resa Bowie did, prior to, and on the 1st day of October, 1800, actually inhabit and cultivate the said tract of land, and was then the head of a family.

Testimony taken, June 15, 1808, at New Madrid, by Frederick Bates, commissioner. William Smith, duly sworn, says that premises were settled in the year 1800; at which time he built two cabins and dug a well; cultivated the land in the following year, and till the year 1803; since which time it has been occasionally inhabited, but not cultivated, that witness knows. Robert Lane, sworn, says that turnips were sown in 1800, and that premises were cultivated by Lloyd for claimant in 1804.

December 4, 1810: Present, a full Board. It is the opinion of the Board that this claim ought not to be confirmed.

CHARLES FINDLEY, assignee of Richard Green, claiming three hundred and fifty arpents of land, situate on Tywappety, district of New Madrid; produces a certificate of permission to settle from Henry Peyroux, commandant, dated 21st March, 1804, and a survey of the same.

Testimony taken, 26th August, 1806. William Smith, being duly sworn, says that the said Richard Green settled the same tract of land in the year 1802, and actually inhabited and cultivated it until the latter end of 1803, when claimant having purchased the same, put a person on it, who actually inhabited and cultivated it to this day; Green had a wife and three children.

Testimony taken at New Madrid, June 15, 1808. William Smith, duly sworn, says that premises were cultivated and inhabited in the year 1802; at which time a house was built, and a field of a few acres cleared, enclosed, and cultivated; constantly inhabited and cultivated to this time: Green had a wife and three or four children in 1803.

December 4, 1810: Present, a full Board. It is the opinion of the Board that this claim ought not to be granted.

RICHARD JONES WATERS, claiming from one-half to one arpent of land on each side of bayou St. Ann and bayou St. Martin, district of New Madrid; produces to the Board a petition, dated 22d December, 1796, with a

****

recommendation from Charles D. Delassus, commandant, dated 29th December, 1796; a certificate of survey of eighty arpents, dated 27th February, 1806.

Testimony taken, March 5, 1806. Marie P. Leduc, being duly sworn, says that in the year 1799 he saw the mill, in consideration of the building of which the said concession had been obtained; that the same was then in operation, and two races dug.

Testimony taken at New Madrid, June 21, 1808. George Ruddell, duly sworn, says premises were cultivated on each side of the bayou, below the junction of the two bayous St. Mary and St. Ann, in 1796, and constantly to the present time, and also habited during most of this time; about the year 1799 a mill was built on premises, which continued to work (grind wheat and corn) till the year 1801, when it fell into the river, with the bank on which it was erected.

On examination of sundry documents now before the Board, and stated by the recorder to have been received by him while on a mission from the Board to the lower districts, and surrendered to him by the recorder of New Madrid district, on a *subpœna duces tecum*, directed to said recorder of New Madrid, which writ issued by him in capacity of commissioner authorized by the Board to take testimony in said lower districts, there is found a petition of Richard Jones Waters, dated 15th April, 1796, for said tract of land, with a decree of Baron Carondelet, Governor General, dated 23d July, 1796, that the same shall not be allowed.

March 5, 1806: Present, Clement B. Penrose and James L. Donaldson, commissioners. The Board confirm to the said claimant his tract, as per his concession.

April 1, 1811: Present, a full Board. It is the opinion of the Board that this claim ought not to be confirmed.

ANDREW SUMMERS, claiming two hundred and twenty-five arpents of land, situate on the Mississippi, district of New Madrid; list No. 1369 is produced by claimant as permission to settle, on which claimant will be found No. 213, for two hundred and twenty-five arpents; said list on file; a plat of survey, dated 10th February, 1801.

Testimony taken, March 14, 1806. George Wilson, being duly sworn, says that the said claimant did, prior to and on the 20th day of December, 1803, actually inhabit and cultivate the said tract of land.

March 14, 1806: Present, Penrose and Donaldson, commissioners. The Board grant the said claimant two hundred and fifty arpents of land, situate as aforesaid, provided so much be found vacant there.

May 10, 1806: Present, Lucas, Penrose, and Donaldson, commissioners. The Board revoke their grant made to Andrew Summers on the 14th day of March last, of a tract of two hundred and twenty-five arpents of land, situate at the Little Prairie, district of New Madrid.

The following testimony in this claim taken at New Madrid, June 15, 1808, by Frederick Bates, commissioner. Jacob Waggoner, duly sworn, says that the said premises were inhabited and cultivated in the year 1801; premises constantly inhabited and cultivated to this time; claimant had a wife and slave in 1803; thirty or forty acres in cultivation, and a good orchard.

October 6, 1810: Present, a full Board. It is the opinion of the Board that this claim ought not to be granted.

It is within the recollection of two of the members of this Board, to wit, John B. C. Lucas and Clement B. Penrose, that George Wilson, who gave testimony in the above claim on the 14th March, 1806, did again appear on the 10th May, 1806, before the Board, and acknowledged that the testimony given on the said 14th March was materially incorrect, in consequence of which the Board revoked the grant made on the 14th March, as stated.

The Board remark that the following testimony given by James Earl, in a claim which the Board have this day granted to said Andrew Summers, shows that the inhabitation and cultivation, proved by Jacob Waggoner, as stated, could not have been personally done by Andrew Summers.

Testimony, as follows. James Earl, being duly sworn, says that the said claimant did move from the Little Prairie, in the district of New Madrid, to Cape Girardeau, in the spring of 1802; that he settled said tract of land in the same year, and did, prior to and on the 20th day of December, 1803, actually inhabit and cultivate the same, and had then a wife and child.

FRANCIS JACOBS, claiming two hundred arpents of land, situate at Tywappety, district of New Madrid; produces to the Board a certified list of permissions to settle, formerly given, No. 1369, on which claimant is No. 158.

Testimony taken, at New Madrid, June 16, 1808. George Hacker, duly sworn, says that claimant cut house logs in 1802; premises inhabited and cultivated in the year 1805, and until the end of the year 1807; no family; about forty years of age; ten acres in cultivation the present year, and three cabins.

December 12, 1810: Present, a full Board. It is the opinion of the Board that this claim ought not to be granted.

FRANCIS MICHEL, claiming one thousand seven hundred and twenty arpents of land, situate on the northeast side of Turk bay, district of Arkansas; produces to the Board a plat of survey, dated 7th April, 1806.

July 23, 1811: Present, a full Board. It is the opinion of the Board that this claim ought not to be granted.

HARDY WARE, assignee of David Helderbrand, claiming nine hundred and sixty arpents of land, situate on the Merrimack, district of St. Louis; produces to the Board a notice of claim to the recorder.

Testimony taken, October 27, 1808. John Cummins, sworn, says that David Helderbrand settled on the tract claimed in 1801, and inhabited and cultivated the same for three years, to wit, 1801, 1802, and 1803; then sold to claimant for two hundred dollars in property; afterwards heard said Helderbrand acknowledge to have received payment for the same: Hardy Ware then moved on the same in January, 1804, and inhabited and cultivated it that and the next year.

August 24, 1810: Present, a full Board. It is the opinion of a majority of the Board that this claim ought not to be granted. The reasons for which the majority of the Board are of opinion that this claim ought not to be granted, are, because no written transfer of David Helderbrand to claimant has been produced; secondly, because the claimant, Hardy Ware, has not produced any evidence of permission granted to David Helderbrand to settle, and that the permission to settle which was granted to David Helderbrand, as appears by the sworn certificate of James Mackay, formerly commandant, hath been applied and made use of by said Helderbrand in a claim which he has on record, and is acted upon. Furthermore, the said majority states that it appears that Hardy Ware was present at the time the testimony in his claim was given in; that the same testimony was closed in his presence; that the said claimant made, at the same time, several declarations which were then taken down on the minutes, wherein nothing appears or is suggested concerning any permission to settle.

Frederick Bates, commissioner, is of opinion that one hundred arpents ought to be granted to David Helderbrand, or his legal representatives, as the permission to settle, believed to be the only alleged defect in this claim, has been improperly adduced in evidence in another claim of the said David Helderbrand, on which such inhabitation and cultivation as the act of Congress requires, have not been proven.

****

October 27, 1808. Hardy Ware, being present, declares that in 1803 he lived at the mines; that he inhabited and cultivated the place which James Smirl claims in 1799, and continued to inhabit and cultivate it until the spring of 1803; then went to the mines and rented a tract of Abraham Baker, and raised a crop; returned to Smirl's place in the fall of 1803, and continued on the same until the spring of 1804; then went to the place which he bought of David Holderbrand.

DAVID FINE, claiming one thousand and forty acres of land, situate on the river Mathias, district of St. Louis; produces a plat of survey, dated the 25th and certified the 28th February, 1806.

Testimony taken, May 6, 1807. William James, being duly sworn, says that he has known the said claimant, David Fine, for these four years last past; that he has raised four crops on said land, and was four years ago actually inhabiting the same; and that in the fall and winter of the following year he was on said tract.

Elijah Baker, being also duly sworn, says that he knew the said claimant about twenty-six years ago; that he arrived with him in the country in April of the year 1802; that either in February or March of the year 1803 he saw him on the said tract; that, in the month of June or July following, he saw a field on said tract and corn growing on it; that, about the 1st day of November of that year, claimant was cribbing corn on the same; that he saw him on the same at different times; that he, the witness, commonly went by said tract two or three times a year, and always saw corn in the field or crib.

Testimony taken, October 13, 1807. Philip Fine, being duly sworn, says that, speaking with the Spanish Lieutenant Governor, Mr. Delassus, early in the year 1802, on the subject of settling on vacant land, he was informed by said Lieutenant Governor that no concessions could be granted at that time, but that any person coming to the country might settle on vacant land; that his brother, the claimant, arrived shortly after in Louisiana, and was informed by him, the witness, of what had passed between him and the Lieutenant Governor, in consequence of which his brother settled on the land claimed: in the year 1803 he built a cabin, and raised a crop that year, and has inhabited and cultivated the same ever since; and had at that time a wife and six children.

John Romine, being duly sworn, says that the claimant has lived on the land claimed five seasons, and raised five crops.

August 20, 1811. Present, Clement B. Penrose and Frederick Bates, commissioners. It is the opinion of the Board that this claim ought not to be granted.

MANUEL LISA, assignee of Francis Lacombe, claiming four hundred arpents of land, situate on the Merrimack, district of St. Louis; produces to the Board a concession from Charles Dehault Delassus, Lieutenant Governor, to Francis Lacombe for the same, dated August 1st, 1799; a deed of conveyance from said Lacombe to claimant, dated 14th May, 1804.

Louis Menard, sworn, says that in the fall of the year before Adam House was killed on the Merrimack, that François Lacombe and his wife were residing on the tract claimed; that the whole neighborhood abandoned their land immediately after said House was killed.

July 9, 1810: Present, a full Board. It is the opinion of the Board that this claim ought not to be confirmed.

ALEXANDER McNAIR and BOYD DENNY, assignees of James Rankin, who was assignee of John Lafleur, claiming four hundred arpents of land, situate in Bonhomme settlement, district of St. Louis; produces a concession from Charles D. Delassus, dated 14th December, 1799, and a survey of the same, dated the 2d and certified the 15th November of the same year, together with a deed of sale from Lafleur to said James Rankin, dated 10th January, 1804, and another deed of sale from said Rankin to claimants, dated the 28th September of the same year.

James Mackay, being duly sworn, says that the aforesaid survey is one of the first he took in this country; that the said Lafleur, having gone with him, the witness, on a voyage of discovery up the river Missouri, at his return, he, the said James, obtained from the Lieutenant Governor the aforesaid concession for the said Lafleur, as a compensation for his services on that expedition.

September 8, 1810: Present, a full Board. It is the opinion of the Board that this claim ought not to be confirmed.

AUGUSTE CHOUTEAU, attorney of Peter Fouche, attorney of Madame Delore Sarpy, representing Charles Dehault Delassus, claiming twenty thousand arpents of land, thirteen thousand one hundred of which are situated on the river Cuivre, and six thousand nine hundred on the Saline river, district of St. Charles; produces to the Board a concession from Zenon Trudeau, Lieutenant Governor, to said Delassus, dated 18th June, 1796, and registered with Narcissus Brouten, notary public at New Orleans, the 16th May, 1807; a plat of survey of thirteen thousand one hundred arpents, dated 15th April, 1801, and certified 20th May, 1801; also a plat of survey of six thousand nine hundred arpents, dated 30th March, 1801, and certified 20th May of the same year; a deed of transfer from said Delassus to Lille Sarpy, dated 30th January, 1804.

Tuesday, July 10, 1810: Present, full Board. It is the opinion of the Board that this claim ought not to be confirmed. [See Appendix for copy of an official letter from Baron de Carondelet to Zenon Trudeau, dated 8th May, 1793; also a copy of a letter from Delassus to Soulard, dated 17th June, 1797.]

JOSEPH SPENCER, Jun. and THOMAS ORME, who claim, as assignees of John Capheart, four hundred arpents of land, being one half of a tract of eight hundred arpents, situate at Murphy's settlement, district of St. Genevieve; produce to the Board a concession for the same from Carlos Dehault Delassus, Lieutenant Governor, to John Capheart, dated 18th December, 1801; also a plat of survey of the same, dated 22d February, 1804, and certified 3d March, same year. John Smith T., produces a notice to the recorder, and an assignment from said Capheart to John Smith T., dated 13th June, 1806.

Testimony taken. October 26, 1808. David Murphy, sworn, says that John Capheart inhabited and cultivated the tract claimed in 1802; in 1803 rented it to one Davis, who did not inhabit or cultivate it, but paid rent in presence of witness; says that John Capheart was a single man.

June 26, 1810: Present, a full Board. It is the opinion of the Board that this claim ought not to be confirmed.

HEZEKIAH P. HARRIS, assignee of Joseph Boyce, assignee of William and Elizabeth Fitzgibbons, claiming five hundred and seventy-eight acres and sixty poles of land, situate in Bois Bruile, district of St. Genevieve; produces to the Board an assignment from William and Elizabeth Fitzgibbons to Joseph Boyce, dated 20th March, 1804; a conveyance from William Boyce, for Joseph Boyce, to claimant, dated 23d September, 1805; a plat of survey, dated February 5, 1806, certified 27th February, 1806.

Testimony taken. October 22, 1808. Alexander McConohon, sworn, says that in 1803 William Fitzgibbons built a house on the tract claimed, inhabited and cultivated it that year, and one year afterwards; that it has been inhabited and cultivated ever since by John Smith, Sen.; that in 1806, witness was informed by the mother of Fitzgibbons, that said Fitzgibbons was of age in 1803; says that Mary Fitzgibbons, the mother, William Fitzgibbons and a brother and sister, lived on the place at the same time.

John Smith, Sen., appears before the Board as the representative of Isaac Devee, and enters a caveat against the confirmation of this tract. William Girty, the agent of Hezekiah P. Harris, being also present, and each party declaring that they are ready to go into an investigation.

Reuben Middleton, sworn, says that William Fitzgibbons acknowledged to this deponent, in the year 1804, that the work done by himself and mother, on the place claimed, in 1803, was done for John Smith, Sen., and that said Smith had paid them for it, and that he had leased the place of said Smith for that year; in the fall of 1804, John Smith, Sen., sowed a crop of wheat on the tract claimed.

John Ross McLaughlin, sworn, says that Isaac Devee, about the year 1800, told witness that he had sold his concession to John Smith, Sen.; that in 1803, Mary Fitzgibbons inhabited and cultivated said land; afterwards saw John Smith, Sen., at two different times pay her property for inhabiting and cultivating said land for him, and holding the property in his name; says that Joseph Boyce told him, deponent, in the fall of 1804, that himself, said Boyce, and a number of others, had joined in a determination to take Smith's place from him, and had a bill of sale from William Fitzgibbons for the same, which was antedated; says that he heard William Fitzgibbons's mother say that said William was but eighteen years of age in 1803; also heard the wife of Alexander McConohon say the same.

Christopher Barnhart, sworn, says that he has heard Mary Fitzgibbons say that she had received payment for her labor done on the tract for John Smith.

Alexander McConohon, questioned, says that Isaac Devee got the concession about eight years ago.

June 4, 1810: Present, a full Board. It is the opinion of the Board that this claim ought not to be granted.

ANDREW BURNS, claiming one thousand and fifty arpents of land, near the Brushy Prairie, district of New Madrid; produces to the Board a notice to the recorder.

Testimony taken, at New Madrid, June 18, 1808. William Coxe, duly sworn, says that premises were inhabited and cultivated from the 1st March, 1803; cleared about four acres in that year, and continued to inhabit and cultivate to this time; a wife and five children in 1803; eight or ten acres in cultivation.

December 22, 1810: Present, a full Board. It is the opinion of the Board that this claim oughtn ot to be granted.

JOSEPH LEGRAND, claiming eight hundred arpents of land, situate in portage of the river St. Francis, district of New Madrid; produces a certificate of a permission to settle, from Charles D. Delassus, dated in January, 1803, and a certificate of survey of the same, dated February 27, 1806.

Testimony taken, March 15, 1806. Richard Jones Waters, being duly sworn, says that the said Legrand did, prior to and on the 20th day of December, 1803, actually inhabit and cultivate the said tract of land, and had one child.

Testimony taken, at New Madrid, June 17, 1808. John Baptiste Olive, duly sworn, says that premises were inhabited and cultivated since 1798 or 1799 till this day; twelve or fifteen arpents now in cultivation; a wife and child in 1803.

March 15, 1806: Present, Penrose and Donaldson, commissioners. The Board grant the said claimant eight hundred arpents of land, as per the said certificate of permission to settle.

January 17, 1811: Present, a full Board. It is the opinion of the Board that this claim ought not to be granted.

JESSE CAIN, by his agent, Rufus Easton, claiming one mile square of land, situate in the district of St. Charles; produces to the Board a notice of claim.

Testimony taken, December 15, 1808. James Piper, sworn, says that in 1799 or 1800, claimant planted corn and raised a crop on the tract claimed.

July 12, 1810: Present, a full Board. It is the opinion of the Board that this claim ought not to be granted.

JOSEPH THOMPSON, Sen., the representatives of, claiming two hundred and thirty-four arpents of land, situate on Ramsay's creek, district of Cape Girardeau; produce to the Board, as a special permission to settle, list A, on which Joseph Thompson, Sen., is No. 156.

Testimony taken at Cape Girardeau, June 3, 1808. James Cottle, duly sworn, says that improvement commenced in 1807; in the spring eight or ten acres in cultivation, and a cabin built.

June 6, 1808. Joseph Worthington, sworn, says that some trifling improvements were made on this land in 1803, but no inhabitation; the improvement was continued until the year 1805, when he removed; built two good houses, and cultivated about ten or twelve acres, and continued to live there until his death; his widow and family still inhabit and cultivate.

Wednesday, March 14, 1810: Present, a full Board. It is the opinion of the Board that this claim ought not to be granted.

ZACHANAH DOWLY, heirs of, claiming four hundred and fifty arpents of land, situate on the waters of Hubble's creek, district of Cape Girardeau; produce to the Board an affidavit of permission to settle from Louis Lorimier, commandant, dated 3d June, 1808.

Testimony taken at Cape Girardeau, June 2, 1808. John Summers, Sen., duly sworn, says that this land was improved and settled in 1800 or 1801; built a cabin, cleared, enclosed and cultivated a small spot; cultivated and inhabited in the year 1803, and ever since; upwards of twenty acres in cultivation; a peach orchard; Elizabeth Dowly died and was buried on the premises.

October 6, 1808. It being asserted that the testimony heretofore taken was false, the Board examine the following witnesses on the part of the United States.

Alexander Summers, sworn, says that Elizabeth Dowly, about the year 1800, built a camp on said tract, and that he (witness) ploughed a small piece of ground on the same for her, and sowed turnips; says that he has seen the place every year since, and that nothing has been done on the same by her, her representatives, or any person for her.

John Weaver, sworn, says that he has known the land claimed about seven years; that there never has any thing been done on it by Elizabeth Dowly or representatives since that time.

November 26, 1810: Present, full Board. It is the opinion of the Board that this claim ought not to be granted.

LAND GRANTS IN MISSOURI TERRITORY - 1805 - 1812   205

****

BENJAMIN JOHNSTON, claiming four hundred and fifty arpents of land, situate on Sandy creek, district of St. Louis; produces a petition to Francis Valle, commandant of St. Genevieve, dated in 1801; a concession from Charles D. Delassus, Lieutenant Governor, dated September 2, 1799; and a certificate of survey, dated 15th January, 1804.

Testimony taken, April 4, 1806. William Moss, being duly sworn, says that the said tract of land was settled in 1799; and prior to and on the 1st day of October, 1800, actually inhabited and cultivated for the use of the claimant.

April 4, 1806: Present, Lucas and Penrose, commissioners. It appearing to the Board, after comparing the dates both of claimant's petition and his concession, that the latter is antedated, they reject this claim; they, however, discharge him of any intention of fraud, and observe that he claims no other lands in his own name in this territory.

October 23, 1810: Present, a full Board. It is the opinion of the Board that this claim ought not to be confirmed.

JACOB BOGARD, claiming four hundred arpents of land, situate in the district of New Madrid; produces a warrant of survey from Henry Peyroux, dated November 25, 1800; and a certificate of survey of the same.

Testimony taken, April 18, 1806. John Friend, being duly sworn, says that claimant began the improvement of said land in the year 1801, and cleared about two arpents of the same; and further, that he did, in the year 1805, actually inhabit and cultivate the same, and has continued thereon to this day; he claims no other land in his own name in this territory.

Testimony taken at New Madrid, June 21, 1808. Edward Robertson, duly sworn, says that premises were inhabited and cultivated in 1800, and constantly to the last of the year 1806; fifteen or sixteen acres then in cultivation; a wife and six or seven children in 1803.

April 5, 1811: Present, a full Board. It is the opinion of a majority of the Board that this claim ought not to be granted, Frederick Bates, commissioner, voting for the granting thereof.

FRANCIS LESIEUR, claiming a lot of one arpent of land, situate in the district of New Madrid, village of Little Prairie; produces to the Board the same papers and the same testimony as in the claim of John Baptiste Barseloux, reported page 602.

July 9, 1811: Present, a full Board. It is the opinion of the Board that this claim ought not to be confirmed.

HENRY MASTERS, claiming seven hundred and fifty arpents of land, situate on lake St. Marie, district of New Madrid; produces a certificate of survey, dated 27th February, 1806.

Testimony taken, March 21, 1806. George Wilson, being duly sworn, says that the said claimant did, prior to and on the 20th day of December, 1803, actually inhabit and cultivate the said tract of land, and was then of the age of twenty-one years and upwards.

Richard J. Waters, being also sworn, says that he knows that claimant had obtained an order of survey for two hundred arpents.

March 21, 1806: Present, Lucas and Donaldson, commissioners. The Board grant the said Henry Masters two hundred arpents of land, situate as aforesaid.

August 15, 1811: Present, Penrose and Bates, commissioners. It is the opinion of the Board that this claim ought not to be granted.

MANUEL GONZALES MORO, claiming eight hundred arpents of land, situate in the district of St. Charles; produces the record of a concession from Charles D. Delassus, Lieutenant Governor, dated 20th June, 1800.

November 27, 1811: Present, a full Board. It is the opinion of the Board that this claim ought not to be confirmed.

DAVID TROTTER, claiming five hundred arpents of land, situate on Tywappety, district of New Madrid; produces a certificate of permission to settle, in 1802; and a certificate of survey of the same.

Testimony taken, March 21, 1806. Jacob Myers, being duly sworn, says that the said claimant did, prior to and on the 20th December, 1803, actually inhabit and cultivate the said tract of land; and was then of the age of twenty-one years and upwards.

Testimony taken at New Madrid, June 16, 1808. Jacob Myers, duly sworn, says that premises were settled in 1800; a cabin built, a well dug, and a small field of about two and a half acres, cleared, enclosed, and cultivated; constantly inhabited and cultivated till the spring of 1804, at which time there were about ten acres prepared for cultivation; claimant had a wife, about eight children, and five or six slaves.

March 21, 1806; Present, Lucas and Donaldson, commissioners. The Board grant the said claimant five hundred arpents of land, as per said certificate of permission to settle.

December 13, 1810: Present, a full Board. It is the opinion of the Board that this claim ought not to be granted.

ALEXANDER McNAIR, claiming four hundred arpents of land, situate near the village of Flourisont, district of St. Louis, as assignee of Jeremiah Connor, sheriff of St. Louis district, who sold the same as the property of Gregoire Sarpy; produces to the Board a concession from Zenon Trudeau, Lieutenant Governor, dated 17th December, 1796, and an assignment from one James Williams, dated 2d March, 1797; also the deed of sheriff Connor to claimant, dated 29th June, 1808.

This claim interfering with the following; the parties being present, agree that they shall be taken together by the Board and adjusted jointly, to wit: William Whitesides, assignee of James Williams, assignee of Thomas Wilkinson, claiming four hundred and forty arpents of land, situated as above; produces to the Board a notice to the recorder, dated 16th June, 1808; also a deed from Wilkinson to Williams, dated 1st February, 1797; a conveyance from Williams to claimants, dated September, 1805, receipt dated 12th September, same year, for consideration money.

Testimony taken, October 26, 1808. Elisha Hemington, sworn, says that Wilkinson gave Williams a cow and calf to build a house on the tract about eleven or twelve years ago; said Wilkinson lived in the house one winter, then sold to James Williams, who moved into the house and cleared some land.

June 26, 1810: Present, a full Board. It is the opinion of the Board that this claim ought not to be confirmed.

WILLIAM GIRTY, claiming seven hundred and forty-eight arpents sixty-eight perches of land, situate on Bois Bruile, district of St. Genevieve; produces a plat of survey dated 5th and certified 27th February, 1806.

Testimony taken, June 24, 1806. Alexander McConohow, being duly sworn, says that one Michael Burns settled the said tract of land in the year 1797; raised two crops on the same; that one Robert McLaughlin cultivated the same in the year 1799, and raised a crop; that, in running the lines, a cabin which stood on Noel Hornbeck's land, adjoining said tract, was taken in the same; that the said Hornbeck caused the said tract to be cultivated and a crop raised on the same in 1800, after which he sold the same to claimant.

Camille Lassus, being also duly sworn, says that he was present when permission to settle was granted to the above claimant.

June 22, 1810: Present, a full Board. It is the opinion of the Board that this claim ought not to be granted.

ELIAS BATES, claiming four hundred arpents of land, situate on Little Mine river, district of St. Genevieve; produces a concession from Charles D. Delassus, Lieutenant Governor, dated 15th January, 1800; a plat of survey, dated 3d February and certified 2d March, 1800.

Testimony taken, December 2, 1807. John Steward, being duly sworn, says that he knows the tract; that it joins the Old Mine; that in 1803 he saw corn raised on the place by one Hypolite Robert; that in the fall of 1804, there was a house built on the place by Manuel Blanco, as a tenant for claimant; that the nearest place where the mineral was got from the claim, was a few rods from the said tract; raised a crop in 1804, and has been cultivated ever since for claimant.

December 30, 1811: Present, a full Board. It is the opinion of the Board that this claim ought not to be confirmed.

ST. JAMES BEAUVAIS, claiming sixteen hundred arpents of land, situate at Mine à la Motte, district of St. Genevieve; produces a concession from Zenon Trudeau, Lieutenant Governor, dated September 2, 1796; and a survey of the same, taken April 25 and certified October 1, 1805.

Testimony taken, June 20, 1806. Francis Valle, duly sworn, says that claimant did, about five or six years ago, being then engaged in working his mines, cut wood on said tract of land, for the melting of the mineral.

December 30, 1811: Present, a full Board. It is the opinion of the Board that this claim ought not to be confirmed.

PETER ABAR, claiming six hundred and forty acres of land, situate in the district of St. Genevieve; produces to the Board a survey of five hundred and ninety acres, situate on the Fourche à Curtois, a water course of the Merrimack; also one other survey of fifty acres, situate near the village of the Mine à Breton, district aforesaid, both surveys dated February 8 and certified February 18, 1806.

Testimony taken, June 25, 1806. Amable Partney, being duly sworn, says that one Hypolite Robert settled the said tract of land in 1799; fenced in and cleared about five or six acres of the same; that he sold the same in 1801, to the above claimant, who built a house on it, moved his family, and has actually inhabited and cultivated it to this day; that the claimant is a Canadian, and was, on the 20th day of December, of the age of twenty-one years and upwards.

Monday, December 30, 1811: Present, a full Board. It is the opinion of the Board that this claim ought not to be granted.

PETER BOYER, claiming six hundred and thirty-nine and three quarter acres and twelve perches of land, situate on the west bank of the Old Mine creek, district of St. Genevieve; produces to the Board a notice of said claim to the recorder, dated May 8, 1807; also a plat of the same, without date, and surveyor not named.

Testimony taken, August 16, 1808. Jean Portell, sworn, says that claimant settled on said land in 1802, and has inhabited and cultivated the same to this day.

December 30, 1811: Present, a full Board. It is the opinion of the Board that this claim ought not to be granted.

ABRAHAM BRINKER, assignee of Andrew Miller, assignee of Francis Thibeauld, claiming five hundred arpents of land, situate near the village of Mine à Breton, district of St. Genevieve; produces to the Board a notice to the recorder; an assignment from Francis Thibeauld to Andrew Miller, dated 4th December, 1806; an assignment from said Miller to claimant, dated 27th June, 1808.

Testimony taken, October 14, 1808. Peter Abar, sworn, says Francis Thibeauld inhabited and cultivated the land claimed in 1802, and until the spring of 1808; and, from the commencement of the improvement, had at least six arpents enclosed and under cultivation; in 1803 Francis Thibeauld had a wife and one child.

Francis Thibeauld, sworn, says that after he bought of Lacroix, about nine or ten years ago, he went to the commandants, Francis Valle and Deluziere, to obtain a concession for the same; that they told him that the best concession he could have was to go and work the land.

December 30, 1811: Present, a full Board. It is the opinion of the Board that this claim ought not to be granted.

CAMILLE DELASSUS, claiming six thousand arpents of land, situate at Terre Blue, district of St. Genevieve; produces the record of a concession from Charles Delassus, Lieutenant Governor, dated 19th September, 1802; record of a plat of survey, dated 18th December, 1805, and certified 20th February, 1806.

December 30, 1811: Present, a full Board. It is the opinion of the Board that this claim ought not to be confirmed.

GEORGE FALLIS, assignee of Joseph Rivet and Louis Aler, claiming a tract of two arpents in front, running from the river St. Ferdinand to the Missouri, containing one hundred and thirty-four arpents ninety-three perches of land, district of St. Louis; produces a letter of office from Zenon Trudeau, Lieutenant Governor, dated 22d February, 1797; and two transfers of the same, the one from Joseph Rivet, and the other from Louis Aler, dated October 6, 1802; produces, also, a connected plat of survey of St. Ferdinand fields.

Testimony taken, July 22, 1806. Francis Dunnegant, being duly sworn, says that the said tract of land was first cultivated in the year 1795, and has continued so, yearly, to this day; that in 1801 the above claimant built a house on the same, which he has actually inhabited to this day.

December 30, 1811: Present, a full Board. It is the opinion of the Board that this claim ought not to be confirmed, because the original claimant on the plat accompanying the letter of office is not connected with this claim.

GEORGE FALLIS, assignee of Augustin B. Lagasse, claiming eighty-eight arpents thirty-two perches of land, situate as aforesaid; produces a letter of office and plat as aforesaid; also, a certificate of a public sale, at the church door, of the effects and property of the said Augustin B. Lagasse, by Francis Dunnegant, commandant, dated December 12, 1802.

Testimony taken, July 22, 1806. Francis Dunnegant, being duly sworn, says that the above claimant cultivated the said tract of land in the year 1804, and to this day; that the said Augustin B. Lagasse was a single man, and of age, and claims no other land in his own name in the Territory.

December 30, 1811: Present, a full Board. It is the opinion of the Board that this claim ought not to be confirmed. The Board remark that, from the situation of the tract of land claimed, the same lying parallel with the other tracts represented in the connected plat, the grant and measurement being of the same date, and the whole having been under one enclosure, this cultivation, from the general run of testimony, has taken place about the same time. From this circumstance, the Board are induced to believe that there is a clerical error in taking down the testimony of Francis Dunnegant, and that 1804 ought to have been 1794.

GEORGE FALLIS, claiming eighty-eight arpents fifty-nine perches of land, situate as aforesaid; produces a letter of office and plat as aforesaid, and a bill of sale for the same, dated 7th February, 1803.

Testimony taken, July 22, 1806. Francis Dunnegant, being duly sworn, says that one Laducier, who was the original proprietor of said tract or out-lot, sold the same to one Hubert Talbot, who began the cultivating of it in the year 1794, and has cultivated it to this day; that the said Talbot was of the age of twenty-one years and upwards.

December 30, 1811: Present, a full Board. It is the opinion of the Board that this claim ought not to be confirmed, because the original claimant on the plat accompanying the letter of office is not connected with this claim.

GEORGE FALLIS, assignee of Elisha Henington, assignee of the widow Rigoche, claiming one arpent and a half front, on St. Ferdinand creek, running back to the Missouri, situate as aforesaid; produces a letter of office and plat as aforesaid; also a deed of transfer from the widow Rigoche to said Henington, dated January 11, 1803; a deed of transfer from said Henington to claimant, dated 1st March, same year.

Testimony taken, July 22, 1806. Francis Dunnegant, duly sworn, says that one Quebeck L'Evecque was the original proprietor of the said tract of land; that he sold the same to one William Hebert, who again sold to one Baptiste Presse; that the said Presse settled the same in 1792, and cultivated it until the year 1802, when he sold to the widow Rigoche, and that it has been actually cultivated to this day; and further, that the said Presse was the head of a family.

December 30, 1811: Present, a full Board. It is the opinion of the Board that this claim ought not to be confirmed, because the original claimant on the plat accompanying the letter of office is not connected with this claim.

GEORGE FALLIS, assignee of Dennis Tool, claiming one and a half arpents front, on St. Ferdinand creek, running back to the Missouri; produces a letter of office and plat as aforesaid.

Testimony taken, July 22, 1806. Francis Dunnegant, being duly sworn, says that the said tract of land was originally owned by one Nicolas Lecompte; that the said Nicolas sold it to one Francis L'Europeen, who sold it again to one Charles Dejarlais; that the said Charles sold the same to the aforesaid Dennis Tool, who sold it again to the aforesaid claimant; and further, that the same was cultivated in the year 1796, and has been actually so to this day.

December 30, 1811: Present, a full Board. It is the opinion of the Board that this claim ought not to be confirmed, because the original claimant on the plat accompanying the letter of office is not connected with this claim.

PAUL DEJARLAIS, assignee of Joseph Lacroix, claiming one arpent front, on St. Ferdinand creek, running back to the Missouri; produces a letter of office and plat as aforesaid; also a deed of transfer of the same, dated July 11, 1803.

Testimony taken, August 19, 1806. Baptiste Crely, being duly sworn, says that the said tract of land was cultivated about sixteen years ago, and has been so to this day, without interruption.

December 30, 1811: Present, a full Board. It is the opinion of the Board that this claim ought not to be confirmed, because the original claimant on the plat accompanying the letter of office is not connected with this claim.

BAPTISTE CRELY, assignee of Jacque Marechal, claiming sixty-nine arpents three perches of land, situate as aforesaid; produces a letter of office and plat as aforesaid, and a deed of transfer for the same, dated 15th February, 1800.

Testimony taken, August 19, 1806. Louis Ouvre, duly sworn, says that the said land was cultivated about twelve years ago, by the aforesaid Jacque Marechal, and that the same has been actually cultivated to this day; that the said Marechal lived in the aforesaid village, and was, at the time of obtaining the same, the head of a family.

December 30, 1811: Present, a full Board. It is the opinion of the Board that this claim ought not to be confirmed, because the original claimant on the plat accompanying the letter of office is not connected with this claim.

LOUIS DUBRIEUL, assignee of Joseph Presse, claiming one arpent front, on St. Ferdinand creek, running back to the Missouri; produces a letter of office and plat as aforesaid; also a deed of transfer for the same, dated 24th November, 1803.

Testimony taken, August 19, 1806. Louis Ouvre, being duly sworn, says that the said Presse cultivated the said tract or lot about twelve years ago, and was, at the time of obtaining the same, of the age of twenty-one years and upwards, and resided in the village aforesaid; that the said lot has been actually cultivated to this day.

December 30, 1811: Present, a full Board. It is the opinion of the Board that this claim ought not to be confirmed, because the original claimant on the plat accompanying the letter of office is not connected with this claim.

MANUEL A. ROCQUE, assignee of Augustin Buron and Francis Mendell, claiming one hundred and five arpents of land, situate as aforesaid; produces the letter of office and plat as aforesaid; also a deed of transfer of the same, dated 20th July, 1804.

Testimony taken, August 19, 1806. Louis Ouvre, being duly sworn, says that the said Buron and Mendell, who were of age when they obtained said land, cultivated the same about twelve years ago, and that the same has been actually cultivated to this day; and further, that they resided in the aforesaid village.

December 30, 1811: Present, a full Board. It is the opinion of the Board that this claim ought not to be confirmed, because the original claimant on the plat accompanying the letter of office is not connected with this claim.

MANUEL A. ROCQUE, assignee of Michel Hebert and Marie, his wife, claiming seventy arpents of land, situate as aforesaid; produces the letter of office and plat aforesaid; also a deed of transfer of the same, dated 15th August, 1804.

Testimony taken, August 19, 1806. Louis Ouvre, being duly sworn, says that the said tract of land came to the said Hubert by marriage; that he cultivated the same twelve years ago, and to this day, and lived in the aforesaid village.

December 30, 1811: Present, a full Board. It is the opinion of the Board that this claim ought not to be confirmed, because the original claimant on the plat accompanying the letter of office is not connected with this claim.

FRANCIS ST. CYR, claiming 118 acres and $\frac{35}{100}$ of land, situate at St. Ferdinand, district of St. Louis; produces a letter of office from Zenon Trudeau, Lieutenant Governor, dated 22d February, 1797, and a connected plat of survey accompanying the same, on which claimant is No. 2.

John Jarrot, claiming 76 acres and $\frac{95}{100}$, No. 6; produces as above.
Louis Moreau, claiming 80 acres and $\frac{69}{100}$, No. 10; produces as above.
Joseph Couder, claiming 116 acres and $\frac{86}{100}$, No. 11; produces as above.
Alexis Cadot, claiming 115 acres and $\frac{92}{100}$, No. 14; produces as above.
Bonin, claiming 138 acres and $\frac{85}{100}$, No. 15; produces as above.
Louis Laroche, claiming 153 acres and $\frac{76}{100}$, No. 23; produces as above.
Joseph Lamer, claiming 77 acres and $\frac{37}{100}$, No. 27; produces as above.
Baptiste Lachasse, claiming 51 acres and $\frac{84}{100}$, No. 28; produces as above.
Joseph Calais, claiming 72 acres and $\frac{38}{100}$, No. 30; produces as above.
Baptiste Delisle, claiming 85 acres and $\frac{51}{100}$, No. 32; produces as above.
Pierre Payant, claiming 48 acres, No. 38; produces as above.
Francis Bernard, claiming 46 acres and $\frac{72}{100}$, No. 40; produces as above.
John Baptiste Tourville, claiming 119 acres and $\frac{35}{100}$, No. 47; produces as above.
Isaac Crosby, claiming 61 acres and $\frac{29}{100}$, No. 49; produces as above.
Etienne Labonte, claiming 121 acres and $\frac{65}{100}$, No. 50; produces as above.
Antoine Ladoucier, claiming 55 acres and $\frac{45}{100}$, No. 55; produces as above.
Louis Liret, claiming 56 acres, No. 56; produces as above.
Joseph Lagrave, claiming 112 acres and $\frac{12}{100}$, No. 57; produces as above.
John Baptiste Noel, claiming 84 acres and $\frac{31}{100}$, No. 58; produces as above.
Amable Montrieul, claiming 55 acres and $\frac{76}{100}$, No. 59; produces as above.
Augustin Bernard, claiming 55 acres and $\frac{69}{100}$, No. 60; produces as above.
Guillaume H. Lecompte, claiming 111 acres and $\frac{28}{100}$, No. 61; produces as above.
Antoine Marechal, Jr. claiming 83 acres and $\frac{24}{100}$, No. 62; produces as above.
Nicholas Leconte, claiming 83 acres and $\frac{32}{100}$, No. 63; produces as above.
Claude Panelon, claiming 61 acres and $\frac{9}{10}$, No. 64; produces as above.

It is the opinion of the Board that the twenty-six foregoing claims ought not to be confirmed. And the Board remark, that the claimants in the foregoing twenty-six claims are original grantees; it is supposed that if the connexion of the claims commencing at George Fallis, assignee of Rivet and Aler, page 659, and ending at Manuel A. Rocque, assignee of Michel Hebert, above, inclusively, could have been made with the respective original grantees, this number would have been deducted from the aforesaid twenty-six; but the identification, from the limited information which the Board possesses, cannot be made; this difficulty and inconvenience arises, in part, from land-holders bearing different appellations or names in acts of sale or transfer, and in original grants or concessions; and, also, from want of due formalities, to wit, from change of possession having taken place, without written evidence. Justice might be done these claimants by confirming their claims by the outer lines of the connected plat; but, as the law stands, the commissioners do not think themselves justifiable in exercising that power.

INHABITANTS OF THE TOWN OF ST. LOUIS, claiming four thousand two hundred and ninety-three arpents of land as a common; produce a certificate of survey of the same, dated 23d February, 1806; a set of regulations of the inhabitants, having for object the keeping in order or repairing of the enclosures of said common, and imposing penalties on such as should neglect or refuse to repair the same; said regulations signed by the then Lieutenant Governor Cruzat, and dated September 22, 1782.

Testimony taken, May 10, 1806. Auguste Chouteau, being duly sworn, says that the inhabitants never had a concession for said common; that he has always known it as such, although of a much smaller extent at first; that it was first fenced in in the year 1764, at the expense of the inhabitants, who always kept it in repair; and further, that every person, inhabitant of the village, was in the habit of pasturing his cattle in the same, and of cutting wood; and further, that he has known the said common, as surveyed and fenced, for upwards of fifteen years hence.

Gregoire Sarpy, being duly sworn, says that he arrived in the country about nineteen or twenty years ago; that he has always known said common as such; that the same had then acquired its present size; that when he arrived he found the same fenced in, and that every inhabitant was obliged, under certain penalties, to attend to and make such repairs as the said enclosure or fence required; and further, that Sylvester Labadie having, in the year 1792, obtained a concession for lands forming part of said common, and having, in consequence thereof, began his improvement of the same, the inhabitants remonstrated against it to the Lieutenant Governor, who prevented him from cultivating the same, until such time as the Intendant should have decreed otherwise.

William H. Lecompte, being duly sworn, says that he has been an inhabitant of the country for upwards of forty-four years; has known the common from his first arrival in St. Louis; that said common has increased in proportion to the population of the village; that he has known it of the size it now is for upwards of ten years; that the old common is included in the present one, and that the regulations passed respecting the same were always considered as laws, and enforced as such; and further, that other regulations were made respecting the same and also put in force.

June 14, 1806. Present, Lucas, Penrose, and Donaldson, commissioners. The Board remark, that this claim originated under the French Government; that as grants of commons were usual under the French and Spanish Governments, and in conformity with their respective laws, they deem it to be equitable under Spanish law.

January 2, 1812: Present, a full Board. It is the opinion of a majority of the Board that this claim ought not to be granted; Clement B. Penrose, commissioner, voting for a confirmation thereof, under the usages and customs of the Spanish Government.

INHABITANTS OF THE VILLAGE OF ST. CHARLES, claiming, as common, fourteen thousand arpents of land, situate on Marais Croche, district of St. Charles; produce a survey of the same, taken 27th February and certified 2d March, 1804; produce, also, the record of a petition from Charles Tayon to Zenon Trudeau, Lieutenant Governor, for part of said tract; a declaration from Zenon Trudeau, that the same cannot be granted, as all lands in that quarter are reserved for commons for the said villages, dated 23d January, 1797.

Testimony taken, August 29, 1806. Antoine Lamarche, being duly sworn, says that he is no way interested in the event of this claim; that the said village is composed of upwards of eighty families, whose only dependence for fuel and fencing the aforesaid common is; that the most part of the same is unfit for cultivation, to wit, the Crooked swamp, which is sometimes overflown by the Missouri; and further, that the said claimants have no wood on their out lots.

Pierre Bissonnett, being duly sworn, says a certain proprietor of said land, lying between the said Crooked swamp and the Missouri, and on which there is no wood, has been actually inhabited; that the inhabitants of said village, who are all of them cultivators, would be obliged to abandon the same, had they not the said common for their supply of fuel, &c.

January 2, 1812: Present, a full Board. It is the opinion of a majority of the Board that this claim ought not to be granted. It is the opinion of Clement B. Penrose, commissioner, that this claim ought to be confirmed, under the usages and customs of the Spanish Government.

INHABITANTS OF THE VILLAGE OF VIDE POCHE, or CARONDELET, claiming six thousand arpents of land, as a common, situate adjoining said village on the lower side, district of St. Louis; produce to the Board a notice of said claim to the recorder, dated 7th June, 1808; a petition from John Baptiste Gamache to Don Zenon Trudeau, Lieutenant Governor, praying for a grant of land below said village, dated 6th December, 1796; and the decree of the said Lieutenant Governor thereon, stating that the land demanded is within the limits of land reserved for the purpose of furnishing wood necessary for the use of the village of Carondelet; and that the demand which is made by Gamache cannot take place, nor any other concession be granted in the direction of a line taken from the end of the field-lots of the village, and running parallel with the Mississippi, further down said river one hundred and fifty arpents, dated St. Louis, December 7, 1796.

Testimony taken, June 15, 1808. Auguste Chouteau, Sen., sworn, says that he knows the inhabitants of Vide Poche, since the year 1770, have made use of the land lying below the field-lots and village of Vide Poche along the Mississippi, as their common, and ever since that time have taken therefrom their fencing and fuel, but does not know the extent of the claim; that, twenty-five years ago, a man by the name of Andre, built from the wood of said common and on the same a boat; that he commenced the building of another; complaint was then made by the inhabitants of said village to the Lieutenant Governor, who ordered said Andre to desist from his work, as the land belonged to said inhabitants; that, about twenty-five years ago, there were about thirty families of farming people, who had no other pursuits; that since that time until 1803, there continued to be about the same number of families; that the land which each of the said inhabitants possesses individually, would not be sufficient to furnish them with fuel, and that without said common they would be obliged to desert said village; that the land held individually was purposely chosen for cultivation, and without fire-wood.

Testimony taken, June 24, 1808. Jean Baptiste Provenche, sworn, says that the village of Carondelet was, to his knowledge, established at least forty years ago; that the village contained, twenty-five years ago, about forty families, all farmers, and about thirty-five or thirty-six years ago the said families have been using wood from the land now claimed, and ever since made use of the same as a common. In the year 1803 there were about forty families; that on the land claimed individually by said families there is no fuel, and that they have no other place to get fuel or fencing from but said common.

January 2, 1812: Present, a full Board. It is the opinion of a majority of the Board that this claim ought not to be granted; Clement B. Penrose, commissioner, voting for a confirmation thereof, under the usages and customs of the Spanish Government.

JAMES MCDANIEL, claiming eight hundred arpents of land, situate on the Missouri, district of St. Louis; produces the record of a plat of survey, dated 14th and certified 26th February, 1806.

January 2, 1812: Present, a full Board. It is the opinion of the Board that this claim ought not to be granted.

ANTOINE REYNAL, assignee of Hyacinth St. Cyr, claiming a lot in the village of St. Charles, district of St. Charles, one hundred and twenty by one hundred and fifty feet; produces a certified copy of a transfer from St. Cyr to claimant, dated 20th January, 1800.

The following testimony was given in a claim of Antoine Reynal, for two hundred and forty by three hundred feet, in which claim the lot above claimed is included, to wit: August 20, 1806. Pierre Becquet, being duly sworn, says that the said lot is situate fronting the main street, and divided from one lot, the property of one Pettit, by a cross street; that claimant did build a house on a lot which had not been conceded, and did afterwards apply for and obtain a concession on the lots adjoining; and that the had a garden on the lots adjoining; and that the same were actually inhabited and cultivated prior to and on the 15th day of October, 1800. August 6, 1807. Isidore Savoy, duly sworn, says that Gagnon claimed part of the abovementioned square, and that he authorized John B. Grazer to build a barn thereon eighteen years ago, which barn he built; that said Grazer sold said land to Bissonnett, and that he, Bissonnett, built a house twelve years ago on the same, and that the same has been occupied ever since by, through, or for, Bissonnett; the witness also says that there were no deeds of sale passed between Gagnon and Grazer, nor between Grazer and Bissonnett, to the best of his knowledge and belief, but that they were mere verbal sales; he also says, that he knows that part of the above claim which was formerly claimed by Paneton; that a barn was built on the same seventeen years ago by Charles Cardinal, who sold, verbally, the said part to Claude Paneton, and that the said Claude Paneton has possessed the said part of this claim, and used the said barn thereon built, for three years; that he also knows that part of the said claim formerly owned by Hyacinth St. Cyr; that St. Cyr sold the same, verbally, to the above named Grazer, but he cannot say in what manner the said part again came into the possession of the said St. Cyr; knows, however, that it was several times bartered with no formal deed of sale; that he also knows the upper part of said square, on which he had permission to settle, was enclosed and kept possession of by him ever since, and that there is now thereon a valuable orchard.

August 21, 1811: Present, Penrose and Bates, commissioners. It is the opinion of the Board that this claim not to be confirmed.

AUGUSTE GAMACHE and JOHN BAPTISTE GAMACHE, claiming ten hundred and fifty arpents of land, situate on the Mississippi, below the mouth of the Merrimack river, district of St. Louis; produce the record of a plat of survey, dated 15th November, 1805, certified 22d February, 1806. Alexander McNair, claiming five hundred and twenty-five arpents of this tract, as assignee of the sheriff of St. Louis district, who sold the same, as the property of John Baptiste Gamache; produces the record of a deed from the sheriff to McNair, dated 4th February, 1807.

Tuesday, November 19, 1811. It appearing to the Board, from the rough minutes of April 3, 1806, that testimony was taken in this claim, and was not entered on the fair minutes, and the same being within the recollection of two of the commissioners, to wit, John B. C. Lucas and Clement B. Penrose, it is therefore agreed to receive testimony on this day.

Auguste Chouteau, sworn, says that he knows the tract claimed; that in 1776, or near that time, the commandant of St. Louis thought proper that a ferry should be established on Merrimack, that a regular intercourse should be kept up between St. Louis and St. Genevieve; that John Baptiste Gamache, father of claimants, hearing of this, agreed to undertake the same; that the commandant, who this deponent believes to be Cruzat, acceded to the proposals of Gamache, to wit, that he should keep a ferry and hold land at the said place; deponent cannot say any thing as to quantity of said land; said Gamache immediately went and settled on said land; cleared land, built a house, and cultivated thereon, and continued to cultivate and inhabit until 1780, when he was ordered away by commandant on account of Indian disturbances; that said Gamache returned to the place claimed one or two years after, as soon as tranquillity was restored, and continued thereon four or five years longer until the death of his wife; that about 1790 the sons of said Gamache, to wit, the claimants, inhabited and cultivated said land about eight years.

Charles Sangurnett and John Baptiste Provenche, sworn, depose to the same as the foregoing witness.

November 19, 1811: Present, a full Board. The Board order that this land be surveyed agreeably to the possession, provided it does not exceed one thousand and fifty arpents; survey at the expense of the United States, and to be returned within ten days.

January 6, 1812: Present, a full Board. It is the opinion of the Board that this claim ought not to be granted, because the survey which has been ordered by the Board contains a much greater quantity of land than is actually claimed, and also because, from the notes contained in the report of survey, it does not appear that the lines of said survey run with boundaries of ten years' standing before the year 1803.

The five following claims, being of so peculiar a nature as not to be susceptible of registry, are specially reported.

INHABITANTS OF NEW BOURBON, assignees of John Dodge, who was assignee of Francis Valle, claiming forty arpents by such quantity as may be found within the following limits, to wit: forty arpents fronting the foot of the hills; running from said hills to a water course or spring on which one Israel Dodge's mill is built; thence, on each side of said spring or run, twenty arpents back, quantity as yet undetermined; produces a certified copy of a concession from Francis Cruzat to Francis Valle, granted on certain conditions expressed in the petition of said Francis Valle, to wit, the building of a mill, said concession, dated 10th March, 1787, and a confirmation of the same by the Baron de Carondelet, under the date of the 8th May, 1793.

Testimony taken, June 25, 1806. Joseph Pratte, being duly sworn, says that the said Francis Valle built a mill on said land prior to the confirmation of said grants by the Baron de Carondelet.

June 25, 1806: Present, Penrose and Donaldson, commissioners. The Board ascertain this claim to be a complete Spanish grant, made and completed prior to the 1st day of October, 1800.

August 17, 1811: Present, Penrose and Bates, commissioners. The Board decline revising this claim, and order a translation of the record to accompany the report. Originals not now produced.

CLEMENT B. PENROSE, assignee of Joseph Brown and wife, assignees of the representatives of Gabriel Cerre, deceased, claiming a certain tract of land, as described within certain boundaries mentioned in a concession from Zenon Trudeau, dated 18th April, 1798, and granted for the purpose of cutting wood; produces the aforesaid concession, dated as aforesaid, and a survey of ninety-eight arpents contained in the said boundaries, dated 5th April, 1798, and certified 10th January, 1800; an act of public sale of the effects and property of the late Gabriel Cerre, deceased, dated 28th July, 1805; a deed of conveyance from Joseph Browne and wife, dated 8th October, 1807.

Testimony taken, 8th July, 1806. Auguste Chouteau, being duly sworn, says that the aforesaid Gabriel Cerre, being possessed of a tract of four hundred and a half arpents of land, on which he had no wood, applied to the Lieutenant Governor for a concession for the above ninety-eight arpents, adjoining the same, that it was granted him; that accordingly he did, from the time of obtaining the same to the time of his death, make his wood on said land.

Testimony taken, November 21, 1808. Louis Braseau, sworn, says that he knows the land claimed, and that it was, fifteen or sixteen years ago, reputed to be the property of Gabriel Cerre, and that said Cerre cut his wood from said land from that time to his death.

July 9, 1810: Present, Lucas and Bates, commissioners. It is the opinion of John B. C. Lucas that this claim ought not to be confirmed; Frederick Bates, commissioner, voting for the confirmation of ninety-eight arpents.

FRANCIS CLARK, claiming two hundred and fifty arpents of land; produces to the Board a notice to the recorder as follows, to wit: " Francis Clark claims two hundred and fifty arpents of land, on a branch of the river St. Francis, by virtue of a settlement and cultivation made in the year 1804, on the west side of said river, and including the place whereon he now lives. May 30, 1808. Francis Clark."

May 30, 1808: Present, Lucas and Penrose, commissioners. The Board are of opinion that this case does not come within their jurisdiction, and therefore decline to act.

LOUIS LABEAUME, claiming eight thousand arpents of land, situate on Portage des Sioux, district of St. Charles; produces the record of a grant from Juan Ventura Morales, dated 5th July, 1802, with condition for the compliance with the 3d, 4th, 6th, 7th, and 9th articles of the instructions, and is found in the abstract of all the concessions and patented grants of land, appertaining to the district of Louisiana, recorded in the registers kept by the Spanish and French Governments of the province of Louisiana, since the 2d July, 1756, until the 23d April, 1802, transmitted to this Board by the Secretary of the Treasury.

January 11, 1812: Present, a full Board. A majority of the Board decline acting on this claim, the original title paper not being produced. John B. C. Lucas, commissioner declares that he cannot act, as no original title paper is produced.

DELAWARES and SHAWANEES, claiming a tract of country between the river St. Coure and Cape Girardeau, and bounded on the east by the Mississippi, and west by White Water, district of Cape Girardeau; produce to the Board as follows, to wit:

****

El Baron de Carondelet, Caballero de la religion de San Juan, Coronel de los reales exercitos, Gobernador, Intendente General, Vice Patrono de las provincias de la Luisiana, Florida Occidental, e Inspector de sus tropas, &a.

Faisons savoir à tous ceux qui la présente liront, qu'en considération des bons et fidels services que le nommé Louis Lorimier a rendu à l'état depuis qu'il s'est rendu sujet de Sa Majesté Catholique, nous lui permettons de s'établir avec les Loups et Chaouanons qui sont sous sa conduite dans tels endroits que bon lui semblera, de la province de la Louisiane, sur la rive droite du Mississippi, depuis le Missouri jusqu'à la rivière des Arkansas, qui se trouveront sans propriétaires, comme également d'y chasser et semer, pour y maintenir leurs familles, sans qu'aucun commandant, officier, ni sujet du roy, ne puisse s'y opposer, ni occuper les terreins par lui et par les dits Indiens semés, plantés, ou établis, tant qu'ils jugeront à propos de s'y maintenir; bien entendu qu'au cas qu'ils les abandonnent pour se transporter ailleurs, ils seront censés rester vacantes; et quant à la maison que le dit Sieur Louis Lorimier a bati au Cap Girardeau, il sera maintenu dans sa possession, sans qu'aucun motif ne puisse l'en tirer, les seules causes de commerce illicite ou correspondance avec des ennemis de l'état excepté.

En foi de quoi, nous avons donné la présente, signée de nôtre main, sous le contreseing du Secrétaire de ce Gouvernement, et à icelle fait apposer le cachet de nos armes, à la Nouvelle Orléans, le 4 Janvier, 1793.

LE BARON DE CARONDELET.

Par mandement de sa seigneurie: ANDRES LOPEZ ARMESTO.

St. Louis, le 1 Mai, 1793.

Ci-joint est le permit que vous donne Monsieur le Gouverneur Général pour faire vôtre commerce avec les nations Loups et Chaouanons, assez étendu pour que vous n'ayez plus rien à désirer, sans crainte que vous soyez troublé par auqu'un officier du roy, lorsque vous vous comporterez comme vous l'avez fait jusqu'à ce jour. Il vous est recommandé de maintenir l'ordre entre les Sauvages, et d'en attirer autant qu'il se pourra sur cette partie en les faisant poster le plus à porter de nos établissemens, afin de nous prêter secours dans un cas de guerre avec les blancs, comme ils seront à même contre les Osages, avec qui je vais déclarer la guerre incessamment, et ce que je n'ai pas encore fait parceque j'ai quelques précautions à prendre avant que cela parvienne à eux. Dites aux Loups, Chaouanons, Peorias, Pouatamis, et aux autres nations qui m'ont présenté un memoire au mois de Septembre dernier, que c'est en vertu des maux qu'ils ont soufferts que Monsieur le Gouverneur Général s'est déterminé à la guerre, afin de procurer la tranquillité sur nos terres; les Osages, privés présentement de secours, et harcelés par eux et par nous, se mettront sûrement à la raison; que, conséquemment, toutes les nations rouges doivent s'entendre de prêter la main; c'est leur bien que le Gouvernement cherche, et c'est ce que vous devez leur persuader, pour que les nations offensés fassent des demarches envers les autres, pour en avoir du secours; et surtout pour que les Ayoas, Saquias, et Renards ne consentent pas à laisser venir les Osages traiter sur la rivière des Moins, et encore moins qu'ils permettent aux Anglais de s'introduire chez eux par cette rivière, comme it est possible.

Protegé par le Gouvernement, vous lui devez vos services en veillant exactement sur tout ce qui peut le faire prosperer, et en avertissant de tout ce qui lui est contraire. Dans ce moment on a des craintes, non pas du Congrès, mais des mal-intentionnés qui en dependent, postés dans un lieu avantageux pour donner des avis du moindre rassemblement de monde. J'ai la confiance que sitôt que vous en aurez connaissance, vous le ferez savoir à tous les commandants dont vous êtes apportés, tant pour nôtre sûreté que pour nôtre défense.

Monsieur le Gouverneur a approuvé la dépense des vingt mille grains de porcelaine que j'ai donné aux Loups, et auxquels vous avez contribués; mon intention avait toujours été de vous en faire le rembourssement, et aujourdhui je le puis faire avec plus de facilité, puisqu'on m'en offre les moyens sans le chercher ailleurs, ainsi vous pouvez tirer sur moi à raison de six piastres le millier, comme le Roi est convenu de me le payer.

On m'a dit que vous deviez venir à St. Louis avec vos Sauvages; comme je suis dépourvu des toutes marchandises, leur visite me serait un peu honteuse; c'est qui fait que je vous engage à venir seul, (si vôtre présence est nécessaire ici,) et attendre que les bateaux soient arrivés, pour être de même de faire un présent honnête à les Sauvages. Dieu vous ait en sa sainte garde.

ZENON TRUDEAU.

A. S. Je garde vôtre permis jusqu'à une occasion à qui je puisse le confier; il porte que vous ne serez pas troublé depuis le Missouri jusqu'aux Arkansas dans vôtre commerce, comme dans les établissemens ou campement qui vous y pourriez former avec les Sauvages Chaouanons et Loups, &c., et que celui fait au Cap à Girardeau vous soit conservé.

Mr. LOUIS LORIMIER.

St. Louis, le 19 Juin, 1797.

MONSIEUR:

Monsieur le commandant militaire me charge de vous dire qu'il a reçu la lettre d'office que vous lui avez adressée pour lui rendre compte de la nouvelle qui vous a parvenu d'un rassemblement de monde destiné, soi disant, pour prendre possession des postes du Mississippi; il vous répondra par M. Sarpy, qui va passer chez vous incessamment, et celle-ci est plutôt pour vous faire des amitiés de sa part que toute autre chose.

Par la même occasion je répondrai également à toutes celles que j'ai reçu de vous, pouvant vous dire dès à présent, malgré la précipitation qu'il me parait très juste de conserver aux Chaouanons un arrondissement raisonable pour leur village de la rivière à la Somme, vous verrez vous-même ce qu'il convient pour n'y laisser placer aucun Américain ni autres, &c.

Vous ferez très bien d'adresser vôtre compte à Monsieur le Commandant Général de la province, et même de ne pas perdre de temps, parcequ'on dit qu'il va être relevé, et je suis certain que vous serez parfaitement bien payé.

Les nouvelles reçues du poste sont à peu près les mêmes que celles que vous avez détaillées par le haut du Mississippi, ainsi que par la rivière des Illinois, où nous avons des agens; il n'y a rien de nouveau.

J'ai l'honneur d'être, avec attachement, monsieur, vôtre très humble obeissant serviteur,

ZENON TRUDEAU.

January 11, 1812: Present, a full Board. It is the opinion of the Board that this claim ought not to be confirmed, not being embraced by the fourth section of the act of the 3d of March, 1807.

****

REPORT OF THE TITLES AND CLAIMS TO LEAD MINES.

The sealed packet which was delivered to the Board by the clerk, on the 28th September, 1811, addressed to the commissioners, and styled, by a letter enclosed in the same, signed William C. Caw, agent for the United States, to be a collection of evidence respecting the claims to, and value of, the lead mines within the Territory of Louisiana, accompanied with a list of the documents submitted. The whole stated to have been made in pursuance of the sixth section of the act of Congress for ascertaining and adjusting the titles and claims to land within the Territory of Orleans and district of Louisiana, passed the 2d March, 1805.

DOCUMENT A.

JULIAN DUBUQUE and AUGUSTE CHOUTEAU, claiming a tract of one hundred and forty-eight thousand and one hundred and seventy-six arpents of land, situate on the river Mississippi, at a place called the Spanish Mines, about four hundred and forty miles from St. Louis, forming in superficies an extent of about twenty-one leagues. They produce, first, a petition by the said Julian Dubuque to the Baron de Carondelet, praying for the peaceable possession of an extent of land of about seven leagues on the west side of the Mississippi, beginning at the heights of Maquanquetons to the heights of Mesquanbinangues, being in front on said river about seven leagues, by a depth of three leagues, the whole forming the said tract called the Spanish Mines; together with a reference by the Baron de Carondelet to one Andrew Todd, an Indian trader, of the above demand under date of the 22d October, 1796, the assent of said Andrew Todd to the granting of the same; provided the said petitioner should not interfere with his trade; the same dated the 29th October, same year.

The decree of the Baron de Carondelet is in the form following: "Concedido como se solicito baxolas restricciones que el comerciante, Don Andres Todd, expresa en sa informe." 10th November, 1796.

EL BARON DE CARONDELET.

The translation of which is as follows: " Granted as it is demanded, under the restrictions mentioned by the merchant, Don Andrew Todd, in his information."

September 20, 1806: Present, Lucas, Penrose, and Donaldson, commissioners. A majority of the Board, the honorable John B. C. Lucas dissenting, ascertain the above claim to be a complete Spanish title.

December 19, 1811: Present, a full Board. On a question being put by John B. C. Lucas, commissioner, Clement B. Penrose and Frederick Bates, commissioners, declined giving an opinion. It is the opinion of John B. C. Lucas, commissioner, that this claim ought not to be confirmed.

DOCUMENT B. (not of record.)

MARTIN DURALDE. Livre Terrien, No. 1, page 24, from which the concession is translated, is dated prior to Livre Terrien, No. 2, which contains the words stated in document marked B, No. 2.

December 20, 1811: Present, a full Board. It is the opinion of the Board that this title ought not to be confirmed.

DOCUMENT C.

Clement B. Penrose, commissioner, retired from the Board, in consequence of his having become interested in this claim since the decision of the former Board.

JAMES RICHARDSON, claiming under Gabriel Cerre four hundred arpents of land; produces a petition, signed Gabriel Cerre, directed to Baron de Carondelet, Governor General, praying for a concession for four hundred arpents of land, including a mine; an information from Zenon Trudeau, Lieutenant Governor, dated 29th March, 1796; an official letter from Baron de Carondelet to Zenon Trudeau, Lieutenant General, dated 28th April, 1796; a concession from Baron de Carondelet, Governor General, for the same, dated 25th April, 1796; a plat of survey of the same, dated 25th January, 1800, certified 28th January, 1800; an extract of an act of partition of the estate of Gabriel Cèrre, by which it appears that the said four hundred arpents of land fell to the share of Antoine Soulard, in right of his wife, as heir of Catherine Geard, deceased, in her life time the wife of Gabriel Cerre.

December 20, 1811 : Present, Lucas and Bates, commissioners. Frederick Bates, commissioner, forbears giving an opinion. It is the opinion of John B. C. Lucas, commissioner, that this claim ought not to be confirmed.

DOCUMENT D.

JOHN BAPTISTE FRANCIS MENAUD and EMILY JOSEFA RENAUD, of the empire of France, heirs of Mr. Renaud, claiming, as a complete title, one and a half leagues in front by six leagues in depth of land, situate on the Little Merrimack, district of St. Genevieve; produces a certified copy of a grant from Boisbriant and Desursins, dated 14th June, 1723.

December 21, 1811: Present, a full Board. A majority of the Board ascertain that this title is not a grant made and completed prior to the 1st of October, 1800. Frederick Bates, commissioner, forbears giving an opinion. Claimants have entered caveats stating that this claim is interfered with by a number of other claims.

The claims alluded to are duly recorded and some of them confirmed.

JOHN BAPTISTE FRANCIS MENAUD and EMILY JOSEFA RENAUD, of the empire of France, heirs of Mr. Renaud, claiming, as a complete title, two leagues of land, situate at Mine la Motte, district of St. Genevieve; produce a certified copy of a grant from Boisbriant and Desursins, dated 14th June, 1723.

December 21, 1811: Present, a full Board. A majority of the Board ascertains that this title is not a grant made and completed prior to the 1st of October, 1800. Frederick Bates, commissioner, forbears giving an opinion. Claimants have entered caveats stating this claim is interfered with by a number of other claims.

The claims alluded to are duly recorded and some of them confirmed.

WALTER FENWICK and ANDREW HENRY, assignees of Francis Azor, alias Breton, claiming four arpents square of land, situate at Mine à Breton, district of St. Genevieve; produce a certified copy of a concession from Francis Cruzat, Lieutenant Governor, dated 20th March, 1782, certified by Francis Valle, 8th April, 1800; a transfer from Francis Azor, alias Breton, to claimants, dated 27th May, 1806. This tract said to be claimed by the representatives of Francis Moreau.

December 21, 1811: Present, a full Board. It is the opinion of a majority of the Board that this claim ought not to be confirmed. Frederick Bates, commissioner, forbears giving an opinion.

DOCUMENT E.

BAZIL VALLE, claiming four hundred arpents of land, situate at Old Mines, district of St. Genevieve; produces a concession from Charles D. Delassus, Lieutenant Governor, to thirty-one inhabitants of the Old Mines, dated 4th June, 1803; a connected plat of survey, on which Basil Valle is No. 1, dated 3d February, 1804, certified 25th February, 1806.

****

December 21, 1811: Present, a full Board. It is the opinion of a majority of the Board that this claim ought not to be confirmed. Frederick Bates, commissioner, forbears giving an opinion.

P. C. H. F. AUGUSTE VALLE, claiming four hundred arpents of land, No. 2; produces same concession and plat as in the claim of Basil Valle.

December 21, 1811: Present, a full Board. It is the opinion of a majority of the Board that this claim ought not to be confirmed. Frederick Bates, commissioner, forbears giving an opinion.

MANUEL BLANCO, claiming four hundred arpents of land, No. 3; produces same concession and plat as in the claim of Basil Valle.

December 21, 1811: Present, a full Board. It is the opinion of a majority of the Board that this claim ought not to be confirmed. Frederick Bates, commissioner, forbears giving an opinion.

JOHN PORTELL, claiming four hundred arpents of land, No. 4; produces same concession and plat as in the claim of Basil Valle.

December 24, 1811: Present, a full Board. It is the opinion of a majority of the Board that this claim ought not to be confirmed. Frederick Bates, commissioner, forbears giving an opinion.

PIERRE MARTIN, claiming four hundred arpents of land, No. 5; produces same concession and plat as in the claim of Basil Valle.

December 21, 1811: Present, a full Board. It is the opinion of a majority of the Board that this claim ought not to be confirmed. Frederick Bates, commissioner, forbears giving an opinion.

JACOB BOISSE, claiming four hundred arpents of land, No. 6; produces same concession and plat as in the claim of Basil Valle.

December 21, 1811: Present, a full Board. It is the opinion of a majority of the Board that this claim ought not to be confirmed. Frederick Bates, commissioner, forbears giving an opinion.

JOSEPH PRATTE, claiming four hundred arpents of land, No. 9; produces same concession and plat as in the claim of Basil Valle.

December 21, 1811: Present, a full Board. It is the opinion of a majority of the Board that this claim ought not to be confirmed. Frederick Bates, commissioner, forbears giving an opinion.

FRANCIS MANICHE, claiming four hundred arpents of land, No. 10; produces same concession and plat as in the claim of Basil Valle.

December 21, 1811: Present, a full Board. It is the opinion of a majority of the Board that this claim ought not to be confirmed. Frederick Bates, commissioner, forbears giving an opinion.

AMABLE PARTINAIS, claiming four hundred arpents of land, No. 11; produces same concession and plat as in the claim of Basil Valle.

December 21, 1811: Present, a full Board. It is the opinion of a majority of the Board that this claim ought not to be confirmed. Frederick Bates, commissioner, forbears giving an opinion.

JOSEPH BLAY, claiming four hundred arpents of land, No. 12; produces same concession and plat as in the claim of Basil Valle.

December 21, 1811: Present, a full Board. It is the opinion of a majority of the Board that this claim ought not to be confirmed. Frederick Bates, commissioner, forbears giving an opinion.

FRANCIS ROBERT, claiming four hundred arpents of land, No. 13; produces same concession and plat as in the claim of Basil Valle.

December 21, 1811: Present, a full Board. It is the opinion of a majority of the Board that this claim ought not to be confirmed. Frederick Bates, commissioner, forbears giving an opinion.

BAPTISTE PLACIT, claiming four hundred arpents of land, No. 15; produces same concession and plat as in the claim of Basil Valle.

December 21, 1811: Present, a full Board. It is the opinion of a majority of the Board that this claim ought not to be confirmed. Frederick Bates, commissioner, forbears giving an opinion.

VEUVE COLMAN, claiming four hundred arpents of land, No. 16; produces same concession and plat as in the claim of Basil Valle.

December 21, 1811: Present, a full Board. It is the opinion of a majority of the Board that this claim ought not to be confirmed. Frederick Bates, commissioner, forbears giving an opinion.

CHARLES BOYER, claiming four hundred arpents of land, No. 18; produces same concession and plat as in the claim of Basil Valle.

December 21, 1811: Present, a full Board. It is the opinion of a majority of the Board that this claim ought not to be confirmed. Frederick Bates, commissioner, forbears giving an opinion.

ANTOINE GOVREAU, claiming four hundred arpents of land, No. 19; produces same concession and plat as in the claim of Basil Valle.

December 21, 1811: Present, a full Board. It is the opinion of a majority of the Board that this claim ought not to be confirmed. Frederick Bates, commissioner, forbears giving an opinion.

NICHOLAS BOILVIN, claiming four hundred arpents of land, No. 20; produces same concession and plat as in the claim of Basil Valle.

December, 21, 1811: Present, a full Board. It is the opinion of a majority of the Board that this claim ought not to be confirmed. Frederick Bates, commissioner, forbears giving an opinion.

T. ROSE, claiming four hundred arpents of land, No. 21; produces same concession and plat as in the claim of Basil Valle.

December 21, 1811: Present, a full Board. It is the opinion of a majority of the Board that this claim ought not to be confirmed. Frederick Bates, commissioner, forbears giving an opinion.

L. LACROIX, claiming four hundred arpents of land, No. 22; produces same concession and plat as in the claim of Basil Valle.

December 21, 1811: Present, a full Board. It is the opinion of a majority of the Board that this claim ought not to be confirmed. Frederick Bates, commissioner, forbears giving an opinion.

F. B. VALLE, claiming four hundred arpents of land, No. 23; produces same concession and plat as in the claim of Basil Valle.
December 21, 1811: Present, a full Board. It is the opinion of a majority of the Board that this claim ought not to be confirmed. Frederick Bates, commissioner, forbears giving an opinion.

F. MILHOMME, claiming four hundred arpents of land, No. 24; produces same concession and plat as in the claim of Basil Valle.
December 21, 1811: Present, a full Board. It is the opinion of a majority of the Board that this claim ought not to be confirmed. Frederick Bates, commissioner, forbears giving an opinion.

JACQUES GUIBORD, claiming four hundred arpents of land, No. 25; produces same concession and plat as in the claim of Basil Valle.
December 21, 1811: Present, a full Board. It is the opinion of a majority of the Board that this claim ought not to be confirmed. Frederick Bates, commissioner, forbears giving an opinion.

F. THIBEAU, claiming four hundred arpents of land, No. 26; produces same concession and plat as in the claim of Basil Valle.
December 21, 1811: Present, a full Board. It is the opinion of a majority of the Board that this claim ought not to be confirmed. Frederick Bates, commissioner, forbears giving an opinion.

A. PARTINAIS, claiming four hundred arpents of land, No. 27; produces same concession and plat as in the claim of Basil Valle.
December 21, 1811: Present, a full Board. It is the opinion of a majority of the Board that this claim ought not to be confirmed. Frederick Bates, commissioner, forbears giving an opinion.

J. BECQUETTE, claiming four hundred arpents of land, No. 28; produces same concession and plat as in the claim of Basil Valle.
December 21, 1811: Present, a full Board. It is the opinion of a majority of the Board that this claim ought not to be confirmed. Frederick Bates, commissioner, forbears giving an opinion.

B. COLEMAN, claiming four hundred arpents of land, No. 29; produces same concession and plat as in the claim of Basil Valle.
December 21, 1811: Present, a full Board. It is the opinion of a majority of the Board that this claim ought not to be confirmed. Frederick Bates, commissioner, forbears giving an opinion.

HYPOLITE ROBERT, claiming four hundred arpents of land, No. 30; produces same concession and plat as in the claim of Basil Valle.
December 21, 1811: Present, a full Board. It is the opinion of a majority of the Board that this claim ought not to be confirmed. Frederick Bates, commissioner, forbears giving an opinion.

PIERRE BOYER, claiming four hundred arpents of land, No. 31; produces same concession and plat as in the claim of Basil Valle.
December 21, 1811: Present, a full Board. It is the opinion of a majority of the Board that this claim ought not to be confirmed. Frederick Bates, commissioner, forbears giving an opinion.

JOHN SMITH T., assignee of Charles Robar, claiming four hundred and twenty acres of land, situate as aforesaid; produces as aforesaid; a notice to the recorder, and the same concession wherein Charles Robar is found to be one of the thirty-one inhabitants; also the plat aforesaid, in which plat said Robar is No. 8; a deed of transfer from said Robar to claimant, dated 24th August, 1805.
Testimony taken. October 22, 1808. Peter Boyer, sworn, says that Charles Robar was settled in the village of the Old Mines five years ago, and inhabited and cultivated a part of said tract of twelve thousand four hundred arpents for three years.
December 21, 1811: Present, a full Board. It is the opinion of Clement B. Penrose, commissioner, that this claim ought not to be granted, being embraced by the second section of the act of the 2d March, 1805, and claims with as slight testimony have been granted.
It is the opinion of John B. C. Lucas, commissioner, that this claim ought not to be granted, because the testimony of Peter Boyer, concerning the inhabitation and cultivation of Charles Robar is indefinite, and does not apply more to the part of the connected plat to which his claim refers than to any other part of the twelve thousand four hundred arpents represented by the connected plat. Frederick Bates, commissioner, forbears giving an opinion.

JOHN SMITH T., assignee of Alexander Duclos, claiming four hundred and twenty acres of land, situate as aforesaid; produces a notice to the recorder. The same concession as aforesaid, wherein Alexander Duclos is found to be one of the thirty-one inhabitants; also the plat aforesaid, in which plat said Duclos is No. 7; a deed of transfer from said Duclos to claimant, dated 24th August, 1805.
Testimony taken, October 22, 1808. Peter Boyer, sworn, says Alexander Duclos was settled in the village of the Old Mines, and inhabited and cultivated a part of said tract of twelve thousand four hundred arpents five years ago, and for three years.
December 21, 1811: Present, a full Board. It is the opinion of Clement B. Penrose, commissioner, that this claim ought to be granted, being embraced by the second section of the act of 2d March, 1805, and claims with as slight testimony have been granted.
It is the opinion of John B. C. Lucas, commissioner, that this claim ought not to be granted, because the testimony of Peter Boyer, concerning the inhabitation and cultivation of Alexander Duclos, is indefinite and does not apply more to the part of the connected plat to which this claim refers than to any other part of the twelve thousand four hundred arpents represented by the connected plat. Frederick Bates, commissioner, forbears giving an opinion.

****

JOHN SMITH .T., assignee of Louis Boyer, claiming eight hundred and forty arpents of land, situate as afore-said; produces a notice to the recorder. Same concession as aforesaid, wherein Louis Boyer is found to be one of the thirty-one inhabitants; also, the plat aforesaid, in which plat Louis Boyer is No. 14; an assignment from said Louis Boyer to claimants, dated 25th August, 1805.

Testimony taken, October 22, 1808. Peter Boyer, sworn, says that Louis Boyer was settled in the village of the Old Mines, and inhabited and cultivated a part of said tract of twelve thousand four hundred arpents five years ago, and for two years.

December 21, 1811. It is the opinion of Clement B. Penrose, commissioner, that this claim ought to be granted, being embraced by the second section of the act of the 2d March, 1805, and claims with as slight testi-mony have been granted.

It is the opinion of John B. C. Lucas, commissioner, that this claim ought not to be granted, because the testi-mony of Peter Boyer, concerning the inhabitation and cultivation of Louis Boyer is indefinite, and does not apply more to the part of the connected plat to which this claim refers than to any other part of the twelve thou-sand four hundred arpents represented by the connected plat. Frederick Bates, commissioner, forbears giving an opinion.

JOHN SMITH T., assignee of Joseph Boyer, claiming one thousand one hundred and ninety acres of land, situate as aforesaid; produces a notice to the recorder. The same concession as aforesaid, wherein Joseph Boyer is found to be one of the thirty-one inhabitants; also the plat aforesaid, in which plat Joseph Boyer is No 17; an assignment from said Boyer to claimant, dated 9th January, 1808.

Testimony taken, October 22, 1808. Peter Boyer, sworn, says that Joseph Boyer was settled in the village of the Old Mines, and inhabited and cultivated a part of said tract of twelve thousand four hundred arpents eight years ago, and ever since until last year.

December 21, 1811: Present, a full Board. It is the opinion of Clement B. Penrose, commissioner, that this claim ought to be granted, being embraced by the second section of the act of the 2d March, 1805, and claims with as slight testimony have been granted.

It is the opinion of John B. C. Lucas, commissioner, that this claim ought not to be granted, because the tes-timony of Peter Boyer, concerning the inhabitation and cultivation of Joseph Boyer, is indefinite, and does not apply more to the part of the connected plat to which this claim refers than to any other part of the twelve thou-sand four hundred arpents represented by the connected plat. Frederick Bates, commissioner, forbears giving an opinion.

DOCUMENT F.

MOSES AUSTIN, claiming seven thousand one hundred and fifty-three arpents thirty-two and two-thirds feet of land, situate adjoining Mine à Breton, district of St. Genevieve; produces to the Board a grant for the same from Don Juan Ventura Morales, Intendant of Louisiana, dated 25th July, 1802, and is found in "the abstract of all the concessions and patented grants of land appertaining to the district of Louisiana, recorded in the registers kept by the Spanish and French Governments of the province of Louisiana, since the 2d July, 1756, until the [23d April, 1802," transmitted to this Board by the Secretary of the Treasury; which grant the Intendant declares to be founded on an official letter from the Baron de Carondelet to Zenon Trudeau, Lieutenant Governor, dated March 15, 1797, ordering the said Zenon Trudeau to grant one league square; and an order of survey from said Zenon Trudeau, dated 14th January, 1799; declaration of its having been surveyed by Antoine Soulard, and registered in the book of surveys, No. 52; and a declaration on the part of said Antoine Soulard that the land was occupied by claimant at the time of survey, granted on condition that claimant shall comply with the third, fourth, sixth, seventh, and ninth articles of the ordinances of his Intendancy, dated 17th July, 1799.

December 21, 1811: Present, a full Board. A majority of the Board ascertain that this title is not a grant made and completed prior to the 1st October, 1800. Frederick Bates, commissioner, forbears giving an opinion.

REPRESENTATIVES OF FRANCIS MOREAU, assignee of Francis Azor, alias Breton, claiming four arpents square of land.

December 21, 1811: Present, a full Board. It is the opinion of Clement B. Penrose, commissioner, that this claim ought to be confirmed, being embraced by the fourth section of the act of the 3d March, 1807. It is the opinion of John B. C. Lucas, commissioner, that this claim ought not to be confirmed. Frederick Bates, commis-sioner, forbears giving an opinion.

ST. JAMES BEAUVAIS, claiming sixty feet in circumference round every hole where he may find mineral.

December 21, 1811: Present, a full Board. It is the opinion of a majority of the Board that this claim ought not to be confirmed. Frederick Bates, commissioner, forbears giving an opinion.

FRANCIS VALLE, representative of, claiming sixty feet in circumference round every hole where he may find mineral.

December 21, 1811: Present, a full Board. It is the opinion of a majority of the Board that this claim ought not to be confirmed. Frederick Bates, commissioner, forbears giving an opinion.

F. SALUMANDIERE, heirs and representatives of, claiming sixty feet of land in circumference round every hole where they may find mineral. This claim is not of record.

December 21, 1811: Present, a full Board. It is the opinion of the Board that this claim ought not to be con-firmed.

AMABLE PARTINAIS, claiming five hundred arpents of land, situate adjoining Mine à Breton, district of St. Genevieve; produces a concession from Charles D. Delassus, Lieutenant Governor, dated 5th September, 1799; and a plat of survey, dated February 20, 1800, certified 10th June, 1800.

December 21, 1811: Present, a full Board. The testimony of Baptiste Valle and Jean Lemoine, stated in the report of the agent to have been taken on the 12th August, 1806, and copied by the said agent, together with the opinion of the Board, from the rough minutes, (which must be understood from the rough minutes of the Board,) is not deemed by the present Board to be proper and legal evidence, inasmuch as the said testimony and opinion never were entered on the fair minutes of said Board, which are the sole minutes known in law, and acknowledged by the commissioners. The Board remark that no kind of testimony suggests or makes it appear that the land claimed includes a lead mine; and the Board would have confirmed the same had it not been included in the agent's report. It is the opinion of the Board that this claim ought not to be confirmed.

CHARLES BECQUETTE, claiming thirty-four arpents of land.
December 23, 1811: Present, a full Board. It is the opinion of the Board that this claim ought not to be granted. The Board remark that no kind of testimony [suggests or makes it appear that the land claimed includes a lead mine, and the Board would have granted the same had it not been included in the agent's report.

LOUIS MILHOMME, claiming twenty arpents of land.
December 23, 1811: Present, a full Board. The Board remark that no kind of testimony suggests or makes it appear that the land claimed includes a lead mine.
It is the opinion of the Board that this claim ought not to be granted, said claimant not having produced permission to settle.

LOUIS GRINEJA and FRANCIS THIBEAULT, assignees of Louis Lacroix, claiming forty arpents of land.
December 23, 1811: Present, a full Board. The Board remark that no kind of testimony suggests or makes it appear that the land claimed includes a lead mine. It is the opinion of the Board that this claim ought not to be granted.

PETER MARTIN, claiming twenty-six arpents of land.
December 23, 1811: Present, a full Board. The Board remark that no kind of testimony suggests or makes it appear that the land claimed includes a lead mine. It is the opinion of the Board that this claim ought not to be granted, claimant not having produced permission to settle.

JACOB WISE, claiming thirty-seven and a half acres of land, situate adjoining Mine à Breton, district of St. Genevieve; produces a plat of survey, dated 26th February and certified 28th February, 1806; produces also permission to settle, sworn to by Joseph Decelle, syndic.
The following testimony in this claim is taken from testimony perpetuated and attested by two of the commissioners, October 24, 1808.
Francis Thibeault, sworn, says that Jacob Wise cultivated the land claimed nine or ten years ago and ever since; built a house the first year, which was rented to Mr. Decelle for two years; has not since been inhabited, but had always been used as a barn; claimant lived adjoining the tract with one Charles Becquette; claimant is a single man.
December 23, 1811: Present, a full Board. The Board remark that no kind of testimony suggests or makes it appear that the land claimed includes a lead mine. It is the opinion of the Board that this claim ought not to be granted, claimant not having inhabited the same on the 20th December, 1803.

THOMAS RUSS, claiming eleven hundred and forty-six arpents forty-one perches of land.
December 23, 1811: Present, a full Board. It is the opinion of the Board that this claim ought not to be granted. The Board remark that no kind of testimony suggests or makes it appear that the land claimed includes a lead mine; and that the claim has been acted on by the Board a long time prior to the report of the agent delivered to the Board.

WIDOW MOREAU, assignee of John Baptiste Labreche, claiming five hundred arpents of land, situate on the waters of Grand river, district of St. Genevieve; produces a concession from Charles D. Delassus, Lieutenant Governor, dated 5th September, 1799.
December 22, 1811: Present, a full Board. It is the opinion of a majority of the Board that this claim ought to be confirmed. Frederick Bates, commissioner, forbears giving an opinion.

DOCUMENT G.

AUGUSTE CHOUTEAU, Jun., claiming eight hundred arpents of land.
December 23, 1811: Present, a full Board. It is the opinion of a majority of the Board that this claim ought not to be confirmed. Frederick Bates, commissioner, forbears giving an opinion.

DOCUMENT H.

REUBEN SMITH, assignee of James and Nicolas Keeth, assignees of Nicolas Boilvin, claiming eight hundred arpents of land, situate on the waters of Grand river, district of St. Genevieve; produces an order of survey from Zenon Trudeau, dated 25th January, 1798; a plat of survey, signed Boyd Denny, dated 26th February, 1806; a transfer from Boilvin to James and Nicolas Keeth, dated December, 1804; a transfer from James and Nicolas Keeth to claimant, dated 20th May, 1804.
December 23, 1811: Present, a full Board. The Board remark that no kind of testimony suggests or makes it appear that the land claimed includes a lead mine. It is the opinion of the Board that this claim ought not to be confirmed.

DOCUMENT J.

JOHN BAPTISTE PRATTE, Sen., claiming one thousand arpents of land.
December 23, 1811: Present, a full Board. It is the opinion of a majority of the Board that this claim ought not to be confirmed. Frederick Bates, commissioner, forbears giving an opinion.

DOCUMENT K.

RUFUS EASTON and JAMES BRUFF, assignees of Joseph Gerrard and Patrick Flemming, claiming eight hundred and forty arpents of land, situate on the second fork of the Grand river, district of St. Genevieve, comprehending and including the Mine à Joe; produces a certified copy of an order from Manuel Perez, Lieutenant Governor, to Peyroux de la Coudriniere, commandant, to grant said tract, dated 7th July, 1790; a certified copy of a concession from Peyroux de la Coudriniere, commandant, to Joseph Gerrard, père, Patrick Flemming, Jr. Joel Maccagne, and Laurent Maccague, for seven arpents by thirty to each of them, dated 17th July, 1790; an order of survey from Charles Delassus, Lieutenant Governor, to Joseph Gerrard and Patrick Flemming for eight hundred and forty arpents, stating the aforesaid concession from Peyroux, commandant, in consequence of the same not having been surveyed before, dated 25th September, 1799; a transfer from Patrick Flemming to claimants, dated 14th September, 1805; a transfer from Joseph Gerrard to Rufus Easton, dated 12th December, 1804; a plat of survey of eight hundred and forty arpents, dated 28th September, 1799, certified 10th January, 1800; an acknowledgment signed by Rufus Easton and James Bruff, and dated 15th November, 1805, by which it appears that said claimants are equally concerned in said tract.

December 24, 1811: Present, a full Board. The testimony of James Keeth and Ezekiel Eastridge, stated in the report of the agent to have been taken on the 2d of December, 1807, and copied by the said agent from the rough minutes, (which must be understood from the rough minutes of the Board) is not deemed legal evidence, inasmuch as the same was ordered by the Board not to be transcribed, and was not transcribed for the following reasons: that the Board had established a rule not to receive evidence partially, but to receive all the testimony at one time, unless, from the peculiar situation of the parties, the testimony offered could not be produced again; in that case, the same was attested on the rough minutes, by the signature of a majority of the commissioners. The object of the rule was, generally, not to let the testimony be open to be improved and enlarged by the parties, the Board conceiving that this opportunity might have been greatly abused. It is the opinion of a majority of the Board that this claim ought not to be confirmed. Frederick Bates, commissioner, forbears giving an opinion.

Document L.

Camille Delassus, claiming two thousand four hundred arpents thirty-four and a half perches of land, situate on the waters of Big river, district of St. Genevieve; produces the record of a concession from Charles D. Delassus, Lieutenant Governor, dated 12th October, 1799; a plat of survey, dated 1st November, 1799, certified 10th January, 1800.

December 24, 1811: Present, a full Board. The Board make the same remarks as in the claim of Amable Partinais, page 678, as respects the rough minutes, and same remarks as in the claim of Easton and Bruff, page 579, as respects the testimony taken on the 1st and 2d of December, 1807. It is the opinion of a majority of the Board that this claim ought not to be confirmed. Frederick Bates, commissioner, forbears giving an opinion.

Document M.

Louis Labeaume and Charles Fremon Deloriare, claiming ten thousand arpents of land, situate near Prairie à Rondo, district of St. Genevieve; produce the record of a concession from Zenon Trudeau, Lieutenant Governor, dated 17th January, 1797; certificate of a plat of survey, signed and sworn to by Antoine Soulard, and dated 15th March, 1808.

December 24, 1811: Present, a full Board. The Board remark that no kind of testimony suggests or makes it appear that the land claimed includes a lead mine. It is the opinion of the Board that this claim ought not to be confirmed.

Document N.

John Smith T., assignee of Jacque St. Vrain, claiming ten thousand arpents of land; original papers not produced; the record of the concession much compressed; thirty-three words are interlined with different ink; the words Louis Labeaume apparently. The heading of said Labeaume's notice of claims occupies one-third of the paper, in the direction which four lines of the record of said concession stands in, so that two-thirds of said paper, in the direction of the said lines, is covered on each side with the said four lines, and the remaining one-third in the middle is occupied by the said words Louis Labeaume. It appears from the records that John Smith T. claims under this concession as follows: One thousand arpents at a place called the New Diggings, about two miles from Mine à Breton; a place known by the name of Mine à Robina, three hundred arpents; on the branch above Renault's Mines, three hundred arpents; three hundred arpents, including Doggit's Mines; two hundred arpents on the first branch emptying into the Mine Fork on the south side above its junction with Big river; two hundred arpents, including a place called McKee's Discovery, about a mile and a quarter from the last mentioned place; fifty arpents, including a mill seat on the second creek emptying into Big river, above the junction of the Mineral Fork, on the west side.

December 27, 1811: Present, a full Board. It is the opinion of a majority of the Board that this claim ought not to be confirmed. Frederick Bates, commissioner, forbears giving an opinion.

Joseph Decelle, claiming six hundred and thirty acres of land.

December 27, 1811: Present, a full Board. In the testimony of David Shaw, copied from the minutes of the Board by the agent, there is an error. It is there stated "about three or four hundred yards from the fields," whereas, in the original, it is "two or three hundred."

It is the opinion of a majority of the Board that this claim ought not to be granted. Frederick Bates, commissioners, forbears giving an opinion.

Document O.

Pierre Charles Dehault Delassus Deluziere, claiming seven thousand and fifty-six arpents of land.

December 27, 1811: Present, a full Board. It is the opinion of a majority of the Board that this claim ought not to be confirmed. Frederick Bates, commissioner, forbears giving an opinion.

Document P.

John Baptiste Pratte, St. James Beauvais, Francis Valle, and John Baptiste Valle, claiming two leagues square of land, situate at Mine à la Motte, district of St. Genevieve; produce the record of a petition and recommendation for a concession from Charles D. Delassus, Lieutenant Governor, dated 22d January, 1801; record of a power of attorney to James Maxwell to obtain said concession; record of a petition of said Maxwell to the Intendant, dated 29th April, 1802; an order from Morales to Peter Derbigny to translate the documents and petitions, dated New Orleans, 30th April, 1802; record of a plat of survey of twenty-eight thousand two hundred and twenty-four arpents, dated 22d February, 1806, certified 26th February, 1806.

December 27, 1811: Present, full Board. It is the opinion of a majority of the Board that this claim ought not to be confirmed. Frederick Bates, commissioner, forbears giving an opinion.

The foregoing claims, from A to P, inclusive, contain the whole of the report made to this Board by the agent of the United States.

John Perry, assignee of Basil Valle, claiming six hundred and thirty-nine acres of land, situate at the Mine à Breton, district of Genevieve; produces a notice to the recorder, dated October 3, 1807; and a deed of conveyance from said Valle to claimant, dated 18th March, 1806.

Testimony taken, December 5, 1807. Joseph Pratte, being duly sworn, says that between the years 1792 and 1795, Basil Valle built a cabin on the claim, cultivated a garden, and cleared six acres of land in 1796; continued to inhabit and cultivate the same till sold to claimant, and has been inhabited and cultivated ever since; said Valle considering said tract not to be more extensive than his improvements; that there has been mineral found within two rods of the enclosure, but does not know of any being found on the land; that the house stands on the street of the village at the Mine à Breton.

December 27, 1811: Present, a full Board. It is the opinion of a majority of the Board that this claim ought not to be granted, because it appears Basil Valle claims another tract of land under concession. Frederick Bates, commissioner, forbears giving an opinion.

THOMAS ALLEY, claiming sixteen arpents of land, situate at Alley's Mine, district of St. Genevieve; produces the record of a petition and recommendation from Francis Valle, commandant, dated 18th August, 1801; a reference from Charles D. Delassus, Lieutenant Governor, to the Intendant, dated 28th August, 1801.

December 27, 1811: Present, a full Board. It is the opinion of a majority of the Board that this claim ought not to be confirmed. Frederick Bates, commissioner, forbears giving an opinion.

ABRAHAM ARMSTRONG and RUFUS EASTON, claiming six hundred and forty acres of land, situate on Big and Platte rivers, district of St. Genevieve; produce a notice to the recorder; record of a transfer of one-half of this tract to Easton, dated 13th December, 1806; said tract called in said notice and transfer Armstrong's Diggings.

December 27, 1811: Present, a full Board. The Board remark that the term diggings is generally understood in this part of the country, when applied to designate a tract of land, diggings of lead mineral. It is the opinion of a majority of the Board that this claim ought not to be granted. Frederick Bates, commissioner, forbears giving an opinion.

The three foregoing claims to land containing lead mines, although not included in the report of the agent, are subjoined to the same.

JOHN B. C. LUCAS,
CLEMENT B. PENROSE,
FREDERICK BATES.

CLAIMS TO LAND, INCLUDING SALT SPRINGS.

CHARLES TAYON, claiming three hundred and twenty arpents of land, situate on the river Dardennes, district of St. Charles; produces a concession from Zenon Trudeau, Lieutenant Governor, for said quantity of land, to include a salt spring; a plat of survey of three hundred and twenty arpents, dated 1st December, 1799, and certified 8th January, 1800; said concession dated 7th March, 1796.

Testimony taken, July 30, 1806. John Lafleur, being duly sworn, says that the said tract of land was settled for claimant's use by one Harrington, in the year 1801; that a house was built on the same.

December 27, 1811: Present, a full Board. It is the opinion of a majority of the Board that this claim ought not to be confirmed. Frederick Bates, commissioner, forbears giving an opinion.

JACQUE CLAMORGAN, assignee of Thomas Tyler, assignee of John Helderbran, claiming eight by forty arpents of land, situate near the Merrimack, district of St. Louis; produces a duly registered concession from Ferdinando de Leyva, dated November 24, 1779; a plat of survey, dated 28th and certified 29th February, 1806; and two deeds of transfer, one from said Helderbran to Tyler, dated November 22, 1788, and another from said Tyler to claimant, dated September 17, 1791. Charles Gratiot produces a deed of conveyance (not on record) from Jeremiah Connor, sheriff of St. Louis district, for the above land, to Edward Hempstead, dated 11th June, 1808, but stating in the body of the same to have been sold by said sheriff to said Hempstead on the 7th day of July of the same year; said deed was afterwards acknowledged in open court on the 11th July, 1808: produces also an acknowledgment from Edward Hempstead and wife, that said property was purchased by him for Charles Gratiot, and by said Hempstead and wife conveyed to said Gratiot, dated November 25, 1808. It is acknowledged by Charles Gratiot that there is a saline on this claim which has been worked for many years.

Testimony taken, July 30, 1806. John Boli, being duly sworn, says that, about eighteen or nineteen years ago, the time at which he arrived in this country, the said Thomas Tyler lived about one mile below the fork of a run on said land, and had then about eighty arpents of the same under fence, forty of which were then planted in tobacco and corn, and then considered the largest farm in the country; that he remained on it about six or seven years; that about two years after his, the witness's, arrival, the settlers being obliged, on account of the Indians, to fortify themselves, they chose the middle of the settlement, in consequence of which the said Tyler moved up to the fork; that about four or five years afterwards he moved again, and settled himself about two miles from the aforesaid place down the creek, towards the saline, made a field and garden, and built a house, and that the said tracts have been actually cultivated to this day, either by the said Tyler for his use, or for claimant's use by his agents, and that this tract was actually inhabited and cultivated prior to and on the 1st day of October, 1800.

November 29, 1808. Peter Chouteau, sworn, says that John Helderbran inhabited and cultivated the land claimed in 1774, and that he found him still inhabiting and cultivating the same in 1780, when deponent, by order of the Lieutenant Governor, went on the premises to warn said Helderbrand to abandon the same, on account of Indian depredations. This order was obeyed by Helderbrand, as well as by all the inhabitants of the settlement of the Merrimack.

July 30, 1806: Present, Lucas, Penrose, and Donaldson, commissioners. The Board confirm to the said claimant as per his concession.

December 27, 1811: Present, a full Board. It is the opinion of a majority of the Board that this claim ought to be confirmed. Frederick Bates, commissioner, forbears giving an opinion.

CHARLES GRATIOT, assignee of Pierre Chouteau, who was assignee of Benito Vasquez, claiming seven thousand and fifty-six arpents of land, situate on the river Merrimack, district of St. Louis; produces a duly registered concession from Francis Cruzat for the same, dated 8th September, 1784, and certified by Charles D. Delassus on the 9th March, 1803, (the same was granted for a *vacherie*, and on the condition of establishment within a year and a day;) a survey of the same, dated the 15th and certified the 17th February, 1806, together with a deed of transfer of said land, executed by Victoire, the wife of said Benito Vasquez, dated 26th September, 1785, and passed before the commandant, Francis Cruzat; a ratification of said transfer by said Benito Vasquez, dated the 31st January, 1805; and also a deed of transfer from the said Peter Chouteau to claimant, dated 4th May, 1804.

Testimony taken, August 29, 1806. Louis Bourse, being duly sworn, says that he has known the said tract of land established as a farm; that it was settled under Francis Cruzat, by the aforesaid Benito Vasquez, who made a park on the same; that there is on said tract a salt spring, distant from said park about three arpents; that he went through said land at two different times; that the same was then actually inhabited and cultivated; saw a great number of cattle, but could not say to whom they did belong.

Hyacinth St. Cyr, being duly sworn, says that he was on the said tract of land about twenty-one years ago; that the same was then actually inhabited and cultivated for the use of the said Benito Vasquez, who then had salt works established at the aforesaid salt spring; and further, that it was prior to and on the 1st day of October, 1800, actually inhabited and cultivated for the said Peter Chouteau.

October 25, 1808. Pierre Lajoy, sworn, says that claimant made an establishment on the land claimed about twelve years ago, when it was inhabited and cultivated for him, and that the same has been inhabited and cultivated for him ever since.

December 27, 1811: Present, a full Board. It is the opinion of Clement B. Penrose, commissioner, that one league square ought to be confirmed. It is the opinion of John B. C. Lucas, commissioner, that this claim ought not to be confirmed. Frederick Bates, commissioner, forbears giving an opinion.

PASCAL CERRE, claiming, as devisee of Gabriel Cerre, eight hundred arpents of land, situate on the Merrimack, district of St. Louis; produces a duly registered concession from Francis Cruzat, for eight by forty arpents, dated the 12th October, 1782; together with an order of survey for the same, with an addition of twelve by forty arpents, to be included in the same survey, said order dated 10th January, 1798, and signed Zenon Trudeau.

Testimony taken, August 30, 1806. Auguste Chouteau, being duly sworn, says that the said Gabriel Cerre settled the said tract of land in the year 1782; and that the same has been actually inhabited and cultivated to this day.

August 30, 1806: Present, Lucas, Penrose, and Donaldson, commissioners. The Board confirm to the said claimant the said tract of eight hundred arpents, as per the said concession.

December 27, 1811: Present, a full Board. It is the opinion of Clement B. Penrose, commissioner, that this claim ought to be confirmed. It is the opinion of John B. C. Lucas, commissioner, that eight by forty arpents ought to be confirmed. Frederick Bates, commissioner, forbears giving an opinion.

CHARLES FREMON DELORIARE and LOUIS LABEAUME, claiming ten thousand arpents of land, situate on Salt river, district of St. Charles; produce the record of a permission from Zenon Trudeau, Lieutenant Governor, to choose a salt spring, dated 13th May, 1799; record of a concession from Charles D. Delassus, Lieutenant Governor, dated 26th March, 1801; record of a plat of survey, signed Antoine Soulard, dated 15th November, 1807.

December 26, 1811: Present, a full Board. It is the opinion of a majority of the Board that this claim ought not to be confirmed. Frederick Bates, commissioner, forbears giving an opinion.

PIERRE CHOUTEAU, claiming thirty thousand arpents of land, situate on Saline river, district of St. Louis; produces a concession from Charles D. Delassus, Lieutenant Governor, dated 20th November, 1799; a paper purporting to be a gift from sundry Indians to claimant, dated 19th March, 1792.

December 27, 1811: Present, a full Board. It is the opinion of a majority of the Board that this claim ought not to be confirmed. Frederick Bates, commissioner, forbears giving an opinion.

HENRY PEYROUX, claiming seven thousand seven hundred and sixty acres of land, situate on Saline creek and Mississippi river, district of St. Genevieve; produces the record of a duly registered concession from Manuel Perez, Lieutenant Governor, dated 24th December, 1787; a plat of survey, dated 22d and certified 26th February, 1806.

December 27, 1811: Present, a full Board. It is the opinion of a majority of the Board that this claim ought not to be confirmed. Frederick Bates, commissioner, forbears giving an opinion.

CHARLES GRATIOT, assignee of Maturin Bouvet, claiming twenty arpents of land, on which there is a saline, situate on the river Ha Ha, district of St. Charles; produces a concession (duly signed) from Zenon Trudeau, dated 1st June, 1795, and an act of public sale of the effects and property of said Bouvet, dated 7th December, 1800.

Testimony taken, July 8, 1806. Francis M. Benoit, being duly sworn, says that he has known a saline established on said land for eleven or twelve years since; that the same was established by said Bouvet; that he died about five years ago by fire; that his house was then destroyed, and that he worked said mine to the last moment.

July 8, 1806: Present, Penrose and Donaldson, commissioners. The Board reject this claim. They observe that the aforesaid concession is duly registered; that the conditions on which said concession was granted have been complied with, but that the same was not actually inhabited and cultivated prior to and on the 1st day of October, 1800.

January 9, 1812: Present, a full Board. It is the opinion of a majority of the Board that this claim ought not to be confirmed. Frederick Bates, commissioner, forbears giving an opinion.

> JOHN B. C. LUCAS,
> CLEMENT B. PENROSE,
> FREDERICK BATES.

INHABITANTS OF THE TOWN OF ST. LOUIS, claiming nine hundred and twenty toises in length, one hundred and fifty in breadth to the north, two hundred in the centre, and one hundred and fifty to the south; produce a notice to the recorder, and a plat of said town, dated in 1780.

January 15, 1812: Present, a full Board. It is the opinion of Clement B. Penrose, commissioner, that this claim ought to be granted, under ten years' possession prior to 20th December, 1803, if not exceeding two thousand acres, under the second section of the act of the 3d March, 1807.

It is the opinion of Frederick Bates, commissioner, that this claim ought not to be granted in manner as claimed.

It is the opinion of John B. C. Lucas, commissioner, that this claim ought not to be granted, because several lots represented by the said plat have already been granted; others confirmed to individual claimants; because the notes of the plat represent or identify, by the letters A, B, C, D, E, F, G, H and I, different species of property, to wit, property of the King, property of the Roman Catholic congregation, such as church, &c.; also a lot marked with the letter G, called Place, which is understood to be La Place d'Armes; and also other lots under the letter I, styled *emplacemens des particuliers*, which would, if granted generally by the plat to the inhabitants, contravene the note of the said plat, by granting generally in common that which appears to be owned severally, and under various species of rights; because, also, the said plat does not appear to be duly authenticated.

Clement B. Penrose, commissioner, observes that no part of the property marked by said letters A, B, C, D, E, F, G, H and I, appears to have been the property of the King except the Place d'Armes.

January 15, 1812. On motion of Clement B. Penrose, commissioner, as follows, to wit:

The Board having acted on all the claims on record, except fifteen claims which were ordered to be surveyed for the purpose of ascertaining the quantity of land claimed, and which have not been returned, although ordered so to be long since; therefore, resolved, that the said claims be reported, with the opinion of the commissioners thereon.

A question being taken on the resolution, Clement B. Penrose and Frederick Bates, commissioners, voted in the affirmative, and John B. C. Lucas, commissioner, in the negative.

The fifteen claims above alluded to are the following, to wit:

JOSEPH BECKETT.—A claim for two arpents front on the Mississippi river, thence to the concession of Madame Lasourse, district of St. Genevieve.

April 19, 1810: Present, a full Board. The Board grant to Joseph Beckett the above tract of land, provided it does not exceed two thousand acres, under the second section of an act of Congress, entitled An act respecting claims to land, and passed 3d March, 1807; and order that the same be surveyed conformably to his possession.

AUGUSTE CHOUTEAU, claiming, under Paul Lacroix, a tract of land, situate in the lower fields of St. Charles, three hundred and twenty-four arpents, more or less, district of St. Charles.

January 15, 1812: Present, a full Board. A majority of the Board declare that they would have confirmed this claim had it been found not to have exceeded three hundred and twenty-four arpents.

John B. C. Lucas, commissioner, declares that he cannot give an absolute vote, under the present circumstances, upon the claim, inasmuch as the Board have heretofore ordered a survey to be made under the foregoing concession, for the purpose of ascertaining the quantity; and inasmuch as the same reasons which induced the Board to make said order previous to the decision of the claim still exists, and the said order remains in force, not having been rescinded; he further remarks, that the claim ought to be confirmed, without being able at present to say what quantity.

MANUEL A. ROCQUE, claiming under John Coontz, a lot of ground in the town of St. Charles, with a mill-dam and race; district of St. Charles.

November 27, 1809: Present, a full Board. The Board grant to Manuel A. Rocque the above tract of land, provided it does not exceed two thousand acres, under the second section of an act of Congress, entitled An act respecting claims to land, and passed the 3d March, 1807, and order that the same be surveyed agreeably to his possession.

JOSEPH M. PAPIN.—A claim for eight arpents front on the Mississippi, and back to the road leading to Carondelet, district of St. Louis.

January 15, 1812: Present, a full Board. A majority of the Board declare they would have confirmed this claim had it been found not to have exceeded eighty arpents.

John B. C. Lucas, commissioner, makes the same remarks as in the claim of Auguste Chouteau, above.

CHARLES GRATIOT, claiming under Maturin Bouvet, eighty-four arpents front on the Mississippi, and in depth from the river back to the hills, district of St. Charles.

January 15, 1812: Present, a full Board. A majority of the Board declare that they would have confirmed this claim had it been found not to have exceeded a league square, and if the same be not situate above the mouth of the river Jeffreon.

John B. C. Lucas, commissioner, makes the same remark as in the claim of Auguste Chouteau, above, with this addition, "provided, also, that the said claim is not situate above the mouth of the river Jeffreon."

BERNARD PRATTE, claiming, under John Baptiste Pugol, six by forty arpents, situate on the Merrimack, district of St. Louis.

January 15, 1812: Present, a full Board. A majority of the Board declare that they would have confirmed this claim had it been found not to have exceeded two hundred and forty arpents.

John B. C. Lucas, commissioner, makes the same remarks as in the claim of Auguste Chouteau, above.

ANTOINE V. BOUIS, claiming under Louis Boury, a barn lot in the town of St. Louis, district of St. Louis.

January 15, 1812: Present, a full Board. A majority of the Board declare that they would have granted this claim under the provisions of the second section of the act of the 3d of March, 1807, had it been found not to have exceeded one hundred and twenty by one hundred and fifty feet.

John B. Lucas, commissioner, declares that he cannot give an absolute vote, under the present circumstances, upon the claim, inasmuch as the Board have heretofore ordered a survey to be made for the purpose of ascertaining the quantity, and inasmuch as the same reasons which induced the Board to make said order previous to the decision of the claim still exists, and the said order remains in force, not having been rescinded; he further remarks, that the claim ought to be granted, without being able at present to say what quantity.

MANUEL LISA, claiming, under one Amiot, six hundred arpents of land, situate on Creve Cœur, district of St. Louis.

January 15, 1812: Present, a full Board. A majority of the Board declare that they would have granted this claim, under the provisions of the second section of the act of the 3d March, 1807, had it been found not to exceed six hundred arpents.

John B. Lucas, commissioner, makes the same remarks as in the above claim of Antoine V. Bouis.

JOHN BAPTISTE PRATTE, claiming, under Paul Deruisseaux, one and a half arpents front by the usual depth, situate on Common Fields, district of St. Genevieve.

January 15, 1812. A majority of the Board declare that they would have granted this claim, under the provisions of the second section of the act of the 3d March, 1807, had it been found not to have exceeded two thousand acres.

John B. C. Lucas, commissioner, makes the same remarks as in the above claim of Antoine V. Bouis.

JOSEPH BRASEAU.—A claim for ten arpents front, on the Mississippi, running back to the road leading from St. Louis to Carondelet, district of St. Louis.

January 15, 1812: Present, a full Board. A majority of the Board declare that they would have confirmed this claim had it been found not to have exceeded one hundred arpents.

John B. C. Lucas, commissioner, makes the same remarks as in the claim of Auguste Chouteau, page 683.

JOSEPH BRASEAU, claiming, under Benito Vasquez, two arpents front on the Mississippi, running back to the road leading from St. Louis to Carondelet, district of St. Louis.

January 15, 1812: Present, a full Board. A majority of the Board declare that they would have confirmed this claim had it been found not to have exceeded twenty arpents.

John B. C. Lucas, commissioner, makes the same remarks as in the claim of Auguste Chouteau, page 683.

SUSANNAH DUBRIEUL, claiming, under Sylvester Sarpy, four arpents front on the Mississippi, back to the road leading from St. Louis to Carondelet, from six to eight arpents, district of St. Louis.

January 15, 1812. A majority of the Board declare that they would have granted this claim under the provisions of the second section of the act of the 3d March, 1807, had it been found not to have exceeded thirty-two arpents.

John B. C. Lucas, commissioner, makes the same remarks as in the claim of Antoine V. Bouis, page 683.

PETER DELUZIERE, claiming under Bartholomew Tardiveau, ten arpents front between the Mississippi and the Common Fields, district of St. Genevieve.

January 15, 1812: Present, a full Board. A majority of the Board declare that they would have confirmed this claim had it been found not to have contained more than the quantity of land contained in a league square.

John B. C. Lucas, commissioner, makes the same remarks as in the claim of Auguste Chouteau, page 683.

JACQUES CLAMORGAN, claiming, under Sumande and others, a lot in the town of St. Louis.

January 15, 1812: Present, a full Board. A majority of the Board declare that they would have confirmed this claim had it been found not to have exceeded one hundred and twenty by one hundred and fifty feet.

John B. C. Lucas, commissioner, makes the same remarks as in the claim of Auguste Chouteau, page 683.

JACQUE CLAMORGAN, claiming, under Dupuy and others, a lot in St. Louis, district of St. Louis.

January 15, 1812. A majority of the Board declare that they would have granted this claim, under the provisions of the second section of the act of the 3d March, 1807, had it been found not to have exceeded one hundred and twenty by one hundred and fifty feet.

John B. C. Lucas, commissioner, makes the same remarks as in the claim of Antoine V. Bouis, page 683.

The foregoing decisions are respectfully submitted.

JOHN B. C. LUCAS,
CLEMENT B. PENROSE,
FREDERICK BATES.

JANUARY 20, 1812.

APPENDIX.

MARIE P. LEDUC's claim, (see page 464.)

ST. LOUIS OF THE ILLINOIS, *December* 30, 1799.

To Don Charles Dehault Delassus, Lieutenant Colonel of the armies of His Catholic Majesty, Lieutenant Governor of Upper Louisiana and its dependencies, &c.

Marie Philip Leduc, who has had the honor that Government had enough confidence in him to be employed by Mr. Thomas Portell, and now by you, as chiefs of said Government, as well at New Madrid as at this place, since your arrival, having shown his zeal and affection in fulfilling the duties of translator of the English language, there being no one particularly appointed for this place, and that it is well known to you, sir, that he has made it his duty to discharge it without any reward or compensation: your petitioner, therefore, prays you, sir, to be pleased to grant him fifteen thousand arpents of land, in superficies, to be taken on the left bank of the river Missouri, on any of the vacant lands of the King's domain, in the views to establish on the same a vacherie, and to form a settlement corresponding to a farm; also, in the views to secure in future a livelihood, in order to support his numerous family, and to be secured from the accidents and adversities so frequent in the other branches of this present life; your petitioner having no other prospects but those of continuing to live a peaceable and faithful subject of His Majesty, and to be submitted to the generous Government from whom he has already experienced the kindness. Your petitioner hopes that you will pay regard to his demand in a favorable manner, promising to make the necessary improvements, as soon as you will permit him, of remaining assiduously ready to translate when required by your orders.

M. P. LEDUC.

ST. LOUIS, *January* 7, 1800.

Having regard that the petitioner is ancient in this country, and that his merit, personal qualities, and capacities are well known and recommendable, being certain of the truth of his petition; and whereas he has more than the necessary means to put the land solicited in value, I do grant to him and his heirs the land by him demanded, if it does not prejudice any body; and the surveyor, Don Anthony Soulard, shall put the petitioner in possession of the quantity of land demanded, on the place mentioned; after which he will deliver the corresponding certificate to the party, together with this, in order that it may serve him to obtain the concession and title in form from the Intendant General, to whom, by royal order, appertains the exclusive right of granting all classes of vacant lands.

CHARLES DEHAULT DELASSUS.

TERRITORY OF LOUISIANA:

I do hereby certify the above to be truly translated from the original.

M. P. LEDUC,
Translator to the Board of Com'rs of Lou. Ter.

LOUISIANA TERRITORY, *District of St. Louis:*   *January* 16, 1812.

Before me, one of the Judges of the Court of Common Pleas and Quarter Sessions for the district of St. Louis, has appeared M. P. Leduc, who has presented to me an original concession for fifteen thousand arpents of land, in the French and Spanish languages, of which said concession I do certify the above to be a true and accurate translation. In witness whereof, I have hereunto subscribed my name.

                                                                    L. LABEAUME.

May 2, 1806. Antoine Soulard being duly sworn true answers to give, &c., in a claim of David Delauney:
Question. Were you the surveyor of Upper Louisiana under the Spanish Government?
Answer. Yes.
Question. Was it any part of the duties imposed on you by the Spanish law and the functions of your office to obey the orders of the Lieutenant Governor of the province, without any regard to their legality or illegality?
Answer. Yes; the Lieutenant Governor was accountable for it.
Question. From whom did you derive your appointment?
Answer. From the Governor General of Lower Louisiana, Baron de Carondelet.
Question. Is that your hand-writing? (showing him the aforesaid concession.)
Answer. I believe it is.
Question. Do you recollect when that was written, and is it your belief that it was written at the time it bears date?
Here the witness refused to answer; whereupon, he was asked by the Board whether he meant to give similar answers to the questions in all similar cases; and answered yes.

JAMES MACKAY's claim for two hundred and eighty-two arpents, (see page 465.)
July 22, 1806: Present, a full Board. The Board, from the above testimony, are satisfied that the aforesaid concession is antedated.

WILLIAM REED, Jun., (see page 505.)
Testimony taken, December 3, 1807. William Murphy, being duly sworn, says he was present when old William Reed obtained permission to settle himself and friends and connexions on vacant land, from Mr. Deluziere, late commandant of New Bourbon, in the year 1798 or 1799; and that witness always understood that said William Reed was brother's son of said William Reed, Sen.
John Lewis, being also sworn, says that claimant raised a crop on said tract in 1806 and 1807.

MANUEL LISA, claiming under Philip Baccane, (see page 546.)
Testimony taken, November 24, 1808. Antoine Soulard, sworn, says that he had the concession in this claim in his possession, to make a survey, some time in 1797; that it was one of the concessions which interfered with the Portage des Sioux; in consequence of which information, the Lieutenant Governor, Delassus, ordered them to be surveyed on the vacant domain. Order dated 18th November, 1803.

DAVID DELAUNEY's claim of eight hundred arpents, (see page 553.)
May 2, 1806: Present, Lucas and Penrose, commissioners. The Board, still not being satisfied, required further proof of the date of the above concession; which not being adduced, they reject this claim.

LEMUEL WAKELY's claim, (see page 563.)
September 1, 1810: Present, a full Board. It is the opinion of the Board that this claim ought not to be granted.

MACKAY WHERRY's claim, (see page 570.)
Testimony taken, September 20, 1806. James Mackay, being duly sworn, says that he knows of claimant claiming no other land in his own name in the Territory; that he has known him in the country for upwards of ten years, and heard him say, long prior to October, 1800, that he had obtained the aforesaid concession; and further, that he was, at the time of obtaining the same, the head of a family.

DANIEL STRINGER's claim, (see page 575.)
August 25, 1806: Present, Lucas and Penrose, commissioners. The Board grant the said claimant three hundred and seventy arpents of land, situate as aforesaid, provided so much be found vacant there.

PHILIP SHACKLER's claim, (see page 576.)
March 21, 1806: Present, Lucas and Penrose, commissioners. The Board grant the said claimant seven hundred and fifty arpents of land, situate as aforesaid, provided so much be found vacant there.

FRANCIS MICHEL's claim, (see page 577.)
December 19, 1810: Present, a full Board. It is the opinion of the Board that this claim ought not to be granted.

FRANCIS B. CORVAISSER, claiming under Isaac Thompson, (see page 581.)
Testimony taken, June 19, 1808, at New Madrid. Peter Dumay, duly sworn, says that premises were inhabited and cultivated from 1794 or '95 to present day; fifteen acres now in cultivation; a wife in 1803.

CHARLES ELLIS's claim, (see page 590.)
June 25, 1806: Present, Penrose and Donaldson, commissioners. This claimant appeared before the Board in order the more fully to establish his claim, and produced Richard Moore, who, being duly sworn, says that claimant caused a crop to be raised on said land in 1803; that one-half of the same was reaped by him, and consumed on said land; and further, that he did, prior to and on the 20th day of December of that year, actually inhabit the same, and had then a wife, who died towards the latter end of that month. The Board grant the said claimant two hundred arpents of land, situate as aforesaid, provided so much be found vacant there.

JOSEPH MATTHEWS's claim, (see page 600.)
September 30, 1811: Present, a full Board. It is the opinion of the Board that this claim ought not to be granted.

LAND GRANTS IN MISSOURI TERRITORY - 1805 - 1812
****

223

B. Martin's claim, (see page 606.)

June 20, 1806: Present, Penrose and Donaldson, commissioners. The Board reject this claim, and remark, that, from the terms of this grant, it appears to have been granted, not as a commons for wood, but as a park for cultivation, to be distinctly apportioned among the inhabitants of the town of St. Genevieve.

Charles Findley, claiming under William Patterson; (see page 664.)

August 26, 1806: Present, Lucas and Penrose, commissioners. The Board confirm to the said claimant, assignee as aforesaid, four hundred arpents of land, as per the said warrant of survey.

St. James Beauvais's claim, (see page 669.)

June 20, 1806: Present, Penrose and Donaldson, commissioners. The Board reject this claim, and observe that the above concession is neither antedated nor fraudulent, and that the above claimant had in 1800 ten children and thirty slaves.

Auguste Chouteau, attorney of Peter Fouche, &c. (see page 666.)

Nueva Orleans, 8 *de Mayo*, 1793.

Como tengo insinuado á vuesamerced, en oficio separado, participandole la contrata hecha por el caballero Don Pedro Carlos Delassus, para la subministracion anual de treinta mil libras de plomo en bala ó galapago, le concedera vuesamerced la porcion de terreno que necesite para beneficiar una mina de aquel metal en el parage que señale como tambien otra regular concesion, para que sus hijos y yerno formen sus plantaciones, conforme las fuerzas con que se presenten y la instruccion dada por los nuevos colonos.

Dios guarde á vuesamerced muchos años.

EL BARON DE CARONDELET.

Señor Don Zenon Trudeau.

San Luis de Illinois, *á* 23 *de Enero de* 1804.

Don Carlos Dehault Delassus, Coronel de los reales exercitos, Teniente de Gobernador de la Luisiana Alta y sus dependencias, &a.: Certifico que la presente es copia de su original que se halla depositado en el archivo de este mando de mi cargo.

DELASSUS.

Nouvelle Orleans, *le* 16 *de Mai*, 1807.

Enrégistré en nôtre office sous la date du treize du présent mois.

NARCISSUS BROUTIN, *Not. Pub.*

Mon cher Monsieur: Nouvelle Madrid, *le* 17 *Juin,* 1797.

Lorsque j'ai obtenu une concession de M. Zenon Trudeau, en date du 7 Juin, 1796, que je vous ai remise, en vous disant que j'esperais bientôt retourner à St. Louis pour être présent à l'arpentage que vous deviez faire, je ne croyais pas que les affaires de service de ce petit poste etaient aussi exigeantes. Imaginez vous que depuis que j'ai reçu le commandement de M. Portell, je n'ai cessé d'être continuellement occupé, soit par les procès, ou avec les passagers de toutes nations, &c. qui arrivent par l'Ohio, et à présent avec le passage de Messieurs les Américains, que j'attends de ce jour, et les ordres de M. Howard, qui m'empêchent de bouger d'ici, ne me laissent aucune espérance de pouvoir aller à St. Louis de long-temps; ainsi je vous prie, lorsqu'il vous sera possible de vouloir bien aller arpenter ma concession citée, qui est de 20,000, à prendre dans les deux endroits mentionnés dans la requête décretée que je vous ai laissée. Vous connaissez les endroits que j'ai choisis, ainsi malgré que je ne serai pas présent, j'approuve d'avance vôtre opération, ne doutant nullement que vous ferez pour le mieux, et vous offrant mes services sincères dans le peu qu'offre ce petit bout de brout.

J'ai l'honneur d'être, très cordialement, vôtre affectionné serviteur,

CHARLES DEHAULT DELASSUS.

Mes respects et amitiés à vôtre aimable famille.

Mons. Antoine Soulard.

St. Louis, *le* 1 *Février*, 1804.

Certifions à tous ceux à qu'il appartiendra, que la lettre ci-dessus est une copie fidèle de l'original qui m'a été adressée par Don Charles Dehault Delassus, lieutenant colonel agrégé au régiment six de la Louisiane, et commandant du poste de la Nouvelle Madrid, laquelle est déposée à l'archive de l'arpentage de cette Haute Louisiane à ma charge.

ANTOINE SOULARD.

Nouvelle Orleans, *le* 16 *May*, 1807.

Enrégistré en nôtre office sous la date du treize du présent mois.

NARCISSUS BROUTIN, *Not. Pub.*

January 23, 1806: Present, Lucas, Penrose, and Donaldson, commissioners. A claim of James Pritchett, under the second section of the act of the 2d March, 1805, being before the Board.

In this case, the honorable the commissioners being undetermined as to the quantity of arpents to be granted to actual settlers under the second section of the act of Congress, agreed to make a case of the same; which being argued on the part of the United States, by their agent William C. Caw, Esq., and, on the part of the actual settler, by Jesse Bledsoe, Esq., the opinion of the Board stood as follows:

Clement B. Penrose and James L. Donaldson are of opinion that the whole quantity of land which may be granted to a settler, in virtue of his having cultivated and inhabited on the 20th of December, 1803, may exceed the quantity of eight hundred arpents, the amount to which the laws and usages of Spain restrained the new settler; this opinion they found on the following reasons, to wit:

1st. That the words of the second section of the act, "providing for the other and further allowance to the wife and family of the claimant," would be rendered inoperative and void by a construction which restrains the whole amount to eight hundred arpents, as the mile square English measure; that is, six hundred and forty acres make seven hundred and fifty arpents, leaving only fifty arpents for the *wife and family;* when, under the Spanish usage and law, the allowance for the wife alone would exceed the quantity by fifty arpents, and the family be entirely unprovided for; which would be to say that the words " other and further allowance for the wife and family of the claimant" had sound but not sense.

2d. That it appears satisfactorily to us to have been the liberal intention of Congress to grant land to the settler in proportion to the number of his family, and that that body were of opinion that an individual who had to support by his labor a wife and large family, was entitled to more indulgence than a single unconnected man; and this was also the principle of the Spanish law, which granted to the man only one hundred arpents in his own right, but, in his capacity of husband, gave him one hundred more, and, in that of father, fifty for each child; that the act commutes the one hundred arpents, the man's allowance, for a quantity not to exceed a mile square, and leaves the residue for wife and family to be determined by Spanish law and usage.

3d. According to the other construction which has been given to the words of the second section of the act, a settler with one child and no wife would be entitled to the same quantity of land as a settler with a wife and twelve children, which would be absurd.

4th. The other and further allowance, according to the laws, usages, and customs of the Spanish Government, was intended as a future provision for a family of children, according to its extent; and this principle entirely accords with our impression of the liberal and benevolent view of Congress in this donation.

5th. Even a law of national bounty should be construed favorably for the citizen, if the construction do not favor speculation, and amount to an imposition on the generosity of the public, which, on the grounds above mentioned, we do not think would be the case in this instance.

6th. The majority of the Board the more readily give the law this construction, because, if mistaken, the honorable body to whom the opinion will be referred will set us right, and have it always in their power to give what they may deem a correct construction to their own language.

We are therefore of opinion that a settler on the 20th December, 1803, under the provision for his wife and family of the second section of the act is entitled to more land in his double capacity of husband and father, and that this additional quantity is to be regulated by, and not to exceed, the measure of the Spanish usage; and as, according to such usage, the whole quantity could not exceed eight hundred arpents, of which one hundred were given to the man himself; being of opinion that the quantity, not to exceed a mile square, given by the act to the actual settler, should be taken to be in lieu of the husband's allowance, we find seven hundred arpents remaining, to which, by the Spanish law and usage, we think "the other and further allowance for the wife and family" of such settler is to be limited.

John B. C. Lucas, one of the commissioners, enters the following reasons and opinion as his protest against the foregoing opinion and decision of the majority of the Board, to wit:

It appears to him necessary to premise that the actual settler, who, by the second section of the act under which this Board act, is the object of the liberality of Congress, must have had the permission of a Spanish officer to make a settlement, in conformity with the laws, usages, and customs of the Spanish Government. This Board have liberally presumed a general permission, when the actual settler hath not been able to show a special permission; but this general permission, which is thus presumed, cannot exceed the bounds of the power of the Spanish officer; and, as by the official instructions of Governor Miro, the regulations of Governor Gayoso, and those of the Intendant Morales, the maximum of donations to new settlers is limited to eight hundred arpents, thus all permissions given to new settlers are limited either by the Spanish officer, or by the laws and customs of the Spanish Government. It also appears to him that the intention of the Legislature of the United States hath been to put the Spanish actual settler by permission in the best possible situation, without abandoning Spanish laws and usages; indeed, all the essential qualities of a Spanish donation to an actual settler are preserved in the second section of this law: he is to have one tract of land, one part of which he is to receive in consideration of his person, the other in consideration of his wife and family; the part which he receives in consideration of his person is no more nor less his own than that which he receives in consideration of his family. The minimum, or least quantity of the Spanish grant, is changed, but the maximum, or greatest quantity, remains untouched; the whole together is but one grant, and that grant is made to him, as a new settler, by Spanish permission. Now let it be examined: what is the quantity of land that hath been heretofore allowed for the wife and family of an actual settler, in conformity with the laws, usages, and customs of the Spanish Government? There is no certain quantity, inasmuch as when an actual settler had more children and slaves than could be satisfied at the common ratio of fifty arpents for each child, and twenty arpents for each slave, out of eight hundred arpents, the number of children and slaves ceased to be counted, and the maximum, to wit, eight hundred arpents, was allowed; dividing, then, the quantity of land allowed for the children and slaves, upon the whole supernumerary number of children and slaves, the dividend for each child and slave becomes less than the ratio of fifty and twenty arpents; that there is no quantity invariable and determinate, in conformity to the Spanish laws, but the quantity of eight hundred arpents; this quantity regulates the variable quantity, but is never regulated. From these, a grant to a new settler is not made according to the laws, usages, and customs of the Spanish Government, if it exceeds eight hundred arpents; but, whilst the language of the law justifies that construction, the reason of it coincides also perfectly—what merits hath a new settler by permission more than a new settler by concession? Why should Congress be more liberal towards the actual settlers authorized by Spain, after she had parted with her right of domain, than to settlers before she had parted with the domain? The former liberality exercised by Congress in the Territory of Mississippi towards Spanish actual settlers in circumstances perfectly similar to those provided for by the present second section, ought also to be taken into view; no more than six hundred and forty arpents have been granted to them, without any addition in consideration of their family. It is also observed that this donation hath been sued for by the donee, and not made *gratia principes*, as the books of law term it; therefore, the act of Congress ought not to be construed against the donor, to wit, the United States.

The opinion of said commissioners is, that no donation under the second section of the act alluded to ought to exceed eight hundred arpents, let the number of the family be what it may.

May 1, 1806: Present, John B. C. Lucas, Clement B. Penrose, and James L. Donaldson, commissioners.

The Board having maturely considered and examined certain communications from the Secretary of the Treasury, containing directions from the President, instructions from the Secretary, and the observations of the Attorney General, together with the opinion of the latter on the same subject, believe, that a certain part of the second section of the law of Congress, under which it acts, is so worded as to admit the construction put upon the said part of the law by the Attorney General, to wit, that the second section of the said law restrains the right of settlement to the quantity of land heretofore allowed to new settlers for themselves, wife, and family, agreeably to the laws, usages, and customs of the Spanish Government; therefore, they have come to the determination to depart from their former decisions on the subject of grants made to settlers under the second section, and now resolve, that the quantity of land to be granted to each actual settler shall, in future, be in the same ratio as is provided for by Spanish law and usage, and shall be restrained to one mile square. They beg leave to refer Congress to the former opinions and reasons of the majority of the Board, and of one of the commissioners on that subject, which have been entered on their minutes of the 23d January last, and may be now considered as remarks.

Jacob Collins's claim, (see page 540.)

Testimony taken in the claim of John Wideman, July 5, 1806. Michael Horine, being duly sworn, says that Francis Valle, when commandant of St. Genevieve, informed him (the witness) that he had permitted the Widemans, consisting then of eight or ten families, to settle on vacant lands.

Jacque St. Vrain, claiming under Louis Lajoy, (see page 592;) produces a survey, dated 19th January and certified 20th March, 1804.

Testimony taken, on behalf of the United States, May 28, 1806. Louis Lajoy, being duly sworn, says that he never applied for a concession; that, about two years ago, in the winter, Louis Labeaume called on him, and informed him that he was ready to give concessions to such as wanted some; that he (the witness) went to Gregoire Sarpy's, where Labeaume lived at that time; that being there, Labeaume showed him some papers which he deemed to be concessions, but did not give him the same; that, not knowing how to write, he made his cross to a paper; that he never received any thing for the land he made over to claimant; and further, that he does not know where the said land lies; was, at the time of the above application to him (the said witness) by said Labeaume, of the age of twenty-two years; had a wife and one child, and claims no other land in his own name in this Territory. Louis Lajoy claims two hundred and fifty arpents of this land, which makes a tract of eight hundred arpents.

List A is a list of one hundred and sixty-four names of persons, to whom land is granted by a general concession from Charles D. Delassus, Lieutenant Governor, dated 30th January, 1803. This concession has been taken by the Board as a special permission to settle, and several grants made under the same.

List B is a list of the names of fifty persons, to whom permission to settle was granted by Louis Lorimier, while commandant of Cape Girardeau, and certified by him 28th July, 1804; and several grants have been made by the Board under the same.

JOHN B. C. LUCAS.
CLEMENT B. PENROSE.
FREDERICK BATES.

columns of "Quantity," denote the quantity to which the claim has been extended by the Recorder of Land Titles, agreeably to the provisions of the 4th section of the act of "An act allowing further time for delivering the evidence in support of claims to land in the Territory of Missouri, and for regulating the donation grants therein," as appears from

sued in the month of December, 1808, by the Commissioners for ascertaining and adjusting the titles and claims to land in the Territory of Louisiana.

n under whom land was claimed.	In whose favor issued.	Nature of the claim.	Water course.	Number of acres.	Number of arpents.	District.
ck, - -	David Musick, - -	Concession, -	St. Ferdinand, - -	-	400	St. Louis.
ck, - -	George Smith, -	Concession, -	St. Ferdinand, - -	-	400	St. Louis.
Cyr, -	Ellen St. Cyr and children, -	Concession, -	Mississippi, -	-	800	St. Louis.
"	Thomas Witherington, - -	Order of survey, -	Marais des Liards, -	-	170	St. Louis.
	Adam Martin, - - -	Order of survey, -	Marais des Liards, -	-	200	St. Louis.
alias John Whitesides,	Representatives of, - -	Order of survey, -	Marais des Liards, -	-	146	St. Louis.
,	Phœbe Wallace and the children of John Whitesides.	Order of survey, -	Marais des Liards, -	-	200	St. Louis.
de, alias Isaac Helder-	Thomas Witherington, - -	Order of survey, -	Marais des Liards, -	-	80	St. Louis.
, - -	James Mackay, - -	Concession, -	Gravois, - -	-	800	St. Louis.
r, - -	Isaac Hosteller, - -	Concession, -	Cuivre, - -	-	400	St. Charles.
ier, -	John Wealthy, - -	Concession, -	Cuivre, - -	-	400	St. Charles.
, -	Noel Antoine Prieur, - -	Concession, -	Upper fields of St. Charles, -	-	40	St. Charles.
, -	Noel Antoine Prieur, - -	Concession, -	Upper fields of St. Charles, -	-	40	St. Charles.
art, -	Joseph Haines, - -	Concession, -	Femme Osage, " -	-	200	St. Charles.
h, -	Edward Hempstead, - -	Concession, -	Upper fields of St. Charles, -	-	40	St. Charles.
Senior, -	William Stewart, - -	Concession, -	Missouri, - -	-	400	St. Charles.
er, -	Samuel Griffith, - -	Concession, -	Mississippi, - -	-	400	St. Charles.
n Boone, -	David Darst, Senior, - -	Concession, -	Femme Osage, -	-	600	St. Charles.
, -	Isaac Vanbibber, - -	Concession, -	Femme Osage, -	-	400	St. Charles.
	Daniel Morgan Boone, - -	Concession, -	Femme Osage, -	-	600	St. Charles.
	James Piper, - -	Concession, -	Missouri, - -	-	450	St. Charles.
re, -	Isidore Savoy, - -	Concession, -	Lower fields of St. Charles, -	-	53	St. Charles.
Belland, -	Toussaint Cerre, - -	Concession, -	Missouri, - -	-	400	St. Charles.
an, -	James Morrison, - -	Concession, -	Upper fields of St. Charles, -	-	80	St. Charles.
	James Morrison, - -	Concession, -	Upper fields of St. Charles, -	-	80	St. Charles.
	James Morrison, - -	Concession, -	Upper fields of St. Charles, -	-	80	St. Charles.
	James Morrison, - -	Concession, -	Upper fields of St. Charles, -	-	40	St. Charles.
	James Morrison, - -	Concession, -	Upper fields of St. Charles, -	-	40	St. Charles.
	James Green, - -	Concession, -	Waters of Missouri, -	-	800	St. Charles.
is & Joseph Genereux,	Antoine Janis and Pierre Chouteau,	Concession, -	Dardenne, -	-	240	St. Charles.
ette, -	François Duquette, - -	Concession, -	Village of St. Charles, -	-	2¾	St. Charles.
ette, -	François Duquette, - -	Concession, -	Village of St. Charles, -	-	2¾	St. Charles.
ette, -	François Duquette, - -	Concession, -	Village of St. Charles, -	-	2¾	St. Charles.
ette, -	François Duquette, - -	Concession. -	Village of St. Charles, -	-	2¾	St. Charles.
ette, -	François Duquette, - -	Concession, -	Lake Tempsclair, -	a lot 140 ft.	240 by 300 ft.	St. Charles.
ette, -	François Duquette, - -	Concession, -	Village of St. Charles, -	-	2¾ arps.	St. Charles.
ette, -	François Duquette, - -	Concession, -	Village of St. Charles, -	-	40	St. Charles.
ette, -	François Duquette, - -	Concession, -	Lower fields of St. Charles, -	-	40	St. Charles.
ette, -	François Duquette, -	Concession, -	Lower fields of St. Charles, -	-	80	St. Charles.

der whom land was ...ed.	In whose favor issued.	Nature of the claim.	Water course.	Number of acres.	Number of arpents.	District.
-	François Duquette, - -	Concession, -	Lower fields of St. Charles, -	-	40	St. Charles.
-	François Duquette, - -	Concession, -	Lower fields of St. Charles, -	-	50	St. Charles.
-	François Duquette, - -	Concession, -	Lower fields of St. Charles, -	-	53	St. Charles.
., -	James Morrison, - -	Concession, -	Upper fields of St. Charles, -	-	40	St. Charles.
-	Henry McLaughlin, - -	Concession, -	Missouri, - -	-	600	St. Charles.
-	Manuel A. Rocque, - -	Concession, -	Village of St. Charles, -	20 by 50 toises,		St. Charles.
-	Pierre Rondin, - -	Concession, -	Lower fields of St. Charles, -	-	40 arps.	St. Charles.
-	Antoine Janis, - -	Concession, -	Missouri, - -	-	549	St. Louis.
tles, -	Alexander Clark, - -	Concession, -	Near fields of Marais des Liards	-	400	St. Louis.
"	Alexander Clark, - -	Concession, -	Near fields of Marais des Liards	-	240	St. Louis.
-	Philip Fine, - -	Concession, -	Mississippi, - -	-	400	St. Louis.
-	William Boli, - -	Concession, -	Merrimack, - -	-	400	St. Louis.
of Christopher, -	Vincent Carrico, - -	Concession, -	Missouri, - -	-	500	St. Louis.
lt, Senior, -	Peter Sommalt, son of Christopher, -	Concession, -	Peruque, - -	-	300	St. Charles.
"	Christopher Sommalt, Senior, -	Concession, -	Peruque, - -	-	550	St. Charles.
-	Jacob Sommalt, - -	Concession, -	Peruque, - -	-	450	St. Charles.
-	Perry Brown, - -	Concession, -	Dardenne, - -	"	300	St. Charles.
-	Peter Hoffman, - -	Concession, -	Dardenne, - -	-	300	St. Charles.
-	Nicholas Coontz, - -	Concession, -	Dardenne, - -	-	400	St. Charles.
-	John Linsay, - -	Concession, -	Waters of Missouri, -	-	500	St. Charles.
-	Squire Boone, - -	Concession, -	Cuivre, - -	-	700	St. Charles.
Leonard Price, -	Conrad Price, alias Leonard Price, -	Concession, -	Dardenne, - -	-	650	St. Charles.
son of Jacob, -	Henry Crow, - -	Concession, -	Missouri, - -	-	400	St. Charles.
-	Andrew Sommalt, son of Jacob, -	Concession, -	- - -	-	200	St. Charles.
-	James Flaugherty, - -	Concession, -	Missouri, - -	-	600	St. Charles.
-	John Baptiste Belland, - -	Concession, -	Missouri, - -	-	160	St. Louis.
Groves, -	Joshua Fisher, - -	Concession, -	Cape Cinqhomme, -	340½ acres,	-	St. Genevieve.
, -	John Walker, - -	Concession, -	Dardenne, - -	-	400	St. Charles.
, -	Jaduthan Kendal, - -	Concession, -	Mississippi, - -	-	400	St. Louis.
-	Representatives of, -	Concession, -	Village St. Genevieve, -	49 by 90 toises,		St. Genevieve.
-	William Patterson, - -	Concession, -	Grand river, -	-	300 arps.	St. Genevieve.
-	Abraham Eads, - -	Concession, -	Grand river, -	-	600	St. Genevieve.
-	John Andrews, - -	Concession, -	Grand river, -	-	400	St. Genevieve.
-	Abraham Baker, - -	Concession, -	Grand river, -	-	240	St. Genevieve.
-	Richard Hawkins, - -	Concession, -	Bois Bruile, -	-	400	St. Genevieve.
-	Daniel Merrideth, - -	Concession, -	Mississippi, "	-	312	St. Genevieve.
-	Daniel Merrideth, "	Concession, -	St. Laurent, -	-	288	St. Genevieve.
-	James Wright, - -	Concession, -	Bois Bruile, -	-	400	St. Genevieve.
-	William James, - -	Concession, -	Au Vase, -	-	600	St. Genevieve.
"	Julian Ratté, - -	Concession, -	Gabourie, -	-	60	St. Genevieve.
-	Thomas Alley, - -	Concession, -	Grand river, -	-	400	St. Genevieve.
-	Ezekiel Able, - -	Concession, -	Bois Bruile, -	-	400	St. Genevieve.
-	Henry Paggett, - -	Concession, -	Grand river, -	-	300	St. Genevieve.
-	William Alley, - -	Concession, -	Grand river, -	-	300	St. Genevieve.
-	John Alley, -	Concession, -	Grand river, -	-	300	St. Genevieve.

...sued in the month of January, 1809, by the commissioners for ascertaining and adjusting the titles and claims to lands in the Territory of Louisiana.

n under whom land was claimed.	In whose favor issued.	Nature of the claim.	Water course.	Number of acres.	Number of arpents.	District.
...ald,	Jas. McDonald 600, Rufus Easton 200,	Concession,	Missouri,	-	800	St. Louis.
...ensie,	Farquar McKensie,	Concession,	St. Ferdinand,	..	400	St. Louis.
...n,	John Brown,	Concession,	St. Ferdinand,	-	600	St. Louis.
	John Patterson,	Concession,	St. Ferdinand,	-	600	St. Louis.
	Sarah James,	Concession,	Missouri,	-	400	St. Louis.
	Representatives of,	Concession,	Waters of St. Ferdinand,	-	400	St. Charles.
...away,	Flanders Callaway,	Concession,	Femme Osage,	-	600	St. Louis.
...per,	His legal representatives,	Concession,	Creve Cœur,	-	400	St. Louis.
	John Allen,	Concession,	Waters of Maline,	-	611 50 pr.	St. Louis.
	Elias Metz,	Concession,	Maline,	-	610	St. Louis.
...l,	Seth Chitwood,	Concession,	Maline,	..	400	St. Louis.
...vood,	Richard Chitwood,	Concession,	Mississippi,	-	610 87 pr.	St. Louis.
...wood,	Isabella Chitwood,	Concession,	Mississippi,	-	400	St. Genevieve.
...h, alias Burts,	John Basye,	Concession,	Mississippi,	-	401 60 pr.	St. Genevieve.
	Barn Burns,	Concession,	Bois Bruile,	-	400	St. Genevieve.
	Thomas Cochran,	Concession,	Bois Bruile,	-	300	St. Louis.
...s,	Michael Burns,	Concession,	Bois Bruile,	-	499	St. Louis.
...cDonald,	Thomas Johnston,	Concession,	Grand Glaize,	-	500	St. Louis.
	Thomas Johnston,	Concession,	Missouri,	-	432	St. Louis.
...ge,	Henry Groff,	Concession,	Missouri,	-	240	St. Louis.
	John Bear,	Concession,	Bonhomme,	-	400	St. Louis.
	Heirs of Lawrence Long,	Concession,	Missouri and Bonhomme,	-	400	St. Louis.
...amilton,	Ninian Bell Hamilton,	Concession,	Bonhomme,	-	450	St. Louis.
...k,	Richard Caulk,	Concession,	Missouri and Bonhomme,	-	800	St. Louis.
	Thomas Caulk,	Concession,	Bonhomme,	-	400	St. Louis.
	Thomas Caulk,	Concession,	Waters of Missouri,	-	300	St. Charles.
...e,	Thomas Mason,	Concession,	Grand Glaize,	-	400	St. Louis.
...u,	Pierre Chouteau,	Concession,	Missouri,	-	299 44 pr.	St. Louis.
...er,	William Palmer,	Concession,	Waters of Missouri,	-	240	St. Louis.
...r,	Emilian Yosty,	Concession,	Waters of Missouri,	-	800	St. Louis.
...lson,	James Richardson,	Concession,	Bonhomme,	-	400	St. Louis.
...son,	John Richardson,	Concession,	Bonhomme,	-	240	St. Louis.
...aham,	Alexander Graham,	Concession,	Wild Horse creek,	-	292	St. Louis.
...lias Sheepe,	George Sip, alias Sheepe,	Concession,	Merrimack,	-	400	St. Louis.
	George Sip, use of Joe Sip,	Concession,	Merrimack,	-	160	St. Louis.
...arpenter,	James Mackay,	Concession,	Missouri,	-	550	St. Louis.
	James Clay,	Concession,	Waters of Missouri,	-	350	St. Charles.
...Cyr,	Antoine Soulard,	Concession,	Fields of St. Charles,	-	40	St. Charles.
...ot, dit Lachance,	Pascal Dutchmandy,	Concession,	Big Marsh,	-	240	St. Genevieve.
	John Graham,	Concession,	Mississippi,	-	·471	St. Louis.
...Laughlin,	James Burns,	Concession,	Bois Bruile,	-	547 75 pr.	St. Genevieve.
...ock,	Forrest Hancock,	Concession,	Waters of Missouri,	-	400	St. Charles.
	Alexander McNair,	Concession,	Milk creek,	-	400	St. Louis.
..., alias McKay,	John McCoy,	Concession,	Cuivre,	-	·450	St. Charles.
...ll,	Michael Placit,	Concession,	Mississippi,	-	299 2 pr.	St. Genevieve.

COMMISSIONERS' CERTIFICATES—Continued.

r whom land was 1.	In whose favor issued.	Nature of the claim.	Water course.	Number of acres.	Number of arpents.	District.
t, - -	Andrew Baker, - -	Concession, -	Grand river, - -	-	606	St. Genevieve.
	Thomas Donnahoe, - -	Concession, -	St. Laurent, - -	-	496	St. Genevieve.
-	Thomas Donnahoe, - -	Concession, -	Mississippi, - -	-	406	St. Genevieve.
-	William Flynn, Senior, - -	Concession, -	Mississippi, - -	-	360	St. Genevieve.
-	Widow and reps. of Andrew Cox, -	Concession, -	Bois Brule, - -	-	400	St. Genevieve.
-	Widow and reps. of Andrew Cox, -	Concession, -	St. Laurent, - -	-	400	St. Genevieve.
t, ·iel and Antoine	Joseph Donnahoe, - -	Concession, ·	St. Laurent, - -	-	209	St. Genevieve.
	Louis Lacroix one-third, & François Kenner two-thirds.	Concession, -	Saline, - -	-	442	St. Genevieve.
-	Benjamin Strother, - -	Concession, -	Saline, - -	-	400	St. Genevieve.
-	John Duval, - -	Concession, -	Cape Cinqhomme, - -	-	200	St. Genevieve.
-	Thomas Donnahoe, - -	Concession, -	Mississippi, - -	-	575	St. Genevieve.
-	Representatives of, - -	Concession, -	Gabourie, - -	-	86 35 pr.	St. Genevieve.
-	Peter Dorlac, - -	Concession, -	Lower fields of St. Genevieve,	-	40	St. Genevieve.
J, u, & Jos. Motard,	Uri Musick and Absalom Link, -	Concession, -	Missouri, - -	-	400	St. Louis.
-	Silas Bent, - -	Concession, -	Mississippi, -	56a. 2r. 20p.	-	St. Louis.
-	George Smith, - -	Concession, -	St. Ferdinand, - -	-	192½ ¼pr.	St. Louis.
- .	William Campbell, - -	Concession, -	Waters of St. Ferdinand, -	-	400	St. Louis.

nd one commissioners' certificates, issued by the Board of Commissioners for adjusting the titles and claims to lands in the Territory of Louisiana, is truly me, as clerk of said Board.

Given under my hand, at St. Louis, the 6th of January, 1809.   THOS. F. RIDDICK.

* Patented.

COMMISSIONERS' CERTIFICATES—Continued.

n under whom land was claimed.	In whose favor issued.	Nature of the claim.	Water course.	Number of acres.	Number of arpents.	District.
Conohon, - -	Alexander McConohon, - -	Concession, -	Mississippi, - -	-	604	St. Genevieve.
ah, - -	Leonard Farrah, - -	Concession, -	Fox river, - -	-	400	St. Louis.
ir, -	Michael Crow, - -	Concession, -	Peruque, - -	-	450	St. Charles.
ick, -	Abraham Musick, - -	Concession, -	Bonhomme, .. -	-	400	St. Louis.
-	Aaron Colvin, - -	Concession, -	Missouri, -	-	400	St. Louis.
ghlin, - -	Alexander McCourtney and Henry McLaughlin.	Concession, -	Waters of Wild Horse creek,	-	310	St. Louis.
w, -	William Massey, - -	Concession, -	Waters of Bonhomme, -	-	400	St. Louis.
-	John Lewis, - -	Concession, -	Missouri, - -	-	562 35 pr.	St. Louis.
widow Rigoche, -	James St. Vrain, - -	Concession, -	Waters of Missouri, -	-	400	St. Louis.
l, -	Charles Sanguinett, - -	Concession, -	Waters of Mississippi, -	-	80	St. Louis.
-	Ezekiel Rogers, (use of Frederick Bates.)	Concession, -	Missouri, - -	-	557 5 pr.	St. Louis.
uebec, -	Auguste Chouteau, - -	Concession, -	Lower fields of St. Charles, -	-	60	St. Charles.
mp, -	Auguste Chouteau, - -	Concession, -	Lower fields of St. Charles, -	-	40	St. Charles.
d, alias Megar, -	Auguste Chouteau, - -	Concession, -	Mississippi, - -	-	615 25 pr.	St. Louis.

ficates, commencing at number one hundred and two, and ending at number one hundred and sixty, issued in the month of January last by the Board of Commis- e titles and claims to lands in the Territory of Louisiana, is truly transcribed from the book of registry kept by me as clerk of said Board.

Given under my hand at St. Louis, February 3, 1809.

THOS. F. RIDDICK.

in the month of February, 1809, by the Commissioners for ascertaining and adjusting the titles and claims to lands in the Territory of Louisiana.

er whom land was ...ed.	In whose favor issued.	Nature of the claim.	Water course.	Number of acres.	Number of arpents.	District.
-	The children of John Ridenhour, to wit: Henry, Mary, Betsey, John, Barnet, and Jacques, and Christiana, his widow.	Concession, -	Martigny, - -	-	500	St. Louis.
- -	William Massey, - -	Concession, -	Mississippi, - -	..	405	St. Louis.
n, alias McKinney	Theoph's McKinnon, alias McKinney	Concession, -	Bonhomme, - -	-	400	St. Louis.
-	John Murphy, - -	Concession, -	Bonhomme, - -	-	400	St. Louis.
-	George R. Spencer, - -	Concession, -	Missouri, - -	-	450	St. Charles.
-	James Richardson, - -	Concession, -	Marais des Liards, - -	..	240	St. Louis.
-	James Richardson, - -	Concession, -	Marais des Liards, - -	-	240	St. Louis.
-	James Richardson, - -	Concession, -	Marais des Liards, - -	-	120	St. Louis.
-	Representatives of Hugh Stephenson, -	Concession, -	Bonhomme, - -	-	400	St. Louis.
-	Auguste Chouteau, - -	Concession, -	Waters of Mississippi, -	-	160	St. Louis.
-	Auguste Chouteau, - -	Concession, -	Lower fields of St. Charles, -	-	60	St. Charles.
-	Auguste Chouteau, - -	Concession, -	Lower fields of St. Charles, -	-	120	St. Charles.
Sen.	Andrew Ramsay, - -	Concession, -	Grand Marais, - -	-	479 90 pr.	Cape Girardeau.
-	Andrew Ramsay, Sen. - -	Concession, -	Ramsay's creek, - -	-	479 68 pr.	Cape Girardeau.
-	Representatives of, to wit: Margaret, William, and Benjamin Tipton.	Concession, -	St. François, - -	..	232 74 pr.	Cape Girardeau.
Sen.	Andrew Ramsay, Jun. -	Concession, -	Waters of St. François, -	-	240	Cape Girardeau.
., -	Joseph Neyswanger, - -	Concession, -	White Waters, - .	-	370 39 pr.	Cape Girardeau.
-	John Probst, - -	Concession, -	White Waters, - -	-	645	Cape Girardeau.
-	Thomas Bull, - -	Concession, -	Hubble's creek, - -	-	239 40 pr.	Cape Girardeau.
-	Enos Randall, - -	Concession, ..	River Charles, - -	-	480	Cape Girardeau.
-	Antoine Roy, - -	Concession, -	Mississippi, - -	-	11 58 pr.	St. Louis.
-	Conrad Stotler, - -	Concession, -	White Waters, - -	-	500 .	Cape Girardeau.
-	Henry Hand, - -	Concession, -	Hubble's creek, - -	-	400 48 pr.	Cape Girardeau.
-	Allen McKensie, - -	Concession, -	Randall's creek, - -	-	239 92 pr.	Cape Girardeau.
-	Hugh White, or his legal represent's,	Order of survey, -	Caney creek, - -	-	800	Cape Girardeau.
-	Medad Randall, - -	Concession, -	Waters of Hubble's creek, -	-	240	Cape Girardeau.
-	James Randall, - -	Concession, -	Charles creek, - -	-	240	Cape Girardeau.
-	Anthony Randall, - -	Concession, -	Randall's creek, - -	-	235 68 pr.	Cape Girardeau.
-	The heirs of Samuel Randall, -	Concession, -	Randall's or Charles creek, -	-	240	Cape Girardeau.
-	Daniel Duggan, - -	Concession, -	Charles creek, - -	-	300	Cape Girardeau.
en. -	John Shepherd, - -	Concession, -	Randall's or Charles creek, -	-	300	Cape Girardeau.
-	Jacob Jacobs, - -	Concession, -	Randall's or Charles creek, -	-	240	Cape Girardeau.
. -	Heirs and representatives of, -	Concession, -	Gibany's creek, - -	-	480	Cape Girardeau.
-	Jonathan Stoker, - -	Concession, -	Gibany's creek, - -	-	350	Cape Girardeau.
-	John Gibany, - -	Concession, -	Waters of Randall's creek, -	-	239 89 pr.	Cape Girardeau.
-	Thomas S. Rodney, - -	Concession, -	Foster's creek, - -	-	200	Cape Girardeau.
-	John and Robert Gibany, -	Concession, -	Mississippi, . -	-	240	Cape Girardeau.

...umber one hundred and sixty-one to number one hundred and ninety-seven, inclusive, issued in the month of February, one thousand eight hundred and nine, ...ng and adjusting the titles and claims to lands in the Territory of Louisiana, is truly transcribed from the book of registry kept by me as clerk of said Board. Given under my hand at St. Louis, this 3d day of March, 1809.   THOS. F. RIDDICK.

...sued in the month of March, 1809, by the Commissioners for ascertaining and adjusting the titles and claims to lands in the Territory of Louisiana.

...n under whom land was claimed.	In whose favor issued.	Nature of the claim.	Water course.	Number of acres.	Number of arpents.	District.
...ey, - -	Lemuel Cheney, - -	Concession, -	Mississippi, - -	-	240	Cape Girardeau.
...en. - -	The representatives of, - -	Concession, -	Byrd's creek, - -	-	240	Cape Girardeau.
... - -	Joseph Young, - -	Concession, -	Waters of Byrd's creek, -	-	240	Cape Girardeau.
...Sen. - -	Jacob Foster, Sen. -	Concession, -	Foster's creek, - -	-	400	Cape Girardeau.
...iams, - -	William Williams, -	Concession, -	Randall's creek, -	-	250	Cape Girardeau.
...h, - -	Jonathan Ditch, -	Concession, -	Randall's creek, -	-	229 80 pr.	Cape Girardeau.
...ey, - -	Martin Rodney, -	Concession, -	Hubble's creek, -	-	480	Cape Girardeau.
... - -	John Tayon, - -	Concession, -	Waters of the Mississippi, -	-	400	St. Charles.
... - -	John Ward, - -	Concession, -	Waters of Creve Cœur, -	-	400	St. Louis.
... - -	Judith Cordell and the representatives of John Cordell.	Concession, -	Waters of Creve Cœur, -	-	800 80 pr.	St. Louis.
...n, - -	Joshua Dodson, - -	Concession, -	Femme Osage, -	-	400	St. Charles.
... - -	John Lard, - -	Concession, -	Spanish Ponds, -	-	400	St. Louis.
...erson, - -	William Patterson, - -	Concession, -	Cold Water, (waters of,) -	-	600	St. Louis.

...ficates, from number one hundred and ninety-eight to two hundred and ten, inclusive, were issued by the Board of Commissioners for ascertaining and adjusting ...rritory of Louisiana, and is truly copied from the book of registry kept by me as clerk of said Board.

Given under my hand at St. Louis, this 5th day of April, 1809.

THOS. F. RIDDICK.

...y of the Treasury, Washington City.

-	-	Jeremiah Thomson,	-	-	Concession,	-	Waters of river Charles,		
-	-	John Summers,	-	-	Concession,	-	Hubble's creek,	-	-	..	479 98 pr.	Cape Girardeau.
-	-	James Dowty,	-	-	Concession,	-	River Charles,	-	-	-	240	Cape Girardeau.
-	-	Matthew Scruggs,	-	-	Concession,	-	Big Swamp,	-	-	-	800	Cape Girardeau.
-	-	John Johnson, or his legal representatives.	-	Concession,	-	Mississippi,	..	-	-	238	Cape Girardeau.
-	-	Edward Hall,	-	-	Concession,	-	Hubble's creek,	-	-	-	250	Cape Girardeau.
-	-	Simon Kenyon 240, and James Cox 336 arpents.	Concession,	-	Randall's creek,	-	-	-	576	Cape Girardeau.
-	-	John Weaver,	-	-	Concession,	-	Ramsay's creek,	-	-	300	Cape Girardeau.
-	-	Robert Green,	-	-	Concession,	- -	Hubble's and Byrd's creek,	-	-	750 24 pr.	Cape Girardeau.
，	-	-	William Dougherty,	-	-	Concession,	-	Hubble's creek,	-	-	444	Cape Girardeau.
-	-	William Dougherty,	-	-	Concession,	-	Hubble's creek,	-	-	240	Cape Girardeau.
-	-	Andrew Ramsay, Sen.	-	Concession,	-	Waters of Cape La Cruche,	-	-	162	Cape Girardeau.
of Amos,	-	Abraham Byrd, son of Amos,	-	Concession,	-	Byrd's creek,	-	-	480	Cape Girardeau.
-	-	Representatives of,	-	-	Concession,	-	Waters of Byrd's creek,	-	-	600	Cape Girardeau.
-	-	Peter Derbigny, use of John B. C. Lucas.	Concession,	-	Missouri,	-	-	-	400	St. Louis.

ficates, from number two hundred and eleven to two hundred and twenty-five, inclusive, is truly transcribed from the book of registry kept by me as clerk ...ing and adjusting the titles and claims to lands in the Territory of Louisiana, and contains a list of all certificates issued by the Board during the month of

Given under my hand, in the commissioners' room at St. Louis, this 3d day of April, 1809.

THOS. F. RIDDICK.

ry of the Treasury, Washington City.

issued in the month of May, 1809, by the Commissioners for ascertaining and adjusting the titles and claims to lands in the Territory of Louisiana.

son under whom land was claimed.			In whose favor issued.			Nature of the claim.		Water course.			Number of acres.	Number of arpents.	District.
ss,	-	-	William Ross,	-	-	Concession,	-	Mississippi,	-	-	-	420	Cape Girardeau.
ger,	-	-	Philip Bollinger,	-	-	Concession,	-	White Waters,	-	-	-	550	Cape Girardeau.
llinger,	-	-	Matthias Bollinger,	-	-	Concession,	-	White Waters,	-	-	-	500	Cape Girardeau.
d,	-	-	Stephen Byrd,	-	-	Concession,	-	Byrd's creek,	-	-	-	600	Cape Girardeau.
tt,	-	-	Heirs of Elijah Averett, alias Elisha,		-	Concession,	-	Fork of Byrd's creek,	-	-	-	250	Cape Girardeau.
rows,	-	-	Representatives of,	-	-	Concession,	-	Hubble's creek,	-	-	-	400	Cape Girardeau.
on,	-	-	Lewis Dickson,	-	-	Concession,	-	Waters of Hubble's creek,	-	..	400	Cape Girardeau.
ssell,	-	-	William Russell,	-	-	Concession,	-	Byrd's creek,	-	-	-	400	Cape Girardeau.
Jun.	-	-	James Cox, Jun.	-	-	Concession,	-	Waters of Randall's creek,	-	-	158 34 pr.	Cape Girardeau.
er,	-	-	Joseph Waller,	-	-	Concession,	-	Randall's creek,	-	-	-	478 95 pr.	Cape Girardeau.
artgrove,	-	-	Nicholas Seavers, Sen.	-	-	Concession.	-	Randall's creek,	-	-	501 20 pr.	Cape Girardeau.
nks,	-	-	Louis Lorimer,	-	-	Concession,	-	Randall's creek,	-	-	-	400	Cape Girardeau.
	-	-	James Boyd,	-	-	Concession,	-	Caney creek,	-	-	-	400	Cape Girardeau.
	-	-	John Boyd,	-	-	Concession,	-	Waters of Byrd's creek,	-	-	251 27 pr.	Cape Girardeau.
pson,	-	-	Webb Hayden,	-	-	Concession,	-	Randall's creek,	-	-	-	260	Cape Girardeau.
ad,	-	-	John Drybread,	-	-	Concession,	-	Waters of Hubble's creek,	-	-	240 24 pr.	Cape Girardeau.
bble,	..	-	John Strong,	-	-	Concession,	-	Hubble's creek,	-	-	-	400	Cape Girardeau.
bble,	-	-	John Strong,	-	-	Concession,	-	Hubble's creek,	-	-	-	235¼	Cape Girardeau.
nsay, Jun.	-	-	John Guething,	-	-	Concession,	-	Hubble's creek,	-	-	-	240	Cape Girardeau.
	-	-	Stephen Byrd,	-	-	Concession,	-	Randall's creek,	-	-	-	240	Cape Girardeau.
rd, Sen.	-	-	Stephen Byrd,	-	-	Concession,	-	Hubble's creek,	-	-	-	560	Cape Girardeau.
ews,	-	-	John McCarty,	-	-	Concession,	-	Byrd's creek,	-	-	-	240	Cape Girardeau.
helow,	-	-	John Hays,	-	-	Concession,	-	Byrd's creek,	-	-	-	240	Cape Girardeau.
ell,	-	-	Hugh Creswell,	-	-	Concession,	-	Randall's creek,	-	-	291 90 pr.	Cape Girardeau.
	-	-	Heirs of Joseph Fight,	-	-	Concession,	-	Hubble's creek,	-	-	240 24 pr.	Cape Girardeau.
	-	-	Edward Robertson,	-	-	Concession,	-	Hubble's creek,	-	-	-	240	Cape Girardeau.
mitt,	-	-	Renna Brummitt,	-	-	Concession,	-	Hubble's creek,	-	-	-	550	Cape Girardeau.
reau,	-	-	Representatives of,	-	-	Concession,	-	Mississippi,	-	-	-	717	St. Genevieve.

' certificates, from number two hundred and twenty-six to number two hundred and fifty-three, inclusive, issued in the month of May, one thousand eight hundred ertaining and adjusting the titles and claims to lands in the Territory of Louisiana, is truly transcribed from the book of registry kept by me as clerk of said Board.

Given under my hand at St. Louis, this 9th of June, 1809.

THOS. F. RIDDICK.

y of the Treasury, Washington City,

der whom land was hed.		In whose favor issued.	Nature of the claim.	Water course.	Number of acres.	Number of arpents.	District.
-	-	John Bannister, or his legal representatives.	Order of survey, -	Mississippi, - -	-	300	New Madrid.
k, -	-	Richard Westbrook, - -	Concession, -	Lake St. Mary, - -	-	350	New Madrid.
-	-	Peter Saffray, or his legal representatives.	Concession, -	Lake St. Isidore, - -	-	240	New Madrid.
-	-	Jacob Myers, - -	Concession, -	Lake St. Ann and St. Francis,	-	80	New Madrid.
-	-	Arthur Mellon, - -	Concession, -	Lake St. Ann, - -	-	160	New Madrid.
-	-	Richard Jones Waters, - -	Concession, -	Mississippi, - -	-	191	New Madrid.
ters, -	-	Richard Jones Waters, - -	Concession, -	Mississippi, - -	-	332	New Madrid.
-	-	Richard Jones Waters, - -	Concession, -	Mississippi, - -	-	120	New Madrid.
-	-	Richard Jones Waters, - -	Concession, -	Mississippi, - -	-	240	New Madrid.
-	-	Richard Jones Waters, - -	Concession, -	Mississippi, - -	-	240	New Madrid.
i, -	-	Richard Jones Waters, - -	Concession, -	Lake St. Ann, - -	-	100	New Madrid.
-	-	Richard Jones Waters, - -	Concession, -	Mississippi, - -	-	240	New Madrid.

cates, from number two hundred and fifty-four to number two hundred and sixty-five, inclusive, issued by the Board of Commissioners for ascertaining and e Territory of Louisiana, during the months of June and July last, is truly copied from the book of registry kept by me as clerk of said Board.

Given under my hand at St. Louis, this 5th day of August, 1809.

THOS. F. RIDDICK.

ary of the Treasury, Washington City.

e Board of Commissioners for ascertaining and adjusting the titles and claims to land in the Territory of Louisiana, during the months of August, September, October, and November, 1809.

on under whom land was claimed.			In whose favor issued.	Nature of the claim.		Water course.			Number of acres.	Number of arpents.	District.
lly,	-	-	Jaduthan Kendal,	Concession,	-	Mississippi,	-	-	-	439	St. Louis.
elin,			Antoine Gamelin, or his legal repr'ves	Concession,	-	Lake St. Ann,				200	New Madrid.
1an,			Richard Jones Waters,	Concession,	-	Lake St. Ann,				148	New Madrid.
, Sen.			Joseph Leduc, - -	Order of survey,	-	Lake St. Mary,				300	New Madrid.
ous,			Legal represent'ves of Jos. Hunot, Sr.	Concession,	-	Lake St. Mary,				77	New Madrid.
			Richard Jones Waters,	Concession,	-	Cape La Cruche,	-	-	-	240	Cape Girardeau.
ey,			George Unerous,	Concession,	-	Lakes St. Eulale and St. Mary,				85	New Madrid.
			Richard Jones Waters, -	Concession,	-	Lake St. Eulale,	-	-		234	New Madrid.
n,			Samuel Dorsey, -	Concession,	-	Lake St. Mary,	-	-		184	New Madrid.
cent Bouis,	-		Legal representatives of Azor Rees,	Concession,	-	Bayou St. Thomas,	-	-		75	New Madrid.
			Charles Gratiot,	Concession,	-	Missouri,	-	-	-	575 76 pr	St. Louis.
ffin,	-		Antoine Vincent Bouis, -	Concession,	-	Mississippi and Gengras,				200	St. Louis.
			Kincaid Caldwell, 271 arpents, and Asa Musick, 312 arpents 22 perch.	Concession,	-	Waters of Missouri,				593 22 pr	St. Louis.
ffin,			Wm. Griffin, or his legal repres'ves,	Order of survey,	-	Waters of Missouri,				36 50 pr	St. Louis.
n,			Isaac Weldon, or his legal repres'ves,	Concession,	-	Dardenne,	-	-		400	St. Charles.
Cyr,			Joseph Hebert, - -	Concession,	-	Mississippi,				175	St. Louis.
ms,			Joseph Williams, - -	Concession,	-	Missouri,	-	-		800	St. Louis.
sdale,			Joshua Stocksdale, -	Concession,	-	Tuque,	-	-		240	St. Charles.
etter,			Representatives of Francis Hostetter,	Settlement right,	-	Cuivre,	-	-		500	St. Charles.
			Legal represent'ves of John Coontz,	Settlement right,	-	Dardenne,	-	-		600	St. Charles.
),			John Mullanphy, "	Concession,	-	Mississippi,	-	-		48	St. Louis.
			Jacob Zoornalt,	Settlement right,	-	Missouri,	-	-		350	St. Charles.
h,			John Haun,	Settlement right,	-	Tuque,	-	-		500	St. Charles.
y,			Francis Smith,	Concession,	-	Missouri,	-	-		250	St. Charles.
			George Gatty,	Concession,	-	Dardenne,	-	-		450	St. Charles.
			John Cook,	Concession,	-	Dardenne,	-	-		600	St. Charles.
Connell,			William McConnell,	Settlement right,	-	Dardenne,	-	-		800	St. Charles.
nan, Jun.			George Hoffman, Jun. -	Settlement right,	-	Dardenne,	-	-		400	St. Charles.
alt,			Adam Zoomalt,	Settlement right,	-	Cuivre,	-	-		600	St. Charles.
bet,			William Tarbet,	Settlement right,	-	Cuivre,	-	-		300	St. Charles.
nalt, Sen.			Andrew Zoomalt, Sen. -	Settlement right,	-	Dardenne,	-	-		580	St. Charles.
dge,			James Baldridge,	Settlement right,	-	Dardenne,	-	-		400	St. Charles.
			Lagal represent'ves of John Coontz,	Concession,	-	Village of St. Charles,	-	Lot 20 by	26 toises,	St. Charles.
laway,			Flanders Callaway, -	Concession,	-	Femme Osage,	-	-		200 arps.	St. Charles.

n to certificate No. 108, issued for 600 arpents by mistake, when it ought to have issued for 800 arpents.

e Board of Commissioners for ascertaining and adjusting the titles and claims to land in the Territory of Louisiana, do certify that the foregoing list of certificates, * to number two hundred and ninety-nine, inclusive, issued by the Board during the months of August, September, October, and November, one thousand eight the book of registry kept by me as clerk of said Board.

Given under my hand at St. Louis, this 6th of December, 1809. THOS. F. RIDDICK.

of the Treasury, Washington City.

ard of Commissioners for ascertaining and adjusting titles and claims to lands in the Territory of Louisiana, during the months of December, 1809, and January and February, 1810.

er whom land was ed.	In whose favor issued.	Nature of the claim.	Water course.	Number of acres.	Number of arpents.	District.
-	Jeremiah Clay, - -	Concession, -	Waters of Missouri, -	-	450	St. Charles.
-	Jonathan Bryant, - -	Concession, -	Femme Osage, -	-	620	St. Charles.
-	Thomas Smith, - -	Concession, -	Waters of Missouri,	-	320	St. Charles.
-	Thomas Smith, - -	Concession, -	Femme Osage, -	-	800	St. Charles.
-	Warren Cottle, - -	Concession, -	Dardenne,	-	650	St. Charles.
-	William Linn, - -	Settlement right, -	Waters of Cuivre, -	-	350	St. Charles.
-	Robert Burns, - -	Settlement right, -	Cuivre, -	-	600	St. Charles.
-	Warner Gilbert, - -	Settlement right, -	Waters of Missouri,	-	500	St. Charles.
-	François Duquetté, - -	Ten years' possess'n	Missouri, -	-	260	St. Charles.
-	Hezekiah Crosby, - -	Settlement right, -	Missouri, -	-	600	St. Charles.
-	David Boyd, - -	Settlement right, -	Cuivre, -	-	350	St. Charles.
wise Stephenson,	Jas. Stephens, otherwise Stephenson,	Settlement right, -	Missouri, -	-	800	St. Louis.
-	Thomas Caulk, - -	Settlement right, -	Waters of Missouri, -	-	400	St. Charles.
-	Thomas Caulk, - -	Settlement right, -	Missouri, -	-	400	St. Louis.
-	Michael Hart, - -	Settlement right, -	Waters of St. Francis,	-	800	St. Genevieve.
-	Thomas Cumstock, - -	Concession, -	Plattin, -	-	700	St. Genevieve.
en. -	Daniel Bollinger, Sen. -	Concession, -	White Waters, -	-	640	Cape Girardeau.
-	Morgan Byrnes, -	Concession, -	Waters of Mississippi, -	-	240	Cape Girardeau.
-	Gilbert Hector, - -	Concession, -	Charles creek, -	-	400	Cape Girardeau.
-	Enoch Evans, - -	Concession, -	Ramsay's creek, -	-	205 24 pr.	Cape Girardeau.
-	James Worthington, - -	Concession, -	Charles creek, -	-	288 52 pr.	Cape Girardeau.
-	Legal reps. of Thos. W. Waters, dec'd	Concession, -	Mississippi, -	-	480	Cape Girardeau.
-	James Earl, - -	Concession, -	River Zeno, -	-	240	Cape Girardeau.
-	John Patterson, - -	Settlement right, -	Hubble's creek, -	-	158 20 pr.	Cape Girardeau.
-	Elisha Whitaker, - -	Settlement right, -	Waters of Hubble's creek, -	-	443 65 pr.	Cape Girardeau.
-	Moses Byrd, - -	Concession, -	Byrd's creek, -	-	240	Cape Girardeau.
-	William Hill, - -	Concession, -	Byrd's creek, -	-	445 5 pr.	Cape Girardeau.
-	John Guething, - -	Settlement right, -	Waters of Hubble's creek, -	-	260 50 pr.	Cape Girardeau.
-	Matthew Hubble, - -	Concession, -	Hubble's creek, -	-	555 27 pr.	Cape Girardeau.
-	Pascal L. Cerré, - -	Concession, -	Mississippi, -	-	800	St. Louis.
-	Lavina Mills, - -	Settlement right, -	Waters of Randall's and Hubble's creeks.	-	231 25 pr.	Cape Girardeau.

of Commissioners for ascertaining and adjusting the titles and claims to land in the Territory of Louisiana, do hereby certify that the foregoing list of com-
ndred to number three hundred and thirty, inclusive, issued by the Board during the months of December, one thousand eight hundred and nine, and Janu-
l and ten, is truly transcribed from the book of registry kept by me as clerk of said Board.

In witness whereof I have hereunto set my hand, at St. Louis, this 20th day of March, 1810,

THOS. F. RIDDICK.

e Treasury, Washington City.

...ued in the month of March, 1810, by the Board of Commissioners for ascertaining and adjusting claims and titles to lands in the Territory of Louisiana.

...on under whom land was claimed.	In whose favor issued.	Nature of the claim.	Water course.	Number of acres.	Number of arpents.	District.
y, - -	Emilian Yosty, - -	Ten years' possess'n	Adjoining town of St. Louis,	-	5 50 pr.	St. Louis.
...illette, - -	William Bouillette, -	Settlement right, -	Lake St. Mary, - -	-	240	New Madrid.
...uguste Follin, -	Alexander Auguste Follin, -	Settlement right, -	Lake St. Mary, - -	-	240	New Madrid.
...bourn, - -	Representatives of Franky Bradbourn,	Settlement right, -	Big Prairie, - -	-	200	New Madrid.
...on, Sen. -	Jaduthan Kendal, - -	Concession, -	Grand Glaize, -	-	800	St. Louis.

...e Board of Commissioners for ascertaining and adjusting the titles and claims to lands in the Territory of Louisiana, do certify that the foregoing list of certificates, ...one to number three hundred and thirty-five, issued by the Board during the month of March, one thousand eight hundred and ten, is truly copied from the book ...Board.

...y of the Treasury.

Given under my hand at St. Louis, this 19th of April, 1810.

THOS. F. RIDDICK.

...ued in the month of April, 1810, by the Board of Commissioners for ascertaining and adjusting titles and claims to lands in the Territory of Louisiana.

...on under whom land was claimed.	In whose favor issued.	Nature of the claim.	Water course.	Number of acres.	Number of arpents.	District.
...uteau, - -	Auguste Chouteau, - -	Order of survey, -	Marais de Liard, -	-	375 40 pr.	St. Louis.
...?, - -	Philip Miller, -	Concession, -	Fémme Osage, -	-	600	St. Charles.
...dges, - -	Daniel and Samuel Hodges, -	Concession, -	Waters of Missouri, -	-	655	St. Louis.
...rphy, - -	William Murphy, - -	Concession, -	River St. Francis, -	-	799½	St. Genevieve.
...hy, - -	Joseph Murphy, -	Concession, -	Waters of St. Francis,	-	550	St. Genevieve.
...s, - -	John Hawkins, -	Concession, -	Saline creek, -	-	400	St. Genevieve.
...ok, - -	Nathaniel Cook, -	Concession, -	Waters of St. Francis,	-	800	St. Genevieve.
...?, - -	James Davis, -	Concession, -	River St. Francis, -	-	400	St. Genevieve.
...et, - -	Joseph Becket, -	Ten years' possess'n	River Au Vase, -	-	71	St. Genevieve.
...ntgomery, -	William Montgomery, -	Concession, -	Big river, -	-	340	St. Genevieve.
...e, - -	Isidore Moore, -	Settlement right, -	Cape St. Comes, -	-	600	St. Genevieve.
...tit, - -	Benjamin Petit, -	Settlement right, -	North fork of St. Francis,	-	800	St. Genevieve.
...ker, - -	Thomas Tucker, -	Settlement right, -	Mississippi, -	-	176 47 pr.	St. Genevieve.

...st of certificates issued by the Board of Commissioners for ascertaining and adjusting the titles and claims to land in the Territory of Louisiana, during the month ...and ten, from number three hundred and thirty-six to number three hundred and forty-eight, inclusive, is truly transcribed from the book of registry kept by me as

Given under my hand at St. Louis, this 23d day of May, 1810.

JOHN W. HONEY.

the month of May, 1810, by the Board of Commissioners for ascertaining and adjusting titles and claims to lands in the Territory of Louisiana.

er whom land was ed.		In whose favor issued.			Nature of the claim.		Water course.		Number of acres.	Number of arpents.	District.
-	-	David Murphy,	-	-	Concession,	-	Waters of the river St. Francis,		-	600	St. Genevieve.
-	-	John Callaway,	-	-	Concession,	-	Waters of the river St. Francis,		-	700	St. Genevieve.
-	-	James F. Piller,	-	-	Concession,	-	Waters of the river Saline,	-	-	400	St. Genevieve.
-	-	James F. Piller,	-	-	Concession,	-	Waters of the river Saline,	"	-	288	St. Genevieve.
-	-	Ira Cottle,	-	-	Concession,	-	River Dardenne,	-	-	400	St. Charles.
-	-	Warren Cottle, Jun.	-	-	Settlement right, -		River Dardenne,	-	640	250	St. Charles.

certificates issued by the Board of Commissioners for ascertaining and adjusting the titles and claims to lands in the Territory of Louisiana, during the nd ten, from number three hundred and forty-nine to number three hundred and fifty-four, inclusive, is truly transcribed from the book of registry kept by

Given under my hand at St. Louis, this 7th day of June, 1810. JOHN W. HONEY.

the month of June, 1810, by the Board of Commissioners for ascertaining and adjusting titles and claims to lands in the Territory of Louisiana.

r whom land was ed.		In whose favor issued.			Nature of the claim.		Water course.		Number of acres.	Number of arpents.	District.
l, -	-	Jean Marie Legrand,	-	-	Concession,	-	Waters of the Saline,	-	-	580 40 pr.	St. Genevieve.
-	-	Isaac Davee,	-	-	Concession,	-	Mississippi,	"	-	300	St. Genevieve.
-	-	Richard Sullens,	-	-	Concession,	-	Missouri,	-	-	450	St. Louis.
-	-	Legal representatives of, -		-	Concession,	-	Waters of Missouri,	-	-	640	St. Louis.
-	-	John Helderbrand, use of Jonathan Helderbrand.			Settlement right, -		Merrimack,	-	-	400	St. Louis.
-	-	Cumberland James,	-	-	Concession,	-	Waters of Missouri,	-	-	400	St. Louis.
-	-	Ebenezer Hodges,	-	-	Concession,	-	Missouri,	-	-	500	St. Louis.
-	-	Jesse Richardson,	-	-	Concession,	-	Bonhomme,	-	-	240	St. Louis.
-	-	Auguste Chouteau,	-	-	Ten years' possess'n		Mill creek,	-	1,031	-	St. Louis.
-	-	Henry Ryley,	-	-	Settlement right, -		Mississippi,	-	-	126 34 pr.	St. Genevieve.
-	-	Jonathan Wiseman,	-	-	Concession,	-	Creve Cœur,	-	-	250	St. Louis.
-	-	Joseph Conway,	-	-	Concession,	-	Creve Cœur,	-	-	400	St. Louis.
-	-	Andrew Kincaid,	-	-	Concession,	-	Creve Cœur,	-	-	800	St. Louis.
-	-	John Stewart,	-	-	Concession,	-	Waters of Bonhomme,	-	-	300	St. Louis.
-	-	Samuel Smith,	-	-	Concession,	-	Creve Cœur,	-	-	450	St. Louis.
-	-	Gabriel Long,	-	-	Concession,	-	Creve Cœur,	-	-	400	St. Louis.

COMMISSIONERS' CERTIFICATES—Continued.

on under whom land was claimed.	In whose favor issued.	Nature of the claim.	Water course.	Number of acres.	Number of arpents.	District.
uitty, - -	Andrew McQuitty, - -	Concession, -	Creve Cœur, -	-	300	St. Louis.
rd, - -	Antoine Soulard, -	Concession, -	Mississippi, -	-	7 80½ p.	St. Louis.
, - -	Antoine Soulard, -	Ten years' possess'n	Merrimack, -	-	480	St. Louis.
son, - -	Jesse Richardson, "	Concession, -	Bonhomme,	-	240	St. Louis.
ds, - -	Zadock Woods, -	Concession, -	Waters of Missouri, -	-	400	St. Louis.
, - -	Auguste Chouteau, -	Concession, -	Waters of Mississippi, -	-	80	St. Louis.
k, - -	Noel Hornbeck, -	Concession, -	Mississippi, -	-	280	St. Genevieve.
Chouteau Papin, -	Marie Louise Chouteau Papin, -	Concession, -	River Des Peres, -	-	3200	St. Louis.
, -	Joseph Cottle, -	Concession, -	Waters of Cuivre, -	-	450	St. Charles.
y, -	Anthony Kelly, -	Concession, -	Waters of Cuivre, -	-	400	St. Charles.
Engle, -	Pascal Detchemendy, -	Concession, -	Gaborie, -	-	44 35 pr.	St. Genevieve.
-	David Bryant, -	Settlement right, -	Tuque, -	-	400	St. Charles.
cock, -	William Hancock, -	Concession, -	Missouri, -	-	600	St. Charles.
ell, -	John McMichell, -	Concession, -	Missouri, -	-	700	St. Charles.
ilton, -	William Hamilton, -	Concession, -	Bonhomme, -	-	450	St. Louis.
, alias McKay, -	Daniel McCoy, alias McKay, -	Concession, -	Cuivre, -	-	300	St. Charles.
n. -	John Long, Jun. -	Concession, -	Lake Creve Cœur, -	-	240	St. Louis.
, -	Davis Hensley, -	Concession, -	Mississippi, -	-	600	St. Charles.
ark, -	Christopher Clark, -	Concession, -	Cuivre, -	-	520	St. Charles.
-	Ira Nash, -	Concession, -	Waters of Mississippi, -	-	325 50 pr.	St. Louis.
ner, -	Frederick Conner, -	Concession, -	Joachim, -	-	506 25 pr.	St. Louis.
-	Walter Jewitt, -	Concession, -	Joachim, -	-	600 25 pr.	St. Louis.
Engle, -	James Rankin 600, and Simon Wood 200 arpents.	Concession, -	River Maline, -	-	800	St. Louis.
-	Legal represent's of Joseph Robidoux,	Concession, -	Mississippi, -	-	240	St. Louis.
ham, -	Jacob Wickerham, -	Concession, -	Merrimack, -	-	700	St. Louis.
n, -	James McClean, -	Concession, -	Mississippi, -	-	300	St. Genevieve.
-	Israel Dodge, -	Concession, -	River Au Vase, -	-	714	St. Genevieve.

ist of certificates issued by the Board of Commissioners for ascertaining and adjusting the titles and claims to lands in the Territory of Louisiana, during the
red and ten, from number three hundred and fifty-five to number three hundred and ninety-seven, inclusive, is truly transcribed from the book of registry kept by

Given under my hand at St. Louis, this 26th day of July, 1810.   JOHN W. HONEY.

and sixty-two and number three hundred and seventy-four are for the same tract of land. The claimant had his claim revised by the present Board, on the
and eight, and again on the twenty-eighth of September, eighteen hundred and eight, which, from the mode of proceeding of the Board in all other cases, must
e claimant. From this circumstance the Board was led into the error. The Board have, therefore, destroyed certificate number three hundred and seventy-four.

JOHN B. LUCAS,
CLEMENT B. PENROSE.

July 26, 1810.

le month of July, 1810, *by the Board of Commissioners for ascertaining and adjusting the titles and claims to lands in the Territory of Louisiana.*

er whom land was d.	In whose favor issued.	Nature of the claim.	Water course.	Number of acres.	Number of arpents.	District.
- - -	Lydia Quick, - - -	Concession,	Spanish pond, - - -	-	550	St. Louis.
- - -	Moses Kinney, - - -	Concession,	Ramsay's creek, - -	-	350	St. Charles.
- - -	James Richardson, - -	Concession,	Waters of St. Ferdinand,	-	120	St. Louis.
- - -	James Richardson, - -	Concession,	Waters of St. Ferdinand,	-	120	St. Louis.
- - -	Legal representatives of, -	Concession,	Mississippi, - - -	-	249	St. Louis.
- - -	Auguste Chouteau, - -	Concession,	Town of St. Louis, -	2 32 per.	-	St. Louis.
- - -	William Hughs, - -	Concession,	Dubois creek, - -	-	500	St. Louis.
- - -	James Richardson, - -	Concession,	Waters of St. Ferdinand,	-	1000	St. Louis.
- - -	James Richardson, - -	Concession,	Waters of St. Ferdinand,	-	704 733 p	St. Louis.
- - -	James Richardson, - -	Concession,	Waters of St. Ferdinand,	-	160	St. Louis.
- - -	James Richardson, - -	Concession,	Waters of St. Ferdinand,	-	120	St. Louis.
- - -	William Burns, - -	Concession,	Bois Bruile creek, -	-	308	St. Genevieve.
- - -	John Mullanphy, - -	Concession,	Waters of St. Ferdinand,	-	400	St. Louis.
- - -	John Violeny, - -	Concession,	Plattin, - - -	-	500	St. Genevieve.
- - -	Thomas Whitley, - -	Concession,	Creve Cœur, - -	-	600	St. Louis.
n. - -	Henry Sommalt, Jun. - -	Concession,	Cuivre, - - -	-	450	St. Charles.
- - -	George McFall, - -	Concession,	Waters of Bonhomme, -	-	400	St. Louis.
- - -	John Long, - - -	Concession,	Bonhomme, - -	-	800	St. Louis.
- - -	John Stewart, - -	Concession,	Plattin, - -	-	440	St. Louis.
- - -	John Parkett, - -	Concession,	Dardenne, - -	-	650	St. Charles.
- - -	Daniel Kieseler, - -	Concession,	Dardenne, - -	-	600	St. Charles.
gton, - -	David McQuitty, - -	Concession,	Mississippi, - -	-	200	St. Louis.
- - -	Bartholomew Herrington, -	Concession,	River Gravoix, - -	-	500	St. Louis.
- - -	John Johnston, - -	Concession,	Sandy creek, - -	-	499 96 p.	St. Louis.
- - -	Auguste Dodier, - -	Settlement right,	Beaver pond, - -	-	500	St. Louis.
- - -	William Null, - -	Concession,	Joachim, - -	-	600	St. Louis.
- - -	Godfrey Kroh, - -	Concession,	Waters of Dardenne, -	-	600	St. Charles.
- - -	William Ewing, - -	Concession,	Sandy creek, - -	-	800	St. Charles.
- - -	Joseph McAllpine, - -	Order of survey,	Bayou St. Thomas, -	-	400	New Madrid.
- - -	Richard Jones Waters, - -	Settlement right,	Lake Richado, - -	-	200	New Madrid.
- - -	Richard Jones Waters, - -	Order of survey,	Waters of Richado, -	-	200	New Madrid.
- - -	Richard Jones Waters, - -	Settlement right,	Bayou St. Thomas, -	-	200	New Madrid.
- - -	William Duncan, - -	Settlement right,	Bayou St. Thomas, -	-	400	New Madrid.
- - -	Richard Jones Waters, -	Settlement right,	Waters of Mississippi, -	-	200	New Madrid.

certificates issued by the Board of Commissioners for ascertaining and adjusting the titles and claims to land in the Territory of Louisiana, during the month from number three hundred and ninety-eight to number four hundred and thirty-one, inclusive, is truly transcribed from the book of registry kept by me as

Given under my hand at St. Louis, this eighth day of August, 1810.

JOHN W. HONEY,

d in the month of August, 1810, by the Board of Commissioners for ascertaining and adjusting the titles and claims to land in the Territory of Louisiana.

on under whom land was claimed.	In whose favor issued.	Nature of the claim.	Water course.	Number of acres.	Number of arpents.	District.
her, - -	Richard Jones Waters, - -	Settlement right, -	Waters of Lake Richado, -	-	250	New Madrid.
eur, - -	Ransom Thacher, -	Settlement right, -	River Pemiscon, - -	-	400	New Madrid.
ell, - -	Joseph Payne, -	Settlement right, -	Waters of Mississippi, -	-	120	New Madrid.
ct, - -	Raphael Lesieur, -	Settlement right, -	Waters of Mississippi, -	-	200	New Madrid.
, .. -	Robert Caldwell, -	Order of survey, -	Lake St. Mary, - -	-	200	New Madrid.
, -	Benjamin Johnson, -	Concession, -	Waters of the Joachim, -	-	240	St. Louis.
ontre, -	John Crow, -	Concession, -	Waters of Missouri, -	-	450	St. Charles.
s, -	Legal reps. of Francis Clark, -	Concession, -	Waters of Mississippi, -	-	600 30 p.	St. Genevieve.
au, -	Legal reps. of James Dodson, -	Concession, -	Mississippi, -	-	450	St. Genevieve.
Gabriel Lachance, -	Uriah and William G. Campbell, -	Concession, -	Waters of Missouri, -	-	400	St. Louis.
alker, - -	St. Jame Beauvais, - -	Concession, -	River Bois Bruile, - -	-	1000	St. Genevieve.
Jun. ;	Legal reps. of Francis Moreau, -	Ten y'rs possession, -	River Au Vase, - -	-	100	St. Genevieve.
Sen., alias Jonas Nu-	Francis Janis, -	Concession, -	River Gabourie, - -	-	96 80 p.	St. Genevieve.
	Antoine and Gabriel Lachance, -	Concession, -	Big Swamp, - -	-	480	St. Genevieve.
	Louis Coyteux, ..	Concession, -	Lake Bois Bruile, -	-	300	St. Genevieve.
	Jonas Nusam, Jun. -	Concession, -	Lake Bois Bruile, -	-	502 50 p.	St. Genevieve.
	Legal representatives of John Nusam, Sen., alias Jonas Nusam, Sen.	Concession, -	Lake Bois Bruile, -	-	505	St. Genevieve.
ce, - -	Samuel Bridge, -	Concession, -	River Saline, - -	-	480	St. Genevieve.
- -	John Duval, -	Concession, -	Waters of the river St. Come, -	-	400	St. Genevieve.

certificates, from number four hundred and thirty-two to number four hundred and fifty, inclusive, issued by the Board of Commissioners for ascertaining and n the Territory of Louisiana, during the month of August, one thousand eight hundred and ten, is truly copied from the book of registry kept by me as clerk of

Given under my hand, at St. Louis, this 14th day of September, 1810.   THOMAS F. RIDDICK.

of the Treasury, Washington City.

e month of September, 1810, by the Board of Commissioners for ascertaining and adjusting the titles and claims to land in the Territory of Louisiana.

der whom land was ed.	In whose favor issued.	Nature of the claim.	Water course.	Number of acres.	Number of arpents.	District.
De Luzierre, -	Pierre De Lassus De Luzierre, -	Concession, -	Waters of the river Aux Vases,	-	400	St. Genevieve.
-	Andrew Cottle, -	Concession, -	River Cuivre, -	-	350	St. Charles.
-	John Howell, -	Concession, -	Waters of river Dardenne, -	-	404 50 p.	St. Charles.
-	George S. Spencer, -	Concession, -	River Missouri, -	-	250	St. Charles.
-	Legal reps. of Isaac Fallis, -	Concession, -	Waters of river Mississippi, -	-	600	St. Charles.
"	George Fallis, -	Concession, -	On the river Cuivre, -	-	350	St. Charles.
-	Jacque Clamorgan, -	Concession, -	On the river Merrimack, -	-	60	St. Louis.
-	Jacque Clamorgan, -	Ten y'rs possession,	Waters of river Gingras, -	-	400	St. Louis.
-	John Colgin, -	Concession, -	River Missouri, -	-	240	St. Louis.
-	Jeremiah Grosjean, -	Concession, -	River Dardenne, -	-	200	St. Charles.
-	Charles Tayon, -	Concession, -	Waters of the Missouri, -	-	40	St. Charles.
-	Legal reps. of Christian Dennis, -	Concession, -	River Dardenne, -	-	400	St. Charles.
-	Charles Tayon, -	Concession, -	Waters of river Missouri, -	-	80	St. Charles.
-	Charles Tayon, -	Concession, -	Waters of river Missouri, -	-	13	St. Charles.
-	Charles Tayon, -	Concession, -	Waters of river Missouri, -	-	40	St. Charles.
-	Charles Tayon, -	Concession, -	Waters of river Missouri, -	-	40	St. Charles.
e, Jun.	John Baptiste Pratte, Jun, -	Concession, -	Waters of Grand river, -	-	800	St. Genevieve.
-	William Byrd, -	Concession, -	River Mississippi, -	-	200	Cape Girardeau.
,	Christopher Clark, -	Concession, -	River Perruque, -	-	240	St. Charles.
-	John Hays, -	Concession, -	Waters of the Mississippi, -	-	278 80 p.	Cape Girardeau.
-	Jesse Cain, -	Concession, -	Waters of Hubble's creek, -	-	256	Cape Girardeau.
-	Antoine Reynal, -	Concession, -	Lake Creve Cœur, -	-	2600	St. Louis.
-	Jacque Clamorgan, -	Ten y'rs possession,	Adjoining town of St. Louis,	-	7 38½ p.	St. Louis.
-	John N. Seely, -	Settlement right, -	River Missouri, -	-	800	St. Louis.
-	Alexander McCourtney, -	Concession, -	Femme Osage, -	-	400	St. Charles.
-	Samuel Hammond, -	Concession, -	Femme Osage, -	-	1000	St. Charles.
-	John Campbell, -	Concession, -	Sandy creek, -	-	800	St. Charles.
-	Pascal L. Cerré, -	Concession, -	Waters of river Missouri, -	-	40	St. Charles.
"	Calvin Adams & Alex. McCourtney,	Concession, -	Waters of Bonhomme, -	-	400	St. Louis.
-	Pelagie Labbadie, -	Concession, -	Waters of Dardenne, -	-	48	St. Charles.
-	Pelagie Labbadie, -	Concession, -	Lower fields of St. Charles, -	-	53	St. Charles.
"	James Mackay, -	Concession, -	Waters of the Missouri, -	-	36	St. Charles.

COMMISSIONERS' ROOM, *October 12, 1810.*

ertificates issued by the Board of Commissioners for ascertaining and adjusting the titles and claims to land in the Territory of Louisiana, during the month d ten, from number four hundred and fifty-one to four hundred and eighty-two, inclusive, is truly copied from the book of registry kept by me as clerk of

e Treasury, Washington City.

Given under my hand at St. Louis,   THOMAS F. RIDDICK.

in the month of October, 1810, by the Board of Commissioners for ascertaining and adjusting the titles and claims to land in the Territory of Louisiana.

n under whom land was claimed.	In whose favor issued.	Nature of the claim.	Water course.	Number of acres.	Number of arpents.	District.
Cyr, - -	Use of James Richardson, -	Order of survey, -	St. Ferdinand creek, -	299 36-100	-	St. Louis.
r, -	Legal reps. of Charles Peltier, -	Order of survey, -	St. Ferdinand creek, -	149 26-100	-	St. Louis.
lias Bochant, -	Beauchamp, alias Bochant, -	Concession, -	On the Marais Croche, -	-	60	St. Charles.
rgan, ..	Jacque Clamorgan, -	Concession, -	On the Marais Croche, -	-	40	St. Charles.
, -	Michael Shell, -	Concession, -	On the waters of Caney creek, -	-	241¼	Cape Girardeau.
n. -	Anderson Nunnelly, -	Concession, -	On Byrd's creek, -	-	240 84 p.	Cape Girardeau.
mers, -	Andrew Summers, -	Settlement right, -	On waters of Hubble's creek, -	237	-	St. Louis.
negant, -	John Mullanphy, -	Order of survey, -	St. Ferdinand fields, -	114 55-100	-	St. Louis.
clais, -	George Fallis, -	Order of survey, -	St. Ferdinand fields, -	83 15-100	..	St. Louis.
delle, -	George Fallis, -	Order of survey, -	St. Ferdinand fields, -	228½	-	St. Louis.
y, -	Baptiste Crely, -	Order of survey, -	St. Ferdinand fields, -	73 65-100	-	St. Louis.
le, -	Baptiste Crely, -	Order of survey, -	St. Ferdinand fields, -	231	-	St. Louis.
e, -	Louis Ouvre, -	Order of survey, -	St. Ferdinand fields, -	208 48-100	-	St. Louis.
ier, -	Charles Mercier, -	Order of survey, -	St. Ferdinand fields, -	184 7-10	-	St. Louis.
e, -	Jean Baptiste Billot, -	Order of survey, -	St. Ferdinand fields, -	94 64-100	-	St. Louis.
	Gabriel Aubuchon, -	Order of survey, -	St. Ferdinand fields, -	47 95-100	-	St. Louis.
on, -	Joseph Presse, -	Order of survey, -	St. Ferdinand fields, -	46 8-10	-	St. Louis.
ané, -	Legal reps. of Claude Paneton, -	Order of survey, -	St. Ferdinand fields, -	92 87-100	-	St. Louis.
	Baptiste Baccané, -	Order of survey, -	St. Ferdinand fields, -	76 82-100	-	St. Louis.
al, -	Pierre Payan, -	Order of survey, -	St. Ferdinand fields, -	74 67-100	-	St. Louis.
uries, -	Louis Dubreuil, -	Order of survey, -	St. Ferdinand fields, -	106 55-100	-	St. Louis.
haitre, -	Joseph Rapieux, -	Order of survey, -	St. Ferdinand fields, -	92 97-100	r	St. Louis.
Billot, -	Joseph Aubuchon, -	Order of survey, -	St. Ferdinand fields, -	118 18-100	-	St. Louis.
1, -	John Baptiste Billot, -	Order of survey, -	St. Ferdinand fields, -	116 13-100	-	St. Louis.
1, -	Auguste Chouteau, -	Order of survey, -	St. Ferdinand fields, -	119 42-100	-	St. Louis.
rmain, -	Auguste Chouteau, -	Order of survey, -	St. Ferdinand fields, -	118 57-100	-	St. Louis.
ie, -	Auguste Chouteau, -	Order of survey, -	St. Ferdinand fields, -	78 69-100	-	St. Louis.
ouceur, -	Peter Ellis, -	Order of survey, -	St. Ferdinand fields, -	61 29-100	-	St. Louis.
ger, -	Madame Ladouceur, -	Order of survey, -	St. Ferdinand fields, -	59 88-100	-	St. Louis.
ux, -	Benjamin Verger, -	Order of survey, -	St. Ferdinand fields, -	121	-	St. Louis.
chal, -	Joseph Robidoux, -	Order of survey, -	St. Ferdinand fields, -	75	-	St. Louis.
hon, alias Yoche, -	Legal reps. of Nicholas Marichal, -	Order of survey, -	St. Ferdinand fields, -	163 9-10	-	St. Louis.
t, -	Joseph Aubuchon, alias Yoche, -	Order of survey, -	St. Ferdinand fields, -	117 93-100	-	St. Louis.
, -	John Mullanphy, -	Order of survey, -	St. Ferdinand fields, -	71 29-100	-	St. Louis.
chal, -	Francois Marichal, -	Order of survey, -	St. Ferdinand fields, -	97 16-100	..	St. Louis.
, -	Legal reps. of John Bodoin, -	Order of survey, -	St. Ferdinand fields, -	70 53-100	-	St. Louis.
, -	Joseph Bodoin, -	Order of survey, -	St. Ferdinand fields, -	47 32-100	-	St. Louis.
enu, -	Pierre Tourville, -	Order of survey, -	St. Ferdinand fields, -	89 35-100	-	St. Louis.
	Pierre Roussel and Pierre Payan, -	Order of survey, -	St. Ferdinand fields, -	101 55-100	-	St. Louis.
chal, -	John Baptiste Lorins, -	Order of survey, -	St. Ferdinand fields, -	72 12-100	-	St. Louis.
lais, -	The reps. of Antoine Dejarlais, -	Concession, -	River Cuivre, -	-	600	St. Charles.
s, Jr. -	Ira Cottle, -					

list of certificates issued by the Board of Commissioners for ascertaining and adjusting the titles and claims to land in the Territory of Louisiana, from number-
er five hundred and twenty-four; inclusive, is truly copied from the book of registry kept by me as clerk of said Board. Said certificates issued in the month of
Given under my hand, at St. Louis, this seventh of November, 1810. THOMAS F. RIDDICK.

of the Treasury, Washington City.

month of November, 1810, by the Board of Commissioners for ascertaining and adjusting the titles and claims to land in the Territory of Louisiana.

er whom land was ed.		In whose favor issued.			Nature of the claim.		Water course.			Number of acres.	Number of arpents.	District.
-	-	John Byrd,	-	-	Concession,	-	Byrd's creek,	-	-	-	800	Cape Girardeau.
-	-	John McCarty,	-	-	Concession,	-	Byrd's creek,	-	-	-	570	Cape Girardeau.
-	-	William H. Ashley,	-	-	Concession,	-	River Zeno,	-	-	-	478 60 p.	Cape Girardeau.
-	-	Joshua Goza,	-	-	Concession,	-	Hubble's creek,	-	-	-	245 52 p.	Cape Girardeau.

f commissioners' certificates issued by the Board of Commissioners for ascertaining and adjusting the titles and claims to land in the Territory of Louisiana nd eight hundred and ten, from number five hundred and twenty-five to number five hundred and twenty-eight, inclusive, is truly copied from the book of

Given under my hand, at St. Louis, this 6th day of December, 1810.   THOMAS F. RIDDICK.

he Treasury, Washington City.

d in the month of December, 1810, by the Board of Commissioners for ascertaining and adjusting the titles and claims to land in the Territory of Louisiana.

son under whom land was claimed.	In whose favor issued.	Nature of the claim.	Water course.	Number of acres.	Number of arpents.	District.
s, - -	Joseph Lewis, - -	Settlement right, -	Lake St. Isidore, - -	-	350	New Madrid.
sters, - -	William Masters, - -	Settlement right, -	Prairie St. Charles, -	-	250	New Madrid.
rs, - -	Jesse Masters, - -	Settlement right, -	Prairie St. Charles, -	-	350	New Madrid.
s, - -	John Masters, - -	Settlement right, -	Prairie St. Charles, -	-	250	New Madrid.
s, - -	Jesse Blanks, - -	Settlement right, -	Tywappety, -	-	200	New Madrid.
ens, Sen. - -	James Clemens, Sen. - -	Settlement right, -	River Pemiscon, -	-	400	New Madrid.
Sen. - -	John Baker, Sen. - -	Settlement right, -	River Pemiscon, -	-	250	New Madrid.
dell, - -	George Ruddell, - -	Settlement right, -	River Mississippi, -	-	600	New Madrid.
rris, alias M. Henagey	Micajah Harris, alias M. Henagey Harris.	Settlement right, -	Big Lake, -	-	200	New Madrid.
', - -	John Hudgens, - -	Settlement right, -	River Mississippi, -	-	200	New Madrid.
ddell, - -	Abraham Ruddell, - -	Settlement right, -	River Pemiscon, -	-	200	New Madrid.
zer, - -	William Frazer, - -	Settlement right, -	Lake St. Mary, -	-	200	New Madrid.
at, - -	Conrad Wheat, - -	Order of survey, -	Lake St. Mary, -	-	450	New Madrid.
', - -	Simon Subtil, - -	Settlement right, -	Little Prairie, -	(640)	100	New Madrid.
s, - -	James Smith, or his legal reps.	Order of survey, -	Big Prairie, -	-	300	New Madrid.
s, - -	John Roberts, - -	Settlement right, -	Bayou St. John, -	-	400	New Madrid.
Jun. - -	John Baker, Jun. - -	Settlement right, -	River Pemiscon, -	-	200	New Madrid.
enie, - -	John Montmenie, - -	Settlement right, -	Waters of Lake Gayoso, -	-	250	New Madrid.
er, - -	Joseph Michel, - -	Settlement right, -	Little Prairie, -	-	120	New Madrid.
er, - -	Joseph Michel, - -	Settlement right, -	Lake Gayoso, -	-	200	New Madrid.
e Hebert, -	Joseph Michel, - -	Settlement right, -	Lake Gayoso, -	-	200	New Madrid.
e Bellefeuille,	John Baptiste Bellefeuille, -	Settlement right, -	Little Prairie, -	-	200	New Madrid.
ayon, -	Hyacinthe Gayon, - -	Settlement right, -	Little Prairie, -	-	200	New Madrid.
ille, -	Luc Bellefeuille, - -	Settlement right, -	Little Prairie, -	-	200	New Madrid.
lais, Femme Lacourse,	Joseph Dejarlais, Femme Lacourse,	Settlement right, -	Little Prairie, -	-	200	New Madrid.
s, - -	Eloi Dejarlais, - -	Settlement right, -	Little Prairie, -	-	200	New Madrid.
nte, - -	Joseph Hunter and Francis Coutely, Jun.	Concession, -	Bayou St. Thomas, -	-	98	New Madrid.
', - -	Joseph Michel, - -	Settlement right, -	River Mississippi, -	-	400	New Madrid.
e Barseloux, -	Joseph Michel, - -	Settlement right, -	River Gayoso, -	-	300	New Madrid.
', - -	Joseph Michel, - -	Settlement right, -	Lake Gayoso, -	-	200	New Madrid.
rtier, -	Baptiste Chartier, - -	Settlement right, -	Near Mississippi river, -	-	250	New Madrid.
oder, -	Toussaint Goder, - -	Settlement right, -	Big portage of riv. St. François,	-	200	New Madrid.
e Maisonville, -	Joseph Legrand, - -	Settlement right, -	Portage of river St. François,	-	200	New Madrid.
cCardle, -	Elizabeth McCardle, - -	Order of survey, -	Big Prairie, -	-	253	New Madrid.
rs, - -	John Lovel, - -	Settlement right, -	Lake St. Ann, -	-	170	New Madrid.
ier, -	Eustace Peltier, - -	Settlement right, -	Little Prairie, -	-	100	New Madrid.
aud, -	Baptiste Ernaud, - -	Settlement right, -	Waters of Mississippi, -	-	200	New Madrid.
n, - -	Arthur Mellon, - -	Settlement right, -	Lake St. Ricardo, -	-	120	New Madrid.

: list of certificates issued by the Board of Commissioners for ascertaining and adjusting the titles and claims to land in the Territory of Louisiana during the : hundred and ten, from number five hundred and twenty-nine to number five hundred and sixty-six, both inclusive, is truly copied from the book of registry kept

Given under my hand at St. Louis, January 24, 1811,   THOMAS F. RIDDICK.

y of the Treasury, Washington City.

the month of January, 1811, by the Board of Commissioners for ascertaining and adjusting titles and claims to lands in the Territory of Louisiana.

...er whom land was ...ed.		In whose favor issued.			Nature of the claim.	Water course.			Number of acres.	Number of arpents.	District.
-	-	Martin Coons,	-	-	Order of survey,	Lake St. Mary,	-	-	-	300	New Madrid.
-	-	James Simpson,	-	-	Order of survey,	Lake St. Mary,	-	-	-	380	New Madrid.
-	-	Peter Noblesse,	-	-	Settlement right,	Little Prairie,	-	-	-	200	New Madrid.
-	-	Richard Secoy,	-	-	Settlement right,	Waters of Mississippi,	-	-	-	200	New Madrid.
-	-	Rheneike and Steinback,	-		Settlement right,	Little Prairie,	-	-	-	120	New Madrid.
-	-	Joseph Jacobs,	-	-	Settlement right,	River Pemiscon,	-	-	-	200	New Madrid.
-	-	Louis Lefevre,	-	-	Settlement right,	On the Mississippi,	-	-	-	200	New Madrid.
n.	-	Francis Trinchard,	-	-	Settlement right,	Lake Gayoso,	-	-	-	300	New Madrid.
s,	-	James Clemens, Jun.	-	-	Settlement right,	On river Pemiscon,	-	-	-	200	New Madrid.
-	-	Representatives of Steward Cummings			Settlement right,	River Gayoso,	-	-	-	400	New Madrid.
-	-	John Hudgeons,	-	-	Settlement right,	Lake Lesieur,	-	-	-	200	New Madrid.
-	-	Richard Jones Waters,	-	-	Settlement right,	Lake St. John,	-	-	-	250	New Madrid.
,	-	Joseph Dorion,	-	-	Settlement right,	Waters of Mississippi,		-	-	200	New Madrid.
,	-	Wilson Cummings,	-	-	Settlement right,	River Pemiscon,	-	-	-	200	New Madrid.
-	-	Richard Jones Waters,	-	-	Settlement right,	River Pemiscon,	-	-	-	700	New Madrid.
-	-	Nicholas Tirart,	-	-	Settlement right,	Big Lake,	-	-	-	200	New Madrid.
-	-	John Viot,	-	-	Settlement right,	Little Prairie,	-	-	-	200	New Madrid.
-	-	Francis Delisle,	-	-	Settlement right,	Waters of river Gayoso,	-	-	-	200	New Madrid.
-	-	Francis Lesieur,	-	-	Settlement right,	Little Prairie,	-	-	-	240	New Madrid.
-	-	Baptiste Delisle,	-	-	Settlement right,	Lake Gayoso,	-	-	-	200	New Madrid.
''	-	James Currin,	-	-	Settlement right,	River Mississippi,	-	-	-	200	New Madrid.
-	-	Nathaniel Shaver,	-	-	Order of survey,	Bayou St. John,	-	-	-	400	New Madrid.
-	-	Jacob Wheat,	-	-	Order of survey,	Lake St. Mary,	-	-	-	600	New Madrid.
-	-	Thomas Brooks,	-	-	Order of survey,	Lake St. Ann,	-	-	-	200	New Madrid.
-	-	Joseph Story,	-	-	Order of survey,	Bayou St. John,	-	-	-	200	New Madrid.
et,	-	Baptiste Grimard,	-	-	Settlement right,	River Gayoso,	-	-	-	200	New Madrid.
-	-	Louis Baby,	-	-	Settlement right,	Lake St. Mary,	-	-	-	250	New Madrid.
r,	-	John E. Hart,	-	-	Settlement right,	Bayou St. Thomas,	-	-	-	240	New Madrid.
-	-	Louis Coignard,	-	-	Settlement right,	Lake Gayoso,	-	-	-	200	New Madrid.
-	-	Joseph Legrand,	-	-	Order of survey,	Portage of river St. Francis,	-	-	-	250	New Madrid.
tier,	-	Peter Sans Quartier,	''	-	Order of survey,	Bayou St. John,	-	-	-	200	New Madrid.
-	-	Peter Labombarde,	-	-	Order of survey,	Bayou St. John,	-	-	-	200	New Madrid.
-	-	Germain Ouillett,	-	-	Order of survey,	Bayou St. John,	-	-	-	200	New Madrid.
-	-	Peter Dapron,	-	-	Settlement right,	Bayou St. John,	-	-	''	207	New Madrid.
-	-	Joseph Michel,	-	-	Settlement right,	Bayou St. John,	-	-	-	200	New Madrid.
-	-	Joseph Michel,	-	-	Order of survey,	Bayou St. Thomas,	-	-	-	240	New Madrid.
-	-	Joseph Michel,	-	-	Order of survey,	Bayou St. Thomas,	-	-	-	273	New Madrid.
-	-	Francis Coutely,	-	-	Order of survey,	Bayou St. Thomas,	-	-	-	246	New Madrid.
-	-	Joseph Michel,	-	-	Order of survey,	Lake St. Mary,	-	-	-	240	New Madrid.
-	-	Peter Sabourin, or his legal repres'ves,			Order of survey,	Lake St. Mary,	-	-	-	300	New Madrid.
-	-	Ambrose Dumay,	-	-	Order of survey,	Lake St. Mary,	-	''	-	240	New Madrid.
-	-	Joseph Michel,	-	-	Order of survey,	Lake St. Mary,	-	-	-	300	New Madrid.
-	-	Joseph Michel,	-	-	Order of survey,	Lake St. Mary,	-	-	-	325	New Madrid.
-	-	John Culbertson,	-	-	Settlement right,	River Pemiscon,	-	-	-	200	New Madrid.
-	-	Anthony Hibernois,	''	-	Settlement right,	Little Prairie,	-	-	-	150	New Madrid.

COMMISSIONERS' CERTIFICATES—Continued.

under whom land was claimed.	In whose favor issued.	Nature of the claim.	Water course.	Number of acres.	Number of arpents.	District.
:er,	William Thacker,	Settlement right,	South fork of Pemiscon,	-	250	New Madrid.
:n,	John Colbertson,	Settlement right,	South fork of Pemiscon,	-	300	New Madrid.
:son,	Alexander Samson,	Order of survey,	Big Prairie,	-	300	New Madrid.
:s,	Hardy Rawls,	Order of survey,	Dry Run of Bayou St. Thomas,	-	400	New Madrid.
:x,	Joseph Genereux,	Settlement right,	Waters of Mississippi,	-	130	New Madrid.
	John Ruddell,	Settlement right,	River Pemiscon,	-	350	New Madrid.
:tson, Sen.	Andrew Robertson, Sen.	Settlement right,	Bayou St. John,	(640)	300	New Madrid.
:it,	Joseph Lafernait,	Order of survey,	Bayou St. John,	-	300	New Madrid.
:isha Winsor,	Thomas and Elisha Winsor,	Order of survey,	Bayou St. Henry,	-	200	New Madrid.
:isha Winsor,	Thomas and Elisha Winsor,	Order of survey,	Bayou St. Thomas,	-	200	New Madrid.
	Robert Trotter,	Settlement right,	Bayou St. Thomas,	-	200	New Madrid.
:Millet,	John Baptiste Millet,	Order of survey,	Lake St. Mary,	-	400	New Madrid.
	Andrew Scott,	Order of survey,	Lake St. Mary,	-	300	New Madrid.

ist of certificates, from number five hundred and sixty-seven to number six hundred and twenty-four, inclusive, issued by the Board of Commissioners for ascer-
:s to lands in the Territory of Louisiana, during the month of January last, is truly copied from the book of registry kept by me as clerk of said Board.
this 14th February, 1811.   THOS. F. RIDDICK.
of the Treasury, Washington City.

:ed *in the month of March, 1811, by the Board of Commissioners for ascertaining and adjusting titles and claims to lands in the Territory of Louisiana.*

:n under whom land was claimed.	In whose favor issued.	Nature of the claim.	Water course.	Number of acres.	Number of arpents.	District.
:ette,	Legal repre's of Francis Pacquette,	Order of survey,	Lake St. Mary,	-	250	New Madrid.
:, Sen.	David Trotter, Sen.	Settlement right,	Lake St. Mary,	-	400	New Madrid.
:eau,	Pierre Antoine Laforge,	Order of survey,	Bayou St. Henry,	-	400	New Madrid.
	Joseph Michel 240, William Deakins 150, Samuel M. Randals 60 arpents.	Order of survey,	Lake St. Mary,	-	450	New Madrid.
:rtson,	Joseph Michel,	Order of survey,	Bayou St. Henry,	-	287	New Madrid.
:Racine,	John Baptiste Racine, "	Order of survey,	Bayou St. Henry,	-	289	New Madrid.
:rd, alias Mimi Lardoise	John Baptiste Olive,	Order of survey,	Open Lake,	-	250	New Madrid.
:nthony Laffond,	Bernard and Anthony Laffond,	Order of survey,	Bayou St. Henry,	-	400	New Madrid.

list of certificates issued by the Board of Commissioners for ascertaining and adjusting the titles and claims to lands in the Territory of Louisiana, from number six
hundred and thirty-two, inclusive, issued during the month of March, one thousand eight hundred and eleven, is truly copied from the book of registry kept by

April 4, 1811.   THOS. F. RIDDICK.
of the Treasury, Washington City.

ths of April, May, and June, 1811, *by the Board of Commissioners for ascertaining and adjusting titles and claims to lands in the Territory of Louisiana.*

hom land was	In whose favor issued.	Nature of the claim.	Water course.	Number of acres.	Number of arpents.	District.
- -	John Tanhill, - -	Settlement right,	Marais des Peches, -	-	200	New Madrid.
- -	David Johnson, - -	Order of survey,	Lake St. Mary, - -	-	200	New Madrid.
- -	Richard Jones Waters, -	Settlement right,	Lake St. Mary, - -	-	234	New Madrid.
- -	William Talbot, - -	Settlement right,	Bayou de Bœuf, - -	-	200	New Madrid.
- -	Alexander Bailly, - -	Settlement right,	Tywappety, - -	-	300	New Madrid.
- -	Charles Friend, - -	Settlement right,	Illinois road, - -	-	400	New Madrid.
- -	John Friend, - -	Settlement right,	Illinois road, - -	-	200	New Madrid.
- -	Jacob Friend, - -	Settlement right,	Illinois road, - -	-	200	New Madrid.
- -	Daniel Hazell, - -	Settlement right,	Ten miles N. New Madrid vil.	-	200	New Madrid.
- --	Richard Hazell, - -	Settlement right,	Ten miles N. New Madrid vil.	-	200	New Madrid.
- -	John Robertson, -	Settlement right,	Bayou St. John, -	-	193	New Madrid.
- --	Richard Jones Waters, - -	Concession, -	On the Mississippi, -	-	240	New Madrid.
iche Dupin,	Samuel Black, or his legal represen's,	Concession, -	On the Mississippi, --	-	240	New Madrid.
- -	Anna Claude Francis Riche Dupin,	Order of survey,	Lake St. Mary, -	-	250	New Madrid.
- -	Daniel Bankson, - -	Settlement right,	Waters of Bayou St. John, -	-	200	New Madrid.
- -	Francis Derousse, or his legal repre's,	Order of survey,	On Bayou St. John, -	-	250	New Madrid.
- -	Jean Simon Geurin, or his legal rep's,	Order of survey,	On the Mississippi, --	-	300	New Madrid.
- -	Peter Van Iderstine, or his legal rep's,	Order of survey,	On the Mississippi, -	-	200	New Madrid.
- -	Joseph McCourtney, or his legal rep's,	Order of survey,	Bayou of Portage St. Francis,	-	240	New Madrid.
- -	Richard Jones Waters, - -	Order of survey,	On lake St. Ann, -	-	150	New Madrid.
- -	Richard Jones Waters, - -	Order of survey,	Bayou St. John, - -	-	50	New Madrid.
- -	John Chambers, - -	Concession, -	Near Marais des Liards, -	-	400	St. Louis.
- -	Barn Burns, - -	Concession, -	Bois Bruile, -	-	600	St. Genevieve.
- -	John Brown, - -	Concession, -	Marais des Liards fields, -	-	600	St. Louis.
- -	Elisha Goodrich, - -	Concession, -	On the Missouri, - -	-	400	St. Charles.
- -	John Watkins, - -	Concession, -	Grand Prairie, - -	-	240	St. Louis.
- -	John Watkins, - -	Concession, -	Little Rock creek, - -	-	240	St. Louis.
- -	John Watkins, - -	Concession, -	River Merrimack, - -	-	160	St. Genevieve.
- -	Legal repres's of John McClenahan,	Concession, -	Mill creek, Bois Bruili, -	-	400	St. Genevieve.
- -	James Burns, - -	Concession, -	Bois Bruile, - -	-	300	St. Genevieve.
- -	Michael Burns, - -	Concession, --	Bois Bruile, - -	-	200	St. Genevieve.
- -	Alexander McNair, - -	Concession, -	Mill creek, - -	-	800 ·	St. Louis. .
- -	Benito Vasques, - -	Concession, -	St. Louis, - -	-	600	St. Louis.
- -	Legal representatives of Adam House,	Concession, -	Fourche à Renault, -	-	400	St. Louis.
ry, -	James McKay, - -	Concession, -	Village St. André, -	-	50 by 50 per.	St. Louis.
- -	The widow of John Henry, -	Concession, -	Missouri, - -	-	160	St. Louis.
s. Maimville,	Julien Chouquette, - -	Concession, -	Fields of Carondelet, -	--	60	St. Louis.
.,	Antoine Roy, - -	Concession, -	Grand Prairie, - -	-	40	St. Louis.
- -	Pierre Chouteau, - -	Concession, -	St. Louis, - -	-	93 1 per.	St. Louis.
- -	Widow and rep's of Antoine Morin,	Concession, -	Mississippi, - -	-	640	St. Louis.
- -	Legal representatives of Jos. Matard,	Concession, -	Adjoining St. Louis, -	-	200 Fr. ft.	St. Louis.
- -	James Carothers, - -	Concession, -	On Hubble's creek, -	-	300	Cape Girardeau.
- -	Widow and rep's of Jacob Slinker,	Concession, -	White Waters, - -	-	550	Cape Girardeau.
- -	Daniel Clinqin Smith, -	Order of survey,	White Waters, - -	-	400	Cape Girardeau.
- -	Anthony Soulard, - -	Concession, -	Adjoining town of St. Louis,	-.	40	St. Louis.

COMMISSIONERS' CERTIFICATES—Continued.

nder whom land was med.	In whose favor issued.	Nature of the claim.	Water course.	Number of acres.	Number of arpents.	District.
otherwise Boining,	Jeremiah Paynish, otherwise Boining,	Concession, -	White Waters, -	-	400	Cape Girardeau.
	William Boner, - -	Concession, -	On Ramsay's creek, -	-	240	Cape Girardeau.
	John Frazer, - -	Order of survey, -	Big Prairie, -	-	300 (310)	New Madrid.
nan, - -	Thomas Twentyman, -	Concession, -	Bayou St. Thomas, -	-	240	New Madrid.
	Francis B. Corvouers, -	Concession, -	Bayou St. Thomas, -	-	240	New Madrid.
	Francis B. Corvouers, -	Concession, -	Bayou St. Thomas, -	-	240	New Madrid.
	Joseph St. Marie, or his legal rep's,	Concession, -	Lake St. Mary, "	-	120	New Madrid.
e,	Joseph Michel, - -	Concession, -	Lake St. Mary, -	-	240	New Madrid.
,	Joseph Michel, - -	Concession, -	Lake St. Mary, -	-	90	New Madrid.
	Peter Dumay, - -	Order of survey, -	Lake St. Mary, -	-	240	New Madrid.
Marie, -	John Baptiste St. Marie, -	Order of survey, -	Lake St. Mary, "	-	240	New Madrid.
	Louis Sojourner, - -	Order of survey, -	Big Prairie, -	-	200	New Madrid.
	Sarah Ruddell, widow of Nic. Anger,	Concession, -	On lake St. Francis, -	-	240	New Madrid.
	Paul Laderoute, -	Concession, -	Lake St. Mary, -	"	240	New Madrid.
	Charles Bonneau, -	Concession, -	Lake St. Mary, -	-	80	New Madrid.
	Isidore Skerritt, -	Concession, -	Lake St. Mary, -	-	240	New Madrid.
	Legal representatives of Jos. Lesieur,	Concession, "	On the Mississippi, -	-	240	New Madrid.
d, -	Henry Peyroux, -	Concession, -	Bayou St. Thomas, -	-	90	New Madrid.
Chisholm,	Henry Peyroux, -	Concession, -	Lake St. Ann, -	-	100	New Madrid.
	Peter Debigny, or his legal repres's,	Concession, -	Bayou St. Thomas, "	-	90	New Madrid.
	Richard Jones Waters, -	Concession, -	Lake St. Ann, -	-	240	New Madrid.
	Richard Jones Waters, -	Concession, -	On the Mississippi, -	-	240	New Madrid.
	Francis Fordonie, -	Concession, -	Lake St. Mary, -	"	240	New Madrid.
	Richard Jones Waters, -	Concession,	Lake St. Ann, -	-	220	New Madrid.
	Joseph Story, -	Concession, -	Lake St. Ann, -	-	240	New Madrid.
k,	Richard Jones Waters, -	Concession, -	Lake St. Mary, -	-	400	New Madrid.
	Thomas W. Caulk, "	Concession, -	Bayou St. Thomas, -	-	400	New Madrid.
	Samson Archer, -	Concession, -	Bayou St. Thomas, -	-	90	New Madrid.
den, -	Joseph Vandenbinden, -	Concession, -	Lake St. Ann, -	-	240	New Madrid.
	Legal representat's of Jos. St. Marie,	Concession, "	Bayou St. Thomas, -	-	90	New Madrid.
	John Hamphill, or his representatives,	Concession, -	Lake St. Francis, -	-	240	New Madrid.
	Peter Lovel, -	[Concession, -	Lake St. Francis, -	-	310	New Madrid.
	Richard Jones Waters, -	Concession, -	Lake St. Francis, -	-	400	New Madrid.
	Richard Jones Waters, -	Concession, "	Lake St. Francis, -	-	240	New Madrid.
	Richard Jones Waters, -	Concession, -	Lake Eulalie, "	-	240	New Madrid.
	George Unerous, -	Concession, -	Lake St. Mary, -	-	240	New Madrid.
	Benjamin Demint, -	Concession, -	Lake St. Ann, -	-	240	New Madrid.
is, alias Meloche,	Richard Jones Waters, - "	Concession, -	Lake St. Ann, -	-	240	New Madrid.
	Richard Jones Waters, - "	Order of survey, -	Lake St. Mary, -	-	90	New Madrid.
saloux, -	John Bap. Bersaloux, or his legal reps.	Concession, -	Lake St. Ann, -	-	240	New Madrid.
	Joseph Story, -	Concession, -	Lake St. Eulalie, -	-	416	New Madrid.
nters, -	Richard Jones Waters, -	Concession, -	Arkansas village, -	-	320	Arkansas.
	Charles Refield, -	Concession, -	Big Lake, -	-	400	Arkansas.
	Legal represen's of François Menard,	Concession, -	Bayou St. Thomas, -	-	400	New Madrid.
	Richard Jones Waters, -					

hom land was	In whose favor issued.	Nature of the claim.	Water course.	Number of acres.	Number of arpents.	District.
-	Richard Jones Waters, - -	Concession, -	Bayou St. John, - -	-	240	New Madrid.
& Co.	Legal represent's of Elisha Jackson,	Concession, -	Bayou St. John and St. Thomas	-	240	New Madrid.
-	Richard Jones Waters, - -	Concession, -	Bayou St. Thomas, - -	-	30	New Madrid.
-	Richard Jones Waters, - -	Concession, -	Bayou St. Thomas, - -	-	90	New Madrid.
-	Isaac E. Kelly, - -	Settlement right, -	Waters of St. Francis, -	(640)	300	Cape Girardeau.
-	Jacques Clamorgan, -	Concession, -	River Gin Grass, - -	-	800	St. Louis.
-	Robert Young, - -	Concession, -	On the Missouri, - -	-	500	St. Louis.
-	Samuel Hibler, - -	Settlement right, -	Creve Cœur, - -	(640)	500	St. Louis.
-	Heirs and repre's of Louis Jeannette,	Settlement right, -	River Dardenne, - -	(640)	100	St. Charles.
-	Anthony Soulard, - -	Concession, -	Prairie near St. Louis, -	-	40	St. Louis.
ere,	Ambrose Bowles, - -	Settlement right, -	On the Missouri, - -	(640)	200	St. Louis.
-	John Mullanphy, " -	Ten years possession	Near the town of St. Louis, -	-	80	St. Louis.
-	John A. Smith, - -	Settlement right, -	Waters of Missouri, -	(640)	300	St. Charles.
-	Jacob Hostetter, - -	Settlement right, -	Mississippi Bluff, - -	(640)	350	St. Charles.
-	Henry Zoomalt, Jun. -	Settlement right, -	River Cuivre, - -	(640)	100	St. Charles.
-	Andrew Edwards, - -	Settlement right, -	River Peruque, - -	(640)	250	St. Charles.
-	Jacob Coontz, - -	Settlement right, -	River Dardenne, - -	(640)	450	St. Charles.
-	Edward Hempstead, -	Ten years possession	Lower Prairie, - -	-	40	St. Charles.
-	Edward Hempstead, -	Ten years possession	Village St. Charles, -	-	lot 120 by 150 ft	St. Charles.
-	Legal repre's of Alexander McClean,	Settlement right, -	On McClean's creek -	(640)	440	St. Charles.
-	John Journey, - -	Settlement right, -	Missouri, - -	-	600	St. Charles.
-	Samuel Griffith, - -	Settlement right, -	District of St. Charles, -	(640)	250	St. Charles.
-	John Mullanphy, - -	Ten years possession	Adjoining town of St. Louis,	, -	40	St. Louis.
-	Legal representatives of John Coontz,	Ten years possession	Village St. Charles, -	-	120 by 120 feet,	St. Charles.
-	John Stewart, - -	Settlement right, -	Grand Glaize, - -	(640)	400	St. Louis.
-	John Baptiste Luzon, -	Settlement right, -	Between Charette and Missouri	(640)	350	St. Charles.
-	John Baptiste Belland, -	Ten years possession	Belland's creek, - -	-	160	St. Charles.
-	Legal representatives of Peter Peltier,	Ten years possession	Creve Cœur, - -	-	80	St. Louis.
-	Isidore Savoy, - -	Ten years possession	Village St. Charles, -	120 front by	150 ft. depth,	St. Charles.
-	Pet. Blanchet, use of John McKenney	Settlement right, -	River Charette, -	(640)	100	St. Charles.
-	Warren Cottle, Jun. -	Settlement right, -	Darderine, "	-	250	St. Charles.
-	William Farnsworth, -	Settlement right, -	River Cuivre, - -	(640)	100	St. Charles.
-	Isaac Cottle, - -	Settlement right, -	River Cuivre, - -	(640)	100	St. Charles.
-	Sylvanus Cottle, - -	Settlement right, -	River Cuivre, - -	-	500	St. Charles.
-	Jonathan Woods, - -	Settlement right, "	River Cuivre, - -	(640)	300	St. Charles.
-	William T. Lemme, -	Settlement right, -	River Tuque, - -	(640)	300	St. Charles.
-	William T. Lemme, -	Settlement right, -	Village Charette, -	(640)	300	St. Charles.
-	Basil Proulx, - -	Ten years possession	Missouri, - -	-	135 feet front,	St. Charles.
-	Edward Hempstead, -	Ten years possession	Lower Prairie, - -	-	80	St. Charles.
-	Etienne Barnard, - "	Settlement right, -	River Dardenne, -	-	500	St. Charles.
-	William McConnell, -	Ten years possession	Missouri, - -	120 front by	150 ft. depth,	St. Charles.
-	Robert Spencer, - -	Ten years possession	Missouri, - -	120 front by	150 ft. depth,	St. Charles.
-	Noel Hebert, - -	Settlement right, -	River Dardenne, -	(640)	300	St. Charles.
-	Ninian Hamilton, -	Settlement right, -	River Merrimack, -	(640)	200	St. Louis.
-	Joseph Baker, - -	Settlement right, -	White Waters, "	-	250 (505)	Cape Girardeau.

COMMISSIONERS' CERTIFICATES—Continued.

...der whom land was ...ned.	In whose favor issued.	Nature of the claim.	Water course.	Number of acres.	Number of arpents.	District.
-	Tillman Smith, - -	Settlement right, -	White Waters, - -	(640)	600	Cape Girardeau.
-	Philip Young, -	Settlement right, -	Byrd's creek, -	(640)	300	Cape Girardeau.
-	James Hannah, -	Settlement right, -	Randall's creek, -	-	600 (719 55½)	Cape Girardeau.
Jr., son of Athamar	John McCarty, -	Settlement right, -	White Waters, -	-	250 (740)	Cape Girardeau.
-	Ezekiel Able, - -	Concession, -	White Waters, -	(640)	240	Cape Girardeau.
-	John and Robert Gibany, -	Settlement right, -	Hubble's creek, -	(640)	400	Cape Girardeau.
-	John Hays and Jeremiah W. Still, -	Settlement right, -	Table river, -	-	250	Cape Girardeau.
-	Charles Lucas, -	Settlement right, -	Mississippi, -	(640)	600	Cape Girardeau.
-	John Tucker, -	Settlement right, -	Tywappety, -	-	250 (686)	Cape Girardeau.
-	John Brooks, -	Settlement right, -	Mississippi, -	-	250 (709)	Cape Girardeau.
-	James Burns, -	Settlement right, -	Sandy creek, -	-	200 (600)	St. Charles.
-	Clement B. Penrose, -	Ten y'rs possession,	Town of St. Louis, -	-	120 by 150 ft.	St. Louis.
-	Robert Baldridge, -	Settlement right, -	River Peruque, -	(640)	450	St. Charles.
-	Jeremiah Connor, -	Ten y'rs possession,	Adjoining St. Louis, -	1 arp. front	by 40 depth,	St. Louis.
-	Francis Vallé, or his legal reps. -	Concession, -	Village of St. Genevieve, -	-	2	St. Genevieve.
-	Legal reps. of Francis Vallé, -	Concession, -	Village of St. Genevieve, -	-	1	St. Genevieve.
...ston, -	James Cunningham, -	Settlement right, -	Grand river, -	-	750	St. Genevieve.
-	Archibald Huddleston, -	Settlement right, -	Waters of the Saline, -	(640)	250	St. Genevieve.
...er	Legal reps. of Archibald Campster, -	Settlement right, -	Mississippi, -	-	500 (550)	St. Genevieve.
...Veidon, -	Susannah Dubreuil, -	Ten y'rs possession,	Cul de Sac, -	1 arp. front	by 40 depth,	St. Louis.
-	Susannah Dubreuil, -	Ten y'rs possession,	Cul de Sac, -	-	80	St. Louis.
-	Robert Reed, -	Settlement right, -	Bellevue settlement, -	(640)	300	St. Genevieve.
-	Jacob Mosteller, -	Settlement right, -	Hazel run, -	(640)	100	St. Genevieve.
-	Jacob Chambers, -	Settlement right, -	-	(640)	250	St. Genevieve.
-	Ananias McCoy, -	Settlement right, -	Bellevue, -	(640)	340	St. Genevieve.
-	Benjamin Crow, -	Settlement right, -	Bellevue, -	(640)	600	St. Genevieve.
-	William Ward, -	Settlement right, -	-	-	100 (700)	St. Genevieve.
-	Joseph Manning, -	Settlement right, -	Mississippi, -	(640)	550	St. Genevieve.
-	Clement Knott, -	Settlement right, -	Cape St. Comes, -	(640)	250	St. Genevieve.
-	William Dunn, -	Settlement right, -	On the Saline, -	-	450 (702 40)	St. Genevieve.
-	John Layton, Jun. -	Settlement right, -	On the Saline, -	(640)	350	St. Genevieve.
f Nicholas Moore,	Jas. Moore, son of Nicholas Moore,	Settlement right, -	On the Saline, -	(640)	200	St. Genevieve.
-	Ignatus Layton, -	Settlement right, -	On the Saline, -	(640)	300	St. Genevieve.
-	John Layton, Sen. -	Settlement right, -	Cape Cinqhommes, -	(640)	200	St. Genevieve.
-	Thomas Ring, -	Settlement right, -	River St. Francis, -	(640)	100	St. Genevieve.
-	Robert A. Logan, -	Settlement right, -	River St. Francis, -	(640)	300	St. Genevieve.
-	David Logan, -	Settlement right, -	River St. Francis, -	(640)	520	St. Genevieve.
, Sen. -	Humphrey Gibson, Sen. -	Settlement right, -	River Plattin, -	-	450 (472 80)	St. Genevieve.
-	Aquilla Hagan, -	Settlement right, -	South fork of river Saline, -	(640)	450	St. Genevieve.
-	Joseph Hagan, -	Settlement right, -	Waters of Bois Bruile, -	(640)	300	St. Genevieve.
-	Charles Lee, -	Settlement right, -	Waters of Cape Cinqhommes, -	(640)	320	St. Genevieve.
-	Peter Tucker, -	Settlement right, -	South fork of river Saline, -	(640)	450	St. Genevieve.
-	Joseph Tucker, -	Settlement right, -	South fork of river Saline, -	(640)	450	St. Genevieve.
-	Michael Tucker, -	Settlement right, -	Saline, -	(640)	200	St. Genevieve.

hom land was		In whose favor issued.	Nature of the claim.	Water course.	Number of acres.	Number of arpents.	District.
-	-	Legal reps. of Thomas Harrod, -	Settlement right, -	River Platine, -	-	300 (531)	St. Genevieve.
-	-	Amos Rowark, " -	Settlement right, -	Waters of Saline, -	-	100 (500)	St. Genevieve.
-	-	Elizabeth Carlin, widow and rep. of Thomas Carlin.	Settlement right, -	Plattin creek, -	(640)	550	St. Louis.
-	-	Camille Delassus and John Hawkins,	Concession, -	Bois Bruile, -	-	800	St. Genevieve.
-	-	James Dotson, - -	Concession, -	River St. Francis, -	-	600	St. Genevieve.
-	-	James Cannavan, -	Concession, -	River St. Francis, -	-	400	St. Genevieve.
-	-	Tunis Quick, -	Settlement right, -	Saline, -	(640)	450	St. Genevieve.
-	-	Samuel Hincks, Sen. -	Settlement right, -	Cape St. Comes, -	(640)	670	St. Genevieve.
-	-	Robert Hinkson, -	Settlement right, -	River Brazeau, -	(640)	550	St. Genevieve.
-	-	Theophilus Williams, -	Settlement right, -	Cape St. Comes, -	(640)	470	St. Genevieve.
-	-	James Berry, -	Settlement right, -	Cape St. Comes, -	-	250 (400)	St. Genevieve.
nes,	-	James Moore, son of James, -	Settlement right, -	Cape Cinq Hommes, -	(640)	300	St. Genevieve.
-	-	William Johnston, -	Settlement right, -	River St. Francis, -	-	410 (680)	St. Genevieve.
-	-	Joseph Girrard, Jun. -	Settlement right, -	Grand river, -	(640)	100	St. Genevieve.
-	-	Mark Wideman, -	Settlement right, -	Negro fork of Merrimack, -	(640)	250	St. Louis.
-	-	John Wideman, -	Settlement right, -		(640)	350	St. Louis.
-	-	Widow St. Franceway, -	Settlement right, -	Chout creek, -	(640)	150	St. Charles.
-	-	Joseph Chartrand, Jun. -	Settlement right, -	Missouri, "	(640)	200	St. Charles.
-	-	Auguste Chouteau, -	Concession, -	Grand Prairie, -	-	40	St. Louis.
-	-	Emilian Yosty, -	Concession, -	Town of St. Louis, -	-	120 by 150 ft.	St. Louis.
-	-	Auguste Chouteau and Antoine Soulard, in right of their wives.	Concession, -	River Merrimack, -	-	1 league sq.	St. Louis.
-	-	James Pritchett, -	Settlement right, -	Forty miles west of St. Louis,	(640)	550	St. Louis.
-	-	Thomas Williams, -	Settlement right, -	" -	-	350 (704)	St. Louis.
-	-	Legal reps. of John Williams, Sen. -	Settlement right, -	Merrimack, -	(640)	450	St. Louis.
-	-	Hug Swan, -	Settlement right, -	Fork of river Cuivre, -	-	100 (740)	St. Charles.
"	-	John Cummins, -	Settlement right, -	Merrimack, -	(640)	400	St. Louis.
-	-	Auguste Chouteau, -	Ten y'rs possession,	St. Charles fields, -	-	40	St. Charles.
-	-	Pascal Detchemendy, -	Concession, -	River Establishment,	-	1 league sq.	St. Genevieve.
-	-	Jonathan Cottle, -	Settlement right, -	Bob's creek, Mississippi, -	(640)	240	St. Charles.
-	-	Robert Bay, -	Settlement right, -	Bonhomme, -	(640)	200	St. Louis.
-	-	Francis Howell, -	Settlement right, -	River Dardenne, -	(640)	700	St. Charles.
-	-	Angus Gillis, -	Settlement right, -	River Peruque, -	(640)	300	St. Charles.
-	-	William Craig, -	Settlement right, -	River Cuivre, -	(640)	200	St. Charles.
"	-	Samuel Bay, -	Settlement right, -	River Merrimack, -	(640)	250	St. Louis.
-	-	William Crow, -	Settlement right, -	Dardenne, -	(640)	300	St. Charles.
-	-	John Wilson, -	Settlement right, -	Little Rock creek, -	-	350 (622)	St. Louis.
-	-	Jeduthan Kendall, -	Settlement right, -	Grand Glaize, -	-	450 (715)	St. Louis.
-	-	Thomas L. Bevis, -	Settlement right, -	River Joachim, -	-	100 (598)	St. Louis.
-	-	William Null, Jun. -	Settlement right, -	River Joachim, -	-	300 (450)	St. Louis.
-	-	John Connor, -	Settlement right, -	River Joachim, -	(640)	550	St. Louis.
-	-	Legal reps. of Peter Heldibrand, -	Ten y'rs possession,	Negro fork of Merrimack, -	-	800	St. Louis.
-	-	Thomas Allen, -	Settlement right, -	- -	(640)	250	St. Genevieve.
-	-	Marie Louisa Papin, -	Ten y'rs possession,	Town of St. Louis, -	-	120 by 150 ft.	St. Louis.

COMMISSIONERS' CERTIFICATES—Continued.

nder whom land was med.	In whose favor issued.	Nature of the claim.	Water course.	Number of acres.	Number of arpents.	District.
-	Leonard Farrow, - -	Settlement right, -	River Dubois, -	(640)	300	St. Louis.
- -	Charles Gratiot, - -	Concession, -	Merrimack, -	-	320	St. Louis.
	Charles Gratiot, - -	Concession, -	Merrimack, -	-	400	St. Louis.
	Legal reps. of widow Camp, -	Ten y'rs possession,	Cul de Sac, -	-	200	St. Louis.
e,	Julian Chouquette, -	Ten y'rs possession,	Mississippi, -	-	640	St. Louis.
	Louis Courtois, -	Ten y'rs possession,	Village Carondelet,	-	150 by 300 ft.	St. Louis.
1,	Heirs and reps. of Joseph Loisel, -	Concession, -	Waters of Mississippi, -	-	160	St. Genevieve.
	Gabriel Cobb, - -	Settlement right, -	Sandy creek, -	(640)	500	St. Louis.
e,	Heirs and reps. of Isaac Helterbrand,	Settlement right, -	Negro fork of Merrimack, -	(640)	100	St. Louis.
	William Bell, -	Concession, -	Horse creek, -	-	800	St. Louis,
e,	Thomas Applegate, -	Settlement right, -	Joachim, -	(640)	100	St. Louis.
,,	Elizabeth Carns, -	Settlement right, -	Bois Brule, -	(640)	500	St. Genevieve.
	Joshua Massey, -	Settlement right, -	Marais-des Liards, -	(640)	450	St. Louis.
e,	Julian Chouquette, -	Concession, -	Carondelet, -	-	150 ft. square.	
,	Julian Chouquette, -	Concession, -	Carondelet, -	-	150 by 150 ft.	St. Louis.
	Charles Gratiot, -	Ten y'rs possession,	Town of St. Louis, -	-	120 by 150 ft.	St. Louis.
e,	Charles Gratiot, -	Ten y'rs possession,	Town of St. Louis, -	-	30 by 130 ft.	St. Louis.
	Julian Chouquette, -	Concession, -	Carondelet, -	-	150 ft. square.	St. Louis.
,	Legal reps. of Gabriel Dodie, Sen. -	Ten y'rs possession,	Prairie de Denoyer, -	-	80	St. Louis.
	John B. C. Lucas, -	Ten y'rs possession,	Town St. Louis, -	-	120 by 150 ft.	St. Louis.
	William Miller, -	Settlement right, -	Grand Glaize, -	-	350	St. Louis.
	Sarah Pruitt, -	Settlement right, -	Negro fork of Merrimack, -	(640)	400	St. Louis.
	James Davis, -	Settlement right, -	Negro fork of Merrimack, -	-	100 (600)	St. Louis.
	Clement B. Penrose, -	Ten y'rs possession,	Creve Cœur, -	-	400	St. Louis.
	James Gray, -	Settlement right,	Joachim, -	(640)	350	St. Louis.
	Pelagie Labbadie, -	Ten y'rs possession,	Missouri, -	-	803	St. Louis.
	Antoine Roy, -	Ten y'rs possession,	Prairie Bœuf Blanc, -	-	162 48 per.	St. Louis.
	Antoine Roy, -	Ten y'rs possession,	Town St. Louis, -	-	120 by 150 ft.	St. Louis.
l,	Antoine Roy, -	Ten y'rs possession,	Town St. Louis, -	-	120 by 150 ft.	St. Louis.
	Legal reps. of Matrom Lewis, -	Settlement right, -	River Peruque, -	-	250 (650)	St. Charles.
e,	François Dupuis, -	Ten y'rs possession,	Town St. Louis, -	-	120 by 150 ft.	St. Louis.
	Milciah Baldridge, -	Settlement right, -	Waters of river Dardenne, -	(640)	100	St. Charles.
	Michael Null, -	Settlement right, -	Sandy creek, -	(640)	400	St. Louis.
	Clement B. Penrose, -	Ten y'rs possession,	Town St. Louis, -	-	120 by 150 ft.	St. Louis.
	Guy Seely, -	Settlement right, -	Cold Water, -	(640)	200	St. Louis.
	Legal reps. of Benjamin Jones, -	Settlement right, -	River Cuivre, -	(640)	250	St. Charles.
	Thomas Henry, -	Settlement right, -	Grand Glaize, -	(640)	250	St. Louis.
	Legal reps. of George Percely,	Settlement right, -	Femme Osage, -	(640)	250	St. Charles.
	John Coons, -	Settlement right, -	Town St. Louis, -	-	120 by 300 ft.	St. Louis.
champ, -	James Richardson, -	Concession, -		-	400	St. Louis.
uette, -	Antoine Soulard, -	Concession, -	St. Louis Prairie, -	-	40	St. Louis.
	Antoine Soulard, -	Concession, -	Prairie St. Louis, -	-	40	St. Louis.
	Auguste Chouteau, -	Concession, -	Prairie St. Louis, -	-	40	St. Louis.
	Auguste Chouteau, -	Concession, -	Prairie St. Louis, -	-	40	St. Louis.
-	Phillip Shults, -	Ten y'rs possession,	Fork of Merrimack, -	-	750	St. Louis.

...whom land was	In whose favor issued.	Nature of the claim.	Water course.	Number of acres.	Number of arpents.	District.
-	John B. C. Lucas,	Concession,	Town St. Louis,	120 by	300 feet,	St. Louis.
-	John B. C. Lucas,	Concession,	Prairie St. Louis,	-	40	St. Louis.
-	Daniel Kichelie,	Settlement right,	River Peruque,	(640)	350	St. Charles.
-	Christian Wolf,	Settlement right,	Dardenne,	(640)	500	St. Charles.
-	Peter Rock,	Settlement right,	Missouri,	(640)	450	St. Louis.
-	Richard Taylor,	Settlement right,	Fork of river Cuivre,	(640)	150	St. Charles,
-	Legal representatives of L. Haff,	Concession,	Mississippi,	-	400	St. Louis.
-	Richard Jones Waters,	Settlement right,	Lake Ricardo,	-	200	New Madrid.
-	Legal representatives of S. Masters,	Settlement right,	-	-	300	New Madrid.
-	Joseph Westbrook,	Settlement right,	Bayou St. John,	(640)	200	New Madrid.
ias Hibernois,	Antony Mesloches, alias Hibernois,	Settlement right,	Little Prairie,	-	200	New Madrid.
-	Simon Duval,	Settlement right,	Saline,	(640)	350	St. Genevieve.
-	William Bellew,	Settlement right,	Wildhorse creek,	(640)	650	St. Louis.
-	Legal representatives of J. Samuels,	Concession,	-	-	800	St. Genevieve.
-	Lewis Layton,	Settlement right,	-	-	300	Cape Girardeau.
-	John Colgin,	Concession,	-	-	400	St. Louis.
-	Alexander Patterson,	Settlement right,	Mississippi,	(640)	400	St. Genevieve.
-	John Burgett,	Concession,	River St. Laurent,	-	600	St. Genevieve.
o woman,	John Mullanphy,	Concession,	Fields of St. Louis,	-	40	St. Louis.
-	John Pruitt,	Settlement right,	Negro fork of Merrimack,	(640)	250	St. Louis.
-	Louis Coyteux,	Concession,	Bois Bruile,	-	500	St. Genevieve.
-	John Baptiste Pratte,	10 years possession,	-	-	1	St. Genevieve.
-	Bernard Smith,	Settlement right,	Cape Cinq Hommes,	(640)	300	St. Genevieve.
-	Legal representatives of J. Chancelier,	10 years possession,	Fields of St. Louis,	-	40	St. Louis.
..	James Morrison,	Settlement right,	River Cuivre,	(640)	200	St. Charles.
-	James Davis,	Settlement right,	Femme Osage,	(640)	250	St. Charles.
-	John Loyed,	Settlement right,	Tywappety,	(640)	350	New Madrid.
-	Joshua Sexton,	Settlement right,	Tywappety,	-	200	New Madrid.
-	John Shorter,	Settlement right,	Cypress swamp,	(640)	250	New Madrid.
-	Thomas Gibson,	Settlement right,	Missouri,	(640)	350	St. Louis.
-	Charles Phillips,	Settlement right,	Missouri,	(640)	350	St. Louis.
-	William Fullarton,	Settlement right,	Pointe Labbadie,	(640)	350	St. Louis.
-	Smith Collum,	Settlement right,	River Dubois,	-	100 (600)	St. Louis.
-	George Cavender,	Settlement right,	-	(640)	250	Cape Girardeau.
-	Legal representatives of M. Reybold,	Settlement right,	Waters of Dardenne,	(640)	500	St. Charles.
Veriat,	Rodolph, alias Rodey Veriat,	Settlement right,	Waters of river St. Francis,	(640)	340	St. Genevieve.
-	Representatives of Antoine Morin,	10 years possession,	Town of St. Louis,	60 by	150 feet,	St. Louis.
-	Louis Lebeaume,	Concession,	Mississippi,	-	356	St. Louis.
-	Joseph Brazeau,	Concession,	Mississippi,	-	4	St. Louis.
-	Pierre Troge,	10 years possession,	-	-	18	St. Genevieve.
-	Jacob Sweenay,	Concession,	Merrimack,	-	400	St. Louis.
-	John Mullanphy,	10 years possession,	Heights of St. Louis,	-	60 feet square,	St. Louis.
-	Guillaume Hebert, dit Lecompte,	10 years possession,	Town of St. Louis,	-	40 feet square,	St. Louis.
-	Guillaume Hebert, dit Lecompte,	10 years possession,	Town of St. Louis,	-	20 feet square,	St. Louis.
-	Guillaume Hebert, dit Lecompte,	10 years possession,	Town of St. Louis,	-	60 feet square,	St. Louis.

COMMISSIONERS' CERTIFICATES—Continued.

...der whom land was ...ned.	In whose favor issued.	Nature of the claim.	Water course.	Number of acres.	Number of arpents.	District.
...phin, -	Guillaume Hebert, dit Lecompte, -	Concession, -	Village of Carondelet, -	150 by	300 feet,	St. Louis.
-	James Beatty, -	Settlement right, -	Bet. Dardenne & Femme Osage,	(640)	100	St. Charles.
...te, -	Nicholas Lacompte, -	Concession, -	River Fifi, -	-	400	St. Louis.
-	Legal representatives of J. Schelen,	Concession, -	North of Merrimack, -	-	400	St. Louis.
-	Gabriel Nicolle, -	Concession, -	Big river, -	-	400	St. Genevieve.
-	Baptiste Deguire, -	Concession, -	Big river, -	-	400	St. Genevieve.
...e, -	Antoine Lachance, -	Concession, -	Big river, -	-	400	St. Genevieve.
-	Peter Veriat, -	Concession, -	Big river, -	-	400	St. Genevieve.
-	Paul Deguire, -	Concession, -	Big river, -	-	400	St. Genevieve.
...s,	Jerome Matis, -	Concession, -	Big river, -	-	400	St. Genevieve.
...ce,	Gabriel Lachance, -	Concession, -	Big river, -	-	400	St. Genevieve.
-	François Lachance, -	Concession, -	Big river, -	-	400	St. Genevieve.
-	Andrew Deguire, -	Concession, -	Big river, -	-	400	St. Genevieve.
-	Michel Lachance, -	Concession, -	Big river, -	-	400	St. Genevieve.
-	Pierre Chevalier, -	Concession, -	Big river, -	-	400	St. Genevieve.
...ce,	Nicholas Lachance, -	Concession, -	Big river, -	-	400	St. Genevieve.
-	Joseph Lachance, -	Concession, -	Big river, -	-	400	St. Genevieve.
-	Josiah Millard, -	Settlement right, -	Bois Bruile, -	-	200 (300)	St. Genevieve.
-	John May, -	Settlement right, -	White Waters, -	-	300	Cape Girardeau.
...n, Jun.	John May, -	Settlement right, -	White Waters, -	-	250	Cape Girardeau.
-	James Mackay, -	Concession, -	Bonhomme, -	-	600	St. Louis.
...a,	James Brady, -	Settlement right, -	Mississippi, -	-	330	Cape Girardeau.
...n,	James B. Hart, -	Settlement right, -	Cold Water, -	(640)	350	St. Louis.
...n, Jun.	Andrew Robertson, Jun. -	Settlement right, -	Waters of lake St. Marie, -	(640)	300	New Madrid.
-	Daniel Mullens, -	Settlement right, -	Seven miles S.W. of Tywappety	(640)	300	Cape Girardeau.
-	E. Coen, or his legal representatives,	Settlement right, -	Wolf fork of river St. Francis,	(640)	450	St. Genevieve.
-	James Williams, -	10 years possession, -	Village of New Madrid, -	-	½	New Madrid.
-	James Williams, -	10 years possession,	Village of New Madrid, -	5	-	New Madrid.
-	James Dowty, -	Settlement right, -	Waters of Hubble's creek, -	-	300	Cape Girardeau.
-	Robert Lane, -	Settlement right, -	On the Mississippi, -	(640)	300	Cape Girardeau.
-	John Randall, -	Concession, -	Randall's creek, -	-	300	Cape Girardeau.
-	John Welborn, -	Settlement right, -	Mississippi, -	(640)	200	Cape Girardeau.
-	John Ferrell, -	Settlement right, -	Waters of Hubble's creek, -	-	500	Cape Girardeau.
...denburg,	Legal rep's of Benj. L. Vandenburg,	Settlement right, -	Waters of Big Lake, -	-	400	New Madrid.
...ay, -	Jeremiah Connoway, -	Settlement right, -	South fork of river Pemiscon, -	-	200.	New Madrid.
...ay, -	William Connoway, -	Settlement right, -	River Pemiscon, -	-	250	New Madrid.
-	George Hacker, -	Settlement right, -	Brushy pond, -	(640)	200	New Madrid.
-	James Simpson, -	Settlement right, -	Mississippi, -	-	200	New Madrid.
-	James Gilbreath, -	Settlement right, -	Mississippi, -	-	250	New Madrid.
-	James Currin, -	Settlement right, -	Mississippi, -	(640)	400	New Madrid.
-	Thomas Clark,	Settlement right, -	Tywappety, -	-	350 (450)	New Madrid.
-	James Smith, -	Concession, -	Big Prairie, -	-	300	New Madrid.
-	Moses Hurly, -	Settlement right, -	Big Prairie, -	-	358	New Madrid.
-	Mary Smith, -	Settlement right, -	Tywappety, -	(640)	250	New Madrid.
...xin, -	John Ordway,	Settlement right, -	Mississippi, -	-	350 (722)	New Madrid.

whom land was		In whose favor issued.			Nature of the claim.	Water course.	Number of acres.	Number of arpents.	Districts.
-	-	Thomas Brown,	-	-	Settlement right, -	Seven and a half miles westwardly of Little Prairie, -	(640)	200	New Madrid.
-	-	John Taylor,	-	-	Settlement right, -	River St. Francis, -	(640)	300	New Madrid.
-	-	Thomas Woolsey,	-	-	Settlement right, -	Tywappety, -	(640)	450	New Madrid.
en.	-	Edward Matthews, Sen.	-	-	Settlement right, -	Tywappety, -	(640)	500	New Madrid.
-	-	Conrad Wheat, Jun.	-	-	Settlement right, -	Lake St. Marie, -	-	450	New Madrid.
-	-	James Y. O'Carrell,	-	-	Settlement right, -	Mississippi, -	(640)	350	New Madrid.
-	-	James Kirkendall,	-	-	Settlement right, -	Mississippi, -	(640)	350	New Madrid.
-	-	Joseph Edwards,	-	-	Settlement right, -	Mississippi, -	(640)	100	New Madrid.
-	-	Joseph Michel,	-	-	Settlement right, -	Big lake, -	-	180	New Madrid.
-	-	Joseph Michel,	-	-	Settlement right, -	Bayou Carondelet, -	-	200	New Madrid.
-	-	Joseph Michel,	-	-	Settlement right, -	Big lake, -	-	200	New Madrid.
-	-	Joseph Michel,	-	-	Settlement right, -	Big lake, -	-	400	New Madrid.
-	-	Joseph Michel,	-	-	Settlement right, -	Big lake, -	-	250	New Madrid.
-	-	John Dorlac,	-	-	Settlement right, -	Big lake, -	-	80	New Madrid.
-	-	Louis Denoyon,	-	-	Settlement right, -	Big lake, -	-	200	New Madrid.
-	-	Louis St. Aubin, Jun.	-	-	Settlement right, -	Big lake, Little Prairie, -	-	200	New Madrid.
-	-	Joseph Payne, Sen.	-	-	Settlement right, -	Near the Mississippi, -	-	300	New Madrid.
-	-	Francis Foisey,	-	-	Settlement right, -	Lake Lesieur, -	(640)	100	New Madrid.
-	-	Dennis Lavertue,	-	-	Settlement right, -	Lake Lesieur, -	(640)	100	New Madrid.
-	-	John Baptiste Dupuis,	-	-	Settlement right, -	Lake Lesieur, -	(640)	100	New Madrid.
-	-	Henry Godair,	-	-	Settlement right, -	Portage of St. Francis, -	(640)	300	New Madrid.
-	-	Peter Grimard,	-	-	Settlement right, -	Big lake, -	(640)	450	New Madrid.
-	-	John Baptiste Olive,	-	-	Settlement right, -	Lake Isidore, -	-	300	New Madrid.
-	-	William Dapron,	-	-	Settlement right, -	Portage of St. Francis, -	(640)	250	New Madrid.
-	-	Thomas Welborn,	-	-	Settlement right, -	Mississippi, -	(640)	500	Cape Girardeau.
-	-	Jesse Baker,	-	-	Settlement right, -	River Pemiscon, -	-	400	New Madrid.
-	-	Peter Noblesse,	-	-	Settlement right, -	Fish lake, -	(640)	400	New Madrid.
-	-	Nicholas Savage,	-	-	Settlement right, -	On the Mississippi, a few miles below the mouth of Ohio, -	-	100 (300)	New Madrid.
-	-	William Brown,	-	-	Settlement right, -	Near Little Prairie, -	(640)	100	New Madrid.
-	-	Noel Burke,	-	-	Settlement right, -	Waters of river St. Francis, -	(640)	100	New Madrid.
-	-	Charles Charters,	-	-	Settlement right, -	Big lake, -	(640)	200	New Madrid.
-	-	John Cummings,	-	-	Settlement right, -	River Pemiscon, -	(640)	100	New Madrid.
-	-	James Martin,	-	-	Settlement right, -	Waters of river St. Francis, -	(640)	100	New Madrid.
-	-	Joseph Ferland,	-	-	Settlement right, -	Gayoso swamp, -	(640)	100	New Madrid.
-	-	John Johnson,	-	-	Settlement right, -	Tywappety, -	-	250	New Madrid.
-	-	Peter Perron,	-	-	Settlement right, -	Lake Carondelet, -	-	200	New Madrid.
-	-	John Baptiste Perron,	-	-	Settlement right, -	Lake Carondelet, -	-	200	New Madrid.
lon,	-	John Baptiste Chandillon,	-	-	Settlement right, -	River St. Francis, -	(640)	100	New Madrid.
-	-	Helen Cummings,	-	-	Settlement right, -	River St. Francis, -	(640)	400	New Madrid.
-	-	Joseph Dumay,	-	-	Settlement right, -	Near river St. Francis, -	(640)	100	New Madrid.
-	-	Stephen Boyeau,	-	-	Settlement right, -	On river St. Francis, -	(640)	470	New Madrid.
-	-	Francis Langlois, Sen.	-	-	Settlement right, -	Bayou St. John, -	-	200	New Madrid.
-	-	Daniel Barton,	-	-	Settlement right, -	Marais des Pechers, -	-	350	New Madrid.

COMMISSIONERS' CERTIFICATES—Continued.

under whom land was claimed.	In whose favor issued.	Nature of the claim.	Water course.	Number of acres.	Number of arpents.	District.
n, - -	Samuel Harrison, - -	Settlement right, -	Big lake, - -	(640)	220	New Madrid.
- -	Francis Gervais, - -	Settlement right, -	Waters of Red Bank bayou, "	(640)	100	New Madrid.
- -	Hezekiah Day, - "	Settlement right, -	- - -	(640)	100	New Madrid.
- -	George Lail, - -	Settlement right, -	Lake Lesieur, - -	(640)	200	New Madrid.
atrimoule, -	John Baptiste Latrimoule, -	Settlement right, -	Mississippi, - "	(640)	250	New Madrid.
as, -	Stephen Nicholas, - -	Settlement right, -	Waters of Mississippi, -	(640)	100	New Madrid.
- -	Hardy Rawls, - -	Settlement right, -	Six miles northwest of New Madrid, - -	-	500	New Madrid.
r, -	Amos Rawles, - -	Settlement right, -	Cypress swamp & bayou St.John	-	200	New Madrid.
- -	Edward Stocker, - -	Settlement right, -	Bayou des Bœufs, - -	(640)	530	New Madrid.
- -	James Trotter, - -	Settlement right, -	Bayou St. Thomas, -	-	200	New Madrid.
educ, " -	Mary Phillipe Leduc, - -	Concession, -	Village of New Madrid, -	-	180 ft. square,	New Madrid.
- -	Ceril Leduc, - -	Concession, -	Village of New Madrid, -	-	180 ft. square,	New Madrid.
- -	Joseph Leduc, - -	Concession, -	Village of New Madrid, -	-	180 ft. square,	New Madrid.
t, - -	Nicholas Hubert, - -	Concession, -	Village of New Madrid, -	-	180 ft. square,	New Madrid.
as, -	Joseph Michel, - -	Settlement right, -	Lake St. Mary, - -	-	200	New Madrid.
, -	Joseph Michel, - -	Settlement right, -	Lake St. Mary, - -	-	250	New Madrid.
- -	Ferman Lesieur, - -	Settlement right, -	Island front of Little Prairie,	(640)	100	New Madrid.
- -	David Gray, - -	Settlement right, -	Highest waters of lake St.Mary,	-	225	New Madrid.
, - -	Richard Jones, - -	Settlement right, -	Marais des Pechers, -	-	400	New Madrid.
- -	Baptiste Lafleur, - -	Settlement right, -	Bayou St. John, - -	(640)	100	New Madrid.
- -	Jacob Devore, - -	Settlement right, -	Bayou St. Jacob, & Mississippi,	(640)	100	New Madrid.
son, Jun. -	Edward Robertson, Jun. -	Settlement right, -	Head of bayou St. John, -	(640)	300	New Madrid.
s, - -	Benjamin Myers, - "	Settlement right, -	Five miles northwest of village of New Madrid, -	(640)	200	New Madrid.
- -	Richard Jones Waters, - -	Concession, -	Lake St. Isidore, - -	-	160	New Madrid.
- -	Daniel Bankson, - -	Settlement right, -	Bayou St. Thomas, -	-	300	New Madrid.
- -	The legal representatives of J. Butler,	Settlement right, -	Cypress swamp, -	-	200	New Madrid.
son, - -	William Robertson, - -	Settlement right, -	Big Prairie, - -	(640)	100	New Madrid.

e Board of Commissioners for ascertaining and adjusting the titles and claims to land in the Territory of Louisiana, do certify that the foregoing list of certificates, ree to number one thousand one hundred and four, inclusive, issued by the Board during the months of April, May, and June, one thousand eight hundred and f registry kept by me as clerk of said Board.

Given under my hand at St. Louis, this 27th June, 1811.

THOMAS F. RIDDICK.

hom land was		In whose favor issued.	Nature of the claim.	Water course.	Number of acres.	Number of arpents.	District.
-	-	Richard Jones Waters, - -	Order of survey,	Lake St. Anne, - -	-	300	New Madrid.
-	-	Richard Jones Waters, -	Settlement right,	Lake St. Anne, -	-	350	New Madrid.
-	-	Charles Crabbin, or his legal repre's,	Order of survey,	Mississippi, - -	-	200	New Madrid.
-	-	Robert Quimby, - -	Settlement right, }	Foot of the hills, - -	(640)	250	New Madrid.
-	-	James Farris, - -	Settlement right,	Lake St. Mary, -	-	232	New Madrid.
-	-	Thomas W. Caulk, - -	Concession, -	Lake St. Mary, -	..	400	New Madrid.
?	-	David D. Wentzell, -	Settlement right,	Waters of bayou St. John, -	-	200	New Madrid.
s,	-	Hyacinth Bertheaume, -	Settlement right,	River St. Francis, -	(640)	300	New Madrid.
-	-	John Baptiste Langlois, -	Settlement right,	Bayou St. John, -	-	200	New Madrid.
-	-	Ric'd Jones Waters, or his legal reps.	Concession, -	Bayou St. Thomas, -	-	90	New Madrid.
-	-	Baptiste Fournier,	Settlement right,	Village of Little Prairie, -	-	2	New Madrid.
-	-	J. Smith, - -	Settlement right,	Village of Little Prairie, -	-	2	New Madrid.
-	-	John Derlan, - -	Settlement right,	Village of Little Prairie, -	-	2	New Madrid.
-	-	Collett Carron, - -	Settlement right,	Village of Little Prairie, -	-	2	New Madrid.
-	-	Alexander Frazer, - -	Settlement right,	Village of Little Prairie, -	-	2	New Madrid.
-	-	Pierre A. Laforge, - -	Concession, -	Lake St. Mary, -	-	400	New Madrid.
?	-	Robert McCoy, - -	Concession, -	Lake St. Isidore, -	-	240	New Madrid.
-	-	Robert McCoy, - -	Concession, -	Lake St. Isidore, -	-	240	New Madrid.
-	-	Robert McCoy, - -	Concession, -	Lake St. Isidore, -	-	40	New Madrid.
-	-	James Ashworth, -	Order of survey,	Road of Big Portage, -	-	200	New Madrid.
-	-	Lewis Worth, - -	Settlement right,	Tywappety, - -	-	250 (300)	Cape Girardeau.
-	-	John Robertson, Jun. -	Settlement right,	Big Prairie, -	(640)	200	New Madrid.
-	-	Joseph Hunot, Jun. or his legal reps.	Order of survey,	Big Prairie, -	-	200	New Madrid.
-	-	Francis Hudson, or his legal repre's,	Order of survey,	Near Lake St. Mary, -	-	200	New Madrid.
-	-	Peter Deroche, or his legal repr'ves,	Concession, -	Lake St. Isidore, -	-	40	New Madrid.
-	-	Philip Lady, - -	Settlement right,	Lake St. Francis, -	-	200	New Madrid.
-	-	George N. Ragin, - -	Order of survey,	Lake St. Mary, -	-	800	New Madrid.
-	-	Robert Rogers, - -	Settlement right,	Lake St. Mary, -	-	240	New Madrid.
-	-	Richard Jones Waters, -	Settlement right,	Waters of bayou St. John, -	-	200	New Madrid.
-	-	Richard Jones Waters, -	Settlement right,	Waters of bayou St. John, -	-	400	New Madrid.
-	-	Richard Jones Waters, -	Settlement right,	Lake Ricardo, -	-	300	New Madrid.
-	-	Richard Jones Waters, -	Settlement right,	Lake Ricardo, -	-	200	New Madrid.
-	-	Thomas Powers, - -	Settlement right,	Big bayou St. John, -	-	200	New Madrid.
-	-	Richard Jones Waters, -	Settlement right,	Lake Ricardo, -	-	200	New Madrid.
-	-	Benjamin Fooy, - -	Settlement right,	Mississippi, -	-	320	Arkansas.
-	-	John Henry Fooy, - -	Settlement right,	Mississippi, -	-	320	Arkansas.
-	-	Nathaniel Spillman, -	Settlement right,	Mississippi, -	-	640	Arkansas.
-	-	William Bassett, Sen. -	Settlement right,	Mississippi, -	-	288	Arkansas.
-	-	William Riggs, - -	Settlement right,	Mississippi, -	-	640	Arkansas.
-	-	Joseph Greenwalt, -	Settlement right,	Back of a lake adjoining Elisha Winters.	-	450	Arkansas.
-	-	Joseph Stillwell, - -	Concession, -	St. Francis, -	..	600	Arkansas.
-	-	William Patterson, -	Settlement right,	Mississippi, -	-	240	Arkansas.
-	-	Chas. Refield, and the heirs of Wolf,	Concession, -	Bayou near river Arkansas,	-	320	Arkansas.
-	-	Joseph Bougy, Sen. -	Ten years poss'n,	Arkansas, -	-	320	Arkansas.

COMMISSIONERS' CERTIFICATES—Continued.

nder whom land was imed.			In whose favor issued.			Nature of the claim.	Water course.	Number of acres.	Number of arpents.	District.
,	-	-	Michel Petersell,	-	-	Settlement right,	Arkansas, - -	-	.34 40 p.	Arkansas.
	-	-	Samuel Treat,	-	-	Settlement right,	Two miles northwest of Arkansas village.	-	416	Arkansas.
	-	-	Peter Lefevre,	-	-	Settlement right,	Adjoining Jacob Bright and others.	-	736	Arkansas.
	-	-	John Bartran,		-	Ten years poss'n,	On a bayou near the lands of Devaugine.	-	132	Arkansas.
	-	-	Peter Lefevre,	-	-	Ten years poss'n,	Bayou ——, - -	-	325	Arkansas.
	-	..	Athanas Racine,	-	-	Settlement right,	Prairie six miles from Arkansas village.	-	181	Arkansas.
	-	-	Charles Refield,	-	-	Settlement right,	Two miles from Arkansas vil.	-	240	Arkansas.
	-	-	Jacob Bright,	-	-	Concession, -	Near the village of Arkansas,	-	20	Arkansas.
	-	-	John Lavergnes,		-	Concession, -	One mile north of Arkansas vil.	-	231	Arkansas.
	-	-	Legal represent's of Peter Jordalles,			Concession, -	Near the village of Arkansas,	-	240	Arkansas.
	-	-	Augustin John Friend, or his legal reps.			Ten years poss'n,	Belle Point, White river, -	-	800	Arkansas.
nte,	-	-	Joseph Michel,	-	-	Ten years poss'n,	White river, - -	-	400	Arkansas.
	-	-	Joseph Michel,	-	-	Ten years poss'n,	River Caches, - -	-	400	Arkansas.
	-	-	Francis Michel, use of Joseph Michel,			Concession, -	Big Lake, - -	-	320	Arkansas.
eruisseaux,	-	-	John Fayac,		-	Ten years poss'n,	Fork of White river, -	-	750	Arkansas.
	-	-	Jean Baptiste Deruisseaux,		-	Ten years poss'n,	Arkansas river, - -	-	268	Arkansas.
gton,	-	-	Jacob Bright,		-	Settlement right,	Adjoin'g claim of Wm. Winters,	-	240	Arkansas.
	-	-	Robert Masters,		-	Settlement right,	Tywappety, - -	-	200	New Madrid.
t,	-	-	Benjamin Dement,	-	-	Settlement right,	Bayou St. Anthony, -	2	240	New Madrid.
	-	-	Richard Jones Waters,	-	-	Settlement right,	Bayou St. John, -	-	200	New Madrid.
	-	-	Richard Jones Waters,	-	-	Settlement right,	Near bayou St. John,	-	250	New Madrid.
	-	-	Richard Jones Waters,	-	-	Settlement right,	Bayou St. John, -	-	300	New Madrid.
	-	-	Richard Jones Waters,	-	-	Order of survey,	Bayou St. John, -	-	110	New Madrid.
	-	-	Richard Jones Waters,	-	-	Order of survey,	Bayou St. John, -	-	250	New Madrid.
	-	-	Richard Jones Waters,	-	-	Settlement right,	Bayou St. John, -	-	200	New Madrid.
	-	-	Richard Jones Waters,	-	-	Settlement right,	Bayou St. John, -	-	200	New Madrid.
	-	-	Michael Ameroux,	-	-	Order of survey,	Lake St. Anne, -	-	240	New Madrid.
Sen.	-	-	Francis Hudson, Sen.	-	-	Settlement right,	Lake St. Isidore, -	(640)	300	New Madrid.
	-	-	Richard Jones Waters,	-	-	Settlement right,	Bayou St. John, -	-	200	New Madrid.
,	-	..	Richard Jones Waters,	-	-	Order of survey,	Bayou St. Thomas, -	-	250	New Madrid.
	-	-	Joseph Brant,	-	-	Settlement right,	Bayou St. Anthony,	-	200	New Madrid.
	-	-	Isaac Thompson,	-	-	Concession, -	Lake St. Mary, -	-	320	New Madrid.
	-	-	Joseph Michel,	-	-	Ten years poss'n,	Lake St. Anne, -	-	170	New Madrid.

Board of Commissioners for ascertaining and adjusting the titles and claims to land in the Territory of Louisiana, do certify that the foregoing list of commissioners' the month of July last, from number one thousand one hundred and five to number one thousand one hundred and eighty two, inclusive, is truly copied from the said Board.

Given under my hand at St. Louis, this 22d of August, 1811. THOS. F. RIDDICK.

of the Treasury.

nths of August, September, October, November, and December, 1811, and January, 1812, by the Board of Commissioners for ascertaining and adjusting titles and claims to lands in the Territory of Louisiana.

hom land was	In whose favor issued.	Nature of the claim.	Water course.	Number of acres.	Number of arpents.	District.
-	Charles Matthews, - -	Settlement right, -	Bayou Bœuf, -	-	200	New Madrid.
-	William McKim, - -	Settlement right, -	Near village of New Madrid,	-	300	New Madrid.
-	John Baker, Sen. - -	Settlement right, -	River Pemiscon, -	-	200	New Madrid.
-	Edward Robertson, - -	Settlement right, -	Lake St. Mary, -	-	200	New Madrid.
-	Jos. Vandenbenden and Wm. Gibson,	Settlement right, -	Lake St. Mary, -	-	350	New Madrid.
-	Edward Hempstead, - -	Concession,	Town of St. Louis, -	-	120 by 150 ft.	St. Louis.
-	Zachariah Tharp, - -	Order of survey, -	Big Prairie, -	-	400	New Madrid.
-	Joseph Matthews, - -	Settlement right, -	Tywappety, -	-	200	New Madrid.
2, -	Nicholas Tanis, or his legal repre's,	Concession, . -	Village of St. Genevieve,	-	4	St. Genevieve.
Louis Bolduc	John Baptiste Vallé and Louis Bolduc	Ten years possession	Marais Potchecoma, -	-	1,000	St. Genevieve.
-	James Thompson, Jun. - -	Settlement right, -	On the waters of Saline, -	(640)	250	St. Genevieve.
-	James Farrell, or his legal represen's,	Concession, -	Waters of Saline, -	-	400	St. Genevieve.
es Liards, -	Louis Brazeau, - -	Ten years possession	Town of St. Louis, -	-	47½ by 150 ft.	St. Louis.
-	Inhabitants of Marais des Liards, -	Concession, -	Marais des Liards, -	-	1,000	St. Louis.
-	John Boly, - -	Ten years possession	River Merrimack, - -	-	320	St. Louis.
-	Jacques Clamorgan, use of Edward Hempstead.	Concession, -	River Missouri, -	-	1,066	St. Charles.
-	Richard Masters, - -	Settlement right, -	Lake St. Mary, -	-	300	New Madrid.
-	Robert Crump, - -	Settlement right, -	- -	(640)	450	Cape Girardeau.
-	John F. Perey, - -	Concession, -	River des Peres, -	-	1,600	St. Louis.
ge of St. Fer-	Inhabitants of the village of St. Ferdinand.	Concession, -	River St. Ferdinand, -	-	5,206¼ p.	St. Louis.
es Liards, -	Inhabitants of the Marais des Liards, or their legal representatives.	Concession, -	Near village of Marais des Liards.	-	1,000	St. Louis.
-	Guillaume Hebert, dit Lecompte, -	Ten years possession	Town of St. Louis, -	-	120 by 150 ft.	St. Louis.
-	Antoine Raynal, - -	Ten years possession	Adjoining town of St. Louis, -	-	80 feet square,	St. Louis.
-	Antoine Raynal, - -	Concession, -	Town of St. Charles, -	-	120 by 150 ft.	St. Charles.
-	Antoine Raynal, - -	Ten years possession	Town of St. Charles, -	-	120 by 150 ft.	St. Charles.
-	Antoine Raynal, - -	Ten years possession	Town of St. Charles, -	-	120 by 150 ft.	St. Charles.
-	Joseph Tibeau, - -	Ten years possession	Town of St. Charles, -	-	120 by 300 ft.	St. Charles.
-	Charles Hogan, - -	Settlement right, -	Fish Lake Tywappety, -	(640)	250	Cape Girardeau.
-	William Hacker, - -	Settlement right, -	Tywappety, -	(460)	300	Cape Girardeau.
-	Representatives of Francis Vallé, -	Ten years possession	Waters of Mississippi, -	-	25 feet square,	St. Genevieve.
-	Antoine Vincent Bouis, -	Ten years possession	Town of St. Louis, -	-	120 by 150 ft.	St. Louis.
-	Pascal Detchemendy, - -	Ten years possession	River aux Vases, -	-	750	St. Genevieve.
-	Pelagie Labbadie, - -	Ten years possession	Town of St. Louis, -	-	4 by 58 feet,	St. Louis.
-	Pelagie Labbadie, - -	Ten years possession	Town of St. Louis, -	-	1 by 150 feet,	St. Louis.
-	Benito Vasquez, use of Alex. McNair,	Ten years possession	Town of St. Louis, -	-	4 by 92 feet,	St. Louis.
-	Benito Vasquez, use of Alex. McNair,	Ten years possession	Town of St. Louis, -	-	150 by 150 ft.	St. Louis.
-	Thomas F. Riddick, - -	Settlement right, -	River Plattin, -	-	800	St. Louis.
-	François Soucier, - -	Letter of office, or order of survey.	Portage des Sioux, -	-	200	St. Charles.
-	Michael Lesage, - -	Letter of office, or order of survey.	Portage des Sioux, -	-	80	St. Charles.

COMMISSIONERS' CERTIFICATES—Continued.

land was	In whose favor issued.	Nature of the claim.	Water course.	Number of acres.	Number of arpents.	District.
-	Francis Lesieur,	Letter of office, or order of survey.	Portage des Sioux, -	..	80	St. Charles.
-	Louis Goe, fils,	Letter of office, or order of survey.	Portage des Sioux, -	-	80	St. Charles.
-	Augustin Clermont,	Letter of office, or order of survey.	Portage des Sioux, -	-	80	St. Charles.
-	Simon Lepage,	Letter of office, or order of survey.	Portage des Sioux, -	-	80	St. Charles.
-	David Eshbough,	Letter of office, or order of survey.	Portage des Sioux, -	-	80	St. Charles.
-	Baptiste Pugol,	Letter of office, or order of survey.	Portage des Sioux, -	-	40	St. Charles.
-	Matthew Soucier,	Letter of office, or order of survey.	Portage des Sioux, -	..	80	St. Charles.
-	Patrice Roy,	Letter of office, or order of survey.	Portage des Sioux, -	-	80	St. Charles.
-	Augustin Lefevre,	Letter of office, or order of survey.	Portage des Sioux, -	-	80	St. Charles.
-	Baptiste Lacroix,	Letter of office, or order of survey.	Portage des Sioux, -	-	40	St. Charles.
-	Solomon Petit,	Letter of office, or order of survey.	Portage des Sioux, -	-	120	St. Charles.
-	Joseph Guinard,	Letter of office, or order of survey.	Portage des Sioux, -	-	80	St. Charles.
-	Julien Roy,	Letter of office, or order of survey.	Portage des Sioux, -	-	80	St. Charles.
-	Basil Picard,	Letter of office, or order of survey.	Portage des Sioux, -	-	80	St. Charles.
-	Abraham Dumond,	Letter of office, or order of survey.	Portage des Sioux, -	-	80	St. Charles.
-	John Baptiste Dofine,	Letter of office, or order of survey.	Portage des Sioux, -	-	80	St. Charles.
-	Alexis Marie	Letter of office, or order of survey.	Portage des Sioux, -	-	80	St. Charles.
-	Antoine Vincent Bouis,	Ten y'rs possession,	Town of St. Louis, -	-	47½ by 150 ft.	St. Louis.
-	Bernard Pratte,	Ten y'rs possession,	Town of St. Louis, -	-	120 by 150 ft.	St. Louis.
-	Francis Racine,	Concession, -	Lake St. Mary, -	-	75	New Madrid.
-	James Alcozer,	Concession, -	Village of New Madrid, -	-	180 ft. square,	New Madrid.
-	Joseph Fenwick,	Concession, -	Cape Cinq Hommes, -	-	3000	St. Genevieve.
-	George A. Hamilton,	Concession, -	Brazeau creek, -	-	1995 71 per.	St. Genevieve.
-	Peter McCormick,	Settlement right, -	Plattin creek, -	-	450	St. Charles.
-	John Zummalt,	Settlement right, -	Femme Osage, -	(640)	400	St. Louis.
.,	Rogers, alias Indian Rogers,	Letter of office, or order of survey.	Marais des Liards, -	-	100	

, was	In whose favor issued.	Nature of the claim.	Water course.	Number of acres.	Number of arpents.	District.
-	James Rogers, - -	Letter of office, or order of survey.	Village of Marais des Liards,	-	150 by 300 ft.	St. Louis.
-	Robert Owens, -	Letter of office, or order of survey.	Marais des Liards, - -	-	120	St. Louis.
-	Elias Metz, or his legal reps.	Letter of office, or order of survey.	Marais des Liards, - -	-	140	St. Louis.
-	Joseph Glover, - -	Letter of office, or order of survey.	Marais des Liards, - -	-	90	St. Louis.
-	Jacque Clamorgan, - -	Ten y'rs possession,	N. W. of the town of St. Louis,	-	40	St. Louis.
-	Widow and reps. of Antoine Morin,	Ten y'rs possession,	Grande Prairie, - -	-	60	St. Louis.
-	Widow and reps. of Antoine Morin,	Ten y'rs possession,	Barriere de Noyer, -	-	60	St. Louis.
-	Widow and reps. of Antoine Morin,	Ten y'rs possession,	Town of St. Louis, -	-	120 by 300 ft.	St. Louis.
-	Widow Hebert,	Ten y'rs possession,	Grande Prairie, - -	-	120	St. Louis.
-	Guillaume Hebert, dit Lecompte, -	Ten y'rs possession,	Town of St. Louis, -	-	120 by 150 ft.	St. Louis.
-	Francis Bissonett, or his legal reps.	Ten y'rs possession,	Grande Prairie, - -	-	40	St. Louis.
e,	Guillaume Hebert, dit Lecompte, -	Ten y'rs possession,	Little Prairie, - -	-	40	St. Louis.
-	René Buet, or legal reps. of,	Ten y'rs possession,	Town of St. Louis, -	-	120 by 300 ft.	St. Louis.
-	John Watkins, - -	Ten y'rs possession,	Big Prairie, - -	-	480	St. Louis.
-	John Watkins, - -	Concession, -	Big Prairie, - -	-	60	St. Louis.
-	John Watkins, - -	Concession, -	Big Prairie, - -	-	60	St. Louis.
-	Pelagie Chouteau, widow of Silvestre Labbadie.	Concession, -	Town of St. Louis, -	-	120 by 150 ft.	St. Louis.
-	Auguste Chouteau, -	Concession, -	Little Prairie, -	-	40	St. Louis.
-	Lewis Tash, alias Eustache,	Concession, -	Randall's creek, -	-	399 84½ per.	Cape Girardeau.
-	John Byrd, - -	Concession, -	Byrd's creek, "	-	450	Cape Girardeau.
-	John Baptiste Barseloux, -	Ten y'rs possession,	Lake St. Mary, -	-	150	New Madrid.
-	John Baptiste Pratte and John Baptiste Beauvais.	Ten y'rs possession,	Common fields of St. Genevieve.	7 arps. front on the Mississippi, back to the hills—1½ front to Pratte and 3½ to Beauvais, if not over 2000 arps.		St. Genevieve.
-	Antoine Baccanne, or his legal reps.	Ten y'rs possession,	Grande Prairie, -	60		St. Louis.
-	Charles Gratiot, -	Ten y'rs possession,	Barriere de Noyer, -	2½ arpents front by 50 depth.		St. Louis.
-	Charles Gratiot and Nicolas Beaugenoux.	Ten y'rs possession,	Barriere de Noyer, -	3 arps. front by 40 in depth—1 arp. front to Gratiot, and 2 arps. front to Beaugenoux.		St. Louis.
-	Merriwether Lewis, - -	Ten y'rs possession,	Little Prairie, -	-	40	St. Louis.
-	John Baptiste Trudeau, -	Ten y'rs possession,	Town of St. Louis, -	-	120 by 140 ft.	St. Louis.
legal	John Baptiste Barseloux, or his legal representatives.	Ten y'rs possession,	Bois Bruile, -	-	320	St. Genevieve.
-	Auguste Conde, or his legal reps. -	Ten y'rs possession,	Big Prairie, -	-	40	St. Louis.
-	Peter Deroche, - -	Ten y'rs possession,	Lake St. Isidore, -	-	235	New Madrid.
-	Jacques Clamorgan, -	Ten y'rs possession,	Little Prairie, -	-	40	St. Louis.
-	Moses Burnett, -	Settlement right, -	Waters of Mississippi, -	-	320	Arkansas.
-	Peter Chouteau, -	Ten y'rs possession,	Town of St. Louis, -	-	120 by 150 ft.	St. Louis.
-	Peter Chouteau, -	Ten y'rs possession,	Town of St. Louis, -	-	120 by 150 ft.	St. Louis.
-	Charles Gratiot, -	Ten y'rs possession,	Barriere de Noyer, -	-	80	St. Louis.
-	Dodier, -	Ten y'rs possession,	Barriere de Noyer, -	-	140	St. Louis.
-	Parfait Dufour, -	Ten y'rs possession,	3 ms. N. W. of St. Genevieve,	-	150	St. Genevieve.

COMMISSIONERS' CERTIFICATES—Continued.

land was	In whose favor issued.	Nature of the claim,	Water course.	Number of acres.	Number of arpents.	District.
oumbrood,	Andrew Drybread, alias Toumbrood,	Ten y'rs possession,	Near village of New Madrid,	-	90	New Madrid.
-	Charles Gratiot, - -	Ten y'rs possession,	Barriere de Noyer, - -	-	80	St. Louis.
-	Francis Hebert, -	Ten y'rs possession,	River des Peres, -	-	80	St. Louis.
-	Veuve Hebert, or her legal reps. -	Ten y'rs possession,	Town of St. Louis, -	-	120 by 300 ft.	St. Louis.
n,	Jeannette, free negro woman, -	Ten y'rs possession,	Barriere de Noyer, -	-	80	St. Louis.
-	Paul Kiercereau, or his legal reps. -	Ten y'rs possession,	Prairie near St. Louis,	-	80	St. Louis.
-	Paul Kiercereau, or his legal reps. -	Ten y'rs possession,	Prairie near St. Louis,	-	40	St. Louis.
-	Widow and reps. of Antoine Morin,	Ten y'rs possession,	Barriere de Noyer, -	-	60	St. Louis.
-	Antoine Saugrain, - -	Ten y'rs possession,	Town of St. Louis, - . -	-	120 by 300 ft.	St. Louis.
-	Bartholomew St. James, -	Ten y'rs possession,	Near town of St. Louis, -	-	80	St. Genevieve.
enne,	Joseph Mainville, dit Dechenne, or his legal reps.	Ten y'rs possession,	Big Prairie, -	-	60	St. Louis.
-	Francis Moreau, or his legal reps. -	Ten y'rs possession,	Near town of St. Genevieve,	-	60	St. Genevieve.
-	Francis Moreau, or his legal reps. -	Ten y'rs possession,	Town of St. Genevieve, -	-	2 by 1½ arps.	St. Genevieve.
-	Legal reps. of Joseph Brazeau, -	Ten y'rs possession,	Town of St. Louis, -	-	120 by 150 ft.	St. Louis.
-	Joseph Brazeau, -	Ten y'rs possession,	Town of St. Louis, -	-	120 by 150 ft.	St. Louis.
-	John Baptiste Provenche, or his legal representatives.	Ten y'rs possession,	South of town of St. Louis, -	-	4½	St. Louis.
-	Francis Pasquin, -	Ten y'rs possession,	Lake St. Mary, -	-	90	New Madrid.
-	Peter Dorion, or his legal reps. -	Ten y'rs possession,	Mississippi, -	-	240	St. Louis.
-	Charles Roy, or his legal reps. -	Ten y'rs possession,	Barriere de Noyer, -	-	40	St. Louis.
-	Charles Gratiot, -	Ten y'rs possession,	Town of St. Louis, -	-	90 by 150 ft.	St. Louis.
-	Charles Gratiot, -	Ten y'rs possession,	Town of St. Louis, -	-	30 by 20 ft.	St. Louis.
-	James Davis, -	Settlement right; see No. 970.	Femme Osage, -	(640)	50	St. Charles.
lemming,	Joseph Girrard, Patrick Flemming, and Auguste Aubuchon.	Concession, -	North fork of Gaboury,	-	1200	St. Genevieve.
-	Jaduthan Kendal, - -	Concession, -	North fork of Gaboury,	-	700	St. Genevieve.
Coy,	Robert McMahon, - -	Concession, -	Mississippi, -	-	250	St. Genevieve.
-	Thomas Rogers & Jaduthan Kendal,	Concession, -	Grande Glaize creek, -	-	320	St. Louis.
-	Edy Musick, -	Settlement right, -	Fify's creek, -	(640)	100	St. Louis.
-	Ely Musick, -	Settlement right, -	Creve Cœur, -	-	100 (300)	St. Louis.
-	James Reynolds, -	Settlement right, -	St. François, -	(640)	400	New Madrid.
-	Auguste Chouteau, -	Ten y'rs possession,	Town of St. Louis, -	-	120 by 150 ft.	St. Louis.
-	Auguste Chouteau, -	Ten y'rs possession,	Town of St. Louis, -	-	120 by 150 ft.	St. Louis.
-	Auguste Chouteau, -	Ten y'rs possession,	Town of St. Louis, -	-	240 by 300 ft.	St. Louis.
-	Auguste Chouteau, -	Ten y'rs possession,	Town of St. Louis, -	-	120 by 150 ft.	St. Louis.
ph Calve,	Anthony Squlard, -	Ten y'rs possession,	Town of St. Louis, -	-	120 by 300 ft.	St. Louis.
ns Soucie,	Antoine Vincent Bouis, -	Concession, -	Town of St. Louis, -	-	120 by 150 ft.	St. Louis.
-	Widow Camp, or her legal reps. -	Concession, -	Town of St. Louis, -	-	120 by 150 ft.	St. Louis.
-	Elisha Belsha, heirs and legal reps. of,	Settlement right, -	Bois Bruile, -	(640)	450	St. Genevieve.
-	Susannah Dubreuil, -	Ten y'rs possession,	Town of St. Louis, -	-	150 ft. square,	St. Louis.
-	Susannah Dubreuil, -	Ten y'rs possession,	Town of St. Louis, -	-	250 by 300 ft.	St. Louis.
-	Charles Gratiot, -	Ten y'rs possession,	St. Louis, -	-	60 by 150 ft.	St. Louis.

COMMISSIONERS' CERTIFICATES—Continued.

as	In whose favor issued.	Nature of the claim.	Water course.	Number of acres.	Number of arpents.	District.
-	Joseph Marie Papin,	Ten y'rs possession,	District of St. Louis,	-	70 ft. square,	St. Louis.
-	Legal reps. of Joseph Pichet,	Ten y'rs possession,	Town of St. Charles,	-	120 by 150 ft.	St. Charles.
-	Levi Wiggins,	Settlement right,	Mouth of Cape Cinq Hommes creek.	(640)	100	St. Genevieve.
-	Francis Shaver,	Settlement right,	Forks of Mississippi and Missouri.	(640)	100	St. Charles.
-	Jacques Clamorgan,	Ten y'rs possession,	Merrimack,	-	40 by 40 arps.	St. Louis.
-	Jacques Clamorgan,	Ten y'rs possession,	Merrimack,	-	20 by 40 arps.	St. Louis.
-	Emilian Yosty,	Ten y'rs possession,	Cul de Sac,	-	2 by 40 arps.	St. Louis.
-	Antoine Soulard,	Concession,	Mississippi,	-	76	St. Louis.
-	Paul Dejarlais,	Settlement right,	St. Ferdinand village,	-	150 ft. square,	St. Louis.
-	Louis Dubreuil,	Ten y'rs possession,	St. Ferdinand village,	-	150 by 300 ft	St. Louis.
-	Auguste Chouteau,	Ten y'rs possession,	Town of St. Louis,	78 square 21 square	perches, and links.	St. Louis.
-	Auguste Chouteau,	Ten y'rs possession,	Town of St. Louis,	-	120 by 150 ft.	St. Louis.
-	Jacob Wickerham,	Ten y'rs possession,	River Merrimack,	630 20 p.	-	St. Louis.
-	Eugenio Alvarez,	Concession,	River des Peres,	462 120 p.	-	St. Louis.
-	Silvestre Labbadie,	Concession,	River Merrimack,	397 106 p.	-	St. Louis.
-	Jacob Wickerham,	Ten y'rs possession,	River Merrimack,	402	-	St. Louis.
-	Louis Brazeau,	Concession,	Mississippi and Gingras,	-	270	St. Louis.

missioners for ascertaining and adjusting the titles and claims to land in the Territory of Louisiana, do certify that the foregoing list of certificates r, November, and December, 1811, and January, 1812, from number eleven hundred and eighty-three to number thirteen hundred and forty-two, me as clerk of said Board, and that the Board have acted on all the claims before them.

iven under my hand at St. Louis, this 20th January, 1812.   THOMAS. F. RIDDICK.

Wedden, John, 103
Wedsay, Juan, 226
Weiland, George, 10
Welborn, John, 256
    Thomas, 257
Welburn, Thomas, 200
Welch, Elijah, 137
Weldon, Isaac, 236
    John, 36
Welker, Jacob, 21
    Leonard, 21
Welsh, Elijah, 19
    Elisha, 22, 29, 30, 31
Wentzell, David, 122
    David D., 259
Westbrook, Joseph, 255
    Richard, 235
Westover, Job, 25, 97, 137
    Joseph, 95
Wheat, Conrad, 246
    Conrad, Jr., 257
    Jacob, 247
Wherry, Mackay, 70, 82, 107, 165,
    190, 222
Whie, Hugh, 231
Whitaker, Elisha, 237
White, Robert, 241, 250
Whitehouse, Joseph, 173
Whitesides, James, 87
    John, 226
    John G., 76
    Phoebe, 76
    William, 205
Whitley, Paul, 87
    Thomas, 135, 241
Wickerham, Jacob, 240, 265
Wickerman, Aquilla, 199
    Jacob, 199
Wideman, Francis, 66, 67, 73
    Francois, 227
    John, 78, 225, 253
    Mark, 67, 253
Wiggins, Levi, 131, 265
Wilborn, Curtis, 160
    James, 160
Wildan, John, 9
Wiley, John, 116
    Robert, 260
    William, 241
Willgate, John, 198
William, Isaac, 18
    James, 203
Williams, James, 87, 199, 205, 256
    John, Sr., 253
    Joseph, 236
    Morris, 200

Theophilus, 253
Thomas, 253
William, 232
Williamson, Sarah, 256
Wilson, Andrew, 184, 250
    George, 109, 110, 114, 115, 116,
        117, 119, 120, 121, 122,
        123, 124, 125, 126, 127,
        128, 137, 138, 202, 205, 250
    John, 77, 253
    Robert, 134
    Samuel, 253
    Samuel, Sr., 238
Winsor, Christopher, 61
    Elisha, 248
    Thomas, 248
Winter, William, 57
Winters, Elisha, 169, 170
    Gabriel, 170
    William, 169, 170
Wise, Jacob, 107, 216
Wiseman, Jonathan, 239
Wishant, Matthew, 105
Wissor, Chrostopher, 259
Witherington, John, 86
    Thomas, 86, 138, 226
Withero, Samuel J., 40
Wolf, Christian, 255
    Michael, 259
Wolverton, Levi, 27
Wood, Abner, 76
    Simon, 240
Woods, Andrew, 126
    Francis, 6, 7
    Jonathan, 12, 251
    Martin, 14
    Zaddock, 132
    Zadock, 12, 240
Woolford, Frederick, 199
Woolfort, Frederick, 48
Woolsey, Thomas, 257
Worth, Lewis, 259
Worthington, James, 237
    Joseph, 27, 31, 204, 243
Wray, Jeremiah, 198
Wright, James, 227
Wyatt, Francis, 90

Y

Yarborough, David, 98, 197
    Swanson, 199
Yon, Amable, 247
Yosty, Emilian, 253, 265
    Emillian, 238
Young, Austin, 26
    Edward, 88, 199

Joseph, 19, 24, 26, 27, 232
Morris, 26
Philip, 252
Robert, 68, 76, 164, 251

Z

Zanes, William, 61, 121
Zanor, Jacob, 159
Zellifrow, John, 29
Zequares, Louis, 174
Zomalt, Henry, 9
Zoomalt, Adam, 236
    Andrew, Sr., 236
    Christopher, 5
    Henry, Jr., 251
Zummalt, John, 262

www.ingramcontent.com/pod-product-compliance
Lightning Source LLC
Chambersburg PA
CBHW081430270326
41932CB00019B/3154